MAKING MARCH MADNESS

SPORT, CULTURE & SOCIETY

DAVID K. WIGGINS, SERIES EDITOR

Other Titles in this Series

Making March Madness

The Early Years of the NCAA, NIT,
and College Basketball Championships
1922–1951

CHAD CARLSON

The University of Arkansas Press
Fayetteville
2017

To Kathi, Brielle, and Bryce—
my championship team

Contents

Series Editor's Preface

Sport is an extraordinarily important phenomenon that pervades the lives of many people and has enormous impact on society in an assortment of different ways. At its most fundamental level, sport has the power to bring people great joy and satisfy their competitive urges while at once allowing them to form bonds and a sense of community with others from diverse backgrounds and interests and various walks of life. Sport also makes clear, especially at the highest levels of competition, the lengths that people will go to achieve victory as well as how closely connected it is to business, education, politics, economics, religion, law, family, and other societal institutions. Sport is, moreover, partly about identity development and how individuals and groups, irrespective of race, gender, ethnicity, or socioeconomic class, have sought to elevate their status and realize material success and social mobility.

Sport, Culture, and Society seeks to promote a greater understanding of the aforementioned issues and many others. Recognizing sport's powerful influence and ability to change people's lives in significant and important ways, the series focuses on topics ranging from urbanization and community development to biographies and intercollegiate athletics. It includes both monographs and anthologies that are characterized by excellent scholarship, accessible to a wide audience, and interesting and thoughtful in design and interpretations. Singular features of the series are authors and editors representing a variety of disciplinary areas and who adopt different methodological approaches. The series also includes works by individuals at various stages of their careers, both sport studies scholars of outstanding talent just beginning to make their mark on the field and more experienced scholars of sport with established reputations.

Making March Madness provides a detailed and nuanced examination of the early years of college basketball and its various postseason championship tournaments. Written by Chad Carlson, an assistant professor and basketball coach at Hope College, the book chronicles in a very interesting and engaging fashion the history of the National Collegiate Athletic Association and National Invitation Tournaments, and other college championships. Based on a combination of primary and secondary source material, Carlson successfully places college basketball in proper historical context and connects it to larger issues in college sport more generally and American society at large. Nowhere in the book is this perhaps more evident than in the discussion on the widespread gambling and point-shaving scandals that rocked college basketball in the mid-twentieth century. We are provided a fresh look at those individuals involved in the scandal and how leaders in college basketball responded to one of the most embarrassing moments in the history of college sport. There are fresh insights, however, on a host of other topics that readers will find interesting, illuminating, and thought provoking.

David K. Wiggins

Preface

The NCAA Men's Basketball National Championship Tournament—"March Madness"—has become one of the highlights of the American sporting landscape. Television ratings remain high and broadcasting rights continue to soar for this event that is nestled in between February's Super Bowl and Daytona 500 and April's Master's Golf Tournament and Major League Baseball's Opening Day.

The setup of this single elimination basketball tournament lends itself to a particular type of second-order participation that is easy and entertaining. Indeed, filling out one's own bracket and entering into a pool to see who can predict the most games accurately has become, along with Fantasy Football, the ways in which we most fully invest in big-time sport in America.

The lure of filling out brackets is that it is so uncertain. Rarely does the top overall seed win the event. Upsets abound, and we are drawn to this type of uncertainty. Rarely does a year go by without multiple mentions of underdogs, Cinderella stories, and upsets. The uncertainty, therefore, is much of the draw.

Uncertainty, luck, and unpredictability are pervasive in sport, and they create a paradox that gives our games much of their allure. Sports are games of skill where the individual, individuals, or team that exhibits the greatest amount of the skill or skills central to the sport have the best chance to win. However, as central as the display of skill is to sport, luck and uncertainty counteract to create a balance between fully deterministic events and fully whimsical events. In other words, we often know which team or individual is best and *should* win, but the outcome does not always follow.

March Madness reveals this paradox as well as any sporting event. With each team given a particular seed, spectators have concrete ways of knowing which team *should* win. But March Madness has its name because of how often the favored team does not win. And in a one-off, forty-minute game to decide who moves on, virtually anything can happen.

Early on, the NCAA tournament benefited from some luck in its infancy. The inaugural 1939 event—well before basketball had become a popular television sport—ended poorly. The tournament had low attendance and lost money. The second year, however, fate intervened. Indiana University won the 1940 Eastern Regional hosted nearby in Indianapolis. Kansas University won the 1940 Western Regional in nearby Kansas City. Thus, the 1940 event benefited greatly from the large local fan turnout for tournament games featuring local teams.

However, this luck—Indiana and Kansas were probably not the favorites going into this tournament even though methods of speculating on relative ability were primitive in 1940—can be explained away. Early basketball even into the 1940s suffered from severe regionalism. The large majority of so-called national tournaments at any level of the game were won by local teams who benefited from local officials, local practices, local equipment, local crowds, and local courts that would have been somewhat foreign to visiting teams. Kansas and Indiana should have won their regionals because the games occurred in their territories. These games were played their way. Such was the nature of the game during its first half century.

The NCAA tournament was third on the scene. In 1939, two events already existed—what is now known as the National Association of Intercollegiate Athletics (NAIA) tournament in Kansas City and the National Invitation Tournament (NIT) in New York City. Thus, sustainability was not a given for the NCAA tournament. After an inaugural event that lost money and a 1942 event that barely made any, the NCAA's future was not certain. Moving to Madison Square Garden in New York City for the 1943 Eastern Regional and Championship Final was the single most important move that put the event on its path to the success that it has today.

And yet this move also came alongside more good fortune for the tournament. In 1943, when the NCAA and NIT champions met immediately after the conclusion of both tournaments in a game for the Red Cross's War Fund, NCAA champion Wyoming pulled off an upset over NIT champion St. John's (a "home" team) in overtime that may have been one of the most thrilling games in the history of basketball. This game firmly branded college basketball in the hearts of local fans, and it proved that the NCAA tournament's quality of participants was at least on par with the NIT, an event that was more prestigious at the time.

One year later, a team of young men from Utah who were either too young or physically unqualified for the military won the NCAA tournament and also knocked off NIT champ St. John's in the Red Cross Classic. The NCAA's champion Oklahoma A&M then beat NIT victor DePaul in 1945. Thus, the NCAA had beaten the NIT in three straight one-off games. Had these games gone to the NIT winner, the legacy of each of these tournaments may have been different. One bounce going a different direction, one nail in the Garden floor raised a millimeter more, or the thick smoke-filled Garden air lowering just an inch may have affected the outcome of early tournament games and, accordingly, the legacy of each event.

Making March Madness chronicles many of the games that made March Madness madness. Indeed, as many journalists reported, so many of the early college basketball tournament games exhibited the thrilling finishes that have come to trademark the obsession we have with the event. *Making March Madness* also chronicles the administration of the early college basketball tournaments. Contrary to popular belief, the National Association of Basketball Coaches (NABC)—the group that created the NCAA tournament—did not give away its tournament to the NCAA for covering its debt after losing money in the inaugural 1939 tournament. The NABC ran the initial tournament only with the blessing of the NCAA in the first place. The NCAA gave its name to the tournament while the NABC leaders ran it. This relationship continued through the early years, but the NCAA slowly took more control—financially and otherwise.

For all the madness on the court during the early years, the NCAA and NABC tournament administrators made some shrewd decisions that helped take its event from a poorly attended afterthought into one of the greatest on the American sporting calendar. Amid the caution of post-Depression America in the late 1930s and the austerity of our nation during World War II, it is quite amazing that any of the three major "national" tournaments survived at all. But that they began and even grew during these times is a testament to both the acumen of their organizers and the overwhelming interest Americans have in sport.

Making March Madness is the story of the inception and early years of men's college basketball postseason tournaments. The history of women's college basketball and postseason tournaments is another, albeit shorter, history that falls outside of the scope of this project because of the time frame studied. However, the histories run parallel in some sense. Indeed, the Association for Intercollegiate Athletics for Women (AIAW) inaugurated a national basketball championship tournament in 1969 only to have it overtaken and essentially killed off when the NCAA began administering a women's basketball postseason tournament in 1982—not unlike the way in which the NCAA overtook the NIT event. The NCAA used its power to leverage its member schools to participate in its events rather than that of its competitors. The NCAA's takeover of the AIAW and NIT events occurred much later than the epoch this book details. And yet, these legally contested changes in the modern college basketball landscape offer evidence of the residue left by the early years of college basketball's postseason history.

Accordingly, *Making March Madness* describes the history of men's college basketball, how its postseason championship tournaments came about, how they grew, and how they dealt with the punch in the gut college basketball received in the form of a widespread basketball gambling and point-shaving scandal in 1951. These "early years" reveal the challenges, struggles, and triumphs that college basketball experienced to gain a foothold for its climb into the American sporting pantheon alongside baseball, football, and everything else we now cherish in the sporting landscape.

Acknowledgments

Someone once told me that it takes a village to raise an idiot. I think this was a conflation of the age-old proverb that it takes a village to raise a child and the common stock character "the village idiot." This confusion made me laugh, but it has stuck with me because it hit home. There is a large village—a metropolis, really—that has raised this idiot into a scholar. And every little bit of help from so many people has me grateful for the communities of which I've been a part.

I am indebted to Professors Scott Kretchmar and Mark Dyreson at Penn State for taking me on as a graduate student. What Dr. Kretchmar and Dr. Dyreson saw in me I will never know, but their passion within the field of sports studies and the excellence with which they studied sport was remarkably inspirational. The time they spent with me to develop writing and research skills must have been a great chore, but they never showed any frustration.

I have grown immensely from the collegial communities at Penn State Altoona, Eastern Illinois University, and Hope College. I have found wonderful and encouraging friends and colleagues at each of these places. My graduate students at Eastern Illinois proved to be valuable assets, including John Pogue, who spent a few months combing through microfilms with me. I am also indebted to the administrators and committees on these campuses who provided me with the internal grant monies to travel to conferences and archives. Jason DeWitt, an undergraduate at Hope College and my cousin, served alongside me as a graduate student would have in a very helpful capacity. Without these gifts and these people, this book would not be possible.

Trying to capture as much information as possible on this topic took me on quite a wild goose hunt. I found a lot of dead ends. Librarians at New York University, City College of New York, Long Island University, New York Public Library, and many other metropolitan universities politely offered their help in my quest despite not being able to find much in their repositories. Other searches were more fruitful. Ellen Summers provided a great deal of assistance in my numerous trips to the NCAA library, while I also found willing assistance at Ohio State University, Kansas University, the Naismith Memorial Basketball Hall of Fame, and the American National Red Cross. Archive and copyright staffs at Kansas, Kentucky, Temple, Oregon, Indiana, Wisconsin, Stanford, Wyoming, Utah, Oklahoma State,

Holy Cross, and City College of New York helped guide me through some of the details with which I was unfamiliar.

Further, the University of Arkansas Press has been a joy to work alongside. Dave Wiggins, the editor of this series, provided a great deal of help. He also introduced me to Larry Malley, who provided invaluable wisdom in the early stages of manuscript development. And on the editing end of things, I am indebted to the professionalism and reliability of David Scott Cunningham and Deena Owens.

I owe more than words can describe to my family. To my wife, Kathi, and my kids, Brielle and Bryce, I especially appreciate your patience, your interest in my work, and the joy you bring into my life.

CHAPTER 1

Prolegomena to the Tournaments, 1901–1937

The story of basketball's creation is as revered as any sporting genesis tale. Dr. James Naismith, instructor of physical culture at the Springfield, Massachusetts, Young Men's Christian Association (YMCA) Training School, created an indoor game to keep the "incorrigible" young men in a physical education class attentive and engaged during the long winter months that forced the students indoors. While the general premise of this creation story is well known, historical accounts ignore a central and overarching fact—Dr. Naismith originally created the game to be part of a *college* physical education curriculum. From its birth, basketball was a college game created by a college instructor for college students to play. Indeed, Naismith wrote in 1892, "Basket Ball is not a game intended merely for amusement, but is the attempted solution of a problem which has been pressing on physical educators." The physical educators of the day worked in YMCA or collegiate settings. Therefore, if tennis is known as the game of royalty because kings, queens, and nobility were the original players; if rugby is the game of English public schoolboys who first played in their free time; and if soccer is the game of the masses; then basketball must be known as the college game.[1]

As the game spread quickly, though, Naismith had grander visions. Since many of the students at the YMCA Training School became messengers of their faith, basketball also could be known as the game of missionaries. Naismith's creation traveled as far and as quickly as the YMCA students took it, catapulting from Springfield to YMCAs and colleges across the country and to Christian mission projects around the world. Yet from the beginning, despite a growing interest from players of all ages, races, creeds, and nations—a manifestation of which Naismith was immensely proud—a college instructor created basketball specifically for male college students so that they would not succumb to boredom and the shenanigans it begets during their winter physical education classes.[2]

Dr. Naismith also created basketball as a recreational activity. It was, in his mind, a means to an end befitting the principles on which the YMCA rested. Basketball players developed good health, vigor, discipline, team-work, obedience, and other character traits that mattered far more to the YMCA instructor than who won or lost. Naismith's poor record as a coach during his tenure at Kansas University provides a case in point—he is the only coach in Kansas's storied basketball history to finish his career with more losses than wins. Naismith did not prioritize the competition in basketball nor did he think teams needed professional coaches who would direct the players and their tactics in attempts to win as many games as possible. As coach at Kansas, when he took his team on the road for away games, he often served as the game's referee instead of his team's coach—and did so impartially, as his poor win-loss record would indicate! Instead, in following the YMCA's ideals, he cared more about character development and playing within the moral framework that existed in his physical education class when he first created the game.[3]

Since winning and losing remained trivial to the instructor, tournaments or championships of basketball teams had no place in his vision. And yet interest in his game became so great so quickly that he could not keep control of it. What Naismith invented as a recreational activity for winter physical education classes quickly became popular because participants enjoyed it. Yet it also became an intensely competitive activity.[4]

The First Competitions and Championships

Many of the eighteen young men who played in the original game four days before Christmas in 1891 took the basket game back to their hometown YMCAs for holiday enjoyment. By spring of 1892, YMCA leaders had introduced the game at Geneva College in Pennsylvania and the University of Iowa. By the 1893–94 season, the New York YMCA branches had established a championship format to close the campaign. Brooklyn Central began a three-year reign as the metropolitan basketball champions. Chicago and Philadelphia bred similar league formats in which certain teams could claim the title of "champions" at season's end. Chicago's Ravenwood YMCA won the 1893 championship and took home a decorative shield—what is probably the first-ever basketball trophy. In the City of Brotherly Love, West Philadelphia won the 1893 and 1894 championships. Winchester Osgood captained the championship team and became an early sports hero of sorts. Osgood had starred as a halfback for Cornell and Penn on the gridiron, and the 5'8" and 183-pound bulldog also claimed national amateur titles in the heavyweight divisions of boxing and wrestling. His legacy grew even more outside of sports, however, as he died in combat while defending the

Cubans against Spanish colonialists two years later. His death is believed to have inspired a rewrite of the song "Just Break the News to Mother," a mega-hit written originally about a heroic fireman by the immensely popular songwriter Charles K. Harris in 1891.[5]

Alexander M. Weyand, a former Olympic athlete and army colonel turned historian, wrote about the feats of successful early teams in a history tome he penned in 1960. The text is an attempt to recognize and perpetuate the legacies of the nation's top teams during basketball's infancy. Weyand mentions that an undefeated team from Cincinnati claimed the championship of Ohio and Kentucky in 1893. A team of "Invincibles" from Pine Bluff, Arkansas, compiled a 39-1 record in 1892 and 1893, making it a top team from that region. A group from Trenton, ranked in local papers as the top New Jersey squad in 1894, played Nanticoke, the supposedly top Pennsylvania team, that year in a game that, after three 20-minute periods, remained tied. A fourth period ensued the following day with Trenton finally breaking the 7–7 tie for a victory. This contest may have been rather unlike today's game, as a Trenton player received praise for "heaving a Nanticoke man over his head." Weyand also notes that Albany claimed the New York championship and San Jose claimed the California championship, in games that also probably did not much resemble the basketball played today.[6]

By 1896, many of the game's instantiations remained brutal. The Philadelphia YMCA League disbanded because basketball "retarded regular gymnasium work, fostered ill feeling among members, and attracted a rowdy element." Camden, New Jersey, acted similarly. However, the game continued to grow in other places. The East District of Brooklyn hosted "the Championship of America" after the New York League season ended. In action that included only two nonmetropolitan teams, the hosts defeated the Brooklyn Central squad that had just lost its three-year reign on the New York City circuit less than a month earlier. Baltimore Central, a team that had just won its fourth straight Charm City title, did not compete in the championship event.[7]

Original College Teams and a Variety of Methods

Compared to the relatively quick organization of competitive basketball in YMCA and community circuits, colleges took much longer. By 1893, the college game reached such schools as Yale on the East Coast, Stanford on the West Coast, and Iowa and Chicago in the middle. A number of early contests mark certain facets of the introduction of intercollegiate basketball. Nine of the players in Naismith's original game went on tour in upstate New York and took on a team of nine YMCA School instructors in the first public game on March 11, 1892. On April 26, 1893, a combined team from the Iowa City YMCA and the University of Iowa played a five-man game against the Cedar Rapids YMCA. The team partially comprised of collegians won, 12–2, in what may have been the first public five-on-five contest. On February 9, 1895, Hamline and Minnesota State School of Agriculture played in what is usually regarded as the first game pitting teams representing two colleges. Hamline, a squad organized by a Naismith colleague from Springfield named Ray Kaighn, lost the contest, 9–3. On March 23 of that same year, a former Naismith student, Charles Williams, organized a team at Temple to play Haverford College of Pennsylvania. Naismith's student also lost this game, 6–4. These two 1895 intercollegiate games included nine players per side on the court at a time, but likely demonstrated the first times that teams comprised only of college players from one school squared off against another.[8]

On March 27, 1897, Yale and Penn played in what was possibly the first five-on-five intercollegiate basketball game, with the Elis winning handily, 32–10. Yale remained strong and may have been as good as any team in the country in the 1898–99 season, finishing with an 8-0 record that included an asterisk. In a game against the Washington Heights YMCA, the two teams got into an argument. Yale refused to continue playing and the referee awarded the game to the other team. Over Christmas of 1899, the Yale squad made the first long-distance road trip to play basketball games. The Elis heavily promoted this western expedition, playing games on the way to Chicago and back. Although many of the scheduled games fell through in response to heavy winter weather, and although Yale lost many other games it did not expect to, this squad implemented a new offensive strategy—the dribble—that would catch on quickly thanks in part to this intersectional endeavor. This turn-of-the-century season also marked the introduction of another prestigious Eastern university—Bucknell—onto the basketball landscape. Sophomore center Christy Mathewson, a three-sport star who would later set the standard for Major League Baseball pitching excellence, led the Bison cagers to prominence over a three-year span.[9]

Cultural historian Neil Isaacs argues that, before the twentieth century, four types of basketball play existed. One was the method in which basketball players became known as "cagers." Building maintenance workers put up a cage around the basketball court through which rowdy spectators could not interfere with play and the ball could never go out of bounds. This created a continuous type of action that only stopped when someone scored. The second was the Yale method that involved no restrictions on dribbling. The Elis promoted this method in the Northeast over the latter half of the

1890s and popularized it in the Midwest during their 1899 excursion. This method, Isaacs notes, "was almost like football," because many offensive players would lower their shoulders, put their heads down, and advance the ball much like a running back would, while dribbling. A player would cut one direction while dribbling until stopped, pick up the ball to change directions before starting to dribble a new way until stopped, and so forth. The third type was probably the most popular across the country. This method involved restrictions on dribbling and placed a premium on passing. Many of the most dominant teams over the following two decades found their success utilizing the pass as the single most effective offensive weapon. Had the dribble been banned during this time, these teams would not have had to change a single part of their intricate short-passing strategies. Last, Isaacs refers to "the so-called 'recreative' game." In this game, the court was split into sections and each player had to stay within his or her section while also performing the skills required of someone in that section. Players would be placed in sections on the right or left side of the court as defenders, halfbacks, or forwards.[10]

Aside from the "recreative" style of play, the most popular types of basketball clearly promoted competition as much as and potentially more than the character development and recreation that Naismith originally envisioned. The dissolution of many YMCA basketball leagues in prominent cities spoke to the ways in which moral corruption through competitive impulses had seemingly taken over the game. Colleges continued to generate interest despite the possible moral misgivings. However, intercollegiate competition remained quite fragmented. In the 1890s, very few college athletic conferences existed, and those that did only convened and governed for the sake of end-of-the-season Track and Field Days or football matchups. The University of Minnesota joined an eclectic league of local YMCA, National Guard, company, alumni, and college teams called the Twin Cities League before the Big Ten opened basketball play in 1906. While records of very few of these types of leagues exist, the Gophers' competition in league play would have mirrored the motley but locally focused scheduling of many other college teams.[11]

Since no local, regional, or national governing body officially oversaw college basketball by the turn of the century, each season had little cohesion. No championships existed, and overall win-loss records provided the best measure of comparison among non-AAU teams. Yet because of the scattered and inconsistent schedules at the time, this measure of comparison provided little help regarding relative measures.[12]

By today's standards, this laxity seems primitive. However, basketball was not all that different from other American sports at the time. Baseball already had two seasoned professional leagues in the 1890s, but their schedules were not as structured or uniform as they are today. Professional and college nines played each other at times during the season and also rounded up games against other amateur or professional teams. Stories abound of college players suiting up for their school teams during the weekends—the times that many college presidents and faculty members mandated for games—and then playing under aliases for professional teams during midweek games.[13]

This underhanded practice occurred even more on the gridiron. The relative anonymity of a heavily armored football player in the trenches of the field far from the eyes of spectators and authorities fostered a breeding ground for "two-timing" players much easier than baseball's focus on individual isolated action. College football stars often played for multiple teams during the year, using pseudonyms to avoid any condemnation—moral or otherwise.[14]

"Two-timers" had much more difficulty getting away with these illicit tactics in basketball. The relatively small number of players on a basketball team and the close proximity of spectators to the court made each player readily identifiable. However, the game was certainly not immune to it. The regionalism of basketball at the time, the lack of photographic coverage of games, and the relatively small spectator base at the turn of the century allowed "ringers" to provide services to more than one team at a time. In fact, the nature of basketball as a fundamentally noncontact sport—despite examples of excessively rough games—allowed players to compete much more often than what they would have in football. The football season always ended when the weather got colder, discouraging extra games and performances. Late-season football games had to be scheduled to accommodate both the winter weather and the toll that a long season had taken on a player's body. Basketball, on the contrary, ends its season just as flowers start to rise. In warmer weather, travel is easier for teams and for individual mercenaries. And in a standard game of basketball that at the time allowed only a certain amount of physical roughness, a player could conceivably play multiple games in a row. These factors encouraged "two-timers." These factors also fostered the commencement of end-of-season tournaments in a way that football could not match.

The First Attempts at National and World Championships

When Naismith left the YMCA Training School in 1895 to pursue a medical degree in Colorado, he gave authority over the game to his boss, Luther Gulick, and the YMCA. They ceded control to the AAU in 1896. End-of-season championships came onto the scene shortly after the AAU took control of the game. These "national" championships marked the first attempts at a true national identity for the game. But the results of these early events showed little national coherence. Not coincidentally, in the first four official AAU national tournaments, local teams dominated the brackets. Indeed, regional variations in how the game was played and officiated affected the outcome. Out-of-town teams, if there were any at these early events, experienced major disadvantages in trying to adapt to local rules and customs.

In 1897, the Amateur Athletic Union (AAU) hosted its first national basketball championship tournament. A team from New York City's 23rd Street YMCA that went 15-0 in the regular season took home the top honor in the round-robin-style championship held in New York City that included almost exclusively local teams. The 23rd Street squad repeated the following year going 33-1 and winning a tournament that replicated the inaugural in 1897 except for its broader geographic scope—which included teams from outside the Big Apple. However, the AAU did not sanction the 1898 tournament. New York's Knickerbocker Athletic Club won back-to-back national AAU titles in 1899 and 1900, also in round-robin style and also in New York City. When only four teams entered the 1900 competition, the AAU decided to change venues. The 1901 tournament and title left the Big Apple for the Windy City. Eight teams competed but two semifinalists withdrew, leaving the Ravenswood YMCA of—not surprisingly—Chicago to defeat the heralded Company E team from Fon du Lac, Wisconsin, in Chicago's Coliseum. This Fon du Lac squad had swept Yale in three straight games during the Ivy Leaguers' seminal trip to the Midwest at the turn of the century and had therefore believed they were the best in the country. The 1901 AAU tournament demonstrated that they may have been among the best teams in the nation. The years 1902 and 1903 passed without any AAU championship competition.[15]

However, this association was not the only group hosting championship tournaments at the time. Buffalo, New York, hosted the Pan American Exposition in June 1901. This showcase included an outdoor basketball tournament. Players battled on a 60' by 40' swath of grass while wearing football cleats. After seven straight victories a local team, the Buffalo Germans, took home the "world championship" title. Frederick Burkhardt, physical director of the Buffalo German YMCA on Genesee Street, had organized this team in 1895 by choosing six boys with an average age of fifteen at the time. Burkhardt molded them into a squad far superior than their peers. And so, when the team began playing against full-fledged senior teams, they dominated. By the 1901 Pan American tournament, this group, whose average age had increased to twenty-one, became virtually untouchable. Their stability at a time in basketball when transience ruled the day gave them a distinct competitive advantage.[16]

In 1904, the team sought to expand its prominence by entering a "world championship" tournament held in its home country. The United States hosted its first Olympic Games in St. Louis to coincide with that year's World Fair. The International Olympic Committee's relative lack of oversight at this point in its existence allowed the United States to dictate much of the Olympic docket and governance. American organizers pushed basketball onto the unofficial schedule of events with both a college and amateur tournament. Hiram College, a small, liberal arts school in eastern Ohio that notes former US president James A. Garfield as a student and instructor shortly after it wrote its charter in 1850, won the gold medal in the college division, becoming college basketball's first "champions." To win this title, Hiram had to defeat only two schools—both small, private institutions known more for their religious affiliation than anything else. Wheaton (Ill.) College came in second while Latter Day Saints University, a business school from Salt Lake City that became affiliated with Brigham Young University, lost both games and came in third place.[17]

The Buffalo Germans entered the Olympics' "open" basketball tournament prepared to face its stiffest competition to date. This outdoor event featured four other worthy opponents. Xavier Athletic Association came in as the top New York City AAU team, Chicago Central YMCA was the top Central AAU team, and the Missouri Athletic Association—the de facto home team—entered the tournament with its only loss of the previous two seasons coming to the Chicago Central YMCA. A Turner Tigers team from Los Angeles that had not lost in six seasons rounded out the formidable field. The Germans took home the "gold medal" and title of "world champions" by beating all four opponents in a round-robin format that included a 77–6 shellacking of the Los Angeles team and a 97–8 pounding of the Missourians. Based on the results, these two teams either did not play worthy competition back home or proved the poor state of the game in their home regions. Therefore, while this tournament was not a world championship like the Olympics of today (the rest of the world later viewed the title of this tournament—the "Olympic World's Basket Ball Championship"—as "pompous" and "arrogant"), it was the first basketball tournament to have truly "national" participation. And it was the first one not to have a local team win.[18]

By 1905, the Germans had become almost invincible as they reigned supreme in the basketball world. But that came to a crashing halt at the hands of a feisty twenty-year-old from Independence, Missouri. Forrest Allen, a hard-nosed young man from a middle-class family, had led the

The Amazing Allen Brothers basketball team in 1904. "Phog" is second from the left. His nephew, Homer, went by the nickname "Little Ham" and served as the team mascot. *Courtesy of University Archives, Kenneth Spencer Research Library, University of Kansas.*

Kansas City Athletic Club's basketball team to a victory over a Naismith-coached Kansas University team that also featured Allen's older brother Pete, on February 18, 1904. The victory gave the younger Allen all the confidence he needed to wire the Buffalo Germans to set up a three-game series that he promoted audaciously as the "World's Championship of Basketball." Allen scheduled this series for March 1905 in Kansas City's Convention Hall, one of the largest buildings in the country at the time. Convention Hall hosted the 1900 Democratic National Convention and could hold 5,000 basketball fans. Allen promised to pay the expenses for the Buffalo Germans but had to drum up a great deal of financial backing from Kansas City businessmen for the Kansas City Athletic Club to approve of the deal.[19]

Allen's promotion of the series brought a great deal of anticipation to the event, so much so that the player-promoter even claimed to have received approval from the AAU to consider the winner of the series the AAU National Champion—a prestigious but somewhat less important claim since Allen dubbed this series the "*World's* Championship of Basketball."

The AAU was in the middle of an eight-year period in which some growing pains prevented it from hosting an annual national basketball tournament. Nevertheless, on March 27, Allen's Kansas City Athletic Club series commenced with the Buffalo Germans squeaking out a close victory, 40–36. The *Kansas City Star* mentioned that "A very questionable decision by Referee Dischinger was responsible for the four points that won the contest for the Buffalo team. Dischinger is a substitute for the Buffalo team." Traveling teams commonly brought a referee along with them on the road to work in tandem with a local official. The following night, Kansas City's tight 30–28 redemption victory drew a similar response from the Germans. The *Star* reported, "Unfortunately in both of the games already played there were repeated squabbles over the decisions of the referees, and the defeated team left the field of battle each night feeling that the victory had not been justly won." Referee Wood, a constant in Kansas City basketball circles, drew the ire from the visitors in that second game. After the perceived injustice, the twenty-five-year-olds from Buffalo threatened to return home unless the officiating changed. Both sides agreed to have Naismith, a spectator at the first two games, officiate the rubber match. Basketball's founder agreed to do so, but he made it well known that he would call the game by his rules— conservatively and with little contact allowed. This return to the old (oldest?) school philosophy of basketball changed the focus of what had been a knockdown, drag-out "World's Championship" series to that point.[20]

The Kansas City Athletic Club had much more experience with Naismith's officiating than the Buffalo Germans. The Father of Basketball, after all, coached Forrest Allen's older brother, thereby indirectly influencing the younger Allen's hoops development. Forrest Allen, the home team's star throughout the series, knocked down 17 free throws in his team's Game 3 victory. Each team could determine one player to take all of the foul shots, and Allen clearly found a rhythm. The home team blew out the visitors, 45–14, and crowned themselves as world champions. The upstate New Yorkers left town still grumbling about the officiating but the final game made one thing clear: the Kansas City Athletic Club played Naismith's game his way much better than the Buffalo Germans. Indeed, local rules mattered, and local teams still ruled the day. Decades later, Allen noted the dirty tactics of the Buffalo squad—that they would kick the heels of the home team when they ran, or they would grab the Kansas City players' thumbs to prevent them from catching the ball. Nevertheless, Allen won and he made money to boot. After an estimated 10,000 tickets sold for the series including a full house for the finale, Allen proclaimed that he sent the Germans home with $600 while he and his financial backers made $5,000. The Kansas City Athletic Club, which would not financially stand behind Allen's event and therefore did not stand to profit from it, prospered nevertheless. The club's membership grew from 410 before the event to more than 1,000 shortly afterward.[21]

Tracking Early College Basketball's Inconsistent Growth

At the end of the 1904–05 college basketball season, the University of Minnesota and University of Wisconsin trekked east, playing games en route to meet Columbia, arguably the best team of the eastern circuit. "The disputed supremacy of the East over the West in basketball was finally decided during the past season," remarked Harry Fisher, a "Well Known College Basket Ball Authority" from Columbia University, in the Spalding athletic company's annual basketball guide. "As had been predicted by the Eastern critics," Fisher noted, only somewhat objectively, "the Westerners could not cope with the accurate passing and shooting, or the speedy play" of the New York quintet. Wisconsin lost 21–15 and Minnesota lost 27–15. Fisher continued, "The victories in these two contests and the winning of the championship of the Eastern colleges, gives Columbia the undisputed title of 'Intercollegiate Champions of the United States.'"[22]

Fisher, from his Columbian viewpoint, offered a slew of discussion points regarding the differences between his school's "eastern" style and that displayed by the "western" teams. "The fundamental difference," he notes, "is in the manner of passing and shooting. In the West all the work is done with an underhand throw, while here in the East the passing and shooting is done with one hand and overhead. As a consequence the Westerners cannot break up our team play at all, while we have no trouble to intercept the low passes they make." However, the Eastern expert concluded that "In the West they play a cleaner game than here; at least there is a stricter adherence to rules and less occasion for calling fouls; that is about the best point of the Western play." In short, "the best Eastern team under present conditions can beat the best Western five."[23]

Wisconsin's coach Emmett Angell offered another description of the differences between Eastern and Western basketball after his team's Eastern foray that provides some corroboration with Fisher's views, but from a distinctly different viewpoint. Angell noted four ways in which Eastern basketball differed from that in the West: "1. The Eastern game is rougher. 2. The officials are less strict. 3. The passing is inferior. 4. The rule regarding 'holding' is not observed and players are seldom penalized." The reality of the East-West basketball displays likely fell somewhere in between Angell's sour grapes report and Fisher's gloating.[24]

Angell concludes his summary on his team's and, more broadly, his region's basketball season with an unusual diatribe that must have been provoked in some way during his team's trip East. "It is characteristic of Western basket ball to enforce the rules," he opines, "and it is certainly true that the game played in the West is cleaner than the Eastern game—*and is not effeminate*—*is not lacking in interest*—and is a man's game, played by men, with science and skill." The Eastern basketball bloc must have equated its roughness to manliness in the game, or at least that is the perception Angell took away from the trip. Angell continues, "If the rules against rough playing, holding, and similar fouls are not strictly enforced the game becomes a game of beef instead of brains." He concludes bluntly, "The West believes in clean ball and strict enforcement of the present rules."[25]

Clearly, basketball in this decade included great deviation and little coherence—a characteristic amplified by the AAU's decision not to host a national tournament from 1901 to 1910. Regional alliances and rivalries ruled the day, and most teams that boasted of championships, like Columbia, did so on the strength of regular season winning percentage or one-off victories over teams with well-known names from other regions. Interested parties have tried to overcome college basketball's regionalism of this time period in the form of retrospective rankings. In 1943, William Schroeder of the Helms Bread Factory in Los Angeles capitalized on the growing amounts of sports-related memorabilia he and the factory had archived into a museum by publishing his first booklet of retrospective college basketball rankings. Schroeder spent two years doing research and contacting college coaches and sportswriters to determine relative rankings dating back to 1920. In 1957, he continued the practice by ranking teams from the 1901–1919 seasons.[26]

Patrick Premo and Phil Porretta took this task a step further in 1995 by publishing the rankings they had compiled over forty years of work. The former professor and former computer programmer ranked the top twenty teams each season as far back as 1896, and also named top teams dating back to the 1892–93 season. However, Premo and Porretta's rankings of basketball's inaugural decade include virtually every team that played an intercollegiate schedule. As evidence, in 1895–96, Temple received the top position with a 15-7 record that seems below par for a top-ranked team. Premo and Porretta gave Bucknell the fifth spot that year despite a 1-3 record. Yale topped this poll in 1896–97 with an 11-5-1 record, in 1898–99 with a 9-1 record, and in 1899–1900 with 9 wins and 6 losses. The Elis fell to fourth in the Premo and Porretta Poll in 1900–01 behind 12-1 Bucknell, 12-0 Purdue, and Penn State at 5-1. Surprisingly, though, their 10-6 record put them at the top of the Helms Foundation Poll that year.[27]

The work that Schroeder, Premo, and Porretta compiled in their retrospective polls, although not perfect, provides a starting point for championship analysis in basketball's early decades. In the years before official college postseason tournaments, trying to determine national champions was futile. The difference of opinion between the two retrospective polls displays the complexity of the process. And without a national governing body at the time, college basketball was far from national cohesion.[28]

Immediately before the 1905–06 basketball season, discussions began that would spark the creation of national authority over intercollegiate athletics. In October 1905, President Theodore Roosevelt invited the presidents of Harvard, Yale, and Princeton—the leaders in higher education and college football at the time—to the White House to discuss growing concerns of the dangers of college football and its rules. Many young men played and sustained serious injuries, sparking public outrage at the nascent game. And yet football did so much for campus morale that alumni wanted no part in its abolition. Roosevelt's discussion with these leaders did little to ensure football safety, but it did spark interest in college administrators uniting to form standard rules for football and, if possible, other sports, too.[29]

In December of that same year, Chancellor Henry MacCracken of New York University invited college administrators from all over the country to join him at a meeting to standardize college football rules and practices. Thirty-one schools participated with others sending in proxies for their absence. This group, which did not include the elite three that had been invited to the White House only months earlier, met again the following month to officially establish a charter. The group adopted the name Intercollegiate Athletic Association of the United States (IAAUS), and increased its vision beyond football rules in 1908. In 1913, the group officially became known as the National Collegiate Athletic Association (NCAA).[30]

Throughout this new organization's early years, basketball was still far from the center of its agenda. However, athletic programs proliferated on college campuses as the IAAUS-turned-NCAA gained its footing in the college sports landscape. While basketball did not figure prominently in public consciousness at this time, it certainly gained interest. The University of Chicago topped both the Premo and Porretta and Helms polls as the top 1907 squad. The team representing the Windy City and a university that was only sixteen years old at the time finished the 1908 regular season at 19-2— good enough for the top Helms spot and second to a 24-0 Wabash team in the Premo and Porretta Poll. Chicago ended that season with a three-game play-off series against a 23-2 University of Pennsylvania team that many at the time believed was for bragging rights as the best team in the country.[31]

The University of Chicago got its start as an institution through financial and in-kind donations from John D. Rockefeller and Marshall Field. William Rainey Harper, the school's first president, opened its doors to students in 1892 with a vision of quickly enhancing the schools national standing by encompassing a first-rate physical education and athletics program, among other things. Harper hired Amos Alonzo Stagg, who had worked with Naismith at the YMCA Training School in Springfield, Massachusetts, to oversee physical education and intercollegiate sport at the new school. Stagg joined Chicago's faculty in 1892 and immediately developed a top-notch athletics program and became a leader in college sport. Although he made the strongest imprint as a college football coach and innovator at Chicago, his legacy is quite robust. While coaching football for forty years, he also coached baseball for nineteen seasons, hosted and administered the NCAA's first postseason national championship event (track and field), coached basketball for one season, and founded an annual postseason national high school basketball tournament.[32]

Despite this multitude of duties, football remained Stagg's true passion. Basketball coaching duties went to Dr. Joseph Raycroft, Stagg's assistant football coach and a professor on campus. Raycroft received a stipend for coaching the Maroon five from 1900 to 1909, making him one of the first professional coaches. Under his direction, Chicago thrived, winning or tying for the Western Conference title four straight seasons from 1907 to 1910. During those years, Raycroft benefited from the services of two early college basketball stars. Guard H. O. "Pat" Page and center John Schommer led the Maroons to this early success. Page, a left-hander who also starred as Stagg's quarterback and defensive end on teams that won the conference gridiron title in 1905, 1907, and 1908, revolutionized the way guards played defense. Schommer, a 6'3" athlete who also starred on Stagg's football team, dominated the paint while leading the conference in scoring for three straight years averaging just more than 10 points per game. While winning twelve varsity letters in four sports throughout his career at Chicago, Schommer was also selected to the 1908 Olympic Track and Field team but declined the trip to London so he could concentrate on his studies. Those studies kept him on campus for a graduate degree after exhausting his eligibility in which he moonlighted as the team's coach for the 1910–11 season. However, his studies won out again, and he gave up coaching for a lifelong career as a professor of chemical engineering and bacteriology at the nearby Illinois Institute for Technology. Schommer never strayed too far from sport, though. He served as his employer's athletic director and refereed college basketball and college and professional football, and is given credit for developing the idea for modern basketball backboards. Schommer's college teammate Page stayed even closer to the game throughout his career. The guard entered the coaching profession full-time, accumulating successful stints at Chicago, Butler, Indiana, and the College of Idaho.[33]

With the advent of conference play, orderliness invaded the previously jumbled college basketball landscape. Conference champions could lay claim to number one rankings of sorts. And since very few prominent basketball conferences existed in the twentieth century's first decade, only a small number of teams could make that claim. In 1908, Chicago finished the regular season tied with Wisconsin for the Western Conference title. Both teams went 7-1 in the league and had two overall losses, even though Chicago had played nine more contests. The Badgers and Maroons squared off in a tiebreaker game the winner of which would go on to play a series against Eastern League champion Penn to informally determine the "national champion." Raycroft's squad traveled up to Madison to face Coach Emmett Angell's Badgers and took home a victory, 18–16, with Page and Schommer starring. This victory set up a best-of-three series with the Penn Quakers in a first-of-its-kind championship series pitting the two most prominent conferences' champions.[34]

Penn traveled west for the series opener and put up a good fight. Yet the Maroons squeaked out a victory, 21–18, as Schommer connected on some clutch shots and Page, the hero of the Wisconsin game, knocked down a late shot in which he released the ball while on his knees amid defensive pressure. The teams traveled to Philadelphia for the second game that was even closer than the first. Penn and its "electrifying dribbler" Charles Keinath came up on the short end again in a 16–15 loss. The third game was unnecessary as Chicago returned home believing they were national champions. The Maroons carried this momentum into a 12-0 conference record in the 1908–09 season but a national championship series with that season's Eastern League champion Columbia "fell through."[35]

College and AAU Connections and Developments

Nothing came of this postseason momentum that pitted the top Western Conference and Eastern League teams but excluded everyone else in the college basketball world. However, the top Eastern and Western teams squaring off provided more display of regional differences. Chicago coach Raycroft noted that his team "was characterized by open passing and evasion of contact, while the Eastern men depended more upon dribbling and a much closer interference game." As such, he argued, "It would seem that a proper combination of these two styles would be more effective than either, while at the same time the game would lose the tendency to roughness which is present in the dribbling game." Clearly, teams in different regions still played the game quite differently.[36]

In the fall of 1910, Harry Fisher of Columbia lamented the inability to schedule the Eastern and Western conference champions in an end-of-season series yet again. Columbia's season ended on February 26, more than two weeks before Chicago's last game, providing scheduling difficulties—the advent of the spring sports season took priority for Columbia over waiting for the Maroons. In an essay to open Spalding's 1910–11 basketball guidebook, Fisher interestingly wrote optimistically about the prospect of this type of "National Championship" series in the future, but also seemed pessimistic regarding championship events in general.

> Although the winner of such a series will be accredited by many with the highest honor in basket ball; nevertheless, there are many adherents of the sport that will challenge the right to decide the National championship without considering other sectional champions. It seems improbable that the sectional champions will ever meet in a series to decide definitely first honors. Even if such contests were possible some outside team would present a claim as they have done in the past. This condition of affairs in college athletics is nothing new, the same proposition has presented itself in every branch of sport, and no matter how conclusively a national championship is decided, there will always be some one that will endeavor to prove the rights of another claimant.[37]

Based on Fisher's rather somber tone, truly national championship events did not fit into his predictions for college basketball's future. Indeed, no college sport was prepared in 1910 to hold this type of event that would bestow the "highest honor."

In 1915, college teams began to make a mark on the AAU championship tournament—a seemingly better route toward national supremacy. Although previous college fives may have participated and it is likely that a number of college basketball players participated in the tournaments with noncollege amateur teams, college squads began to show increasing prowess—but from previously unrepresented regions of the country. National basketball reports focused on the regions surrounding New York City and Chicago at the time, as those regions included the Eastern and Western Intercollegiate conferences and those cities had hosted all of the AAU national tournaments. This new regional representation did not necessarily mean that basketball had recently come to a high level in these areas. Instead, many of these teams had just started competing beyond local schedules.

In 1915, Whittier College finished as runner-up to the prestigious San Francisco Olympic Club in the AAU tournament hosted, not surprisingly, in San Francisco to coincide with the Panama-Pacific Exposition. In 1916, the tournament moved back to Chicago, where the University of Utah's Clyde Packer connected on a late field goal to give the Utes a 28–27 victory, the first AAU championship for a college team, and the first for a team outside the host region. The victory marked the beginning of successful careers in basketball for Coach Nelson Norgren and Utah all-tournament team member Dick Romney. Norgren, who played football, basketball, baseball, and track at the University of Chicago only a year earlier—and who was therefore very familiar with Chicago basketball, helping his team to overcome its opponents' home court advantage—would go on to coach basketball at his alma mater from 1921 to 1957 while serving as president of the National Association of Basketball Coaches in 1942. Romney coached football and basketball at what is now Utah State throughout his long career before becoming the commissioner of the Mountain States Athletic Conference in 1949. The year after Utah's AAU win, the Illinois Athletic Club brought the title back "home," winning the Chicago-hosted event after dominating Brigham Young University, 27–14, in the title game. The Mormons fared the best of any college team in the sixteen-team event, but not by much. Montana State finished third.[38]

The United States' entrance into World War shortly after the 1917 basketball season created a vacuum in the interest and skill level of the college and amateur game. Many young men left their basketball teams to join Uncle Sam and help fend off the central forces in Europe. While most college teams continued to compete, they took great care to cut down on travel and act prudently with resources during the 1917–18 season. Accordingly, the AAU canceled its 1918 basketball tournament. When the championship resumed the following year, six teams squared off in Los Angeles for the AAU title. Utah, the only college team in the event, finished fourth. However, entrance into this event was not meritocratic and the college basketball world remained disjointed. Premo and Porretta did not rank the Utes in its top twenty for that season.[39]

A Banner Year for the College Game

In retrospect, the 1919–20 basketball season was one of the most important for the growth beyond regionalism of the college game. The AAU moved its tournament to a new locale—Atlanta. This move paid dividends as sixteen teams entered the event representing all regions of the country. In this first truly national AAU tournament, NYU defeated Rutgers 49–24 in the first and only all-college final in the history of the event. Howard Cann, who went on to coach NYU for thirty-five seasons including the school's glory years, led the "Violent Violets" to this championship as the team's star. Premo and Porretta ranked this New York squad, at 16-1, fourth in its retrospective poll and Rutgers did not make its top twenty. Premo and Porretta and Helms both ranked Pennsylvania as number one. The Quakers took a 20-0 record into a "national championship" series against Chicago that replicated the series that the Maroons won in 1908.[40]

Chicago won the 1920 Western Conference title with a 10-2 record. Wisconsin, a team that had won five of seven conference titles from 1912 to 1918, fell on hard times, opening the door for other teams to take conference honors. Dr. Walter Meanwell, Badger coach until 1918, took his short-passing method of "scientific basketball" to Missouri where he found immediate success. The Tigers won the Missouri Valley Conference crown in 1918 and again in 1920 under Meanwell, also garnering Premo and Porretta's number 2 ranking that year behind Penn. Without Meanwell's influence on a Badger team, Chicago and the other top Western conference squads thrived.[41]

The Maroons, led on the floor by future Butler coach Paul "Tony" Hinkle and future Princeton coach Herbert "Fritz" Crisler (who is better known for coaching football at Michigan), took the first game in its "national championship" series with Penn. With this home victory, Chicago had visions of another series sweep to match its 1908 feat. But the series opener proved to be Penn's only loss of the season. Game 2 at Penn went to the Quakers quite handily, 29–18. Penn center Bill Grave returned to action in the rubber match after fending off the influenza. He played "a beautiful game" in front of a capacity crowd across the Delaware River on Princeton's court for a 23–21 victory despite seventeen extra seconds of chaotic play at the end because the timer's gun misfired, making no sound. Luckily no scoring occurred, and the game ended fairly. The losers left with dignity, though, knowing they had proven their mettle in a fierce second-half comeback that had fallen just short. Had Chicago not played this series, it may have found greater favor in Premo and Porretta's rankings. Instead, it finished tenth in their poll, four spots behind the Purdue team that had finished 8-2 in the conference—good enough for a close second place. Purdue finished the season 16-4 and Chicago finished 11-4.[42]

In 1921, the AAU tournament moved to Kansas City, settling in the Garden City until 1935. During that time, teams from Kansas or Missouri won or finished second in the tournament in all but two years, continuing the trend that plagued the game since its birth. The 1920s saw the tournament grow to include more teams annually from outside the host region. However, the local teams, not surprisingly, fared better. When Chicago hosts the tournament, for example, it uses local officials. Naturally, then, the "Chicago" way of playing the game becomes the norm for that event. Kansas City during the 1920s was no different. And yet the continuous success of the local teams in AAU tournaments during a period of time in which basketball's regional identities began to flood together established Kansas City as a basketball hotbed.[43]

From 1921 to 1935 four college teams reached the AAU's championship game. In 1921, Southwestern College of Winfield, Kansas, lost in the finals. In 1924, Butler University of Indianapolis won the event, coached by former Chicago standout Pat Page. The following season, Coach Arthur "Dutch" Lonborg—whose career hoops accomplishments included starring at Kansas under Phog Allen, winning the AAU tournament as a player in 1921, coaching at Northwestern, serving as Kansas's athletic director, and running the NCAA tournament for fourteen years—coached the Washburn College squad from Topeka, Kansas, to the tournament title—the last time a college team would win the event. Northwest Missouri State College lost the championship game in 1932 by a score of 15–14.[44]

Indianapolis Hosts a National College Championship

While Kansas's recognition for quality basketball grew based in part because it hosted the AAU tournament, basketball-rich Indiana sought similar prestige. High school basketball earned social capital in the Hoosier state early on like few other places in the country. Indianapolis, then, attempted to reap the benefits of this popularity by hosting a national college basketball tournament at the end of the 1922 season. The Indianapolis Junior Chamber of Commerce raised the issue in January and voted unanimously in February to host the event in March. Officials from four conferences across the country—the Western Pennsylvania–West Virginia, the Pacific Coast, the Missouri Valley, and the Southern Intercollegiate Athletic Association— agreed to send their top teams who would join one invitee each from the "central west" and "east coast" regions for a six-team tournament of night games at Indianapolis's State Fair Coliseum. Organizers promoted this tournament as "an annual affair to determine the real national championship." The subtle meaning behind this statement was that Indiana had many strong small college teams whose qualities rarely received recognition.[45]

By the end of February, the *Indianapolis Star* announced the tournament's first entrant and speculated on others. The selection committee chose

Wabash College from nearby Crawfordsville, Indiana, to represent the central west region. Wabash had fielded strong basketball teams in the past, and the committee chose the Little Giants from among four "finalists" in the Hoosier State. The selection group excluded Butler after it lost to DePauw and split with Wabash; DePauw missed out with losses to Wabash; and Purdue, who won the Western Conference title that season, beat Wabash but lost to DePauw and was not chosen because the Western conference did not sanction the event.[46]

The *Star* also reported that the Southern Intercollegiate Athletic Association and the Southern Intercollegiate Conference set up a twenty-six-team tournament in Atlanta and would send the champion to Indy as the regional representative. By early March, the University of North Carolina had won the southern tournament by defeating Mercer College of Georgia in the finals. The University of Idaho beat out Washington to finish an undefeated season and win the Pacific Coast Conference; West Virginia, Carnegie Tech, Penn State, and Pitt sought the top spot in the Western Pennsylvania–West Virginia Conference; Kansas and Missouri both held out hopes from the Missouri Valley; and Rutgers—AAU runners-up two seasons before—appeared to be the team to beat in the East.[47]

At the beginning of March, Idaho secured an invitation to Indy while Rutgers committed to representing the East. And with an influx of telegrams from interested colleges around the country, the Indianapolis Junior Chamber of Commerce discussed increasing the event from six to eight teams. BYU, noting its top status in the Rocky Mountain region, expressed a desire to participate. Small midwestern schools Illinois Wesleyan, Knox (Ill.) College, and Kalamazoo (Mich.) College sought bids, and the University of Alabama showed a strong interest in competing even though it had lost in the semifinals of the South's postseason tournament.[48]

By Sunday, March 6, only four days before the tournament's tip-off, the Junior Chamber of Commerce had offered only four bids. Wabash, the local entrant, had high hopes after its recent victory over Purdue; Rutgers remained committed from the East; Idaho had already boarded an eastbound train; and North Carolina had earned the right to represent the South by winning its tournament. The Missouri Valley remained undecided as Kansas and Missouri held identical records with losses only to each other. The *Star* noted the possibility of both outstanding teams entering. The Western Pennsylvania–West Virginia Conference picture was even cloudier, as Carnegie Tech, Pittsburgh, West Virginia, Penn State, Grove City College, and Washington and Jefferson Colleges "have all won and lost so many games that it is difficult to get a line on which team is the best." Such geographically random schools, the *Star* noted, as Holy Cross, Brigham Young, New York University, Michigan State, Illinois Wesleyan, or Kalamazoo would be invited "if no definite winner can be picked from (the Western Pennsylvania–West Virginia) district."[49]

Because "there was a large field of contending teams with won and lost records that looked like a Chinese puzzle," the local selection committee navigated the logjam at the top of the Pennsylvania–West Virginia region by asking a group of Pittsburgh sports reporters to decide. They chose Grove City, who sported three losses—all due to early season illness—but won the Tri-State (West Virginia, Pennsylvania, Ohio) League. And by Tuesday, March 8, the selection committee finalized the roster of entrants. Grove City, Wabash, and Idaho remained on the list, but the rest of the teams left major question marks that the *Star* did not answer. North Carolina was out, replaced by the South's runner-up, Mercer. Rutgers did not enter the tournament and neither did Missouri nor Kansas, Missouri Valley co-champions. Instead, the final two bids went to Illinois Wesleyan and Kalamazoo. The selection committee noted in much of its pretournament correspondence that it sought the nation's "fastest" and best teams. Therefore, the entertainment of fast basketball may have played a role in final bids.[50]

The selection committee drew up the tournament bracket by picking teams out of a hat on Wednesday night, the eve of the opening-round games. Wabash defeated Illinois Wesleyan easily in Thursday night's opener, 39–16, while Kalamazoo took down Idaho, 38–31, in the nightcap. The "Kazooks'" speed was too much for the Vandals to handle. Mercer and Grove City looked on during opening night with byes in hand. Yet the extra scouting helped neither squad the following night as Wabash and Kalamazoo continued on hot streaks. The Little Giants scored 62 points in a rout of Mercer while the Kalamazoo Hornets used their fast pace to outrun Grove City. Saturday night's championship game between Wabash and Kalamazoo generated all kinds of local hype, but the game was over quickly. The Little Giants simply outmatched the Hornets, building on a 24–8 halftime lead to finish off the Michigan team 43–23. Despite Kalamazoo's dazzling speed, it could not penetrate Wabash's solid defense nor could it stop the Little Giant's strong attack.[51]

The local team's "national championship" featured prominently in the local press. This victory signified a landmark moment in Hoosier "hysteria" over basketball. However, the tournament received less enthusiasm nationwide. While Wabash's victory received mention as far away as Boston, most outlets decided against promoting Wabash as "national champions," a decision that may have been encouraged by the parochialism, sectionalism, and elitism that continued to pervade college basketball at the time. Basketball remained a regional game in the 1920s. Although a national rules commit-tee created uniform laws for the game that had been largely accepted over the previous six seasons, in 1922 various interpretations of how the rules should be enforced still made intersectional competition difficult on visiting teams. So while it may not have been well known that both officials for the tournament's games—one of which was Butler's coach Pat Page—lived in Indianapolis and had distinctly Midwestern understandings of the game, it certainly would have been easier for Midwestern teams to play by Page and his colleague's interpretation of the rules. It should come as no surprise, then, that two Midwestern teams squared off in the tournament championship and that the local team won.[52]

Regionalism unfortunately hindered this 1922 tournament just as it had with virtually every other "national" basketball tournament up to that time. Clearly, playing at home and in front of a friendly crowd helps a team. That much has always been clear in sport. Yet, since neither rule interpretations nor equipment had been standardized across the country, the home team received even more advantage. Idaho, Grove City, and Mercer, for example, were at a disadvantage by traveling to play in Indianapolis. However, with the relatively naive climate of sports at the time, they may not have known when they laced up their sneakers that they might be using a ball much different from what they usually used, basket rims and nets made of different materials, and officials who interpreted and viewed rules differently from their local customs. Or they may have accepted this simply as a part of the game.

This may or may not have been on the minds of the country's top teams that year that did not participate in this "national championship tourna-ment." North Carolina did not make the trip despite its standing as the top Southern team. Rutgers did not make it, either, even though it was the class of the prestigious and competitive Eastern circuit. Penn, Yale, and Princeton—often the best of their league—usually hesitated to participate in events that were not perfectly to their liking. In football, baseball, crew, basketball, and virtually every other college sport at the time, these "elitist" schools generally participated in sporting events only when they had control and could set the terms. They had the power to dictate events for their teams, and did so generally knowing—or at least believing—that they were the best whether they participated or not.[53]

The Western Conference held similarly elitist attitudes at the time, which may have encouraged them to prevent Purdue's participation in the Indianapolis tournament by not sanctioning the event. An interesting bal-ance of power had fermented throughout college basketball by this time that included two major players. The Eastern League, which would come to be known as the Ivy League, originated intercollegiate sport in America and had always been at the forefront of academic prestige. These schools wielded their power and social prestige as much as they could in the realm of college sport often, during this epoch, backing it up with the nation's top teams. The Western Conference—oppositional in name and in certain philosophies—had not founded college sport in America nor did its schools have the academic prestige of the "Ivies." However, Western Conference schools were the class of the Midwest, and the conference quickly became a leader of the organization and administration of college athletics. Both conferences believed they were the best, and neither was willing to drop its standards for the sake of coherent nationalization of basketball at this time.[54]

A Dry Spell

The absence of a Western Conference or Eastern League team may have been the poison that prevented the Indianapolis tournament from becoming an annual event. Efforts to organize a second National Intercollegiate Championship Tournament in 1923 stalled, and the tournament dissolved. Over the next seven years, the field of suitable events to determine a "national champion" dissipated. Yet, as the "Roaring 20s" produced a wave of increased interest in college sports that included massive stadium and arena construction campaigns on many of the country's most prominent college campuses, this decade prepared the college basketball landscape to overcome its regionalism. And yet, almost paradoxically, national championship tournaments did not aid in this effort. Indeed, the period from 1922 to 1929 may have seen the least amount of college championship events since basketball's initial decade. College fives reached their peak of success in the AAU tournament during this stretch, and it may have been because the country's college cage teams had no other postseason opportunities.[55]

Throughout this decade, many college athletic departments joined, realigned, or reinforced conference affiliations that continually organized and reorganized the college sports landscape. So although no postseason tournament provided national cohesion to the world of college hoops, conference championships—denoted by regular season record—played a major role in determining a team's success. Yet even if a team did not win its conference, the league in which a team participated could also become a source of pride. The Western Conference—which had finally become a "Big Ten" when Michigan joined in 1917—became the elite conference in the Midwest and, in many ways, across the country as its leadership became

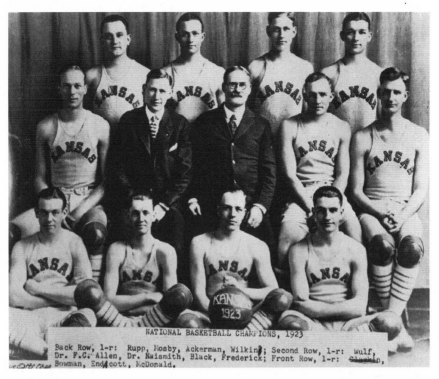

NATIONAL BASKETBALL CHAMPIONS, 1923
Back Row, l-r: Rupp, Mosby, Ackerman, Wilkin?; Second Row, l-r: Wulf,
Dr. F.C. Allen, Dr. Naismith, Black, Frederick; Front Row, l-r: _____,
Bowman, Endicott, McDonald.

The 1922–23 Kansas University basketball team that lists themselves as national champions despite no national tournament. Allen and Naismith sit in the center while future Kentucky coach Adolph Rupp stands in the back row, left. *Courtesy of University of Kentucky Special Collections Research Center.*

almost synonymous with NCAA leadership in the 1920s. However, many independent Midwestern teams also turned in strong performances throughout this decade.[56]

The Eastern League continued as the class of New England and the Middle Atlantic, also alongside many notable independent teams. New York City college teams, most notably, came to national prominence during this time. These teams lacked continuity beforehand since many players moonlighted with other teams in the densely populated metropolis, having to learn multiple systems with high player transience. In the 1920s, many teams stabilized by hiring paid coaches who enjoyed long tenures. One of these, St. John's University, hired James "Buck" Freeman. Freeman recruited a "Wonder Five" who, from 1926 to 1930, went 86-8 and set the standard for metropolitan teams to come. While many New York City teams remained independent of conference alignment, local sportswriters began the annual process of determining the standings of what they called an "intra-city league."[57]

The Dribble Debate and a New National Coaches Committee

In 1927, the regionalism that plagued basketball found its strongest antidote. Kansas coach Forrest C. "Phog" Allen chartered a new national committee of basketball coaches. Allen, who organized the 1905 "World's Championship of Basket Ball" and played for Dr. Naismith at Kansas, heard reports that the National Basketball Rules Committee entertained the idea of banning the dribble. While not a part of Naismith's original vision as he taught the game to his class of "incorrigibles," dribbling had become a valuable and popular skill in the game—one that the early governance and rules committee personnel treated with ambivalence.[58]

Always an activist, Allen began a campaign to defeat the proposed ban. While disagreements on the rules of the game and the ways in which the rules should be interpreted created lively debates among basketball's brass throughout the first two decades of the twentieth century, no other rule split the basketball establishment like this one. Dribbling had a unique history within the game. Early versions of the skill, when accepted by coaches and players as legitimate means of advancing the ball or avoiding defensive pressure, included one-handed dribbling, two-handed dribbling, double dribbling, and even overhead dribbling where a player would continuously toss the ball over his head to himself while advancing the ball—a skill that brought a host of issues along with it and quickly became obsolete. In early April 1927, the Joint Rules Committee that had authority over basketball's rules took action on discussion that had occurred over the past year regarding dribbling codification. Dr. Walter Meanwell, who had returned to Wisconsin to coach after a stint at Missouri and was now head of the rules committee, led a vote that came out 9–8 in favor of abolishing unlimited dribbling and instead allowing one dribble per possession.[59]

Meanwell found great success as a coach with a short, quick passing style of offense that did not require dribbling. Often referred to as the "Little Giant," "Little Doctor," or "Napoleon of Basketball," the diminutive coach ruled with an iron fist in everything he did. Born in England, Meanwell moved to Buffalo, New York, with his family when he was three and grew up in a local basketball landscape dominated by the Buffalo Germans. After receiving a degree from the University of Maryland Medical School, the English immigrant began directing athletics in Baltimore. His basketball teams developed reputations as sound, technical passers out of necessity—the settlement house in which his teams practiced and played did not have much room. When Meanwell took his coaching talents west to the University of Wisconsin in 1912, he implemented his short passing techniques to the midwestern players that had never seen such structured action. His Badger team tried to have him fired immediately for his unorthodox style, but they redacted their plea as the team went undefeated that first season and lost only once in his first three years. This string of success gave Meanwell respect within coaching circles, social capital that he cashed in by joining the authoritative National Basketball Rules Committee. In that position, he led the charge to abolish unlimited dribbling, which would then put a greater premium on offenses like his. After the vote, Meanwell's committee argued that unlimited dribbling offset the delicate balance between offense and defense too much in favor of the offense. An expert dribbler, they thought, was too difficult to stop.[60]

The night of the 9–8 vote to ban unlimited dribbling, the rules committee watched a professional basketball game in which the Original Celtics beat the Cleveland Rosenblums. After the game, Nat Holman, the City College of New York (CCNY) coach who also moonlighted as a player for the Celtics, asked the committee to reconsider implementing the new rule. Holman grew up in and furthered the eastern style of basketball that relied heavily on the dribble. His plea sought to save basketball as easterners had always known it. The committee obliged, offering the 1927–28 season as a deferment period for the rule. This moratorium set off a firestorm of debate on the topic. Meanwell's anti-dribble voice found support from the University of Montana's coach J. W. Stewart and the University of Illinois's Craig Ruby, who played for Meanwell at Missouri. Pro-dribble voices, forced to fight harder because the rule proposal had passed, came out in stronger numbers. Bob Hager of Oregon State, William Reinhart of Oregon, "Hec" Edmundson of Washington, R. V. Borleske of Whitman College, Everett Dean of Indiana, and Harold Olsen of Ohio State all sought to have the vote overturned.[61]

But the strongest advocate of unlimited dribbling was Kansas's Allen. Naismith's former pupil argued that "what the broken-field run is to football, the dribble is to basketball." Allen called a meeting among coaches that coincided with the annual Drake Relays track tournament in Des Moines, Iowa, to discuss this potential rule change. Somewhere between forty and fifty coaches—including those from both sides of the dribble debate—attended the April 29, 1927, meeting. While the coaches came to a consensus at this meeting that the proposed one-dribble rule should be abolished, they also agreed that their collective view in this informally congregated state would not have much impact on the rules committee that would ultimately determine the outcome of the rule. So Allen and his colleagues decided to meet again in the summer to officially incorporate.[62]

On June 10, 1927, the National Association of Basketball Coaches officially met for the first time. The Auditorium Hotel in Chicago hosted this inaugural conference in which Allen presided over the acceptance of a constitution. The purposes of the new organization were

1. To further dignify the basketball coaching profession;
2. To elevate the game to its proper place in the scheme of education;
3. To foster and encourage a better understanding between basketball coaches of the various sections of the United States;
4. To maintain, even to a greater degree, the standards of sportsmanship as outlined in the basketball code.

A vote to accept the constitution passed and Allen set up association officials, a board of trustees, and subcommittees that would navigate the direction of the group in the following years. And in its first order of business, this association successfully worked to maintain unlimited dribbling in the game.[63]

Second Attempts

One of the more progressive-minded coaches at the 1927 NABC convention was the University of Pittsburgh's Dr. Henry Carlson. A former football, basketball, and baseball standout at Pitt, Carlson gained a medical degree and practiced medicine for the Carnegie and U.S. Steel companies that made Pittsburgh America's "Steel City." Carlson came into coaching only part-time in 1922 while still serving the steel industry's workers. The 1927–28 Pitt cage team—Carlson's sixth—went undefeated, topping the retrospective Premo and Porretta and Helms polls in the future but, more importantly, bringing Pitt to national prominence in the present. Carlson's innovative "figure eight" or "continuity" offense, which featured three players sharing the ball and moving in a figure eight while the other two remained stationary, quickly gained popularity and became the basis for many of the patterned offensive strategies that coaches across the country used in the following decades.[64]

Carlson's prominence came from this patterned offense and from his unusual coaching behavior and showmanship that provoked fan reactions. The offensive-minded coach often called upon his team to stall on offense when leading and playing against a zone defense. On the road once early in his career, Pitt led 3–2 shortly after the opening tip-off and had the ball when the home team packed into a zone. Carlson instructed his players to hold the ball for the rest of the half. When the fans began to complain, the coach yawned and threw peanuts at them. When Pitt traveled to West Virginia to play the Mountaineers, Carlson felt betrayed by the referees in one game, repeatedly yelling, "this burns me up!" A Mountaineer fan provided quick remedy by dumping a bucket of water on the coach's head. After a game in which Pitt took a victory over Washington and Jefferson in the southwest corner of the Keystone State, a matronly Presidents' fan repeatedly whacked Carlson on the head with her umbrella. The Pitt coach may have encouraged some of the abuse he incurred, for he often threw the proverbial first stone. After a particularly close and unexpected victory at Notre Dame in overtime, Carlson lamented the unfair treatment his team endured, hyperbolically describing the event as follows:

> The timer, his gun poised in the air, ready to end the game, was interrupted in the performance of his duty by a gentle tap on his arm. He turned toward the interrupter to find a little old lady who said only "Wait!" which he did. There was a fraction of a second's play, a shot was made, the gun discharged, the ball bounced against the bank board and into the basket—two points and a tie game.

Fortunately, this perceived mistreatment only delayed Pitt's victory.[65]

Carlson maintained a strong interest in expanding the reach of his innovative offense and rarely turned down opportunities to play new teams in new areas. As such, he agreed to pit his Panthers against Montana State in a 1930 game staged by the support group for the emerging Basketball Hall of Fame. Organizers picked the teams mostly on merit—Pitt was the retrospective 1928 national champion and Montana State received the same honor from Premo and Porretta and Helms in 1929—and they promoted it as a "championship game." This "championship game" was little more than a one-time spectacle to promote the Hall of Fame, and most knew that it could not live up to its moniker. Pitt's 37–36 victory on a last-second shot by future Hall of Famer Chuck Hyatt—two of Hyatt's game-high 27 points—did, however, help earn the Panthers the retrospective top spot in Helms's 1930 poll despite an increasingly talented and sophisticated world of college basketball teams. The 1930 All-Big Ten first team featured four players who would go on to win NCAA tournament titles or postseason #1 rankings as coaches (Branch McCracken played at Indiana and coached the Hoosiers to 1940 and 1953 NCAA titles, Harold "Bud" Foster played at Wisconsin and coached the Badgers to the 1941 NCAA title, Doug Mills played at Illinois and coached the Illini to a #1 ranking in 1943—his team disbanded at the end of the regular season after losing too many players to the war—and John Wooden played at Purdue and won ten NCAA titles at UCLA).[66]

In the early 1930s, Carlson, Springfield coach Ed Hickox, and Ohio State coach Harold Olsen began evangelizing their NABC peers to invite teams to play showcase games at the NABC convention held every April. Top teams continued to dot the basketball landscape from many different sections of the country, and many of their coaches attended the convention. This proposal would, no doubt, give more publicity to the seasons' top teams. Carlson, Hickox, and Olsen hoped to be able to promote games among top teams from different regions so coaches could witness differing styles of play. In previous years, the convention agenda included different coaches talking about the game, its rules, its administration, and some of their strategies that had been particularly successful. However, with the regionalization that still plagued the game, discussion about strategies and tactics may not have been the most successful way to share ideas. Carlson, Hickox, and Olsen believed exhibition games featuring teams from different regions could better demonstrate differing styles of play.[67]

The NABC agreed to such an event in 1934 when the association reached new territory by convening in Atlanta. Carlson nominated his own team for the exhibition, joining South Carolina, Northern Illinois Teachers College, and Illinois Wesleyan for the first-ever NABC exhibition games. The *Atlanta Constitution*, a daily outlet that covered the convention closely, mentioned that each of the four teams had been chosen based on their standing as the top teams in their respective regions, even though the two Illinois schools were located within 120 miles of each other. Nevertheless, on Thursday night, March 29, the exhibition games tipped off, providing yet another example of intersectional college basketball competition. It is unclear how many of the 200-plus coaches at the convention attended the games.[68]

Attendance across the country had been closely monitored all year. Teams from the South noted a continued decrease in attendance at their games, resulting in financial losses. This trend began, for many of these schools, shortly after the stock market crash in October 1929. Adolph Rupp, coach of the perennially popular Kentucky Wildcats, noted that his team had only played one home game in front of a sellout crowd during the 1933–34 season. Many teams in the East and Midwest, on the contrary, noted increases in their game attendance that season. *Atlanta Constitution* reporters heard that Iowa had broken the Big Ten attendance record with 13,200 fans at one game. Because of these opposing trends, many of the coaches and reporters in attendance attributed the South's attendance decrease not to the Depression but to the poor quality of that region's teams. Thus, the NABC exhibition games could give coaches from the region exposure to tactics that teams across the country successfully employed. The NABC guessed that their exhibition games would thus be successful. They also wanted to reimburse the participating exhibition teams for their travel to Atlanta, and they did so by charging a small fee for the coaches who watched the exhibitions at the Atlanta Athletic Club. The modest admission fee enabled the NABC to reimburse each team an even more modest $11.55 for their travel—a sum that provided a welcome gesture but did not cover travel costs.[69]

The NABC decided on twenty-minute games for the exhibition series in hopes that this would be a good amount of time to showcase different playing styles and proposed rule changes. Pitt and Northern Illinois Teachers squared off on opening night. Pitt, led by the "hallroom boys"—three players who hailed from the Allegheny Mountains east of Pittsburgh and were supposedly so poor that they had to live in an unheated and draughty corner hall room of a "dilapidated war-time building that serves as Pitt's stack house"—possessed outstanding speed that took them to a 24–13 victory over the northerners. The "hallroom boys," probably enjoying a reprieve from their frosty northern lodging, scored 16 of Pitt's points. In the nightcap, Illinois Wesleyan's "hefty" squad overpowered South Carolina, 18–14. Both games included a proposed rule that a fouled player gets the chance to shoot from the spot on the floor in which he was fouled. Those fouled under the basket were allowed to jump when attempting their "foul shot."[70]

The following night the winners and losers squared off. South Carolina defeated Northern Illinois, 17-10, in the third-place game. And Pitt's speed overtook Illinois Wesleyan's brawn in the first-place game, winning 18–15. While Pitt and Dr. Carlson took pride as the class of the demonstration games, no one doubted the modesty of these abbreviated appearances. The implementation of new rule proposals gave the games a clear exhibition feel. Further, while Pitt and South Carolina were big-name schools that had enjoyed some kind of national status—South Carolina ranked second in Premo and Porretta's 1933 poll and first in 1934 and Pitt ranked eighth in Premo and Porretta's 1934 poll—Northern Illinois and Illinois Wesleyan did not have national names. Few could argue that this was a championship of top teams in the country.[71]

However, the NABC enjoyed the experience and immediately afterward its constituents agreed to a second installment with increased emphasis the following year—including two sectional games before a final, increased promotion, and an attempt to turn a profit. Efforts stalled, though, as post-convention excitement waned, and the exhibitions never transpired into a tournament for which many members hoped. In the 1935 NABC convention in Chicago, exhibition games to show proposed rule changes continued, but only two local teams—DePaul and Illinois Wesleyan—received invites. The *Chicago Tribune* only mentioned the two teams once and stated clearly that they engaged in "practice contests." Any momentum from 1934 for a true NABC national tournament fell away.[72]

The year 1934 also marked two other notable national basketball developments. The NABC exhibition was not Pitt's only unique endeavor that year. A group of Atlantic City, New Jersey, businessmen generated the idea of hosting an end-of-season basketball game that would serve as "the Rose Bowl of basketball." They called their contest the American Legion Bowl and invited Carlson's troops to face Louisiana State University (LSU). Although Premo and Porretta retrospectively ranked Pitt eighth in 1934 and LSU did not even make the top twenty, local organizers referred to this as a championship game. The Panthers outplayed the southerners for most of the tilt until, incredibly, the Pitt players began turning the ball over hastily, which resulted in a loss. Their play became so sloppy that newspaper reporters at the game thought these errors occurred purposefully. While point shaving and "throwing" games crippled college basketball in future decades, no moral or legal condemnation ensued.[73]

Carlson took direct blame for his players' sloppy play at the end of the game. Neither gamblers nor bookies encouraged his troops' slovenliness. Instead, he claimed later that he called for the errors. Carlson caught wind before the game of a Sugar Bowl of Basketball to be held in Louisiana at the end of the following season. Knowing the fantastic treatment the visiting football teams always received there, and knowing that the organizing committee was searching for an opponent to face the home team—LSU— the Pitt mentor took a consequentialist approach to the American Legion Bowl. Even though it seemed apparent at the American Legion Bowl that Pitt was the superior team, Carlson believed that if he lost then his team would have better chances of being invited to the following season's Sugar Bowl of Basketball than if his team won. After all, a rematch of the previous season's "championship" game in which Pitt, the clear favorite, sought to avenge a previous upset victory, would have Sugar Bowl promoters salivating.[74]

Carlson's foresight paid off as Sugar Bowl officials invited his team to the inaugural Sugar Bowl of Basketball in 1935. Pitt won the rematch, 52–47, in a game that proved wildly successful. Local organizers built off this success, and the Sugar Bowl of Basketball continued for more than forty years. The American Legion Bowl, on the contrary, found no such success. After Pitt threw the inaugural event in 1934, the game's administrators ceased operations. However, some good for the game of basketball certainly came from the Atlantic City contest. Apparently, a young, entrepreneurial New York City sports reporter named Ned Irish watched the 1934 Pitt-LSU contest with keen interest.[75]

Moving to the Big Stage

Legend has it that while covering local college basketball for the *New York Daily News*, Irish had difficulty gaining admission to many contests because campus gyms were so small. One evening, he arrived just before tip-off to find himself locked out of a gym that was jam-packed beyond capacity. Needing to cover the game to appease his editor, Irish found an open athletic department office window and climbed through, ripping his pants on the way down. Irish vowed then and there never to resort to such embarrassing practices in the future, and propositioned Madison Square Garden to let him promote and host college basketball games there. In 1961, *Sports Illustrated* revealed the reality of this story. Bill Stern, a radio personality "whose fables were imposed on innocent radio listeners some twenty years ago," embellished the story like he did many others. The idealism in the hyperbolic tale became central to Irish's legacy.[76]

In reality, the idea to host basketball games at Madison Square Garden was not Irish's at all. The young journalist had been part of a group of sportswriters who carried out New York City mayor Jimmy Walker's 1931 charge to hold a "college basketball spectacular" in the Garden to raise Depression relief funds. Irish, then making less than $60 a week as a newspaper reporter who also moonlighted as the publicist for football's New York Giants, saw how this January 19, 1931, college basketball triple-header in the Garden attracted a capacity crowd and dreamed of its potential. The initial event's success encouraged Mayor Walker to license another similar event. On February 22, 1933, a seven-game afternoon and evening docket drew 20,000 fans. A year later, Irish contacted John Reed Kilpatrick, then president of Madison Square Garden, and asked if he could host college basketball games in the mammoth arena. Irish asked for leave from his journalism with the *New York World Telegram* to pursue this promotions opportunity. When the newspaper denied his request, Irish quit, showing confidence that this venture would succeed. Yet he continued his publicity work for the Giants just in case. Luckily, Kilpatrick and Madison Square Garden believed Irish would succeed, too. The Garden president had received other such offers from entrepreneurial promoters, but noted that Irish's was different. "Ned Irish was the only one who had a concrete plan and a sound knowledge of what he was doing," Kilpatrick remembered. The president, looking for ways to fill the Garden on cold winter weeknights, agreed to give Irish a shot. The young sportswriter ensured the Garden that he had guaranteed backing from Giants owner Tim Mara to the tune of the $4,000 rental fee the venue charged, but reimbursing Kilpatrick or Mara was not Irish's focus. Having quit his day job, he knew that if his receipts did not cover the rental fee, the Garden would not allow him to return and he would be out of another job.[77]

Irish originally attempted to begin his Garden promotions with a game featuring NYU and CCNY in March 1934. Both teams were at the end of undefeated seasons and likely would have drawn a sizable local crowd, but Irish could not find an acceptable date for all three parties. The young entrepreneur then invited Notre Dame and its star, Edward "Moose" Krause, nine months later to face NYU on December 29, 1934. As insurance, Irish also asked Westminster College of Pennsylvania to take on St. John's of Brooklyn that night, but NYU-Notre Dame was the big draw. Notre Dame, with a football team that had become among the most prominent in the country over the past decade, enjoyed a national sports following—especially among American Catholics—that was unparalleled. "Moose" Krause served as a tight end on the football team, a position that thrust him into nationwide fame. He also starred for the Irish hoops squad. The two-sport star became a centerpiece of Irish's marketing for this unprecedented venture into "big-time" college basketball in New York City. Krause's star power helped the publicity, but it was not enough on the court. NYU fended off the Fighting Irish 25–18. The quality competition justified the invite for the South Bend, Indiana, team to travel all the way to New York for one game, setting up an annual rivalry that lasted twenty-three years. However, the real value of the game lay in the box office statistics: 16,188 fans paid admission, providing the Garden with profits in excess of $4,000, earning Irish more than enough in one night to justify quitting his day job, and relieving Mara of any potential debt obligations.[78]

Irish built on this success, hosting seven more college basketball double-headers that season. Five of these ballgames pitted a local New York City school against a visiting team. Purdue, Kentucky, Temple, and Duquesne provided a top-notch sampling of regional basketball styles at the Garden in 1934–35. Most of these teams played against NYU, and all of them drew more than 6,000 fans to the Garden. These intersectional matchups gave visiting teams a chance to experience New York City's tough and patterned style of basketball while visiting the "Big Apple." It also gave New York City teams a chance to test themselves against the best competition—and potentially different styles of play—across the country. But these were all added benefits. Irish's main selling point to attract local teams to the Garden was its size. NYU, winner against Notre Dame in front of more than 16,000 at the Garden in 1934, had a student population of 7,500 but a gymnasium that could only seat 1,500. CCNY, a squad that Irish had originally sought for a Garden date, enrolled 12,000 students, but its gymnasium seated only 1,200. Fordham's gym, probably the largest on-campus metropolitan venue at the time, sat 2,500 and probably came closest to being able to accommodate its entire student body. Madison Square Garden could accommodate all of the students from any of the local schools who might want a ticket to watch their team play—and no local campus gymnasium could say the same.[79]

Irish hosted ten double-headers in 1935–36 that drew almost 160,000 spectators. This docket of games mirrored the previous season—some intersectional games and some local showdowns. Immediately after the season, Irish and Madison Square Garden hosted the Olympic Basketball Trials, the first postseason championship event the "Big Apple" had hosted since 1900 when a round robin of four local teams comprised the AAU National Championship tournament. Basketball had changed drastically since then, and New York City was now very well prepared to host the nation's top amateur teams.[80]

The 1936 Olympic Trials

The 1936 United States Olympic basketball tournament came about with considerable administrative squabbling. Although basketball had matured since the 1904 Olympic basketball tournaments in St. Louis, the game's administration remained discordant. The AAU and the NCAA both administered amateur basketball circuits, but neither of these circuits had an outright claim to overall national supremacy. Further, the NCAA had no national tournament to establish its top teams. As such, no basis existed by which the Olympic Basketball Committee could determine who should and should not be selected to play on the team that would represent basketball's birthplace at the Berlin Games. The Olympic Basketball Committee, chaired by Dr. Walter Meanwell of Wisconsin and assisted by AAU president J. Lyman Bingham, decided to host an eight-team tournament in April 1936 to determine the makeup of the German-bound squad. The tournament champion would choose seven of its players for the American roster, the runner-up would select six of its players for the team, and the committee would choose one more outstanding player from the tournament to round out the national team.[81]

Meanwell, Bingham, and the committee of NCAA, AAU, and American Olympic Committee officials invited teams to the Olympic Basketball Trials in New York City as fairly as they could. However, without much understanding of the relative ability levels among NCAA teams, AAU teams, and even YMCA teams, this would be no easy task. AAU teams, the committee decided, would receive two of the eight trial tournament spots. AAU officials decided that the association's national tournament champion and runner-up would receive invites to the New York event. The YMCA received one spot that would go to its national champion. The NCAA, then, received the remaining five entries.[82]

While this setup appeared to give a competitive edge to the NCAA, that sort of advantage may not have been the committee's rationale. In fact, although the NCAA had the most teams competing at the Olympic Trials, each of them may have been at a distinct disadvantage. The NCAA had no postseason championship tournament by which it could select its top five teams. The AAU and YMCA did, and so they would have no trouble selecting their representative teams. The NCAA, however, had to create a method by which it would select its five teams. So the association divided its membership into ten districts that would each determine a representative. These ten district representatives would each square off against the representative from a neighboring district. The five winners would move on to the trials in New York City.[83]

One of the reasons that the Olympic Basketball Committee gave the colleges five spots in the tournament had to do with revenue. The AAU and YMCA kept the money from their national tournaments because they were established and would happen even in non-Olympic years. College teams, on the contrary, had no such tournament, and the NCAA had no such contract on the proceedings. Intra-district play-off games and the series of competitions whereby the ten district teams would be whittled down to five had the potential to bring in gate receipts that could help fund the American Olympic Committee in grand style. Thus, the Olympic Basketball Committee doled out five college bids in an attempt to raise funds for the overall Olympic team's travel eastward.

The district qualifying process was a medley of games, tournaments, and decisions. In District 3 of the southeast and District 8 of the Rocky Mountains, committees simply chose the representatives. District 9 of the Pacific Northwest and District 10 of the Pacific Coast created a tournament for the top two teams in both the Pacific Coast Conference's North and South divisions. District 4 of the south-central United States, District 6 of the north-central, and District 7 of the American heartland all held four-team play-off tournaments. District 1 of the northeast and District 2 of the mid-Atlantic hosted five team tournaments. And District 5 of the Great Lakes held a ten-team play-off.[84]

A Temple team that would win the inaugural National Invitation Tournament two years later earned the District 2 selection and defeated District 1 representative Niagara for one trials slot. An Arkansas team that started its basketball program on campus only ten years earlier won the District 4 entry and beat District 3's Western Kentucky. Giant-slaying DePaul, a team that was becoming the bane of the Big Ten by frequently taking down its top teams, earned the District 5 nod and beat yet another Big Ten team, District 6 representative Minnesota, for a trials slot. Washington earned the right to move on from Districts 9 and 10. And Utah State, representing District 8 defeated District 7's Kansas in a three-game series. The Kansas-Utah State series amplified some of the administrative difficulties in pulling this Olympic Trials event together. Coach Phog Allen of Kansas led much of the dialogue regarding American Olympic basketball at the time. Allen was the leading proponent of the NCAA's participation in the Olympic Basketball Trials and, so he thought, in getting basketball onto the Olympic docket. He was also firmly behind this district play-off system as a way in which the college teams could generate funding for the American Olympic contingent.[85]

Kansas had ended the regular season 18-0 with great form. In the District 7 play-off, the Jayhawks took down Washburn College and Oklahoma A&M to win the right to face Aggies of another state. Utah State came to Kansas City for the interdistrict play-off series only conditionally. Allen agreed to pay the Aggies $500 from the gate to cover their travel expenses. Kansas took the first game in overtime, 39-37, but surprisingly lost the second, 42-37. And the tide continued Utah State's way in the rubber match as Kansas could do nothing to stave off elimination, losing 50-31. Despite Allen's disappointment at the losses, he was relieved that the series generated $10,000. However, that relief quickly turned to anger when he found out that all of that money would go to the AAU before it could help the Olympic basketball team, leading him to refer to the AAU as "quadrennial oceanic hitchhikers who chisel their way across the oceans every four years on the other fellow's money."[86]

The Olympic Basketball Trials commenced in Madison Square Garden on April 3, a date that coincided with the end of the NABC annual convention also in New York City that year. Many NABC members stayed to watch the proceedings of the trials, which ended with the two AAU teams in the championship game. That meant that, of the fourteen-man roster that would be going to Berlin, only one player—Ralph Bishop of Washington, who was chosen as the alternate by the committee—came from college fives. This bothered the coaches of the NABC, who felt that they had provided the impetus for getting basketball into the Olympics in the first place. The

Olympic Basketball Committee shared an equal amount of disappointment, but for a different reason. The Olympic Trials and the college district and interdistrict games leading up to the trials had not produced nearly the revenue the American Olympic Committee expected. Olympic Basketball Committee secretary Bingham reported, "The games were an unqualified success from the point of view of excellence of competition, but were a complete failure from the standpoint of attendance and raising money to send the team to Berlin," adding that the committee "would have been money ahead had the final games not been played." Bingham had expected college district games to generate between $100,000 and $200,000 for the Olympic cause. The actual amount generated did not reach that estimate, and the Madison Square Garden tournament lost money. In fact, the final profit was so small that the players chosen for the Olympics—many who hailed from California and Kansas—had to fund their own travel to New York City in August to board the Berlin-bound ship.[87]

Through this administrative mess, the NABC coaches realized a few things. First, college basketball was popular, powerful, and full of potential. If Olympic Basketball Committee officials believed that a series of play-off games could generate between $100,000 and $200,000, then they believed in the power of that sport at that level to amass excitement and enthusiastic fan support. Second, the addition of the still-burgeoning NCAA would be crucial to the success of a postseason endeavor. Since the NCAA did not license or oversee the interdistrict play-offs, there was little coherence to it, and it flopped financially. The NCAA's oversight could have changed that by providing start-up funds and authorizing a more "big-time" feel to the events. Third, postseason tournaments could be successful. Because of the cost of travel and the uncertainty of crowd support in some areas of the country, holding a postseason tournament that earned a financial profit would not be easy but was a definite possibility. Last, in order for a postseason tournament to reach its potential, it had to include the nation's top teams. This was not the case in the 1936 Olympic Basketball Tournament. Many teams did not participate for academic reasons—players had already missed enough class time. Others did not participate on political grounds. Long Island University, for instance, finished the 1935–36 season undefeated, and many believed they were the top quintet in the country—at any level. However, since the majority of the Blackbirds were Jewish and the Olympics were hosted by the Nazis, the team and its coach, Clair Bee, decided not to participate in the trials. This omission marred the event, as many believed that LIU could have beaten any of the eight participants.[88]

Premo and Porretta listed LIU as the top 1936 team, and Helms had

Notre Dame on top. Neither of these teams participated in the trials, and this hurt the event. But both figured prominently in Ned Irish's regular season schedules at Madison Square Garden. Despite the low spectator turnout, the Garden received a boost in national prominence when it hosted the Olympic Trials, and its standing increased even further eight months later.

Star Power

On December 30, 1936, Irish, the Garden, college basketball, and New York City hit the jackpot. The promoter invited Stanford to the Garden on its coast-to-coast road trip to face the undefeated Long Island Blackbirds. The locals had a 43-game winning streak on the line that the West Coast quintet busted in fine fashion. Stanford guard Hank Luisetti put on a dazzling show for the season-high 17,623 New York City fans who paid admission. His 15 points led the way to a 45–31 Indian (then Stanford's nickname) victory. While the scoring seems relatively modest, newspapers the next day gushed over his ballhandling wizardry and, more importantly, his cutting-edge one-handed jump shot. "It seemed Luisetti could do nothing wrong," sportswriter Francis J. O'Riley reported. "Some of his shots would have been deemed foolhardy if attempted by any other player, but with Luisetti doing the heaving, these were accepted by the crowd as a matter of course." Although Luisetti had been shooting that way for West Coast audiences for years, demonstrating his unique skill in the media capital of the world catapulted his fame and the reverence for his unorthodox skill.[89]

Irish hosted more and more college basketball soirees at the Garden as loyal local fans continued to grease the turnstiles. Twelve nights of college basketball in the Garden in 1936–37 drew more than 140,000 fans. In order to ensure large crowds, Irish usually scheduled two and sometimes even three games per night as he brought college basketball into the massive arena. In the middle of the 1930s, the Garden had room for college basketball on its docket, as the building was occupied "maybe 30 percent of the time." Kilpatrick usually had weeknights available during the winter for college hoops showcases. And yet, basketball came at just the right time. Indeed, by 1941, the regular Garden weekly schedule had no vacancy with tennis on Mondays, hockey on Tuesdays, basketball on Wednesdays, hockey on Thursdays, boxing on Fridays, and a dance on Saturdays. Thus, as Irish increased the amount of basketball games in the Garden each year, it was not to simply fill an empty Garden. College basketball's popularity, led by Luisetti and the like, forced Kilpatrick to grant the promoter more nights because the Garden leaders could not ignore the profits that came from the hoops double-headers.[90]

While local matchups in the Garden brought in large partisan crowds, intersectional contests in these early years created the momentum to revolutionize the game. These contests had a lot to offer: visiting teams enjoyed the "New York experience," local fans appreciated seeing the visiting talent, and Ned Irish made loads of money. They also began the process of creating a national basketball consciousness. The college game, which generated rabid enthusiasm in certain parts of the country, remained regionalized at the time. In 1934, *Time* magazine noted as much, stating, "A winter sport which in some parts of the U.S. amounts to a seasonal hysteria, (basketball) is played almost entirely within regional leagues." While Irish's intersectional games began changing this malady, *Time* also explained that "The argument of each league that it has the best team in the land is more footless than most such controversies." By early 1937, Irish had not yet fully rectified this perceived knock on college basketball.[91]

Championships and Titles in Hindsight

While hosting tournaments like the AAU's model seems now like it would have been an easy decision for college basketball administrators at the time, it certainly was not. Single-elimination tournaments were not the only models of determining a "champion." Indeed many early AAU events followed the round-robin format. Yet not every "championship" considered itself a tournament. Pitt participated in the American Legion Bowl in 1934 and the Sugar Bowl in 1935—both games in which the winner claimed to be a "champion." That many of the early basketball attempts at national title games and events focused on the football bowl model indicates that college basketball desired a national title in any form, and that college basketball envied college football's postseason at least to some extent. Although college football has struggled over the years to find a fair and accurate method of determining its national champion—falling far behind college basketball— bowl games evoked envy in early college basketball administrators. In fact, in the 1940s and 1950s many football bowl games also invited two basketball teams to square off during the winter holidays to add to the local attractions. However, the logistics of most of these games being played in the middle of basketball season precluded them from having much impact on national title discussions. Further, postseason basketball bowl games like Pitt and LSU's matchups in 1934 and 1935 seemed unable to garner much attention outside of the local media. One lone final game between two top basketball teams seemed unable to generate as much national media interest as lone end-of-season football games.

Once national championship tournaments established consistency in the 1940s and 1950s, William Schroeder of the Helms Foundation, and later Premo and Porretta began their quests to retrospectively crown national championship teams in both football and basketball. In football, the relatively small number of powerhouse teams each season and the small number of bowl games that the top teams attended made this practice palatable. Basketball, however, presented a difficult task for these ambitious individuals.

Schroeder published his rankings and retrospective "titles" in booklets that were not widely disseminated or accepted at the time. The obvious difficulties in the task he undertook provided college basketball fans with little reason to believe that his efforts represented anything more than an interesting side project for a very avid sports fan. Premo and Porretta often agreed with Schroeder by choosing the same top team, but also showed a great deal of discrepancy. These differences provide evidence of both the difficulty of the task that Schroeder and Premo and Porretta undertook and the ways in which, without a national championship tournament or play-off, determining a national champion is very difficult (a complication college football realized much, much later), especially considering the regionalization that plagued basketball even beyond the 1930s. Despite the obvious limitations to these retrospective polls, they remain the simplest and therefore the most popular way to understand college basketball's primitive national landscape before 1938.[92]

The Helms and Premo and Porretta polls show biases that demand further analysis. Both polls heavily favored large schools that played reputable regular season schedules as they made their retrospective rankings. Although relatively obscure schools often staked their claims to early basketball "championship game titles," the retrospective pollsters rarely gave much weight to these one-off end-of-season events or their unfamiliar champions. For instance, in 1904, although Hiram College won the college division title of the Olympics, Schroeder and Premo and Porretta identify Columbia as the season's top team. In 1915, even though Washburn won the AAU tournament, Schroeder and Premo and Porretta both give the nod to an undefeated Illinois squad. In 1922, Wabash won the National Intercollegiate Basketball Tournament in Indianapolis, but Schroeder names Kansas as the top team, even though the Indianapolis tournament's selection committee had a difficult time determining whether or not Kansas was even that region's top team. Premo and Porretta's top choice of Missouri seemed to be just as formidable, and both teams generated discussions regarding tournament invitation even though neither participated.[93]

How these small schools and others like AAU champion Butler in 1924 would have stacked up against Schroeder's or Premo and Porretta's top picks is anyone's guess. These small schools all won tournaments while the retrospective picks did not. The retrospective pollsters' picks showed strength throughout the entire regular season. It may be more appropriate to think of these retrospective picks as receiving an end-of-the-season #1 ranking rather than a "championship" title. Even by today's standards, finishing the regular season as the #1 team is somewhat prestigious, but it matters little if a team cannot win a postseason tournament. History shows that very few overall #1 teams at the end of the regular season win postseason tournaments in college basketball, and we tend to remember tournament champions rather than top regular season teams. Therefore, had Hiram played Columbia in 1904, Washburn played Illinois in 1915, or Wabash played Kansas in 1922, for example, who knows which team would have won in a one-off game to determine supremacy much like we see in today's March Madness format.

Schroeder's and Premo and Porretta's picks fell rather closely in line with whatever general consensus existed in 1908 and 1920. At the end of these two seasons, Chicago and Penn determined that they were the top teams in the West and East, respectively, and faced off in best-of-three series for the title of national champion. While Chicago won in 1908 and Penn won in 1920, it serves as no coincidence that Schroeder chose Chicago in 1908 and Penn in 1920. Premo and Porretta had Chicago second and Penn third in 1908, and Penn first and Chicago tenth in 1920. Schroeder also chose Pitt as the top team in 1930 most likely based on its Hall of Fame–sponsored "title" victory. In this contest, promoted as the "national championship," Pitt defeated Montana State—a team Schroeder identified as the previous season's best. Premo and Porretta ranked Pitt third that year and did not even have Montana State in the top 20.[94]

Between 1901 and 1943—the years that Schroeder made retrospective choices—Premo and Porretta's picks match those made by Schroeder in the top spot twenty-five times. On the one hand, this consistency is remarkable considering the fragmented nature of college basketball during those years. On the other hand, the fact that eighteen of the forty-three choices differed serves as a reminder of just how futile retrospectively determining a champion in the wilderness of early college basketball can be. The retrospective rankings are most helpful in determining which teams were among the best in these early seasons rather than which team was number one. Therefore, since Premo and Porretta ranked twenty teams, they provide a much more robust indication of which teams were best even if the actual rank of each team came about relatively arbitrarily. However, Premo and Porretta published their rankings in 1995—one hundred years after the first season they analyzed. In this sense, Schroeder's rankings may be more reliable since he conducted his research by interviewing coaches and media members who had actually seen many of these teams play.

Regardless of the interpretation of these retrospective rankings, they provide context for discussing the prowess of early college basketball teams. They also underscore the need for a formal basis to determine superiority. Interestingly, using a postseason single-elimination tournament to determine the season's champion like the college basketball establishment does today may not be a perfect method either. After all, what makes March Madness so captivating to fans is the fact that it encompasses so many upsets. The NCAA basketball tournament, for instance, so appeals to fans because so many lower-ranked teams beat higher-ranked teams. While this creates viewer excitement, it decreases our ability to understand who the best teams are each year. There is never any question regarding who wins the NCAA tournament each year, and we endow that team with the label of "national champion" without any argument. Indeed, the history of the NCAA tournament has proven that the regular season's best team rarely wins the NCAA tournament. In fact, in some seasons, teams have won the NCAA championship without even winning their conference title. Schroeder and Premo and Porretta, without the help of a season-ending national tournament, ranked teams based on their overall season record. With the NCAA tournament continually growing today, overall season record means much less than it did in the days before championship tournaments. What matters most today is how hot a team is at the end of the season.

While the current method may not be perfectly fair—if only one team across the country ends the season undefeated after having played a difficult schedule, that team has no right to the national title unless they win the national tournament—this style of tournament caught on very quickly in the late 1930s not because of its equitability but because of its uncertainty and excitement that has always been of such interest to fans.

CHAPTER 2

Genesis of the Kansas City and New York City Tournaments, 1937–1938

Ned Irish's promotion of intersectional college basketball games at Madison Square Garden occurred in unlikely circumstances. America in the 1930s provided great difficulties for businessmen and entrepreneurs alike. The Great Depression produced a backdrop of financial insecurity and frugality among a generation of Americans who quickly learned the limits of their willingness and ability to save and persevere through difficult times. Saving, securing, and stabilizing became the key economic model across the country.

In this unlikely context, Irish's events at the Garden enjoyed growth and success. The depressed economy, it seemed, was no match for college basketball. New Yorkers had no problem reaching deep into their pockets to find the spare change they needed to fill a seat at a Wednesday night double-header in New York City's prized venue. Spectator sporting events have time and again proven their immunity to the human symptoms of mass economic recession. Indeed, even in the midst of America's greatest economic downturn, citizens continued to show interest in sporting events. Baseball became the strongest antidote in the 1930s across the country. The national pastime entertained Americans on the long, hot summer afternoons, diverting their attentions away from job losses, slashed incomes, and debt accrual. By the middle of the 1930s, Ned Irish's college basketball double-headers did the same thing for New Yorkers during the long, cold winter weeknights.[1]

Early Basketball Geography

Although New York City had the population, media, and sights to attract college basketball teams from all over the country like no other city could, it was not the exclusive hub of hoops. The early success and growth of numerous college, scholastic, and AAU teams across the country produced pockets of passion for the basket game. In its first forty-five years of existence, basketball had become more than simply a stopgap between football and baseball season like the YMCA Training School instructors originally intended. In certain regions of the country, it turned into a way of life. Dr. Henry Carlson of Pitt and Charles "Chick" Davies of Duquesne promoted basketball heavily at their universities in the Steel City and its surrounding western Pennsylvania mining towns. Carlson and Davies set the standard that produced many stars throughout the first half of the twentieth century. Coach John Bunn built a strong program at Stanford, encouraging the creativity and instincts of playmakers like Hank Luisetti, who captivated audiences in the Bay Area and wherever he played. The phrase "West Coast basketball" had a certain exotic connotation that captured the innovative techniques of the ruthless westerners. Chicago became an early basketball haven, too. The Windy City's strong Catholic, Eastern European immigrant community found favor with the hoops game, and its sons—toughened from the hard knocks of living as low-class citizens on the street—dotted the rosters of the successful early DePaul, Loyola, and Notre Dame squads. Chicago's protestant sons found fame at the University of Chicago, Northwestern, or nearby Purdue.[2]

Purdue enjoyed a geographic location ideally situated near Chicago's blossoming basketball establishment and also amid the growing Hoosier Hysteria for the hoops game. Purdue, Indiana, Butler, and Indiana State benefited in no small way from the statewide interest in local hoops, as did smaller schools such as Wabash and DePauw. The Hoosier State's passion for the hardwood game became the exemplar for midwestern interest in basketball that paralleled New York City's hoops fervor but had different characteristics. Indeed, the game that Indiana boys played in the open spaces and relative isolation of farm lots, school gyms, and barns differed greatly from that played by New York City boys in the crowded, tight spaces of back alleys, dance halls, and settlement houses—even though the basketball zeal of these two groups may have reached the same levels.[3]

Indiana's passion for the game in its early decades found competition nearby. Ohio State coach Harold Olsen presented perennially strong teams matched by Toledo and Bowling Green that promoted basketball interest in the Buckeye State. Kentucky coach Adolph Rupp set off hysteria for hoops in the Bluegrass State as his early teams dominated the American South. Despite Rupp's dictatorship over the state's hoops, Western Kentucky also came to national recognition. Illinois coach Craig Ruby put forth strong early teams that provided an attractor for young athletes downstate in the Land of Lincoln. Much smaller schools such as Illinois Wesleyan, Northern Illinois Teachers College, and Wheaton also made blips on the national radar.

Farther into the American heartland, Missouri, Oklahoma, and Kansas caught the fever. Hoops in the heartland became among the most popular activities to withstand the bitter winds and frigid temperatures characteristic of winters across the plains.[4]

Back along the Eastern Seaboard, New York City was not the lone basketball-mad metropolis. Philadelphia provided the Big Apple with its closest regional peer. The City of Brotherly Love seemed to match New York City in its hoops popularity, but the former did not have the massive media engine to promote itself in the same way. Rochester, Buffalo, Syracuse, and other middle-market cities in the East also became prodigious basketball locales, growing in the image of the Empire State's most famous city. These towns, just outside the sight of Lady Liberty but within the Empire, could not match the national interest that only Gotham could generate. Indeed, no other city affected the evolution of basketball in its early years like the Big Apple. In fact, the next most basketball-revolutionizing city came from halfway across the country and promoted a basketball character expected of a town nestled in the center of the American heartland. Kansas City did more to promote early basketball than any other city outside of the Big Apple.[5]

Kansas City and Muscular Christianity

Kansas City's emergence as an early national hoops leader had three main forces. First, the prominent Kansas City Athletic Club (KCAC) under the direction of Dr. Joseph A. Reilly initially provided great support for the game. The KCAC produced first-rate teams and hosted early championships. Dr. Reilly was influential in bringing the AAU national championship tournament to Kansas City in 1921. However, the Garden City may not have had the chance to host these tournaments if it had not successfully hosted the 1905 "World's Championship" tournament between the host KCAC team and the 1904 Olympic champion Buffalo Germans. While Dr. Reilly played a part in this event, its sine qua non was a twenty-year-old native of the Kansas City suburb of Independence, Missouri. Phog Allen became the second main force behind the basketball status of Kansas City. Allen, an entrepreneur throughout his life, served the Kansas City area well and became much better known nationally than Reilly because of the former's coaching feats. Allen's early coaching, however, occurred against the wishes of his college coach, Dr. James Naismith—Kansas City's third main hoops force. Nearby Kansas University hired Naismith in 1898 to be on its faculty, a position he held until his retirement in 1937. Naismith evangelized for the game until the day he died, and the region in which he worked for thirty-nine years benefited greatly. Allen was one of Naismith's students and players, and the bold young Missourian took local interest in the game to a whole new level—one with which the founder of the game may not have ever expected.[6]

Allen and Naismith present a system of contrasts that, together, allowed basketball to reach ever-increasing audiences. Naismith, by all accounts a humble, conscientious, and idealistic man of strong faith and moral character, believed in the extrinsic benefits of the game above all else. While basketball was fun to play, the founder believed his game's great contribution to society was that it promoted vigorous health and its players developed moral characteristics that contributed positively to greater society. This emphasis on moral development in sport categorized Naismith as a "Muscular Christian." Muscular Christianity emphasized sports and physical activity as a way to create tough yet moral-minded men in the Protestant Church who would carry the gospel of Jesus Christ with strength, courage, and conviction. This cultural crusade provided an antidote to what many feared as the negative trends of an increasingly industrialized society—men of the church were no longer farmers or laborers but had become weak, effeminate, and poor examples of godly men. Indeed, weak and effeminate men would be of no help in the calls to action so central to the teachings of Jesus Christ.[7]

As such, in the late 1800s and early 1900s, Muscular Christianity took root in greater American society. YMCAs opened all across the country and promoted moral and spiritual development through sport and physical activity. The hub of this crusade became the Springfield, Massachusetts, YMCA Training School. Headmaster Luther Gulick guided a program of higher education that taught young men the principles of the Bible and the ways in which sport could help them learn and transmit those principles. Naismith taught at this school and espoused its ethos. In the fall of 1891, Gulick had two prized pupils on his staff—Naismith and Amos Alonzo Stagg, a football and baseball star at Yale in the 1880s. When the two men met, Naismith reminisced, "Stagg grasped my hand with a grip that he was accustomed to use on a baseball, and I retaliated with a grasp that I had learned in wrestling. Our friendship has been a lasting one." Gulick chose Stagg to travel the country that year evangelizing Muscular Christianity at every church, school, and YMCA he could find. Naismith, however, remained in Springfield where he invented basketball that winter. When Stagg returned from his sojourn, he learned Naismith's game and quickly realized its value. The following summer, Stagg left Springfield to join Dr. William Rainey Harper at the upstart University of Chicago. Harper inaugurated the school as president and Stagg became the school's director of the Department of Physical Culture and Athletics, a tenured professor, as well as the head baseball, football, and track coach.[8]

Stagg was gregarious, strong willed, opinionated, confident, forceful, and persuasive. His talents, no doubt, increased the standing of "Muscular Christianity" during his 1891–92 evangelization journey. His talents also served him well in his new position at the University of Chicago as he spent great amounts of energy recruiting and motivating players as well as persuading the faculty of the benefits of sport. Naismith, on the other hand, was a conscientious teacher. While he had the capacity for firmness and conviction just like Stagg, basketball's founder espoused much more genteel manners than his colleague. Naismith was more naturally a teacher and Stagg more naturally a salesman, coach, and director.[9]

Phog Allen and Kansas City

As the Father of Basketball's protégé, "Phog" Allen probably held a disposition more like Stagg's than Naismith's. However, Allen learned a great deal about the game from Naismith, his coach. And yet, for all of Naismith's passion for the game of basketball, he coached Allen and his other players with little interest in winning. The game was meant to invigorate young men's health and create in them godly moral character. It was not, in Naismith's mind, meant to be professionalized. Naismith's record as a coach was below average—the worst in Jayhawk history. But that did not detract from his influence on the game. It merely serves as irony in the game's history. Naismith enjoyed overseeing the game and guiding young men toward it for the health-related and moral benefits, but his interests were different from other coaches in that he did not prioritize winning.[10]

While a student at Kansas and a member of its basketball team in 1905, Allen discussed with his coach—Naismith—the possibility of coaching at a nearby college, Baker University. Allen would practice in the afternoon at the university with his teammates before hopping on a train to Baker for its evening practices. The stipend Allen would obtain would help him pay for his education. In a story that Allen often told later in his life, Naismith approached him and said, "I've got a good joke on you, you bloody beggar. They wanted you to coach basketball down at Baker." "What's so funny about that?" Allen replied. Naismith's supposed response, which he may or may not have actually said because of his unique views on sport, has become an epitaph for his life as much as any other thing he said. According to Allen, Naismith replied, "Why, you can't *coach* basketball. You just play it." In spite of Naismith's puritanical misgivings about Allen's endeavor into coaching, the Kansas student found great success in the profession. In 1907, Allen became Kansas University's first paid basketball coach, taking the reins of the team from his mentor. Naismith cared little about the intricate tactics of the game that other coaches began employing. The game, in that sense, had already passed him by.[11]

Allen took up the tactical torch of basketball as ardently as any coach in the 1910s—so much so that Naismith referred to his pupil as "The Father of Basketball Coaching." Growing up in a middle-class family with five brothers, Allen developed a toughness of character that he carried with him—to a fault, some would say. The Allen brothers started a basketball team when Phog was ten, and the boys grew up playing basketball and boxing between their hard labor jobs that helped augment the family's income. While education was important and blue-collar work was respectable, Allen had a love for basketball and physical activity that drew him to the physical education program that Dr. Naismith taught at Kansas. Allen then followed in his mentor's footsteps by earning a medical degree while also coaching basketball—two professional interests that Allen maintained for the rest of his career.[12]

Allen coached at Kansas from 1907 to 1909 before leaving the profession temporarily to obtain his degree in osteopathic medicine. He returned to the sidelines in 1912, coaching Central Missouri State for seven seasons. In 1919, Allen moved back to Lawrence to once again coach the Jayhawks. At the end of the second year of Allen's second stint with the Jayhawks, nearby Kansas City took a crucial step in its rise as a basketball-prominent city. The AAU tournament that was attracting an increasingly national following found its home in the Garden City. From 1921 to 1934, this tournament brought the best amateur teams in the country into America's heartland to battle for what few doubted was the premier amateur championship. Many college teams participated in this event—especially those within geographic proximity to Kansas City. The 1924 and 1925 championship teams came from the college ranks. Yet college basketball never fully embraced this amateur event because the AAU would not give the colleges their own bracket that would separate the young players from the "tramp" athletes and seasoned veterans on noncollege teams whose skills naturally exceeded those of college players because of their extra years of work on the game.[13]

The AAU, Rules, and Administration

In basketball's early years, Naismith and Gulick maintained at least nominal authority over basketball, despite its wildly growing popularity, by printing an annual pocket-sized rules brochure that became an actual rulebook. In 1895, Naismith moved to Denver and left authority of the game in Gulick's hands. By 1898, this task had become too large for the YMCA School director and his associates, and they ceded governance of the game to the AAU. Almost immediately, the AAU implemented registration requirements for all amateur teams that included paying an annual fee. The AAU, in effect, began ruling amateur basketball with an iron fist. Any team interested in playing AAU-sanctioned games had to register with the organization. Those who did had to receive clearance from the AAU before playing any other AAU-registered teams. Further, AAU-registered players were not allowed to play in any non-AAU games or events.[14]

These draconian restrictions provided enough disincentives that the majority of college teams did not register with the AAU. And while the college teams that existed in basketball's early years generally were not very selective about which teams—college, AAU, or otherwise—they would play during the season, the AAU restriction provided some major barriers within the college ranks. In early 1905, a highly anticipated matchup between Yale and Penn spurred discussion about the AAU. Penn was not an AAU member and the association had disqualified Yale. College basketball brass at this game suggested that colleges break away from the authoritarian governing body and, therefore, away from the mainstream of basketball. That spring, thirty-five college representatives met and founded a seven-person College Basket Ball Committee that created a set of rules for college basketball that differed from those of the AAU.[15]

In 1909, this committee became part of the Intercollegiate Athletic Association of the United States—the original name of the NCAA—and its rules became so popular that the YMCA and AAU adopted many of them. In 1914, the disparate organizations unified in a new Joint Rules Committee comprised of three YMCA representatives, three college representatives, and four AAU representatives. Years later, Naismith noted that the rules this committee adopted were much more in line with what the colleges had been using than either of the other two groups.[16]

Certain tensions remained among these factions—especially between the colleges and the AAU—into the 1920s. In 1927, the Joint Rules Committee added two representatives from the Board of Approved Basketball Officials, making it a twelve-person committee. That same year, the committee decided to take action on the highly controversial dribble rule proposal that would change the course of basketball's governance forever. The Joint Rules Committee proposed banishing unrestricted dribbling and implementing a one-dribble maximum. With loads of grassroots activism, the committee eventually voted down this proposal in 1927. This grassroots activity brought together college coaches from all over the country that, under the leadership of Allen, incorporated their activities to strengthen their voice, taking the title of National Association of Basketball Coaches.[17]

By 1929, the NABC had grown to 123 members and its annual discussions of basketball rules and governance had already impacted the game in a major way. So when the group convened for its third annual meeting on April 5 of that year, the AAU sent representation as well. AAU president Avery Brundage addressed the coaches by campaigning for the unification of colleges and the AAU regarding basketball rules and game action. The AAU leader argued that it would be in basketball's best interest for the NABC to become a part of the AAU.[18]

This diatribe naturally provoked the ire of the NABC membership, providing a glimpse of the controversial views Brundage openly expressed throughout his career as the AAU president, American Olympic Committee president, and International Olympic Committee president. Phog Allen took particular offense to the AAU president's comments, and the Kansas coach's feelings regarding Brundage intensified with two subsequent slights—the AAU chose football instead of basketball as the domestic exhibition sport at the 1932 Los Angeles Olympic docket and the AAU took credit for getting basketball onto the schedule for the 1936 Berlin Olympics. Allen felt as though his work went unnoticed and unrewarded.[19]

Allen's efforts received great recognition outside the AAU, though. By 1934, he had established himself as among the world's authorities in basketball. Much of this came from his commanding character, but his blustery presentations came alongside undeniable logic around which coaches and players rallied. His teams featured prominently in the Midwest, annually finishing among the tops in the Missouri Valley Conference and the nation. And his influence among his peers grew parallel to that of the NABC.[20]

Kansas City Born Again

In the summer of 1934, the AAU took its annual season-ending tournament from Kansas City to Denver. According to C. E. McBride, the city manager of Kansas City at the time, the AAU wanted a greater percentage of the gate receipts from the tournament. Kansas City, which had lost money in the 1933 tournament, disagreed with the new terms, and so the AAU found a city that would accommodate its increased demands. This decision did not please locals who believed their city had become one of the foremost in national basketball circles. Finding themselves suddenly without a tournament, city officials reassessed the Garden City's identity. A couple of local businessmen spurred discussions to construct a new arena that would attract new events and reinvigorate Kansas City's tourism.[21]

In 1936, more than 20,000 local citizens joined President Franklin D. Roosevelt to dedicate the new $6.5 million Municipal Auditorium that served as the centerpiece of a ten-year civic plan to increase Kansas City's national status. With this new venue that could seat 10,000 basketball fans, the Garden City was even better prepared to host basketball tournaments. However, with the AAU moving to Denver and the Garden City's effort to re-attract the amateur tournament failing, Municipal Auditorium needed to find suitors quickly to help finance the arena. Further exacerbating the problem, Municipal Auditorium officials decided against structuring the edifice to accommodate hockey when it was originally built. Without the ability to fill weeknight openings with hockey like Madison Square Garden could, basketball had to provide an answer.[22]

Dr. Reilly of the KCAC came to the rescue. Reilly and city manager McBride, discussed hosting a new event to fill the void created by the AAU's departure. Without the amateur association in town anymore and with the AAU's unwillingness to grant college teams their own bracket within the AAU tournament structure, Reilly and McBride believed that the colleges now had an opportunity to host their own tournament in a city that was basketball-mad and tournament-prepared. McBride put Reilly in touch with Emil S. Liston, basketball coach at nearby Baker University, to continue the discussion of a possible Kansas City college basketball national championship tournament.[23]

The legacy of this early discussion often omits Reilly and McBride. When they asked Liston to come on board for a new tournament, they were merely prominent Kansas Citians looking to replace an event that had become a celebrated part of the Garden City's annual social and athletic calendar. McBride knew he needed events in Municipal Auditorium for it to satisfy its financial and social obligations, and Reilly knew that any national athletic events in Kansas City meant an increase in the status of and interest in the KCAC. Liston, however, as a basketball coach and athletic director, actually had a concrete plan of action. The Baker coach dreamed of hosting a week-long thirty-two-team tournament much like the AAU's that brought teams in from every part of the country. The dream was not his alone, though. Liston's reverie had been shaped by discussions with his friend, Dr. James Naismith.[24]

An All-College Tournament

In late 1935, when the Olympic Basketball Committee decided to allow five college teams into its eight-team qualifying tournament for the 1936 Berlin Games, the method of qualification for those five slots became a source of conflict within the college ranks. Since the NCAA did not take the reins of the process, competition for possible play-off spots became rather Darwinian—the big schools won out because of their big names, and small schools received no chance. This injustice bothered Liston, who believed in the prowess of small college teams. Liston penned a letter to J. Lyman Bingham, Brundage's AAU assistant and the secretary-treasurer of the American Olympic Committee, to argue his case. The Baker coach pleaded with members of the Olympic Basketball Committee regarding the equitability of the event, too, but without success. Thus, at the end of the 1935–36 season, Liston and sixteen other college coaches from Missouri, Kansas, Nebraska, Oklahoma, and Texas met during the Southwestern Invitation Basketball Tournament in Winfield, Kansas, to discuss this issue. The coaches present named Liston as the head of their ad hoc protest committee. The group's campaigning, though, fell short of their goal and no small college gained entrance in the Olympic Trials.[25]

Shortly before Naismith shipped off to watch the inaugural Olympic basketball tournament in the summer of 1936, basketball's father spent some time in Baldwin, Kansas, discussing this problem with Liston. A national college basketball tournament seemed to be the answer, but neither of these men could pull off such an event on their own. Frank Cramer, founder of Cramer Sports Medicine, also joined Liston and Naismith in their dialogue, providing a voice from outside the basketball establishment. Liston, Naismith, and Cramer agreed on two philosophical points in particular about this proposed tournament. First, that it should not be run for a profit. Naismith's high moral values fit with this ideal. The three men had seen enough individual businessmen profit from college basketball "bowl" games and intersectional contests at neutral sites. They read accounts of these games with disdain, believing that potential profiteers tainted the purity of college basketball. Second, they believed that the tournament should be truly meritocratic. In other words, any team that qualifies should be eligible to compete regardless of the size or prestige of the school. Liston's awareness of the quality of small college basketball especially in his region provided this personal dictum that size and name recognition did not matter.[26]

Liston inaugurated the National Intercollegiate Basketball Championship Tournament as a sixteen-team event in 1937 in Municipal Auditorium. Publicity via the *Kansas City Star* indicated on February 28 and March 3, 1937, that the tournament would host sixteen teams on the evenings of March 9, 10, 11, and 13—Tuesday, Wednesday, Thursday, and Saturday. However, on the eve of the event, the *Star* noted that the tournament would commence with only eight teams. This scaled-back entry size, the *Kansas City Times* noted, was due at least in part to the fact that Municipal Auditorium was no longer available on Saturday night. Auditorium manager George Goldman booked a tennis exhibition featuring the world's number-one player for Saturday, March 13. Further, many of the competing teams needed the entire weekend to travel to Denver for the AAU tournament the following week—the AAU had scaled back its rigid eligibility requirements. Thus, when Drury College and Westminster College of Missouri wired in their entries three days before the event, Liston cut them off. Although he thought he could still get to sixteen teams, he did not have enough Auditorium dates and he did not want to risk losing teams if he scheduled weekend games. He also did not want to water down the quality of his tournament. While Kansas City had supported the AAU tournament for fourteen years, the city's fan support waned in the latter of those years as the tournament field grew and the quality of entrants diminished.[27]

The midweek scheduling of the event was not ideal, but Liston could do no better. Despite these sizable snags, local reporters believed that the tournament "in all likelihood will become an annual attraction, and quite possibly . . . preclude any chance of the National AAU tournament ever returning to this city." Because of the dearth of entries, though, the local media remained realistic about the event. The *Kansas City Times* reported, "The birth of what the future may bring as the national collegiate basket ball championships will be in the Municipal Auditorium tonight." The 1937 National Intercollegiate Basketball Championship Tournament became a trial run for Liston's future plans, but it remained a competitive event nonetheless.[28]

The Inaugural National Intercollegiate Championship Basketball Tournament

On Monday, March 8, seven conference champions—Southwestern of Kansas, South Dakota Wesleyan, Liston's Baker squad of Kansas, Morningside of Iowa, Central Missouri State Teachers, Luther of Iowa, and Central Arkansas State Teachers—and independent St. Benedict's of Kansas arrived in the Garden City for three nights of action beginning with opening-round games at 7, 8, 9, and 10 the following evening. The basketball-savvy fans of Kansas City had to wait until the nightcap for much excitement in the first-round games. The opener was a blowout, local favorite Baker lost in the second, and the third was a rout before the crowd could impartially enjoy a close game—Central Arkansas State Teachers' one-point win over St. Benedict's.[29]

The relatively disappointing action on opening night compelled the local media to pump up the potential competitiveness of the following night's semifinal action. Liston lamented to the *Kansas City Journal-Post* that he sold only $250 worth of tickets for the opening night dud, but the *Kansas City Times* promoted the upcoming semifinal action, describing that "a 2-game salute will be fired tonight with the gunpowder potent in each of the two battles." Central Missouri State's height and ballhandling advantages outweighed the aggressiveness of the Southwestern, Kansas, squad in a 4-point victory. Morningside of Iowa used lockdown defense to overcome a massive deficit in the first half to defeat the State Teachers of Conway, Arkansas, in the evening's other game. Semifinal action, therefore, did provide some fireworks with two competitive games, but only few spectators attended the spirited action. More fans attended Thursday night's final, which pitted the Central Missouri State Teachers against Morningside College. The Missouri squad's height won out again as its stifling second-half defense shut down the Iowa team's numerous long-distance marksmen. The modest crowd—larger than the semifinal attendance but still much below capacity—hung around after the game to see Dr. Naismith present the championship trophy to the Central Missouri cagers. With his wife, Maude, having passed away less than two weeks prior, basketball's inventor had mixed emotions while presenting the new trophy named in her honor.[30]

During the tournament, Liston met with numerous coaches and administrators to discuss the event's future. By the time of the finals, these men settled on an official name for the tournament—the National Intercollegiate Basketball Championship Tournament—and a governance structure. Liston secured a fifteen-member board of management that represented a wide geographic reach. This group included coaches or athletic directors from the universities of Oregon State, Stanford, Colorado, Oklahoma A&M, Northwestern, Kentucky, and Long Island University (LIU) alongside those from smaller schools across the Midwest and Great Plains. The selection of big-name university staff to comprise almost half of the board of management may have seemed counterproductive. After all, the underlying philosophy of this event was to provide opportunity for all schools, especially the smaller ones. Yet Liston seemed to realize that he needed the support of the "name" coaches to give credibility to the event.[31]

The inaugural National Intercollegiate Basketball Championship Tournament took in only $700 at the gate and netted just $28. While this represents a modest sum, Liston worried little. Teams participated knowing in advance that no one would make money on this tournament—a principle on which Liston, Reilly, Naismith, and Cramer based the entire affair. How much money each team had to pay for participation, though, was not so clear. Before the tournament, Liston explained that the event had been underwritten to such an extent that each competing team would have their expenses paid once they arrived in Kansas City, but they would have to pay for their own travel. Further, Liston noted that Auditorium president George Goldman allowed the event to use his facility free of charge, thereby relieving the tournament and its entrants of a normal financial burden. Yet the actual dispersal of the modest financial intake remains cloudy. Twenty years after the event, Goldman remembered each team receiving accommodations, lodging, and entertainment funding while in Kansas City just as he and Liston promised before the gala. However, tournament publicist George Bowles and Baker University publicist Thomas Evans—who helped Liston run the event—both remembered twenty years later that each team paid for everything on their own, with the understanding that they would be reimbursed if there was money left in the purse. The $28 tournament profit does not clarify this discrepancy. Twenty-eight dollars may have been the remaining sum after Liston provided some reimbursement to each team. It also may be what was left after he covered tournament operations, leaving such a small sum that was not worth dividing up among the eight teams. What is clear is that no one made more than $28 profit on the tournament.[32]

A Bigger Postseason in 1938

Shortly after the event, Liston began receiving interest from coaches about the next year's affair. In early 1938, the Baker coach encouraged that interest by writing letters to college coaches around the country and high school coaches in the area to visit Kansas City during the championship and share in the collection of basketball minds that would be huddled in the Garden City for the event. With anticipation growing, Liston convinced a handful of local businessmen to promise to cover the meals and lodging of participating teams. While this left entrants to cover their own travel fare, the compensation made tournament participation a reality for many small schools that had been financially handcuffed for the past decade by the economic depression.[33]

After hearing from a qualified pool of applicants interested in the tournament, Liston offered bids to 32 teams, all of whom accepted by Friday, March 4. On the following Sunday, Liston's friend George Edwards, who fulfilled dual roles as Missouri coach and NABC president, finished seeding the teams in the tournament, splitting them into two 16-team brackets and ranking the top four in each cohort. After finalizing the opening-round pairings, Edwards and Liston received three unfortunate messages. One came from the East—Western Kentucky's squad could not secure the funding to travel and would not make the trip; and one came from the North—the Dakota

Wesleyan team got into a car accident on their southbound travels and, while still intending to play, would do so with a few banged-up players. The final message came from the rest of the tournament field that had arrived in Kansas City on time. Liston and auditorium organizers had attached a sensor to the basketball hoops that ignited a red light above the backboard to reaffirm to fans that a basket had indeed been scored. During pretournament practices, players unanimously agreed that the new mechanism was more bothersome than anything else. "All day yesterday," the *Kansas City Times* descriptively admitted, "the teams used the floor for their warm-ups and many were the ejaculations of surprise as the young collegians first saw the arena." The invention—one that hockey teams would deploy almost sixty years later— experienced death before it ever had life in the sport of basketball as Liston ordered the sensors to be removed only minutes before the opening game.[34]

Shortly after noon on Monday, March 7, the six-day tournament featuring thirty-one teams from eighteen states as far away as Virginia, Minnesota, Oregon, New Mexico, and Mississippi began. First-round games on Monday and Tuesday in front of an estimated 3,000 fans the latter night preceded eight second rounds of games on Wednesday, 4 quarterfinals on Thursday, 2 semifinals on Friday, and the championship on Saturday. This taxing schedule dismissed twenty-nine squads and wilted the two finalists by Saturday. Only Central Missouri State Teachers, the defending champion, and Roanoke, a college of fewer than 1,000 students from Virginia, made it through. While the small Virginia school, which featured only one player taller than six feet, had toppled giants earlier in the week, the rangy Central Missouri Mules won going away, 45–30, for back-to-back National Intercollegiate Basketball Championship Tournament titles. The local media, however, did not seem to see things that way. After the tournament's less-than-impressive debut in 1937, sportswriters seemed to gush about the 1938 event almost as if the 1937 event did not occur, proclaiming that "Central State Teachers of Warrensburg, Mo., became the first intercollegiate basketball champions of the United States."[35]

This claim may have been premature in the eyes of certain basketball fans, however, as the basketball season was not over yet. Halfway across the country, a second postseason championship began only days after Central Missouri captured its second straight "title." Ned Irish, director of basketball at New York City's Madison Square Garden, hosted the inaugural National Invitation tournament in March 1938. This championship, founded and directed by the Metropolitan Basketball Writers Association (MBWA), provided strong counterpoints to Liston's tournament. Kansas City, in certain ways a cultural hub for America's heartland, obviously differed from New

York City, which was a hub of macro-American culture in its own right. Liston's tournament was theoretically open to any team in the country that finished with a good enough record and, by 1938, he accepted thirty-two of them while turning many others away who did not make the cut. Most of Liston's entrants were small schools that had little name recognition outside their geographic regions. The *Kansas City Times* reported that Oklahoma A&M and Drake planned to enter the event less than two weeks before it began. The inclusion of these two "name" schools would have helped the draw, but their inclusion represented little more than hearsay. Thus, while Liston's tournament grew immensely from 1937 to 1938 in size and geographic reach, it was not well recognized or publicized outside of Kansas City or the home areas of participating teams.[36]

The MBWA tournament, on the contrary, was an "invitation" event. In other words, the scribes' selection committee initiated contact with potential entrants whereas Liston had schools contact him first and then he would distribute bids based on the records of the interested pool of teams. Further, the MBWA kept its tournament small initially by hosting only six teams, all of which were large and well-known schools. While the MBWA invited teams from different parts of the country, the association made no attempt to host a "national championship." Instead, the National Invitation tournament simply brought teams in from around the country to play against each other and against the top teams from New York City. So while Liston's 1938 "open national championship" tournament hosted thirty-one teams that hailed from eighteen different states, the National Invitation in New York City held fast to its exclusivity by only hosting a few teams from outside the Big Apple.

While each tournament received official oversight and administration from groups of basketball experts, Ned Irish and Emil Liston garnered the most publicity for their central roles in each of these events. And philosophically, Irish and Liston could not have been more different in their tournament endeavors. Liston was an educator and coach who created his tournament for the benefits of players and small colleges. His interests remained closely attuned to what was best for the game of basketball and its players in the college ranks. He also held conservative moral views that could be developed through basketball play that paralleled the idealism of his friend and mentor, James Naismith. Irish came to his position as a sportswriter, promoter, entrepreneur, and businessman. As a part of New York City's vast media machine, he understood sports as a commodity for which the public was willing to pay—even though his moral may have been pure. Irish, as Madison Square Garden's host, provided the means that made a trip to the Big Apple financially worthwhile for visiting teams, but he also personally profited from these games—a fortune that allowed him to found, own, and operate the professional New York Knicks a decade later and also, consequently, help keep the fledgling National Basketball Association (NBA) afloat.[37]

The First Annual National Invitation Tournament

On February 1, 1938, while Liston sifted through applications for his upcoming tournament, Irish met with the Metropolitan Basketball Writers' Association and agreed to host a "national intercollegiate invitation basketball tournament" at Madison Square Garden. The sportswriters would oversee and administer the event, and Irish would host it. Everett B. Morris, president of the scribes' group and columnist for the *New York Herald-Tribune* sports section, scheduled the first round of games with Irish for Wednesday, March 9. This double-header, Morris noted, would feature four outstanding teams selected from the metropolitan area. A semifinal slate of games would ensue on Monday, March 14, between the preliminary round's winners and two teams of distinction from outside the Atlantic Seaboard. The championship and consolation games would pit the same four semifinalists re-paired two days later.[38]

Morris also noted that, in another difference from Liston's tournament, the selection committee for the New York event would consist of a small group of sportswriters from the MBWA. Morris oversaw the team selection along with *Herald-Tribune* colleague Irving Marsh, the *New York Times*'s Arthur Daley and Joseph Sheehan, Lew Burton of the *New York Journal-American*, and Ed Dooley of the *New York Sun*. The selection committee would closely monitor the top major teams around the country before making their decisions.[39]

Two weeks later, the *New York Times* noted organizational developments to the tournament. In an effort to increase college representation in its governance, the MBWA invited Asa S. Bushnell, executive director of the Eastern Intercollegiate Athletic Association, and H. H. Salmon, a local businessman who chaired the NCAA basketball committee. While not on the selection committee, Bushnell and Salmon provided experience in college basketball matters to guide the administration of the tournament.[40]

The *Times* noted twenty-one teams under consideration for invitations on February 16 but cut that number to twelve by February 22. Local newspapers tried to keep up with the changing decisions governing selection of teams in the lead-up to the tournament. While Morris noted at the beginning of the month that four local squads would compete, within three weeks the *Times* wondered if more than one would qualify for an invitation. New York

University (NYU), City College of New York, and LIU seemed to have the inside track on the local competition. Colorado appeared to have secured an invite at this time, but it seemed contingent upon their winning the "Big Seven" conference.[41]

By Monday, March 7, the selection committee completed the field. Colorado did indeed garner an invitation with its Rocky Mountain Conference co-championship. Oklahoma A&M became the other "Western" entrant with its Missouri Valley Conference title. The two Western teams received byes into the semifinals. While the MBWA's schedule for this six-team tournament suggested that the two teams receiving first-round byes might be considered the top seeded teams, Morris, Irish, and their colleagues gave no indication that this was the case. Travel logistics seem to present the major factor in team scheduling. The MBWA gave the two squads that had to travel the farthest the benefit of not having to wait around New York City between the Wednesday openers and Monday's semifinals.[42]

Even though no sportswriters alluded to rankings before the tournament tipped off, the *Times* considered Bradley Tech of Peoria, Illinois, "a dark-horse entrant." Bradley matched up with Temple in its first-round action while NYU and LIU received what ended up being the only two local bids. NYU topped the local city standings with the best record against local foes. LIU, who rarely played local metropolitan teams, won a bid based on its superior record when compared to that of the other local teams. In fact, the *Times* gave the LIU Blackbirds a slight pregame edge because of its strong season output and star-studded lineup that featured African American Dolly King. A three-sport standout at LIU, King ended the regular season as one of five Blackbirds within the top six individual scorers in the metropolitan area.[43]

A total of 13,829 fans came out on Wednesday night, March 9, to watch the opening double-header. Temple sent a "stage-frightened" Bradley Tech team home early in the opener. Despite their continued success, the Owls had to fight fan perceptions all season long. Tournament game programs described the team as "a most un-athletic group . . . emaciated as they appear to be." The Owls could relax and watch the second game of the night—an extremely overdue local affair. "Four years of wrangling may be settled in 40 minutes tonight, when Long Island U. and New York U. basketballers clash," the *Brooklyn Daily Eagle*'s George E. Coleman wrote, adding that, "Many hours of the past four seasons have been spent by the Violet and Blackbirds' supporters relating to each other what (NYU coach) Cann's cagers did to this club while (LIU coach) Bee's outfit only did this and so on." NYU put this banter to rest as it upset LIU to take the "unofficial city crown" away from the Blackbirds. The NYU Violet's win came against further odds as starter

Jerry Tarlow informed his coach that he refused to play in the game. Without speculating on Tarlow's decision, Arthur Daley of the *Times* noted that this made NYU's "victory all the sweeter."[44]

NYU lost a heartbreaker in its semifinal against Colorado, however, in "a hair-raising battle" that "was the most spectacular fray that the Garden ever has seen." The lead changed hands three times in the final forty-five seconds with Colorado finishing on top by one point. The dazzling finish left the crowd "limp and exhausted," as "much too much had happened." Temple had opened the evening by defeating Oklahoma A&M by 12 in front of 12,000 fans. The "most un-athletic group" continued to show its basketball prowess. While Temple's overall record made it the favorite in the final, Colorado developed strong metropolitan support during its pulsating semifinal win. Local fans had become mesmerized with Colorado's appropriately nicknamed guards Jim "Swisher" Schwartz and Byron "Whizzer" White. At the time of the tournament, White was already a three-sport Buffalo star, which included All-American honors in football. Intellectually, he was a star, too, having obtained a Rhodes Scholarship that would help catapult him to a career as a future United States Supreme Court justice. Schwartz, on the other hand, was a basketball player to the core—an accurate shooter among the best in the country. These two nationally recognized Buffaloes provided a counterpoint to the "un-athletic" and "emaciated" Owls. "Swisher" Schwartz and "Whizzer" White scored half of their team's points in the final game, but it was not nearly enough against "the giant Temple five." An estimated 14,500 fans watched the 60–36 blowout victory. With a 33–18 halftime lead, Temple coach Jimmy Usilton graciously began substituting his reserves early in the second half.[45]

In the consolation game that night, Oklahoma A&M defeated NYU easily 37–24, leaving the best local team in fourth place of the tournament. While New York City fans loved seeing local teams show their prowess in intersectional events, they also maturely appreciated good basketball from visiting teams—even when they beat local favorites. Therefore, Arthur Daley's recap of the National Invitation tournament's final night focused on the prowess of the two games' winners. Oklahoma A&M "had such speed that they could have rolled up any number of points," the writer gushed. But Daley bestowed the most praise on the champion Owl quintet. "Not since the McPherson Oilers displayed their collective skill in the Olympic tryout tournament two years ago," Daley opined, "has there ever been anything that could quite compare with the giants in Temple's red." The reporter continued his praise, writing, "It is doubtful that Stanford or any college team could have stemmed the furious scoring outbursts of the Owls." This

The 1938 NIT Champion Temple team, a "most un-athletic group," according to the *New York Times*. *Courtesy of Special Collections Research Center, Temple University Libraries, Philadelphia, PA.*

comment reflects a humility regarding the National Invitation tournament after its inauguration. The mention of Stanford and the way in which Daley refers to the Indians means that he realized that not all of the best college basketball teams competed in the tournament. Indeed, while Temple received the title of National Invitation tournament champion, no one referred to this event as a "national championship" like the sportswriters in Kansas City did after Liston's tournament the week before. The poor showing of its local entrants may have affected the New York writers' humility regarding this tournament's status.[46]

Nevertheless, the Helms Foundation's retrospective ranking service listed Temple as its "national champion." The Premo-Porretta retrospective index also ranked Temple first, with Stanford second, MBWA tournament consolation champ Oklahoma A&M fifth, MBWA entrant Bradley sixth, National Intercollegiate Basketball Tournament drop-out Western Kentucky seventh, Kansas City champ Central Missouri eleventh, and runner-up Roanoke twelfth. No local sportswriter claimed that the National Invitation champion Temple quintet won a national championship even though more recent experts have offered them that title seemingly by virtue of their New York tournament victory. Central Missouri State Teachers College, on the contrary, received praise from the local Kansas City press as "United States national champions" at the time but retrospective expert analysis has ranked them no higher than eleventh.[47]

The Racial Climate

On the day Temple defeated Colorado for the first National Invitation crown, the National AAU tournament commenced in Denver. Central Missouri State justified its National Intercollegiate Basketball Championship Tournament title by winning the newly formed college portion of the AAU bracket, making the Missourians the only college team to reach the AAU quarterfinals. A team named the "Collegians" reached the round of 16 in the noncollege side of the bracket. This team of African Americans from Chicago may or may not have gone to college, but they took the moniker nonetheless. The Chicago Collegians lost to the Antler Club of Colorado Springs in the third round and left Denver bitterly. The *Chicago Defender* noted that the team received a harsh lecture from the referees regarding their conduct before their loss. The referees clearly impacted the game, as this speech made the Collegians "afraid in their guarding." Despite the players' wariness, three Chicago starters fouled out of the game while the referees only disqualified one player from the Antlers.[48]

The *Chicago Defender*, a black weekly newspaper, informed its readers of the news differently from a mainstream daily like the *Chicago Tribune* or *Chicago Daily Times*. Indeed, the *Defender* mentioned that "A.A.U. officials are charged with having decided not to allow the Collegians to win in the tournament." Any direct accusations of racism in the mainstream newspapers may have offended a public that still accepted a segregated military and all-white professional baseball, and was still twenty-six years away from the Civil Rights Act. This factor in the nation's racial climate coupled with the poorly recorded history of the early years of the AAU tournament have left the racial integration of the event less than clear. Nevertheless, historian Adolph Grundman notes the Chicago Collegians' participation in the 1938 tournament, implying that, if they were not the first African American team to participate, a black team was at least rare enough to deserve mention. Four years earlier, when Kansas City hosted the tournament, it may have been more difficult for an all-black team to compete. Missouri had a unique racial climate that stemmed from its role within the political maneuverings before the Civil War.[49]

The 1820 Missouri Compromise set the stage for the "Show-me State's" unique cultural heritage. American lawmakers allowed the Missouri territory to become the only region of the Louisiana Purchase above Missouri's now southern border to hold slaves. In 1854, Kansas and Nebraska, Missouri's western neighbors, received popular sovereignty regarding slavery in the Kansas-Nebraska Act. Longtime Lincoln nemesis Stephen Douglas drew up this statute as a way to allow western territorial citizens to determine their own fate and allow him to delay having to take a stance on slavery—a political decision he dreaded. After a great deal of bloodshed in Kansas on this issue, both territories drafted state constitutions disallowing slavery. Legally mandated abolition of slavery after the Civil War forced Missouri to change its ways. Yet the Thirteenth Amendment to the United States Constitution gave rise to a new kind of racism in these areas—Jim Crow. *Plessy v. Ferguson* accomplished one of its two mandates, creating separate yet unequal customs that led to a racial hierarchy not altogether different from the pre–Civil War era in the South.[50]

Liston grew up and lived in such a complex climate on the Kansas side of the Missouri border. The Baker coach, who hosted his second annual National Intercollegiate Basketball Championship Tournament across the river in Missouri, knew no other way of life. By the late 1930s, Jim Crow laws regulated Kansas and Missouri, but were not as rigidly enforced as they were in the Deep South. Liston's first tournament did not include a single minority athlete, and his second included only one—Kiko Martinez, a light-skinned Mexican National Team star who also headlined the New Mexico State squad, scoring 33 points in his team's two tournament games. Inclusion of the Aggie "floor general" in the event came and went with little mention.[51]

Martinez's light skin color likely aided his assimilation into the otherwise all-white event. Skin color mattered in Kansas City at this time, but degrees of separation and ethnicity mattered, too. Martinez's skin was indecipherably different from many of the "white" players in the rest of the tournament field. He was not black, and so his appearance was not strikingly different from the rest of the players and fans. Further, he was part of an ethnic group seen as much less threatening than many others at the time. Thus, Martinez's race registered little in Liston's event; it remained as comfortable as if it had been an all-white tournament.[52]

The homogeneity of this tournament was the only way the event could occur. Local customs would have had a strong influence on Liston's views and policies, thus dictating the gala's racial composition. And yet, no team—not even the New Mexico State Aggies—forced the director's hand. Martinez's Mexican heritage was not an issue; a black player's African American heritage would have been. Fortunately for Liston and his event, very few mainstream college basketball teams were integrated at the time—especially in America's heartland. Of all the teams that showed interest in qualifying for the Kansas

City tournament, it is likely that not one of them included an African American or any other player with skin dark enough to raise eyebrows.[53]

Even halfway across the country in New York City—America's most diverse region at the time—an all-white basketball tournament would not have struck fans as unusual. It may have been more unusual that the 1938 National Invitation tournament included a black athlete—Long Island's Dolly King. Like New Mexico State's Martinez, King was a standout on his team. Indeed, the "six feet three, 220-pound, all-sport athlete from Alexander Hamilton High in Brooklyn" starred in football, basketball, and baseball for LIU (sometimes in two of these sports on the same day), and was "one of the finest athletes (LIU Coach Clair Bee) . . . ever had."[54]

New York City newspapers, however, wasted little ink giving special mention to King's race or skin color. This may be attributed to New York City's progressiveness, for the Big Apple has often been at the forefront of cultural change. NYU had an integrated football team even before World War I, and Coach Nat Holman of CCNY, the other metropolitan basketball power, would soon find himself ahead of the curve in his acceptance of black players. It might be attributed to New York City sportswriters' comfort with King—after all, they covered the Blackbird all year long—in basketball, football, and baseball. It might be attributed to LIU coach Clair Bee's unique philosophy of coaching. Bee rarely scheduled local opponents, instead playing a national schedule each year, and he wrote children's novels to perpetuate moral virtues in sport. So why would anyone be surprised that he neglected unjust social mores to carry an integrated squad? The exceptionally noiseless mention of King integrating the National Invitation also may have been because LIU exited the event in the first round, leaving only a small imprint on the first New York tournament.[55]

Indeed, Long Island's first-round loss to NYU seemed to make a big splash in metropolitan newspapers for a reason other than its integrated racial composition. Sportswriters seemed to enjoy how the tournament pitted New York City's top two teams of the season and determined by virtue of head-to-head competition which one was best. Many sportswriters also enjoyed how this event provided a crescendo to the season. On a national scale, the tournament provided a bit of aid to postseason rankings regarding which teams were the best. The *New York Times* noted after the season that Temple, by winning the National Invitation, "took rank with Stanford, Notre Dame, and Purdue as America's standout teams" for the season. The *Times* also added that Temple and Stanford were "perhaps a shade superior to the other two."[56]

The recently completed National Invitation provided local scribes with some objectivity. Temple's postseason feats were the freshest in their minds.

The Owls impressively defeated Bradley, Oklahoma A&M, and Colorado—three of the top teams from their respective regions—to take home the tournament's inaugural title. But sportswriters of the time did not have the ability to watch many games from these or any other teams around the country. They had two lenses through which they could rank teams—a squad's overall record and seeing them perform firsthand. Indeed, metropolitan sportswriters usually praised as season's best the squads and individuals who performed best in front of their eyes on Madison Square Garden's big stage. Thus, Temple received special mention from its tournament performance alongside Stanford, whose slick one-handed shooter, Hank Luisetti, captivated the Garden crowd every time he traveled there to play. Despite not playing in the National Invitation, Luisetti and his teammates had captured the hearts of the New York City basketball aficionados nonetheless.[57]

Setting a Legacy

The inaugural National Invitation tournament helped the 1937–38 basketball season end with a bang, a fitting apex to college basketball in the Garden. College hoops had become a prominent part of the Garden's annual schedule, and the Garden had become a prominent feature of college basketball —especially now with the postseason event. Ned Irish hosted twelve collegiate double-headers that season, selling 162,039 tickets in the process. This sum outdid the previous record attendance from the 1935–36 season by 2,000. Irish noted that the double-header featuring Stanford-CCNY and Minnesota-LIU set a Garden basketball attendance record, attracting 18,148 fans on December 27. The westerners won a "double defeat of the locals." Two nights later, 18,124 fans witnessed another double western triumph as Stanford beat LIU and Minnesota overtook NYU. Despite these visiting victories, Irish also noted that in the twelve Garden games on the season that pitted a local team against a nonlocal team, metropolitan fives won six and lost six of the local intersectional contests. In a world that had little national basketball cohesion, this record mattered. New York City believed it had the best basketball around, and results like this gave Ned Irish and others from the New York City basketball establishment a statistic from which they could argue that if not the best, their geographic pocket of teams could at least compete on an even playing field with the best of the rest of the nation.[58]

The record-setting 1937–38 regular season attendance totals meant that about 13,500 spectators greased the turnstiles for each night of college basketball action. However, the unsurpassed interest in the intersectional double-headers between the holidays suggests that on other nights the

Garden bill attracted many fewer than the average number of fans during that season. Yet while the Garden could hold a few hundred more than 18,000 fans for basketball contests, this meant that Irish had his arena more than two-thirds full on average. His ticket totals were impressive and record-breaking, but there was still more room to grow.

The inaugural National Invitation provided a glimpse of how Irish's spectator totals could grow. This postseason gala achieved a large portion of the success that the MBWA dreamed it would. MBWA president Everett Morris reported that the tournament ended with "approximately" 40,000 ticket stubs, which would mean an average of around 13,333 for each of the three nights. Irish, however, claimed that the tournament drew 45,000 fans—an average of 15,000 per night.[59]

Regardless of the exact totals, the inaugural National Invitation was a success. Two days after the Temple victory, Morris announced the dates for the following season's tournament and added that, with the success of the first go-round, the tournament would expand to include eight teams over four nights in 1939. The *New York Times* stated that the tournament was "a signal success," and that the MBWA was "suddenly prosperous as a result of the national invitation tournament it sponsored."[60]

While Ned Irish and the MBWA did not disclose their financial reports, the newspaper reports and the interest in scheduling the following year's event made it clear that the inaugural tournament's revenue was high enough to cover the Garden's steep rental fee—a portion of which went directly into Irish's pocket—and have enough left over to send each team home with a cash prize that, while also undisclosed, became enough to entice these teams back again if invited. Further, the MBWA presented each member of Temple, runner-up Colorado, and fourth-placed NYU—by virtue of its metropolitan crown—with brand-new wristwatches. Third-place Oklahoma A&M received medals for their victory in the tournament's consolation game.[61]

This financial success caught the attention of basketball coaches and administrators around the country. Clearly, a postseason tournament featuring a small number of large, prominent university teams from across the country could succeed. The success of Liston's Kansas City–based tournament also created waves in the basketball world. Although his first two tournaments ended with much less inspiring financial records, his participation rate skyrocketed from the first to the second National Intercollegiate Basketball Championship Tournament. Clearly, a postseason tournament much different from that in the Garden—with a large amount of small college teams from across the country—could also succeed. A market had been created, but its scope was yet undefined.

CHAPTER 3

The NABC and the Inaugural
NCAA Tournament, 1938–1939

The success of Madison Square Garden's National Invitation tournament captivated local fans and had the powerful media smitten. Kansas City Municipal Auditorium's National Intercollegiate Basketball Championship Tournament had more difficulty drawing fans, but its participation had grown considerably from year one to year two. College basketball teams around the country took notice of these opportunities, wondering how they could get involved in a postseason event.

Less than a month after Central Missouri State Teachers College won its second straight Kansas City tournament and Temple won the inaugural National Invitation—a crown that provided the Owls at least a stake in the national media's subjective determination of the country's top teams—the National Association of Basketball Coaches held its twelfth annual convention. The Chicago venue for this early April gathering and the reduced membership fee—down from $5 to $2—enabled the largest attendance to date. At least 109 of the 136 official members traveled to the Windy City to discuss basketball matters.[1]

Many coaches at the convention anxiously awaited discourse on annual postseason basketball tournaments like the New York City and Kansas City championships. Many hoped the NABC would throw its hat in the ring to host its own event, while many others had no interest in the association putting its energies toward an event for only a select few elite teams. Outgoing NABC president George Edwards of Missouri, who oversaw the team selection process in Liston's 1938 tournament, offered the Baker coach a chance to discuss his tournament in front of the membership. Edwards also offered the Metropolitan Basketball Writers' Association president Everett Morris the chance to speak, but Morris could not be found when called upon. Liston knew that, despite his championship's modest bottom line, certain coaches envied his event and its potential. And the Baker coach had a bone to pick with the coaches. He wondered why no big schools showed any interest in his tournament. To be sure, he built his gala around equal opportunities for small schools to showcase their teams, but in no way did he ever prohibit large schools from participating. Did the bigger schools look down their noses at the smaller schools and "their" tournament? If so, Liston would have resented that condescension.[2]

With his ear to the ground regarding the coaches' specific concerns about the existing postseason championships, Liston spoke diplomatically. The Baker coach allayed the delegation's largest fears by underscoring the fact that his tournament was run by college personnel and the money remained with the tournament, the teams, and schools. This financial methodology distinguished Liston's tournament from New York City's National Invitation, the success of which went directly to the MBWA and Madison Square Garden. Liston knew that the majority of the NABC members cringed at the thought of private entities profiting from basketball games played by college teams—and he did, too.[3]

Liston further appeased the membership by noting that virtually all of the coaches helping him direct his tournament were NABC members. The coaches' association, under this logic, should have no fears of Liston's tournament, for it was already coexisting with the NABC. Liston's event could succeed and grow without taking anything away from the coaches' organization. The Baker coach, after all, was not a maverick trying to generate a quorum to secede from the NABC. On the contrary, he seemed interested in running his tournament with the support—nothing more and nothing less—of the NABC.[4]

NABC Discussion of a New Event

Beyond Liston's clarifying remarks, he was not willing to have the NABC either overtake or determine the course of his tournament regardless of the coaches' thoughts on the matter. And the coaches did have a lot of thoughts on the matter. In fact, this topic dominated discussion at the 1938 convention like no other topic had outside of the rules of the game. Stanford coach John Bunn appeared to be the coach who brought up this idea, and the Indian mentor would have been a likely candidate. Bunn's 1938 squad was recognized as one of the top two teams in the country at season's end. Led by senior Hank Luisetti, the Indians had achieved great success all over the country—including stops in New York City. Bunn believed his team could have matched up well against any squad in the country in postseason play. However, Stanford's conference, the Pacific Coast Conference (PCC), did

not sanction the New York City event. Many other prominent college conferences such as the Big Ten and Big Six (now Big Twelve) had to approve
any of their members participating in postseason events. None of these three
conferences approved the National Invitation, and Stanford felt disadvan-
taged because of it.[5]

The Big Ten, Big Six, and PCC were all NCAA members, though. Thus,
when Bunn's colleagues at those conference schools caught wind of his
thoughts, they jumped on board. The NCAA's member schools and conferences would likely sanction a tournament run by the association. Therefore,
while Bunn may not have had the support of the majority of NABC members, his brainchild certainly resonated with a vocal group of prominent,
big-name coaches. One of those was Ohio State's Harold Olsen. While much
of the conversation regarding postseason events was impromptu, Olsen had
prepared a point-by-point statement delineating his and Bunn's views to the
delegation. NABC president Edwards read the following on Olsen's behalf:

> There is quite a definite development along the line of invitational
> national college basketball championships, such as the one sponsored
> by the Metropolitan Basketball Writers Association, held in Madison
> Square Garden, and the one held in Kansas City. If there is to be a
> development of this kind, it would seem that the National Association
> of Basketball Coaches, acting as an affiliate of the National Collegiate
> Athletic Association, might very well promote and manage such com-
> petition. The N.C.A.A. now sponsors a national collegiate track and
> field meet, a swimming meet and, this year, a tennis meet, with the
> strong prospect of doing the same in golf next year. If such champi-
> onships are held, it is altogether proper that the N.C.A.A. should run
> them rather than some less desirable sponsor.
>
> There are some very good reasons why the National Association
> of Basketball Coaches might well give serious thought to inaugurat-
> ing such championships, decided by tournaments in each of the eight
> N.C.A.A. districts and then by a final tournament of eight teams at
> some favorable spot:
>
> 1. There appears to be a demand for deciding by some means a
> national collegiate championship basketball team. The proper group
> to sponsor such championship play is the Coaches Association.
>
> 2. Revenue. The chance of such championships bringing in some
> very welcome revenue to the National Association of Basketball
> Coaches is very good. (No outside promoters to get their first
> "cut" etc.)
>
> 3. Such a championship set-up will give a fine chance to demon-
> strate a means of insuring proper collegiate representation in the next

Olympic game try-outs. Many colleges who were not interested in the try-outs before the last Olympic games, will be decidedly interested in a set-up which gives them a chance to compete for a place on the Olympic team with strictly college opposition.

4. The final tournament in this championship set-up, if held in conjunction with our annual convention, would be the finest sort of a "tie-up" that we could possibly have.[6]

Olsen's written diatribe connected with the audience because of its logic and timing. His document was a "slam dunk" as it perfectly characterized the shortcomings of the existing tournaments. While it did not persuade every NABC member, it found great support and revealed much of the nexus of power in college athletics.

Olsen, who grew up in Rice Lake, Wisconsin, played college basketball at the University of Wisconsin under the direction of Dr. Walter Meanwell before the Great War. Olsen teamed with future NABC president and Marquette coach Bill Chandler to win the 1916 Big Ten title while both players earned all-conference honors. Both retrospective polls ranked this Badger team as tops in the nation. Their mentor, one of the most influential early coaches, developed a very successful "short-pass system" that took many of his teams to conference championships. Meanwell held fast to this "short-pass system" when Olsen and Chandler played for him at Wisconsin. After World War I, the Badger coach joined basketball's Joint Rules Committee and took a leadership role in that group just in time to lead the contentious 1927 discussions about banishing the unlimited dribbling allowance. Meanwell became the voice of the anti-dribbling faction as it fit his system perfectly and prohibited his pet peeve—players who dribbled too much.[7]

By 1927, Olsen already had one conference title under his belt at Ohio State and had moved geographically and philosophically away from Meanwell. Olsen vocally opposed his mentor, giving the pupil much credibility among the mostly pro-dribbling future NABC brass and also around the Western conference. The Western, or Big Ten, Conference hired Major John L. Griffith, a former University of Illinois associate director of athletics, as its commissioner in 1922. Although the Big Ten began as the leader among the nation's intercollegiate athletic conferences, Griffith pushed the Big Ten to new levels of influence. In basketball, this influence was unmistakable.[8]

Early in the history of American intercollegiate athletics, elite institutions on the East Coast ruled the day. Harvard, Yale, and Princeton, the country's most enviable institutions of higher learning, dictated the administration of sports such as crew, football, and baseball. With power and prestige in these three sports, any others that came onto the scene also assumed a natural submission to the influence of the three future Ivy League schools. And yet basketball changed this hierarchy quickly. Harvard, Yale, and Princeton participated prominently in hoops much like they did with other sports. However, they did not generate a following beyond the aristocracy like they did with the other sports.[9]

Baseball and football required nine and eleven players, respectively, but did not always require or generate star players. The team, often, was the star. With high enrollment numbers and high admissions interest, the Eastern elites could oftentimes easily field outstanding football and baseball teams filled with loads of high-quality athletes. Basketball, with only five players to a side, lent itself much more to individual feats and stardom. In that sense, it was easier for schools outside the East Coast elite to compete with the best teams in the nation. All it took was a star player or two, and any inner-city playground or small farm town could produce that.

Olsen was raised in this latter context. The future Ohio State coach's matriculation at the University of Wisconsin meant that he was not an elitist. On the contrary, Wisconsin and its Big Ten peers embodied the dignified middle-class ambition for which the Midwest came to be known. In college athletics, the Big Ten did in the 1920s and 1930s what the "Ivies" had done in previous decades—they set the bar in terms of athletic quality and success, which gave them an important influence within college athletics. This influence was reaffirmed at the end of each basketball season. No matter how the season had gone across the nation, the champion or co-champion of the Big Ten usually gained mention in discussions about the season's top teams.[10]

The Big Ten's overlapping administrative relationship with the NCAA also gave it a great deal of influence on organizational matters. Within this context, Olsen presented his argument for why the NABC should implement a national championship tournament. His first reason for doing so—that there appears to be a demand for a means to determine a national champion and that the NABC should be the group to make that determination—appeared a bit parochial, naïve, or arrogant. When Olsen wrote these words, two postseason tournaments already existed. New York City's National Invitation did not claim to be a "national championship" tournament; it simply invited top teams from across the country to compete for a tournament title and prize in an envious locale. Liston's National Intercollegiate Basketball Tournament Championship did claim to crown a "national champion," or at least that is what the local media promoted despite the homogeneous composition of small, and at the time, mostly midwestern schools.[11]

And yet Olsen's argument that the NABC should host such a

determination of a national champion is not without solid rationale. He believed that the coaches' association had the best interests of basketball and college students in mind. Therefore, his second argument—that an NABC-hosted national championship would bring much appreciated money into the association's coffers, which could be used to better the game of basketball—was a direct attack on the Madison Square Garden tourney. Ned Irish and the MBWA, he knew, profited handsomely from the first National Invitation just recently completed. Irish and his venue took the "first cut" that Olsen condemned. The teams received whatever was left—and, reportedly, this was no paltry sum.

This line of argumentation resonated well with many of the coaches in attendance at the 1938 NABC convention—especially those from the Big Ten and American heartland that constituted a majority of the association's membership. Their wholesome views regarding basketball finances differed greatly from those of Irish and the MBWA. And yet, National Invitation organizers could afford to more aggressively commodify college basketball—New York City provided the media market and dense population to drive profits on previously un-capitalized practices of which promoters outside the Big Apple never dreamed. In fact, the MBWA was "financially embarrassed" that it had so much money after its 1938 event. "It isn't the income tax man who has the (writers) scared," George E. Coleman of the *Brooklyn Daily Eagle* wrote in a hyperbolic tone, "it's the responsibility of doing the right thing with the money." Coleman noted that the scribes discussed such options as a scholarship to a poor student or a postgraduate course for basketball players. However, they ended up simply putting the extra money into a treasury.[12]

The Olympic Issue

While Olsen's fourth argument—that a postseason national championship tournament held in conjunction with the NABC convention would be amenable to the association's interests—provided practical justification, it remained contingent upon the strength of his other arguments. It was little more than an appeal to the rational sympathies of the association's members. A tournament held in conjunction with the annual NABC convention would be a fine "tie-up," just the sort of event that would build on the attempts to showcase top teams in front of the coaches in 1934 and 1935.

Thus, Olsen's first argument, about the demand for a tournament that should be run by the coaches, provided some strength but was too idealistic to carry the day. His second argument—about revenue—was strong but

remained a bit too ideological to persuade all coaches. His third argument—
that an NABC-sponsored national championship tournament would provide
college basketball with a better opportunity for representation in the United
States Olympic Basketball Trials—struck a chord with a powerful faction of
the NABC. Kansas's Phog Allen, notably, saw great merit in this third line
of reasoning.

The Kansas coach had argued forcefully for the inclusion of basketball on the Olympic docket. When the United States received approval to
host the 1932 Olympics in Los Angeles, International Olympic Committee
(IOC) rules stated that the host country could choose one sport to put on the
Olympic schedule of events that was not an official Olympic sport but would
become a medal sport for that particular Olympic Games. In the 1930s, the
AAU ruled amateur athletics in the United States and was awarded local
control of the Los Angeles Games. Allen immediately lobbied AAU president
Avery Brundage—who had offended Allen and NABC members in 1929 by
orating at the coaches' convention that the NABC should submit its influence
on basketball to the AAU—to include basketball as the local exhibition sport
for the 1932 Olympic Games.[13]

Brundage, a former University of Illinois and Olympic decathlete, chose
American football instead. The AAU president argued publicly that football, because it would be played in the new Los Angeles Coliseum in front
of large crowds, would be a better choice. Basketball organizers had their
skepticism, though. The hoop game had become much more internationally
accepted than the gridiron game by the early 1930s and Allen argued that
this international appeal would be better than showcasing football—a game
that had yet to catch on outside America's borders.[14]

Allen and the coaches believed that underlying Brundage's choice of
football over basketball was his jealousy that the NABC had accumulated
such influence in amateur basketball that had originally—at least at the turn
of the century—been the AAU's domain. Yet Allen would not give up his
dream of having basketball become a full-fledged Olympic sport. Between
1932 and 1936 he spent a great amount of energy promoting basketball's
international merits. Brundage, however, came under intense scrutiny over
that same time period that would come to characterize his professional
career administrating amateur sport. When the IOC gave Nazi Germany the
1936 winter and summer Olympic Games, Brundage defied the public out-
cry to boycott because of Adolph Hitler's theories of Arian supremacy and
his termination of Jews. While many Americans—especially ethnic minority
groups—believed that a boycott would be justified, Brundage downplayed
Nazi ideology and practices. Hitler invited the former Illinois trackster to

Berlin, and Nazi propaganda overwhelmingly convinced Brundage that America should not boycott the games. Many Americans, however, thought differently.[15]

Basketball's international reputation took a major leap while the Third Reich prepared for this international spectacle. In 1932, European basketball officials founded the International Basketball Federation (FIBA) to govern the sport at an international level. In 1935, this group sponsored its first international basketball tournament, the European Basketball Championship. While only seven teams attended and the small Baltic nation of Latvia took home the title, this tournament seemed to give basketball the international awareness needed for the IOC to implement hoops in the 1936 Olympics as an official medal sport.[16]

While FIBA and its tournament played a major role in convincing the IOC to add basketball, Americans believed they helped promote the game abroad, as well. Allen and the AAU both believed that their efforts are what eventually persuaded the IOC to include the hoops game—a misunderstanding that further deteriorated relations between Allen's NABC and Brundage's AAU. Yet matters got worse in the lead-up to the Berlin Games.[17]

The AAU was in charge of sending America's delegation of athletes to Berlin for the 1936 Olympics. In sports such as track or swimming, the determination of athletes to represent America evolved naturally—winners from among the nation's best at a national meet would go. In basketball, determining team members was not so easy. Thus, Allen and college basketball administrators worked hard to encourage the AAU that college teams and players deserved an opportunity to compete alongside AAU teams and players for the right to hold the limited roster spots allowed in the American basketball delegation.[18]

Creighton coach A. A. Schabinger oversaw the collegiate portion of the Olympic Trials qualifying play-offs and tournament that determined selection of the national team. The Olympic Trials ended with only one of the five college district champions reaching the semifinals even though most of the money earned throughout the trial process came from the college district play-off games. Indeed, that is why the Olympic Basketball Committee gave five of the eight slots to college teams. The selection committee secured the roster and coaching staff from this tournament. Six players from the runner-up McPherson Oilers—whom local metropolitan journalists noted used "reverse lay-up shots" in which they threw the ball down through the rim instead of shooting it up at the rim—joined seven players from the champion Universal Pictures, the coach from both teams, and two alternate players to comprise the predetermined cut. Allen expected to be the eighteenth member who would oversee the organization and administration of the other seventeen to help ensure that the team was well represented and at its best.[19]

However, in the lead-up to Berlin, AAU president Avery Brundage notified Allen that the basketball contingent would include only seventeen representatives, and he was the odd man out. This sent the Kansas coach into a rage that spilled into the news media. Allen publicly referred to Brundage and the AAU leaders as "quadrennial oceanic hitchhikers who use other people's money for their own enjoyment." Brundage and his colleagues responded that Allen had only weaseled his way into a red herring Olympic position and should not take credit for work he did not do.[20]

The American Olympic hoopsters did not need Allen in Berlin as they coasted to a championship in which North America swept the medals. The Berlin basketball tournament took place outside on a court made of clay—a primitive locale compared to what the Americans experienced domestically. The United States was years ahead of the competition any other country could muster. Indeed, the 19–8 score in the gold medal match against Canada did not reflect how much better the American squad was than its adversaries. The satisfaction of national success, however, meant little to Allen in light of the bureaucratic slight Brundage had given him.[21]

Two years later, at the 1938 NABC Convention, Allen was still stewing. And the third argument Ohio State's Harold Olsen presented for creating a new collegiate national championship tournament gave Allen the ax he needed to grind with the AAU. While the New York and Kansas City tournaments existed already, neither of them seemed fit to provide college basketball with the kind of be-all, end-all determination of a national champion that might challenge the AAU for the right to represent the United States in the 1940 Olympics scheduled for Tokyo. The Kansas City tournament saw itself as a true national championship because it was open to schools of all sizes. Critics, though, pointed out that while it was unrestricted in nature, the entrance of small and virtually unknown schools discouraged many of the large, prestigious university teams from competing. After all, they had little to gain from competing against small, parochial institutions. The New York tournament also seemed inadequate to Allen and the NABC. While it attracted big-name teams to the media mecca of the world, it remained an invite-only tournament with a philosophical foundation of inviting some of the best teams around the country to compete against New York City's best. This method, as popular and successful as it was at the time, found detractors who called it a showcase put on by profiteers. The lily-white amateur values of the AAU brass would never appreciate the National Invitation tournament's champion as king of the college basketball world.

Allen grabbed onto Olsen's third argument for why the NABC should initiate a postseason championship tournament with enthusiasm. If the NABC and NCAA—two organizations promoting college basketball's amateur values—could collaborate and put on a "national championship" tournament, the college coaches could persuade the AAU to forego the cumbersome college district and interdistrict play-off games that dissuaded so many teams from competing in the Olympic Trials. If the NCAA could crown a "national champion," then college basketball could better identify the best team or teams at season's end and simply slot them into the Olympic Trials. This would give AAU officials a much clearer hierarchy of college teams at season's end to invite to the trials. Notre Dame or Purdue, for instance, would not have to miss an extra week or two of classes to play in district and interdistrict games before the trials. This would appease their administrators and taper their players in preparation for the big stage. Further, this would prevent a team like Kansas from having to play games against seemingly inferior opponents such as Utah State in which the Jayhawks would be susceptible to upset.

Tournament Executive Decisions

Luckily, Allen and his NABC colleagues only had to seek NCAA approval to host a national championship tournament in 1939. Any discourse with the AAU likely would have been explosive, and no conversations occurred until early 1940. New NABC president Bill Chandler of Marquette created an Olympic and Tournament Committee immediately after the 1938 convention that included himself, Olsen as chair, Allen, and Stanford's Bunn. This committee immediately put forth an official proposal to NCAA president W. B. Owens, professor at Stanford. In this proposal, Olsen and his committee sought to have the NCAA "take basketball 'under its wing' in much the same way as it has sponsored national collegiate championship contests in track and field, swimming, wrestling, tennis, and golf." Thus, Olsen specifically proposed:

> That the N.C.A.A. assume responsibility for the conduct of a National Collegiate Basketball Tournament in the Spring of 1939. This championship play to be so arranged that any lengthy, time consuming district play-offs be avoided. One team to represent each of the eight N.C.A.A. districts might very well be chosen by a selection committee from each district. The teams representing districts 1, 2, 3, and 4 (East of the Mississippi River) might play a four team tournament at some point where interest would be high, travel expenses low and time away from school negligible. For example,

Indianapolis, Indiana. The other four teams from districts 5, 6, 7 and 8 (West of the Mississippi River) might meet in a four-team tournament at Kansas City or Denver. Then the two winners could play at some central point for the N.C.A.A. Basketball Championship.

It is the belief of our committee that such a plan for 1939 would be feasible and practical. It should produce enough revenue to pay all expenses and it is not likely to meet with strenuous objections from conferences and from individual schools who frown on post-season contests, etc. In 1940, the Olympic year, a more ambitious and comprehensive program of elimination tournaments in each district might well be considered.[22]

The NCAA took five months to review Olsen's proposal before giving approval. And it was no rubber stamp. The NCAA deliberated thoroughly on the merits of the proposal. This tournament would be much more complex than the NCAA's other national championships because of its scope and volume. Each of the existing NCAA national championship events included teams, to be sure, but they were in individual sports. This, in certain ways, simplified logistics, as full squads did not need to travel together to participate. Further, the NCAA in 1939 was not the colossal operation it is today. Indeed, it had little manpower to staff the proposed event and little money to sink into it. Thus, the NCAA accepted conditionally. It would sanction and lend its name to the event, encouraging its member schools and conferences to participate if chosen, but the NABC had to administer it and assume the financial risk.[23]

The NABC received news of victory in October 1938 and immediately got to work. Olsen obtained approval to put together an official NCAA tournament committee and a selection committee for each of the NCAA's districts. The tournament committee largely resembled the NABC's Olympic and Tournament Committee. Olsen was chair, NABC president Chandler was a de facto member, and Bunn and Allen would serve. However, the NCAA encouraged Olsen to seek New York City representation. After some discussion, H. H. "June" Salmon, a prominent New York City businessman, came onto the committee as appointed by the NCAA. Salmon had long been involved in amateur basketball in the Big Apple, and was serving on the prestigious Basketball Rules Committee of the United States and Canada at the time. Further, and more importantly for the NCAA's purposes, Salmon served as the chair of the NCAA section of the national rules committee. Olsen also recommended that Salmon serve as the District 2 selection committee chair. Olsen's committee thus included the NABC president and the selection committee chairmen from District 2 (Salmon), 5 (Allen), and 8

(Bunn). This representation was both geographic and strategic, for Olsen had committee members from across the country and from within the key regions of the other tournaments—New York City and Kansas City.[24]

Olsen, Bunn, Allen, Salmon, and Chandler had to work quickly. Once they and each of the other five district selection committee chairmen accepted their posts, only four months remained until the event. The Ohio State coach wrote to each committee chair with general instructions for putting together an equitable and powerful committee. Olsen urged Bunn to choose for his District 8 committee one coach from the Pacific Northwest and one from Los Angeles, thereby providing fair geographic representation. Olsen's conversation with Allen regarding the District 5 Selection Committee composition revealed major obstacles the tournament would come up against. Olsen encouraged Allen to select a committee of individuals who have "some standing in the basketball world." This could include coaches or athletic administrators, and, importantly, they have to be "NCAA men." However, Olsen also mentioned that "in some of the other districts the chairmen are going to put on their committee one outstanding newspaper man."[25]

The "newspaper man" issue came with complexity. In one sense, Olsen and the NCAA wanted this to be a tournament run by college men for college teams and for the good of college basketball. Newspapermen ran the National Invitation—a setup that in some ways spawned the creation of this NCAA event. And yet newspapermen controlled much of the media. With the scribes' approval, the tournament could receive a great deal of publicity. If they felt excluded, the scribes could ignore the event in their columns and the tournament would suffer. Allen understood this dynamic and responded to Olsen with ambiguity. "The one outstanding newspaper man in this vicinity is Clyde E. McBride (of the *Kansas City Star*)," Allen opined. Beyond his faithful and fair sports reporting, McBride had also been "friendly to" the AAU tournament when Kansas City hosted the event. As Allen recalled, "It was his support that really put that tournament over." After all of these praises, Allen described his hesitation in asking McBride to serve with him— Liston's Kansas City tournament.[26]

"Mr. McBride has been very friendly in aiding in the promotion of (Liston's) tournament," Allen acknowledged, adding that he was "just a little afraid at this time" to approach McBride. Allen's hesitation had to do with the tournament committee's second order of business—the tournament sites. Olsen and Allen favored Kansas City to host the Western Regional and the National Final. However, with Liston's tournament in the Garden City's Municipal Auditorium from March 13–18, 1939, the NCAA event would have to schedule the Western Regional before and the National Final after that optimal week if it were to utilize Kansas City's premiere venue. Allen believed that bookending Liston's tournament would diminish support for the older event—a change he could accept but McBride would dislike. If McBride saw or sensed a conflict between the two tournaments, he would honor his prior commitment to Liston while declining Allen's offer.[27]

Thus, Allen recruited McBride by having coaches from his district write letters expressing what the Kansas City scribe's inclusion in the selection committee would mean to the tournament. Allen further expressed his and McBride's shared interest in having Kansas City become a major focal point for college basketball. Hosting the inaugural NCAA tournament would provide a large step toward this goal. And yet the tricky issue of the dates remained.[28]

John Bunn's voice from the West Coast came forth to provide an answer of sorts. "I suppose that Kansas City is the best place to hold the tournament," the San Franciscan allowed, "however, we shall run into competition with the Liston party." Indeed, this presented certain scheduling problems, but those were potentially surmountable. Of equally great concern, though, was the confusion of two "national college" basketball tournaments occurring simultaneously. Carl Lundquist of the *Kansas City Journal-Post* queried Allen on this issue. "In what respect will (the NCAA tournament) differ from (Liston's event)?" the reporter asked, and, "Will these two tournaments conflict in any way?" These questions forced Olsen and company to reconsider using Kansas City as a host site.[29]

Bunn, as a former Kansas Jayhawk hoopster under Allen, knew the region and amateur basketball very well. He also knew Olsen's second option out west: Denver. "If you were to hold the tournament in Denver," Bunn argued, "you would compete with the A.A.U. affair." Based on previous tensions between the NABC and AAU, this would also represent a less-than-ideal arrangement. What made the decision for this committee, though, came from a different issue that Bunn raised. "The date you have [unofficially] chosen for the play off for the western districts [March 6–11] is in conflict with the Pacific Coast Conference championship series," Bunn mentioned. Stanford's conference—the premiere athletic league in District 8 and potentially much of the American West—planned to play part of its conference championship series the week after that. Thus, if Olsen chose March 6–11 for the Eastern regionals, he could get Kansas City, but he probably would not get McBride and definitely would not get the Pacific Coast Conference champion. If Olsen chose the final days of the following week for the Eastern and Western Regionals, he would not get Kansas City but he would definitely get the Pacific Coast champion and might still get McBride, too.[30]

"I believe we could build up considerable enthusiasm for the tournament if you saw fit to bring it to San Francisco," Bunn added at the end of his note to Olsen on December 16, 1938. The City by the Bay had many redeeming qualities that perked Olsen's ears. It was becoming a tourist destination, it was near Bunn's office at Stanford, and it was a region that had been captivated by college basketball and the likes of Hank Luisetti in recent years. Further, the San Francisco Fair would coincide with the mid-March dates, and the exposition promised to cover the expenses—including team travel— of the games it would host. Thus, the committee chose San Francisco and its Sports Coliseum—nicknamed the Cow Palace—on man-made Treasure Island to host the Western Regional.[31]

Olsen chose Chicago for the Championship East-West Final game, and did so without much discussion. The Windy City offered a large population and a geographically central hub that would make East and West travel as easy as possible. Olsen did, however, survey his committee regarding the date and venue. Chicago offered a large venue in Chicago Stadium, yet it was available only on Monday, March 27. Nevertheless, it could hold 13,000 fans and had "reasonable rent." Olsen, however, had publicized Northwestern's Patten Gymnasium for the night of Saturday, March 25, in his earlier press releases. Despite the allure of possible "prominence and finances" that could result from Chicago Stadium, the committee agreed that the March 25 date was much better—it was a Saturday, which would garner more spectator interest and require participating teams to miss less class time than a Monday championship.[32]

Allen was not pleased with any of the Chicago decisions. Under the impression that Kansas City would be the host of the national East-West final, the coach griped, "It seems to me that there has been too little communication between the members of the committee to have made a decision so peremptorily." Further, when the Western Regional was scheduled for March 20 and 21, he believed that the March 25 championship provided the Western representative in the final with too little travel time. With less than two months until the tournament began, Olsen put forth his best diplomatic efforts to appease Allen's complaints. Chicago remained the host city; Patten Gymnasium in Evanston remained the venue; but after weeks of discussion, Olsen pushed the date back to Monday, March 27. At the time of this decision, Chicago Stadium no longer had its vacancy.[33]

In the East, site determination proved just as difficult. New York City would provide the natural geographic counterpart to San Francisco. Olsen's original proposal to the NCAA mentioned Indianapolis, but the committee knew that New York City held much more promise. However, with the

MBWA tournament tentatively scheduled in Madison Square Garden when the NABC hoped to squeeze its way in, logistics became a concern—and so did the fate of the New York tournament. Olsen and his committee discussed the matter with Everett Morris and the other MBWA officials. As late as January 21, 1939, the *New York Times* sports editor announced that, "Due to the N. C. A. A.'s announced intention of holding a national collegiate championship, the plans for the Basketball Writers Association tournament are being held temporarily in abeyance." Thus, despite its riches from the 1938 event, the MBWA still publicly pondered shutting down its operations to accommodate the NCAA.[34]

The abeyance did not last long. Two weeks earlier, the MBWA had commissioned a study to determine the advisability of continuing its tournament in light of the new and similar NABC event. The results came back positive. "Several colleges have signified their willingness to send teams (to the National Invitation tournament)," *New York Times* sportswriter Francis J. O'Riley noted. Several NABC members scoffed at this supposed research, noting that the MBWA asked coaches if they would still be interested in playing while feting them with a lavish meal. These local coaches, the skeptics argued, wanted to appease the MBWA because the scribes were the source of their teams' marketing. O'Riley also publicly proclaimed what had become the company line, stating, "The (MBWA) voted to give the National Collegiate Athletic Association all the help possible in the conduct of its national championship tournament in March."[35]

While MBWA members gave public support for the start-up NABC tournament in their news columns, the goodwill was not enough to alter Ned Irish's schedule at Madison Square Garden. Irish was not willing to bump any of the Garden's late March events to accommodate the new and unproven tournament. The MBWA was also unwilling to cede its Madison Square Garden tournament dates. In looking elsewhere, the NABC chose the next best thing. But this meant a step outside of the Big Apple—a move that had gigantic implications. Philadelphia's Palestra hosted the Eastern Regional tournament dates. The City of Brotherly Love could not match New York City, but it was a basketball-mad conurbation and it would be the only game in town in late March 1939.[36]

District Decisions

With the dates and sites set, district selection committees began preparing to choose the top team in each of the NCAA's eight geographic regions. However, with the MBWA tournament also seeking out top talent, this would be no easy task. Each tournament was only as good as the teams that entered it. Therefore, securing acceptance from the invitations that went out became a high priority.

Olsen and his committee, therefore, went to great lengths to publicly explain which teams were eligible. This inaugural event was officially an NCAA championship—of that, Olsen wanted no ambiguity, even though the NABC administered and staffed it.[37] Uncertainty remained because the NCAA stayed behind the scenes and let the coaches do all the work in running the event. As such, only NCAA member institutions could participate. Schools like LIU, the committee noted, were not eligible because they were not NCAA members. The association enjoyed far fewer members in 1939 than it does today—only 221 schools total. Its strict guidelines for member schools often discouraged independent institutions from joining. One guideline in particular—freshmen eligibility—became a major dividing line. As Olsen, Allen, and crew discussed this matter, they reminded one another that NCAA membership prohibits freshmen to play on varsity teams. This "year in residence" rule by itself would have also excluded schools like LIU.[38]

This rule limited the scope of teams that Olsen's selection committees could choose. However, it did not mean that NCAA teams had to choose the NCAA tournament. Indeed, NCAA members could, based on merit, choose between any of the three postseason events. Thus, Olsen had to promote his event to the association's membership. Most of this early communication came within the NCAA's fifth district—the region in which Liston held his tournament. Dr. F. H. Ewerhardt, vice president of the NCAA's fifth district, wrote a letter to each of the twenty-three NCAA member schools in his region. "Your active support is needed in order that the development of so-called national tournaments by non-collegiate interests be retarded," the professor urged, continuing, "We members of the Fifth District should give (the NCAA tournament) our unlimited support to the exclusion of any other national tournament." Ewerhardt spoke in no uncertain terms against Liston's tournament. Four NCAA District 5 schools had played in Liston's event already. Rallying cries were less forceful outside of the Kansas City region.[39]

While Ewerhardt's underlying arguments focused on the purity of the NCAA event—the money would go back to the association, the schools, and the coaches' organization—the tournament committee also went to great lengths to rectify the logistical complaints of the other existing tournaments. Olsen and his committee tried to keep the number of games at a minimum to avoid the charge that "competing in the NCAA tournament involved a lot of 'post-season' play." District 7, a region with only ten NCAA member schools, asked Olsen if it could host a play-in tournament. The chairman responded gently but clearly, stating, "If we can possibly select representatives from each of the eight N.C.A.A. districts without resorting to play-offs within each district then that is the thing which should be done." Olsen relayed to his committee that, if it is "impossible to make a final selection . . . and you find that (the top) teams are willing to play off to see who will represent the district, then I can see no objection to such a procedure." Any extra play-off format or play-in games would potentially be seen as a deterrent if it forced teams to miss more class time. After all, many prominent conferences were just beginning to allow any postseason play because of the NCAA's new event. Thus, the new tournament remained conscious of its scope.[40]

As a result of this directive, selection committees out west in Districts 6, 7, and 8 simply chose what they thought were the best teams—Texas, Utah State, and Oregon, respectively. Yet these decisions did not come without complexity. In District 7, Colorado won the premier conference—the Mountain States Conference, also known as the Big 7. Colorado had traveled to New York and finished second in the inaugural National Invitation in 1938 and had also voyaged back to the Big Apple in December for a set of holiday games. Thus, the Buffaloes were exhausted. Accepting an NCAA bid would mean that they would be extending their season at least two weeks beyond their last regular season game, and so the team opted out of all postseason play. The district selection committee then chose the next best team.[41]

District 5 had a more difficult time choosing its team. This region included two similarly prominent athletic conferences—the Big Six and the Missouri Valley—the winners of which could not be fairly compared. The four-person selection committee, which included Kansas's Allen, decided that they needed a play-off to decide their representative. Missouri, the top Big Six team and one of four play-off selections, opted out at the last minute and so the Big Six's Oklahoma and Oklahoma A&M and Drake from the Missouri Valley battled for the coveted spot. Oklahoma won the play-off and took home the honor of representing the district in San Francisco.[42]

In the East, Districts 1, 2, and 3 chose Brown, Villanova, and Wake Forest as their representatives in the same fashion as Districts 6, 7, and 8—a panel of experts analyzed the top teams and chose from among them, just as Olsen had hoped. Wake Forest was the Southern Conference champion that the selection committee chose over a strong Kentucky squad and Clemson, the Southern tournament champions. This was the first of many contentious District 3 Selection Committee decisions. This district included eleven states in Dixieland and the District of Columbia. Two prominent athletic conferences would continually make this a difficult district to oversee. Villanova accepted its bid, but the Wildcats lamented in hindsight that they would have rather played in the National Invitation. The committee in District 1 chose Brown after Eastern Intercollegiate Basketball League champion Dartmouth decided against postseason play. District 4 chose Bradley Tech of Peoria, Illinois. However, the Peorians turned them down in favor of a National Invitation bid they received from New York. Bradley had bowed out in the first round of the National Invitation the previous year and felt it had unfinished business in Madison Square Garden. The NCAA's District 4 selection committee then went down its list to the next best team and chose Big Ten champion Ohio State. This change in District 4 plans started a trend of Big Ten teams representing District 4 that became touchy. Bradley's snub of the NCAA offer unknowingly and unfairly demonstrated what would become an accusation of the event—that it favored conference-affiliated teams over conference-independent teams. This accusation would grow immensely in the future.[43]

The Third Annual National Intercollegiate and the Second Annual National Invitation Tournaments

On March 13, nineteen conference champions and thirteen other teams tipped off the third annual National Intercollegiate Basketball Championship Tournament in Kansas City. Liston amped up the promotions for his event in light of the additional tournament on this postseason's slate. Associated Press columnist Whitney Martin wrote favorably on February 2 about the Kansas City event, arguing that it "would seem the most representative and consequently carry more prestige" than the other two. Martin's logic was that Liston's event was open to all accredited four-year colleges whereas only NCAA members could play in the NCAA tournament and only invited teams could play in the New York City event. The counterargument to Martin's case had to do with the belief that bigger schools—those who played in the NCAA and National Invitation tournament—were naturally better than the smaller schools that played in Liston's event.[44]

However, the *Kansas City Journal-Post* denied that claim as it promoted the 1939 National Intercollegiate tournament. "Only a scattered few of the 32 colleges in the brackets represented colleges of more than 1,000 students," the daily reported, but "they came as giant killers." The article continued, stating, "almost every small college on the list has won its way into the tournament by bowling over a team from a school many times as large." Yet the major source of pride for the locals who supported Liston's event was that "many of the coaches voiced the belief that the 'major league' colleges

which might have been eligible stayed away to avoid the possible humilia-
tion of being beaten in the first round by a team from Waxahachie, Texas,
Natchitoches, La., or perhaps Menominee, Mich." This jab had unique reso-
nance. It carried some weight in that big-name teams seemed to have little to
gain from an appearance in Kansas City. But the message had a detrimental
long-term effect, that a big school should be humiliated by losing to a team
from Waxahachie, Natchitoches, or Menominee. More helpful and long-
sighted dialogue would have argued that there's nothing embarrassing about
losing to teams from obscure towns because they are very good.[45]

The high quality of teams attracted twice as many ticket sales—30,000—
as the 1938 tourney. The Central Missouri State Teachers' quest for a third
straight championship fell short as the Mules lost to Peru Teachers College of
Nebraska in the quarterfinals. Peru lost in the semifinal to San Diego State,
a team who traveled 2,200 miles to get to the event. The Aztecs then fell
one point short in the finals, missing a last-second desperation shot to lose
the crown to Southwestern College of Kansas. The title, therefore, stayed
in region.[46]

On March 9, the MBWA finalized its six-team roster when out-of-region
fives from Bradley and New Mexico A&M—an entrant in Liston's 1938
event—accepted their invitations to the New York City event. Local sportswriters kept a close record of the selection process noting the broad and
successful teams the MBWA had considered for invites. Indeed, local scribes
thought more broadly about this year's participants because it thought more
highly of its event. "The tourney is not two years old and it is already considered the top championship of the country," one local paper reported, adding
boastfully that, "The winner of the competition on Ned Irish's midtown
court will be recognized as the champion, while the victors in the other play-
offs will be known as the winners of just so many play-offs." Among this
elite group of potential participants were Southwestern of Kansas, Washburn
of Missouri, and Roanoke of Virginia. The New York tournament's selection committee publicly stated that they "refused to allow themselves to be
entranced by 'name colleges,' but have insisted on getting teams of undisputed class." Roanoke and Washburn had strong showings at the previous
year's National Intercollegiate Basketball Championship Tournament in
Kansas City, and Southwestern was weeks away from winning Liston's third
annual event. By considering these teams, the MBWA may have believed in
the quality of small college teams present in Kansas City, or it may have been
trying to steal the Kansas City event's top teams.[47]

The MBWA only invited Roanoke out of the three, and it may have been
a result of Coach Gordon White's promotional tour of the Big Apple early

in the season. White hobnobbed with the local newspapermen quite successfully. The Virginia squad's "Five Smart Boys" would face local St. John's in
the first round. The "Johnnies" gained their invite by virtue of having the
top record in the city. At 17-2, they outmatched all local competition except
for LIU, who rarely played local opponents and ended with a 19-0 record in
a national schedule. LIU faced New Mexico A&M. The Aggies entered the
National Invitation as newcomers, but they had a history of success. They
traveled east as three-time defending Border Conference champs that had
not lost a league game in thirty-eight attempts and reached the quarterfinals
of Liston's event the previous season. Further, they brought a team that
averaged 6'4" in height.[48]

New Mexico A&M's Kiko Martinez entered the tournament as his
team's leading scorer. New York newspapers identified him as the "ace"
of a high-scoring team. These scribes also mentioned that Martinez had
led his home country to the bronze medal at the 1936 Olympic basketball
tournament. Therefore, Mexican American Martinez would line up against
LIU African American Dolly King in the first postseason college basketball
game featuring two integrated squads. Both stars led their teams into this
tournament with postseason experience, and local writers gave little mention
to this racial breakthrough.[49]

King's entrance in the inaugural New York event the previous year
came and went with little hoopla. The Long Islanders lost in the first round,
and New York City writers did not focus on King's skin color as the story.
Martinez's inclusion in the 1939 event also received little attention. New
York City again showed progressive attitudes toward race, and Martinez's
light skin color would have evoked less antipathy throughout most of the
country at the time. The inclusion of these minority athletes in New York
City proves that the MBWA assessed each possible participating team on its
merit, when in many other athletic competitions around the country at the
time, merit mattered only if skin was the right color.[50]

On Wednesday, March 15, the New York invitational tournament began
with the MBWA proudly declaring, "Two games is the most any tournament quintet has lost" in the regular season. A crowd of 14,443 tickethold-
ers watched as the local teams stole the show. King's LIU pulled away at
the end to defeat Martinez's New Mexico team, 52–45, while St. John's
simply outmanned Roanoke while coasting to a 71–47 win. Disappointed
by their teams' showings, the Roanoke and New Mexico coaches pleaded
for another chance to woo the local crowd. The gracious New York City
hosts allowed the visiting teams to stay and open up a triple-header in the
National Invitation's next scheduled date.[51]

New Mexico's "Crimson Cavalcade" and Roanoke's "Five Smart Boys" squared off in an exhibition game on Monday, March 20, to open the semifinal evening of the National Invitation. The triple-header started at 7 p.m. and an estimated 15,000 showed up to watch New Mexico hold off Roanoke in a game for little more than pride. Thus, Roanoke, indirectly representing all small schools in this major event, left with two unfortunate losses. New Mexico A&M made the long trek home having salvaged some dignity in the last game, but their 1939 postseason ended much like 1938—with a loss that kept them out of the semifinal round of a national tournament.[52]

By the time St. John's squared off with Loyola of Chicago that evening in the first semifinal, 18,206 fans had gained entrance, making this Madison Square Garden's third largest basketball crowd ever. The Chicago squad remained unbeaten on the season by taking down the Johnnies in overtime, 51–46. In the nightcap, LIU also kept its unbeaten season in tact by holding off Bradley Tech. After racing out to a 23–11 halftime lead, the LIU Blackbirds weathered numerous Bradley attacks and hung on to win 36–32.[53]

Thus, a battle of unbeatens ensued two nights later for the second National Invitation title; 18,033 spectators watched the consolation and final games. In the opener, semifinalists Bradley and St. John's squared off. Bradley won its first National Invitation game in its third try, downing the Brooklyn squad, 40–35. In the finals, LIU took home top honors with a surprisingly easy 44–32 win. Loyola's 6'9" Mike Novak had dominated the tournament to that point on both ends of the court. However, Blackbird coach Clair Bee had his troops prepared. On defense, LIU employed an innovative tactic whereby they never had less than two men covering Novak—one of the original "double teams." On offense, to neutralize Novak's ability to "tend the goal" by swatting away shots near the rim (at a time when goaltending rules did not exist), Bee had his men shoot high arcing shots off the backboard all night. Novak batted away nine shots in Loyola's semifinal victory against St. John's but he could not reach even one against the Blackbirds. Gordon White, the Roanoke coach, summed up the victory most aptly by saying, "Any team that can change its style of shooting overnight and still click deserves to win." Coach Bee's reputation rose quickly after this game.[54]

Two days later, the MBWA hosted an awards banquet that all four semifinal teams attended. LIU received the championship trophy, both finalists were awarded brand-new wristwatches, and every participating team received gold medals—even LIU's mascots. The parting gifts showed the MBWA's prosperity. While each participating team had its expenses covered and then some, the watches and medals additionally induced players to return to this tourney if invited.[55]

The Inaugural NCAA Tournament

While the season was over for the only undefeated team in the country—National Invitation champion LIU—one game remained on the schedule. On Monday, March 27, Northwestern University's Patten Gymnasium hosted the NCAA championship game between Ohio State and Oregon. Both teams reached the finals without any major scares in earlier round match-ups. In the East, Ohio State pulled away late against Wake Forest on Friday, March 17, with a 64–55 first-round win in front of 2,036 fans before rolling over Villanova—a hometown team of sorts—53–36 in the sectional final among a paltry crowd of 1,489 at Philadelphia's Palestra. Oregon played even more dominantly in its sectional, blowing out Texas 56–41 and Oklahoma 55–37 in front of a two-night total of more than 6,000 spectators in San Francisco.[56]

Oregon had won the right to enter the NCAA tournament by winning the Pacific Coast Conference with a 14-2 league record. With a 10-2 league record, Ohio State sneaked in as the Western Conference champs with the help of some late-season losses to the league's top teams—and Bradley's lack of interest in the event. Since Ohio State was not even the top choice of its district selection committee, its success in the tournament came with complexity. If the second best team in District 4—which encompassed Ohio, Michigan, Indiana, Illinois, Wisconsin, and Minnesota—could reach the tournament finals, then it must be a strong district. However, Bradley placed third in the six-team National Invitation tournament. It stood to reason, then, that Bradley may have been the top team in the NCAA field had it accepted its bid. It certainly would have been among the top two teams, at least on paper. And so its finish behind unbeaten LIU and previously undefeated Loyola of Chicago—also geographically within District 4, but not an NCAA member—meant that the New York tourney may have had higher-quality teams, at least at the top.

Bradley's spurning of the NCAA for the National Invitation probably did not strike many as unusual at the time. Indeed, Ohio State was not even that excited about the event despite having a coach who founded it. Buckeye captain Jimmy Hull recalled, "Our ball club was so tired at the end of the Big Ten season that we were not interested in playing in this tournament." Hull continued, "It was a new tournament—unheard of. There was no publicity about it. And we didn't get any publicity in our town of Columbus until we won the Eastern championship." In fact, Hull and his teammates did not even know about the tournament until after the regular season. "Olsen never said a word to us about going to the NCAA tournament all season,"

Hull remembered. Ohio State's late rise in the Big Ten standings came unexpectedly—so much so that the university held a celebration in which 1,500 students showed up to praise their team for its conference title. Thus, Olsen may have had no reason to tell his troops about the opportunity any earlier.[57]

Oregon played a regular season schedule much more suited to postseason preparation. "I believe the making of our team came in December 1938 when we pioneered an Eastern trip for teams from the northwest," Oregon coach Howard Hobson surmised. The Ducks made stops in Portland, Philadelphia, Cleveland, Buffalo, Detroit, Peoria, Des Moines, and San Francisco on their sojourn to New York City and back, playing ten games in twenty-two days. "Because of playing all through the rest of the country, we were ready for any kind of officiating," Hobson noted, indicating how his team overcame the difficulties of basketball's regionalism that had plagued so many other teams seeking championships in the game's past.[58]

The NABC held its 1939 convention in Chicago on the weekend of the tournament final. Four hundred coaches attended and stayed as part of the "near-capacity crowd of 5,500" to watch the Ohio State-Oregon matchup on Monday night. Oregon's "Tall Firs" had three starters with more height than Ohio State's tallest player and used this advantage along with some versatile and quick guard play to win a fast-paced game, 46–33. Ohio State's Hull had an ankle injury that limited his effectiveness in the championship. Further, Oregon had prepared better. Hull explained, "We were blind all the way through this thing. We knew practically nothing about Oregon. We had no idea they had all that height. We had nothing to practice against." Olsen either took Oregon lightly, was too busy with tournament operations, or feared the awkwardness of setting up a tournament that his team won, leading him to neglect his scouting duties. Hobson, however, had done his homework. Oregon forward John Dick recalled that they "had some knowledge about Ohio State" that gave them the confidence they needed.[59]

Before the game, Hobson told his captain Bobby Anet "to make Ohio State call the first timeout and not to call any until we were really tired." Ohio State called five and Oregon did not call any. So Hobson asked Anet after the game why he did not call any timeouts when the game was in hand. Anet responded, "You told me not to call a timeout unless we were tired, and hell, we're not tired." The throng of coaches in attendance noticed Oregon coach Howard Hobson's unique use of his players' talents. His two guards on offense played as forwards on defense. This raised Hobson's stock among coaches. Ohio State coach Harold Olsen, the tournament committee chairman, had neither the athleticism nor the versatility on his team to match the "Webfoots." Thousands of fans back in Eugene enthusiastically greeted

Oregon's Bobby Anet receives the championship trophy. The statuette at the top of the trophy had been cracked off during the game when Anet chased after a loose ball and crashed into the trophy table. *March 27, 1939, University of Oregon Archives Photographic Collection, Special Collections & University Archives, University of Oregon Libraries, Eugene, Oregon.*

Hobson and the "Tall Firs" upon their triumphant return. The Ohio State players, returning to a campus vacated by spring break, received no such welcome for their second-place finish.[60]

The 1939 NABC Convention

During NABC meetings that championship weekend, Olsen and his committee presented a report to the general assembly regarding their work. They made plain to this aggregation that most of the individuals whom they had chosen as district selection committee members were also NABC members. This ensured the association that this NCAA tournament that spawned from the NABC maintained a strong coaches' presence. Olsen and his colleagues assured the membership that his "committees have functioned in a very fine manner," saying that they were "faced with a good many of the problems which a pioneer in any event is sure to run into." And even though "there are no doubt some 'bugs' in the program as carried out this season," he made sure to mention that the "tournament gives promise of becoming a very outstanding event in basketball."[61]

With that said, Olsen offered three suggestions that he and his committee believed would enhance the tournament in future instantiations:

> 1. That if the N.C.A.A. Basketball Tournament is to be the success that it should be, it must have the whole-hearted support of every single member of the Coaches' Association. In this connection it seems that the Coaches' Association as such might well have a larger measure of the direction of the tournament. For example, we should like to propose that the N.C.A.A. agree that a considerable number of the members of the tournament committee be appointed by the Coaches' Association rather than the N.C.A.A. and, further, that the Coaches' Association may share directly in the profits of the tournament. Such a participation in the net proceeds of the tournament would give the Coaches' Association more funds with which to do some of the things that they can do for basketball better than any other organization.[62]

While this suggestion begins as a call to arms for the NABC to unite and fight against the Kansas City and New York City tournaments, Olsen does not follow through in that way. Instead, he offers his thoughts on negotiations with the NCAA on tournament setup and profit sharing. The distribution of proceeds would continue to be an issue in the years to come.

Olsen's second suggestion finished the inference he made to other tournaments in the first suggestion:

> 1. That the Coaches' Association go on record as believing that the conduct of collegiate basketball events should be in the hands of the colleges or some association of colleges and not in the hands of any outside promoters.[63]

This is a clear jab at the National Invitation and, to a lesser extent, the National Intercollegiate Basketball Championship Tournament. Olsen was not comfortable with the way these three tournaments had coexisted in the previous months. The Ohio State coach ruefully noted, "Because of the late start and because of opposition in some quarters by other agencies interested in conducting so-called 'national basketball tournaments,' there was considerable difficulty experienced in arranging the set-up" of the tournament. Olsen directed this lamentation at both the New York City and Kansas City events, neither of which was willing to cede its prized venue or its dates to the NCAA.[64]

Kansas City and New York City may have been better host sites for NCAA sectional competition. Madison Square Garden's seating capacity far outnumbered what any other venue could offer, and the National Invitation prospered because of it. The two nights of competition in Philadelphia's Palestra attracted fewer than 3,600 fans total—just a fraction of what the Garden drew in a single night of National Invitation action. San Francisco fared a bit better, totaling 6,000 fans over two nights. While still a small number compared to what New York City and Kansas City regularly drew, the Western Sectional did not lose money for the NCAA tournament as the San Francisco Fair covered the full expenses of the four teams and tournament operations.[65]

Olsen's third argument strayed from the first two but dealt with the Olympic representation issue that had been so high on Phog Allen's priority list:

1. That the Coaches' Association register a protest at the decision
   to drop basketball from the 1940 Olympic games and that it
   take steps to secure reconsideration by the Olympic Committee
   for this event.

As early as 1932, the Japanese delegation had promised Allen that when it hosted the 1940 Olympics, basketball would be on the docket as a medal sport. As European interest in basketball increased from 1932 to 1935, basketball took an important step by gaining entrance into the Berlin Games. However, the aftermath of that American-dominated tournament presented new problems. Shortly after 6'8" Joe Fortenberry and 6'5" Frank Lubin led the American team to the gold medal, Japanese basketball officials made a proposal. They believed that it was unfair for nations with taller players to compete with nations whose citizens do not grow as tall. Therefore, they circulated a petition seeking a 6'3" height limit on further international basketball competition. Mexico and China joined Japan in this proposal but an official ban never reached legislation. This injustice did succeed, however, in moderating the growth in the game's popularity worldwide. The "shorter" nations to which Japan referred began to think twice about promoting interest in a sport that so heavily favored taller players. By 1939, the International Olympic Committee had stripped Tokyo of the Games for political reasons and awarded them to Helsinki, Finland. However, because of the increased threat of war and the financial belt-tightening that accompanied, officials dismissed a number of other sports, too.[66]

With the official onset of war in Europe in 1939, the NABC did not have to worry about basketball's status in the Olympics as the International Olympic Committee decided to cancel the 1940 games. The NABC could then focus its efforts on a more central problem to its existence—its ailing financial state. After Oregon beat Ohio State to take home the NCAA "national championship," the tournament ended with expenses totaling $2,573 and revenues of only $42.54. Low ticket sales and high travel costs produced a debt that the NABC would not be able to repay.[67]

The NCAA graciously forgave this debt, but not without implications for the future. Olsen had less bargaining power to ask for more of the future proceeds, and the NCAA would provide greater oversight. Yet these implications were contingent upon whether the event would even continue—a questionable proposition based on the poor bottom line from the inaugural tournament.

CHAPTER 4

Toward Sustainability and Financial Solvency, 1939–1940

The inaugural 1939 NCAA basketball tournament left its organizers with plenty of work to do to ensure its future. Harold Olsen offered the most positive public pitch he could despite the tournament's financial shortcomings, but the Ohio State coach and his tournament committee had a Herculean task on their hands to convince the NABC and NCAA to continue the affair. Olsen's committee made changes, but not before intense discussion and shrewd policy moves that allowed the tournament more time to grow.

Olsen garnered every bit of public relations expertise he had for his assessment of the inaugural tournament as he spoke to the media, the NCAA, and his coaching colleagues. Knowing that his tournament was younger, attracted fewer fans, and had a bottom line much worse than both the National Invitation tournament in New York City and the National Intercollegiate Basketball Championship Tournament in Kansas City, the Ohio State coach assessed his tournament in the best light possible.

Shining any positive light on the inaugural gala was not easy. In theory, the NABC Basketball Tournament Committee—including Olsen, Phog Allen of Kansas, John Bunn of Stanford, Marquette's Bill Chandler, and New York City's H. H. Salmon—organized the tournament in a way that would serve the NABC's aims of promoting basketball at the collegiate and amateur levels. The tournament's financial goals were unclear from the start. The NABC wanted money to go directly toward basketball and hoped that would happen in a variety of ways. The coaches hoped to provide some surplus into an Olympic Basketball Fund, they hoped to give some money to the NCAA, and they hoped to reimburse participating team expenses. Then, if any money remained, it would go to the participating teams and to the NABC for the betterment of basketball. The Western Regional was the most certain. As the San Francisco Fair promised to cover team expenses the NABC had nothing to worry about. However, they also had fewer rights to any potential distribution of profits.[1]

When the tournament ended with red financial ink, payouts could not be made to the intended stakeholders and the NCAA had to assume the debt incurred. Yet Olsen stated that the "National Collegiate Athletic Association Basketball tournament made a very satisfactory debut." And his counterparts at the NCAA concurred, despite having to indemnify the tournament. NCAA president W. B. Owens proclaimed that the tournament would "provide a great national contest" and speculated that "The National Collegiate Athletic Association Basketball tournament should become a classic, a fitting annual climax in the program of this great American sport." Owens also sent a subtle message that identified the source of his pleasure. "It is entirely fitting that the 'prestige' of college basketball should be supported, and demonstrated to the nation, by the colleges themselves," Owens argued, "rather than that this be left to private promotion and enterprise." Stanford's John Bunn, Olsen's colleague on the tournament committee, agreed with Owens and Olsen when he optimistically wrote, "This NCAA tournament undoubtedly will develop into the main basketball event of the season."[2]

Yet not everyone in the NABC or in college basketball circles held such rosy views of the tournament's future. Oregon's championship coach Howard Hobson lamented that there was a lot of opposition from coaches about continuing the tournament. Coming out of the Great Depression and with escalating political tensions across both oceans, the NABC did not like the thought of being indebted to the NCAA or anyone else. This fiscal prudence and the uncertain future induced Olsen to ponder his next moves. "There is some question about the advisability of us continuing (the tournament)," the tournament committee chair admitted frankly within months of his team's loss in the inaugural championship game.[3]

Early NCAA-Sponsored Championships

Despite the tournament's tenuous future, Olsen had surprisingly little trouble convincing the NCAA to carry on with the tournament. However, the NABC offered a major concession. The NCAA had overseen the inaugural tournament even though it had been run by the NABC. After the 1939 tournament, the NCAA took greater control. Very little actually changed, though, as the NCAA maintained NABC aristocrats Olsen and Allen as the heavyweights on its tournament oversight and operations committee, and maintained similarly structured district selection committees. The most noticeable changes had to do with Olsen and his committee better promoting the NCAA's mission as part and parcel of the tournament.[4]

In 1939, the NCAA basketball tournament was one of a growing number of postseason NCAA-sponsored events. That year, the NCAA also hosted national championship events in men's gymnastics, boxing, track and field, cross country, and golf. The association worked with host schools and venues to fund each of these culminating events differently and, like in basketball's case, revenues did not always cover expenses.[5]

Since the inaugural national intercollegiate track meet in 1921, the NCAA had played an increasing role in hosting national championships, but change occurred slowly. The University of Chicago and its legendary football, baseball, and track coach, Amos Alonzo Stagg, put on the 1921 track meet as an NCAA event. This became the first of its kind and slowly sparked interest in postseason championship events. Many of these championships occurred with very low overhead costs. Oftentimes schools covered the costs for their teams or individuals to participate. More often, and especially in Olympic years, participants paid their own way to the event. But most often, the host site or school covered the expenses that went beyond revenue. Some NCAA championship events, however, ended with profit. If so, participants often received a ceremonial award that had some cash value or a cut of the profits to relieve the cost of expenses.[6]

With all of these different methods, the NCAA was not altogether worried about turning a profit from each event. The association's main focus at this time was not to conduct championship events but to provide cohesiveness to intercollegiate athletics around the country most specifically in the form of game rules. Indeed, rules committee reports dominated the NCAA annual proceedings and had been so since the association's inception in 1905. More recently, addresses on health, safety, and best practices augmented rules committee reports. The inclusion of these reports from faculty members, medical doctors, and university presidents showed a keen interest in the well-being of the students.[7]

When issues regarding end-of-season championship events came to the fore, the focus remained the same—the fairness, health, safety, and well-being of the participating students. Turning a profit or even meeting budget did not seem to be a high priority for the NCAA at this time. Therefore, Olsen and his NABC colleagues followed suit and focused on providing a fair and nonexploitative event in which students would miss as little class time as possible in order to participate. This event, they also hoped, would become the most prestigious and would determine a true national champion. With this prestige, profits would doubtlessly follow.[8]

Even though money did not drive the NCAA's sponsorship of these events, the association encouraged and appreciated financial stewardship and prudence. The red ink of the 1939 basketball tournament's bottom line did not represent poor oversight or a lack of responsibility on Olsen's or anyone else's part. In fact, outside of the tournament's accounting and lack of revenue, every other aspect followed a logical path—even if they encountered bumps in the road. The NCAA wanted to oversee the NABC in hosting a tournament that would provide a formal and nationally recognized ending to the mostly regional competition in which schools took part throughout each season. The NCAA was a willing participant in this endeavor—after all, they were in the nonprofit business of amateur athletics—and they saw the potential of this event. However, NABC members worried about when the NCAA's goodwill might run dry.

Deciding to Continue the Event

Making money on a tournament actually mattered more to the intensely competitive coaches of the NABC. The tournament deficit gave the tournament a shoddy reputation in certain ways, especially compared to its more established peers. As such, the financial deficit hit Olsen and his peers the hardest when compared to the financial solvency of Liston's Kansas City tournament and the financial prosperity of the Madison Square Garden event. Nobody in the NABC wanted their tournament to be the least prominent postseason championship, and financial records after March 1939 put the NCAA event in third place.

Thus, Olsen and his tournament committee had greater difficulty convincing their peers in the NABC that continuing the event was a wise and prudent move. Indeed, the membership of the coaches' association did not uniformly stand behind this tournament after its initial installment. Many NABC members helped run and even participated in Emil Liston's Kansas City tournament or the National Invitation in New York City. To these coaches, both of the privately run tournaments provided a fitting challenge to end the season, even if they may not have been full-fledged national championship events according to the NCAA's moral and academic ideals. But they were enough. If two tournaments saturated the basketball postseason market, then so be it. One tournament existed for small schools and one for big schools. If the NABC tournament did not fit in, then the association could drop the event and redirect its efforts to other endeavors.

Therefore, Olsen and others who sought a second instantiation of the event had to campaign vigorously within their association. Knowing that internal unrest could be the downfall of the event, Olsen set out to convince his NABC colleagues to continue the tournament. While many coaches hesitated to follow him in this tenuous endeavor, he found one ally that proved to be all he needed. Kansas coach Forrest "Phog" Allen enthusiastically supported the tournament's continuation to anyone with whom he could gain an audience. His efforts and promises allowed the tournament to continue.[9]

In fact, Allen wanted to host it. He had a history of successfully running basketball events. Most recently, the Kansas coach had organized and overseen the 1939 NCAA District 5 play-off in Oklahoma City. This two-game, two-night event, which hosted three teams, made $457. Allen also proudly promoted his role in two other prominent basketball events: the 1905 "world's championship" series between the Kansas City Athletic Club and the Olympic champion Buffalo Germans, and the 1936 Olympic Trial play-offs in his region. These three highlights provided evidence that he had a perfect record of hosting successful basketball tournaments in or near Kansas City. Granted, he was aware of Liston's growing tournament of small schools in the Garden City, but did not show any public concern over it. Allen believed in his own abilities to run a profitable event, the philosophy of the NABC tournament, and the willingness of local fans to support such an affair.[10]

Yet the presence of Liston's event continued to generate complications because it would not go away. In the middle of its 1939 event, Liston and his peers took an important step to overcome criticism and solidify its standing. Olsen and others within the NABC and NCAA spoke pejoratively about the other postseason events run by individuals and businessmen rather than the schools themselves. Thus, Liston diminished the role of the Kansas City Chamber of Commerce businessmen who had been helping him and officially joined forces with other coaches in a new "intercollegiate" organization. They called themselves the National Association of Intercollegiate Basketball (NAIB).[11]

With all of this college basketball interest and activity in Kansas City coupled with the popularity of the annual AAU national championship that the Garden City hosted from 1921 to 1934, Allen thought that if he brought the NCAA tournament there, it would be a sure success. "You give me this tournament in Kansas City," he preached to the NABC in the wake of its 1939 convention, "and I will not only pay back the deficit, but we will make you some money." Olsen responded in favor, stating, "The more I think about it the more I am convinced your suggestion of Kansas City is the one to which we should turn." With this response, Allen made it his personal mission to ensure this tournament's success in 1940 and its enduring legacy. The coach put his neck on the line to save the event, and put his heart into ensuring its success and prosperity. As such, the NCAA would be forever indebted.[12]

Once the NCAA accepted Allen's proposal, the coach went to work with great pugnacity. The former boxer did everything short of drawing battle lines to evangelize for the NCAA tournament. Since each of the postseason events was so young, many schools remained open to the possibility of entering any of the events and sought the best one they could. So Allen, a prolific letter writer, began penning his missives on behalf of the NCAA tournament to drum up loyalty among coaches. But this was no mean feat.[13]

National Invitation Changes

The National Invitation tournament required only little effort to perpetuate its event after the 1939 gala. Yet its role in the college basketball postseason remained unclear. Therefore, Madison Square Garden president of basketball Ned Irish and the MBWA acted diplomatically on behalf of college basketball. The National Invitation ended its second annual tournament in much better shape than the NCAA and potentially could have changed its philosophy from a season-ending "invitation" tournament that showcased local teams and some of the best in the country to a national championship format. The MBWA and its invitation tournament likely had the power to do so, and yet such a drastic move would have been imprudent. The college basketball postseason landscape was still very tenuous—many schools hesitated to participate in postseason events when it would mean more lost class time for its players and some schools and conferences had bans on postseason play—and if the MBWA wanted to rope in the nation's top teams, it knew that it would have to play by their rules.

Like Liston and his newly formed NAIB, the MBWA took steps to dampen criticism from the NABC and NCAA. Irish and the local sportswriters profited greatly all winter long from the massive influx of teams around the country visiting Madison Square Garden to play local teams. Irish scheduled these intersectional games as frequently as he could and local sportswriters covered them with great interest. NYU professor and future NCAA president Philip O. Badger argued as much in a letter to Olsen, stating, "(Irish) is anxious to cooperate with us here at New York University and with the N.C.A.A. in every way possible and realized that in certain respects the future of the intercollegiate basketball program at the Garden is related to the matter of maintaining friendly relations with (the NCAA and NABC)." Had Irish and the MBWA tried to grow and overtake the college basketball postseason in 1939 to push out the NCAA tournament, they may have risked a Madison Square Garden boycott from the NABC-member coaches and NCAA schools.[14]

Therefore, instead of attacking, Irish and the MBWA stepped back and heeded the advice from those in power in college basketball administrative circles. The MBWA had been called "obstructionists" and "profiteers" who had no business exploiting college basketball teams for their own personal gains. While the National Invitation's existence may have obstructed the early success of the NCAA tournament and the MBWA may have profited from the tournament, the writers believed they were acting out of good faith and a vested interest in the betterment of college basketball. To prove this goodwill, MBWA president Everett Morris announced in April of 1939 that the MBWA would cede control of the National Invitation basketball tournament to the local colleges, thus killing off the NABC's major criticism that it was run by a private organization that took a cut of the profits. Instead of the writers organizing and administering the tournament, all power would now be vested in the newly created Metropolitan Intercollegiate Basketball Committee (MIBC) comprised of City College of New York, Fordham, Long Island University, St. John's University, Manhattan College, St. Francis University, Pratt Institute, Brooklyn Polytechnic Institute, Brooklyn College, and Hofstra. The president of the newly formed group, Professor Walter Williamson of CCNY, selected representatives from three of the ten member institutions—CCNY, Manhattan, and Brooklyn College—that would likely not qualify to play in the 1940 tournament and one MBWA member to serve on the tournament selection committee. Eastern Intercollegiate League commissioner Asa Bushnell served as the final member of the oversight group.[15]

One school notably missing from the MIBC was New York University. Despite the school's participation in the inaugural National Invitation, their conspicuous absence from the MIBC came with context. Ever since Chancellor Henry MacCracken of NYU called a meeting in December 1905 that led to the creation of the NCAA, the Violet athletic teams remained loyal to the association. This made little difference in most sports, but the landscape of college basketball forced their hand. NYU played mostly local competition and seemed to value its relationships with other metropolitan universities. And yet regarding college basketball's postseason, they chose differently than did their metropolitan counterparts. Professor Philip O. Badger, chair of the NYU intercollegiate athletics oversight board, wrote to Ned Irish and lobbied other metropolitan basketball leaders on philosophical grounds that promoted the amateurism espoused by the NCAA. Badger explained to Irish, "I believe that the function of the writers is that of reporting the games and should not be that of promoting them. The conducting of tournaments in which college teams play should be in the hands of the colleges."[16]

The creation of the MIBC seems to have occurred along these lines. If the colleges wanted tournaments conducted by the colleges, then the MBWA would rather give their tournament to the local colleges who would maintain its operations rather than discontinue it. After all, the National Invitation was quickly becoming a prominent late-winter feature for all New York City newspapers. All of the local schools except NYU carried this torch.

Metropolitan basketball leaders continued to show their willingness to adapt to political pressures while also ensuring their event's survival. The previous year they had informally queried coaches across the country to gauge their interest in participating in the National Invitation. Results came back positive, so they continued the tournament. The writers publicly promoted this interest, but not without opposition. Badger, in particular, believed that political rhetoric had become involved in these discussions. "The coaches in their energy to get favorable publicity for their teams are very likely to play up a bit to the writers." With this continued criticism of their professionalized and exploitative practices, Irish and the MBWA turned their tournament over to the local schools. The popularity of the tournament would not miss a beat under the new administration. In fact, local college athletic programs and the sportswriters who covered their contests remained so closely wedded that the change in the tournament's administration went largely unnoticed.[17]

One of the factors providing confidence in this event was that the metropolitan basketball power structure believed it had better teams than the other postseason events. Based on the 1939 tournament scores, the New York event appeared to have stronger teams. Bradley Tech from Peoria, Illinois, was the top choice of the NCAA's District 2. However, they spurned the NCAA tournament in favor of a bid to the National Invitation. Therefore, the top team in the Midwest—one of college basketball's strongest regions—came to Madison Square Garden and lost its first game on the way to a third-place finish out of six. Ohio State, Bradley's replacement in the NCAA District 2, powered its way through the Eastern Regional to finish as runner-up in the NCAA tournament. Further, National Invitation champion LIU finished the season undefeated while NCAA champ Oregon accumulated five losses throughout the season before hitting its stride late in the winter. On paper, then, the New York invite appeared to have stronger participating teams.[18]

Ned Irish built on this discussion as he designed the slate of regular season college basketball games in the Garden for the 1939–40 season. Irish started the season's fifteen double-headers on December 16 with a matchup of the 1939 NCAA and National Invitation champions. Oregon and LIU both entered the contest having lost multiple stars to graduation but also having suffered no losses in the early season schedule. Spectators clearly understood the importance of this matchup as 17,852 fans paid entrance into the Garden for this pre-Christmas thriller. The Webfoots led most of the way until LIU's furious finish in regulation initiated by Dolly King, its "220-pound Negro Hercules," who "became a double-barreled hero." King made the game-winning shot in overtime for the Blackbirds to triumph by one, 56–55. Arthur J. Daley's *New York Times* postgame write-up proudly declared that the "winners of the national invitation tournament last season (turned) back the champions of the National Collegiate A. A."[19]

Early Relationships among the Tournaments

The victory marked the fortieth in LIU's ongoing win streak that put them at the top of the season's rankings. Eight days after the victory over Oregon, the *New York Times* announced in its calendar year-end sports wrap-up that LIU had been the top team of the previous season. While this seems like a safe choice based on overall records, the Blackbird victory over Oregon in Ned Irish's Garden opener certainly reaffirmed what the local basketball establishment had believed throughout the past season—that LIU was the best in the country. Not surprisingly, then, the Premo and Porretta retrospective poll listed LIU as the top team, too.[20]

In its year-end wrap-up, the *New York Times* referred to the Garden tournament as "the basketball Rose Bowl classic." This analogy perfectly fit the event's philosophy. The National Invitation sent out bids for its event with preconceived notions of who should participate—the best local teams and some of the top "big name" teams from across the country—just like college football's Rose Bowl game. Both of these events provided interesting intersectional competition at the end of their respective sport seasons, but neither gala was nor claimed to be a "national championship."[21]

Official designation as "*the* national championship" continued to elude all three postseason basketball events at the end of 1939 even though the NCAA and NAIB tournaments claimed to be so. They could call themselves "national championships," and their organizers seemed to believe they were, but national consensus did not fall heavily enough on any of the three tournaments to have official possession of that title. The NCAA event seemed best suited for the task, for it hosted a national championship of its association members. However, since NCAA members Bradley Tech and Colorado turned down its invites, the NCAA champ was not necessarily the best of the association. Olsen and his colleagues hoped and believed that the college basketball tournament landscape would change in their favor. But this outcome seemed unlikely at the time, considering the tripartite situation at hand. The NCAA clearly saw both tournaments as thorns. The New York gala invited top-tier teams and played in front of massive crowds and a powerful media. Of this event, the NCAA was envious. Toward Liston's event, the NCAA was less envious than irritated. The newly formed NAIB drew NABC members, wrote a mission statement similar to that of the coaches' association, and most frustratingly for Olsen and Allen, would not fold like the NABC had hoped.

The relationship between the NABC and the NAIB was complex. Liston, a founding father of the NABC and close friend of Allen's, did not start his tournament in secret. He had nothing to hide from the NABC with his brainchild. In fact, he ascertained the help of certain NABC members as his tournament grew to a thirty-two-team field between 1937 and 1938. However, he did not ask for the help of the coaches' association to run the affair. The NABC included enough high-powered coaches from big-name schools that any association-level help likely would have forced Liston to change his tournament's philosophy, especially before the existence of the NCAA tournament. Although Liston would have welcomed big-name schools, he was not prepared to have them commandeer his event.[22]

By the spring of 1939, Liston enjoyed the help of a number of prominent basketball coaches whose teams would likely never seek inclusion in his tournament. George Edwards of Missouri, Clair Bee of LIU, Adolph Rupp of Kentucky, and Henry Iba of Oklahoma A&M were among the cohort of coaches who helped the NAIB officially charter and draft a constitution. Outside of Edwards, who helped in team selection and also played the role of local supporter, the reason the other coaches offered help is unclear. Bee's role is especially befuddling. The LIU coach had no explicit connection to Liston, Kansas City, or the American heartland. His teams often featured prominently at Madison Square Garden and the National Invitation tournament —which seemed to be the antithesis of the NAIB event. Nevertheless, Bee was also known for his progressivism and willingness to try new things. This may have simply been a curious novelty choice for him.[23]

Despite this support, many NABC members looked down upon Liston's event once he created the NAIB. The 1939 NABC president Edward Hickox became the voice of this discontented bloc. Once Liston began publishing an association bulletin entitled, "Intercollegiate Basketball," and sending it to NAIB members—many of whom were also NABC members—Hickox acted on behalf of his organization. The NABC president sent a letter out to all his members except Liston with a fiery denunciation of the new NAIB organization. Questioning what purpose the NAIB has and why it feels the need to charter when the NABC serves similar purposes, Hickox wrote, "I note that the five objectives stated for this proposed organization differ very little from those of our own Association . . . I am frankly puzzled then as to the necessity or desirability of a second organization of this sort." Hickox goes on with his appeal:

> I am disturbed that members of our Organization should wish to ally themselves with what might well become a devisive [sic] movement. If the N.A.B.B.C. [an alternate term for the NABC] is doing the job I think it is, there is no need for a raw organization covering the same ground—instead there will tend to be competition destructive to the strength and influence of both . . . I appeal to you, therefore, to give your best interest and efforts to the N.A.B.B.C., and to consider carefully before giving encouragement or aid to a movement that might well weaken the power and influence of the Basketball Coaches in the United States.[24]

After catching wind of this letter from a number of colleagues, Liston felt the need to respond to Hickox's criticisms. So, despite the ongoing basketball season in which each of these coaches presumably found little free time, Liston replied carefully. In noting the associations' differences, he stated that "The National Association of Intercollegiate Basketball membership is institutional, not individual." This point, while not enough to appease Hickox and his faction alone, became a major component of the future of the NAIB. Liston also simply disputed many of Hickox's charges:

> The National Association of Intercollegiate Basketball is not a "devisive [sic]" organization. The National Association of Intercollegiate Basketball has not, through its membership or through representatives of its membership, sought to discourage or to alienate members of the National Association of Basketball Coaches or any other organization or individual members of such organization.[25]

Liston then goes on to speak of the ways in which the organizations should coexist. In these lines of reasoning, his logic is not airtight and his thoughts hint at the competition inherent in these two organizations that Hickox noted originally. However, Liston's arguments also note that he is in no way apologizing or backing down from his commitment toward the NAIB. He states:

> It is not unlikely that the programs of two national organizations interested in basketball would engage in overlapping activities. I am sure that the National Association of Intercollegiate Basketball is not envious of the accomplishments of the National Association of Basketball Coaches. In fact, many of us are cooperating in the work of the National Association of Basketball Coaches and in its program. If the main controversy is that of determining the national

champion, my suggestion is that the teams qualifying for the N. C. A. A. playoffs or those that can qualify compete in the National Intercollegiate Championship Tournament (NAIB tournament). Or allow those teams that qualify for play in the National Intercollegiate Championship Tournament, or those that can qualify, to participate in the N. C. A. A. playoffs. This would settle once and for all the controversy. Until that is done, there will be a National Intercollegiate Champion (Open Championship), and an N. C. A. A. Champion (Closed Championship) . . . Then in the spirit of cooperation . . . wouldn't it be better to go along in these respective fields, working in the interests of the game without fear that one association will do what the other has not yet been able to do?[26]

The NAIB tournament had been able to attract considerable interest from small schools around the country. The NCAA and National Invitation had been able to garner growing interest from large schools across the nation. The NAIB competed with no other tournament for small schools to compete in its championship. The 1938 NAIB runner-up Roanoke College had been invited to the 1939 National Invitation, giving this "David" a chance to vicariously test the mettle of all small schools against the "Goliaths" who regularly played in the Garden. Roanoke, coming off a twenty-game winning streak and returning much of its 1938 NAIB roster, was trounced by St. John's 71–47 in the opening round of the "Goliath" tournament. The undersized underdogs then lost a consolation game to New Mexico State, the other opening-round loser and, coincidentally, the other past National Intercollegiate participant. The Aggies came to New York City as a novelty act, clad in cowboy boots and ten-gallon cowboy hats during their stay. The MBWA brought these two teams in because of stellar records, but also to diversify the brackets. However, early losses for the exotic southwesterners and the "Five Smart Boys" reaffirmed local prejudices.[27]

Team Selection for the 1940 Tournaments

Competition among small schools remained intense for the limited spots in Liston's "open" tournament. By 1940, the NAIB leader had attracted teams from twenty-four different states in the tournament's four-year history. While this group included teams from every state in the American heartland—the region and culture in which Liston created the tournament—California, Oregon, and Idaho teams represented the Pacific West and North Carolina, Virginia, West Virginia, and Kentucky teams represented the Middle Atlantic and Appalachia. And yet the fourth annual event ended with yet another local champion. Tarkio College of Missouri shot at a "blistering pace" with a new white basketball without seams that Converse launched for the event to defeat San Diego State University in the final.[28]

Competition among large schools became more visible with the two seemingly parallel tournaments. Large schools had to indirectly compete against each other for tournament bids, and the NCAA and National Invitation tournaments competed against each other to see who could attract the best teams. With many of the country's top teams traveling to Madison Square Garden throughout the regular season, competition for the tournament's roster spots would be fierce.

The National Invitation tournament committee met for the first time on February 28, 1940, to begin discussions about team selection. MIBC president Walter Williamson of CCNY led a board comprised of Asa Bushnell of the Eastern League, Everett Morris of the MBWA, Herb Kopf of Manhattan College, and Lou Oshins of Brooklyn College in the selection process. By March 4, Joseph Sheehan of the New York Times announced that Duquesne received the first invitation to the New York event. Duquesne, whose coach Chuck Davies was on the NAIB's board of directors in 1940, had captivated the metropolitan crowd by beating LIU in early February. Sheehan also noted the competition for metropolitan teams to receive National Invitation bids. St. John's and LIU appeared to be in a battle for one invite, and NYU seemed to have a major right to the other. However, Sheehan questioned whether NYU would even accept a bid, arguing that "they may prefer the N. C. A. A.'s Kansas City event."[29]

NYU brought its 18-0 record into a March 5 contest against a struggling CCNY team at Madison Square Garden. Fans, 15,187 of them, viewed an upset that "had to be seen to be believed, and even then it strained credence." NYU's shooters went cold and CCNY's got hot as the latter ended the regular season on a surprise victory, 36–24. The outcome put both CCNY and NYU at 4-1 atop the intra-city standings despite their differing records outside the Big Apple. NYU still expected to receive a bid to the New York invite.[30]

Two days later, NYU announced that it would be ending its basketball season without postseason play. The university's board of athletic control, chaired by Professor Philip O. Badger, noted that "the stress of a strenuous schedule was one of the chief reasons for the committee's final vote." Sportswriters surmised that the strain of maintaining a long winning streak throughout the season also factored in to the decision. The MIBC had extended a formal invitation to NYU, which the Violets subsequently declined. The NCAA's District 2 had not yet chosen its representative to that event, and so NYU took itself out of the running.[31]

This decision had major implications. Not only was NYU the best metropolitan team, the Violets were also Harold Olsen's ticket into New York City. "As I see it," the coach wrote to Philip Badger, NYU's professor in charge of the athletic committee, "New York University can't miss receiving the selection as the N.C.A.A. team to represent District 2" on February 26, less than two weeks before the Violets took themselves out of contention. The coach added, "I feel definitely that if we can't secure a team like New York University . . . that the whole idea of the National Tournament ought to be thrown right out the window." Olsen copied this letter to Allen with a scribbled note at the bottom: "Dear 'Phog'—This will 'make' us—if N.Y.U. will come thru [sic]!" Unfortunately, they did not come through, substantially lowering Olsen's hopes for the event. However, NYU's total escape from postseason play meant that the National Invitation's card lost some luster, too.[32]

March 7 left only four days until tournament action began, and only four teams had accepted bids to the National Invitation. Colorado, St. John's, Oklahoma A&M, and Duquesne prepared to vie for the title. The Oklahomans, in the midst of a twenty-five-game winning streak, tested their mettle more than any other team ever had in one postseason. Coach Henry Iba's Aggie squad accepted their bid to the National Invitation tournament, but only entered on the condition that it not interfere with the team's participation in the NCAA District 5 play-off. Iba and his troops planned to fly to New York for their opening game—a semifinal—on Wednesday, March 13. Win or lose, the team would play again on the final night of competition, Friday, March 15. Ned Irish assured Iba that the Aggie game that night would be over in time for a police escort to lead his team to the airport to catch an 11:10 flight from New York City back to Oklahoma City. The following day, the Aggies would put their Missouri Valley Conference title to the test against the Big Six champion in the NCAA's District 5 qualifying tournament.[33]

Iba noted the local sentiments of his fan base regarding the two tournaments, as he explained, "We're going to keep faith with our followers at home and enter the N. C. A. A. play-offs, but we're going to New York, too." Clearly the local fans valued the postseason action that was occurring very nearby the Aggies' Stillwater campus, and the NCAA meant more in that section of the country than the National Invite. And yet the New York tournament probably carried more prestige at the time, especially among inner basketball circles. It certainly captivated the Aggie squad, as Iba noted that "my seniors want to make the trip East and it may be the last time that an A. and M. team ever has such an opportunity." This last phrase hinted at a future trend in athletic conferences throughout the Midwest. Many of these groupings prohibited or were about to prohibit their annual champion from competing in any event outside of the NCAA tournament.[34]

Allen responded to Oklahoma A&M's entry into the National Invitation with warranted concern. "The ridiculous has happened," he wrote to Olsen in early March, "the winner of the Southwest Conference (Rice), the winner of the Rocky Mountain Conference (Colorado) and the winner of the Missouri Valley Conference (Oklahoma A. & M.) are all entering the promotional tournament in New York." Allen may have jumped to a hasty conclusion, as Rice never actually obtained a bid. Further, Colorado and Oklahoma A&M greatly reduced his fears when they accepted invites to the NCAA Western Regional and District 5 play-off, respectively, in the following days. Still, his logic when complaining to Olsen spoke volumes about the NCAA tournament's inferiority. "There is no justifiable reason for (these teams to compete in the National Invitation) except that these N.C.A.A. teams are entering for the money," he surmised. "This will cause confusion in the minds of the academicians who will resent our tournament. Ours is an educational project and the other is nothing but a promotional venture which strikes at the heart of our tournament." Allen's rhetoric became much more fiery and polemical as the tournaments neared.[35]

On March 8, the MIBC had rounded out its field. LIU—the second local squad—accepted a bid for the third straight season. It became the only team to play in each of the first three New York invites. DePaul, a Catholic school from Chicago, became the last acceptance, entering the tournament for the first time. The MIBC selection committee chose LIU only after NYU shut down its basketball operation for the season, and DePaul received the nod over "Rice Institute" of Texas after great deliberation.[36]

Lou Oshins of Brooklyn College explained the selections with great transparency. "Our problem was more in getting dates at the Garden than in picking the teams," the coach explained, speaking specifically about the Friday night final. Friday nights had become sacred in the Garden as prize-fight boxing demonstrations rarely ceded the venue to any other event. Ned Irish convinced his boss, Colonel John Reed Kilpatrick, to release the date to the MIBC. Had he not, the group was prepared to host only a two-night affair.[37]

Madison Square Garden's scheduling continued to affect the New York and NCAA tournaments. As the MIBC worked with Irish on the 1940 dates, a few possibilities arose, including March 20 and 22. The MIBC needed only one of these, and when NYU's Badger heard of this, he immediately lobbied to get Olsen's event in on the other date. Olsen agreed without hesitation that, if the NCAA could get even one date at the Garden, it should do so—especially when NYU was still in the running for a tournament spot. Since the Eastern Regional required two nights of action, this would complicate matters, but Olsen was willing to send the first-round winners elsewhere for their regional final. Such was the allure of the Garden. Unfortunately for the NCAA, though, Irish scheduled hockey in the Garden on those empty dates before Olsen had a chance to make a decision. And when Badger heard that the MIBC was unwilling to give up any of its secured dates in the Garden, the NCAA was shut out of the premier venue yet again.[38]

With three dates secured, the NYU situation rose to the top of the MIBC's issues. Oshins noted that, had NYU finished the regular season unbeaten, the New York event simply could not have occurred without the Violet team. Oshins implied that there was a possibility of NYU playing in only the NCAA tournament. A New York tournament without the undefeated New York University participating would have lost credibility. "But Nat Holman's City College team helped us out of that dilemma by beating New York," Oshins mentioned, "so we don't need them anymore."[39]

The third annual National Invitation was shaping up to be another successful event. Oshins and his colleagues paired the teams as best they could, candidly speaking about this process, too. Oklahoma A&M and Colorado, as the teams traveling farthest to New York City, received first-round byes, thereby guaranteeing their inclusion on the docket for the final night, too—whether in the championship or consolation games. The Aggies started their season with a loss to Kansas before avenging that setback during a twenty-five-game winning streak that proffered their bid to New York. Colorado went 15-2 on the season, splitting a pair of games with Utah State and losing to Duquesne.[40]

Duquesne went 17-1 on the regular season, beating Colorado and LIU in the process but losing to Indiana. Its first-round opponent would be St. John's, who finished with a 15-4 record. The other first-round game pitted LIU and DePaul—two teams that had split games against each other during the season. With nearly identical records of 20-3 and 21-4, respectively, and similar losses to Southern California, this matchup seemed the most enticing. DePaul also, notably, had lost to the Indiana squad that gave Duquesne its only blemish.[41]

Despite their transparency about the teams they chose, Oshins and his colleagues offered very little regarding the teams they left out. Inviting only six teams to a national tournament excluded many worthy teams. And inviting two local teams every year further complicated the matter. In New York City, and to an only slightly lesser extent in the surrounding region, teams put great stock in tournament invites. Certain excluded teams, then, always finished the season feeling snubbed. Seton Hall University found itself in an especially unique situation seemingly year after year. From 1939 to 1941, Bob Davies led the Tommies with his deft playmaking and scoring abilities. Davies, blessed with blond hair, blue eyes, and fine features, starred in football, basketball, baseball, and track and field. The Boston Red Sox lined up the scholarship at Seton Hall for him to hone his diamond skills, but the "Harrisburg Houdini"—a moniker given for his Pennsylvania hometown and his magical ballhandling abilities—decided to focus on basketball. At 6'1", 175 pounds, with an innocent face and superior talent, Davies became the quintessential All-American boy. These features shone through so much, in fact, that LIU coach and future author of a series of adolescent sports novels, Clair Bee, modeled his overwhelmingly popular title character Chip Hilton after the Tommies' star.[42]

Seton Hall perennially put forth a top-notch basketball team, but the school's location in East Orange, New Jersey, put it on the wrong riverbank. It was not officially a metropolitan team even though it was nearby and often played many metropolitan teams. After winning twenty straight games to finish the season, many Seton Hall fans felt their team deserved a bid—especially over a seemingly inferior 15-4 St. John's squad. Spectators bombarded the *New York Times* with letters to such an extent that the editor responded, saying, "The tournament selectors will do well to avoid New Jersey for a while."[43]

Nevertheless, local sportswriters hailed the third annual National Invitation tournament field as among the best. The *New York Times* furthered the selection committee's ideals when it wrote that the six competing teams "are pretty much the pick of the nation's top-ranking combinations. With the possible exceptions of Southern California and New York University, they have few superiors from coast to coast. Hence the tournament victor will come pretty close to recognition as America's No. 1 team." This speculation reeked of local bias and exaggeration to which many sportswriters were inclined, but there was some substance to these claims. Indeed, history was on the side of the National Invitation, albeit a history that was in some part written by these local sportswriters. "In 1938, Temple won and was bracketed with Hank Luisetti's Stanford team as national champion," the daily went on to argue, and "in 1939 unbeaten Long Island University triumphed in the tournament and was acknowledged as the court power of the United States."[44]

On opening night, the *Times* further promoted the tournament by noting, "For the first time since this postseason classic started there is no tournament favorite. Two years ago Temple was the choice and triumphed. Last year it was L. I. U. that moved right through to victory." Hindsight certainly aided in these claims. In fact, Temple and LIU were not overwhelming favorites before their championships. However, sportswriters focused on the fact that this year, any number of evenly matched entrants could take home the prize without much surprise.[45]

The 1940 National Invitation

When the opening games began on Monday, March 11, 10,551 fans witnessed a visiting sweep. In two slow-paced contests, beat writers noted very little interesting action as Duquesne came on late to beat St. John's 38–31 and DePaul held off LIU 45–38. The relatively low scoring of both contests spoke to the deliberate but effective offensive methods of both teams moving on to Wednesday night's semifinals.[46]

New York Times columnist Louis Effrat chose the two newcomers as favorites for the semifinal matchups. Colorado flew in early enough to scout DePaul in its Monday night encounter. Further, the Buffaloes were no strangers to Madison Square Garden, having lost in the finals of the original National Invitation in 1938 and making a return trip in December of the previous season. Effrat chose Oklahoma A&M as favorites against Duquesne simply by virtue of its overall season record.[47]

The Aggies' methodical style of basketball was not as effective as Duquesne's similarly deliberate tactics. The Dukes won 34–30. Despite the slow pace that attracted only 10,771 fans to the Garden on a night when not a single local team played, Oklahoma guard Jesse Renick proved his worth. The Aggie floor general, whom the *New York Times* noted was "a Choctaw Indian," netted 10 of his team's 30 points. Alongside LIU's Dolly King, who had participated in two National Invitation tournaments, and New Mexico A&M's Mexican star Kiko Martinez from the 1939 invite, Renick represented a third minority group in the New York tournament's third year of existence.[48]

Outside of one attempt to describe his race, the half-Choctaw, half-Chickasaw Renick competed without incident. The Oklahoman found very little resistance in his home state where Native Americans resided in large numbers. New York City, on the contrary, did not have as high a concentration of Choctaws, Chickasaws, or any other native tribe. Martinez fell into a similar situation the year before. His ethnicity rarely registered in New Mexico, a state that was home to plenty of Mexican Americans. New York was different. LIU's Dolly King, a New York native, experienced the

National Invite in a way that showed similarities to and also stark differences from Renick and Martinez. The African American forward captured a few more racially focused descriptions of his outstanding play for Coach Clair Bee than either the Native American or the Mexican American. Interestingly, even though New York City's African American population was higher than its Native American or Mexican American populations, King's race garnered the most attention. While this attention was admirably small in New York for the racial climate around the rest of the country in 1940, King's darker skin tone made a difference in a country still coming to grips with skin color variations.

Eight years later, Renick traveled back to New York City as part of the first integrated United States Olympic basketball team. However, he was not the minority of note on that team. African American Don Barksdale provided many of the socially based storylines because of his ethnicity. While Barksdale's inclusion on the national team generated relatively little national attention in 1948 even though he participated with many southern team-mates and an assistant coach, Adolph Rupp, who became vilified as a racist, Barksdale's personal triumphs with his team in the lead-up to the Olympics provides interesting insight into American attitudes on race. The African American received death threats while touring with the American contingent. Renick, the Native American who was also chosen as captain of the 1948 US cage team, rarely even received mention of his race. Even as the team took gold in the London Games, making Renick the first Native American to win a gold medal since Jim Thorpe's rescinded decathlon victory at the 1912 Stockholm Games, Renick captured little publicity as a Native American.[49]

A victory in the semifinals of the 1940 National Invitation tournament may have generated more headlines regarding Renick's Native American heritage, but the New York crowd and writers seemed to care more about his on-court play rather than his race. And his play, while admirable, was not enough to push the Aggies past Duquesne. The Pittsburgh crew met Colorado in the Friday night final. The Buffaloes had deliberately milked its second-half lead against DePaul in the semifinals and coasted to a 52–37 victory.[50]

Sportswriter Arthur J. Daley noted that the final "should be as close to a toss-up as the tournament has had thus far" even though "Colorado may find itself a slight favorite." The Buffaloes appeared vulnerable in its semi-final victory, but the Dukes had even more question marks resulting from a semifinal injury to guard Moe Becker. Nonetheless, 15,201 fans turned up for the final—an increase of almost 50 percent from the previous two evenings' totals. The larger crowd saw Colorado take control late to win the title, 51–40. More intense action came in the consolation game. Oklahoma A&M led DePaul by a "miserly" 12–7 at halftime. Both teams loosened up slightly in the second half as the Demons took a 22–21 lead late before Renick hit the game-winning shot with a minute left to help his team to a one-point victory.[51]

While the tournament seemingly ended without any major setbacks, Ned Irish could not have been happy with the outcome. Attendance fell dramatically from the 1939 event—something to which Irish was not accustomed. Local fans did not seem as attracted to the 1940 invitation as was expected. The new management of the event could not have been the reason, for the MIBC ran the tournament exactly as the MBWA had. The only difference was the composition of the selection committee. And sportswriters, who had been virtually left out of the 1940 selection process, continued to promote the event just as they had in the past.

Local fans provided two lamentations once Colorado left with the crown. The first was obvious and parochial. When NYU declined its invitation, local fans may have had some wind taken out of their sails. The Violet team was clearly the cream of the local crop—at least until its upset at the hands of CCNY in late February—and had fared the best against intersectional competition. One local fan described the attitude of many metropolitan basketball fans when he wrote, "I think N. Y. U. would have won (the tournament) hands down." NYU may or may not have been able to live up to its regular season standards in tournament action. The "lose and go home" character of the NIT—and all college basketball postseason action—left the results of many championships up to chance. So any assumption that NYU would have won the invite was no more than hopeful speculation.[52]

NYU, however, would have much more likely appeased the other complaint from local fans after the 1940 National Invitation: the slow pace of play. "While Duquesne, Colorado, Oklahoma A. and M. and De Paul all deserved invitations to the national basketball tournament at the Garden, I think the selection committee hurt the attractiveness of the show by bringing on these four particular teams," one fan argued, stating that "all play an ultra-deliberate, slow-breaking, set-play type of game . . . (that is) hardly calculated to keep the spectator on the edge of his seat." While NYU was no run-and-gun team, its pace was less snail-like than the 1940 visiting entrants. Local fans, with plenty of entertainment options in the Big Apple outside of basketball, wanted to be thrilled when they paid admission to an event. Thus, in the future, the MIBC and Ned Irish had to bring in the top teams in the country *and* make sure that those top teams played an exciting brand of basketball.[53]

The 1940 NCAA Tournament

On Saturday, March 16, only twenty-four hours after its one-point victory over DePaul for third place in the National Invitation, Oklahoma A&M was on a different court halfway across the country with hopes of extending its season even longer. The NCAA District 5 play-in game featured the Missouri Valley champion Aggies and the Big Six conference champion Kansas. The Aggies gave all they had in front of the Oklahoma City crowd before bowing to the Jayhawks in overtime, 45–43. Kansas became the last entrant in the NCAA tournament, joining the Southern California team that had beaten two National Invitation teams during the regular season and had been hailed as one of the top two teams in the nation, the Colorado squad that had just won the National Invitation, and the Rice quintet that had been left out of the National Invitation at the last minute in favor of DePaul. The NCAA Western field could not have been any stronger.[54]

Rice played with an ax to grind for its New York snub. A small and relatively unknown school that played among the major name universities in Texas and the American Southwest, Rice may have developed a bit of an inferiority complex. And yet this was a talented team. The NCAA game programs featured a picture of two "Rice Institute Stars." Picture captions identified Frank Carswell as a two-time All-Southwest Conference guard and Placido Gomez as a forward. Gomez's inclusion in the event gave the NCAA tournament its first ethnic minority player. As a Mexican American, Gomez received even less attention for his ethnicity than New Mexico A&M's Kiko Martinez, for the latter played with the Mexican national team. Nevertheless, the NCAA game program notes that "Both (Rice stars Carswell and Gomez) are Houston boys." This may have been a simple description to indicate that they were both hometown boys—in fact, they played high school ball together at Houston's Jeff Davis High—or it could have been reassurance that Gomez is indeed an American.[55]

Rice's two Houston stars struggled shooting in the NCAA opening round, and the Owls could not catch Kansas after an early deficit. They were outmatched, and the Jayhawks had played the entire season with motivation provided from Coach Allen regarding the NCAA tournament hosted in its own backyard. This motivation, and 21 points from forward Howard Engleman, helped Kansas hold off the Houston team, 50–44. Most of the full house of 8,380 spectators stayed for the nightcap between Southern California and Colorado. The Trojans lived up to their hype and defeated Colorado by six, 38–32. The Buffaloes may have been emotionally drained from their New York championship.[56]

In the Western Regional final, Southern California gave the Jayhawks all they could handle and treated the crowd to a breathtaking finish. Kansas trailed 42–41 late in the game when Bobby Allen, the Kansas coach's son, stole the ball and sent a crosscourt pass to an open teammate. "The thunder of 7,500 screaming voices carried to the West Coast and back as Howard Engleman, K.U. forward, nailed a set shot from the corner with eighteen seconds remaining in the finals, to defeat Southern California, 43 to 42," one local reporter wrote. Kansas guard Dick Harp, who would go on to become Allen's assistant and successor in the 1950s, paced the Jayhawks with 15 points. Rice finished off the deflated Colorado Buffaloes in the consolation game, 60–56.[57]

Kansas's opponent in the NCAA final came from the Eastern Regional hosted by Butler coach Tony Hinkle in Indianapolis. Although Indianapolis was a great basketball city and Hinkle an able manager in Butler's prized gymnasium, the event weathered a small storm to remain in "The Crossroads of America." On March 8, only two weeks before the event would commence, the Eastern Regional "struck a new snag." The Indianapolis Ministerial Association protested that the tournament would be held during Good Friday and Saturday of Holy Week, and asked Hinkle to "cancel the affair." Hinkle and his local organizing crew called Olsen in to "look over the situation." The Ohio State coach visited and decided to continue the event as scheduled.[58]

Indianapolis News sports editor William F. Fox Jr. wrote that the four participants in this event represented "the rising tide of Southern basketball, the known strength and craftiness of the East, the comparative weakness of the New England states, and the omnipresent omnipotence of the Hoosier brand of court-cavorting." Western Kentucky demonstrated the "rising tide of Southern basketball" in a close loss to National Invitation runner-up Duquesne—a team that proved the "known strength and craftiness of the East." Western Kentucky may have overcome the Iron Dukes had it not been for the foul trouble of its aptly named center, Carlyle Towery. The big southerner tipped in a rebound to bring the Hilltoppers within one, 30–29, late in the game, but fouled out immediately after. Chaotic play ensued with no more scoring until the buzzer sounded.[59]

Springfield College of Massachusetts demonstrated the "comparative weakness of the New England states" in its tournament opener. Indiana University crushed the team representing basketball's birthplace 48–24, and the 30–11 halftime score indicated that the game was out of reach early. Fox's appraisal of the Springfield team as representative of a weak region may have been unfair, for the region boasted some strong quintets. However, Springfield had no excuses. Basketball's founder and patron saint, Dr. James

Naismith, had passed away at the beginning of the 1939–40 season, and Springfield's entrance into the NCAA tournament was a fitting tribute to the school's former physical education instructor. Therefore, with sentiment on its side, Springfield had all the motivation it needed to beat the odds.[60]

Indiana was simply too good. The Hoosiers, who finished second in the Big Ten to a Purdue squad that continued to abide by a no postseason policy, took down Duquesne in the Eastern championship, 39–30. A biased local crowd may have aided the Hoosiers to victory. Indeed, the Hoosier state's flagship institution had a strong following in the state capital that was only fifty miles from Bloomington. Enough Hoosier fans attended the two nights of regional action for the event to gross $6,405.75 in ticket receipts and turn a profit of $1,200. Aside from the one-sided crowd support, another possibility for the outcome is that the Iron Dukes may have simply run out of gas after a relatively long and emotional postseason. However, since it made the Eastern Final, Duquesne qualified to travel to Kansas City for the consolation game against Southern California, the Western Regional's runner-up.[61]

Local Kansas University squaring off against a popular and regionally based Indiana squad in the NCAA National Final virtually guaranteed the tournament to be a success. Since ticket sales drove almost the entire revenue stream, tournament organizer "Phog" Allen could not have chosen two better teams. While it may have been disappointing to basketball sentimentalists that Springfield College did not qualify to pay tribute to Dr. Naismith's death, Allen expected large and enthusiastic crowds of Jayhawk and Hoosier supporters.[62]

Allen appeased basketball sentimentalists—especially those in the Kansas City area that knew Dr. Naismith well from his career in Lawrence—with a tribute to basketball's fallen founder. And he did so to a packed house. Partisan fans greased the turnstiles with abandon and were treated to a gem. Most of the Hoosiers' games that season sent crowds away amazed. The carefree "Laughing Boys" from Indiana played a fast-paced game that often left the crowd and their coach breathless. Indeed, the Hoosiers whimsically referred to Branch McCracken as the "Head Coach of Worry."[63]

McCracken did not worry about ball possession. Allen, the championship opponent, told McCracken that if his team could gain possession for 60 percent of the game, then the Jayhawks would win. McCracken replied that Kansas could "have it for 90% of the time, as long as I outscore you." Indeed, tactics played a strong role in the outcome of this game. McCracken's nerves heightened the day before the game when he begrudgingly allowed his wife to take his players to the local cinema to see Gone With the Wind. The coach's wife knew her husband thought that being in a dark room for

Kansas's Allen congratulates Indiana's McCracken after the championship game. *Courtesy: Indiana University Archives (P0028871).*

so long would hurt the players' vision, and so she made up for it by having the team go outside during intermission to run wind sprints.[64]

Later that day, McCracken ran into colleagues Sam Barry of USC and Everett Dean of Stanford. They asked him if he had scouted Kansas and he replied in the negative. Then they asked what type of defense he would use. McCracken disclosed that he planned to employ a shifting man-to-man defense. Barry and Dean suggested a full court press, and, after more discussion, the Indiana coach obliged. The "Hurryin' Hoosiers" used their fast-paced break and a full court press to outplay the Jayhawks, 60–42. "We pressed them from the moment the ball changed hands," McCracken remembered, joyfully. The full court pressure "took stamina and condition . . . for 40 minutes," he recalled, "but it wrecked Kansas' set shots and let us play our fireball game." Local fans, NABC members, and the Joint Rules Committee of the United States and Canada members who were in attendance were all "astonished" by "Indiana's breathtaking antics on the court." One major key to the Indiana victory was the Hoosier hot hands. Indiana hit on one-third of its shots in the first half and 36.1 percent in the second half "to finish the game with an amazing 34.6 percentage." While numbers like these today would prove defensive superiority, in 1940 they showed great offensive efficiency.[65]

Indiana University president Herman B. Wells congratulated the team on its championship, stating, "The game which you played at Kansas City was to the glory of yourselves, to Indiana basketball and to Indiana University," adding that, "(McCracken) and the boys have seen to it that Indiana still is the leading basketball state." With the Hoosiers winning the NCAA title while finishing second place in the Big Ten to in-state rival Purdue, the Hoosier state looked mighty strong in hoops.[66]

The Kansas University marching band provided the Kansas City Municipal Auditorium with the feel of an on-campus gymnasium. The massive amounts of students who made the fifty-mile trek from Lawrence furthered this atmosphere. And it was just what the tournament officials wanted. Tournament director Harold Olsen made it clear from the start that he believed this was part of the morality of college basketball. In other words, not only should the colleges run a college basketball "national championship" tournament, but the games should also be played on college campuses. The 1939 NCAA Regional tournaments both occurred off campus, and the tournament committee waffled on whether the East-West Final should be on or off campus. Olsen and his colleagues debated the merits of the potential profits of hosting the game at Chicago Stadium. However, fate intervened. By the time they decided on a date, Chicago Stadium was booked and Northwestern University hosted the game.[67]

The 1940 championship also had a mix of on- and off-campus locations. Butler University coach Tony Hinkle hosted the Eastern Regional at his campus's home gymnasium. Much like Northwestern's Patten Gymnasium, Butler's Fieldhouse is near the heart of a major metropolitan area that could easily attract large amounts of local fans. The 1940 Western Regional and Championship Game occurred off campus. Allen felt so strongly that he could generate a profit for the tournament if he hosted it in Kansas City— without the help or hindrance of an on-campus gymnasium—that the tournament committee believed it had no better option. After losing money in 1939, Olsen and his committee were in no position to develop idealistic moral theories that required the tournament host venues to be on-campus facilities. This tournament needed to turn a profit.

And they did. The second annual NCAA Basketball Tournament finished with great success. Olsen wrote months later that "The success of this second N.C.A.A. tournament unquestionably establishes it as the outstanding basketball event in the country." The Ohio State coach also gave great praise to site managers Allen and Hinkle for their efforts. Dan Partner of the *Kansas City Star* offered further praise, claiming, "The greatest attraction in the history of basketball—a tournament including the five top teams of the nation—provided a banner year for the National Collegiate Athletic Association." Partner also noted that tournament organizers "erased the red ink from the books as 25,880 fans paid $22,228.65 to see what truly was the world series of basketball."[68]

Partner ended his quote by offering an appropriate analogy for the tournament organizing committee's marketing efforts. On the cover of the game programs sold at Kansas City Municipal Auditorium for the Western Regional and East-West championship game, tournament director Allen printed the subtitle, "The World Series of Basketball." The allusion to professional baseball was fitting. Baseball's world series brought together the best team from the National League to face the best from the American League. The NCAA basketball tournament similarly featured the best team from the West against the best from the East. This creative rhetoric encouraged spectators to view the tournament as a true championship in the direct mold of America's national pastime—and in direct opposition to the National Invitation's "Rose Bowl" approach. Such was Allen's promotional genius.[69]

The result of Allen's promotions and rhetoric was a tournament balance sheet that looked totally different from the previous season. The Indianapolis games grossed $6,405.75 and, after expenses totaling $5,224.44—which included $2,486 of guarantees and travel expense reimbursement to the four participating teams—netted $1,200. This profit was respectable. The real money, however, came from Kansas City. The Garden City brought in $23,069.55 from ticket sales and program receipts. Its expenditures—which included guarantees and travel expense reimbursement to the five participating teams totaling $5,366.07—ran only to $13,479.49, meaning that Allen generated $9,590.06 of profit. Once general administration expenses were subtracted, the tournament ended with a positive overall balance of $9,522.55—more than $12,000 different from the previous year's bottom line. While this change provided great relief for both the NCAA and NABC, a one-year positive fluctuation did not provide much stability yet. Therefore, of the profits, the NCAA allowed the NABC to keep $300 as an advance for the work the 1941 tournament operating committee had ahead of them and kept $9,222.55 for itself.[70]

The NABC could not argue too much with the NCAA's allocation of the profits. The NCAA clearly had leverage after bailing the NABC out the previous season. The NABC found more satisfaction in putting on a profitable tournament than dissatisfaction over being able to keep so little of the profits. The $300 cash advance the NCAA gave to the 1941 tournament committee was small consolation, but a diplomatic gesture nonetheless.

The $9,222.55 that the NCAA took provided it with more cash than each of the other six association championships combined. The 1940 boxing tournament and swimming championship each broke even. The golf championship also broke even because it required the host course to pay a guarantee up front. The tennis and gymnastics events made $458.90 and $316.50, respectively, but did not pay for the participants' travel nor did they prorate profits to the schools. Finally, cross-country lost $456.24, track lost $5,759.53, and wrestling lost $1,073.92. It would not be long before the NCAA began using basketball's profits to counteract net losses for the other championship events—a method the association continues today.[71]

The travel reimbursement and guarantee that each basketball team received for participating offset any losses each team would have otherwise incurred, but it did little else. Allen and Olsen originally assumed they would reimburse each team's travel and expenses for twelve people, but with the profits, they extended that to fifteen. And yet the issue remained as to where the profits would go. Allen had his mind made up that each team should receive some of the profits, and he queried the coaches for their thoughts on the matter. He believed that the NCAA should be reimbursed its $2,500 from the previous season and should receive another $5,000 on top of that as a cash advance in case a future tournament bombed financially. However, he and the tournament committee were unaware of an NCAA rule stipulating that the profits of any NCAA event must all go toward the association's general fund—and none can be given to participating teams or individuals. This clause spurred a lot of heated debate over the summer, and it soured Allen to the administration of this tournament.[72]

When the NCAA Executive Committee met in early September 1940, they agreed to more lenient financial terms than they previously had on the books. While Allen still did not get what he wanted, the association at least set a policy that took steps toward encouraging teams to participate in the NCAA and not the National Invitation tournament—and that was the crux of this issue. The NCAA decided that, after expenses and travel costs went back to participants, the profits would split as follows: 10 percent off the top to the NCAA general fund, 50 percent of the remaining profits also to the NCAA general fund and 50 percent prorated to the participating teams.[73]

While financial payouts today help fund a university's athletic department, the 1940 profits that each team received did not have nearly the reach that profits do today. Then, as now, football bowl games provided a great deal of cash inflow to university athletic departments. The *Chicago Tribune* noted disappointment in December 1940 that the Big Ten faculty committee voted to retain its bowl ban first initiated in 1938. In doing so, the league prevented its participating team from receiving the $100,000 receipt with which the visiting team usually returned home. Even if it were to be split evenly among the Big Ten teams, each team would have received more money than the entire basketball tournament earned. Clearly, football reigned as king, but basketball was coming into its own.[74]

The *New York Times*'s calendar year wrap-up in December 1940 provided summary of a basketball season in which "general progress overshadowed individual progress." The daily argued that "Nine quintets seemed to be the nation's leaders." Colorado won the National Invitation—referred to in the *Times* as the Rose Bowl of college basketball—but lost in the first round of the NCAA tournament. Duquesne lost to Colorado in the National Invitation finals and lost to Indiana in the NCAA semifinal. Indiana won the NCAA tournament but did not even win the Big Ten conference. Kansas lost to Indiana in the NCAA finals and ended the Big Six season in a three-way tie. NYU tied for metropolitan honors amid a one-loss season but did not participate in any postseason competition. Purdue won the Big Ten but also chose to sit out of the postseason. Southern California lost in its NCAA opener despite a season record that many believed put it with NYU as the nation's best. And, illogically, the *Times* mentions Rice and Santa Clara as the final two possibilities. Rice lost in the NCAA semifinal to Kansas and barely missed out on a National Invitation bid. Santa Clara joined NYU and Purdue as the top teams that did not participate in postseason action. College basketball's three national postseason tournaments clearly had not provided immediate clarity to the college basketball landscape, but it would not be long before a hierarchy began to take shape.[75]

CHAPTER 5

Early Peaks and Valleys, 1940–1942

With the success of the 1940 NCAA tournament, the NABC and event organizers rode a wave of momentum into the 1940–41 season. Tournament committee chair Harold Olsen of Ohio State, site director Phog Allen of Kansas, and their colleagues had established the NCAA tournament as a premier postseason event that, if handled correctly, had the potential to generate financial profits and sustainability. New York City's National Invitation tournament, on the contrary, had to make changes. The slow pace of play from the participating teams and the inability to attract two of the nation's top teams—NYU and Southern California—had deterred fans from flocking to the Garden like they had the previous two seasons. In three nights of action, the Madison Square Garden tourney averaged only 12,000 fans in attendance—much more than the other tournaments but also much less than its attendance in the past. Emil Liston's NAIB tournament fell somewhere in between. His event continued successfully in 1940, but its reputation remained a bit too parochial for a so-called national organization that put on a "national championship" tournament. The decisions made by these three tournaments' organizers over the next two seasons allowed the events to persevere through a tenuous time in United States history. The tournament organizers further hinted at policy decisions that would set each tournament down the path toward its ultimate characterization within the college basketball landscape.[1]

Administrative Changes

The NCAA tournament organizing committee needed little prodding to determine its 1941 site. Allen's success in managing the Kansas City–hosted Western Regional and Final Game while also leading his team to the Final Game in 1940 made the Garden City a unanimous choice to host again. And although Butler's Tony Hinkle managed the Eastern Regional respectably in Indianapolis, generating a healthy profit after two nights of competition, the NCAA looked elsewhere in 1941. University of Wisconsin officials had attracted a great deal of attention in 1939 as they hosted the NCAA boxing championship tournament. This event, which was theretofore little more than a demonstration, attracted sellout crowds of rowdy spectators at Wisconsin's on-campus gymnasium. With this ability to attract local interest, the NCAA chose Madison, Wisconsin, to host its Eastern Regional. Madison and Kansas City would open their doors for regional action on March 21 and 22, with the East-West Final scheduled for March 29.[2]

The Metropolitan Intercollegiate Basketball Committee made two changes in order to overcome both the lackluster display of basketball at its 1940 event and the lack of interest from its local fans. Total renovations, though, were not in order because the tournament had great potential and solid appeal in its first two years. The MIBC may have seen the 1940 gala as an anomaly. And yet to ensure it was not the beginning of a downward trend, the organization worked hard to set itself up for certain success.

On December 18, 1940, the *New York Times* noted in passing that the organization decided to expand its tournament from six to eight teams for the 1941 event—its fourth annual affair. But this was no small change. Expanding the tournament had major implications. First, it provided for a more fair and objective bracket of teams. In a six-team event, two entrants received a free pass into the semifinal round. The MBWA and MIBC generally acted graciously in this regard and allowed the teams who had to travel the farthest to receive the byes. First-round games often occurred as much as five days before the semifinals. With the cost of travel and the amount of classes that basketball players miss throughout a long season, traveling across the country to participate in the tournament's opening round may not have been enticing. If a western team were to win its first-round game, it would have had to either stay in New York City for as much as a week waiting for its next games (and, after winning in the first round, a team is guaranteed two more games—a semifinal and either the championship or consolation game), or the team would have to travel home before making the same trip back a few days later. If the team lost in the first round, then its cross-country travel would have been just for one game.[3]

With a six-team tournament the onus fell on the local and regional teams who had to play the extra games. Without the luxury of a first-round bye, these teams had to win an extra game against teams who were considered among the best in the nation. By adding two teams, the MIBC overcame this inherent unfairness. With four opening-round games, every team started on equal footing, needing three victories to take home the crown.

By adding two teams, the MIBC put its tournament more in line with the

NCAA Championship event. The inherent equality and relative cleanliness of putting eight teams in a bracket seemed to be part of the draw of the NCAA event. Since Harold Olsen's NCAA tournament had enjoyed great success in 1940, the MIBC sought ways to stay popular. The addition of two teams to increase the number of games from which it would generate ticket revenue seemed a natural alteration.

Indeed, by adding two teams, the MIBC increased its potential profits in a major way. Hosting four instead of two opening-round games meant that Ned Irish would have to open Madison Square Garden for four nights of National Invitation action instead of the three that the tournament had used in the past. This meant one more night of ticket proceeds. The MIBC and Irish scheduled opening-round action for Tuesday and Wednesday, March 18 and 19. The semifinals would ensue three nights later on Saturday, March 22, with the finals following on Monday, March 24. The scheduling of these dates meant that the four opening-round losers could leave immediately after their loss thereby minimizing the amount of classes their players would miss. The four quarterfinal winners were guaranteed two more games, but had an option in the meantime. For regional teams, they could travel the short distance home over the three- or four-day respite between the quarterfinals and semifinals. The semifinal and final rounds were only separated by one day so that, when the regional teams did travel back, they would not have much down time in between rounds. And the entire event lasted only six days.[4]

The March 1941 dates that the MIBC and Irish chose also demonstrated a policy change. The 1940 National Invitation occurred a week earlier and coincided with the NAIB tournament dates. This allowed a team such as Oklahoma A&M to participate in the New York tournament and then return home to compete in a district play-off for the right to compete in the NCAA tournament that commenced a week later. The NCAA tournament, then, while not necessarily seen uniformly as the capstone or culminating event of the college basketball season, at least enjoyed status as the final event on the college basketball schedule. And with this status came at least some prestige. After all, a championship event should occur at the absolute conclusion of a season. Therefore, the MIBC postponed its event a week on the March calendar to coincide with the NCAA event. While it then shared the conclusion or final dates of the season with the NCAA, it also provided an important implication for the future of the tournaments—it all but precluded any team from entering both events.[5]

Emil Liston and his NAIB colleagues maintained their existing tournament schedule for the fifth annual Kansas City event in 1941. But Liston also made some changes in an effort to enhance his tournament's status. The opening-round loss by Roanoke College in the 1939 National Invitation tournament after finishing as runner-up in the 1938 NAIB tournament gave critics some objective measure to prove the NAIB's inferiority due to its small college focus. And yet the event remained well attended.

During the 1940 NAIB tournament, Liston and his organization met to discuss future plans. More than one hundred delegates from thirty-five states attended. The Baker coach attempted to build on this administrative geographic diversity by pleading for even better geographic diversity among participating teams. A fully national tournament—more easily demonstrated in a thirty-two-team tournament than an eight-team event—set the NAIB apart from the NCAA and MIBC events, at least in Liston's mind. Schools from twenty-four states had participated in the first four events, leaving half of the states unrepresented in the actual action. Further, no team outside of Kansas and Missouri had won the championship, giving it an even more insular feel.[6]

By March of 1941, the NAIB tournament committee had selected a roster of participating teams that mollified some of its critics. The tournament field included teams from nineteen states, two of which—Maryland and Montana—had never been represented. With San Diego State entering yet again, the tournament had a true coast-to-coast participation for the first time ever. Adding credibility to the growing tournament, Liston and the NAIB board of directors hired Dick Dunkel Sr., an "expert who rates the nation's basketball teams" from New York, to help seed the teams. Dunkel began the practice of ranking college football teams in 1929. In doing so, he joined a handful of others interested in similar football postseason honors. In 1937, Dunkel began ranking college basketball teams at season's end, too. The dopester's knowledge of college basketball across the country was unparalleled at the time, as William Schroeder was still two years away from establishing the Helms retrospective rankings. Dunkel's expertise provided the tournament with a bit more balance and excitement, ensuring that pre-tournament favorites would not meet each other until late rounds.[7]

San Diego State reached the finals of the previous two NAIB tournaments and, therefore, came in as one of the pretournament favorites, according to Dunkel and local sportswriters. Dunkel ranked the Aztecs sixth, behind West Texas State, Murray State, Superior College of Wisconsin, Stephen F. Austin of Texas, and Baltimore University. The Californians struggled through their early games before meeting West Texas State in the semifinal round. The Texans, hailed as "the tallest team in the world," averaged 6'5" per player and had blown through their early round games, looking nearly invincible.[8]

San Diego State literally rose to this challenge, however, taking down the tall Texans before taking home its first NAIB title by defeating Murray State in the championship game. Thus, the fifth NAIB championship trophy became the first one to leave Missouri or Kansas, traveling all the way back 2,200 miles to California with the Aztecs. However, San Diego State's celebration came with some criticism of the event among other Golden State teams. The day after the San Diego State victory, the *Pittsburgh Courier*— among the most prominent and reputable black daily newspapers in the country—reported that the team from Santa Barbara College just up the California coast who lost in the early rounds of the NAIB tournament was asked to leave its lone African American player at home. NAIB officials justified this racism descriptively: with so many teams from the Jim Crow South, the participation of integrated teams would repel enough other tournament regulars that the tournament may have had to fold. Amid this thin but potentially accurate logic, the *Courier* also reported that San Jose College in California turned down an NAIB bid because its two black stars would have been forbidden.[9]

Metropolitan Basketball

This racial policy stood in stark contrast to that of the New York City invitational tournament. LIU's "negro Hercules" Dolly King had participated in each of the first three Madison Square Garden postseason events, and the Blackbirds seemed to be on track to make it four in a row. However, NYU seemed to be the class of the metropolitan squads again, at least before the season started. Ned Irish scheduled the Violets for nine games in the Garden. St. John's and King's LIU had seven dates, while CCNY received six. These teams would meet up with the twenty-one squads representing every other part of the country that Irish had invited to regular season Garden contests.[10]

LIU won eleven of its first twelve games leading up to a January 29, 1941, meeting with Butler in the Garden that was publicized as a going-away party of sorts for King. The multitalented Blackbird had decided in midseason to try his hand at professional basketball and baseball, thus forfeiting his remaining collegiate eligibility at LIU—a school, critics argued, that had fewer eligibility standards than other colleges in the first place. He would begin with a new basketball team immediately. Madison Square Garden officials presented King with an honorary trophy before the game.[11]

The Blackbirds won King's send-off and continued on a tear without him. On February 19, the *New York Times*'s Arthur J. Daley remarked that LIU was "virtually definite" to receive a bid to the National Invitation alongside the possibility of NYU, CCNY, or Fordham—the darkhorse of the race. Outside of metropolitan New York, the MIBC had the difficult task of inviting six other teams. In theory, Daley noted that the MIBC hoped that four teams would be selected from around the country and two would be chosen from the East. "There are so many good Eastern combinations this season," the writer lamented, "that it might not be wise to have too rigid a sectional rule. An extra college from the Atlantic Seaboard might be preferable to a lesser one from elsewhere." On March 1, a local sports fan concurred in a letter to the *Times*'s sports editor, opining, "With so many fine basketball teams in the East, it hardly will be necessary to go outside this section in order to select eight teams for the national invitation tournament." The editor responded that "the East will be fully and ably represented but," he added, "it is a 'national' tournament." Clearly, although interest in national tournaments and competition remained high, many New Yorkers simply enjoyed high-quality in-region competition. Further, many thought the best competition came from nearby.[12]

Local metropolitan basketball heated up as March rolled around. Intracity games at this time of year often had tournament implications. These local games provided the MIBC with hard evidence of which teams should receive bids to the National Invitation and which ones should not. With all of the local games throughout the season, choosing the top two for the postseason invitational was often among the least disputed decisions the MIBC made. Since most of the local schools squared off against each other at least once per season, the selection committee had objective measures to back up their invitations. LIU did not play local competition, though. Coach Clair Bee instead had his teams play a fully intersectional schedule of games every season thus excluding the Blackbirds from the mythical intra-city standings on which sportswriters eagerly reported.

Since 1938, LIU had been so dominant that National Invitation selection committees could not keep them out. They became the top local drawing card at the Garden. Choosing the second local team for the National Invitation did not seem as easy, though, especially in 1941. By March 10, the MIBC had unofficially narrowed the list of local possibilities to join LIU in the National Invitation from three down to two—CCNY and NYU, who squared off in the final regular season game. Attendance had been good all year at college basketball double-headers for Ned Irish. He revealed that the Garden averaged 14,538 fans per night of college basketball—a new Garden record. This number grew thanks to the March 10 showdown between the "ancient rivals" of NYU and CCNY; 17,886 local fans came out for what was reportedly no less than a National Invitation play-in game. The highly competitive game that resulted in a 47–43 CCNY victory meant that the Beavers had won 12 of their last 13 games and ended the season with a 14-4 record. The MIBC immediately "went into a quick huddle" after the game "and emerged with the news that City College had been invited to play in the (National Invitation) tournament."[13]

The following day, the *New York Times* announced that the tournament field had been set. Long Island, Rhode Island State, and Seton Hall had previously accepted bids, while City College, Duquesne, Westminster, Virginia, and Ohio University accepted the final invitations. This octet of teams meant that no squad west of Athens, Ohio, or south of Charlottesville, Virginia, would be competing in the event. The MIBC decided to set up the brackets in a way that would prevent the two New York City and two Pittsburgh teams from meeting their local opponents until the finals. MIBC officials picked the rest of the bracket out of a hat. Joseph M. Sheehan of the *Times* noted that this lineup looked like "the best of its kind ever staged here." The reporter also made comparisons to the coterminous NCAA tournament. "The eight competing teams, independents from comparatively near-by places in contrast to the N. C. A. A.'s geographically balanced set-up of conference champions," Sheehan noted, "are representative of the best there is in the game and the winner will have as much right as any quintet to national supremacy." Thus, many of the differences between the two tournaments became more precise. The National Invitation was "the Rose Bowl of college basketball." The MIBC invited teams that it thought were the best, regardless of geography. Sheehan also noted that most invited teams were conference-independent rather than conference teams and that, while the National Invitation was not a "national championship," its champion would doubtlessly represent the class of the country.[14]

The 1941 National Invitation and the NABC Convention

On Tuesday, March 18, the fourth annual National Invitation opened with one of the pretournament favorites Duquesne sporting a 17-2 record and squaring off against a 16-3 Ohio squad that "is capable of bothering any club." The Tuesday night docket finished with CCNY facing Virginia, who had won 17 and lost 3 throughout the season. CCNY easily vanquished the Cavaliers 64–35 and Ohio pulled a 55–40 upset victory over the Dukes in relatively mundane action in front of 15,751 spectators.[15]

The second night of opening-round action featured a Seton Hall team that had been aching for a Garden invite for the past three years and was in the midst of a three-season 42-game winning streak. "Seton Hall is determined to show the basketball world that its team is as good as any in the country," the *Brooklyn Daily Eagle* reported. The Pirates would face the "high flying" Rhode Island State squad that finished the season 21-3. The evening's other battle featured 22-2 LIU against undefeated Westminster. Seton Hall backed up its lobbying efforts for a Garden bid as they "cut a swashbuckling path through the first round" with a 70–54 win over the Rhode Islanders. LIU walked all over Westminster, winning 48–36 in a "drab contest." However, the anticipation of these matchups attracted a record Garden crowd of 18,341.[16]

That Garden record did not last long as the crowd for Saturday night's semifinal action toppled it by sixteen fans. Ohio continued its upset streak by eking past CCNY 45–43. "Five minutes from the end," Arthur J. Daley reported, "Ohio wrestled the lead away from City, the eleventh time in this see-saw encounter that the advantage whipped back and forth. And the Bobcats hung tenaciously to their margin right to the game-ending horn." In the other semifinal, Long Island ended Seton Hall's forty-three-game winning streak in bold fashion, outscoring the Pirates 49–26.[17]

In Monday night's final, yet another record Garden crowd watched the tournament final; 18,377 fans watched favored LIU rout Ohio, a team that had become "the people's choice," 56–42, for the Blackbirds' second National Invitation championship in the tournament's four years of existence. In the consolation game, future NBA champion New York Knicks coach Red Holzman capped off his sophomore season at City College by leading his team to a 42–27 victory over a deflated Seton Hall squad.[18]

The final night of the fourth annual National Invitation coincided with the fifteenth annual NABC convention. The coaches' group met in Chicago in 1939 and Kansas City in 1940—both times in conjunction with the NCAA basketball tournament that it spearheaded—before choosing New York City for 1941. This marked a drastic change in philosophy, for one of Harold Olsen's four original reasons for initiating the NCAA tournament in the first place was to have an end-of-season event that would occur at the same time and site as the coaches' convention. Now, only three years removed from Olsen's arguments, the coaches decided to hold their convention in conjunction with the New York City tournament—their biggest postseason competitor.[19]

Nevertheless, this change of plans spoke to the relative amicability between the two tournaments. While there may have been plenty of opponents to this decision on the NABC's side, the New York contingent seemed interested in closer relations. In 1941, the MIBC, along with running the National Invitation, decided to offer an annual award at the NABC convention. This honor, which would exalt the person who made the most "outstanding contribution to the game of basketball," would be awarded at the end of the two-day convention. MIBC president Walter Williamson, professor at City College, presented the first annual "outstanding contribution award" to his school's coach, Nat Holman. While on the outside this reeked of bias, the choice did not seem to have many opponents. Holman had done a great deal for the game around the world and was just finishing his term as NABC president, disclosing why New York City hosted the coaches' convention that coincided with the New York event.[20]

The schedule of the coaches' convention on Monday and Tuesday, March 24 and 25, made it more difficult but certainly not impossible to participate in or at least attend NCAA tournament games while also witnessing the National Invitation final. Olsen scheduled the NCAA tournament Regionals for Friday, March 21, and Saturday, March 22, with the championship game a week later. While these overlapping schedules spoke to a possible interest in having these two tournaments at similar times but not so similar that teams squared off on the same night, they also spoke to local patterns of entertainment. In New York City, where basketball was very popular but far from the only mode of entertainment, the MIBC played its games on a Tuesday, Wednesday, Saturday, and Monday—not exactly prime days of the week aside from the Saturday semifinals. And yet the National Invitation attracted more than 70,000 fans throughout its four nights. The NCAA, however, was able to corral Friday and Saturday night openings in Madison, Wisconsin, and Kansas City for its tournament.

The 1941 NCAA Tournament

Local fans reached a fever pitch once tournament organizers selected the teams. Each 1941 NCAA tournament entrant was a conference champion, leading Olsen to remark, "This year's tournament definitely stamps the N.C.A.A. tournament as the 'World Series' of collegiate basketball." Indeed, tournament administrators believed it had finally reached a level of competitive parity with the National Invitation event. West of the Mississippi River, Pacific Coast Conference champion Washington State, Missouri Valley winner Creighton, Rocky Mountain conference leader Wyoming, and Southwest Conference victor Arkansas squared off on March 21 and 22 in Kansas City. The inclusion of these four teams "showed the basketball world it isn't necessary to have a home team on hand for an N.C.A.A. tournament to be a success." An excited 10,095 fans watched the two-night Western Regional in Kansas City's Municipal Auditorium. Even though this two-night total was far lower than each of the four single-night attendance figures from Madison Square Garden and paled a bit below NAIB numbers, NCAA excitement remained high. Two rather uninspiring opening-round games in which Washington State took down Creighton 48–39 and Arkansas beat Wyoming 52–40 did little to dispel excitement. The following night, the Cougars from the Northwest defeated pretournament favorite Arkansas 64–53 on a "sizzling" 40 percent shooting mark from the field to win the regional. In the consolation game, Creighton edged Wyoming in a back-and-forth game that eventually came down to free throws. The Blue Jays made 7 of 8 charity tosses to the Cowboys' 6 of 14 to win by one, 39–38.[21]

A ways north, the Eastern Regional featured four conference champions, as well. Dartmouth broke an Ivy League trend of sitting out postseason play by traveling to Wisconsin to join the local Badgers, who won the Big Ten, Southern Conference champion North Carolina, and Eastern League winner Pittsburgh. Henry J. McCormick, sports editor for the *Wisconsin State Journal*, referred to this four-team event as "the finest exhibition of the sport" that local fans had ever seen. On opening night the Badgers edged Dartmouth 51–50 and Pitt defeated the Tar Heels 26–20. Wisconsin then held off the Pittsburgh squad 36–30 to avenge an earlier loss to the Panthers and take home regional honors in front of a home crowd. Around 10,000 fans witnessed the first-round games and almost 13,000 crammed in for the finals.[22]

The Badgers departed for Kansas City as underdogs publicly, but the team lacked no confidence. At the train's stopover in Chicago during the southern voyage, a throng of Wisconsin students met the team at the platform to wish them good luck, to which reserve guard Ed Scheiwe replied, "Oh hell, we've forgotten how to lose." The train brought the Badgers the rest of the way, where they joined Fred Wegner, their assistant coach, in Kansas City. Head coach Bud Foster had dispatched Wegner a few days earlier to scout the Western Regional. The assistant witnessed Washington State's 6'7" star center Paul Lindeman score 14 points as the Cougars took down pretournament favorite Arkansas.[23]

This scouting negated the supposed inferiority that the press threw on the Badgers' shoulders. "The Badgers lack the manpower and the ability to reach the heights achieved by Indiana in the 1940 Finals against Kansas," noted one newspaper. Another wrote, "Their only hope is to control the ball against Washington State, thus dictating the style of play." The *Kansas City Times* put these speculations most objectively, stating, "(Washington) State holds the physical advantages and is expected to capitalize on them to the fullest extent." This advantage included a one-inch average height difference and a 15-pound average weight difference.[24]

The University of Wisconsin's Fieldhouse filled to capacity during the champion-ship 1941 season. *Courtesy of the University of Wisconsin-Madison Archives.*

Bud Foster ordered his team to continue the ball control offense he had learned from his mentor, Dr. Walter Meanwell, former Badger coach. But the real genius of the Wisconsin game plan was on defense. Wegner encouraged Foster to double-team Washington State's Lindeman, with Wisconsin's All-American center Gene Englund in back and forward Johnny Kotz in front. The strategy worked, and Lindeman ended the game with only three free throws to his credit.[25]

A crowd of 7,219—fewer than half of the National Invitation finals crowd but more than both Western regional nights—entered the Kansas City Municipal Auditorium to watch the Badgers lockdown Lindeman and his teammates for the third annual NCAA National Tournament crown. The Badger defense held Washington State scoreless for a nine-minute stretch in the middle of the first half that allowed the Cheese Staters to take a 21–17 halftime lead. The Badgers used a mix of fast breaks and slow-paced set offense in the second half as pivot man Gene Englund and sophomore for-ward Johnny Kotz led their team to victory, shutting Lindeman down and scoring 25 combined points in a 39–34 win. Kirk Gebert's sharpshooting paced the Cougars with 21 points. He was "the only Cougar cager who hit the nets with the adeptness exhibited in previous games."[26]

Wisconsin coach Foster attributed his team's win in part to Cougar overconfidence. "They had done such a fine job against Arkansas the week before that they were the favorite sons of all the Kansas City fans," Foster surmised, adding that the Cougars may have been a bit cocky because "the papers praised them highly." Clearly, since Washington State had not scouted Wisconsin, they only had the local press accounts from which to prepare.[27]

Kotz, Wisconsin's star forward, thought a bit differently. "I think they had a better ball club than us, but I think what hurt them is that they had to stay in Kansas City that whole week leading up to the finals," he suggested, assuming that the Cougars "were a little pooped" from being around the Garden City all week. The slow means of transportation for the Pacific northwesterners required this arrangement. The Badgers, however, "came in a day ahead of time after spending the week at home," and Kotz thought they "were the better for it."[28]

Once the Badgers and Cougars departed Kansas City, tournament directors announced the financial report of the event. The Wisconsin-hosted Eastern Regional made a net profit of $6,685.71—a total more than five times the amount that the 1940 Eastern Regional in Indianapolis earned. The sum included $15,093.47 in total receipts from ticket and program sales along with $8,407.76 in disbursements. The largest disbursement line item included the guarantees and travel expenses for the competing teams. Wisconsin did not have to travel, cutting down on this cost, and the association reimbursed North Carolina, Dartmouth, and Pitt a total of $3,896.39.[29]

The Western Regional in Kansas City earned $9,071.10 in receipts from tickets, programs, and the NCAA tournament's first broadcasting rights deal. A local Kansas City radio station paid $70 to broadcast the game on the airwaves. The Western Regional incurred $6,471.10 in expenses, which included the guarantees and travel costs of the participating teams. Since all four teams came to Kansas City from out of the area, it would follow that the total Western disbursement would be greater than the Eastern's. Yet this was not the case. Creighton and Arkansas did not have to travel far to get to the Garden City, but Wyoming and Washington State did. So the $2,836.97 in reimbursement to the teams—roughly $1,000 less than the Eastern Regional—seemed low. Much of this may be attributed to Kansas City's generosity when hosting basketball teams. The Garden City had a lot of experience with this and local businessmen often offered to cover certain lodging and dining expenses. Much more of it could be attributed to the relative ease of travel to Kansas City—a central node among many cross-country railways—as opposed to the difficulty getting to the northern and lesser-known outpost of Madison, Wisconsin. Once disbursements had been deducted from the total receipts, the Western Regional made $2,600.[30]

The final game generated twice the broadcasting rights revenue as the Western Regional: $140. This marked only a small percentage of the $6,956.84 of overall receipts collected. After $5,304.78 in disbursements, the final game netted $1,652.06. In sum, then, the tournament's net receipts totaled $9,043.92. This amount was a few hundred dollars less than the previous year's total, but was a welcome profit nonetheless. The Wisconsin regional provided a very positive balance and, despite no "home" team in the Western Regional or Final Game, both of those events also made money. Thus, Olsen and his organizing committee were very happy to learn that the local Kansas City fans supported the event even without the serendipity of a local team participating. Of the $9,043.92 total, the NCAA took 10 percent off the top. The remaining 90 percent was then split in half. The NCAA received one half and the participating teams split the other half. Tournament organizers divided the teams' shares up into eighteenths. Finalists Wisconsin and Washington State each received 3/18—$678.28—while the other six teams each received 2/18—$452.20. Although these totals remained modest, the tournament showed some durability. The 1940 success was no one-hit wonder. Two consecutive years' worth of similar profits mattered. And, although it was still finding its identity, Olsen remarked that the event "was very successful."[31]

1941 Postseason Round-up

Each of the three postseason college basketball events had great success in 1941. The NCAA tournament enjoyed participation from the championship teams of eight different basketball conferences across the country. Further, Kansas City fans showed their support of the tournament despite no local team participating in the Western Regional or Final. The National Invitation tournament enjoyed record crowds for its fourth annual event that included eight teams for the first time. This growth from three nights of games to four nights occurred with an overflow in the coffers of Ned Irish's box office. Local LIU's second National Invitation championship delighted local fans and may have encouraged local supporters to come out in record numbers. The NAIB tournament continued to grow in scope, too, including participating teams from two new states and loyal repeat participation from a number of other teams that spanned most of the country. Further, San Diego State's championship marked the first time that a team from outside Missouri and Kansas won the event, helping Emil Liston's event to shed its seemingly parochial nature.

The *New York Times* recapped the 1940–41 basketball season by identifying National Invitation champion LIU and NCAA winner Wisconsin as the undisputed top teams in the country. While the previous campaign's postseason events had not clarified the national scene much—the *Times* noted nine teams that were at the top at the end of the 1939–40 season—this season's picture was much crisper. In fact, the *Times* voiced what most metropolitan fans would have believed, that, "if an edge were to be awarded (between the two teams), it probably would have to be given to L. I. U. on the strength of its work against more powerful opposition." This speculation would have been disputed by most in the Midwest. After all, Wisconsin won the Big Ten, a conference many believed was the best in the nation. Indeed, in the previous season Indiana won the NCAA tournament and had not even finished first in the Big Ten.[32]

Notably absent from the discussion of the season's top teams, yet again, was the NAIB champion. San Diego State, although champion of the event, garnered no publicity in New York City. Less notably absent from the *New York Times*'s end-of-season wrap-up was the winner of the National Collegiate Basketball Association tournament. Cincinnati hosted this inaugural tournament at the end of March, which pitted the best African American college teams against each other. The five-round elimination event ended with Louisiana's Southern University defeating North Carolina Central in the championship game, 48–42. Southern had to beat West Virginia State, North Carolina A&T, Kentucky State, and Clark University of Atlanta to reach the finals of this rookie event. The tournament took place with some primitive characteristics compared to the growing excellence of the NCAA, NAIB, and New York events. Most teams traveled north to Cincinnati, and the racism in terms of facilities, dining, and lodging that ensued prevented the teams from enjoying the luxuries of postseason tournament participation that athletes in the other postseason galas enjoyed. National Collegiate Basketball tournament participants slept overnight in the gymnasium and ate wherever their short funds would be accepted. The unreimbursed amounts of money that each team spent in this event and the red financial ink at the end of the tournament extinguished this championship before it could set up a second annual occurrence.[33]

The NAIB and Inauspicious Conditions for Basketball's Jubilee

Although money played a role in the quickly evolving landscape of college basketball postseason tournaments, the nation's foreign relations also altered each of the college basketball postseason events. The first week of December

1941 marked the beginning of the 1941–42 basketball season. It also marked the official entry of the United States into World War II. After the Japanese bombed Pearl Harbor, the United States acted quickly in ways that had a major impact on the lives of college-aged men. Less than four weeks after the attack, with a defenseless Pacific Coast and perceived threats of further assault, the US military would not allow Pasadena, California, to hold its cherished Rose Bowl football game or surrounding festivities. In order to maintain the football tradition, though, Eastern invitee Duke offered to host Oregon State in the only Rose Bowl not played at the Rose Bowl.[34]

The basketball tradition remained popular, too, despite all of the domestic complications and uncertainty that came along with the war. NABC president Nels Norgren of the University of Chicago understood as much. In an article to the membership entitled, "Basketball and War," Norgren relayed to the coaches association about the drafting of college-aged men, "The military authorities have said that they are not primarily concerned with the military knowledge of the recruits, but that they would be thankful if the recruits were in adequate physical condition and appreciated the value of the proper health habits which are necessary to maintain efficient physical and mental health." All of this is to say that "it is our duty to continue to promote basketball contacts and to encourage as many of the boys of our schools as we can to participate in this sport, which develops so many attributes that may be useful to the fighting man." With the onset of war, basketball would continue, but priorities would change.[35]

The 1941–42 season marked basketball's fiftieth year of existence. A founding member of the NAIB referred to this season as basketball's "Golden Jubilee"—a biblical reference that underscored a growing characteristic of the Kansas City–based tournament. In the heartland, such religious references in public discourse remained acceptable and influenced the NAIB's evolution. As a friend of the righteous Dr. Naismith, Emil Liston created his tournament with philosophical underpinnings that made basketball's founder proud. The expression of high morality and character in the Kansas City meet had always been a priority, but without players and coaches who embody such values, the promotion of character and morality in a competitive sporting event is simply empty rhetoric. Fortunately, many of the players and coaches from the small colleges that participated in the NAIB's first five affairs did in fact embody the character and morality that Naismith and Liston believed produced basketball of the highest order. And the local Kansas City fans appreciated those affective qualities as much as the style of play.[36]

San Diego State entered the NAIB tournament in 1942 for the fourth straight season. In the previous three the Aztecs had finished as runners-up twice and took home the crown in 1941. This West Coast team had become the Garden City favorite by 1942 because of its "fighting spirit, outstanding play and sportsmanship." The *Kansas City Times* explained that, "No home team could be more popular than the West Coasters," on the eve of the event. In the 1942 tournament, the Aztecs came in as favorites based only on their work the previous three seasons. The team, unfortunately, was only a skeleton of its past. Its previous star and fan favorite Milky Phelps had graduated and enlisted in the US Air Force, leaving a major void that went unfilled. Phelps's former teammates lost in the second round of the 1942 NAIB, but local fans believed the Californians deserved more. Thirty locals contributed money toward a plaque that the Aztecs received in the middle of the quarterfinal action of the tournament. The award was given for "their play and their fighting spirit until the final gun," despite their poor showing that season.[37]

Mixed with this appreciation for and development of high character and morality was the reality that, for the NAIB to have the influence it wanted, it had to grow and compete with the NCAA and National Invitation tournaments. Liston's most imminent competitor was the NCAA tournament with which he shared a venue. The NCAA scheduled its 1942 tournament for late March while Liston maintained his early March affair. Once the Baker University coach scheduled the fifth annual NAIB event for March 9–14, he urged Kansas City to adopt these dates as "National Sports Week." In doing so, Liston may have been trying to corral Garden City interest in his tournament and also take interest away from the NCAA tournament that had become a feature of Kansas City's sporting landscape.[38]

Liston and his colleagues knew that they received condescending looks among others in the basketball industry for running a small-school tournament. However, they did not let those glances deter them from trying to make their tournament supreme. Indeed, the philosophy behind hosting a tournament that was truly "open" to all teams—as long as those teams only brought white players along—seemed to follow in the democratic and meritocratic fashion that America was in the process of fully espousing. Liston and his colleagues, therefore, continued to believe that their tournament best fit the bill as the most appropriate way to end the college basketball season.

Eugene Kiffibrell, athletic director at Westminster College in Missouri and NAIB president in 1941–42, commented similarly in a letter to the association's membership at the beginning of that season. "If baseball prospers through a world series, if football needs its bowl games, if golf can use a National Open, if track can find a profit in a national meet, why shouldn't the most popular American sport top off its season with a great national intercollegiate championship open to all, large or small?" the president opined rhetorically. Kiffibrell further argued, "All other collegiate sports groups have developed their seasons to wind up in a finely drawn peak. Why should the sport with the greatest base of all sports wind up the season with a figure flat across the top?" This may have been a question that college basketball organizers of each postseason tournament were asking themselves at this same time. With four tournaments that officially ended the 1940–41 season, college basketball certainly did not end with a "finely drawn peak."[39]

The peak of the NAIB's Golden Jubilee of Basketball tournament in 1942 occurred with thirty-two teams representing twenty-one different states. Dick Dunkel again ranked the teams so tournament officials could produce fair brackets that increased interest as the event progressed. Luther College of Iowa received the top spot, but not by much—only a small margin separated Luther from Wisconsin-Steven's Point, the lowest-seeded team. The event culminated after six days of action with 5,500 fans watching Hamline College of Minnesota take home the crown by defeating Southeastern Oklahoma 33–31—the tournament championship's closest final game. This small school in the Twin Cities came onto the basketball scene in 1895 as a participant in what is widely regarded as the first intercollegiate basketball game. Forty-seven years later, the Minnesotans gained their second entry into the basketball annals. After the event, newly elected NAIB president Lois Means of Beloit College in Wisconsin remarked that "the N.A.I.B. has made progress." Means also avidly proclaimed, "The tournament has become a national success, and the organization back of it is growing along with it. Many coaches come here to see what the tournament is all about, and they go away convinced it is the nation's finest court event."[40]

Means had only anecdotal evidence for this strong claim. And yet no one could deny that the tournament continued to grow and attract attention from a wider geographic swath. Although two of the four finalists had to travel less than two hours to get to Kansas City, having two straight champions from outside the Missouri-Kansas region and having crowds of 4,000–6,000 per night helped the tournament's national credibility.[41]

The 1942 National Invitation

In New York—a market the NAIB had not yet broken into—the National Invitation tournament was also growing. The previous season's record-setting attendance figures and enlarged listing of teams gave it great momentum heading into the 1942 gala. Yet the MIBC was not ready to rest on its laurels. In January 1942, the group announced that Eastern Intercollegiate Athletics Central Office director Asa Bushnell would be executive chairman of the tournament committee. This began the crucial role Bushnell played in the tournament's administration for a critical period in its existence and growth. The Princeton graduate would oversee the three college representatives chosen from the ten MIBC-member schools and one MBWA member who comprised the tournament committee.[42]

By late February, the local press noted the race for the two local bids to the tournament. It came as no surprise that the local scribes were most familiar with the metropolitan teams and their comparative abilities. Joseph M. Sheehan of the *New York Times* noted on February 23 that Long Island would probably be in because of its nationalized schedule. The other spot remained up for grabs among CCNY, NYU, St. Francis, and St. John's. One week later, Sheehan reported that LIU and City College had "virtually assured themselves of berths in the national invitation tournament." The following day, Sheehan also advised that St. John's had not been ruled out. The Johnnies joined LIU and CCNY as local tournament eligible teams along with Toledo, Rhode Island State, West Texas State, Rice, Colorado, Oklahoma A&M, Creighton, Kentucky, Duke, and Western Kentucky from around the country. Penn State, with a 15-2 record that included a defeat of a 14-3 West Virginia squad the previous week, took its name out of contention by accepting the District 2 bid to the NCAA tournament.[43]

By March 11, six teams had accepted bids to the National Invitation. West Texas State, the "tallest team in the world" which had entered the NAIB the previous year, accepted the first bid. They finished the season as Border Conference Champions. At 28-2, their only losses came to traditional powers Bradley Tech and LIU. The Blackbirds, with a 24-2 record, accepted another bid. Rhode Island State at 18-3, Toledo at 22-3, Missouri Valley Conference champs Creighton at 17-4, and Western Kentucky at 26-3 took the other early bids. Bushnell and his committee proffered the final two spots on March 13. Intra-city champs CCNY at 14-2 and the West Virginia team that had been previously ruled out by its loss to Penn State was revived based on an 18-4 record.[44]

With the eight teams set, Bushnell's tournament committee decided to seed each team for the first time in the event's history. The three 2-loss teams received the first three seeds—LIU at one, West Texas State at two, and CCNY at three. Of these three, the tall Texans had the most wins—twice as many as City College and two more than LIU—but the Blackbirds had beaten the Texans during the regular season. The three 3-loss teams ranked next with Toledo at four, Rhode Island at five, and Western Kentucky at six. The two 4-loss teams—Creighton and West Virginia—received the seventh and eighth ranks, respectively. The tournament committee also publicized, accordingly, that first-round pairings would be arranged so that the top seed would play the bottom seed, the second would play the seventh, the third would play the sixth, and the fourth would play the fifth.[45]

As the tournament opened on Tuesday, March 17, Arthur Daley noted that "a double bombshell exploded," setting "the show off to an uproarious start." The top two seeds fell. LIU lost by double digits to West Virginia and Creighton held off West Texas State by one in front of 16,585 fans. Two nights later, the highest remaining seed lost again. In this evening's action, 17,860 fans watched third-seeded CCNY lose to sixth-seeded Western Kentucky and fourth-seeded Toledo—a team with two African American starters—take down fifth-seeded Rhode Island in a game that many believed was a toss-up from the start. However, the *New York Times* also indicated that Toledo had been favored by the simple virtue of its higher seed.[46]

Despite the top three seeds—including local squads CCNY and LIU—falling in the opening round, local fans flocked to the Garden for the semifinal action on Monday, March 23. After first-round action, fourth-seed Toledo looked to be the top team still eligible for the tournament crown. And again, every one of the 17,935 spectators witnessed the top remaining seed knocked out. Arthur Daley noted the embarrassment of the tournament selection committee as eighth-seed West Virginia took down fourth-seed Toledo in the opener, 51–39, and sixth-seed Western Kentucky outplayed Creighton, 49–36, in the nightcap.[47]

The season's record crowd packed into Madison Square Garden on Wednesday, March 25, for the tournament final; 18,251 excitedly filled the venue to watch Western Kentucky and West Virginia battle for the fifth annual National Invitation title. The Mountaineers had been underdogs throughout the tournament and the Hilltoppers, despite a six seed and even after defeating City College in the first round, entered both of its games as perceived underdogs, too. In the final, the *New York Times*'s Arthur Daley eloquently quipped, "Thus was the last crushing blow delivered to the selection committee that had seeded the eight combatants. For it was West Virginia, the last-ranking quintet, that came through to a triumph over the seventh-seeded contestant in the final." Although Western Kentucky was listed as the six seed before the tournament, the *Times* referred to them as the seven seed. Further, Toledo, which was listed at four before the event, was referred to as five during the tournament. This confusion and lack of detail surrounding the new method of pretournament seeding showed the total unfamiliarity the media had with such an undertaking. Nevertheless, the lowest seed prevailed with a 47–45 nail-biter in the final game, showing the difficulty in ranking teams that played relatively regional schedules. This final upset came at the hands of a team that only received a bid to the tournament as an afterthought. Penn State would have theoretically received the bid after beating the Mountaineers but chose the NCAA tournament instead. Thus, West Virginia's resurrection provided some thrilling madness to the New York postseason games. Yet it also forced the tournament selection committee to reassess its new practice of seeding entrants.[48]

The 1942 NCAA Tournament

The NCAA tournament, because of its geographically equitable setup, continued without the need for seeding teams. Districts 1–4 always comprised the Eastern Regional, and the site director chose first-round opponents out of a hat. Districts 5–8 did the same in the West. In 1942, that meant that district designees Dartmouth, Penn State, Kentucky, and Illinois made the long trek down to New Orleans for the Eastern Regional. The Big Easy hosted the NABC convention that normally coincided with the regional. With the onset of war, New Orleans felt the effects just like every other major city. When the US Navy took over the Big Easy's biggest auditorium, Olsen had to move the event to Tulane University's on-campus gym—a considerable reduction in seating capacity. This move did not dissipate local interest in the event. The *New Orleans Times-Picayune* promoted the ensuing action for days leading up to the event. "Points are going to flow like water . . . if the teams follow their past season's performances," the daily predicted on March 18, while promoting that "The classiest bunch of basketball teams ever to meet for a series in the Deep South gets together here tonight."[49]

While first-round tournament action sizzled, this location proved to be a major setback to the tournament. On Friday, March 20, Dartmouth dropped Penn State and Kentucky took down Illinois in first-round action—thereby eliminating the Big Ten's chances at a third straight NCAA championship and a fourth straight finalist. Dartmouth finished off Kentucky in the Regional Final the following night, easily winning by a score of 47–28. Unfortunately, local interest from the Big Easy could not offset the costs of getting the four teams down to New Orleans. Indeed, while the Regional brought in $5,623.95 in gross ticket revenue, its receipts did not cover its expenses. With each participating team requiring more than $1,000 in guarantees and travel reimbursement, the Regional ended up losing $1,972.48—a drop of $8,658.19 from what the Madison, Wisconsin, Regional of 1941 made.[50]

Unfortunately, the Western Regional in Kansas City lost a bit of its luster, too, despite unprecedented local interest. Fans continued to show their faithfulness to college basketball in the opening round as 8,200 spectators took in first-round action. "Stanford's towering lads" defeated Rice 53–47, and Colorado knocked off local favorite Kansas 46–44. The Stanford crew, which averaged a lengthy 6'3½", easily took down the Buffaloes in the Saturday night final. While ticket revenues came in at an all-time high for the Western Regional, so did expenses. The expenditures totaling $10,405.79 mostly offset the $14,223.21 in receipts generated throughout the two nights of action. Costs increased across the board due to wartime rationing, but team travel expenses came in especially high—it cost Stanford more than $2,000 to participate—and a nearly 50 percent increase in the building and grounds expense charged by Kansas City's Municipal Auditorium.[51]

Stanford's regional title meant they would stay in Kansas City for the week—a fate that doomed Washington State the previous year. But Stanford coach Everett Dean received a reversal of fortune. Dean had "universal recognition of being one of the finest gentlemen in the game," and many of his coaching colleagues considered him a close friend. His friendship and kindness paid off during the week between the regionals and the final game. The Eastern Regional site, which also hosted the 1942 NABC convention, doomed the NCAA tournament's profits because it was so far out of the way during the early uncertainty of war. But this site meant that many of Dean's coaching colleagues from the Pacific Northwest would be traveling back by train through Kansas City during the week. Four of those coaches—University of Washington's Hec Edmundson, Washington State's Jack Friel, Oregon's Howard Hobson, and Oregon State's Slats Gill—stopped in the Garden City to spend time with Dean. Two of these coaches had experience in the NCAA championship game, and all four had watched Dartmouth in the Eastern Regional very closely on their friend's behalf. "Those coaches gave us details about the players that were invaluable," Dean recalled, but the coach was no stranger to Dartmouth himself. Stanford had played the northeasterners twice in the previous three years and, more importantly, Dean had coached Dartmouth coach Ossie Cowles when the latter played and the former coached at Carleton College in Minnesota.[52]

Dean used every ounce of "dope" he received from his friends as the week off between games almost derailed his team. The down time allowed the boys to reflect. "We had a lot on our minds," forward Howie Dallmar remembered years later, "what were we doing there playing games when guys our age were defending their country?" Questions lingered among many of these young men, but others had more pressing issues. Stanford forward Jim Pollard, a future Hall of Famer, caught a Kansas City strain of the flu, and starter Don Burness further aggravated an ankle injury. Lady Luck had both given and taken away regarding these westerners.[53]

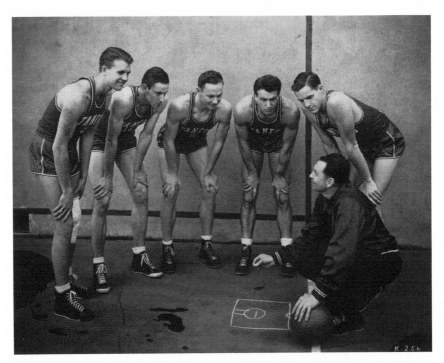

Coach Everett Dean's 1941–42 starting five, depleted for the championship game.
Courtesy of Stanford Historical Photograph Collection (SC1071).

On Saturday, March 28, the depleted West Coast squad met Dartmouth from the East Coast to determine the NCAA champion. Local fans again greased the turnstiles in greater numbers than the previous season despite the war and the distance each competing team traveled. The lanky Stanford Indian squad ran away with the title—even though Pollard sat out in street clothes and Burness played ineffectively and sparingly—by beating the Dartmouth Indians 53–38. The final game generated $1,302.78 in net profits as more than 6,000 fans took in District 8's second title in four years.[54]

After the tournament, Harold Olsen and his tournament committee assessed the event's fourth year of action. "In spite of war conditions the Fourth N.C.A.A. Basketball Tournament was in many respects more successful than any which preceded it," the Ohio State coach opined. He justified this remark by noting the quality of teams, "No national tournament could hope to have a finer 'field' than this one had." Mark Cox of the University of Missouri argued that "The World Series of Basketball" was gaining momentum and that the fourth annual tournament "included the greatest collection of Collegiate cage personnel ever assembled in the 50-year history of the game." Cox also noted that "Veteran tournament observers called the Stanford team the greatest ever to appear in N.C.A.A. competition."[55]

While the field may have been strong and the tournament may have been managed hospitably and effectively, attendance numbers remained well below the National Invitation tournament. While Ned Irish packed 70,000 fans into Madison Square Garden for four nights of tournament action, the NCAA tournament generated only 24,372 over the course of its tournament. Even the much smaller NAIB tournament attracted more spectators—more than 35,000—albeit with thirty-two competing teams and over a span of six days.[56]

Nonetheless, since ticket revenue presented the majority of the overall income, this hindered the NCAA event's bottom line. The overall profits of $1,361.85—only a percentage of what the previous two NCAA tournaments earned—meant that the NCAA and each participating team received much less prize money. Stanford and Dartmouth took home $93.75 each, a total that represented a prize only nominally. When considering it took both Indian squads around $2,000 to participate in the final game—a sum that was reimbursed—the award money appeared paltry. The other six teams took home just $50.59. These totals paled in comparison to what the competing teams had taken home the previous two seasons. They also paled in comparison to what the National Invitation participants received.[57]

Phog Allen's Disillusionment

One of the coaches privy to these prizes, Phog Allen, became especially disillusioned by the NCAA's financial stewardship. The Kansas coach played a large part in the tournament's viability by convincing the NABC to hold a second annual event in 1940—and to do so under his watch in Kansas City. His administrative expertise in hosting the 1940 Western Regional and Final Game brought riches to the tournament much quicker than expected. However, Allen's disillusionment began shortly after that 1940 event.[58]

Prior to the 1940 NCAA tournament, the tournament committee— Olsen, Allen, Edmundson of Washington, James W. St. Clair of Southern Methodist, and B. T. Grover of Ohio University—decided on a financial plan. With the potential profits generated from the event, they would pay the NCAA back for the 1939 loss, cover their current expenses, and use the rest to "promote the game of basketball" as they saw fit. This promotion would include prize money to the participating teams, an allocation for the NABC, and a portion to help fund the travel for teams competing in the upcoming

Olympic Basketball Trials. However, Olsen apparently could not convince the NCAA on this matter. So when the 1940 event finished, the NCAA had its own method of dividing up the financial plunder. The NCAA took 10 percent of the net profits, and then another 50 percent of what was left. That left the NABC in control of 45 percent of the profit—a far cry from the 80 percent Allen thought they should have.[59]

Despite the success of the 1940 tournament, Allen became disenchanted through a series of discussions with the NCAA. He had promised the NABC and the tournament's participating teams a large profit back in 1939 and, while the tournament did generate a healthy bottom line, the NCAA would not let him disburse the funds in such a way that he could uphold his promise to the NABC and its members. So he and the NCAA tournament committee parted ways. The NCAA claimed that he resigned, and yet he told many of his colleagues that, "After I had served (the NCAA) for thirteen years, it was felt by some members that it would be a good idea to" move in a different direction. "The nominating Committee selected (Missouri coach) George Edwards as Representative of this (Fifth) district and he automatically becomes the Manager of the Western and the National N.C.A.A. Tournament." Consequently, Allen's criticism mounted.[60]

The 1940 financial disagreements gave Allen a growing distrust of Olsen's leadership of the tournament. Was the Ohio State coach trying to run the best tournament possible, or was he trying to appease the NCAA? When Wisconsin qualified for the 1941 Eastern Regional tournament that Olsen had chosen the Badgers to host, Allen's complaints continued. The Kansas coach argued that this decision "gives Wisconsin an eight- to 10-point advantage and the whole idea of the playoffs is to give every team an equal advantage." He argued further that Olsen was "selling fair play rights for gate receipts." Olsen, who called Allen "a toe-dancing, shadow-boxing politician" for his actions in guiding the tournament, replied that Allen's logic was duplicitous. The Kansas coach, after all, had brought the Western Regional and Final Game to within forty miles of his campus, giving him a perceived advantage in fan support. Yet Allen did not buy this argument. Traveling forty miles and across a state line does not make for home court advantage, he claimed.[61]

Despite Allen's misgivings about the administration of the tournament, the Kansas coach continued to enter his team. Allen and Edwards, his successor in tournament management, exchanged barbs in the *Kansas City Times* in March 1942, regarding the tournament. Allen declared that NCAA teams "receive nothing but bare expenses" for their participation in the tournament—a statement that the coach knew was inaccurate. Thus was Allen's tendency toward hyperbole. Edwards responded that the first cut that the

NCAA took from the profits was put into a fund "with which the N.C.A.A. seeks to insure the financial safety of future tournaments and to finance American basketball teams in the Olympic games." Both of these uses of the money fell directly in line with what Allen originally wanted. His beef remained with the first 10 percent cut the NCAA took, and, indirectly, with the fact that he was excluded from the event's leadership.[62]

Allen took a precarious position regarding the NCAA tournament. While he was a vocal, outspoken, and public critic of the way the tournament operated, he was also more than willing to enter his team into its brackets despite the option of competing in either of the two other tournaments—one of which occurred in Kansas City and the other that reportedly provided participating teams with thousands of dollars of prize money. Kansas's athletic conference, the Big Six, prohibited the Jayhawks' participation in any other event, but Allen would have had the audacity to push the limit of the conference's power. Indeed, he mentioned as much when he turned down a National Invitation bid for his team. Relaying his reply to Ned Irish, he explained, "Even if there wasn't a Big Six rule (prohibiting extra-NCAA play), I wouldn't abandon the N.C.A.A. as long as Kansas has the chance to compete. N.C.A.A. schools should stand behind their own tournament and not enter privately promoted 'affairs.'" Allen cemented his thoughts by adding, "I insist the N.C.A.A. does not give the competing schools their share of the money, but I'm loyal to the organization and always have been."[63]

Tournament Battle Lines

The battle lines that Allen had originally drawn in 1940 to ensure that certain coaches and teams would avail themselves if asked to participate in the NCAA tournament continued to grow. Near the end of the 1942 season, *New York Times* sports editor John Kieran called this divide "Class Warfare." Kieran noted that the National Invitation "featured the best available teams from all the countryside." He explained that he used the word "available" because some teams would not come if invited. "The Big Ten and the teams in the Eastern Intercollegiate Basketball League won't come out and play in the Madison Square Garden parties," he reported. Big Ten officials constituted much of the NCAA power nexus at this time and Big Ten coach Harold Olsen had been running the tournament, so that conference's alliances came as no surprise. Many of the Eastern teams that neglected the New York City event were among the original elite universities in the country and held amateurism views that precluded their entrance into any postseason event, much less one that filled the pocketbooks of private promoters. Indeed, Dartmouth, among the leaders in the NCAA's First

District, did not even consider the NCAA tournament until 1942. Eastern Intercollegiate League director Asa Bushnell's inclusion on the MIBC tournament committee went a long way toward influencing eastern collegiate views on the postseason—and especially the New York event.[64]

In February 1942, Kieran noted that Ned Irish did not seem too bothered by the "Class Warfare" that had permeated college basketball postseason events. If Illinois or Dartmouth did not want to play in Madison Square Garden, Kieran relayed that Irish "hints that it's their loss." He believed that the Eastern Intercollegiate and Big Ten teams "are about as good as the teams" who play in the Garden invite, "but no better."[65]

Describing each tournament's alliances with teams and conferences as "battle lines" seemed appropriate considering the social context of the time. War efforts changed everything, including the allocation of resources that had gone to college athletic departments in the past. And yet Americans continued to believe that elite sporting events provided a welcome diversion from the horrors of war. Many in the metropolitan area believed that sports could promote war efforts even further.

Late in the 1941–42 season, fans began writing letters to the *New York Times* asking for a matchup of the top two teams in New York City—LIU and CCNY—in a charity match. Calls for this type of war fund charity game had come the previous season, too, but they did not reach the newspapers until April—after each team had disbanded. This season, however, was different. The United States was at war, and the nation's consciousness included collective war funding as a high priority. Further, this matchup had great appeal. LIU and CCNY did not meet during the regular season, and both lost in the first round of the National Invitation.[66]

On March 28, the same night as the NCAA tournament final in Kansas City, LIU and CCNY squared off at Madison Square Garden for a game to benefit the Army Emergency Fund. That same day, Kieran suggested that National Invitation champion West Virginia stay around to meet Dartmouth in a charity game if the Eastern quintet won the NCAA final that night. They did not, and the idea garnered no more interest. LIU and CCNY, however, received a great deal of interest. City College upset the Blackbirds 42–34 in a second-half rally that excited the 16,251 fans in attendance. The game generated a "considerable sum of money for the Army Emergency Relief." This connection between college basketball's postseason and American war efforts would become much stronger in the years to come.[67]

Even though the basketball season officially ended in the Garden after the charity game and in Kansas City the same night, discussion of the college basketball landscape continued. The NCAA and National Invitation tournaments received obvious comparisons because both occurred with large, prestigious university teams. Therefore, many took to juxtaposing the two events. One way to compare them was based on attendance figures. Since ticket sales were by far the majority of each tournament's revenues at the time, and since the MIBC and Ned Irish's private organizations did not have to disclose its financial records, attendance figures provided the best indication of overall profitability. On this mark, the National Invitation clearly outclassed the NCAA tournament. The other method of comparing the two tournaments was by the quality of participating teams.

Shortly after the season, a fan from Schenectady, New York, filed a complaint about the National Invitation's quality of teams to the *New York Times*. "Comparing the teams entered in the N. C. A. A. tournament with those in the New York event makes the latter look pretty bad," the fan commented, "however, the field was not as bad as last year, when L. I. U. gained a hollow triumph." The author used strength of schedule arguments to underscore his main points. Coming from New York, this thesis was heresy. While local sportswriters who accepted and printed this letter remained diplomatic, metropolitan fans took issue with this argumentation.[68]

A week later, two fans from Brooklyn shot back. The first argued that the Schenectady author "appeared to be misinformed and not up to par in his knowledge of basketball when he tried to belittle the national invitation basketball tournament." This fan theorized that, when "comparing the N. C. A. A. and Garden events, one must give the nod to the local affair. Dartmouth, which went to the final of the N. C. A. A. tournament, was soundly trounced by Toledo, which could do no better than fourth here." These types of derivative and hypothetical arguments were not new. In fact, this line of argumentation had been offered on behalf of both tournaments in years past. However, as this Brooklyn fan noted bluntly, "the gentleman from Schenectady is all wrong." The second Brooklyn fan concurred, calling the original arguments "very hollow." He underscored his arguments with the attendance issue, which figured prominently into comparative arguments but was beside the point of this particular discussion. "I believe the Garden tournament was every bit as good as, if not better than, the N. C. A. A. event," he opined, "the attendance figures at both certainly indicate the local affair was the greater attraction." The sports editor compiling and printing these letters ended the discussion peacefully, concluding, "all the teams in the two tournaments were good. Let it go at that."[69]

Unfortunately, no one let it go at that. In fact, NCAA and National Invitation tournament comparisons were only beginning. And as sportswriters around the country named National Invitation champ West Virginia and NCAA champ Stanford as the top two teams in the country at season's end, the matter of which tournament was best was far from over.[70]

CHAPTER 6

New York City and True National Championships, 1942–1945

NCAA tournament officials moved into the 1942 off-season with major concerns about their championship event. The gala, it seemed, had lost much of its steam. Increased calls for war support certainly played a role in this ebb tide, and the NCAA decided to call off its championship events in wrestling, fencing, cross-country, and gymnastics for 1943 because of the war. Basketball, however, continued on, as NCAA administrators believed that wartime austerity was no excuse for a poor showing.[1]

New York City's National Invitation and Kansas City's NAIB tournaments continued to grow in tangible ways despite having to deal with the same suppressing wartime conditions. Olsen and his colleagues had to make changes in order for the NCAA tournament to survive the nation's austerity, and they did so. The Ohio State coach, who had lobbied Ned Irish to let him have some Madison Square Garden dates to conduct the Eastern regionals of the NCAA tournament for a number of years, was finally able to gain admittance into basketball's mecca. This venue change became the single most important decision in the tournament's history, catapulting the event into the early phases of the spectacle that it is today.

The 1942 postseason tournaments ended with many teams disbanding so that the athletes could enlist in the military. Indeed, intercollegiate athletic programs across the country fell apart as team rosters fell prey to service rosters. A 1943 survey of 148 of the nation's teachers colleges found that 38 of them had "eliminated entirely" their athletics programs. Thus, the welcome home for tournament teams was bittersweet. Both 1942 NCAA finalists—Stanford and Dartmouth—lost key players after the season to the war. Thus, the joy of accomplishment and the relief of returning home upon the completion of yet another season quickly waned, overtaken by the reality that leisure time spent training for the game of basketball and its faux combat would be replaced by training for life-and-death battle in World War II. However, while many young men were forced into choosing international combat and its accompanying perils instead of intercollegiate athletic competition, those who stayed at home continued to be delightfully distracted with the "serious non-seriousness" of elite sporting events. Such is the power of sport.[2]

While basketball and many other sports offered delightful distractions from the grim realities of war, the men who organized these tournaments found their jobs increasingly difficult. The business of running a successful sporting event was no easy economic chore in normal conditions. With a nation focused on a two-front war, running a sporting event became even more difficult.

Despite the fact that Americans had been asked to give much more time, energy, and money to support the war than they ever had before— time, energy, and money that normally could have been spent attending elite sporting competitions—Olsen believed that he knew the answer to the NCAA tournament's problems. The event had floundered because it lacked what the National Invitation tournament had—a mega-sized arena and the fan base to fill it. In this time of war, a large venue and an eager fan base became absolute necessities for an event to persist.[3]

A New Venue

On January 20, 1943, the *New York Times* announced that the NCAA "tournament finals probably will be staged at Madison Square Garden." This indecisive proclamation came alongside many other unconfirmed possibilities for the end of the 1942–43 season. The *Times*, via the Red Cross's National Sports Advisory Committee chairman A. J. Ditman, also reported two other possibilities. First, the MIBC hoped to offer a special postseason charity tournament among local college teams. All eleven members of the MIBC and NYU had agreed to participate in this event that would donate its proceeds to a war fund.[4]

The other possibility was for the NCAA tournament champion to meet the National Invitation champion in Madison Square Garden after both tournaments had concluded. The unconfirmed reports of this possible event had been brewing for quite some time. Sportswriter John Kieran had suggested such a game immediately following the conclusion of the 1942 championships. The proposed game would feature the two teams that would have the greatest claim to being the nation's best. Over the past two seasons, the National Invitation and NCAA tournament champions had been the consensus top two teams as reported by many newspapers nationwide. Thus, the two tournaments were seen as equals, or at least similar enough to generate interest in a head-to-head face-off. By 1943, the NCAA no longer referred to its tournament as the World Series of Basketball and the National Invitation no longer referred to itself as the Rose Bowl of Basketball. The tournaments had become too similar and competition for participating teams had become manifest. Therefore, the NCAA's use of Madison Square Garden and the encouragement from nonprofit organizations for teams to play more games to support the war created a wave of momentum to have a better climax to the college basketball season.[5]

The *New York Times*'s Kingsley Childs confirmed the NCAA's Garden dates on January 21, 1943. The sportswriter speculated on the NCAA's reasons for this change of venue, arguing, "Although the transfer of the . . . N.C.A.A. event to the Garden was made largely in the interest of transportation conservation and with an eye toward sparing the four Eastern regional participants the problem of traveling to and from Kansas City, the switch may prove more beneficial to them financially." These arguments seemed sound, and the speculation was definitely prescient. Olsen, his tournament committee, and the NCAA may have argued that hosting the Eastern regionals and tournament final in New York City would conserve travel, but any savings would have been negligible. Of the teams that had participated in the previous Eastern regionals and tournament finals, at least half of them would have had to travel farther to get to New York City than Kansas City. Therefore, while travel conservation sounded good during this wartime period, actual conservation was certainly not assured. Attracting more tickets and their accompanying receipts—that is, making more money and becoming more prominent—seemed to be the soundest argument for the tournament's move to New York City. Olsen and the NCAA did not appear to hide this rationale.[6]

The move put the NCAA and National Invitation tournaments on a head-to-head crash course. On February 11, the *New York Times* reported the dates of each tournament. The National Invitation reserved the Garden for its quarterfinals on Thursday, March 18, and Monday, March 22; its semifinals on Saturday, March 27; and its final game on Monday, March 29. The NCAA received the Garden's open nights of Wednesday, March 24, and Thursday, March 25, for its Eastern regional games. The Western Regional games, which had more leverage in the smaller market that Kansas City's Municipal Auditorium served, would be held on Friday, March 26, and Saturday, March 27. The NCAA reserved Tuesday, March 30, for its East-West tournament final in the Garden—the day after the National Invitation tournament wrap-up. Notably absent on this schedule was a Friday night in the Garden. Prizefighting had a stronghold there that college basketball had yet to overcome. Also absent were Sunday games, demonstrating the religious climate of the country—especially when at war.[7]

On February 19, the *New York Times* also reported that a "Red Cross benefit game" had been scheduled between the NCAA tournament and National Invitation tournament champions for April 1. The logistics of both championship events was such that it would be easy for both victors to stay in New York City for a couple more days. This "mythical national championship" would be played in a fashion that theoretically would bring Americans together to support a good cause. And yet the fierce competitiveness that sport embodies allowed other implications of this game to arise.[8]

Competition for the Competition

With the addition of this head-to-head matchup, tournament selection committees felt increased pressure to put together strong brackets of teams. These groups went right to work. The MIBC noted on February 25 that they were considering thirty-eight teams: fifteen from the East (including five from New York City), seven from the South, eight from the Midwest, three from the Southwest, one from the Rocky Mountains, and four from the Pacific Coast. And if previous traditions held true, the final eight teams would include two from New York City.[9]

Repeat contenders Western Kentucky and Creighton accepted the first two bids to the Garden tournament. Toledo also accepted a repeat bid. While the Ohioans had lost many seniors including its two African Americans from the previous season's squad, it came in with a new star in African American Davage Minor. Rice Institute and Washington and Jefferson College rounded out the visiting teams at the Garden while three local teams received invitations—the highest number of local quintets to date. St. John's came in as a favorite, and locals Fordham and Manhattan received their first bids by way of outstanding regular season records.[10]

Creighton, with a 19-1 season record, earned the top seed. The Blue Jays certainly merited this ranking, and yet the MIBC may have taken special delight in this decision. Creighton, champions of the Missouri Valley Conference in the NCAA District 5, chose the New York event over the NCAA championship. On March 4, Blue Jay coach Ed Hickey told the NCAA's District 5 selection committee that his team was out of the running. They had not officially been offered an NCAA bid yet, and did not want to miss out on postseason play overall. So they chose the National Invitation. The concurrent dates of the two events precluded any team from entering the NCAA Western Regional and the MIBC tournament. Creighton's decision was such a blow to the NCAA that Kansas coach Phog Allen—at that point quite ambivalent toward the NCAA event—offered to withdraw his team as a potential District 5 representative in favor of the Blue Jays. Creighton opted for the certainty of the National Invitation bid.[11]

Four teams with two losses followed Creighton in the National Invitation rankings. St. John's was second with 18 wins and Western Kentucky was third with 24 wins. The inconsistency here may have indicated, like in previous seasons, some local bias. The fourth-seed Toledo had 19 wins while local Manhattan, entering its first National Invitation, was fifth with 18 wins. The other new local entrant, Fordham, came in as the six seed with a record of 15-4. Rice, a "bubble" team that was left out of the field in previous seasons, finally made its first appearance in the tournament and was seeded seventh with a 16-7 record. Washington and Jefferson, the runt of the litter, rounded out the field as the eight seed after finishing the season at 16-3.[12]

Selection of the NCAA tournament teams occurred at the same time. Because each district chose its own representative, the NCAA's selection process was not as streamlined. And without a centralized office and the local media to promote it, the NCAA selection process received less attention than that of the National Invitation. Nevertheless, the Eastern participants found their way onto New York newspapers' sports pages, perhaps mostly because NYU accepted the bid to represent the NCAA's second district in the tournament. Dartmouth would represent District 1; Georgetown represented District 3; and DePaul received a surprise bid to represent District 4. The fourth district had been the strongest over the past four years, having sent a team to the finals in each of the first three NCAA tournaments. This 1943 selection, though, was different. Each of the previous District 4 representatives had been members of the Big Ten conference. The Big Ten was the cream of the crop in terms of college athletic conferences. They were leaders, they directed national policies, and they were successful in the most popular sports. So when previous District 4 selection committees had to choose their representatives, they naturally went with the top Big Ten team. In 1939, Bradley received the district's invite but the independent team chose the New York invite for a second straight year, believing it had unfinished business at the Garden. In 1940, the district selection committee chose Indiana, the second-best Big Ten team, as conference champion Purdue continued its policy of abstaining from all postseason play.[13]

This selection method may not have been as narrow-minded as it appeared. After all, the Big Ten usually sported the top teams in the region. Therefore, many top independent teams and those from other conferences in the region realistically had little shot at making the tournament. However, in

1943, DePaul became the first non–Big Ten District 4 representative. Illinois, the season's Big Ten champ, declined a bid and so did the nationally prominent Notre Dame basketball team. With these refusals and with wartime austerity, the District 4 selection committee gained its first commitment from a non–Big Ten team. In the past, independents like DePaul, Loyola of Chicago, Bradley, Ohio, and Toledo naturally chose the National Invitation tournament in part at least because they believed they did not stand much chance of receiving the District 4 bid to the NCAA tournament. They certainly did not have any chance of gaining a bid in years where they were not NCAA members.[14]

DePaul's entrance provided hope for the future for independent schools in District 4. The Big Ten did not have a monopoly on District 4 bids. And yet this region's selection committee did not act much differently than did certain other regions. Many other NCAA districts also found themselves bound by a limited number of NCAA in-region members and only one major athletic conference. In the West where fewer well-known independent teams resided, conference-aligned teams received the only NCAA bids. For the 1943 NCAA tournament, conference champion state schools Oklahoma, Texas, Washington, and Wyoming accepted bids to the Kansas City regional.[15]

Kansas City and the 1943 NAIB

With the NCAA tournament final moving to New York City, the NAIB tournament enjoyed status as the only Kansas City "national" championship in 1943. Its early March tip-off that occurred well before the NCAA and National Invitation tournaments, though, reaffirmed that it remained much less heralded nationally than the National Invitation and the NCAA tournament. Emil Liston's tournament continued to progress, however, attracting teams from as far away as both coasts despite evolving wartime austerity. The first game of the sixth annual affair showed the attitudes of the participants all around. While each team wanted to win, the small schools that participated seemed to have a healthy understanding of college basketball's place in greater society at the time. Southeast Missouri State and Dakota Wesleyan squared off in the opening game of the tournament to move on to the round of 16, but they also played for blood. The teams agreed before tip-off that the members of the losing team had to donate blood afterward to the war drive.[16]

Dakota Wesleyan came up short and quickly found their way to the blood bank after the buzzer. Southeast Missouri State could have made that friendly wager—which seemed to fit nicely within the NAIB's interest in promoting competition within the confines of good character—in any of its games during its week in the Garden City and not lost any blood. In the finals on March 13, the Southeast Show-Me Staters took down the Northwest Missourians for the title, 34–32, thus bringing the championship back to Kansas or Missouri for the fifth time in seven years.[17]

The 1943 National Invitation and NCAA Championship

Five days after the NAIB final, the National Invitation tipped off its first-round action in the Garden. The NCAA sat waiting for a few more days. But both of these tournaments for larger schools would overlap in the coming days. The *New York Times*'s Arthur Daley noted the difficulty in following the parallel action. "The championship phase of the campaign is upon us and it is a bit on the confusing side," he complained, "With two interlocking tournaments under way simultaneously a bewildered fan has to study time schedules carefully in order to discover who plays whom and when."[18]

On Thursday, March 18, the National Invitation tipped off first-round action in front of 16,265 fans in the Garden. Fourth-seed Toledo met fifth-seed Manhattan. "Both teams moved about the court with special finesse and eye-opening players prominent," sportswriter Louis Effrat explained. However, Toledo's Davage Minor made the difference in the ball game. "Without the Negro ace Toledo is a good team," Effrat noted of the Rocket who would star at UCLA after the war and become an early NBA racial pioneer, "with him in the line-up is superb."[19]

However, the night's most thrilling action came as eighth-seed Washington and Jefferson "sneaked through with a 43–42 upset triumph over top seeded Creighton as the Blue Jays lost four players on personal fouls." This first-round dismissal of the top team marked the second straight year that this had happened. Sportswriters indirectly lamented that the MIBC tournament committee should be embarrassed by what became poor seeding, especially because of the overwhelming amount of upsets in the 1942 event, but this criticism may not have been fair. Before seeds, every team entered the National Invitation not having an explicit rank attached to them. In this way, no team came into the event with any extra motivation to win that would have come from being seeded lower than expected. However, with seeds now being made public, certain teams may have used a low seed as extra fuel on the court. Further, as was the case in both the 1942 and 1943 opening nights, the top seed may have believed it did not have to play as hard because, in the eyes of the selection committee that used relatively subjective methods to seed teams, they were much better than their first-round opponents. Such is the nature of tournament competition.[20]

Four nights later, the event continued, and 18,135 fans came to see two local quintets take on visitors. On Monday, March 22, second-seeded St. John's, the top remaining seed, held off Rice Institute, 51–49. St. John's reserve guard Hy Gotkin missed a set shot with six seconds remaining. Yet he was able to snag his own rebound and score with one second left for the win. "Too much credit . . . cannot be accorded Gotkin, the smallest man on the floor," Effrat relayed in his assessment. "He was all over the floor, and though he tallied only 10 points, his value to the squad was immeasurable."[21]

In the other contest, sixth-seeded Fordham upset third-seed Western Kentucky, 60–58. This matchup, in Effrat's eyes, "unquestionably was the better game"—a bold claim considering the buzzer-beater from the Johnnies' Gotkin. Effrat explained that Fordham and Western Kentucky were equal in every way except that the former "made their shots count." The writer noted that the first-, third-, fifth-, and seventh-seeded teams were out after the first round of competition. That left only the even seeds remaining, and meant that two of the four games were upsets based on the subjective seeding methodology the selection committee used.[22]

On Wednesday, March 24, the NCAA opened its Eastern Regional tournament at Madison Square Garden for the first time. Harold Olsen anxiously awaited his tournament's ability to finally squeeze into Ned Irish's venue. DePaul and Dartmouth opened the evening's action as the Chicagoans easily handled the New Englanders, 46–35. Giant sophomore center George Mikan paced the Blue Demons with 20 points. Georgetown upset local favorite NYU in the nightcap with a blowout score of 55–36. The Hoyas had a big man of their own, agile 6'8" center John Mahnken, who led the charge with 20 points to match his fellow skyscraper.[23]

The following night, the NCAA concluded its Eastern Regional action with a battle of the big men. Georgetown came from behind to win by four, 53–49. Mahnken outplayed his Blue Demon counterpart, scoring 17 to Mikan's 11. But the real difference in the game involved tactics rather than personnel. The Hoyas, after watching the Blue Demons' "ace 'goal-tender'" in his opening-round game, opted to shoot "over and around, instead of at the versatile DePaul pivot." Although Georgetown, by knocking DePaul out of the tournament, gained entrance into the East-West Final game, the Garden would see plenty more of Mikan in years to come. In two nights of action, 30,576 fans had come to appreciate all that the DePaul center brought to the court.[24]

The Western Regional at Kansas City on Friday and Saturday commenced the day after Mikan's Thursday night exit from the Garden. Texas's "lanky" forward, John Hargis, took center stage in the Garden City, winning the individual scoring honors with his sharpshooting. In the Longhorns' opening-round game against Washington—the fourth-place team from the Pacific Coast Conference—Hargis ran "wild early" and "supplied the early fireworks" by scoring 13 points in the first ten minutes. The Longhorn finished with 30 points. And yet another Longhorn won the hearts of the crowd on this night; 5'8" seventeen-year-old red-head Roy Cox won the game for Texas with three quick field goals at the end to turn a 2-point deficit into a 4-point victory. With three of its stars having exited on fouls, Washington was susceptible defensively and the diminutive Cox capitalized.[25]

In the other opening-round game, Oklahoma also suffered from foul trouble. Its standout center, "Big Gerald" Tucker went over the foul limit late in the first half with the Sooners leading Wyoming. Milo Komenich, star Wyoming center and "a tremendous physical specimen," then went on a rampage with Tucker out of the game, scoring 16 points to lead his team to a 53 to 50 victory.[26]

On Saturday, March 27, Kansas City action wrapped up for the season with the NCAA Western Regional and Consolation Final. Oklahoma beat Washington in the consolation match, 48–43, while the Wyoming "Wranglers" defeated Texas, 58–54. Wyoming's size, speed, and ballhandling overtook the Longhorns. Senior Kenny Sailors struck awe into the Kansas City crowd with his "change-of-pace dribble." The Cowboy "had a knack of speeding down the floor, stopping suddenly and then continuing with his dribble." An estimated 13,000 fans witnessed the weekend action. Wyoming would continue its one-loss season by traveling east to New York City for the NCAA championship game against Georgetown—the first NCAA championship game that did not include either a Pacific Coast Conference or a Big Ten team.[27]

However, before any championship could be settled, the NIT had rights to the Garden floor for its semifinal round. For the first time in the tournament's history, two local teams reached the penultimate round. Unfortunately for local die-hards, the two had to face each other in the semifinals. Therefore, St. John's and Fordham headlined the semifinal action; 18,419 fans—an all-time Garden basketball record crowd at the time—came to see the Redmen outplay the Rams. While Fordham started out strongly in the first three minutes of action, "the next thirty-seven minutes of play told an entirely different tale" as St. John's pulled away 69–43. "Big Boy" Harry Boykoff, at 6'9", presented a problem that the Rams could not solve, as the center scored 22 points in the victory. Toledo's win over Washington and Jefferson became only an afterthought to the local matchup that night. The Presidents led at halftime and maintained a 7-point advantage early into the second half until their most dependable forward went down and out with an ankle injury. Toledo seized the opportunity by scoring 7 straight and then took control a few minutes later for a 7-point victory, 46–39.[28]

Interestingly, the subtitle of the semifinal newspaper report in the *New York Times* referred to the tournament as the "U.S. Invitation." The National Invitation tournament, which reporters always referred to by its official title or as the Metropolitan or New York tournament, had never been referred to as the "U.S." tournament. Quite obviously, the term "national" that was used referred to the US, but the difference is worth mentioning. The "U.S." term used may have been a simple variation employed by the editor to spice up the text. However, it also may have been a strategy to further promote the New York–based tournament. After all, its organizers may have felt the effects of the NCAA tournament sharing its prestigious venue for the first time. So the MIBC may have felt the need to set the National Invitation apart from the NCAA tournament. By employing a new title, they may have done so, while also playing on American citizens' patriotic wartime emotions. More likely, sportswriter Louis Effrat and his editor, Arthur Daley, used the term to separate the alliterative confusion between the *National* Invitation and the *National* Collegiate Athletic Association tournaments. Nevertheless, the new moniker did not stick.[29]

On Monday, March 29, the "National" Invitation Final featuring St. John's and Toledo attracted 18,233 spectators. The intense semifinal-round action demonstrated the zeal with which these teams competed. Harold Parrott of the *Brooklyn Daily Eagle* alluded to one reason for the intensity —rumors swirled that Toledo was using players who were not amateurs. However, Parrott was in no mood to get to the bottom of this hair splitting. "Squeamish colleges aren't forced to compete," he reminded his readers, "They could decline—but they are all in there for the moolah as well as the glory. Team that wins tonight will be assured of nearly $15,000." The potential profits for winning apparently meant more for the team that was not accused of playing professionally. After a 22-all tie early in the second half, the Redmen took over and coasted to an easy 48–27 victory, becoming the second local team to win the championship in the event's six-year history. The following night, the NCAA staged its first New York City final, featuring Wyoming and Georgetown. The westerners came out of the blocks quickly but Georgetown found its stride, catching up and hanging with the Cowboys for most of the game. However, with six minutes left, Wyoming found a new gear. The Cowboys overcame a 5-point deficit by outscoring the Hoyas 20–3 the rest of the way for a convincing 46–34 victory.[30]

The inaugural NCAA championship game in Madison Square Garden attracted 13,206 spectators. This became the largest crowd for an NCAA championship game in the tournament's five-year history—a welcome trend. However, this attendance figure was well below the National Invitation's crowd tally. At this point, however, the difference between these two figures followed logically. The local New York crowd was more accustomed to the local tournament. After all, only one metropolitan team had even competed in the NCAA affair to this point, and this was the NCAA tournament's first season holding games in New York City. Further, the National Invitation included three local teams, the semifinals included two, and the championship went to local St. John's. The NCAA Eastern Regional games—which averaged just over 15,000 fans per night of action—included just one local team and the NCAA championship game featured none at all. Clearly, in America's #1 media market—New York City—the National Invitation tournament reigned supreme.[31]

A Championship of Champions, in the Name of Charity

Wyoming continued its postseason success two nights later. This team was accustomed to intense basketball competition both at home and on the road. The Cowboys' 5,000-seat home gym in Laramie earned the nickname "Hell's Half-Acre" for its intimidation to visiting teams. Coach Ev Shelton's "eccentric sideline behavior" always riled the crowd into a frenzy.[32]

In 1939, Shelton had a special group of freshmen that beat the varsity squad. So the coach began scheduling his team in big media markets across the country to promote them early. Thus, although the team came from "Hell's Half-Acre" in the sparsely populated high plain town of Laramie among the Rocky Mountains, star Kenny Sailors, enforcer Milo Komenich, and the rest of the Cowboys entered New York City with a superb reputation. Indeed, after winning the NCAA Western Regional and East-West Championship Game, and after reaching the semifinal round of the AAU National Tournament that occurred before the NCAA events, the Cowboys entered the Red Cross charity matchup with the National Invitation champion St. John's squad on a hot streak. Local journalists noted that this game was "for what amounts to the unchallenged college leadership of the country."[33]

Sport for charity was nothing new. American athletes and sports fans had shown their willingness to donate their time, effort, and money to sporting events in the name of charity over the previous decades. The money fans paid for admission to a charity event made them feel good about their disbursement, and they received entertainment in return. The athletes got to ply their trade in front of large, adoring crowds and, while not getting paid to do so, they generated large amounts of goodwill in the process.[34]

The problem with these events, however, was with the promoters. The formula for hosting a successful sporting event in the name of charity was easy to manipulate. Getting headlining athletes to perform was the first step. When secured, the crowds would naturally show up in large numbers. This part was easy. It was usually the closed-door negotiating between the money-grubbing promoters and the naïve charity organizations that became problematic.

For many years, the methods by which promoters divided the profits with charities for these "feel good" sporting events were not disclosed. Promoters found ways to hide their profits and charity organizations simply fell prey to the fine print of their contractual obligations. However, as the Great Depression and World War II put the United States on a collision course with austerity and utility that forced Americans to seek the public good over individual gain, ideologies changed. No longer were the profits of the Roaring Twenties large enough to disburse in a way that made everyone happy. No longer was personal gain acceptable if it meant the public good suffered.

Early in the Second World War, sportswriter John Kieran brought to light the evils that had beset sport for charity. He lamented the historical boxing matches held in the name of charity in which promoters "chiseled" the profits away from the nonprofit organizations. Kieran noted that, in these sporting events, "Charity got everything except the money." These heinous procedures, which found amnesty in the economic boom of the 1920s, became heretical by the beginning of World War II.[35]

By the early 1940s, the Red Cross had taken a stand against the ways in which event promoters "chiseled" at the profits of their events. The aid organization ruled that if any sporting event was to be held in its name, then all revenues would go directly to them without any cut for event promoters. With all that goes into putting on a major sporting event, this naturally meant that much more volunteerism would be required to put on charity sport for the Red Cross.[36]

The worldwide aid organization was large enough that it could handle missing out on potentially lucrative sporting events to maintain the reverence and prestige of its name. The American Red Cross became the primary beneficiary of "the greatest free will offering in history" during the war. More than 150 million Americans donated almost $785 million in memberships and subscriptions from 1942 to 1946. The Red Cross noted, "No other single cause save that of the country itself has received contributions that approach such magnitude. The membership is greater than the votes cast by either of our political parties in the 1944 Presidential election or than the membership of any of our great religious faiths."[37]

The success of individual and family subscriptions and memberships allowed the Red Cross to take a hard-line stance regarding public sporting events in its name. The organization was clearly not hurting for money, and so it passed on potentially profitable events to ensure it played no role in promoters' corrupting influences. The Red Cross's demand if its name was to be attached to sporting events, was that they receive all revenues without any expenses deducted. This all-or-nothing stance made it difficult for individual sport athletes especially to donate their performances to the aid organization's cause, for if an athlete was to do so, he or she would have to pay for travel and related expenses to get to the venue to even allow for the event to occur.[38]

Within months of the attacks on Pearl Harbor, athletes began showing a willingness to provide such a donation to the Red Cross. Norwegian figure skater Sonja Henie helped change athletes' attitudes as she embarked upon a skating exhibition in Madison Square Garden in January 1942 in which she fronted all of the event's expenses. The three-time Olympic gold medalist and ten-time world champion had already started an American acting career that had catapulted her fame in the United States. Her exhibition was a great success.[39]

Two months later as the 1942 basketball season was wrapping up, a local metropolitan basketball fan wrote a letter to the *New York Times* sports editor asking if it would be possible for the top two metropolitan college quintets to square off in a postseason game for charity. CCNY and LIU, the two teams at hand, had not played each other during the regular season, and both lost in the first round of the National Invitation that year.[40]

This was not the first call for postseason basketball in the name of charity. Fans had made similar pleas to the press a year earlier, describing a donation method whereby the proceeds would go to an international aid organization that could help the allied nations in their war efforts. Unfortunately, these 1941 calls were too late. One year later, they were right on time. Sportswriter John Kieran carried the torch of these fan propositions and helped orchestrate the LIU-CCNY showdown within one week that occurred in the name of the Army Emergency Fund. "It took a war to get them together," Kieran noted of the collaboration between the usually hostile rival metropolitan squads.[41]

The game was a huge success, hosting 16,251 fans and generating more than $7,000 for the Army Emergency Fund. Had the charity followed the

Red Cross's all-or-nothing financial regulations, it might have generated even more money. However, the reason the Army Emergency Fund became the beneficiary of the event in the first place was because of its less rigid financial restrictions. Nevertheless, with expenses paid off, promoters and event officials happy, and the charity much richer than it was before, this goodwill game became a model of sorts. And in Kieran's column discussing the game, he suggested casually that the top two college postseason tournaments ought to follow this model and offer their respective champions in a game to fund the Red Cross.[42]

Throughout 1942, Madison Square Garden held a litany of sporting exhibitions to help sponsor the Red Cross's war efforts. Henie's figure skating got the ball rolling on this method of support. However, baseball and horse racing events for charity were where the big money rolled in. Madison Square Garden could not host those sports. The best it had been doing in terms of gate receipts was in college basketball. Ned Irish was making money hand over fist in this sector of the industry, and the Red Cross, with its strict financing ideals, was missing out.[43]

By early 1943, the aid organization became willing to alter its hard-line stance on funding. Apparently, a matchup between the NCAA and National Invitation tournament champions in Madison Square Garden was too much to pass up for the Red Cross. Ned Irish orchestrated the setup, now that the NCAA tournament played its final game in the Garden, and had cooperation from both events. He was also able to convince the Red Cross to dismiss its all-or-nothing creed.[44]

Irish had some help in doing so. By 1943, metropolitan sportswriters realized the power of sport for charity and set up a sports committee that served as an arm of the New York City chapter of the Red Cross. This group set out to generate as much money as it could for the aid organization through sporting events. And these sportswriters knew the powerful way in which college postseason basketball events could attract viewership.[45]

In late January 1943, Irish set up the logistics for the NCAA champion and runner-up to stay in New York City for two extra days to square off against the National Invitation's champion and runner-up on April 1. With the history of two parallel tournaments providing the nation with two "champions" at year's end and the speculation that ensued from this plateau, a game to finally determine the champion of champions was hailed as a "dream game" and a "mythical national championship."[46]

The 1943 Red Cross War Fund Benefit Game represented the first time that the NCAA and National Invitation tournaments connected on-court. And the game occurred with great local buildup. Fans, as promoters expected, took great interest in watching this "game of champions" while helping the Red Cross with their ticket receipts. As the National Invitation champion, St. John's found local favor and attracted a strong crowd against the visiting Wyoming Cowboys. Local headlines in the lead-up to the game indicated the prowess of each team seemingly without bias. Local metropolitan fans would have been much more familiar with St. John's than Wyoming, and they would have been more familiar with the National Invitation than the NCAA event. This likely would have bred some favoritism. The *Brooklyn Daily Eagle* reported that St. John's was confident it could beat Wyoming. "Cowboys and Indians perform for the American Red Cross War Fund at the Garden tomorrow night. And the St. Johns U. Redmen, after watching the towering Wyoming U. Cowboys down Georgetown, 46–34, for the National N.C.A.A. title on the midtown court last night, are confident they can scalp those Westerners."[47]

On April 1, St. John's and Wyoming squared off in the "national collegiate championship." National Invitation and NCAA tournament runners-up Toledo and Georgetown met in the evening's opener, and the Hoyas made easy work of the Ohioans, 54–40. That game quickly became little more than an appetizer once the nightcap began. "I don't believe Madison Square Garden has ever gotten so excited about any basketball game nor do I believe there was ever a better basketball game played in this country than the one between St. John's and Wyoming," gushed A. J. Ditman of the American Red Cross. An 18–18 tie thirteen and a half minutes into the game became a 30–23 Wyoming advantage at intermission. The Cowboys maintained a seemingly comfortable 8-point lead, 46–38, with two minutes remaining when the Redmen turned on the heat. Guard Al Moschetti scored a backdoor layup, forward Fuzzy Levane connected on a free throw, center Harry Boykoff put back a rebound, and forward Larry Baxter hit another free throw to close the gap to 2 points with thirty seconds remaining. On Wyoming's ensuing possession, Johnny point guard Hy Gotkin stole the ball and started a fast break that led to a Moschetti layup to tie the game with ten seconds left. St. John's tried calling timeout as Wyoming took the ball out of the hoop to begin its last-ditch counterattack. The din of the 18,316 fans in the Garden muted the referee whistles and game action continued while star Cowboy forward Kenny Sailors drove the length of the court and scored just as the buzzer sounded. The refs convened and agreed to negate the basket and award St. John's a timeout. Wyoming's ensuing attempt to prevent overtime failed.[48]

Even though it had given up an 8-point lead in less than two minutes, its game-winning basket had been recalled, and the game's leading

Wyoming's Kenny Sailors protects the ball against St. John's defenders in the first Red Cross game. *Courtesy of University of Wyoming.*

scorer—Cowboy star center Milo Komenich, who had 20 points—had just been disqualified on fouls, Wyoming did not throw in the towel. The two-minute extra period went scoreless until forty-five seconds remained. Komenich's replacement, Jim Weir, scored a bucket and Wyoming was awarded a foul shot at the same time. The try was good, but St. John's added a free throw at the other end to get to 49–47. St. John's would not convert again, as Weir added another basket and a free throw to ice the game and finish with a score of 52–47.[49]

"When it was over," Louis Effrat noted, "the Cowboys claimed the national collegiate championship, and none in the crowd could dispute their right to the crown." Effrat continued to heap praises, arguing that "this crew of rip-roaring, swashbuckling big men merited every honor, every handshake and every backslap that came their way. And there were plenty on all sides." With the victory, Wyoming had as much stake to claim in speculating the nation's top team as anyone ever had—in any season. The *Brooklyn Daily Eagle* called them the "Real National Champion." The Red Cross game provided a steeply pitched crest to what had been an end-of-season plateau of at least two teams claiming the title of season's best after the postseason.[50]

While Wyoming received "undisputed" honors immediately after its thrilling overtime Red Cross win and continued to receive more recognition than any other team after the 1943 season, they were not the only team mentioned at the top of the season's rankings. St. John's, without surprise, received some mention as a potentially top team. The Redmen, after all, had a terrific season and local reports of their Red Cross loss mentioned that they simply had an off-night. Surprisingly, the University of Illinois also received recognition at the end of the season as a team that deserved mention among the top tier. The Illini, Creighton, and Kansas all received commendation for finishing their conference schedules undefeated, and Creighton lost only one overall. Illinois and Kansas had shut down their teams after the regular season for military reasons. The Illini passed up the tournament "in a move of war-time austerity" and the Jayhawks lost many of their players to the military. Surprisingly, Ned Irish and Orlo Robertson, general sports editor of the Associated Press, mentioned in *The Official National Basketball Committee Basketball Guide* that Illinois "shared national title honors with Wyoming." Even though Illinois declined their NCAA tournament bid, the "whiz kids" had captivated fans throughout the season by breaking numerous scoring records as they paced the Big Ten conference. Over time, however, Wyoming's NCAA and Red Cross championships have overshadowed Illinois's regular season feats.[51]

Despite this delayed ambiguity in ranking 1943 college basketball teams, the Red Cross game was a major success both within the college basketball world and among the nation's generosity to the war effort. It cleared up the postseason plateau, at least among those teams who entered a postseason event. But, more importantly in the larger picture, it provided a great deal of much-needed funding to the Red Cross War Fund. The day after the game, Effrat noted that the game generated around $24,000 for the aid organization from ticket sales. This number grew because of the generous offers in the halftime auction for the game ball. A $1,000 bid won the ball among a total pool of $4,665 in attempts, putting the unofficial total donation from the game at more than $28,000. The *New York Times* reported in its end of the month audit of giving that the Red Cross received a check in the amount of $26,244 from the college basketball benefit night. This modified sum may have reflected an actual ticket revenue sum less than original estimates. At the end of the 1943 calendar year, the Red Cross's Eddie Dooley reported that the game's "resulting cash contribution" to the organization ended at $30,909.98. This augmented total would have included residual donations in honor of the game and pledges that had been unrealized at the time of earlier reports.[52]

College Basketball in Austere Conditions

This Red Cross War Fund Benefit basketball game capped the 1942–43 season on a high note. Wyoming and St. John's provided high-quality basketball and a thrilling finish, and the substantial proceeds helped American war efforts abroad. And these donations were sorely needed, as Uncle Sam dug deeper into the trenches across both oceans. President Roosevelt continually asked more of American citizens, and the customary routines of normal life became more and more difficult. Every activity of daily life changed as wartime rations, taxes, and social capital went directly to the government and its armed forces.

Colleges and universities across the nation, which thrived on the matriculation of young adult males, found the wartime to be especially difficult. The American military draft system snatched young men of college age out of the comfort of daily life—college life, for many. The enrollment numbers at universities and colleges across the country plummeted as their male students went to war. This presented numerous challenges that each individual campus had to address. Many schools began offering women opportunities on campus that they had previously been denied. Other schools totally altered their focus, turning from academic training to military training. The US Navy, in this way, came to the rescue of the many colleges and universities that saw their enrollments dive. The navy set up a V-5 program on college campuses to train young men to become pilots, a V-7 program of officer training on select college campuses, and a V-12 program that vastly increased the amount of colleges that could educate naval trainees to become officers. Commencing on July 1, 1943, the navy sponsored V-12 programs at 131 colleges and universities across the country, reaching an estimated 80,000 trainees. Accordingly, many male college students were forced to transfer from one university to another according to the navy's regulations and the stations at which they trained their new soldiers. And, in a twist that would provide plenty of complication, the NCAA recognized these transfer athletes as eligible immediately.[53]

Unfortunately for college athletics, the US Army—the country's largest military organization at the time—prohibited its trainees from engaging in athletic competition. This difference in philosophy meant that any of the nation's top athletes who joined the army could not "compete in any organized sports that might interfere with their military training." Soldiers could, however, play on unit and base teams once they had been assigned following their training. Athletes who wanted to continue to compete in intercollegiate athletics had to enroll in the navy at their own volition and take advantage of its forty-eight-hour leave allowance to travel to away competition.[54]

These changes put an obvious crimp in college athletics. The tenuous nature of normal life for college athletes and their teams forced college sport administrators to reassess the prudence of carrying on as they had in the past.

Americans loved their sports at the time, as indicated by the overwhelming turnout to the 1943 Red Cross game, but that was a one-off game. Was sport played for charity a better use of resources than disbanding sport altogether to allocate all of the original resources to the war or its aid organizations?

On November 9, 1943, Ned Irish announced a scaled-back college basketball schedule at the Garden for the 1943–44 season. The sixteen regular season double-headers he had on the docket represented a figure two less than the previous season. This became the first time in the ten seasons that college basketball had been played at the Garden that the number of dates had diminished. Irish scheduled only five local teams among these sixteen dates and one of them—LIU—would be playing short-handed. The Blackbirds' legendary Coach Clair Bee opted to join the military after the 1943 season. The *New York Times*'s Louis Effrat, in reporting on Irish's schedule and Bee's military service, also proudly noted that the pared-back Garden schedule of visiting teams reduced normal basketball travel by more than 250,000 "man miles."[55]

The pared-back schedule was certainly not for lack of interest. The Garden had developed a loyal base of visiting teams who found a visit to the basketball mecca to be the pinnacle of their seasons. Western Kentucky coach Ed Diddle, for example, expressed the views of a number of coaches when he said at the end of 1943, "There's no question about (it), we always want to come back to New York." The Hilltopper coach's remarks referred to the regular season, but also insinuated the postseason National Invitation bids his teams had received in 1942 and 1943. Western Kentucky seemed to have a goal of playing in the Garden every season, whether it was in the regular season or postseason.[56]

Unfortunately, because of the war, many teams did not get to realize their goals in 1943 and 1944. Western Kentucky did not receive an invite to the Garden's 1944 postseason event. By the standards set across the country, however, they may have been lucky to even field a team. In the 1943 football season, many schools simply shut down their squads. More than three hundred schools across the country did so, including contemporary powers Fordham and Santa Clara and perennial powers Alabama, Tennessee, and Stanford. Many other schools such as Harvard and Boston College went on with their seasons, but only did so "informally."[57]

The smaller rosters on basketball squads made fielding teams easier than football. However, many schools eliminated hoops on campus. The 1942 Mountain States Conference champion and NCAA tourney participant Colorado was among the first to do so. Many schools disbanded hoops because its players were drafted or enlisted in the military. Others did so because they had given up their gymnasiums to house military trainees or equipment.[58]

As the 1944 calendar year began, the NCAA felt the need to address this ebbing wartime tide. In 1943, the association held seven of its ten postseason championship events. Yet their continuation in 1944, along with regular seasons occurring as they normally had, came into question. The association drafted a resolution that stated:

> The National Collegiate Athletic Association—with a membership of more than 200 colleges, universities, and intercollegiate athletic conferences—reaffirms its method of encouraging the continued development of competitive athletics as a vital element in the training of young men for service in the armed forces of the United States. At the beginning of the war our member institutions pledged their facilities and staffs to the war effort. They were used as completely and effectively as national authorities found plausible. We believe the experience of last year has confirmed the practical wisdom of that policy, and the armed forces have made active use of the facilities and fields of member institutions. We believe that continuation of competitive athletics throughout the period of the war is vital to the total training of the individual. We believe that competition is an essential element in any active program of physical training and recreation. We believe that additional use of existing facilities and staffs should be made in order to include all elements in our college institutions in competitive intercollegiate and intramural sports. We believe that competitive sports are an integral part of American life in time of war and time of peace and, therefore, we have an obligation not only to expand the present uses of facilities but to prepare for the period following the war when problems must be faced.

The NCAA's statement set the tone for the 1944 athletic seasons. The organization and its members would make concessions to accommodate war needs, including many scaled-back sports, travel restrictions, and facility use, but intercollegiate athletics would continue.[59]

Because of its need for high participation numbers, football experienced noticeable problems as it persisted through the war. The University of Utah held on to its intercollegiate athletics program, but only with the participation of seventeen-year-olds who were too young to enlist and 4-F qualifiers—those who did not pass the military's physical condition testing. Ute football coach Ike Armstrong reportedly was so disgusted with the youth of his 1944 team during its early practices that, after having them line up, he asked which of them shaved that morning. Those who stepped forward became the starters.[60]

Tulsa, one of the top college teams in 1943, went 6-1 despite having a team of misfits, too. Of their forty-two-man roster, nine were underage and twenty-four were 4-F. Partway through the season, *Time* remarked, "The tailback has osteomyelitis. Another back, the best ground gainer, has a severed achille's tendon. One tackle has two bad knees, another has only one lung. A guard has only one arm. But somehow the team's not beaten." The lamentations from basketball coaches and teams were much less publicized.[61]

Setting Up Scaled-Back Tournaments

By the first of February, basketball's postseason title events had been scheduled. The National Invitation secured the Garden for quarterfinal action on Thursday, March 16, and Monday, March 20; semifinal games on Wednesday, March 22, and the finals on Sunday, March 26. "Scheduling the final on Sunday," the *New York Times* noted, "places it in free time for trainees" who could make up a sizable portion of the crowd. The NCAA scheduled its Eastern Regional in the Garden for Thursday, March 23, and Saturday, March 25—the latter a prime weekend date. Its East-West final would occur two days after the MIBC's final, on Tuesday, March 28. The date for the highly anticipated second annual Red Cross event was not yet scheduled.[62]

Notably absent in the postseason lineup was the NAIB tournament. Emil Liston, the "father of the seven-year-old event," had a rough off-season that put the tournament in doubt. The Baker coach had heart troubles that confined him to bed rest for much of the summer at his vacation home in Denver. Back to full health by the fall, Liston hit another bump in the road as he suffered a knee injury getting caught in a pile-up while officiating a Kansas City high school football game. Complications arose in the hospital throughout his medical treatment, and Liston had to spend most of the winter in St. Luke's Hospital in Kansas City.[63]

Liston would not let his health get in the way of the eighth annual NAIB tournament, and so he continued to publicize the event as he always had. Unfortunately, the matter ended up out of his hands. At a special meeting of the NAIB executive in mid-February, the group decided to cancel the tournament because of the war. Enough small schools had canceled their seasons, and enough players on the teams that continued would be joining the war effort immediately at season's end that the executive board thought it would be wise to take a year off. Publicly, Liston stated that the tournament "had been cancelled because the Navy's 48-hour ruling made it impossible for high caliber teams to enter the competition."[64]

The war forced the NAIB to cancel its 32-team tournament, but the two 8-team events in the Garden carried on. And even though some schools canceled their teams' seasons and others remained, all college athletic departments faced notable day-to-day changes in all sports. Arthur Daley reported on these developments in his February 11, 1944, column in the *New York Times*. Daley wrote that "the sports picture" had been "jumbled . . . almost beyond recognition." The scribe lamented that "The old cry, 'You can't tell the players without a score card,' is truer now than it ever was before." Since some colleges shut down their athletic departments and others offered their facilities as military training bases, many college athletes ended up competing for different teams than they had before the war. The NCAA's transfer rules allowed players from one team who had been forced to relocate to a training base at another school to participate in intercollegiate athletics for their new "school." Thus, six schools identified as Navy V-5 and the 131 schools marked as Navy V-12 prospered with new waves of talent. But this also meant assimilating unfamiliar teammates.[65]

Daley described a couple of events that underscored his point. The University of Rochester basketball team, as it had recently suited up against NYU, started three cagers who had played at Fordham and two that had played at Syracuse the year before. A Rochester track relay team that same year included three former Fordham Rams and one former Violet runner. Daley also ran through a litany of track athletes who had changed colors, so to speak—from Minnesota to Notre Dame, from Columbia to Dartmouth, from Virginia to Siena, from NYU to Dartmouth, and so on.[66]

Daley also noted the potentially doubled admission tax on sporting event tickets. President Roosevelt planned on putting the measure into action on either March 1 or April 1 of 1944. The tax increase, from 10 percent to 20 percent, would change the sacred and traditional baseball ticket price from $1.10 to $1.20. If the bill went into effect on March 1, the college basketball postseason events would be affected, as well. And with wartime rations, it became difficult to predict how many fans this would deter.[67]

Ned Irish, the MIBC, and the NCAA agreed to schedule the 1944 Red Cross game for March 30, thus avoiding the tax increase if it was enacted in April. This announcement came as part of a master plan by the Greater New York Red Cross committee to raise $22,386,000 over twelve months beginning March 1. And this committee hoped that sporting events would play a major role in generating this ambitious level of financial support. A tennis exhibition tournament was scheduled in Madison Square Garden for March 14, the college basketball championship game would be on March 30, Major League Baseball's Dodgers and Phillies would meet the following day at Ebbets Field for charity, baseball's Yankees and Giants would meet on April 13 at the Polo Grounds, and soccer, bowling, and dog race events were also scheduled for later in the spring. Promoters were in the process of lining up golf, track, squash, boxing, and other sports for charity.[68]

The Red Cross was able to generate quite a docket of sports to help fund its local metropolitan chapters' financial goal. Among the events hosted, baseball and basketball became the most noteworthy from a sporting perspective. Major League Baseball was nearing the peak of its popularity as the national pastime, and games between the Dodgers, Phillies, Giants, and Yankees would draw large crowds regardless of where the profits went. New York City was also feverishly into college basketball, and so the second annual Red Cross "mythical national championship game" would also attract large crowds. However, this charity event's success was based on that of the two competing tournaments that sent their winners for the "dream game" crown.

Naming Teams

On February 17, a full month before it would commence, the National Invitation announced its first participants. Adolph Rupp's Kentucky squad would make its first appearance in the tournament, having won thirteen of fourteen games to that point. Its lone loss came to Illinois's 1944 "Whiz Kids." Oklahoma A&M became the other early entrant, making its second National Invitation appearance. Three days later, Utah accepted the third bid while also declining an invitation to the NCAA tournament to represent the seventh district. The Utes did not provide a reason for this choice at the time, and their inclusion in the New York meet meant that they would travel the farthest east to Madison Square Garden of any team in the tournament's history. Years later, however, the Utes admitted that everyone knew that the National Invitation paid its participating teams much better than the NCAA tournament. So going to the MIBC event was an easy choice for them.[69]

Utah was in the midst of an unusual season. With wartime needs, the team had no home facility available to play in nor did it have any regional college competition. The school offered its gymnasium to the Army Specialized Training Program as barracks and so the Utes practiced every day in the women's gym and played any home games in Deseret Gym in downtown Salt Lake City. Most teams in the region disbanded because of war needs. Accordingly, their only collegiate competition during the regular season came from Weber State, Idaho State, and Colorado. So the Utes packed their schedule with games against "the West's strongest service teams." These service team opponents provided a stark contrast to the Ute squad. They were literally in a different league since they were made up of the best basketball players on each respective service base. Further, they included men of all ages. The Utes, however, had an average age of eighteen and a half years old. This was, no doubt, a young squad. Most of Coach Vadal Peterson's troops were freshmen, as the upperclassmen from the previous season had traded in hoops uniforms for military get-up. These battles of young men against military men seasoned the young Utes very quickly. This would pay dividends for the westerners in their postseason journey, an odyssey that became even more unusual than that of the regular season.[70]

St. John's of Brooklyn became the fourth team to accept a bid to the New York Invite on February 24. They constituted the only local team in the tournament, the first time the affair did not include at least two metropolitan squads. With the emphasis on cutting down team travel, this trend—and Utah's inclusion—came with questions. The best answer is that St. John's was the top team in the Big Apple that year without question. To include another local team would have watered down the tournament's prestige. Further, the local crowds would get to see plenty of local talent when military trainees returned with their new teams.[71]

DePaul was the fifth Garden invite, and its acceptance came with drama. The Blue Demons squared off against Big Ten champion Ohio State on Friday, February 25, for a battle that would unofficially determine which team would receive the NCAA District 4 berth. DePaul won 61–49, thus surmising that they would receive an invite. However, Coach Ray Meyer told the district selection committee—who were all at the game—that he needed to receive the invite by 10 a.m. the following day because he had already received an invitation to the MIBC's New York event. Meyer did not receive a call by his deadline and so he wired Ned Irish immediately after 10 a.m. to notify him that the Blue Demons would compete for the National Invitation prize. The NCAA District 4 selection committee called Meyer twenty minutes later to make their offer. However, as the *Chicago Tribune* noted, "When the Demons announced their selection of the Madison Square Garden offer, Ohio State was named to represent the 4th district." Muhlenberg College of Allentown, Pennsylvania, also accepted an offer to the National Invitation tournament that day. By March 2, Canisius and Bowling Green accepted the last two bids to fill the tournament's brackets. Canisius's inclusion came into question after a crushing loss at home two days later at the hands of Cornell, 51–29. This late blowout loss coupled with the fact that only one local team got a bid to the National Invitation gave local sportswriters reason to second guess the selection process.[72]

Don Leighbur, sportswriter for the black newspaper, the *Philadelphia Tribune*, also questioned the selection process. Leighbur identified Ned Irish as the culprit for the apparently racist practices of team selection for the National Invitation. While Irish was not on the MIBC tournament selection committee, he did play a powerful indirect role in team selection. Irish was the one who invited visiting teams to the Garden during the regular season—an honor that gave particular teams a tryout of sorts in front of the local basketball establishment for the postseason tournament. Leighbur argued that Irish "has persistently declined to recognize the ability of Negro College basketball teams and issue an invitation to leading clubs among them to participate in his annual National Invitational Collegiate Tournament." Leighbur pointed out the success of Long Island's point guard and captain, African American Eddie Younger, that season. He also argued that two black colleges—North Carolina College and Lincoln University of Pennsylvania—were so much better than the rest of the black schools they played that each deserved a bid to the MIBC event.[73]

Leighbur's outburst may have missed its target. Irish, as director of basketball at Madison Square Garden, did not have a direct role in tournament team selection. Further, the National Invitation tournament was the only nationwide college basketball championship tournament that had included any African American athletes up to that time. The NCAA and NAIB had both included Mexican American participants—both of whom had assimilated easily among white players because of their light complexion—and the NAIB was, by this time, operating with an unwritten but spoken racial exclusion policy. Leighbur could have spit his venom at either of these tournaments, but he chose to confront the National Invitation. This choice demonstrates the viewpoint of many along the Eastern Seaboard at the time. The National Invitation tournament was the premier college basketball postseason event throughout the region that included America's densest population.

The NCAA understood that it played second fiddle in New York City in the broad and densely populated East Coast. However, it also knew that it was gaining ground. The 1943 Red Cross victory for NCAA champ Wyoming over National Invitation champ and local St. John's had put the prowess of NCAA tournament teams on the map. In order to capitalize on this growth in America's largest media market, the NCAA had to draw a top team from that region into its tournament.

The first two NCAA districts to name their representatives to the postseason event were Districts 1 and 2—the New England states and the Mid-Atlantic states. District 2, which included New York City, chose

Temple—a strong squad that had been on the MIBC's radar. District 1 selected Dartmouth, a top Eastern team over the past couple of years that had recently accepted Navy V-12 trainees on campus. One of these transfers included St. John's guard Dick McGuire.[74]

McGuire was a New Yorker to the core. The middle of three brothers, he honed his point guarding skills each summer as the McGuire boys took over the Coney Island basketball courts. Dick was the most talented of the three, and he generated a cult-like respect in the city. McGuire would enter college at St. John's to play for Coach Joe Lapchick before embarking on a Hall of Fame career in the NBA with the New York Knicks and Detroit Pistons. Younger brother Al also starred at St. John's and played in the NBA before coaching Marquette to an NCAA championship in 1977. After an outstanding 1943–44 freshman regular season at St. John's, Dick McGuire was drafted into the navy and stationed at Dartmouth for his officer training. Wartime laxation in the NCAA's rules made him eligible immediately. St. John's great loss then, as it entered the 1944 National Invitation tournament, was Dartmouth's great gain as it began the NCAA tournament.[75]

Joining Dartmouth and Temple in the Eastern NCAA Regional tournament were Catholic University of Washington, DC, and Ohio State, who received the District 4 bid when the selection committee failed to call its first choice, DePaul, on time. West of the Mississippi River, the NCAA had loads of trouble with team selection. Pepperdine of Malibu, California, would represent District 8—that much was clear. But difficulties brewed in the other three regions. District 7, comprised of Montana, Wyoming, Utah, Colorado, and New Mexico, sent no representative. Utah had been invited but declined, and very few other teams existed in the region that year. District 5, however, seemed to have too many representatives. Iowa State and Oklahoma tied for the Big Six conference championship, but with the conference rule "that the team with the best offensive and defensive record should be the circuit's representative," Iowa State became the nominee. The Cyclones declined, ruling themselves out on March 6. "After an investigation in which it developed that the personnel of the Iowa State team could not be held together for the entire tournament," athletic director George Veenker announced, the team and players "regret they would have to decline any invitation to compete, since we do not feel it fair to start play, when we know we could not go all of the way." However, three days later, after Oklahoma had also ruled itself out due to the navy's forty-eight-hour rule, Iowa State reconsidered upon the urging of the District 5 selection committee. The Cyclones accepted, "for the sake of the tournament."[76]

Iowa State's decision answered some questions, but many remained.

District 7's vacancy remained, and for the sake of cost, District 5 assumed it could and should fill the void. The University of Iowa, a Big Ten team that resided in District 5, availed itself if needed. Iowa's board of athletics control originally prohibited the team from postseason competition but relented after player protests. So on March 8 the *Kansas City Times* announced that the Hawkeyes would be the District 7 replacement. However, five days later, the team found out that its two leading scorers would be drafted and therefore "was forced to withdraw." That same day, District 5 extended District 7's bid to Missouri, the Big Six Conference's third best team. Missouri coach George Edwards had been instrumental in conducting the Kansas City Western Regionals since 1941 and would not have his team pass on a chance to play in the tournament he helped develop.[77]

District 6—comprised of the noncontiguous states of Arkansas, Texas, and Arizona—had no trouble deciding on the University of Arkansas as its team. The Razorbacks had an outstanding regular season, led by future Olympic pivot man Gordon "Shorty" Carpenter. However, the team received a literal death whip. Twenty miles from Fayetteville on the way back from a pretournament exhibition game, a station wagon full of players pulled to the side of the road in a rainstorm with a flat tire. A car came over a hill behind the station wagon and smashed its backside, pinning two Razorback players between the vehicles and killing a team instructor. The two injured players received such severe lower body injuries that doctors debated amputation. As the team mourned the death and awaited word on the injuries, Coach Eugene Lambert determined that the team would not compete in the event. The NCAA would have to act quickly to find a replacement.[78]

The 1944 National Invitation and NCAA Tournament

On the eve of postseason action, the Associated Press remarked that "the rafters in Madison Square Garden will be thoroly (sp) dusted off during the next two weeks as a dozen of the nation's outstanding college teams, many of them featuring skyscraping centers, seek basketball's highest honors in two tournaments." The *Times*'s official schedule of the postseason, printed on March 14, listed the National Invitation's three rounds, and the NCAA's two eastern rounds and the East-West final. The *Times* also listed the Red Cross game featuring the NCAA and National Invitation tournament champions as the "National Championship Game."[79]

As the National Invitation commenced on Thursday, March 16, many skyscraping teams felt that they had a chance to win it all. In the opening night of action, Bowling Green and its 6'11½" center Don Otten took on

St. John's while DePaul and its 6'9" center George Mikan faced Muhlenberg College. Arthur Daley sounded off on this skyward trend in basketball in his column that day by referring to these big men as "giraffes." He used Otten, Mikan, and Oklahoma A&M's 7-foot Bob "Foothills" Kurland as exhibits A, B, and C to demonstrate how the game is changing. "Once the discovery was made that a good big man is better than a good little man in basketball as well as in every other sport, things began to happen," Daley remarked. Tall men had not always ruled the game. In fact, this era marked the beginning of the true recognition of the value of height. "The giraffes speedily acquired larceny in their finger-tips and began deflecting 'certain' baskets by the simple expedient of stretching out full length, leaping daintily off the floor and, in effect, clamping a lid over the net." This "goal-tending" ability came to the great disgust of most coaches across the country. Oklahoma coach Bruce Drake conducted a poll of fifty-four coaches, and fifty of them believed that "goalies" should be banned from the game. "The remaining four, while not identified," Daley surmised, "probably have pet giraffes of their own."[80]

That night's action proved, however, that "giraffes" were not invincible. Fans, 18,197 of them, entered the Garden's gates to see the first-round action. In the opener, defending champion St. John's—who managed to come into their game against Otten and Bowling Green as underdogs—held off the tall Ohioan and his teammates 44–40. The Redmen held Otten to 4 points, only half as many as he accounted for on defense as he tipped in four St. John's shots while trying to block them. The Falcon giraffe also had seven successful blocked shots, but it was not enough as his team exited early.[81]

In the second game of the night, George Mikan's height and ability proved too much for Muhlenberg. Even though the Allentown, Pennsylvania, squad benefited from the help of V-12 mercenaries on the court, Mikan and his teammates "literally poured it on the Navy and Marine trainees from Muhlenberg, running to a score of 68 to 45." Mikan made a statement that he was a giraffe to be reckoned with, scoring 27 points against the undersized and outmatched Mules.[82]

After the weekend off, in which the Garden booked prizefighting, first-round action resumed on Monday, March 20. Oklahoma A&M's giraffe, Bob "Foothills" Kurland, was on strong display in the opener. The Aggies' offense and defense featured the seven-foot sophomore, and it proved to be too much for Canisius to handle. Kurland and company coasted to an easy 43–29 victory that was never in doubt. Kentucky held off Utah, 46–38, in the nightcap. Yet Utah, the "mystery team of the tournament" based on its unfamiliarity with the Garden crowd, won the favor of the locals with its one-handed shooters and its "brimful of color and pride." This strong showing in defeat would pay off very soon.[83]

At midnight, only hours into the Utes' pity party for their season-ending loss, Coach Vadal Peterson received a phone call in his New York City hotel room. On the other end of the line was the NCAA Western Regional tournament director offering the Utes a chance to rise from the dead and continue their season in Kansas City as Arkansas's replacement. The Utah squad seized the opportunity for new life. After an ad hoc team meeting and vote, the Utes boarded a train for Kansas City to tip off against Missouri—another relatively late entry—in the first round of the NCAA Western Regional on Friday, March 24.[84]

As Utah headed to the Garden City, the Garden in New York City continued its basketball tournament action, and 18,353 saw two thrilling semifinal games. In the first, St. John's captured victory from the grips of defeat, overcoming a late 8-point deficit and controversy to outlast Kentucky. Late in the game, referee Pat Kennedy accidentally impeded a Wildcat's attempt to retrieve a loose ball. Kennedy's interference allowed the ball to fall past the boundary line, giving St. John's possession at a crucial point late in the game. Kennedy received an earful from Kentucky players after the game in what stained an otherwise well-played ball game. In the curtain call, "Foothills" Kurland dueled with "Mountainous" Mikan as Oklahoma A&M squared off with DePaul. Both giraffes played too aggressively in this epic battle of height, as Mikan fouled out four minutes into the second half and Kurland exited with ninety seconds left and the game still in the balance. The Aggies had to finish with only four players on the floor, giving the Blue Demons just the advantage they needed to win by three, 41–38.[85]

The NCAA kicked off its postseason competition with prime-time reservations in the Garden. While the Eastern Regional originally booked the Garden for Thursday, March 23, and Saturday, March 25, military leave rules would have prevented Dartmouth's squad of naval and marine trainees from participating. So Ned Irish arranged for a Friday–Saturday Eastern Regional at the Garden that coincided with the Western Regional in Kansas City. This marked the first Friday tournament game in the Garden's history. No one celebrated this milestone, and few even noticed. Domestic wartime needs thwarted many sacred social traditions. Wartime rations on travel forced Ohio State and Catholic University to arrive only a day before their first-round games while Temple and the majority of the Dartmouth squad arrived on the day of their games.[86]

Thus, on Friday, March 24, four travel-weary teams squared off in first-round action. Dartmouth showed no ill effects from its last-minute travel as the "Indians threw aside their traditional headdress and tomahawks, and called upon their expert marksmen from the marines and their navy trainees to aid them" to an easy 63–38 victory over Catholic. Ohio State finished the evening by holding off Temple, 57–47. Less than twenty-four hours later, the Buckeyes and Indians met in the Eastern Regional final. Dartmouth continued its hot streak by jumping out to an early 14-point lead before Ohio State cut the deficit to 6 at halftime. In the second stanza Dartmouth V-12 trainees Harry Leggat from NYU, Aud Brindley from LIU, Bob Gale from Fordham, and Dick McGuire from St. John's showed their metropolitan mettle by holding off the Buckeyes for an Indian Regional title.[87]

Halfway across the country, the NCAA Western Regional provided fans with thrilling postseason action that same weekend. Without an NAIB tournament this March, Garden City fans had only this tournament to support. Utah was back in action on Friday night against Missouri, but the Utes were playing short-handed. Center Fred Sheffield was out with an ankle injury. Nevertheless, the "Wonder Boys" from Utah "played a spirited brand of ball" all weekend, beating the Tigers by a score of 45–35 and then taking down Iowa State 40–31 in the Western final. The Cyclones had downed Pepperdine 44–39 in their opener before falling to the Utes before 6,000 fans. Sheffield surprisingly reemerged against the Cyclones, aiding his teammates to victory. Utah freshman Arnie Ferrin, who "was brilliant at dribbling left-handed although he is right-handed . . . lost his touch at the art of goal making against Iowa State." Sheffield came to the rescue, and so did Wat Misaka, "a Utah-born Jap" who was "a mite of a fellow at 5 feet, 8 inches in height, with speed to spare."[88]

The NABC Convention and Money Matters

While Utah and Dartmouth garnered regional honors, the NABC hosted its convention in New York City. The annual coaches' event had not found the rhythm in recent years that its tournament founders envisioned. Indeed, it had not always coincided with the date and site of the NCAA championship game. The 1944 convention coincided instead with the NCAA's Eastern and Western Regional tournaments. The NABC choice to hold the convention in New York City further established movement of power from Kansas City in the early 1940s to New York City. The NCAA had followed the National Invitation to the Big Apple and now appeared to enjoy New York City as its base. Part of this gradual shift may have been pragmatic. With the war, many of the country's resources—including manpower and tangible travel necessities—had been pooled around the country's bases that were in the best geographic position to support the war. This included military bases and coastal areas closest to both the eastern and western fronts of battle. College basketball, if it wanted to sustain its annual postseason championships, had to make accommodations. The NAIB, a Kansas City–based tournament with mostly American heartland teams as its prized constituents, could not offer a tournament in 1944. The National Invitation and NCAA—both relying heavily upon New York City and teams along the Atlantic Seaboard—found ways to acclimate themselves to the austere war conditions.[89]

The 1944 NABC convention attracted only fifty voting members in a drastic decrease from the association's numbers before the war. Nevertheless, a quorum was present and Harold Olsen had one very important item on which he needed association support. Although his original tournament committee members had resigned their service under unfavorable conditions, Olsen maintained his reign over the event. He had ruffled feathers, no doubt, but he had steered the ship into the smooth waters of sustainability. However, much of the basketball-loving public continued to view the NCAA tournament as realistically below the National Invitation in terms of prestige and popularity. Olsen and his colleagues could make a case that their event was just as good as the New York City event—after all, 1943 NCAA champion Wyoming had beaten National Invitation champion and local leader St. John's in the Red Cross benefit game. Yet most other rationale favored the MIBC's event. The NCAA tournament saw gold at the end of the rainbow when it moved its Eastern Regional and East-West Final to the Garden in 1943 and benefited greatly. This move may have been the most important in the tournament's history. However, in the mid-1940s it came at a price. The NCAA profited handsomely from the large crowds that supported college basketball of any sort in the Garden, but the NCAA played a clear secondary role to the National Invitation in the latter's home. Two number comparisons provided clear evidence.[90]

First, attendance figures advantaged the National Invitation. In its four nights of action—a Thursday, a Monday, a Wednesday, and a Sunday—it attracted more than 71,000 fans for a per night average of just fewer than 18,000. The NCAA, on the other hand, generated only 44,000 tickets sold for its three nights of action—a Friday, a Saturday, and a Tuesday—for an average of fewer than 15,000. These 1944 figures largely paralleled the 1943 totals. Local fans may have supported the National Invitation more because they were simply more familiar with it, but other factors mattered. The New York event featured a local team and three teams featuring theretofore unmatched height. While the NCAA Garden games featured local players, they were only local expatriates biding their time at Dartmouth on Navy V-12 assignments before deploying to war.[91]

The second figure by which the National Invitation could claim superiority over the NCAA tournament was a source of soreness for Olsen. The New York event, originally run by a private association of sportswriters and now run by a private association of metropolitan college administrators, promised its participants a much greater financial reward for competing than the NCAA tournament did. The *Chicago Tribune* relayed that the NABC "suggested that the National Collegiate A.A. should give a larger share of the proceeds of the annual championship tournament to the colleges participating in it." Olsen and the fifty coaches in attendance "voted to appoint a committee which will take up the subject with the N.C.A.A." The newspaper went on to report, "It was pointed out that the basketball tournaments had contributed largely to the N.C.A.A. funds and that many colleges preferred playing in the National Invitation tournament . . . with the assurance of getting a sizable cut in the gate receipts, to playing in the N.C.A.A. tourney with less certain financial returns." Olsen also proposed that the NABC "be granted a percentage of the receipts to finance its activities."[92]

While the amount that the MIBC gave as a parting gift to its competitors is unknown, the NCAA's cash prize was clearly lower. The NCAA had dealt with this issue since the inception of its tournament in 1939. Dispersal percentages had varied, and the NCAA continued its fickle and ambiguous methods of financial oversight. The percentage given out to the teams had been as high as 81 percent and as low as nothing—the year the tournament lost money. The NCAA was slowly settling in on dividing up between 45 and 55 percent of the profits to the teams, but Olsen and his crew thought that was still too low. Utah and DePaul's quick decisions to accept MIBC invites with NCAA bids still in doubt proved this inequality.[93]

Redmen Repeat, and Cinderella's Appearance

In the Garden, the war-ravaged St. John's squad upset George Mikan and DePaul on Sunday, March 26, for the National Invitation title before 18,374 fans as the big man again exited early in the second half on fouls. Two days later, 14,990 fans watched Utah upset war-aided Dartmouth for the NCAA title. The difference in attendance at these two games provides an entry into the issues that Olsen dealt with on behalf of profit disbursement for his tournament. The NCAA finals' attendance put it 800 fans below the reported regular season average attendance for college basketball double-headers in the

Garden, and put it well below the National Invitation's average. Therefore, Olsen and the NCAA had fewer profits to disburse. With less overall ticket revenue, they likely had less money to offer to competitors regardless of the percentage allocated into the NCAA's coffers. Further, the NCAA was a large national organization that showcased an entire docket of sports and championship events. The MIBC was a group of eleven local men who put on one basketball tournament. Clearly, the operational costs for these two associations were much different. The NCAA likely needed a much greater percentage of the profits from its basketball tournament because it ran a more expensive operation. The MIBC could function on a shoestring budget and send just about all of its profits to the competing teams. In this sense, the NCAA clearly faced a disadvantage.[94]

A more imminent difficulty for the NCAA came to light on the day of the Utah-Dartmouth final. Louis Effrat reported that the US Navy banned leave extensions for its trainees, making Dartmouth—the favorite for the NCAA title—unable to compete in the Red Cross benefit game against National Invitation champion St. John's. "Behind the decision that barred further competition for Dartmouth," Effrat noted, "is the Navy's objection to extended leaves from school, cutting in on the classroom work of the athletes—all Navy and Marine trainees." This ruling meant that Utah, a team that had lost in the first round of the National Invitation, was now guaranteed a spot as the NCAA's representative in the Red Cross "National Championship Game" against the National Invitation champ. Effrat noted the disappointment for the fans and for the Red Cross if Dartmouth took the NCAA prize and could not play in the de facto national championship game. "That became an interesting pressure for us in the NCAA finals," Utah's Arnie Ferrin recalled, "We didn't want to play the NIT champion as a loser. That would've been just terrible."[95]

Luckily, none of this mattered, as Utah upset Dartmouth. The Utes had been through a lot as a team—not having a home gym, playing most of its games with last-minute scheduling, losing all but one of its letterwinners from the previous season to war duties, losing in the first round of the National Invitation, and now playing its way into the finals of the NCAA tournament. Dartmouth, on the contrary, had not even been through an entire month together. At the close of the regular season, it lost five of its ten regulars to the war and gained five V-12 transfers. It was less a team than it was an all-star aggregation. And when the stakes were highest, the cohesive team outplayed the all-stars.

Utah, described as a "young, colorful" team with "speed and spectacular one-handed shooting," had been given all kinds of labels throughout

Arnie Ferrin passes to Wat Misaka in Utah's NCAA championship victory.
*Courtesy of Special Collections Department, J. Willard Marriott Library,
University of Utah.*

the season. Their coach reported nicknames such as the "Blitz Kids, Kids of
Destiny, Cinderella Kids, Live Five with the Jive Drive, Squeeze Kids, and
anything you'd care to add to the list." As their descriptions and nicknames
indicate, they were young, successful, and energetic. However, their description as "colorful" deserves special attention. The team roster includes nine of
the eleven team members as white and of Anglo-Saxon heritage. This type of
persona rarely generates descriptions as "colorful" unless there is something
unique and special about their personalities. This team must have had great
charisma and fun on the court to be labeled as "colorful."[96]

Interestingly, the other two members of the Utah squad were not white.
Masateru Tatsuno and Wat Misaka stand out in the team picture as Japanese
Americans. Tatsuno received no publicity throughout the year in large part
because he did not play. The University of Utah agreed to accept 150 qualified
students from the Japanese American internment camps, and Tatsuno was
one of them. He left his family at the Topaz camp and joined the university

and its basketball team. However, Tatsuno was the eleventh and final man on the roster. And in this time of war, the team could only travel with nine players. Tatsuno was left behind. And yet Coach Peterson did all he could to make the young man feel included. Tatsuno was not the only player who did not see the court, as Peterson strictly used a six-player rotation. Misaka, whose family avoided the internment camps because they did not live on the West Coast, found himself as the sixth man in this rotation, providing a spark off the bench. While the term "colorful" was not usually used to describe Asian Americans at the time, and it was rarely used to describe any integrated team, Misaka's on-court play was "colorful." He was a speedster on the court who used his unique acceleration to lock down opposing guards and score on occasion when the defense let its guard down.[97]

Misaka's basketball experience provided an interesting counterpart to his life off the court. In 1944, the United States was still in the process of determining how to handle its relatively large domestic population of ethnic Japanese. With the Pearl Harbor massacre still fresh in the nation's consciousness, American distrust of Japanese Americans remained high. Misaka's father—an orphan in Japan—immigrated to Ogden, Utah, in 1902 and became the town barber. Twenty years later, he returned to his homeland to marry Wat's mother and bring her back to the United States. When Wat's father passed away in 1939, his mother expressed an interest in returning to Hiroshima with Wat and her two younger kids. After all, their apartment was in the middle of "a notorious gantlet of gambling joints, brothels, opium dens and bars" in Ogden. But Wat said no, and the family stayed on "the toughest street in Utah."[98]

Misaka became the second gear of a team that had not yet realized its potential. All but one of the players grew up within thirty-five miles of the campus; and only one, forward Dick Smuin, was recruited to play for the team—the others simply responded to a call for tryouts. Yet it was a group that had athleticism and talent. Besides Misaka, Smuin, and Ferrin—who went on to become Utah's athletic director—the Utes enjoyed the services of center Fred Sheffield, who was the reigning NCAA high jump champion; forward Herb Wilkinson, who would place fourth in the same event in 1945; and guard Bob Lewis, who would become an NCAA tennis semifinalist in doubles competition and eventually defeat Pancho Gonzales.[99]

Misaka remained as the outlier of this team to outsiders and therefore received extra attention. "The Japanese-American jumping jack" figured prominently in his team's postseason run and in the media representations of his team. In the NCAA final, "Little Walter [sic] Misaka" scored to put the Utes up by 4 with four minutes to go. Utah then stalled and Dartmouth pressed. The Utah lead remained at 4 with a minute to go when Dartmouth's pressure resulted in two baskets to tie the score at 36 as time expired. In the overtime period, the teams exchanged baskets until the score was knotted at 40 with twenty seconds left. Utah had possession and worked the ball around until Herb Wilkinson "took aim and let go" of a "tricky angle set shot" that bounced around the rim and went in for a Utah victory, sending the Indians back north as NCAA runners-up and securing a true, deserved spot in the Red Cross National Championship Game for the Utes.[100]

Two nights later in the Red Cross game, Utah capped off its season with "a distinct Horatio Alger flavor throughout." Because of their poor showing in the National Invitation, no one gave Utah much of a chance against the Redmen. "The long, lean, leaping youngsters from Salt Lake City are inspiring court performers, but they lack polish and the smart attack of the Redmen," George E. Coleman surmised. The *Brooklyn Daily Eagle* reporter added, "One hates to see the plucky kids from the West lose, but after all, St. John's has brought much prestige to Brooklyn, downing all comers, including army and navy trainee rivals." However, Coleman was wrong. The first half ended with the teams tied at 19. Utah exited the locker room after the intermission and its players "were greeted by a deafening ovation" from the metropolitan crowd that had fallen for the Utes. In the second half, Arnie Ferrin "provided the inspiration and the playmaking" and "Misaka contributed the perspiration on defense," as the Utes took down the favored St. John's squad 43–36 "before a howling audience of over 18,125." Ferrin scored 17 points to pace the Utes with Wilkinson chipping in 11. Experts noted that Misaka "never seemed to tire and he was a leech on defense the entire night" while scoring 5 points.[101]

Utah's victory against all odds provided a resounding storyline for Americans in the midst of war. It also gave the entire Salt Lake State a reason to rejoice. University president Leroy E. Cowles said, "I'm simply breathless after hearing the University of Utah team win the national collegiate crown. Not only in basketball skill, but in scholastic ability these young representatives are right at the top. The scholastic average of the team is above B." Utah governor Herbert B. Maw said, "We're all mighty proud of the boys. They have brought a great honor to the state of Utah, and I hope our citizens will welcome them back enthusiastically, as they deserve the best." And Salt Lake City mayor Earl J. Glade chimed in saying, "In copping the national basketball championship, Utah's phenomenal team last night did our great commonwealth a priceless service. To set it down as a million dollars in constructive community advertising is to understate." Glade also put words to the burgeoning wartime attitude, "Utah showed America that our youngsters do not belong to any lost generations."[102]

This Red Cross Benefit Game's war aid also generated strong headlines. The massive crowd at the game provided the Red Cross with more than $41,000. This total provided a large step up from the previous year's sum and made the game a major success for the second year in a row. Further, Utah's victory—the second straight for an NCAA team in the Red Cross game—provided a bit more momentum for the shifting of power in the college basketball postseason from the National Invitation to the NCAA tournament.[103]

The Best of Times, the Worst of Times

Utah's miraculous postseason run provided the most prominent early Cinderella story for college basketball. A team that was down and out after losing in the first round of the National Invitation received the fairy godmother's blessing to enter the NCAA tournament after Arkansas's misfortunes. Shortly after this magic, however, came an indication of the harsh realities of college basketball's seedy underbelly. In October 1944, Phog Allen cited Utah coach Vadal Peterson when offering a harsh criticism of point shaving that many believed tainted college basketball games in New York City. "There hasn't been enough publicity given known cases where bribes were taken," Allen asserted.[104]

Problems with gambling were not new. But college basketball in the Garden had become especially vulnerable. In the midst of the second annual National Invite in 1939, *Brooklyn Daily Eagle* sports editor Jimmy Wood asked, "what about all the whispers around town, about the peculiar point system of betting, the bulk of wagering on Garden games, the peculiarity of some final scores, following half-time tallies that indicated a far different result?" Wood was speaking broadly about college basketball and not necessarily about National Invitation games. "No one wishes to go about with nose in air, sniffing at every rumor. But the Garden basketball situation has passed the stage where one has to sniff for rumors," he added, "They bat one right in the beak." This was clear publicity that there was a problem, and Wood seemed to indicate that no one was willing to address the problem that was clear to everyone. Nevertheless, he offered advice to the MBWA: "Perhaps it would be a splendid idea for the basketball writers to pull their name off the tournament before the storm breaks." The wisdom in this suggestion would become clear in a few years.[105]

The secret had gotten out by that time that gamblers and bookies would approach players or coaches and ask them to alter the final outcome in one form or another. The gambling scene was based on a point spread for each game. When Kentucky played Utah in the National Invitation's first round, for instance, the point spread was 10—meaning that the odds were that Kentucky would win by 10 points. Local newspapers published the point spreads for many of the games. So if local fans wanted to gamble on the games, they could bet one of two ways. First, they could bet that Kentucky would cover the spread, meaning that Kentucky would win by 10 or more. If the Wildcats did so, the gambler would make his money back and whatever premium was offered on top. Second, a gambler could bet that Kentucky would not cover the spread, meaning that they would either win by less than 10 or lose the game. If this occurred, then the gambler would also win his money back along with a premium.[106]

The point shaving that had begun coming to light, then, occurred in two forms. A gambler or bookie could approach members of the favored team—such as Kentucky—and ask them to keep the game close so that Kentucky does not cover the spread. Gamblers could downplay the ramifications of this method to the players and coaches they attempted to infiltrate. Indeed, gamblers would tell players that they are not asking them to throw the game. They are simply asking them to miss a few shots, make a few turnovers, or play some poor defense at the end of the game so that the point spread is not covered. A victory is what really matters to a team, and the team could still attain that by shaving points. All a gambler cares about is whether the point spread is reached or not. And so if a gambler colludes with a player on the favored team to keep the game's final score under the spread, both parties can win.

A gambler or bookie could also approach an underdog team—such as Utah—and ask them to lose by more than the point spread. In this method, a gambler might approach a Utah player and say that, since the team is expected to lose anyway, why not just play a little worse throughout the game to ensure that the team loses by more than the point spread. This tactic was not as popular as infiltrating the favored team. Players were less willing to try to lose than to win by less, whether they were favored or not. While ethical guidelines may have been blurred throughout this process, players seemed to indicate that they were less willing to simply not try at all to win. Playing poorly to ensure a closer victory for a favored team seemed more acceptable within a player's moral compass while engaging with gamblers.

At the time, rumors circulated that gamblers often placed tens of thousands of dollars on games in Madison Square Garden. With such amounts of money invested, they wanted to ensure victory. And so, they would lure players or coaches in by offering an amount of cash if players shaved points in such a way that the gambler would win. This amount usually came to only a fraction of what the gambler stood to make, but it was often hundreds or thousands of dollars—large sums at the time, especially to college students who could not make legitimate money from playing basketball otherwise.

On October 21, 1944, Allen told the Associated Press that when Kentucky beat Utah in the National Invitation seven months earlier, "a spectator ran out on the floor and kissed a Utah player who had made a last-minute goal . . . because the goal had saved the man $15,000." Allen continued by saying, "The betting boys had laid 10 points on Kentucky and that last-minute score gave the Kentuckians only an 8-point margin." While there was no speculation that either team had engaged with gamblers to shave points in the game, this was not the Utes' only brush with gamblers during their Cinderella run. The night before Utah's NCAA championship game against Dartmouth, a gambler approached Peterson in his hotel room and asked how much it would cost to have his squad lose to the Indians. Peterson told Allen that he immediately closed the door in the man's face, abruptly ending the conversation.[107]

Allen, from his perch in Kansas, also reported that gamblers had successfully bribed two players to "throw basketball games in Eastern intercollegiate tournaments," and predicted that this problem would "create a scandal that will stink to high heaven" if it is not squelched immediately. Allen aimed his declaration at basketball on the East Coast, especially that in New York City. Because of his distance from the eastern basketball establishment and because of his lack of details, Ned Irish responded in print the following day, asking Allen to relay "any proof that he may have that games were thrown in Madison Square Garden so that the information may be conveyed to the proper police authorities and to the heads of the schools involved." While any such behavior would certainly go against all ethical codes and would lose the public's trust in the purity of college basketball, its legal ramifications were not so clear. The state of New York had laws against such behavior, leading Irish to follow up with Allen's comments. Yet many other states did not have laws precluding point shaving in spectator sports. Therefore, the Empire State's jurisdiction may or may not have come into play depending on Allen's details.[108]

Allen's response to Irish came with great ambiguity. The Kansas coach, who mentioned two players a day earlier, now reported that he was unwilling to disclose "the name of the player," and did not mention anything about the second player he alluded to the day before. But Irish wanted names and answers so that he could protect the integrity of the entity that had become the crown jewel of his lucrative business. While describing the difficulty of obtaining actual legal proof, Allen explained his argument, "I have obtained much information from coaches who told me things honestly and frankly, but who now refuse to take responsibility for their statements." Speculation also circulated that Allen received information from his son who had relayed a story about a Temple player throwing a game in New York. However, further investigation into this matter by eastern authorities revealed that the player in question did not even travel to this game for health reasons.[109]

Irish and the eastern authorities that Allen implicitly accused of poor oversight seemed to know that this type of activity was potentially going on in their venues and tournaments. "It has not taken a statement from Lawrence, Kansas or Denver for me to realize the seriousness of gambling on college sports," the Garden executive responded, idealistically adding that, "It is extremely unlikely any gambling can emanate from the building here." However, Allen's accusation added a specific element to an issue that had not been publicly discussed much to this point. Nothing questioning the purity of college basketball had ever come publicly from the coaches before. Although Irish and his local colleagues were not naïve to this practice, they did feel unfairly called out by Allen. The Kansas coach tried spreading the blame by arguing that "gambling is rampant in the Garden and every other auditorium where tourneys are held," but his beef remained with Irish and the Garden. Utah's Peterson publicly offered his thoughts, diplomatically reporting "that the betting by fans in New York is no different than the betting by fans in Kansas or Utah." Peterson may have been generating goodwill with the metropolitan basketball establishment that had treated his team so well and that he hoped would invite his young and talented team back in the future. After all, his was the only name Allen had mentioned as squealing on gamblers.[110]

Allen had a keen ability to make public statements that polarized the listening audience, and this was a case in point. Many responded favorably to Phog's accusations. Statements of support came from journalists in Lincoln, Nebraska, Denver, the *Saturday Evening Post*, and from Andy Rooney in *Stars and Stripes*—the wartime newspaper on matters affecting the United States armed forces. Many also responded negatively. Irish's patience with Allen's critical foreboding seemed to wane as he lamented, "(Allen's) been doing this sort of thing for years now, and the mystery to me is that people take him seriously in light of his previous false prophecies." Red Smith, a prominent journalist in Philadelphia, put forth a vicious ad hominem attack, sarcastically criticizing the coach's character to disprove his accusation, saying, "Dr. Phog Allen, who has made a career out of proving that he would have invented basketball if James Naismith hadn't thought of it first, is an extraordinarily fortunate man gifted with many talents, rare personal charm and a reverent admiration for the sound of his own voice. Out in Kansas . . . schoolchildren are taught that Dr. Allen invented the very peach basket that Naismith first tacked up on a pole." A different New York journalist called Allen, "a well-known loud mouth" and a "bumpkin of no particular standing and of questionable ability as a basketball coach" who "has managed through phony publicity to build himself into some kind of character in basketball."[111]

These comments represented Allen's polarizing personality and the feelings that certain prominent sportswriters had about him. On the Eastern Seaboard, he clearly had many detractors. However, the harshest rebuke of Allen's comments on the matter came from fellow Kansan Emil Liston. The NAIB founder "deplored what he termed Allen's lack of faith in American youth and meager confidence in the integrity of the coaches of intercollegiate basketball." A day later, Allen responded, "I find Mr. Liston's childlike faith very touching, and I hope nothing ever happens to enlighten him." Liston's views did prove naïve in the years to come, but at the time of his rebuke his voice resonated with many Americans across the majority of the country. While those in and around New York City and other eastern cities knew the abilities of gamblers to infiltrate amateur sport, most of the country wanted to believe in the purity of college athletics especially during this time of war when patriotism and national faith reached a pinnacle.[112]

The connection between gambling and amateur sports was serious to those who worked in the administration of college athletics. For these leaders, the problem was real and its growth could lead to major disasters in the amateur sporting establishment. However, to those outside of the world of college sport, gambling was still a rather lighthearted topic. Arthur Daley proved as much when, in looking back on the year 1944 in sports, he made an analogy to gambling. "Perhaps the sports fans' reaction [to the season] is the same as that of the gambler who was warned that the roulette wheel was crooked. 'Maybe so,' he said cautiously, 'but it's the only wheel in town.'" The columnist meant that sports had not been at their best that year because of the war. "Every sport suffered tremendously from manpower shortages," he argued. And yet spectator attendance thrived. "Attendance boomed in football, baseball and in practically everything else which had a turnstile," Daley noted, adding that basketball fans "bought tickets in unprecedented numbers." Daley's critique, then, was not that the sports action was any less thrilling—quite the opposite. Indeed, he noted that Utah's Cinderella basketball story was not the only tale that could have included help from the fairy godmother. "The manufacturers of glass slippers had to work overtime to provide for [all of the teams]," he reported, tongue-in-cheek, while listing all of the baseball and football teams that had unexpected success. Daley's theme, then, was that many of the best athletes were not on display because they were wearing uniforms of a different sort while serving the United States military. This reality did not hinder the thrills of the action, the journalist argued, but the drop-off in talent was noticeable.[113]

Basketball Continues under War Conditions

The games continued in 1945 despite uncertain conditions. As the war continued, "Uncle Sam" required even further domestic resources. In February, the Office of Defense Transportation (ODT) inherited the power to cancel anything unnecessary in the country in order to redirect the previously used resources toward the war effort. Word from Washington, DC, came on February 21 that the ODT "was asking all forms of sports to curtail travel by 25 per cent and to play on a 'home field' basis only." Basketball and track events came under question since they were the most likely to be held at neutral sites. In this type of event, teams "use more than the usual amount of transportation." The ODT warned sport administrators that certain neutral site events might be canceled, but that threat proved hollow.[114]

A more real threat to the perpetuation of postseason college basketball tournaments came not from "Uncle Sam," but from the black market. At the end of January, many college basketball administrators' greatest fears became reality when the New York County district attorney's office uncovered a game-fixing scheme involving five Brooklyn College basketball players. These young men accepted bribes from gamblers to throw their upcoming game against Akron in the Boston Garden. When authorities uncovered this scheme, they quickly canceled the game and the rest of Brooklyn College's season.[115]

While rumors of this type of behavior clearly had been brewing for a few years by this time, nothing—not even Allen's accusations—had ever gotten beyond mere speculation. This hard evidence provided college basketball's critics with cannon fodder and forced its administrators to respond. Many wondered if this revelation meant that college basketball's postseason tournaments—two of which were based in New York City where the gamblers got to the Brooklynites—would cease their operations to help ensure that the game would remain pure.

Harold Olsen immediately squelched any discussion of the NCAA tournament coming to a halt. "Just because a couple of kids are stupid enough to accept bribes doesn't mean there's anything wrong with basketball," the Ohio State coach argued, "After all, you don't stop going to church because a preacher does wrong." His line of reasoning was the most prominent among coaches across the country at the time. They believed that the problem was not with the basketball establishment so much as it was with greedy players.[116]

Ned Irish, acting president of Madison Square Garden during the war, spoke somewhat on behalf of the MIBC in response to the game fixing. Irish echoed New York City mayor La Guardia's thought, stating that "the Mayor has done basketball a great service in pointing out that the site of the games is not the reason for any evils that exist [in college basketball and its postseason]." The National Invitation tournament would go on, too.[117]

Cutting Travel for the 1945 Tournament Participants

Even the NAIB tournament found new life in 1945. Emil Liston mentioned that his tournament, which had run since 1937 before taking 1944 off, would reemerge as a sixteen-team event in 1945—a bracket size half of what it had become. By February 22, Liston had already received commitments from eleven teams with tentative agreements from five others, putting him close to a full and official bracket for his March 12–17 event in Kansas City. Liston appeased the ODT by explaining that a condensed field of sixteen teams cut the participants' travel mileage from 380,740 for the thirty-two-team field in 1943 to 223,000 for the sixteen-team gala in 1945—a reduction of 157,740 miles.[118]

Pepperdine, the 1943 NAIB runner-up and 1944 NCAA District 8 representative, entered the eighth NAIB championship as the favorite among a list of future small NCAA Division I schools such as Southern Illinois, Eastern Kentucky, and Central Missouri. Pepperdine fit the bill by reaching the finals. Unfortunately, the Waves finished as runners-up yet again, losing to a Loyola University squad from New Orleans. The Louisianans held the pace and locked down Pepperdine's high-powered offense in a 49–36 victory on Saturday, March 17.[119]

That same day, the MIBC kicked off first-round action in the eighth annual National Invitation tournament at Madison Square Garden. The selection committee had spent the past month narrowing its list of invitees down. They pared an original list of thirty-two down to twenty teams on February 26. Army and Navy, both in the midst of outstanding seasons, were on the original list, but MIBC officials dropped them because they "felt neither institution would accept a bid." Many of the other ten dropped from the original list felt a necessary geographic discrimination. "An important factor in the (team selection)," Louis Effrat relayed, "will be the conservation of travel." The February 26 list of twenty teams included only one from west of the Mississippi River—1944 NCAA and Red Cross champion Utah—and only four other teams west of Appalachia. Clearly, the MIBC had already met its mission "to do everything possible to cut down on long trips." And yet Effrat noted that the New York group also did not want to affect "the quality of the participating teams."[120]

Despite the conservation efforts, the MIBC selected only one local team from its list of twenty. Two-time defending National Invitation champion St. John's accepted the first 1945 bid on February 28. The Redmen, led by Coach Joe Lapchick, had become the cream of the local crop the past two years despite losing Navy V-12 trainees and increasingly tough competition from metropolitan teams such as CCNY and NYU. LIU, the first team to win two National Invitations, had fallen on relatively hard times since its coach, Clair Bee, took leave to serve in the military in 1943. Bee would return after the war, and his team would improve because of it.[121]

Muhlenberg College accepted the second bid two days later. The Mules' basketball team had benefited greatly from its status as a Navy V-7 school, receiving loads of court talent that would not have otherwise come to Allentown, Pennsylvania. Muhlenberg's success over the past two seasons with this military talent propelled its coach, Alvin "Doggie" Julian, into elite coaching circles. Before the 1945 National Invitation started, Julian had already accepted the head coaching position at the College of the Holy Cross in Worcester, Massachusetts. However, Julian would remain with the Mules to see his team through the postseason.[122]

Over the next three days, Tennessee, Rhode Island State, and DePaul all accepted bids to the New York invite. Capturing the Blue Demons was a major coup for the MIBC. Many experts listed the Chicagoans as the best team in the country that season. "Giant" George Mikan had become quite a force. College basketball beat writers had referred to Mikan and his stock by a number of somewhat derisive but playful monikers. Arthur Daley chose the term "Galloping Goons," referring to big men who were "ruining" the game with their height and prowess. However, Daley backed off his stance on the Blue Demon, stating, "Large George qualifies as a 'Goon,' but he also is a mighty slick performer as well. He'd be a star if he were only a midget of six feet in height."[123]

Bowling Green, with its own giant of a center—6'11½" Don Otten—accepted the sixth National Invitation bid. The 1942 MIBC champion West Virginia accepted next. When NYU accepted a bid to the NCAA tournament, the MIBC offered its last invite to Rensselaer Polytechnic Institute of Troy, New York. Once the final teams accepted their bids, Asa Bushnell and the MIBC tournament committee went to work ranking and scheduling the teams. Bushnell and his colleagues only seeded half of the teams, citing the lesson they learned three years before. In 1942, the committee ranked all eight teams. Only one higher seed held court in the first round, and eight-seed West Virginia defeated fourth-seed Toledo in the championship game. Bushnell's humbled committee gave DePaul the top seed in 1945 despite the Chicagoans sharing an 18-2 record with St. John's—who the committee seeded second. Bowling Green ranked third and Tennessee received the fourth spot. The three and four seeds would open first-round action on March 17 and the top two seeds would not have to commence until two days later. This tournament setup, Bushnell stated, complied with ODT guidelines and cut travel by 50 percent compared with the 1944 tournament.[124]

NYU's decision to enter the NCAA fray instead of the MIBC event dampened excitement for the New York tournament only slightly. Indeed, George Coleman—one of the more locally biased newspapermen—immediately speculated on the possibility of the Violets matching up with St. John's in the Red Cross game. NYU, the only metropolitan school to play in the NCAA tournament, continued to show loyalty to the national organization that it founded forty years earlier. NYU professor Philip O. Badger served as president of the NCAA in 1945 and 1946, a position that may have given him some influence over the postseason decisions of the Violets' prized basketball team.[125]

NYU represented the NCAA's second district, joining District 6's Arkansas and District 5's Oklahoma A&M in the field. District 5, having suffered from many invitation denials in 1944, offered the Aggies and seven-footer Bob "Foothills" Kurland a chance to participate in its event. Reigning champion Utah joined Oklahoma A&M and Arkansas in the Western Regional. District 7 may have suffered from manpower shortages as much as any district during the war. A vast and sparsely inhabited area covering the western plains and Rocky Mountains, Utah represented this region in both major events in 1944 and again in 1945 because of its zeal and because many other teams in the region could not field a team. However, since the war had taken the services of many of the heralded freshmen from the 1944 championship team, this Ute squad looked much different. The 1939 NCAA champ Oregon rounded out the Western field.[126]

The University of Kentucky, a growing basketball force in the football-crazed region of the country south of the Mason-Dixon Line, garnered the NCAA District 3 bid. The third district covered a lot of territory and included a lot of schools—eleven states from Louisiana to Florida to Maryland—but it was geographically and culturally still far away from the NCAA's nexus of power in the Midwest and American higher education's elitism and prestige in the northeast. Kentucky, a team representing a state on the northern edge of the Deep South, became a bridge of sorts between the basketball establishment and Dixie.[127]

Tufts College in Boston, a small, academically prestigious institution, represented District 1, leaving the NCAA Eastern Regional with a relatively weak field of teams. However, NYU brought some prestige to the association's event. Metropolitan sportswriters noted with a touch of condescension that the NCAA event would benefit from having a Big Apple team participate. NYU became that team. But Kentucky came from a region that had not produced much good basketball by that time and Tufts was certainly not a well-known team. Further, the NCAA had a chance to attract DePaul and Mikan to represent District 4, but an MIBC invite reached Coach Ray Meyer well before the NCAA district selection committee chose its favorite. Without DePaul, the top independent team in NCAA District 4 and potentially across the entire country, the next desirable squad would naturally be the winner of the Big Ten conference. Unfortunately, conference champion Iowa fell geographically outside of District 4. The states of Iowa and Minnesota, by virtue of their residence on the western banks of the Mississippi River, were a part of District 5 at this time. However, the war had previously forced the NCAA to soften its district lines to obtain the most quality teams and it would continue to do so. The Hawkeye basketball team, however, decided to reject any postseason bids it might receive. Unlike the 1944 decision, this one came unanimously. Athletic director E. G. "Dad" Schroeder said, "The boys have decided they have had enough basketball for one season. The team has been disbanded." This seemingly unusual proclamation from a group of elite young athletes at the prime of their athletic careers seems wasteful and short-sighted. Yet this decision reveals how much the war affected everyday American life. The Hawkeyes' decision stemmed, no doubt, from the way in which wartime austerity put life and mere games into perspective. Perennial NCAA contender Ohio State and Coach Harold Olsen subsequently drew the District 4 bid.[128]

On the eve of opening-round National Invitation action at Madison Square Garden, the New York Times's Arthur Daley promoted the continually high caliber of play in the MIBC event despite the war. "Perhaps there were not quite as many top-flight teams to choose from this campaign as in normal pre-war years," Daley wrote, "but they'll do." The scribe mentioned further that basketball was less susceptible to manpower shortages than other team sports, giving two reasons. First, "it requires fewer stars than most" other sports. Second, "it has less of a gap in ability between schoolboys and collegians than other forms of athletics," meaning that young players have nicely fit in when teams have lost veterans to the war.[129]

Daley also promoted the increasing value of the Red Cross charity game as the event "which decides the national championship." Indeed, the following day the *Times* referred to college basketball's "two tournament affair leading to the crowning of the champion" as a "so-called world series." This comparison to professional baseball's denouement relayed the ways in which college basketball's tournaments had come to be known. The local New York City basketball establishment, at least, saw the National Invitation and NCAA tournaments as similar to the pennant races for Major League Baseball's National and American leagues. The winners of the competing events would then face off in a final to crown the official champion. The NAIB tournament in Kansas City, to New Yorkers, was little more than a minor league event.[130]

The Tall Boys Reach the Top

On Saturday, March 17, National Invitation quarterfinal action began. Five Rhode Island starters went the distance, upsetting fourth-seeded Tennessee 51–44. In the second game, Big Don Otten led Bowling Green with 27 points to defeat upstart and previously undefeated Rensselaer Polytechnic Institute 60–45; 18,142 fans poured into the Garden for this opening double-header. Two nights later, before 18,061 fans, St. John's held off Muhlenberg 34–33. The Johnnies' reserve, Tommy Larkin, knocked down a side court set shot with two minutes to play that held up as the game winner. In the loss, Muhlenberg sent Coach Julian off to his new job at Holy Cross. The college clearly had intercollegiate sports in perspective. While graciously and amicably parting ways with Julian, Muhlenberg's president also reported that the school would be donating all of its basketball profits from the 1944–45 season to charity.[131]

In Monday night's second game, Mikan and DePaul "overwhelmed" West Virginia, 76–52. Mikan, who moonlighted as a baseball pitcher and had been offered professional contracts by the Indians, Cubs, and White Sox, led the way. "Big George" broke the Garden season scoring record set two nights earlier by Otten with a 33-point outing. In an arrangement pitting seemingly unequal teams together because of the two standout big men, Saturday night winners Rhode Island and Bowling Green would square off against Monday night winners DePaul and St. John's, respectively, on Wednesday.[132]

Mikan continued to dominate in Wednesday night's semifinal action. "Amazing Mr. Mikan" stunned Rhode Island and the entire 18,253 spectators by scoring 53 points in a blowout victory. The Blue Demons tallied 97 points, and the entire Rhode Island team could only match Mikan's total, even though the big man played only thirty-eight minutes. Mike Santoro, 5'7" center on the fast-breaking Rhode Island team, gave up fourteen inches to his counterpart. Nevertheless, Louis Effrat mentioned in his post-game article that Mikan wrote nine new scores into the Madison Square Garden college basketball record book. The curtain-closer was anticlimactic. Nothing could rival Mikan's feats, and a St. John's defeat did not help. The locals lost 57–44 despite a pedestrian night for Bowling Green's center. Otten could only muster 8 points as his "hard-driving" teammates kept the Redmen on their heels.[133]

While Otten's ordinary performance in the semifinal reduced the publicity potential of a "Giant" final matchup, the stage was set nonetheless. Otten's uninspiring semifinal game provided a better understanding among local fans of his team's overall strength. He was no one-man show. And, in a stroke of misfortune, DePaul would have to prove that it was not a one-man show, either. On Friday, March 23, the "high-scoring ace" injured his left leg in a practice session. The Blue Demon trainer reported that Mikan had a deep bruise in his leg and that the "bespectacled" star would probably play and could potentially even start the game, but would not be at full force. Luckily for the Blue Demons, MIBC officials pushed the finals date back a day because it had originally fallen on Palm Sunday. The MIBC, made up of a number of athletic directors who governed at Catholic institutions, had the conscientiousness to move the game off the religious holiday. This decision provided Mikan with an extra day to recover from his injury.[134]

The day before Mikan's injury—Thursday, March 22—the NCAA opened its regional action in New York City. In the Eastern Regional, local NYU began its tournament trek by defeating Tufts College. The Boston school, who was not given much of a chance from the local press even before the game began, put up as much fight as they could in a 59–44 loss to the Violets. Ohio State ended Kentucky coach Adolph Rupp's first NCAA tournament entrance early, putting the Wildcats to rest, 45–37.[135]

In the Eastern final on Saturday, March 24, NYU and Ohio State battled in "one of the most sensational finishes in the history of the seven-year tournament." George Shiebler, NYU's publicity chairman and a member of the

NCAA's basketball tournament committee, noted in a postgame recap that "Coach Howard G. Cann of N.Y.U. turned in a masterful job in his handling of the Violet players during the exciting final minutes." Late in regulation, Ohio State's 6'9" star center, Arnold Risen, fouled out after having scored a game-high 26 points. NYU responded with "a wild scramble of running, scoring and substituting right up to the final gong." Down 5 points when Risen left, NYU knotted the score as time expired and then took over in the extra period, winning 70–65 in front of 18,161 fans. Four NYU players scored in double figures, including future professional football standout Sid Tanenbaum and future professional basketball standout Adolph Schayes.[136]

Out west, the Friday–Saturday Regional also coincided with Mikan's injury, and another "Galloping Goon" showed his court prowess. Oklahoma A&M's Bob "Foothills" Kurland led the Aggies with 28 points in a first-round blowout win over defending champion Utah, 62–37. Utah boasted not one regular from its six-player rotation in 1944 that won the NCAA tournament and the Red Cross championship game. All five starters from the previous season entered the military. Sixth man Wat Misaka, a Japanese American, also served in the military. In the other first-round game, Arkansas squeaked past Oregon, 79–76, to win "one of the wildest scoring games ever witnessed in the (Kansas City) Auditorium." The "Porkers" and "Webfoots" set three single-game scoring records in their free-for-all in front of 5,623 fans.[137]

Approximately 7,000 fans came out to Saturday night's final. The fast-paced Razorbacks and the seven-foot Kurland provided more than enough storylines to attract a savvy local basketball crowd. Arkansas and Oklahoma A&M had squared off three times already that season with the Aggies winning twice. In this fourth encounter, the Aggies found their largest margin of victory, 68–41. "The Razorbacks concentrated their efforts on . . . Kurland," Paul O'Boynick of the *Kansas City Star* reported, but the big center would pass off to his teammates who hit with precision. Kurland, "an answer to any coach's prayer," controlled the boards and anchored a stout Aggie defense that the Porkers were unable to penetrate. "Those Cowboys," O'Boynick mentioned, "made few, if any, wrong moves on the floor" in their victory.[138]

Kurland and company immediately traveled east for the NCAA title matchup against NYU. The big Aggie arrived in time to see his fellow "Goons" Don Otten and the ailing George Mikan square off in Monday night's National Invitation final. Otten's Bowling Green Falcons came racing out of the gate to an 11–0 start and the DePaul Blue Demons did not score a field goal for the first eight and a half minutes. However, once the Chicagoans came to life there was no stopping them. Mikan dominated despite his leg contusion, scoring 34 points and holding his counterpart to only 7, as Otten fouled out with eight minutes to play. The final attracted 18,166 fans, putting the four-night total at 72,622 spectators—an average of 18,155 that set a new National Invitation tournament record.[139]

The following night, the other "Goon" took center stage and outshined his fellow performers in "an awfully, awfully rough game." Kurland wowed the 18,035 fans by scoring 22 points as his Aggies slowed the game down to defeat the fast-breaking New Yorkers. The Violets, made up of "a bunch of poor neighborhood kids who thought they could beat anybody," had no match for Kurland. For all of his offensive highlights, the Aggie center may have been more impressive on the other end, scoring "a 100% rating for defensive play." Shiebler wrote, "the Aggie 'giant' planted himself in the right spot every time a N.Y.U. rally started." Kurland, who would virtually take over elite amateur basketball in the years to come, was greatly aided by teammate Cecil Hankins, an Aggie football standout, who scored 15 points in the final. With Kurland and Hankins, and NYU's Tanenbaum and Schayes—who combined to score only 10 points—this game displayed a great deal of future talent and star power in postcollegiate basketball and football.[140]

This game also solidified the fact that the NCAA tournament was continually increasing its profits. The Western Regional netted $3,007.65 and the Eastern Regional and Final Game made $53,516.79. While the Garden hosted one more night of action than Kansas City's Municipal Auditorium, the differences in these figures shows just how much New York City meant to the tournament. Kansas City collected $12,106.37 in gross ticket receipts while Madison Square Garden collected $71,794.60. These totals equal roughly $1 per ticket and show just how many more paying customers watched the games in the Garden versus Municipal Auditorium. Further, Kansas City listed $70 in receipts from "broadcasts." New York City had this same ledger item, but it listed $1,500 in earnings from "sale of broadcasting rights." This line item would be pivotal in the NCAA's future growth.[141]

The NCAA had to pay 50 percent of the net receipts from games at Madison Square Garden to Ned Irish and his staff. This princely sum of $26,758.40 cut considerably into the NCAA's profits and emitted a bit of tension into the NCAA's relationship with the Garden. The association knew it needed the Garden to obtain increasing levels of interest and profit—and it needed to have a presence in basketball-mad New York City. But Olsen and his colleagues believed they were getting price-gouged by Irish for the 50 percent rental fee—20 percent of which went directly into the promoters' pocket. Nevertheless, the full $27,666.98 net profit was not theirs to keep either. The NCAA took 10 percent off the top. Both finalists received a flat cash prize of $3,600—roughly ⅓ of the profits when put together—and the other six teams each received ⅑ of the profits that equaled $2,400 each. The remaining $3,300.28 also went to the NCAA.[142]

The Battle of the Skyscrapers

And yet the season was not over. On Thursday, March 29, the Aggies took on the Blue Demons in a battle of the champions for the supreme crown. While this third Red Cross game was the first one that did not include a local metropolitan squad, fan interest ran high. Arthur Daley promoted the action as "the greatest show on earth" that would be "a terrific tussle between towering titans." Indeed, "Mountainous Mikan and Kolossal Kurland" captured the pregame buildup. "Without Mikan his DePaul team would be good without being great," Daley argued, "ditto Oklahoma A&M without Kurland." In their regular season matchup, DePaul took down the Aggies.[143]

New York basketball faithful filled "The Garden" for this highly antic-ipated matchup between "Foothills" Kurland and "Hi-Ho" Mikan in a "Battle of the Skyscrapers." Unfortunately, the game did not live up to its billing. Hampered by some residual effects of his leg injury, Mikan fouled out only fourteen minutes into the game with his team leading 21–14. Kurland's Aggies coasted to a 52–44 victory from there for the NCAA's third Red Cross win in as many tries. Although fans did not get to see much of the anticipated low post battle and without a local team to support, the game still generated $48,499.73 for the Red Cross War Fund, including $5,000 from radio broadcasting rights, $1,000 for game programs, and an $8,000 bid for the game ball at halftime that bumped the overall donation above that of the previous year's Red Cross game.[144]

The 18,158 fans that witnessed Mikan's downfall made the Red Cross Championship game a success for the third straight year. The 1943 event raised $24,256.06 for the aid organization and $44,454.68 in 1944 before the small jump in the 1945 donation. The differences between these totals reflect trends in domestic donations to the war effort. In 1943, the United States had not yet realized the full extent of its citizens' generosity. While private donations and subscriptions aided greatly in the war effort, this trend was just beginning. With the origination of unprecedented generosity in 1943, the Red Cross and other aid organizations evangelized even harder in 1944 for more money. American citizens found depth in their pockets that they did not know existed and were able to meet increased calls for support. However, in 1945 it appeared as though money was drying up. It

Oklahoma A&M's Bob Kurland and the 1945 basketball squad. *1992-052 ICApg141, OSU Photograph Collection, Archives, Oklahoma State University Libraries.*

also appeared that the war was reaching a conclusion. Therefore, calls for support were greatly reduced. Yet sporting events such as the Red Cross Game continued to increase their ability to generate unrestricted funds. Such is the power of sport.[145]

After the war, sport took on a whole new place in American society—one that amateur athletic administrators would be able to cash in on. As the nation came back to a new level of normalcy, college sports presented great potential for growth. The NCAA, MIBC, and NAIB would all try to cash in.

CHAPTER 7

Postwar Boom, 1946–1950

Every sport seemed to benefit from the close of the war. Participation in sports increased as the young men in the physical primes of their lives returned to a country thrilled to have them back. And spectatorship increased, too, as free time and leisure funds proliferated. Those in charge of major sporting events capitalized on this renewed interest. From 1946 to 1950, the NCAA basketball tournament saw its greatest sustained growth in the pretelevision era. As soldiers returned home and took advantage of the GI Bill to spend time on college campuses, intercollegiate sport flourished. More schools sponsored teams, and these teams were better than ever with this influx of mature, veteran talent.

Sportswriter Austin Bealmear opined, "Interest in basketball, already at the highest peak in its history, is going to keep right on mounting as the result of the game's extensive use by the armed forces for both recreational and training purposes." The scribe queried coaches about their thoughts—many of whom served as athletic directors during the war. Blair Gullion of Connecticut said, "I think there will be a tremendous increase in spectator interest in basketball as the result of its use in the service athletic program." John Bunn, former Stanford coach who had just been hired at Springfield College, noted that there were two levels of military basketball: one was a "divisional level" that included outstanding talent and teams, and the other was a "company level" that stressed participation. Butler's Tony Hinkle mentioned that basketball was the most popular sport in the South Pacific and Western Illinois coach Ray Hansen said it was the most popular sport in the Marines."[1]

Ned Irish and the Postwar Proliferation of Basketball in Madison Square Garden

Ned Irish, always the opportunist, made quick work to capitalize on the new interest. Irish had been promoted from director of basketball to acting president of Madison Square Garden during the war. His previous boss had reenlisted at a high rank after serving previously in the military. And yet college basketball had become so prominent in the Garden that few realized the promoter's change in title. While Irish received much more publicity during the war than he had previously, it was not because of his temporary promotion.[2]

Irish became the focal point of the finger pointing after the five Brooklyn College players admitted to shaving points in January 1945. Even though these young men acted seemingly on their own volition to throw a game that was to be played in Boston, the local basketball establishment knew how rampant gambling was at Irish's venue and worried that rumors of thrown games and shaved points occurred in the Garden, too. While local authorities investigated the extent of gambling on college basketball games in New York City, the court called Irish to testify as to his actions. As the promoter of neutral site college basketball games that were of great interest to the public because they often included the country's best teams, and as the face of a private organization seeking to profit from these incredibly popular events, Irish had great power to curtail gambling—at least in theory. And he did try to snuff it out. Irish had his staff compile a list of sixty known gamblers and barred them from attending college basketball games at the Garden. By doing so, he thought he would be separating gamblers from the athletes, thereby ensuring the purity of the games. If gamblers had no access to the players, then they would have a harder time fixing the games.[3]

Within a preliminary hearing, news of Irish's good fortune from college basketball came to light. The promoter was forced to disclose where the money went from these highly popular games in the Garden. While lawyers leading this inquisition were unable to force Irish to give a specific amount of money that he made, the former journalist did reveal his base salary—$12,500, a not-so-modest sum—and the fact that he personally took home 10 percent of the profits of every college basketball event he hosted. Doing the math to determine an exact dollar figure would be difficult, but it was easy to determine that this agreement made Irish a very wealthy man. If Madison Square Garden received a rental fee of about $23,000 for hosting three nights of NCAA tournament action in 1945, then Irish would have made $2,300 from those three nights of work. That sum of money would have been more than many coaches made in an entire year.[4]

In the 1945–46 season, Irish lined up a schedule of twenty-one double-headers in the Garden. The money he stood to make was astounding, but the public was more interested in the increased quality of teams visiting basketball's mecca. With wartime travel restrictions released, Irish invited more teams from the western part of the country including Oklahoma A&M, Utah, Oregon, Oklahoma, Oregon State, Brigham Young, Colorado, Drake, and Wyoming. This diverse docket would indirectly increase the quality of the National Invitation tournament at season's end. The MIBC still saw its event much like a college football bowl game in that it invited the teams it thought was best and most marketable. In year's past, one of the deciding factors used to extend invitations to the event was through the ways in which local crowds reacted to certain visiting teams. Teams that caught the fancy of the Garden crowds during regular season intersectional games seemed to have a greater likelihood of being invited to the postseason event.[5]

With less need to keep travel time in mind now that most of the competitors were no longer active in the military, Irish was free to schedule the postseason events as a businessman would—to maximize profits. As such, the schedule changed. The previous season, the National Invitation and NCAA tournaments overlapped in the Garden. In 1946, that would not be the case. In consultation with the MIBC, Irish scheduled the New York Invite for March 14, 16, 18, and 20. The NCAA would open up its Eastern Regional on March 21 and finish with its East-West final on March 27. By today's standards, this put the NCAA in the driver's seat. The season's final event usually tends to be the culmination and most important part of the season. If the NCAA event was last, then it theoretically would be the most important. And yet this logic did not always follow. Irish's original invitation to the NCAA to use his venue in 1943 came on the heels of the National Invitation, too. At that point, the NCAA event was seen more as an afterthought than a culminating event. Further, with the Red Cross game following both tournaments, it still may have been a part of the lead-up to the season's culmination.[6]

It is unclear exactly why Irish scheduled these championships like he did, but his logic may be retrievable. The National Invitation had traditionally hosted more teams that operated independently of any conference affiliation. The NCAA, which chose its teams through district selection committees, often favored conference champions over strong independent teams. Therefore, many independent teams often accepted a National Invitation bid if offered. The NCAA selection committees often held play-offs or play-in games to determine district representatives, and these games took time to schedule. So the reason the NCAA tournament started in the Garden a week after the National Invitation may have been to accommodate these special games the NCAA hosted to determine district representatives. The MIBC had no such events and no need for the extra time.

Selection Controversy

The MIBC extended the first invitation for postseason play in 1946 to Kentucky—a bid the Bluegrass State's team accepted on February 26. The Wildcats and their increasingly successful coach, Adolph Rupp, had entered the New York event for the first time in 1944 and the NCAA tournament for the first time in 1945, failing to make the finals either time. But the Bluegrass Boys were coming off a 19 and 2 season in which they won the Southeastern conference in convincing fashion to begin a half decade of unprecedented success. Coach Rupp took over the Southeastern Conference, Dixie, and most of college basketball, showing that southerners could play with anyone.[7]

On February 27, Muhlenberg College accepted a bid yet again. This third straight entry showed that it could win even without former coach Alvin "Doggie" Julian and navy trainees. A day after that, Big Don Otten and his Bowling Green teammates accepted an invite to enter the event for a third straight year. St. John's accepted a bid on March 1 and Syracuse and West Virginia did the same on March 2, leaving only two spots remaining with two weeks before the tournament opened. Asa Bushnell, chair of the selection committee, noted informally to local sportswriters that the teams in consideration for the final two entries were the high-scoring Rhode Island State squad, local CCNY, Holy Cross with its new coach Julian, Oklahoma A&M with "Foothills" Kurland, and DePaul with "Hi-Ho" Mikan.[8]

On March 4, with three-quarters of the bracket complete, tickets went on sale for the event. Even without knowing the exact lineup, fans flocked to the Garden's ticket booth with unprecedented interest. Locals started lining up in front of the booth at 5 o'clock in the morning for a sale that started four hours later. By nine, the line had become so long and the applicants so unruly that Irish shut down the sale twenty minutes later until a reserve of mounted and foot police troops could make their way to the Eighth Avenue venue. The length of the queue increased throughout the morning to wrap around the building and spill onto neighboring blocks. By noon, 10,000 tickets had gone and by 3 p.m. 16,000 had been sold with the line still several thousand people long.[9]

Speculation continued over the next few days regarding the last entrants. CCNY coach Nat Holman indicated that his team "would like nothing more than a bid to the Invitation tourney, and a good showing by them on Thursday (against NYU) may get them one." NYU had already accepted a bid to the NCAA tournament and was one of the city's top teams. CCNY was slightly below the Violets and St. John's in terms of win-loss record, and yet Holman thought he had an outside chance. The MIBC selection committee also admitted that it was still considering the Beavers for the field.[10]

On March 7, some of the speculation came to rest. Colorado reported that it had received offers from the MIBC and the NCAA's District 6, and had accepted the NCAA offer. Arizona wired in its acceptance of a National Invitation bid that same day. This left one spot open. The selection committee had not made its final decision by the time CCNY lined up against NYU in what had become the main attraction of the regular season's final double-header. City College beat the Violets, and, with all the speculation surrounding the National Invitation, believed that it had done enough to secure a bid to the local event.[11]

When Bushnell and his committee reported that Rhode Island had accepted the final bid the next day, CCNY students reacted in vigorous opposition. The City College student council immediately wrote a letter to the committee, MIBC schools, and Ned Irish, complaining that they felt exploited:

> Since publicity indicated that a bid hinged on the outcome of the N.Y.U. game and since C.C.N.Y. exhibited skill and prowess with such finality, we are both amazed and discouraged at the absence of an invitation to the tournament . . . The silence of the committee for publicity purposes is nothing short of exploitation. We are resentful. We hope this will not happen again to any school . . . (The silence of the committee) would seem to indicate that the decision was made before the C.C.N.Y.-N.Y.U. game . . . If this is true why were the teams, the students and the fans not informed? City played with the invitation as its goal and interest in the game rose accordingly.[12]

Bushnell responded two days later that no changes would be made in light of this public protest from City College's students and fans. He indicated that every team invited to the tournament had won more games than the Beavers. With a 13-4 record, Bushnell was correct. Even though the City College win-loss percentage would have come close to matching some of the tournament entrants, the fact that it played far fewer games meant that Bushnell had some evidence on which to stand fairly. Nat Holman would have to extend his schedule the following year.[13]

Bushnell received "severe cross-examination" at meetings and press conferences leading up to the tournament. Local sportswriters wondered why the committee passed over Holman's squad, and they had the same feelings regarding the omission of defending champion DePaul. George Mikan was in his senior season and, alongside fellow giant Bob Kurland from Oklahoma

A&M, had become a force unlike anything basketball had ever seen. Bushnell flatly responded that DePaul had five losses and City College had four.[14]

The MIBC selection committee did not change course based on the questioning, and seeded the top four teams three days before the tournament began. Kentucky, with freshmen standouts Ralph Beard and Wallace "Wah Wah" Jones—who also played Wildcat football for Coach "Bear" Bryant— leading Coach Adolph Rupp's charge, received the top spot with a two-loss record and a strong showing in a victory over St. John's in the Garden during the regular season. Bowling Green, defending National Invitation runner-up with 6'11½" center Don Otten, took the second seed. New entrant Syracuse received the third rank, and 1942 surprise champion West Virginia was seeded fourth.[15]

Flowering the Garden

On Thursday, March 14, opening-round action commenced, and the first evening ended with "an all-victorious night for the underdogs" even though fourth-seed West Virginia beat its opponent, St. John's. Local writers knew the seedings, but they were also well aware of the bookmakers' line for the game—and both groups operated with at least a hint of local bias. The bookies favored St. John's by five points heading into the matchup, but the Redmen could not live up to the line in a 12-point loss. The Mountaineers had another victory against the odds.[16]

Local fans had to wait longer than expected that night for the Redmen to play, however, during #2 Bowling Green's curtain raiser against Rhode Island State. A Garden basketball record 18,458 fans jammed into the arena and witnessed a game for the ages. Rhode Island State, because of its lack of height, used a "fire-horse type of play—the Rams never stopped driving." Ram center Ernie Calverley, standing 5'11" and weighing 145 pounds, gave up more than a foot and around 100 pounds to his counterpart, the Falcons' Otten. While Otten seemingly had his way, scoring 31 points, Calverley won the admiration of the crowd with his "poise, speed, steadiness, incredibly perfect passing and a fiery will to win." The diminutive center—who suffered from a heart condition and even collapsed at one point in the second half, scored 16 points, the most important of which came from a fifty-five-foot desperation shot at the buzzer to tie the game at 74 and force overtime. Otten disqualified on fouls with three minutes left in regulation, giving the Rhode Islanders a considerable advantage in the extra period. "Calverley did not score a point in the overtime, but his mere presence on the floor, his excellent feeding, inspired his mates to their most notable conquest," columnist Louis Effrat noted. The Rams won 82–79.[17]

Two nights later, yet another Garden basketball record crowd was on hand. This time, 18,483 fans filled the arena's seemingly limitless capacity. Top-seed Kentucky outmatched Arizona from the opening tip, winning 77–53 and never relinquishing a lead. The Wildcats looked like the class of the tournament. In the second game, Muhlenberg and new coach Lee Croker collected their first-ever postseason tournament victory by holding off the Syracuse Orangemen 47–41 in a physical affair. The referees called fifty-two fouls in the game—thirty-eight of which came "with good reason" against Syracuse.[18]

Semifinal action took place two nights later, on Monday, March 18, in front of another vast crowd of 18,478. Ernie Calverley and the Rhode Island State Rams opened the evening with a 59–49 win over Muhlenberg. While Calverley's performance was spectacular in the opening-round game, his semifinal performance shone brighter. Against the Mules, the big-hearted center carried his team on his diminutive shoulders. Calverley scored 27 points while "generally forcing Muhlenberg to hate his presence." In the second game, West Virginia and Kentucky fought tooth and nail for thirty-eight minutes that saw fourteen lead changes. However, Kentucky scored 8 straight points in the final two minutes to seal the win, 59–51.[19]

The Wildcats entered Wednesday's final as 11.5-point favorites according to the local bookmakers. But Coach Rupp's squad needed all they had to outlast Calverley's cavalry. Rhode Island State stayed tight with Kentucky the entire game, forcing twelve ties. With forty seconds remaining, Calverley committed his fifth and disqualifying foul on Wildcat freshman point guard Ralph Beard. Beard, who had masterfully held Calverley to only 8 points on the night, sank the free throw. Each team scored one more foul shot at the end for a 46–45 Kentucky win. Despite his relatively low point total, Calverley led the Ram offense by setting up his teammates for basket after basket and won the tournament's outstanding player award. After the game, a relieved and impressed Rupp rhetorically responded to the press that had favored his team so highly by commenting, "Who said Rhode Island State had no defense? Who said Rhode Island State had no offense?" Ernie Calverley provided enough of both by himself—and 18,475 witnesses attested to it. As newly crowned National Invitation champs, Kentucky hung around New York City awaiting the fate of the end of the basketball season. The Garden would host more college basketball, and the Wildcats hoped to factor in to it.[20]

NCAA Repeat Champions and Growing New York Interest

The NCAA Eastern Regional opened in the Garden the night after Kentucky's championship. While the MIBC seeded its top four teams, preventing any of them from meeting each other in the first round, the NCAA simply matched teams randomly within each region. In fact, tournament officials chose teams out of a teacup for first-round matchups. On Thursday, March 21, first-round games pitted Ohio State against Harvard in the opener and NYU against North Carolina in the closer. Ohio State earned the District 4 bid by winning the Big Ten in a backdoor fashion. Indiana beat Iowa in the last game of the season, giving Ohio State the title over the Hawkeyes. The Buckeyes also benefited from DePaul's unfathomable five regular season losses. With George Mikan as a senior, the Blue Demons did not live up to the exceptionally high expectations for the season. Ohio State and Coach Harold Olsen, then, represented the district for the second straight year. Harvard earned the District 1 bid with even more good fortune. Dartmouth, who won the 1946 Ivy League championship—giving them eight such titles in the previous nine seasons—decided in mid-February that they would not accept any postseason bids. The Hanover campus was still affiliated with the military, and Coach Cowles's squad would lose four regulars at the close of the regular season. Harvard became the fill-in.[21]

Ohio State had no trouble vanquishing the Crimson. The Buckeyes won 46–38 in front of an NCAA tournament record 18,452 fans. Most of the spectators, however, were more interested in the second matchup of the evening. Southern Conference champions North Carolina earned the District 3 bid since Southeastern Conference champion Kentucky accepted an early bid to the National Invitation tournament. This bid gave the Tar Heels the right to play District 2 representative NYU in the Garden. NYU, a conference independent team and the only New York City team to play in the NCAA event to date, came into the matchup as one of the top metropolitan teams of the season. This matchup had a strong New York City feel to it that generated considerable excitement in the Big Apple. NYU enjoyed a loyal local fan base, but North Carolina did, too. Although southern basketball remained second class to those in most other parts of the country, this District 3 representative came in with a reputation. Tar Heel coach Ben Carnevale played for NYU coach Howard Cann in the late 1930s. Indeed, Carnevale was a member of the 1935 Violet squad that many regarded as "national champions," and he starred on NYU's 1938 National Invitation tournament team. After gaining commission as a navy officer during World War II, Carnevale took over the Tar Heel basketball program in 1944. Lanky 6'6" center Horace

"Bones" McKinney, who would coach Wake Forest to its only Final Four berth in 1956, led the Tar Heels into battle, and the southerners took it to their coach's former team and mentor in a 57–49 opening-round victory.[22]

On Saturday, March 23, North Carolina and Ohio State squared off in the Eastern Regional final. The two "all-star teams" battled hard to the pleasure of the 18,371 fans. The first five minutes of the game elapsed without any scoring, much like two heavyweights marking their territory cautiously while waiting for the other fighter to make the first move. North Carolina shot to a 17–6 lead from there before an Ohio State recovery to within one, 20–19, at the half. In the second period, the Buckeyes shot out to a 34–27 lead until North Carolina closed in and eventually tied the game at 54 at the end of regulation.[23]

NYU publicity chairman George Shiebler wrote that "the overtime period had all the elements of a Hollywood scenario." A hook shot, an angle shot, and two foul shots gave the Tar Heels all they needed to hold off Ohio State, 60–57. The Buckeyes suffered an overtime loss in the Eastern Regional final for the second straight year, and the Tar Heels won the right to stay in the Big Apple to await the Western Regional champion.[24]

Oklahoma A&M, the District 5 representative and defending NCAA and Red Cross champion, came into the 1946 NCAA Western Regional heavily favored. The Aggies won the Missouri Valley conference and defeated Kansas in a district play-in game before 9,045 fans—the largest crowd to ever see a game in Kansas City's Municipal Auditorium. Kansas had no match for Aggie senior center Bob Kurland. Kurland and company's first opponent in Kansas City was District 6 representative Baylor. The upstart team from Waco was just beginning its ascent into basketball's upper echelons, winning the Southwestern Conference title through strong play from sophomore forward Jackie Robinson. Robinson, a white Texan not to be mistaken with the California-raised African American who was in the process of breaking Major League Baseball's color barrier, was the leader of an integrated squad. Mexican American Dickie Gonzales played sparingly in the Bears' opening-round loss to the Aggies. Gonzales, Placido Gomez on Rice's 1940 team, and Japanese American Wat Misaka, who starred defensively on the 1944 NCAA champion Utah team, became the first nonwhite athletes on NCAA tournament team rosters to play in the event. This type of slow and relatively inconspicuous integration went largely unnoticed. Unlike baseball's integration in which a league of all white players suddenly had an African American with dark skin among its ranks, Gonzales, Gomez, and Misaka had much lighter skin and they came from racial ancestry that was markedly less threatening in the collective thought of the white establishment.[25]

Unlike Misaka but similar to Gomez, Gonzales could not aid his team to victory. Kurland proved too much for the Bears, who listed only one player as taller than 6'2". The Aggies steamrolled Baylor, 44–29. The 8,864 fans on hand that night also witnessed Pacific Coast Conference champion California take down District 7 representative Colorado, who had spurned an MIBC invite in favor of the NCAA. The 8,950 fans that came to the final game on Saturday, March 23, saw even more Aggie dominance. Kurland scored 29 points on 52 percent shooting to put his weekend scoring total at 49 points—many of which came on shots he "tipped in or jammed home."[26]

Oklahoma A&M immediately traveled east to take on Eastern champion North Carolina for the NCAA title. The Aggies, after winning the 1945 NCAA title, were eager for an unprecedented back-to-back title run. Kurland and his teammates had enjoyed this postwar success in an unusual way. Most of the regulars from the 1945 championship team graduated. With Kurland back for his senior campaign, the 1946 outlook was not bleak, but the Aggies would need help.

Many teams upgraded their talent with veterans coming back from war. Some of these former GIs transferred to new schools, but many returned to complete degrees at the schools they attended before enlisting. The Aggies welcomed back guards A. L. Bennett and Sam Aubrey onto campus in the summer of 1945. They knew Bennett would help but were skeptical of Aubrey's chances. The latter returned to Stillwater on crutches, having been shot in combat in northern Italy. "Nobody expected him to walk, much less play," Kurland recalled, "But there he was in the lineup later that year."[27]

Kurland and his teammates entered Madison Square Garden with Aubrey's continuing motivation and loads of momentum from two straight convincing victories. North Carolina, meanwhile, looked strong, too, but not as dominant as the Oklahomans. The Tuesday, March 26, encounter attracted an NCAA record 18,479 fans—four more than attended the National Invitation final—to the Garden. The Tar Heels stayed close, but they had no answer for Bob Kurland in the end. The red-headed seven-footer "put on an eye-opening exhibition of feeding and defensive tactics while he helped himself to a total of 23 points—his greatest output on the Garden court in ten appearances." The big man "had his beefy hands in just about everything that night." The 43–40 victory made Coach Iba's squad the first to win two straight NCAA titles. The Tar Heels, in the words of student reporter Carroll Poplin, "deserve a lot of credit for winning the eastern title of the N.C.A.A. which tabs them as the second best team in the country."[28]

"WELL --
Seven-foot Bob Kurland, star
of the Oklahoma A and M cage
team who makes split-second decisions on the floor, puzzles
over an answer to Radio Announcer
Larry Ray, of Kansas City, Mo.,
when interviewed after he had
sparked the Aggies to a 44-29
victory over Baylor University
in the Western NCAA playoffs at
Kansas City March 22.

ASSOCIATED PRESS PHOTO
offered wire/2 pts KB/mag ny/
fcc-7-0115-stf wps

Oklahoma A&M's Bob Kurland analyzes his team's win over the radio. *1992-052 ICApg143, OSU Photograph Collection, Archives, Oklahoma State University Libraries.*

The Uncertain Future of the Red Cross Game

Unfortunately for the Aggies and for the entire college basketball establishment, this game marked the end of the collegiate hoops season. For the past three years, the National Invitation and NCAA champions had met in a "championship" game that benefited the Red Cross War Fund. With the United States now at peace, there was less imminent need for donations to the Red Cross, but there remained a strong interest in determining the official national champion of college basketball. And with two similar tournaments and no matchup between their champions, the college basketball world had to revert back to speculation regarding which team was best.

The omission of the Red Cross game raised plenty of questions regarding the politics of college basketball at the time. Fans and the local media clearly favored this game as a tidy year-end tie-up. In fact, local metropolitan sportswriters had been discussing the feature for months. As far back as January, the *New York Times*'s Louis Effrat speculated on the fate of the game. "The big playoff has proved a most desirable one," the scribe argued, reaffirming that, "with virtually no dissenters, (the winner) was acclaimed the national champion." Effrat's January 28, 1946, column announced a new "East-West all-star college basketball game" at the Garden on Saturday, March 30—four days after the NCAA championship game. Effrat also noted that the circus was due to move in to the Garden immediately after this all-star event, leaving only two dates that the Red Cross Game could be played. Wednesday, March 27, was out because it was the day after the NCAA championship and would be unfair to its titleholder. Thursday and Friday, then, were the only options before Saturday's all-star game and the Sunday onset of the weeklong circus.[29]

Effrat interviewed Ned Irish for his story. The Garden operator relayed that "so far nothing had been done about arranging the play-off," but also that the implementation of the all-star contest would not exclude the possibility of a fourth Red Cross championship game. Effrat had no logical response for Irish's ambiguous answer. Without such a game, the basketball season would end in "a nation-wide muddle" with "numerous title claims." "Why there should be any hitch at all is mysterious," Effrat opined, "but if arrangements are to be made for a championship play-off, the powers-that-be will have to start moving pronto."[30]

Three weeks later, Asa Bushnell, the de facto face of the National Invitation tournament, told the press that "he knew nothing about plans for the annual Red Cross benefit play-off" game. Effrat's plea to tournament organizers to get moving with plans for this contest found no adherents. In fact, Irish's new all-star game began running into glitches. Everett B. Morris of the *New York Herald-Tribune* relayed on March 11 that the individual showcase event was "meeting with considerable opposition." Apparently, Morris, Irish, and other organizers of this all-star event to benefit The Tribune Fresh Air Fund were having difficulty lining up some of the nation's top players for the event. Without big names such as DePaul's George Mikan and North Carolina's "Bones" McKinney, the game would not attract the spectators that organizers desired.[31]

Despite the struggling logistics of the all-star game, the play-off championship game had not been dismissed yet. On March 19, the Red Cross game "was given a new lease on life" as Harold Olsen announced that if NYU, Ohio State, or Oklahoma A&M won the NCAA tournament, "there was a good chance of the classic being held at the Garden." On March 22, the day after the National Invitation final, Arthur Daley offered a ray of hope that the game might go on. The game, Daley noted, is "perched up in midair. The date is being saved, the tickets are printed and the show can go on with no more than ten hours' notice . . . The game should be played in order to keep the chain unbroken and determine an undisputed national champion."[32]

That same day, George Coleman announced that Kentucky had nixed plans for the Red Cross classic. "Kentucky is willing to play the NCAA winner but not for charity," he announced. According to the journalist, the Kentucky board of trustees had mandated after a Duke-Kentucky football game a few years prior that no Kentucky teams would participate in charity contests. The school apparently wanted and in some cases needed the payout from these types of events. Rupp also suggested, as Coleman relayed, that the potential NCAA–National Invite matchup would not have to occur in New York City. Rupp suggested Louisville as another possible site.[33]

Although Rupp's program was on the ascent, he did not garner nearly as much power in the Bluegrass State as he would a few years later, and so he had to abide by the university's policies. "The University of Kentucky has a ruling that bars its teams from playing all traveling charity games," the coach admitted, "We have many charities at home that want us to play benefit games." North Carolina coach Carnevale mentioned a similar submission to institutional policy. When asked about his team's interest in playing in the classic if they won the NCAA event, he responded, "Look, I'm just the coach; any decisions on additional games for our team must come from North Carolina." Hank Iba, coach of the reigning NCAA champion Aggies, had a different viewpoint. "We're always ready to play basketball any time," he averred with a smile, "for the Red Cross or for any other reason."[34]

Four days later, on the day of the NCAA final, Irish put an end to the speculation. The vice president of the Garden stated bluntly, "the mythical national championship . . . would not be held." Adolph Rupp offered yet another suggestion for why the event would not occur. "Rupp, who remained in (New York City) pending a decision (on the fate of the game), said the proposal to stage the game was not advanced until too late to permit satisfactory arrangement," reported Michael Strauss of the *New York Times*.[35]

By staying around New York City, Rupp seemed to be showing his interest in participating in the event even if it could not be for charity. At this early stage in his career, he seemed eager to play in any postseason event he could. Further, his team was young and exceptionally talented. He likely would have jumped at the chance to get his outstanding freshmen another game on the sport's biggest stage against the talented Aggies or Tar Heels. Oklahoma A&M's Coach Iba and North Carolina's Coach Carnevale seemingly would have been willing to participate in the game, too. Iba was coming off a victory in the 1945 game and, with Kurland playing at an unstoppable level, would have had few fears about losing. Carnevale, who may not have been quite as confident coming in, was from New York City and his public comments during the tournament indicated that he enjoyed coaching in front of his "home" crowd. One more game may have been very welcome for him personally. The only negative for these coaches may have been that their teams would have had to stay in the Big Apple for three more nights, which meant three more days of missed classes for their players who had already missed a lot of class.

"Who's to blame?" Coleman asked once the game had been nixed. "That question has not been answered yet. But it should be; the fans demand it." The simplest answer was the University of Kentucky's board of trustees. However, they simply prohibited the Wildcats from playing in a charity game. The classic could go on, but under other auspices. Yet no one stepped in to take control of the event.[36]

Speculation on the opinions of tournament organizers toward a national tie-up would be much more complex. While the event was wildly popular and tournament officials appreciated that, when it could not go on as usual these men were not quick to carry the torch. Three straight wins for the NCAA in Red Cross championship games had given the association's tournament solid footing in basketball's mecca. Metropolitan fans were treated to a heavy dose of the quality of basketball outside the five boroughs. Wyoming and Utah beat St. John's—the best that New York City and the National Invitation could offer—in 1943 and 1944. In 1945, Oklahoma A&M took down DePaul and George Mikan, who was arguably the best player in the country at the time. While New York City basketball and the

National Invitation tournament may not have lost prestige during the three Red Cross games, the NCAA surely gained prestige as a tournament at least on par with the Big Apple event and perhaps even more competitive.

The National Invitation had been consistently popular throughout the war, averaging sellout or near capacity crowds each year but one. The NCAA did not have the same record. However, it did have attendance figures that increased very rapidly. The NCAA made a large jump in attendance figures at the Garden between 1943 and 1944. Wyoming, who came into the 1943 Red Cross game as underdogs to local St. John's, may have changed a lot of local opinions about the quality of basketball west of the Mississippi. The following season, even as Utah—first-round loser in the National Invitation—won the NCAA crown, many more fans came to watch. Part of this increase may have been due to familiarity. The NCAA tournament was no longer a new tournament in the Big Apple—that is, it was no longer simply a Middle American tournament glomming onto the New York City spotlight that gave prestige to the MIBC event. Indeed, as the NCAA consistently rented the Garden, local fans came to see the event as yet another feature in the college basketball landscape in New York City.

Even though it may have entered New York City as second fiddle, no one could deny the NCAA's increasing popularity and record profits when they played in the Garden. The association's profits from the basketball tournament went from $1,361.85 in 1942—the year before the move to New York City—to $10,200.29 in 1943, $26,029.29 in 1944, and $27,666.98 in 1945. Further, as Oklahoma A&M won its second straight title in 1946, the NCAA welcomed in an astounding $50,664.33 in profits. These massive upsurges—a 37-fold increase in four years—allowed the tournament to finally begin awarding its participants cash prizes that would have rivaled what the MIBC had given its participants all along. While this gift increase—which Kansas's Phog Allen had been arguing for since the tournament began in 1939—may not have received public recognition from many coaches, it certainly mattered.[37]

Thus, the NCAA loved being in New York City. The association also loved that it had relinquished its role as an afterthought in the Big Apple by beating the National Invitation champ three straight times. The Red Cross game and the war years had given the NCAA tournament the ability to become an equal with the originally more prestigious National Invitation event. Pete Newell, coach of the University of San Francisco at the time and 1959 NCAA champion coach at California, recalled thirty years after his team's championship that "a lot of people didn't like the idea of playing in New York, but there is no question it helped establish the tournament."[38]

Despite the NCAA's growth in New York City and despite the National Invitation having to share the college basketball limelight in the Big Apple—which it did not publicly complain about—tournament organizers for both events may have shared similar views on the fate of the Red Cross game. The NCAA had won every time and its champion had been crowned "national champ" almost unanimously each time. Therefore, the National Invitation tournament lost out on its champion having at least some right to the "national title" that it had enjoyed before the Red Cross matchups. Despite these differences, by putting such stock in the outcome of the Red Cross game and by continuing the event, both tournaments would have been acknowledging that theirs was not *the* national championship tournament. Indeed, if the Red Cross game determined the "national champion," then neither tournament was a national championship. They were both simply lead-up events. The NCAA, which considered its tournament a "national championship," may not have wanted to relinquish that claim. The MIBC, whose event had originally been the premiere postseason tournament, may not have wanted the Red Cross games to continue because it may not have wanted any further evidence that it was an equal to the NCAA and nothing more than that. What good was such an event if one tournament's teams won it every year? And what good were two separate tournaments, after all, if their winners met every year in a charity game the profits of which neither tournament's administration kept?

Ned Irish's thoughts on the Red Cross game may have been similar. The ambivalence he showed publicly may have been his true feeling toward the event. He too would not see the profits from a "national championship" matchup for charity. Although he generated a great deal of goodwill from hosting the three events, he did not profit financially and even lost out on a night's worth of income. He knew how valuable his venue was to the college basketball postseason, and he knew that he would profit greatly from it whether the Red Cross game occurred or not. Irish did, in fact, host another Red Cross charity game on Thursday, March 29, but it did not involve college teams. Instead, Irish scheduled three-time defending AAU champion Phillips 66 Oilers of Bartlesville, Oklahoma, to play an aggregation of college players representing the New York Athletic Club. While the quality of play was very high in this game, only 6,734 fans attended—a Garden season low—and raised only $12,000. Clearly, the public was not nearly as interested in a one-off game featuring random teams as it was in a meaningful encounter pitting two postseason tournament champs in a "national championship" game. The public was also much less interested in donating money to the Red Cross now that the country was no longer officially at war.[39]

NAIB Growth

Halfway across the country, the NAIB did not even factor into this national postseason discussion, showing the continued evolution of college basketball's national landscape. Emil Liston's event was back on its feet in 1946 after a hiatus in 1944 and scaled-back operations in 1945, but it was not a part of true "national championship" discussions—at least according to the powerful New York City media. After a sixteen-team 1945 event, Liston got back to a full thirty-two-team docket in 1946 in Kansas City—the city where his tournament mattered most.[40]

Even though sportswriters in the Big Apple omitted the NAIB from postseason discussions, Emil Liston was not willing to concede second-rate status to his event. The NAIB founder's claim was that his was not "a tournament of small colleges." And to shed that label, Liston and his colleagues went "all-out" to reinvigorate the tournament as a mainstay of postwar America. Liston and Kansas City's Municipal Auditorium hosted a four-team tournament in December of 1945 which included 1943 NAIB runner-up Pepperdine, 1945 NAIB champion Loyola of New Orleans, and West Texas State—a team that showed great promise in the early 1940s. Yet Valparaiso of Indiana, the least heralded of the quartet, ended the tournament on top. The momentum from this event encouraged many growing state schools to participate in the postseason NAIB. Minnesota State, Eastern Kentucky, Northern Iowa, Arizona State, Nevada, Houston, and finalists Indiana State and Southern Illinois marked only a few of the recognizable teams that accepted bids. These relatively big names negated the fact that Arizona declined an invite in favor of the New York tournament and Marshall University of West Virginia declined an invite because the tournament conflicted with its spring football practices.[41]

However, the 1946 NAIB event had something to boast of that no other event had. Phog Allen would be conducting an exhibition game using twelve-foot baskets. For years, Allen—himself an undersized center—lamented the advantage that tall players received. Bob Kurland, George Mikan, and their fellow skyscrapers could score, rebound, and tend the goal much too easily because they could reach the ten-foot rims with little effort. Allen surmised that raising the baskets would dissipate this advantage.[42]

So Allen recruited two NAIB teams to participate after they had been knocked out of the tournament. He chose, not at random, the tallest and shortest teams in the event. Allen pitted the New Mexico School of Mines—a team that featured 7'1" Elmore Morgenthaler who averaged 22 points per game—against small and short Drury College of Missouri. Morgenthaler still dominated the game, scoring 36 points from the field as the tall team won 84–61. Postgame remarks from those in attendance were not altogether supportive of this new initiative. Most coaches felt that one exhibition game was not enough to settle the matter, but that little changed to neutralize the advantage of a tall player in this exhibition. After all, one coach remarked, "The ball still will fall around the basket." Much of the sentiment behind this and other similar comments provided a bit of omniscience regarding Allen's true motives. The Kansas coach had arguably been the most effective individual regarding the evolution of basketball and its rules. Indeed, he spent a great deal of time and energy evangelizing for the good of the game. However, many of his critics came to cynically believe that what Allen promoted as good for the game also happened to be good for him and his team. And this matter was no different. Allen had not been able to successfully recruit an exceptionally tall and talented player. Further, his Jayhawks had been excluded from the NCAA tournament the past two years by Oklahoma A&M—a team led by 7-footer Bob Kurland.[43]

Luckily for Liston and the NAIB, all of the publicity surrounding Allen's exhibition game and the increasing number of "name" teams in the event produced a smoke screen for a larger problem. The NAIB maintained an unwritten color code for its players. While growing numbers of publicly funded teams featuring war veterans played in the 1946 event, one player had been specifically excluded. Morningside College, a small school on the western edge of Iowa, traveled to the tournament short-handed. The Mustangs received a bid to enter the event, but it was conditional—they had to leave their lone African American, Rosamond Wilson, behind. The Mustangs lost in the second round.[44]

While Southern Illinois defeated Indiana State for the NAIB "national title," neither team featured in the Associated Press's (AP) final season rankings. Determining a hierarchy purely based on win-loss percentage, the AP listed NCAA champion Oklahoma A&M first followed closely in a tie for second by National Invitation champion Kentucky and Ivy League runner-up Yale. The Elis' only loss was to Harvard, who received the NCAA District 1 bid after Ivy League champion Dartmouth declined. Kansas ranked fourth followed by National Invitation entrants West Virginia and runner-up Rhode Island State. Harvard, NYU, Slippery Rock of Pennsylvania, Indiana, and Louisiana State rounded out the top ten. The inclusion of Slippery Rock shows that the AP took at least some smaller schools into account for these rankings, and yet no NAIB team made the list. Thus, while the Kansas City–based tournament returned to full strength in the Garden City, it still made only little waves in the national news media. It had, however, increased momentum locally after its wartime hiatus.[45]

Skin Color in the Postseason Tournaments

The 1947 NAIB brought forth increased interest. Attendance and net income records fell as the event attracted sellout crowds in late-round matchups. Liston, who had relinquished his role at Baker University in the previous off-season to devote his full energies to the NAIB as its first official executive secretary, promoted the event like he never had before. He publicized the wide-open field that was taken over surprisingly by the Thundering Herd of Marshall College in West Virginia. Spring football practice did not conflict with this season's NAIB, and the basketball team was finally able to show its prowess.[46]

Unfortunately, the NAIB policy of racial exclusion came to broader light before the 1947 tournament commenced. The 1946 runner-up Indiana State team became the focal point of this controversy. Glenn Curtis, who had coached John Wooden at Martinsville high school in the 1920s before leaving the Sycamores, left to guide a professional team after the 1945–46 season and passed the torch to his former player. Wooden took over a veteran team that included many of the previous season's regulars. However, Wooden added an African American player to the squad. When the Sycamores ended their season with only two losses, Liston offered a bid—with contingencies. Only the white Sycamores could play. Wooden and his team, through a complicated context and a roundabout rationale, ended up not participating in the event.[47]

The National Invitation and NCAA championships had no such rule, but the racial zeitgeist produced unique experiences in each of the two New York City events. The NCAA tournament also had yet to experience an African American player on the roster of a participating team. Such a record may not have been intentional as most participating teams gained entrance meritoriously. In other words, since most district representatives gained that honor by winning a conference title or a series of play-off games, any racial discrimination from district selection committees potentially would have become public—with the exception of District 2 and District 6, where Jim Crow continued to rule the day. And yet so few teams across the country were integrated at the time that selecting eight all-white teams for the tournament each year occurred commonly and without controversy. The Big Ten, for instance, was just starting to integrate in the late 1940s and only a handful of prominent conference affiliated teams had African American players at the time. So by 1947, the NCAA tournament had included Mexican American and Japanese American players, but no African Americans.[48]

The National Invitation welcomed African Americans from the start. The Big Apple was the cultural center of America's melting pot, allowing LIU's Dolly King and a slew of Toledo African Americans without incident. Further the performances of King and Toledo star Davage Minor overshadowed the color of their skin. Since Minor's appearance in 1943, though, no African American had played in the MIBC event. Such happenstance allowed the University of Kentucky—generally acclaimed as one of the top two teams in the country in 1946 and a candidate for top honors again in 1947—to play in the invite without any worries. At the time, the Wildcats and their legendary Coach Rupp were a season and a half away from playing against their first black player, five seasons away from playing against one in their home gymnasium, and twenty-four years away from having an integrated squad.[49]

Kentucky embodied the racial climate of schools in the American South. Jim Crow laws reigned and intercollegiate athletics became among the most prominent ways in which racial segregation came on public display for all the country to see. No Southeastern Conference team fielded an integrated basketball squad until late 1965—the same season that Kentucky ended by gaining notoriety as its all-white team lost in the NCAA finals to seven black players from Texas Western.[50]

As the Southeastern Conference's northernmost school, the Wildcats were not the racial trailblazers that they naturally could have been. In the late 1940s, the Kentucky football and basketball teams garnered national attention for their success and figured prominently year after year in national rankings. Their coaches—football's Paul "Bear" Bryant and basketball's Adolph Rupp—became legendary in their own rights as strong disciplinarians, coaching geniuses, and possible racists. While the two competed heavily with each other for prominence on campus—Bryant soon left Lexington reportedly because of his second-class status to Rupp—both perpetuated the South's Lost Cause, which included racial segregation. Both nationally renowned coaches eventually integrated their squads, but—like most coaches in the South—they only did so when it became apparent that they could not win as much as they wanted to without African American players.[51]

Strong Fields in the Two New York Events

In 1947, Kentucky entered the National Invitation tournament as defending champions. The event had been scheduled back to its 1945 format as the MIBC and NCAA tournaments again overlapped after a year in which one followed the other. Kentucky came to New York with a 27-2 record and diversity only in its arsenal of talent—the Wildcats had "speed, height and experience." National Invitation veteran teams West Virginia, Duquesne, Utah, LIU, Bradley, and St. John's, along with newcomer North Carolina State, rounded out Kentucky's competition in the field.[52]

The Wildcats took the top seed in the event followed by West Virginia—a team that had thrived on low seeds in the past. Duquesne received the third seed. African American forward Chuck Cooper, a Pittsburgh native who was the first black player drafted into the NBA in 1950, led the Duquesne squad. Cooper's team—the Dukes—came in with a 19-1 record and a penchant for physical play. North Carolina State was seeded fourth. The Wolfpack's entrance gave Dixie two teams in the Big Apple for the first time ever. But new coach Everett Case's team had a decidedly northern feel to it. Case was a native Indianan and had coached high school basketball in the Hoosier state before moving south. When he took over in Raleigh, he was able to transplant a number of northerners with him. With the magic of Hoosier high school hoops in his blood, Case was able to win right away.[53]

The NCAA brackets filled, like the National Invitation's, with the highest quality teams. Most coaches agreed in mid-March that the NCAA and MIBC fields were both the strongest they had ever been. Holy Cross represented District 1. Coach Alvin "Doggie" Julian was having immediate success in Massachusetts just like he had previously at Muhlenberg College. CCNY represented District 2. The Beavers and their legendary coach Nat Holman became the second metropolitan team to compete in the NCAA event. NCAA founder NYU had remained loyal to the large association's event when offered a bid, but the Violets had suffered this season with a 12-9 record. CCNY, however, completed a 16-4 regular season that placed them as third best in the city. National Invitation entrants St. John's and LIU sported better records. Nonetheless, the Beavers took a quality squad into the NCAA event. It also took an integrated squad into the event. Sporting one African American starter and two reserves, the Beavers provided the first African Americans to play in the nine-year-old tournament.[54]

Navy, with a 16-1 record, became the first military school to enter a postseason basketball tournament as the Midshipmen represented District 3. Big Ten champion Wisconsin won the District 4 bid that had traditionally gone to that conference's winner. Although the District 4 selection committee had previously offered the bid to conference-independent Bradley in 1939 and DePaul in the George Mikan days, the committee had always been too late with the Blue Demons. Nevertheless, Wisconsin's bid became their first since the championship 1941 season.[55]

Out west, NCAA veteran Wyoming took the District 7 bid and Oklahoma, another NCAA team from years past, won the District 5 bid by defeating Missouri Valley Conference champion St. Louis University in a play-off game. Oregon State won the Pacific Coast Conference and garnered the District 8 bid, giving the NCAA tournament an unlikely two "Beaver" quintets entering the field for the first time. To round out the brackets, Texas roped the Southwestern Conference title away from Baylor to earn the District 6 representation.[56]

Old and New Tournament Storylines

The National Invite kicked off New York City postseason basketball on Saturday, March 15, with a quarterfinal double-header. Second-seed West Virginia opened against a young Bradley team that started two freshmen and two sophomores. The inexperience showed, as Bradley—although scrappy and hard-working—left a lot of points on the court by missing close-range shots in losing to an uninspiring Mountaineer team, 69–60. In the second game, most of the 18,468 fans rooted for the home team. St. John's took a comfortable lead early against North Carolina State by dissecting Everett Case's zone defense. However, late in the first half, Case subbed 6'9" center Bob Hahn into the game and the freshman from Ann Arbor, Michigan, neutralized the Redmen's seasoned center, Harry Boykoff. Hahn disrupted Boykoff enough that the Wolfpack had cut the lead to 2 points at halftime and, after a seven-minute dry spell for St. John's in the middle of the second half, North Carolina State took over for a 61–55 victory.[57]

Two nights later, the other two opening-round matchups commenced in front of six more fans than the first night of action. Utah and Duquesne raised the curtain with a "rough and exciting" game. The Utes, led by a core of veterans who had won the NCAA title and Red Cross championship game in 1944 as freshmen, held off Cooper and the Dukes, 45–44. After a slow start, the westerners found just enough rhythm to win the "ragged, loosely played affair." Wat Misaka, Utah's Japanese American defensive stopper, scored 8 points and impressed the metropolitan crowd enough to garner a tryout with the Big Apple's new professional team, the Knickerbockers. In the second game of the evening, the Kentucky Wildcats literally ran out to a 49–30 lead early, but their legs began to wear. LIU, outmatched on paper, caught up and tied the game at 62 with thirty seconds remaining, much to the fancy of the local crowd. However, fifteen seconds later Kentucky's Wallace "Wah-Wah" Jones crushed the Blackbird hopes for an upset with a set shot from the corner that swished through the net. Jones paced the Wildcats with 20 points in what ended up as a 4-point victory.[58]

On Wednesday, March 19, even though both local teams had been defeated, 18,472 fans entered the Garden for semifinal action. Kentucky continued its torrid pace with a victory over North Carolina State, 60–42. The Wolfpack stuck with the defending champs for twenty-five minutes before the Wildcats started pulling away. Kentucky sophomore point guard Ralph Beard scored 15 points for the winners. The quick ballhandler became the pulse of the Wildcat team. As Beard goes, so the saying went, so goes Kentucky. In the other semifinal, Utah survived another cardiac finish, outlasting West Virginia 64–62. The Utah trio of Vern Gardner, Arnie Ferrin, and Wat Misaka combined for 47 points that were enough to hold off 8 straight Mountaineer points in the final ninety seconds for a close victory. The Kentucky and Utah victories put the two experienced postseason teams on a collision course for the National Invitation finals set for Monday, March 24. In the meantime, the Utes and Wildcats could relax in the Big Apple and take in the NCAA Eastern Regional tournament scheduled for Thursday, March 20, and Saturday the 22nd.[59]

The 1946 NCAA tournament marked the last installment of the event that founder Harold Olsen directed. The Ohio State coach also stepped down from his position in Columbus to coach the new professional basketball team in Chicago—the Stags. Olsen's impact on the tournament was immense, as he created the idea and then implemented it. He also oversaw the tournament as it went from red to black ink and from Chicago to Kansas City to New York City—and, most importantly, from sustainability to profitability. And yet Olsen could not take all of the credit. Many able and interested coaches assisted him. One of them who played a major role throughout was Arthur C. "Dutch" Lonborg, coach of Northwestern. While Lonborg's Wildcat teams never made it to the tournament, the coach played a major role in the NABC and tournament proceedings. Therefore, Lonborg assumed Olsen's role for the 1947 NCAA tournament. Coincidentally, Olsen ended his career in Lonborg's previous role, coaching at Northwestern from 1950 to 1952.[60]

The 1947 event, Lonborg recapped, "broke all previous records for attendance." In the opening-round games at the Garden, Coach Julian's young Holy Cross team dismissed the Navy Midshipmen, 55–47. Standout forward George Kaftan led the New Englanders most of the season in scoring, but the team's flair came from freshman reserve point guard Bob Cousy, who led the Crusaders' second squad in a platoon system that featured two vastly different systems. Cousy and the reserves—all freshmen—would fast break while Kaftan and the starters kept the pace slow. In the other opener, the integrated CCNY squad took down Wisconsin, 70–56. African American Joe Galiber started at center for the Beavers and scored 4 points while Sonny Jameson, another African American, came off the bench to tally 10 against the Badgers. The victory made CCNY the only metropolitan team to win a postseason game that season. In Saturday's Eastern final, 18,470 fans saw George Kaftan almost single-handedly take down City College. The New Jersey native who prepped in New York City scored 30 points as his team won, 60–45. Few could dispute that the Crusaders were the class of the Eastern quintets.[61]

Back west, NCAA action occurred simultaneously in Kansas City, which included "record-breaking crowds, hair-raising action, and widely diverging types of basketball." Indeed, 17,571 fans came to Municipal Auditorium over two nights to set a new record, even though this two-night total remained less than every one-night total at Madison Square Garden. Wyoming and Texas tangled in the opener. The Cowboys held a 3-point lead at halftime but the Longhorns—a squad that had not played a game in sixteen days—tied the score with two minutes left and, after intercepting a late pass, scored the decisive basket to win, 42–40. Oklahoma and Oregon State produced a similarly thrilling finish. The Sooners held the Beavers at bay in an uncomfortable 56–54 victory despite the presence of 150 zealous Oregon State students who made the trek to the Garden City. The Oklahoma-Texas final pitted teams from opposite banks of the Red River who played widely different styles of basketball. On the one hand, the Sooners employed a deliberate offense and a strong defense. The Longhorns, on the other hand, "were thought by many to be the fastest team in basketball" during the season while utilizing a fast-breaking style. Slater Martin, the Longhorn who made the game-winning shot the previous night, paced Texas with 18 points and helped the team enjoy a lead throughout most of the game. However, future Olympian Gerald Tucker kept his Sooners close with 15 points. With the Longhorns up by one late in the game, Oklahoma's Ken Pryor scored his only points of the game by nailing a "side court shot" to give the Sooners a 55–54 victory. The exciting Western Regional made close to $17,000.[62]

As the Sooners traveled to New York City for the NCAA championship game, the National Invitation tournament crowned its champion. On Monday, March 24, Utah and Kentucky squared off in a rematch of the fateful 1944 first-round invite game in which the Wildcats sent the Utes packing back to Kansas City where they won the NCAA Western Regional before traveling back to the Big Apple to win the NCAA championship and

Red Cross game. Since then, Kentucky had established itself as a perennial powerhouse team. In Dixie and its Southeastern Conference, the Wildcats were nothing short of dominant.[63]

Kentucky's hardcourt success encouraged the *New York Times*'s Arthur Daley to list Wildcat basketball alongside "fast horses, strong whiskey, and fine tobacco" as the Bluegrass State's most popular cultural exports. Coach Rupp, the orchestrator of the basketball team's rise to prominence "is more heavily loaded than a moonshiner's shotgun." Nicknamed "the Colonel," Rupp "reminds you of the Joe McCarthy of old." Because of his dominance, most coaches avoided scheduling his teams. However, Daley sympathized with the Southeastern Conference foes that had to face him every year. The journalist reported sarcastically that, in that season's Southeastern Conference tournament, Kentucky "edged out Vanderbilt in the first round, 98–29; barely beat Auburn in the semi-final, 84–14; and virtually had the blind staggers in nosing out Georgia Tech in the final, 75–53."[64]

Daley relayed a story that revealed the Southeastern Conference's jealousy toward Kentucky. Tennessee football coach General Bob Neyland—a highly successful coach in his own right—sat in the stands watching a Tennessee-Kentucky basketball game. The normally reserved general began cheering his school on with fervor. The woman seated one row back commented to Neyland about his demonstrative favor, saying, "My, but you certainly are for Tennessee, aren't you?" Neyland's reply was, "Madam, I'm for everyone but Kentucky." This quote summed up the feeling among Southeastern Conference teams, but Neyland's remark became evermore amusing when the general found out he was speaking to "none other than Mrs. Adolph Rupp."[65]

Daley gave Utah a fighting chance against Kentucky in the National Invitation final, "but only if the Fairy Godmother still has a powerful lot of magic hidden away in her wand." The Cinderella analogies seemingly followed Utah wherever they went. In 1944, the team set the bar low with their first-round loss to Kentucky, making every subsequent victory seem like an upset. And the Utes' seemingly endless supply of late-game heroics in this tournament reaffirmed the parallels. Further, the roster of pale-skinned, blond-haired Mormon boys who teamed with the "cute" and short Japanese American Misaka, endeared fans to this team, further perpetuating the analogy.[66]

Metropolitan sportswriters indulged in plenty more analogies after Utah took down Rupp's men, 49–45, to win the tenth annual National Invitation title. "Midnight still was an hour away but the clock was wrong—as wrong as all the experts who predicted that Utah didn't have a chance against mighty Kentucky . . . last night," Louis Effrat reported, "for at 11 o'clock last night, the Utes, who back in 1944 were called the 'Cinderella team,' completed their upset victory over the Wildcats." Effrat continued, arguing that, "With this unexpected conquest of an all-powerful court aggregation . . . Utah's undermanned and certainly underestimated squad sealed for all time its right to exclusive ownership of the 'Cinderella' tag." Although Gardner and Ferrin paced the Utes with 15 points each, Misaka was the belle of the ball. The Japanese American "was a 'cute' fellow intercepting passes and making the night miserable for Kentucky." Misaka's defense won the day as he held Kentucky All-American and future Olympic point guard Ralph Beard to one point.[67]

Oklahoma and Holy Cross played to much less hyperbole and literary allusion the following night in the NCAA final. However, this game had an unexpected outcome, too. Holy Cross became the first Eastern team to win the NCAA championship since it had moved to New York City and the first East Coast team to ever win it. This elated the Eastern basketball establishment who had come to see the Crusaders as their own. This team of "orphans" had only a very small on-campus gymnasium, and so they played most home games in the Boston Garden or other public venues, thus endearing themselves to all of Beantown. And when they arrived in New York City and the locals realized that Kaftan and many other Crusaders hailed from the Big Apple, Coach Julian's troops won the hearts of the metropolitan fans.[68]

The Crusaders and Sooners clashed in a keen struggle "between beautifully coached quintets" that stayed close for most of the game, captivating the 18,445 court fans. Kaftan led the Crusaders and was equally matched by Sooner floor leader Tucker. In the end, Holy Cross shut down everyone but Tucker for a 58–47 victory and the ninth NCAA crown. Effrat, in his postgame column, mentioned that "The Crusaders had hoped to play Utah for the mythical national championship tomorrow night, but plans for such a meeting were dropped at dawn yesterday when the national invitation winners, who had upset Kentucky in the final Monday night, boarded a plane for home." Utah coach Peterson told the writer that his players had to get back to Utah for the upcoming term's course registration two days later. Utah and Holy Cross would share national championship honors in the eyes of many experts.[69]

At the end of three nights of NCAA basketball action in the Garden, the tournament brought in $114,807.73 in total receipts. This included ticket sales and $2,550 in the sale of broadcasting rights. After $27,723.51 in disbursements, the Eastern Regional and Final Game had a positive balance of $87,084.22, half of which went to the Garden as a rental fee. This $43,542.11

The 1947 NCAA champion Holy Cross team of "orphans." *Courtesy of College of Holy Cross Photo Archives.*

fee for a three-night event—putting the average nightly fee at just under $14,000—stood in stark contrast to the $3,280.22 that the NCAA paid to rent Kansas City's Municipal Auditorium for two nights. While the Garden City's rental fee was only a fraction of the Garden's, it also only allowed the NCAA to bring in a fraction of the ticket revenue. Of the $57,635.10 that the overall tournament profited, half went to the NCAA and half to the teams as prize money for their participation. Finalists Holy Cross and Oklahoma each received $4,500; semifinalists Texas and CCNY received $4,000 each; and the remaining four teams went home with $3,000.[70]

The National Invitation, in contrast, would have brought in more money in ticket sales and likely had lower disbursements because it was a locally rather than nationally run tournament. Over four nights, the MIBC event averaged 18,472 fans—nine more than the NCAA averaged in three nights at the Garden. The NCAA's two nights of action in Kansas City would have come close to equaling one night of action in the Garden and so the two tournaments'. receipts may have been very similar. However, the NCAA had to pay higher travel costs for its competing teams—more of which had to travel a greater distance to participate—and the NCAA footed the bill for its nationwide tournament and rules committees. Local officials who would have claimed only minimal expenses ran the National Invite. Financially, then, the two postseason events ran somewhat parallel courses. The NCAA had matched and even potentially outstretched the National Invitation in prestige and quality of competition, and now its cash prizes came close to matching the MIBC's.

Basketball's Second Olympic Year

The 1948 college basketball postseason came with added interest because it was an Olympic year. Basketball first entered the Olympic lineup in 1936. However, with the world at war, the 1940 and 1944 Olympic Games were canceled. So 1948 marked only the second official Olympic basketball tournament. The United States used a trial tournament to determine its 1936 Olympic basketball squad. Two AAU teams made the trial finals and were each able to send seven players to Berlin. In 1948, the American Olympic Committee decided on a similar format. Olympic Basketball Committee chairman Louis Wilke of Bartlesville, Oklahoma, chose Madison Square Garden to host an eight-team tournament to determine the roster of the Olympic squad. The AAU—believed by many across the country to have the best amateur basketball teams—received three tournament spots. The top three AAU teams after its national tournament would qualify to compete in the Garden. This representation had become a contentious issue between the NCAA and AAU.[71]

Wilke's home in Oklahoma certainly played a role in his viewpoints. Although publicly diplomatic, the chairman lived in a town that proudly boasted the top AAU team. The Phillips 66 Oilers, five-time defending AAU national champions at the time, presented a lineup of former college standouts that were hired—in the AAU model—by a company to work *and* play basketball for the company squad. The Phillips Oil company welcomed this arrangement, giving its basketball players low-stress supervisory jobs at the company that offered free time in the late afternoons for basketball practice and plenty of time off to travel to away games. The Phillips squad boasted a lineup featuring Gordon "Shorty" Carpenter from the 1945 Arkansas NCAA semifinalist team, rookie Gerald Tucker from the 1947 Oklahoma NCAA runner-up team, Jesse Renick from the 1940 Oklahoma A&M National Invitation squad, Lew Beck of the 1947 Oregon State NCAA tournament squad, R. C. Pitts of the 1941 Arkansas NCAA tournament team, and seven-foot Bob Kurland from the 1945 and 1946 NCAA championship squads. The Oilers were no less than a college all-star team and had strung together virtually unprecedented success.[72]

Wilke and his Olympic Basketball Committee also gave one bid to the National YMCA championship team. These four noncollegiate teams would square off in one half of the tournament bracket. Four college teams would play on the other side of the bracket, ensuring at least one collegiate and one noncollegiate team would reach the final game of the trials. The two finalists, then, would each provide five of its players for the Olympic roster. Since only one collegian was selected for the 1936 US squad, this trial tournament format pleased Kansas's Phog Allen and all the other college coaches who had lobbied hard for better collegiate representation.[73]

On the collegiate side of the Olympic Trials, Wilke and his committee again showed some geographic bias. Living in the American heartland where the NCAA and NAIB tournaments were best known, the NCAA tournament received two of the four slots. The 1948 NCAA champion and runner-up would play for Olympic representation. The NAIB champion and the National Invitation champion would also be admitted to the trials. This arrangement clearly promoted the NCAA as the top intercollegiate postseason basketball tournament. While Wilke's committee did include a New York City representative, most of the other members resided in areas in which many more teams had participated in the NCAA event rather than the National Invitation. The NCAA event had been geographically equitable since its inception in 1939, and this fairness was paying off. Most regions of the country saw the NCAA as the premier college basketball postseason event. The National Invitation tournament, while still likely the main event in New York City's vast market, did not have the backing of a national organization that promoted anything other than basketball. Further, Wilke and his committee—as ardent proponents of amateurism in its staunchest forms—may still have had some lingering resentment over the Metropolitan Basketball Writers' Association profiting from the original National Invitation tournaments.

The National Invitation tournament, run by the newly renamed Metropolitan Intercollegiate Basketball Association (MIBA)—could not have been excited that the NCAA event received two Olympic Trials slots. Yet it must have been somewhat proud to receive one bid. The NAIB, on the other hand, was thrilled to have even one spot reserved in New York City. Emil Liston said as much in personal correspondence to his closest friends. And yet the Kansas City event almost lost its representation.

The NAIB's Quick Policy Change

Liston, in putting on his annual thirty-two-team tournament, attempted to breach the basketball-heavy New York City market for his event in 1948. In doing so, he invited LIU, Manhattan College, and Siena College. All three declined, but LIU and Manhattan did so publicly because of the NAIB's all-white racial policy. In fact, while Manhattan had an all-white team it took a stand on moral grounds. The student body got wind of the NAIB's racial exclusion and petitioned the college's administration to decline the invite because racial exclusion was antithetical to Catholic ideals. Mal Eiken, University of Buffalo basketball coach and chairman of the NAIB's New York/New Jersey district, voiced local concerns. "I will suggest that we don't send a representative from this district" unless the policy is rescinded, he proclaimed, adding that, "as long as Manhattan and Siena (and LIU) have taken this stand it's likely others would do the same."[74]

When Olympic Basketball Committee member Harry Henschel—a businessman from New York City—got wind of the reason for these rejections, he sought to eject the NAIB from representation in the trials. Henschel, who did not have any explicit connection to the MIBA, might have been acting in part on the collective consciousness of New York City's basketball establishment. This consciousness would have felt strongly about two things: that a racially exclusive basketball tournament is weak and unjust, and that the National Invitation held a less than ideal position within the Olympic Trials format. Its one spot made it an equal to the NAIB that any New Yorker would have claimed was inferior to the National Invitation. If the NAIB lost its roster spot, the National Invitation runner-up would be the most natural replacement, giving it equal representation to the NCAA—the tournament it believed was much more its equal.[75]

Indiana State's coach John Wooden found himself in the middle of the NAIB's racial policy, too. Liston offered the Sycamores a bid for the second straight year. This time, without much public discussion, Indiana State accepted, indicating nebulously that the team would take ten of its twelve players. Indeed, the Sycamores' lone African American, Clarence Walker, was not initially allowed to play. This would have been the second time that Wooden took his team on the road without Walker so as to abide by Jim Crow policies.[76]

With all of this publicity and the threat of losing representation in the Olympic Trials, Liston had to act quickly. He phoned or telegraphed his seven-member executive committee a day before they were supposed to embark on their journeys to Kansas City for an immediate "telegraphic" vote on the racial ban. Liston offered his thoughts that the ban should be dropped, and his colleagues followed suit, voting 6–1 to drop the ban. Liston explained that the policy had been discussed at the previous year's executive meeting but no action had been taken. Thus, Liston also had the issue on the docket for the 1948 meeting that would precede the tournament championship game. However, "the telegraphic poll was made to expedite matters," Liston reported. After the vote, Manhattan accepted their bids, LIU stayed out of the tournament, Indiana State's Walker would be allowed to play, and the NAIB retained its Olympic Trials representation.[77]

John Wooden's Sycamores made the most of their opportunity to play in this postseason event. In front of an average of nearly 9,000 fans per day—a new NAIB record—Indiana State almost completed a storybook ending. Walker, a sophomore at the time who, in the words of his coach, "showed great promise," did not see the floor much in the tournament. Yet this integrated squad made an immediate impact, reaching the finals and losing to a Louisville squad that never would have thought to enter the event only a few years earlier. A larger school with a recognizable name, Louisville proved that the NAIB was becoming more popular. No longer were only small, private, midwestern schools competing. Louisville would eventually become a blue blood of college basketball. And yet in this 1948 event, Indiana State gave it all it could handle in the NAIB championship.[78]

Competition for NCAA and National Invitation Bids

A number of schools had established themselves as perennial powers with name recognition that would draw well. Many of these teams were highly sought after by the postseason events that occurred in New York City. Therefore, competition for teams between the NCAA and National Invitation tournament grew. The MIBA sent out a few of its bids before any NCAA district had selected its teams most years, and 1948 was no exception. On February 27, St. Louis, Western Kentucky, and Texas accepted bids to the New York invite. The Billikins and Hilltoppers were not big-name teams, but had established traditions of excellence at their relatively small campuses. Therefore, the large New York City lights enticed them and gave their schools national visibility. Texas, on the other hand, was a big name. Leonard Lewin of the *New York Daily Mirror* provided three reasons why the Longhorns showed promise in the event: "(1) they're from Texas; (2) they were the best rootin' tootin' foul-shootin' bunch of hombres in the nation and (3) they never had lost a Garden game in four appearances." The Longhorns finished second in the Southwestern Conference a year after it had won the league with an undefeated record. The MIBA was happy to host a team from such a large and prominent conference.[79]

The North Carolina State Wolfpack accepted a bid to the National Invitation the following day. With a team of mostly freshmen and sophomores, Coach Everett Case had turned the program around very quickly. "North Carolina State is a southern basketball team with a northern exposure," Sid Friedlander of the *New York Post* reminded locals of the Wolfpack team that was entering the National Invite for the second straight season, "The odor of jasmine and honeysuckle comes out of the bottle only and the flavor of cornpone and chitlins is strictly ersatz." DePaul, LaSalle, and Bowling Green each accepted bids in the following days, too. Both DePaul and Bowling Green had been mainstays in the Garden over the past few seasons with their dominant big men who had since graduated. LaSalle, however, was new to the event and brought the interests of Philadelphia's prominent basketball establishment to New York City. However, the National Invitation scored the most publicity points by roping NYU into its event. The Lavender, one of the four big teams in the Big Apple, enjoyed an outstanding season. This was not unusual, but NYU's entrance into the MIBA event was. The Lavender had been faithful to the NCAA event since it began, playing in both the 1942 and 1946 tournaments.[80]

NYU's acceptance of a National Invitation bid did not exclude it from the NCAA tournament, though. A local metropolitan team would have little trouble playing in both the National Invitation and the NCAA Eastern Regional events. Yet with an 18-1 record, Columbia University received the NCAA's District 2 bid. With so many good teams in the district, the selection committee likely opted against NYU to give another highly successful squad a chance at postseason play. Defending champion Holy Cross won the bid in District 1, Big Ten champion Michigan received the honors in District 4, and Kentucky won the District 3 bid. The Wildcats' entrance in the NCAA tournament was a major victory for the association. Coach Rupp's squad had entered three of the last four National Invitations and won the championship in 1946 with a young team that many also considered the best in the country for much of the 1946–47 season. With every regular from that 1946 championship team still on the roster, many considered Kentucky the best team in the country yet again. The Wildcats' entrance in the NCAA tournament naturally offset any disappointment the association would have had when NYU announced it was entering the National Invitation field.[81]

Out west, Kansas State entered the tournament for the first time, joining 1943 champion Wyoming, Baylor, and Washington. Baylor entered the event as the Southwestern Conference's champion. Baylor star Jackie Robinson, a "20-year old ordained Baptist minister," was "one of the greatest high school players ever to participate in a Lone Star State tournament." Since the National Invitation included no teams from west of Texas, Wyoming and Washington became the only teams from their respective regions participating in either of the two major postseason tournaments.[82]

Wyoming's entrance came with complications. Brigham Young won the Mountain States Conference title and, while most pundits had them slotted for the NCAA tournament, the Cougars unfortunately found out at season's end that they had an ineligible player by NCAA standards. Thus, they accepted an invite to the NAIB and lost to Wooden's Indiana State Sycamores in the second round. The Mountain States Conference found a logjam at second place, a position shared by Denver, Wyoming, and Utah. The Pioneers also entered Liston's event, leaving two possibilities left for the NCAA District 7 bid. NCAA tournament director Dutch Lonborg telegraphed Utah on March 8 that it would engage in a play-off game against Wyoming on Saturday, March 13, in Boulder, Colorado, to determine the district's representative. However, Lonborg's communication with both schools broke down, and Wyoming declined an invite to the play-off game. District 7 then chose Wyoming as its representative on March 9, citing its strong late-season performances, including a victory over Utah. The Utes protested this decision to the NCAA president, Dr. Karl Leib of Iowa, stating that the decision was "inconsistent and unfair."[83]

Utah coach Vadal Peterson reacted with disappointment: "If the N.C.A.A. had picked Wyoming to start with I wouldn't have objected. But to arrange a play off in which Wyoming declined to participate and then invite Wyoming anyway—well, I think we have a kick coming." Clearly, Utah had a point. Wyoming, obviously elated at the committee's choice, reacted diplomatically. Athletic director Glen Jacoby offered no comment on Utah's protest, but remarked, "It is unfortunate that a play-off could not have been arranged between Wyoming and Utah." His rationale for this proposed Saturday event was thin: "Both schools because of academic reasons primarily found it impossible to agree on a mutual play-off date." Utah's protest was "rebuffed," as the NCAA cited that the District 7 selection committee and tournament director Lonborg acted well within association policy in their decision.[84]

The National Invitation Pits Two Cities in the Finals

The MIBA invitational tournament opened on Thursday, March 11. Western Kentucky, seeded in the number-one spot ahead of local favorite NYU, defeated LaSalle, 68–61. However, the "burly" Hilltoppers were less than impressive in a "ragged game that saw both sides suffer from nervousness." Fourth-seed St. Louis provided the best performance of the evening. Future NBA star "Easy" Ed Macauley led the Billikens to a 69–53 victory over Bowling Green. The Falcons, in their first National Invitation appearance since the graduation of center Don Otten, could not get past the first round despite the efforts of Mac Otten, Don's younger brother. A less-than-capacity crowd of 17,147 attended these games.[85]

Two nights later, another prominent younger brother had more success. DePaul's Ed Mikan took over where his older brother George had left off, scoring 23 points in the Blue Demon's 75–64 win over North Carolina State. The younger Mikan set a tournament record by netting eleven free throws in the game, and his team set a record by making twenty-three charity attempts. The 18,467 fans delighted in the result of the other contest that evening. Second-seed NYU snatched a victory from Texas. Down 4 with just less than two minutes remaining, NYU fouled Texas star Slater Martin. Basketball rules at the time stated that, if fouled, a team could choose to shoot free throws or take the ball out of bounds. Normally in this situation, a team with the lead would choose the latter option, but the Longhorns were "rootin', tootin', foul-shootin' hombres." Texas coach Jack Gray wanted the points his star would presumably make at the charity stripe. When Martin missed, NYU had the opportunity it needed. Violet star guard Ray Lumpp fed star forward Adolph Schayes for a basket and, five seconds later, Lumpp stole the ball back and fed teammate Fred Benanti for the tying bucket. Four unsuccessful possessions ensued before NYU reserve Dick Kor scored the game-winning field goal with only six ticks left on the clock for the win, 45–43.[86]

Lumpp continued his strong efforts in the Monday, March 15, semifinals. The guard scored 29 points in the Violets' 72–59 semifinal victory in front of 18,478, overcoming a 20-point effort from the younger Mikan brother. In the other semifinal, Macauley was a "remarkable feeder" to his St. Louis teammates but "still found time to be the high scorer, with 19 points" in a win over the tournament's top-seeded Western Kentucky. St. Louis and New York then squared off in the finals on Wednesday, March 17, for the National Invitation crown and a cherished spot in the Olympic Basketball Trial tournament. In front of 18,491 fans St. Louis displayed "the value of sound, fundamental basketball" in a 65–52 victory over the local squad. "The most talented college basketball team seen here in many a season" enjoyed another outstanding performance by Macauley, who registered 24 points in the win.[87]

The nature of the college basketball scheduling in the Garden that month provided a long break for the National Invitation champion before the Olympic Trials. So after the victory, St. Louis headed back west. Since the Billikens would have to wait for a week and a half before the trials started, Coach Ed Hickey made no promise that his team would return to the Big Apple for a chance to win the Olympic Trial tournament. After all, the top two teams in the trials would only provide five players each to the American contingent. This meant that, if St. Louis was to participate, it would be doing so for the possibility of sending only its starters to the Olympic Games. Hickey mentioned that his players' studies might keep his team from returning. Meanwhile, NYU, who stood to earn the berth if St. Louis defected, lay in wait.[88]

A Ho-Hum Event Shows Kentucky's Class

The night after St. Louis's championship, the NCAA tournament opened in the Garden. Overall favorite Kentucky made easy work out of Ivy League champion Columbia. The Lions, playing in their first postseason event, provided no match for Rupp's squad. The Wildcat trio of All-Americans— Wallace Jones, Alex Groza, and Ralph Beard—scored 21, 17, and 15 points, respectively, to lead their team. In the other opener, a seasoned Holy Cross squad with a coach, Alvin Julian, who seemed at his best in March, made Michigan's entrance into postseason play less than ideal. Flashy sophomore point guard Bob Cousy led the Crusaders with 23 points while star forward George Kaftan added 15 in a victory.[89]

The Garden hosted the Eastern finals on Saturday, March 20. Holy Cross and Kentucky both brought a great deal of tournament experience to the matchup. However, Kentucky had a major edge in height and took advantage. A total of 18,472 fans jammed in to watch a set of fast-breaking teams race against each other. The Kentuckians, in the end, found more success. Jones, Groza, and Beard scored 12, 23, and 13 to outshine Holy Cross's stars. Kaftan tallied 15 but Cousy scored only 5 in an unusually poor shooting display.[90]

Kentucky stayed in the Big Apple, awaiting the champion of the Western Regional, hosted in Kansas City that same weekend. On Friday, March 19, a sellout crowd of 9,700 fans packed Municipal Auditorium for the opening night's action—many of whom were pulling for the "home" team from Kansas State. The Wildcats won their first-ever Big Six conference title and created a wave of crowd support in Kansas City. However, the Baylor Bears showed championship grit by taking down the favored and heavily supported Wildcats, 60–52. In the Western finals, Baylor faced a Washington team that had overcome Everett Shelton's inexperienced Wyoming squad

Kentucky's Ralph Beard drives for a lay-up at the Garden. *Courtesy of University of Kentucky Special Collections Research Center.*

in the first round, 57–47. Baylor overcame a ten-minute first-half scoring drought to eventually overtake Washington in the Western final, 64–62, in a game also played to a capacity crowd. The two-night total of 19,400 spectators set a new tournament record, finally out-drawing in two nights what the Garden regularly attracted in one.[91]

Baylor took its contingent east for a Tuesday, March 23, East-West NCAA Final against Kentucky. If Baylor won, Texas newspapermen reported, Coach Rupp could "take a bow." The Kentucky mentor had spent considerable time leading coaching clinics in the Lone Star State over the previous few years and the Texas basketball establishment knew it was indebted. "Baylor backers won't be surprised if they lick Kentucky anyway." The relatively listless action in Kansas City, however, made this result seem unlikely. Accordingly, only 16,174 came out for the action in New York City in what may have been the saturation point for college basketball in the Garden—the Olympic Trials alongside the MIBA and NCAA events may have given fans too much. The faithful saw an NCAA championship game that followed the speculation. The Kentucky squad "thoroughly outclassed" the Texas team in the victory. Only once did Baylor reach within 9 points of Kentucky in the second half of a 58–42 Wildcat victory. Kentucky's emerging star junior center Alex Groza led the team with 14 points and was named the tournament's most valuable player. Groza, "whose head seemed to threaten the mezzanine every time he outjumped a Baylor man," also took over on the glass, as "he sucked in rebounds like a vacuum cleaner." The tournament's overall Garden attendance of 53,123 in three nights put its nightly average below 18,000—less than it had been one year prior.[92]

This drop in attendance concerned the NABC and the NCAA basketball tournament committee. Net receipts from the Kansas City regional reached an all-time high at $18,501.57 coming solely from ticket and program sales. The Western Regional had not tapped into any possible income from selling the games' broadcasting rights for this season. Uncertain attendance figures at this venue made promoting radio broadcasts a potential box office drawback. The amount of fans listening on the radio would affect the regional's bottom line and would potentially take fans away from Municipal Auditorium.[93]

The NABC and NCAA tournament committee's major concerns were with Madison Square Garden. Ticket sales had gone down slightly from 1947, but the broadcasting rights sales continued to jump. For the 1948 event, the NCAA negotiated $4,075 from local radio stations to broadcast the New York games. This put the New York net profits at $40,199.43— just above what they were in 1947. The tournament's overall balance of

$62,753.34 also edged the previous season's total by about $2,000. But the decrease in growth concerned tournament administrators. Of particular concern was the growing rental fee at Madison Square Garden. Ned Irish and his facility took home $40,199.42 for hosting three nights of games. Ten percent of that—or $4,019.94—went directly into Irish's pocket. That substantial sum represented more than what four of the eight participating teams received as participation prizes. The NCAA listed first-round losers Michigan, Columbia, and Wyoming, along with Western runner-up Washington as having earned cash prizes of $3,137.67. In what may have been a clerical error, first-round loser Kansas State (as listed) and semifinalist Holy Cross took home $4,314.29 each while Baylor and Kentucky both earned $5,098.71.[94]

Therefore, when the NABC convened on March 24 in New York City, the tournament's host site became a major discussion point. Among other prominent issues, NABC members discussed possible sites for the 1949 tournament. New York City had hosted since 1943 and Kansas City had hosted since 1940. Change in venue, then, was not a customary item for this tournament. However, NCAA executives believed the time was ripe for variation. Even though attendance went down in New York City—attendance also dipped slightly for the National Invitation event—the NCAA believed its tournament was still growing. National appeal was up, and so the association sought a different venue for the final game. Dutch Lonborg, tournament committee chair, provided evidence of "a bright picture of player and public interest in the post-season games." The Northwestern coach was given the autonomy to choose a site, but the NCAA brass requested that he and his colleagues "consider a plan calling for rotation of the Final Game among various sections of the country."[95]

Venue change had been on the NCAA's radar even before the 1948 tournament. Association president Karl Leib of Iowa announced in January of that year that his organization had an "ardent desire to take basketball tournaments back to the campuses of the member institutions." Up until this point, "off-campus competition had been necessary to raise funds," but "as soon as some of the colleges complete new and larger field houses, the games would be taken from the hands of private promotional outfits such as the Garden." The NCAA had used the Garden out of necessity. Irish's venue helped the NCAA tournament through a very tenuous time, and allowed it to grow. The tournament may not have survived the war had it not moved to New York City. However, the Garden was "practically an even interest partner in the venture" by receiving 50 percent of the net receipts as rent.[96]

Leib and Lonborg's decision to seek change also stemmed from "the scandalous rumblings attached to big-time basketball promotions by private interests." Organizers of amateur athletics continued to bristle at this most primal reason for the NCAA's inception of its basketball tournament. It had wanted college basketball's postseason out of the hands of private promoters. And yet it had sought Ned Irish and his venue, reaping great financial and status rewards in the process. But the NCAA believed it had grown large enough to stand on its own legs. Thus, the NCAA leaders "intimated that a smaller income (now) would be preferable to the scandal now attached to private promotion."[97]

More Racial Issues, and the Olympic Trials

The moral priorities of the association's leaders remained complex, for just as the organization sought purity in its venues, another moral issue reared its head. Lonborg read a letter "from representatives of several prominent Colored Colleges asking that tournament administration be altered so that their teams could participate in the games." By this time, historically black colleges and universities had established quite a basketball establishment along the eastern corridor of the country. These schools remained, like segregated local school districts, impoverished compared to their white or majority-white state-funded peers. And their basketball programs were no different. However, many coaches at these "Colored Colleges" believed that their teams could compete with the best in the nation. In the early 1940s, these coaches lamented their neglect from Ned Irish and the MIBC. Irish responded that he did not choose the teams. He also implied that the teams chosen for the Garden event had as much to do with their drawing power as anything. In other words, the tournament selection committee invited the teams that had the best chance of filling the arena. Historically black colleges and universities, Irish believed, likely could not do this.[98]

So the attention of these coaches turned to the NCAA event. With its regional basis, the NCAA's acceptance of a historically black college would be complex. Many of these schools resided in the South where Jim Crow still reigned. In NCAA jargon, this was District 3. None of the NCAA teams in District 3 were integrated at this time, and very few had even played against black players. Further, the district selection committee was comprised of white coaches from the region. So black colleges had very little chance of ever being selected for the event—especially with the likes of Kentucky and North Carolina State faring so well in recent postseason play.

The mid- to late 1940s saw a major wave of racial barrier busting in American sport, and basketball was no exception. By 1948, each of the three postseason tournaments had become integrated, and this year marked another major milestone in the integration of amateur basketball. The 1948 Olympic Basketball Trial tournament, held in New York City immediately after the 1948 NABC convention, featured one integrated squad. The Oakland Bittners from California, by virtue of a runner-up finish at the AAU National Tournament, received a spot in the noncollegiate side of the tournament bracket. Don Barksdale, a fiendishly athletic yet undersized center who had become the first African American All-American while playing for UCLA in 1946 and 1947, led the Bittners into New York City. Although his team struggled, Barksdale impressed the metropolitan crowd in the Bittners' first-round exit from the event. Former two-time NCAA champion Bob Kurland's Phillips 66 Oilers, five-time reigning AAU champs, won the noncollegiate side of the bracket.[99]

On the college side, NCAA finalists Kentucky and Baylor qualified alongside NAIB champion Louisville. National Invitation winner St. Louis declined their offer because the school would not allow its players to miss more classes from another trip to New York City. A six-man committee on the Billikens' campus determined that the twelve-day voyage to New York City for the National Invite represented enough missed class time for star Ed Macauley and his teammates. Therefore, National Invitation runner-up NYU filled their spot. Baylor took down local NYU in front of a season-low Garden attendance of 9,251, and Kentucky beat Louisville in front of 15,927 fans in the other night of opening-round action. Then Kentucky outlasted Baylor in the finals. The victory gave Kentucky two important things: a spot in the trials final, which meant that five of their players and their coach would go to London, and the official nod as the season's top college basketball team. Since the Red Cross "national championship" game was a relic of the past, no other means of determining an overall champion through head-to-head play had developed. This Olympic event had become a de facto championship face-off in the college basketball world. And Kentucky showed that they were far and away the best college team in the country—especially since St. Louis declined its invitation. At the end of Rupp's record-setting career, he remarked that this group "was the greatest basketball team of all time."[100]

In the Olympic Trials final, Kentucky put up a good fight but eventually lost to the Phillips squad before 18,475 spectators. The starters for both teams received spots on the Olympic roster along with both coaches. Phillips coach Omar "Bud" Browning would be the head coach and Rupp would be the assistant. The Olympic Basketball committee then met behind closed doors to select two collegiate and two noncollegiate players from the participating teams to fill out a fourteen-player roster. From the college ranks,

Lexington's Union Station welcomes back the Wildcats after the championship 1948 season. *Courtesy of University of Kentucky Special Collections Research Center.*

the committee chose Baylor's Jackie Robinson—the white, long-limbed and defensive-minded forward—and NYU guard Ray Lumpp, who had come on with strong postseason performances. From the noncollegiate teams, the committee chose Vince Boryla—a peripatetic forward who had played two seasons at Notre Dame before joining the AAU's Denver Nuggets for a season and then finishing his college eligibility at the University of Denver before a long NBA career—and Barksdale. Barksdale's inclusion meant that the Kentucky players and coach who represented Dixie's NCAA district and eventually came to be a symbol of the South, would have to team with an African American to represent the stars and stripes abroad. After a contentious series of exhibition games played during the summer in the Jim Crow states of Oklahoma and Kentucky, the team set off for London and won the gold medal without much opposition from other squads and without any overt racial tension from within.[101]

The Greatest Team of All Time

The 1949 season commenced with a number of key organizational changes to the postseason of college basketball. But one thing remained the same—Kentucky had a strong claim to the title of nation's best team. The Wildcats returned Groza, Beard, and Jones—their three All-Americans—and Rupp kept the talent pipeline flowing with the most outstanding prospects from the Bluegrass State and its neighbors. Rupp also benefited from an influx of veterans eager to show the Baron that military service had only increased their abilities. Two of them—Dale Barnstable and Jim Line—figured prominently in the 1948–49 lineup after a few other veterans graduated in 1948. Barnstable and Line supported the three stars, each of whom had his own unusual matriculation story.[102]

Rupp called Beard "the most terrific competitor of all time" in which no one "tried harder to be a great basketball player." The guard almost enrolled at Western Kentucky, but joined Jones at Lexington after the two struck up a friendship during a high school all-star game. Jones, "a rough, tough competitor who never backed off from anybody," according to his coach, "was quick and intelligent, and he had the size and weight to demand respect under the boards." Jones and Beard began their Kentucky careers on football scholarships. The former enjoyed an outstanding gridiron career while the latter quit in his freshman year from shoulder injuries and even filled out paperwork to begin the process of transferring to Louisville before deciding to stay.[103]

Groza, on the contrary, never had interest in playing college football, even though it was in his blood. His older brother Lou played offensive line and kicker at Ohio State before the war and enjoyed a Hall of Fame career afterward. Groza the younger, "who could hold his own with any center in the country at any time," wanted to follow his brother to Columbus but decided on Kentucky when the Buckeyes failed to show any interest. Groza had started at Kentucky a year before Beard and Jones. But Uncle Sam required his services midway through his freshman season and, eighteen months later, he returned to join their class.[104]

After a string of early season victories in December of 1948 for this Odyssean crew, Rupp's charges slipped up in the Sugar Bowl basketball game in New Orleans to St. Louis. The Billikens, who had won the previous season's National Invitation tournament and then declined an Olympic Trials bid, put a bit of doubt in the basketball establishment that Kentucky was the top team in the country. Without a victory over St. Louis in the past two seasons, the press saw Kentucky as the second-best team. Indeed, the weekly national rankings compiled by the Associated Press listed the Billikens first and the Wildcats second for the first three weeks of January 1949. After a St. Louis loss to third-ranked Oklahoma A&M, Kentucky finally overtook the Gateway City squad.[105]

Coach Rupp believed he had the top team in all of college basketball, and he seemed intent on making sure everyone knew it. So after his team's loss to St. Louis—the only regular season loss for the Wildcats—he publicly stated his interest in entering both the NCAA and National Invitation tournaments. St. Louis accepted an invite on March 1 from the MIBA to play in the New York City event and Rupp accepted his the following day. He had unfinished business with the Billikens that could be settled in the finals of the New York tournament. And, as defending champions of the NCAA event, he readily accepted District 3's representation in that tournament, too. By entering both events, the *New York Times* noted, "The N.I.T.-N.C.A.A. 'double' has been attempted before, but never with premeditation." Utah had done so in 1944, entering the National Invitation and then filling in for an incapacitated Arkansas squad after losing in New York City's first round. However, the *Times* had forgotten about the 1940 postseason in which Colorado won the New York event before losing in the first round of the NCAA's Western Regional and Duquesne made the New York finals before losing in the NCAA semifinals.[106]

Talking about the "double" tournament championships that Kentucky sought gave sportswriters reason to begin calling the New York City tournament by its initials. Metropolitan daily newspapers had always referred to the National Invitation by its full name—while utilizing the generic lower-case spelling of the word "tournament"—or calling it the New York invite or simply the invitational tournament. Yet when referring to Kentucky's attempt to win two tournaments, describing the "NIT-NCAA double" seemed far more practical, catchy, and alliterative than using the "NIT's" full name and only the NCAA's initials. The condensed nickname caught on over time.[107]

The NIT's New York Massacre

On March 3, Bradley and Western Kentucky joined St. Louis and Kentucky as NIT entrants. Utah accepted a bid two days later, with the University of San Francisco and CCNY accepting on March 8. The inclusion of CCNY with its unimpressive 17-7 record raised many eyebrows across the basketball world. The MIBA selection committee indicated five days earlier that it would invite two local teams to the event, but CCNY provided little indication of its quality in poor showings late in the season. Ned Irish felt the need to respond to criticism of tournament selection: "It has been reported that I used influence to get the committee to name two local teams in order to help ticket sales." He followed by stating, "The fact is that if I had an influence at all it would have been used the other way—getting out-of-town teams into the tournament. I did not attend any of the committee's meetings."[108]

With all of the criticism of CCNY's selection and one bid still to give, the selection committee made a last-minute decision to extend the tournament field to twelve teams. The committee added Loyola of Chicago, Bowling Green of Ohio, and three local teams—NYU, St. John's, and Manhattan—to its brackets. "Certainly, the committee's action was a surprise," Louis Effrat commented, but "the naming of four metropolitan fives was a *complete* surprise" (emphasis added). The relatively poor records of the usually dominant metropolitan teams demonstrated what looked like a watered-down NIT field. CCNY's 17-7 record made them the top local choice, followed by Manhattan and NYU with seven losses and St. John's with eight. San Francisco came into the tourney with five losses and Bradley had six, so the seven and eight losses were not statistical outliers, but experts had noted all season long that metropolitan teams "did not . . . rate representation in the tournament at all."[109]

This tournament extension meant that the schedule would change for game times, although only slightly. NIT games were originally scheduled with quarterfinals on Saturday, March 12, and Monday, March 14, semi-finals on Thursday, March 17, and finals on Saturday the 19th. The addition of four teams meant that four more games would be included on the docket. The new schedule would feature four games instead of two on Saturday, March 12, in what would now be first-round action. The four winners would advance to the quarterfinals on Monday, March 14. Those four games, like the docket on Saturday, would include two in the afternoon matinee session and two in the evening. The semifinals would remain on Thursday and the finals on Saturday.[110]

The MIBA selection committee seeded the top four teams who would receive byes in the first round and wait until Monday for their first action. Kentucky, St. Louis, Utah, and Western Kentucky got to sit in the stands and scout their opponents in the tournament's initial action. Each of the four local teams was paired with a "favored" visiting team for Saturday's first-round action. Local predictions became reality as all four metropolitan teams lost on opening night in what local fans referred to as the "New York Massacre."[111]

The round of eight followed without a local team for the first time in the NIT's twelve-year history. And, unfortunately, local interest took a dive. But the competition in Monday's four matches did not suffer. Even though a meager 12,592 fans came to the afternoon double-header and 15,587 attended at night, four upsets thrilled the loyal customers. The four unseeded teams that had knocked out the local quartet on Saturday continued their winning ways by unseating all four seeded teams. The Kentucky and St. Louis losses were especially shocking. Both teams came into the event looking unstoppable. Their matchup in the finals seemed inevitable. Coach Rupp took the loss especially hard, stewing over the game in his hotel room until 2 a.m. He kept telling himself, "There's something wrong with this team. I tell them what to do and, dammit, they won't do it." The ultracompetitive "Baron of the Bluegrass" knew that his was a special team. With Groza, Jones, and Beard providing senior leadership and unmatched talent, he thought his team was invincible. Only the 2-point loss to St. Louis over the holidays had tripped his squad, and he believed that was a fluke. Unfortunately, Loyola proved otherwise, and he would not get the chance to avenge the St. Louis loss.[112]

In Thursday's semifinal round, the crowds returned to the Garden; 18,301 fans greased the turnstiles to see San Francisco take on Bowling Green and Loyola square off against Bradley. Unfortunately, "the finesse, tenseness, and over-all excellence that had been looked for were missing" from these games. San Francisco's win over the Ohio squad surprised many. The Dons held the Falcons to 39 points in a 10-point victory. The Loyola-Bradley outcome was no surprise, though. Every member of Loyola's team hailed from Chicago in this all-Illinois contest, and the Windy City Boys got the best of their down-state brethren. Two nights later, San Francisco—"not a great team, but certainly one that ranks among the slickest in the nation"— took home the tournament title. Coach Pete Newell led an inspired group of players to a one-point come-from-behind victory in front of a Saturday, March 19, crowd of 18,297. This total, while around 200 short of the tournament's peak, showed that interest remained high even for an unseeded and out-of-town final matchup.[113]

With two of the four NIT Garden dates—the opening night and the finale—coming on a Saturday, Ned Irish appeared willing to provide the college basketball postseason with prime scheduling. The two tournaments in New York City had originally been allowed to use the facility only in evenings in which the Garden was available. The circus, ice skating exhibitions, hockey, professional basketball, and any other type of indoor exhibition would fill the Garden schedule, leaving only certain days for college basketball. But as the tournaments grew in popularity, Irish seemed to prioritize the game at the Garden. Indeed, college basketball had slowly eclipsed every event outside of boxing at the prized venue.

A Bradley player shoots a free throw in the Braves' National Invitation consolation game against Bowling Green. *Courtesy of University of Kentucky Special Collections Research Center.*

The NCAA Moves Out

After Saturday's NIT final, the NCAA Eastern Regional filled New York's spacious venue on Monday and Tuesday, March 21 and 22. These dates were not ideal, but since the NCAA moved its East-West Final to Seattle and scheduled it for Saturday, March 26, there were no other options. This schedule also marked the first time that the Garden hosted NCAA games on back-to-back weeknights. Kansas City hosted the Western Regional yet again, and followed the Friday–Saturday format it had employed for years.[114]

Fan interest in the Western Regional continued to grow, and so did capacity at Kansas City's Municipal Auditorium. Although crowds had reached capacity the year before, 500 more fans crammed into the venue each night of this tourney to the tune of a 10,200 nightly average. The opening-round action was a tale of two games. Oklahoma A&M, a team accustomed to postseason success, barely overtook District 7 representative Wyoming on a last-second "spinning shot from under the basket" by forward Jack Shelton. The Missouri Valley Conference champion Aggies, who barely made it into the tournament with a close District 5 play-off win over Big Six conference co-champion Nebraska, knocked the Cowboys out 40–39. In the other opening-round game Oregon State had no trouble dismantling District 6 representative Arkansas. The Razorbacks, another team accustomed to the postseason, could not find their shooting touch in a 56–38 loss.[115]

The Saturday night final and consolation game showed a different side of each team. Arkansas, which looked so poor in the opener, manhandled Wyoming 61–40. The Razorbacks found their shooting touch and lit up the scoreboard. The Cowboys, then, who were only one point away from gaining a spot in the regional final, went home as the fourth-place team. In the final, Oklahoma A&M had no trouble defeating an Oregon State squad that look unbeatable just one night earlier. The final score of 55–30 was not even the largest separation the Aggies enjoyed that night. The Oklahomans hit on 47 percent of their shots from the field and 21 of 24 free throws. The Beavers tried everything to stop them including zone defense in the first half, man-to-man defense in the second half, and full squad substitutions, but nothing seemed to work. These two nights of action produced more than $18,000 of net profits, a figure that was almost two times the amount that the entire tournament made just nine years earlier.[116]

The NCAA Eastern Regional games in Madison Square Garden came with a great deal of hype for three individuals. Kentucky's Alex Groza, Villanova's Paul Arizin, and Yale's Tony Lavelli all averaged more than 20 points per game that season and starred in their teams' offenses. In the first round, Lavelli could not spark his team to victory over the much more socialized Illinois offense. Illinois came into the game as the Big Ten champion but, as the *Chicago Tribune* noted, that did not provide them with an automatic berth in the tournament. The Illini only got in because the normally outstanding independents in District 4—DePaul, Notre Dame, Marquette, and Loyola—had not enjoyed their usually dominant ways that season, even though Loyola was strong enough to garner a National Invitation bid and beat Kentucky. Nonetheless, Illinois's berth gave them the task of stopping Lavelli and his Ivy League teammates. The Eli did his best, scoring 27 points, but the Illini took a 71–67 victory with them into the Regional finals. Groza and the future pro Arizin put on quite a show in the second opening-round game. Both stars scored 30 points to lead their teams in a game played at a breakneck pace. The contest's 157 total points set the NCAA tournament record for most total markers in a game and Kentucky's 85 points set a single-team single-game record. Kentucky's 23 successful free throw attempts also set a one-game record. In the finals the next night, Groza paced the Wildcats with 27 points in a blowout victory over Illinois, 76–47. These two nights of action brought in $64,423.64 of gross ticket receipts and broadcasting rights sales of $2,995—less than the previous year because there was no championship game to broadcast locally. After paying expenses and 50 percent of its profits as a rental fee to the Garden, the Eastern Regional netted $25,797.68.[117]

The championship game hosted by the University of Washington at its Edmundson Pavilion admitted a sellout crowd of 12,500 fans, having to turn away many more to this Saturday, March 26, contest. The offensive-minded Kentucky Wildcats faced the defensive-minded Oklahoma A&M Aggies. Kentucky decided on a ball-control offense that would normally have played to the Aggies' favor. However, the Oklahomans were normally the team in control of the ball and found themselves a bit unsettled. Further, Coach Iba went away from his traditional sagging defense to an all-out man-to-man that many questioned afterward. Iba thought his center, Bob Harris, could shut Kentucky's Groza down. A tight man-to-man defense would then prevent Kentucky's other scoring threats from getting open looks.[118]

The Aggies did not score on the Wildcats for the first eight minutes and thirty-five seconds of the second half in the finals as Kentucky slowly built a 12-point lead. Harris fouled out during this time, making it much easier for Groza to score. Alex "The Nose" Groza netted 25 of his team's 46 points in a 10-point win and a second-straight NCAA championship. Coach Rupp, elated that his team had followed their NIT flop with a championship, stated, "It was a tough game all the way. We had to play this one the hard way, almost to the finish. We beat a good team and we're mighty happy about it." The Baron also remarked smugly, "I guess that's an answer to those guys who said Harris would stop (Groza)." Coach Iba, who seemed just as competitive as Rupp—and also as gruff when he lost—lamented, "We just had a bad night; we were away off on our shots." Aggie senior forward Vernon Yates, who guarded Jones, remembered, "what really won the game (for Kentucky) was the fact that we didn't sink back and help out," allowing Groza to have his way. Yates, guarding the other Kentucky big man, would have been the natural defender to help in Iba's normal sagging scheme.[119]

This one night of action produced $32,676 in ticket sales and $1,250 in radio and television broadcasting rights. After expenses, which included a mere $275 for the building and grounds rental, the final game produced $22,558.43 profit. The rental fee at Edmundson Pavilion was little more than 1 percent of what Madison Square Garden received for hosting the Eastern Regional. Overall, the 1949 NCAA tournament made $66,381.59. Half of the money went to the NCAA, and the other half was disbursed among the participating teams, averaging out to just less than $4,000 per team.[120]

The New College Basketball Postseason Landscape

While the NCAA decided to try a new venue for the finals of its growing tournament, the NAIB continued its growth without any major administrative changes. By the time of the 1949 NAIB tournament and convention, Emil Liston tallied 260 members in his association who came from forty-six states and the territory of Hawaii. The NCAA was also growing, and listed 381 members from forty-eight states by 1952. Further, Liston's tournament had hosted teams from thirty-six states. Neither the NCAA nor the NIT could match that total, mostly because they only hosted a fraction of the teams that participated in the NAIB.[121]

The thirty-two-team 1949 NAIB field included heightened excitement because the University of Hawaii, in trying to impress the NAIB brass, offered a fully paid trip to the Aloha State over the 1949 Christmas season for the NAIB champion. Hamline College of Minnesota and its star center, future NBA Hall of Famer Vern Mikkelsen, entered the event with the top seed. Although a number of teams came with individual stars, the *Kansas City Times* surmised "that it's Hamline against the field." With strong play from Mikkelsen and guard Hal Haskins throughout, Hamline took home the crown—and the Hawaii trip—with a culminating 57–46 win over Regis College of Denver.[122]

Little more than a week after Regis's Saturday, March 12, loss to Hamline, the Rangers hosted their own tournament that was new to the college basketball postseason slate. The Denver school hosted fifteen other teams to the new National Catholic Invitational tournament. The NCIT, or NCI tournament, came as a result of the many successful Catholic college and university basketball teams who did not receive bids to postseason action. The Catholic schools would have been ideal candidates for the NAIB event, but that tournament, although much broader in geographic scope now than when it began, still heavily favored schools in the heartland. Further, Liston's tournament was not well recognized outside of that region and other pockets across the country. Many of the country's Catholic schools resided outside the heavily Protestant heartland of America.[123]

Regis College invited fifteen of its Catholic peers from New York, Minnesota, Washington, Kansas, Iowa, Texas, Wisconsin, Ohio, Maryland, and Pennsylvania to compete for a new prize. From March 20 through the 26th, these Catholic schools competed in Denver while the NCAA tournament carried on in Kansas City, New York City, and Seattle. St. Francis College of New York ran through a litany of Holy Names—defeating St. Norbert's of Wisconsin, St. Thomas of Minnesota, and St. Benedict's of Kansas—to reach the tournament final and face the home team. Second-seeded Regis College came out on top 51–47.[124]

Although many games were poorly attended—even those featuring the host Rangers—the tournament was enough of a success that organizers thought it should continue in 1950. Loyola College in Baltimore offered to host. This school was arguably only the third most prominent Loyola campus across the country based on basketball recognition. Loyola of Chicago had twice participated in the NIT, finishing as semifinalists in 1939 and as runner-up in 1949. Loyola of New Orleans won the NAIB tournament in 1942. Unfortunately, Loyola of Baltimore's attempt to get on the basketball map by hosting the second annual NCIT fell through. Racial segregation that regulated public housing in Charm City would have prevented the integrated St. Francis of New York team from living together during the event. So the second annual NCIT moved to Albany, New York, where Jim Crow had much less reign. Loyola would no longer host and did not even play in the condensed event. Only eight teams traveled to New York's capital in late March 1950 for the four-day tournament that included five teams from New England states, one from Pennsylvania, one from Nebraska, and one from Iowa. Creighton, the Nebraska team who received the affair's top seed, gave the tournament the most prestige. The Jays had entered the NIT twice earlier, but only saw little success. The Nebraskans ended with little success in this event, too. Third-seeded Siena, the tournament's official host, beat St. Francis of New York in the finals, 57–50, sending the Franciscans home for a second straight year as the runner-up.[125]

The advent of the NCIT demonstrated the growing interest in the college basketball postseason. Three events had lasted beyond a decade already, but college coaches and administrators seemed to believe that the market allowed for more. Each new tournament onto the college basketball post-season landscape came about to serve a purpose. The NCIT offered an outlet for the top Catholic teams in the country. Many of these often-overlooked squads did not have conference affiliations and were not NCAA members, making NCAA bids nearly impossible; many of them were not big or big-name schools, making NIT invites extremely difficult for all but New York City Catholic schools; and many of them felt lost in the sea of talented small schools from which the NAIB chose its lineup. The college basketball land-scape was evolving.

The NCAA tournament—third on the scene—offered the first truly nationwide event, and it came about as the first tournament officially run by a group of coaches. These men wanted the control of college basketball and its postseason to stay with the colleges and coaches. They saw the NIT as a group of exploitative businessmen in New York City. And they saw the NAIB as a small-scale operation that would not be able to accommodate the grow-ing state universities that many of the powerful NABC coaches oversaw.

The NIT came about second, as the brainchild of New York City sports-writers and Ned Irish, who saw an opportunity to promote and operate a high-profile event. While their initiative may have been innocent and in good faith—to promote the game of college basketball and showcase some of the country's finest teams at season's end—they doubtlessly found extra motiva-tion in the likelihood of this kind of event making loads of money. And they were right. They continued to operate their tournament like a showcase even as other events came on the scene.

Liston and the NAIB

The seed for the NAIB event—college basketball's original postseason tour-nament—was planted through Liston's discussions with basketball's founder, Dr. James Naismith. The two of them and a few close colleagues wanted a way to host an end-of-season tournament that would not be dominated by the high-profile schools that sent teams to Madison Square Garden because of their name recognition. While Liston certainly had no interest in exclud-ing these "name" teams, he wanted the event open to teams like his Baker University Wildcats. Unfortunately, Liston's "open" philosophy came to stig-matize his event as a championship for small schools.

The 1950 NAIB event would be the first without its founder. Emil Liston passed away in October of 1949. The foundation that "Big Liz" had set for the association and its tournament provided an easy transition to his successor. Within a month of his death, the NAIB named Al Duer, athletic director at Pepperdine University, as the new NAIB executive director. Duer, who had recently given up the positions of head basketball coach and dean of men at the Malibu university to focus all of his efforts on directing the athletic department, received approval from his school to take over Liston's responsibilities. Duer had been a prominent NAIB member, working closely with Liston and the executive committee for years and faithfully bringing his team to the tournament when it qualified.[126]

Duer had also overseen a strong and prominent California district—one of the NAIB's thirty-two geographical sections. Pepperdine, Santa Barbara, and San Jose State had all fared well in previous editions of the NAIB event, displaying strong basketball from the West Coast. This district and region had also been involved in a number of contentious issues within the NAIB regarding race, wartime travel, and now—in Duer's first year—financial purity. The University of Nevada team that qualified for the 1950 event found out that their bid had been revoked only days before their plane would leave for Kansas City. Duer and the NAIB brass found out that the Wolfpack trip to the Garden City would be financed by a known gambler from Reno. University officials immediately reallocated funds to prove it could cover the costs without the "dirty money," but the NAIB would not relent. The *Nevada State Journal* noted that the letter the university received officially denying its appeal came on "official stationery from the NAIB (that) bears the printed slogan on its envelopes: 'The Best in Modern Education in a Wholesome Christian Environment.'"[127]

Beyond these issues, the quality of play throughout the tournament's history favored the middle districts. And this trend continued to hold court at college basketball's original event with Duer at the helm. Indiana State and its African American senior forward Clarence Walker found fairy tale justice at the 1950 NAIB. In 1946, under Coach Glenn Martin, the Sycamores finished second in the tourney. In 1947, under new coach John Wooden, the team rejected a bid. Walker, then a freshman reserve, would not have been able to play or even travel to the event with the team. In 1948, Liston and his executive committee reversed the Jim Crow law, allowing Walker to attend with his Sycamore teammates. They did and reached the final game again before losing. In 1949, Coach John Longfellow, who replaced the departed Wooden as head Sycamore coach, took the team to a semifinal finish, losing to eventual runner-up Regis College. Finally, then, with Walker figuring prominently in the team's on-court success in 1950, the Sycamores overcame their late tournament jinx by taking down East Central Oklahoma. After finishing in the top four in three out of the last four tournaments—and abstaining from the fourth—the Indiana State squad finally reached the NAIB peak. Walker scored 6 of the team's final 8 points in a 4-point victory in the championship, 61–57.[128]

College Basketball's Elusive "Double"

Kentucky figured as prominently in the NIT and NCAA tournaments in the late 1940s as Indiana State did in the NAIB. The Wildcats represented the strength of major college basketball. Groza, Beard, and Jones graduated in 1949 having won the 1946 NIT in their freshman campaign and the 1948 and 1949 NCAA tournament in their junior and senior seasons. These titles were marred only slightly by the unsuccessful attempt at winning the "double" in 1949 that their coach thought was so possible. That first-round loss to Loyola shocked many experts. Coach Rupp's players, who had been so consistent for so long, could not execute the way they had all season long, confounding their coach. Rupp and the perplexed experts would have their answer soon enough.

Even without Groza, Beard, and Jones, the Wildcats were very strong, but not the impeccable team that won back-to-back NCAA titles. The 1949–50 team went 25-4, winning the Southeastern Conference title yet again. The Wildcats had been ranked in the Associated Press poll's top ten most of the season but did not crack the top five until late in the season. The last poll had Kentucky at number three. Naturally, then, Rupp assumed that his team would garner yet another NCAA District 3 bid. As conference champions and the third-ranked team in the nation, he would have had strong arguments. But these arguments were not perfectly airtight. North Carolina State won the Southern Conference, the district's other prominent league, and ended with a 24-5 record that was good enough to have the Wolfpack ranked fifth in the country. Even though Kentucky would have a slight edge over North Carolina State on paper with its better win-loss record and its back-to-back NCAA titles, the District 3 selection committee was unwilling to simply give the Wildcats the nod. Virginia's Gus K. Tebell, District 3 selection committee chair, decided with his colleagues that the two conference champions should "play off" for the region's bid. He invited Rupp and Wolfpack coach Everett Case to a winner-take-all contest pitting the two squads.[129]

Rupp, a man who was slowly developing a reputation as a stubborn and outspoken coach who often misdirected the public with his biased proclamations, refused to enter his team into a play-off game. "A play-off on the basis of the teams' records would have been ridiculous," he opined. Without his cooperation, Tebell and his colleagues chose North Carolina State for the district's bid. Tebell had learned from the District 7 debacle in 1948 when Wyoming refused a play-off game and then was given the nod. Rupp and his team—victims in his mind, but hollow martyrs to all others—then put all of their energies into winning the NIT, a tournament he dejectedly claimed was "a better event anyhow."[130]

Kentucky's attempt at the 1949 "double" caught on with other coaches interested in making history. At the end of the 1949–50 season, Bradley was the AP's top team. The Braves, a quintet that reached the NIT semifinal the previous season and returned virtually all of their regulars, showed interest in both crowns, too. The Peorians' 27-3 regular season record was good enough for them to win the Missouri Valley crown and garner an NIT bid.[131]

The 1950 NIT was scheduled, once again, to begin and end in one week. Yet this year's event included one extra date of action. The March 11, 13, 14, 16, and 18 dates included only one matinee session. On March 11, the eight unseeded teams would all square off in preliminary round action. Playing the ensuing quarterfinal matchups over two evenings would likely draw bigger crowds than what the two matinees attracted in 1949. The NCAA event, however, maintained the same format it had since its inception in 1939. It would play its Eastern Regional games in the Garden on March 23 and 25, and then, after a year's hiatus from the Garden, would hold the East-West Final again back in New York City on March 28. The NCAA was apparently interested in moving its championship game around to different parts of the country. It was also apparently not as committed to hosting the games on campus gymnasiums as it was with wooing the powerful New York City media market.[132]

Strategic Team Selection

With five days in between the NIT finals and the NCAA's first round, NCAA selection committees were under no pressure to make quick decisions regarding their district bids. And two districts, in particular, took full advantage. District 5 always hosted a play-off game involving the champions of its two prominent conferences—the Missouri Valley and the Big Seven, formally known as both the Big Six and the Missouri Valley Intercollegiate Athletic Association. The district selection committee scheduled its play-off game for March 20, which fell two days after the NIT finals but three days before the NCAA's first round. Kansas, by winning the Big Seven, would compete in this one-off matchup against Bradley. The Braves, although falling geographically within District 4 in the Eastern Region, would be vying for the District 5 crown in the Western Region by virtue of its conference affiliation. In previous seasons, teams near the upper regions of the Mississippi

River had been grouped into a district based on geography only. Iowa and Minnesota, for instance, two teams in District 5 who were members of the Big Ten conference that was based in District 4, were discussed as potential District 5 representatives. Bradley's attempt to gain the District 5 bid despite its location represented a policy change that gave more clout to a team's conference affiliation than its geography. The prominence of one's conference would continue to increase.[133]

District 2 was the other holdout. This had traditionally been a very strong district. Teams from the basketball hotbeds of New York City, Philadelphia, and Pittsburgh believed that they could play with anyone. And yet the district had never won an NCAA title and had only reached the finals once—NYU's loss to Oklahoma A&M in 1946. Thus, Lafayette College athletic director Bill Anderson chaired a District 2 selection committee that acted shrewdly to enhance its standing in NCAA circles. The committee, realizing that seven District 2 teams were invited to the MIBA event, waited to see how that event shook out before choosing among the seven or any other district candidates.[134]

Indeed, seven teams from New York and Pennsylvania accepted bids to the 1950 Garden tournament. LIU, St. John's, and CCNY comprised the three local entrants. The Blackbirds and the Redmen had both been ranked in the nation's top ten for most of the season until LIU fell to thirteenth in the last poll. CCNY, an ultra-talented team of mostly sophomores was inconsistent, never cracking the top ten because of its erratic play. The 1946 entrant Syracuse and first-time NIT participant Niagara received the other Empire State offers to play in the Garden. Duquesne, a three-time NIT participant led by star African American forward Chuck Cooper, and back-to-back participant LaSalle represented the Keystone State's two major cities. Defending champion San Francisco, Border States Conference champion Arizona, Southeastern Conference champion Kentucky, Missouri Valley champion Bradley, and five-time Garden tourney participant Western Kentucky rounded out the strong field for the 1950 NIT.[135]

Six of these teams finished the season ranked in the AP's top ten, three more finished in the top twenty, and the last three—CCNY, Syracuse, and Niagara—all received at least some votes. The AP poll made seeding for the tournament relatively easy for the MIBA. Bradley, the NIT's top AP-ranked team, received the top seed in the tourney. Kentucky, the AP's number three, received the second seed. Duquesne, AP number six, received the third seed. However, the MIBA committee seeded St. John's, the AP number nine, fourth and left Western Kentucky, the AP number eight, out of its seeding. It was well within the MIBA's rights to do so, and the local tournament committee had favored the Johnnies in past seedings. Thus, this decision came without much controversy within local basketball circles.[136]

"City" Wins

When action opened on March 11, the Hilltoppers "shook off a case of first half jitters" to take down Niagara by seven points while CCNY defeated defending champion San Francisco by 19 in the afternoon session. The matinee provided a bit more entertainment than the night show. However, 18,000 fans paid admission to see Syracuse coast through the second half to beat LIU by 28 and LaSalle pull away from Arizona in the final six minutes to win by 6. Two nights later, St. John's justified their fourth seed by defeating Western Kentucky 69–60 and Bradley ousted Syracuse by 12 in front of 17,500 fans. The following night Duquesne squeaked by LaSalle and the integrated CCNY team astonished the 18,000 fans in attendance by whipping the all-white Kentucky Wildcats, 89–50. This defeat was the worst of Rupp's career, and it led him to address his team in the locker room by saying, "I want to thank you, boys. You get me selected coach of the year and then bring me up here and embarrass the hell out of me." City College continued on its tear, eliminating Duquesne by 10 in front of 18,000 loyal fans. Bradley held its seed by defeating St. John's by 11 points in the other semifinal.[137]

City College was having a truly magical postseason run. This team could boast of being no better than third-best metropolitan team after a regular season in which the squad did not reach its potential. Glowing midseason victories over St. John's, Loyola, and West Virginia showed promise. But losses to Oklahoma, UCLA, Niagara, Syracuse, and Canisius showed that the team was far from invincible—and far from where it could be. Coach Nat Holman—a New York City basketball icon—knew that this team had the talent to be a force. So when the Beavers started to click, Holman was not surprised nor was he in fear of the top-ranked Bradley Braves.[138]

The Peoria squad was coming off its most successful season in school history without question. And the Braves were no strangers to the National Invite. Local fans had become accustomed to the squad's unorthodox attack. In fact, they played "sensationally and refreshingly atypical." Paul Unruh was "a center who can run like a deer." Even though he was "a smallish center" at 6'4" he was "a sleek racehorse," "a relentless driver," and "a defensive stalwart" whose "blazing speed and pogo-stick jumping soon cuts (opposing) giants down to his size." Gene Melchiorre, Bradley's other atypical but effective player, was "a little guy who specializes in close-range pivot shooting." The 5'8½" guard "enthralled observers" with his "amazing number of fakes and feints" and "baffling gyrations." These unorthodox methods gave Melchiorre the nickname, "midget Mikan," referring to DePaul's National Invitation legend George Mikan.[139]

Local fans were at a fever pitch over this matchup. They were also somewhat in shock at the success of their local team. City College was the university most fundamentally representing the people of the Big Apple. CCNY—simply known as "City" to locals—was free to any metropolitan citizen who qualified above the rigorous admissions standards and only served local students. Thus, with public funding and with local players, the team was endeared to the local crowd.[140]

So when the Beavers took down favored Bradley, 69–61, to win the thirteenth annual NIT crown, local fans went wild. CCNY overcame "seventeen minutes of woefully weak work" in the first half to outplay the out-of-towners. The throng of 18,000 who attended the game came bolstered with the announcement the previous day that the NCAA District 2 selection committee had chosen CCNY as its representative based on the Beavers' outstanding play in the NIT.[141]

Locally, however, the NIT victory was a reason for pause. New York City's board of education, "in an action unprecedented for that august body," officially expressed its "extreme pleasure" with City College's NIT championship. And on campus, the president of the college suspended classes on Monday, March 20, for a rally to celebrate the invitation championship. After a congratulatory meeting with New York City mayor William O'Dwyer in the morning that 300 CCNY students and faculty witnessed, 2,000 more students attended a rally at noon. Coach Holman, who was suffering from a viral infection at the time, spoke briefly to the crowd, telling them the team would not rest on its laurels.[142]

The 1950 NCAA Tournament: More of the Same

The Beavers joined the NCAA Eastern Regional with a great deal of momentum and confidence. However, their competition would be difficult. District 1 named Holy Cross as its representative. Although standout George Kaftan had graduated, point guard Bob Cousy had become one of the nation's finest players in his senior season. He was "the answer to every coach's dream" because "there is nothing the lad cannot do on a hardwood floor," gushed sportswriter Louis Effrat. The Crusaders had been ranked as high as number one during a twenty-six-game winning streak during the regular season that was snapped late by Columbia, dropping Cousy's squad to number 4. Everett Case and his North Carolina State Wolfpack received the District 3 bid when Kentucky refused to participate in a play-off game. In four years at the helm, Case had won four Southern Conference championships and had played in a postseason tournament every year. The AP ranked the Wolfpack fifth in the final poll.[143]

Ohio State gained the District 4 bid by winning the Big Ten and outplaying the independent teams in the region. The Buckeyes finished the regular season with a win over Michigan on February 27 to put them in second place in the final AP regular season rankings. However, they still had three weeks until the opening of the NCAA tournament. This extended layoff was not unusual for the Big Ten champ, and the qualifying team usually thought it put them at a disadvantage. So in 1950, the conference faculty committee granted permission for the conference champion to play two extra games in between the regular season and the NCAA tournament. Ohio State struggled to find opponents for these games because league teams were not eligible—a ruling that was quickly overturned for future seasons.[144]

The Kansas City Regional had three of its four participants selected before the NIT championship. Brigham Young entered the NCAA event on the heels of its Skyline Six Conference championship. The Cougars gained the District 7 bid to enter the NCAA tournament for the first time ever. In fact, this marked the first time since 1939 that a team other than Wyoming, Utah, or Colorado represented the Rocky Mountain district. Southwestern Conference champion Baylor continued its string of making the tournament every other year by gaining the District 6 bid. The Bears participated in 1946 and made the finals in 1948. And UCLA won the Pacific Coast Conference title, giving Coach John Wooden his first taste of NCAA tournament action as the Bruins' coach.[145]

The District 5 bid remained up in the air, to be determined by a Missouri Valley–Big Seven play-off game on March 20 in Kansas City. Bradley came into the game with the final AP number-one ranking, having won the tough Missouri Valley title, and having lost in the final of the NIT. However, the Braves' opponent from the Big Seven Conference became a major source of tension. The conference ended in a three-way tie, leaving the selection of Bradley's play-off opponent in the hands of the NCAA District 5 selection committee chaired by Oklahoma coach Bruce Drake. Overall, Kansas State finished 17-7, Kansas finished 14-10, and Nebraska finished 16-7. Drake and his committee unanimously chose Kansas, touching off a firestorm of protest from Kansas State's campus. "This comes as the greatest shock of my coaching career," Wildcat coach Jack Gardner complained, adding without regard for hyperbole, "It's the greatest injustice that ever has been done to a group of athletes."[146]

Drake and his committee responded two days later, affirming that "the decision stands" despite Kansas State's protest. The committee believed it had selected the team "that it considered was the best team at the close of the season and would do the best job for the Big Seven in the playoff." Kansas had won five of its last six games by wide margins. Kansas State, on the other hand, had lost three of its final six games. However, this rationale did not satisfy Gardner. The Wildcat mentor suggested that in following years "he'd just try to win six games—the last six—so his team could be considered" for the postseason. "We made a mistake by winning by such tremendous scores in our early, tough schedule," he added with no small touch of sarcasm. The difficulty of selecting district representatives for the tournament was coming to a head.[147]

The ecstatic Kansas Jayhawks thus came into the game ranked nineteenth—two spots behind conference foe Kansas State. Phog Allen's squad's suboptimal season record, like CCNY, was due to the inconsistency of a sophomore-heavy lineup. Phog Allen's sophomores were resilient and confident, if nothing else. Their talent and character matched any Jayhawk squad Allen had coached. Only three seasons prior, Allen had promoted a twelve-foot basket that supposedly would negate the inherent advantages enjoyed by the big men who had taken over the game. Allen did not have an exceptionally tall or talented center at the time and wanted to equalize the playing field. By 1950, Allen's star sophomore was husky 6'8½" center Clyde Lovellette. The Indiana native originally committed to playing for Coach Branch McCracken and the Hoosiers before changing his mind late in his senior year to join Allen's Jayhawk squad. This historic recruiting battle generated loads of ill will between the two coaches, but disrepute was not unfamiliar territory for either mentor.[148]

By the Bradley play-off game, Lovellette had already rewritten the Big Seven conference scoring records with his season's performances. Indeed, the future pro was tough to handle. The 6'7" Bradley forward Elmer Behnke was assigned the task of guarding Lovellette behind a zone defense and in front of 10,700 fans. Behnke carried out his duties admirably, holding the Kansas big man without a field goal for twelve and a half minutes in the first half. Behnke's four fouls in the first period hindered his ability to stop Lovellette in the second half, and the Jayhawk ended with 21 points. However, Behnke scored an unusually high 17 points of his own to keep the Braves close before All-American Paul Unruh hit four shots in the final four minutes to take the lead and hold on for a 59–57 victory.[149]

With the win, Bradley stayed in Kansas City for three days enjoying a short break from action and awaiting their NCAA first-round game against

UCLA. The lay-off seemed to take the Braves out of rhythm, though, as they came out rusty against the Bruins. While UCLA did not shoot well, Coach Wooden's breakneck pace had UCLA taking eighty-one shots in the game. The Californians maintained a 57–50 lead on the Peorians with six and a half minutes remaining in the game and looked to close things out. However, from that point on the Bruins could do nothing right. Bradley scored 23 points over the final stretch and limited the Bruins to only 2, finishing with an easy 73–59 victory going away. The Bruins had simply run out of gas where the Braves had not. This loss so bothered Coach Wooden that he changed his entire coaching philosophy. He would seek, from then on, to make sure his teams were always better conditioned than their opponents so they would never be outplayed at the end of a game like that again.[150]

The victory for Bradley put the Braves in the Western Regional final—the battle of the B's—against a Baylor team that "staggered" into the game after a one-point defeat of Brigham Young on a late foul shot. Despite being a heavy underdog, Baylor put up its best fight and hung with the Braves. The Bears held the lead until halfway through the second period when a Behnke tip-in—the forward's only points of the night—put the Braves ahead, 47–46. With just over three minutes to play, Bradley led by 8 before a last-ditch effort from Baylor. The Bears came within one at 67–66 with nine seconds remaining, but the Braves sank one free throw at the end to save a victory, 68–66, and earn the right to return to Madison Square Garden for yet another tournament final.[151]

The Eastern Regional in the Garden provided plenty of excitement to rival the action in Kansas City. CCNY and Ohio State raced out to a 40–40 tie at halftime. Ohio State shot above 50 percent and City College shot a warm 43 percent. Fortunes changed in the second half, though, as both teams cooled off considerably. The Buckeyes only hit on five of twenty while the Beavers made six of twenty-one shots. This difference was just enough to give the Lavender a one-point victory. In the other opener, North Carolina State overcame an injury to its star center, future Duke coach Vic Bubas, to outplay Holy Cross. Cousy overcame early shooting struggles to post 24 points, but most of them came too late as the Wolfpack won 87–74. City College held Bubas to 2 points and no field goals in the Eastern Final, sending Case's squad home by a score of 78–73.[152]

The victory meant that CCNY and Bradley would square off for the second time this postseason in a tournament championship. It also meant that CCNY's improbable run of postseason victories could potentially conclude with an unprecedented feat. "So the stage is now set for the most important contest of the season," Michael Strauss of the *New York Times* promoted, "with C.C.N.Y. slated to come into the game as a four or five point favorite. This, not because the Beavers are considered greatly superior to Bradley, but primarily because the New Yorkers now are looked upon as a team of destiny."[153]

One day later, CCNY was listed in the *New York Times* as only 2-point favorites. The *Times* made a point to regularly list the betting line for important college basketball matchups. And that line often changed in the lead-up to a game. The odds-makers would change the line based on the money that had been bet. When City College had been 4- or 5-point favorites, enough gamblers must have placed money on Bradley that bookies changed the line so that more people would put money down on City College to even out the ledgers. This was common in the lead-up to a big game. And local sportswriters promoted the point spread because they knew how common gambling was.[154]

Despite the shrinking point spread, CCNY came into the game with great confidence. This Beaver squad, despite the task it had in the upcoming game, did not think it could lose. When asked about their ability to beat the nation's top-ranked team for the second time in a championship game in the span of eight days, the team's consensus reply was, "We did it before and we'll do it again." Louis Effrat tried to rationalize this logic for a Beaver squad that was on an eight-game winning streak—its longest streak of the season. He noted that City would have a height advantage and benefit from playing on its "home floor." The Beavers had played thirteen of their twenty-two regular season games at the Garden.[155]

Bradley started the game off in a "surprise zone defense" that had the Beavers perplexed and impatient but also aggressive. This assertiveness kept them in the game early, as the lead changed hands nine times and was knotted six times. Late in the first half, City began piercing the Braves' zone and took a 7-point lead into halftime, 39–32. The Lavender slowly increased its lead in the second half to an 11-point margin with nine minutes to go before the Braves switched to a man-to-man defense that changed the course of the contest. Despite a number of players getting into foul trouble, Bradley staged a comeback that put City College on its heels. With two minutes remaining the Beavers were up, 66–61. One minute later City led 69–63 before Bradley made a mad dash. Guard Joe Stowell scored his only point of the night on a free throw and ace Gene Melchiorre scored twice to make the score 69–68 with only forty seconds remaining. Melchiorre looked poised to score again on a drive to the hoop when Beaver Irwin Dambrot stripped him of the ball. "Melchiorre drove to the middle, and the entire CCNY team converged on him," the Braves' Paul Unruh remembered, "It was a hatchet job." Unruh

Madison Square Garden is packed for a CCNY game. *Courtesy of Archives, City College of New York, CUNY.*

had fouled out and was on the bench to watch the controversial play. "The films later showed him being ripped apart."[156]

Dambrot grabbed the ball and then spotted teammate Norm Mager wide open. Mager had been involved in a head-to-head collision near the end of the first half that had left both him and Bradley's Aaron Preece unconscious while blood streamed from the Beaver's head. After a halftime suture, the City star recovered fully and scored an "unmolested" basket off Dambrot's pass in the closing seconds to secure a 71–68 victory for the local five. "It was a really traumatic experience for us," Unruh recalled thirty years later. The Bradley basketball yearbook shortly thereafter explained that all of "Peoria was heartbroken . . . it felt its team was the victim of injustice." One local theater that showed the film of the game wrote on its marquee: "Was Squeaky [Melchiorre's nickname] Fouled? You Be The Judge!"[157]

New York City's reaction could not have been more different. "It was 'Allagaroo' through the canyons, the side streets, on Times Square, Fifth

Avenue, and all over the borough of Manhattan through the night and late into the afternoon yesterday," journalist Irving Spiegel reported in the *New York Times* of the celebration that followed City's unprecedented success. "Allagaroo" had become the keyword in the school's identifying cheer that had captivated the metropolitan community throughout the Beavers' unimaginable postseason run, and went as follows: "Alla-garoo, garoo, garah; Alla-garoo, garoo, garah; ee-yah, ee-yah, sis, boom, bah; team, team, team!" While the exact origin of the cry was not known, some on campus believed that "Allagaroo" was a term that came from the French command "allez guerre," meaning "off to war." Others believed it was simply a fun word to say that was a mix between alligator and kangaroo. Regardless of the origin, the cheer of school pride "echoed over a wide range of streets at St. Nicholas Heights" throughout the night.[158]

The following morning school president Harry N. Wright canceled classes starting at noon. Two thousand students streamed out of the school of business and paraded to the main campus where they joined 4,500 more Beavers in the quadrangle for a celebration rally. One professor at the school remarked that this was the "greatest thing that ever happened in the 102-year history of this venerable institution" while snake dances, conga lines, and waving banners engulfed him in the celebration. Wright brought order to the rally by orating from atop a makeshift podium, announcing, "This is one of the proudest days of my life. This team came here to study, not to play basketball. I am proud of the team and what it has done for the college. I want to point out that they are given no scholarships to play ball, and they have not been imported to play ball . . . I am particularly proud of their high scholastic rating."[159]

Clearly, although winning has a special cohesive effect on crowds, Wright and the university were proud of this team because it had done things the right way. In a time in which more and more scandals involving the excesses of college athletics and the incompatibility of big-time athletics on college campuses came to light, Wright and the entire CCNY community was proud of their basketball team for three reasons. First, CCNY did not give athletic scholarships. Since it was a free school, scholarships were unnecessary, but Wright and others promoted it because it represented the fact that every Beaver basketball player was a student first and none was brought onto campus with an athletic subsidy. Second, all were good students. Every student that got into New York City's free university—and it was open to anyone in the Big Apple—was required to have an outstanding academic record. The Beavers who played basketball were believed to be no different. And third, it was a totally local team. Much of the social ills demoralizing college athletics at the time came from the recruitment of athletes. College coaches and boosters spent a great deal of time and energy to import players who were little more than athletic mercenaries to a school at which a student-athlete had no ties. This was not the case with CCNY. All of its basketball players—indeed all of its student body—hailed from the five boroughs.[160]

Wright ordered the Main Building tower bell to ring for five minutes—a call normally reserved only for "extraordinary occasions"—after his speech. Coach Nat Holman spoke, loyally attributing his team's victories not to luck but to "their cooperation and wonderful C.C.N.Y. spirit." And each member of the team stepped onto the podium individually to roaring applause from the gathered throng. However, the hero of the NCAA championship game, Norm Mager, was conspicuously absent. The forward, perpetuating the student-athlete ideal that Wright so vehemently proclaimed, was taking a midterm exam.[161]

A week later, Mager joined his teammates in Wright's office for a ceremony led by the Manhattan Borough president Robert F. Wagner Jr. Wagner presented each player with an engraved scroll from the borough for their accomplishments and designated Coach Nat Holman as an "Honorary Deputy Commissioner of the Borough of Manhattan." Wagner praised the team, stating, "The people of Manhattan are very proud of the fine job you have done at City College." All of the celebrating and praise was not hollow rhetoric. New York City and the borough of Manhattan clearly saw this unprecedented feat as their own, a remarkable achievement accomplished by their sons in their town. College basketball in New York City, which had always been prominent and popular, had never been as unanimously endeared to the metropolitan citizens as it was after City's "grand slam" championship titles that March.[162]

CHAPTER 8

The Scandal, Damage Control, and Alternate Options, 1950–1951

The unprecedented "grand slam" postseason run by the CCNY Beavers brought great joy and pride to New York City and local college basketball fans. City College, after all, was the free university that the local taxpayers funded. It was their team, and stars Al Roth, Ed Roman, Ed Warner, Floyd Layne, and Irwin Dambrot were their boys. City's NIT and NCAA championship runs reaffirmed to the Big Apple basketball establishment what its members had believed all along: that college basketball in New York City was as good as it gets.

CCNY was the third metropolitan team to win the NIT. LIU took the crown in 1939 and 1941 and St. John's won back-to-back titles in 1943 and 1944. NYU was the only other team to place, finishing second in 1948. A few other local fives had participated—Fordham, Manhattan, and St. Francis—but these were all second-tier metropolitan teams. St. John's, LIU, CCNY, and NYU represented the strongest local college basketball heritage. St. John's was the premier Catholic institution in the city, and Coach Joe Lapchick had built a basketball team to match and even exceed the school's reputation. Coach Clair Bee built LIU into a national basketball powerhouse that far exceeded the small school's reputation. A visionary without peer, Bee treated his team as no other coach had before. LIU rarely played top-flight local competition. Indeed, Bee took his teams all over the country to play and invited only out-of-town or small-scale local fives to play against his squad at home. Bee's teams played the first truly national schedules. Part of the LIU mentor's unique scheduling was out of necessity. His success—and that of other metropolitan coaches—spurred intense animosity and an unwillingness to schedule the Blackbirds. LIU, like many other schools at the time, found itself accused of impropriety on a number of fronts.[1]

CCNY mentor Nat Holman came to represent an institution that was antithetical to LIU and Bee. "Mr. Basketball," as the Beaver coach was affectionately nicknamed, also built a basketball team with a reputation that reached farther than that of the institution itself. Yet Holman, a Gothamite himself and a former basketball star for the Original Celtics, led a hoops team that stood for much of what LIU did not. The coach rarely took his team outside the region. Instead, his team of local boys stayed local and played local. Although intersectional games at the Garden dotted the Beavers' schedule, Holman and his team embodied New York City and its culture.[2]

Since the early 1940s, CCNY and NYU had squared off in the last regular season game at Madison Square Garden in what had become a prominent fixture in the college basketball landscape. Often one or both of the teams played in this game with a spot in one of the two postseason championships hanging in the balance. Until 1947, CCNY had participated only in the NIT. New York City was a small part of the NCAA's second district, and the region's selection committee had not felt the need to choose a metropolitan school in the past—even though it had selected NYU three times by 1950. The Violets reached the NCAA finals in 1945 and earned a spot in the NIT's final game in a 1948 loss to St. Louis.[3]

All four of these premier Big Apple teams—alongside Columbia University, a Manhattan school that by 1951 had taken over prominence in the Ivy League—became perennial powerhouses by the end of the 1940s. CCNY, St. John's, and NYU usually ended the season atop the "intra-city" rankings, and LIU usually garnered an asterisk saying that it had an exceptional record but did not play local teams and therefore could not figure into the local standings.

The Evolving Basketball Landscape

Many other cities and regions across the country also boasted a multitude of perennially talented college basketball squads. Philadelphia had put LaSalle, Temple, and Muhlenberg—from nearby Allentown—into the NIT and Villanova and Pennsylvania into the NCAA event, with Princeton having turned down a 1950 offer. Further, in 1951 LaSalle was in the process of recruiting a local star, Tom Gola, who would take the Explorers to the 1954 NCAA title. The City of Brotherly Love was also, at the time, in the process of developing an agile 7-foot star center at Overbrook High School named Wilt Chamberlain, who would forever change the game.[4]

Many believe that Pittsburgh, a city much smaller than New York City and Philadelphia even during its peak years in the first half of the twentieth century, has been much more of a football than basketball town. Yet the Steel City provided high-quality basketball during this time. Pitt, the city's most recognizable team, figured prominently in national rankings before any of the postseason championships began and then participated in the 1941 NCAA tournament. Tiny Westminster College and Washington and Jefferson College—both just outside Pittsburgh—entered early NIT fields, and the Presidents even reached the 1942 final. Further, Duquesne had a distinguished postseason history. The Dukes reached the NCAA Eastern Regional final and NIT championship game in 1940, made the NIT quarterfinals in 1941 and 1947, and reached the NIT semifinals in 1950 with the outstanding play of Chuck Cooper, who, by late 1950 had become the first African American to be drafted by an NBA team.

Going west across the Rust Belt, Ohio became a prominent basketball state. Although the Buckeye State is better known for football, too, Ohio produced very successful college basketball teams. Ohio State had participated in more NCAA events than any other team by 1950 and, a decade later, a Buckeye team of local players finally won an NCAA championship. From the southeast section of the state, Ohio University reached the 1941 NIT finals. And in the northwest section of the state, Toledo and Bowling Green had proven their quality while featuring in many of the 1940s NIT fields.

Kentucky had quickly become a basketball state with "Colonel" Rupp's regional and national success. By 1950, Rupp had won the Southeastern Conference crown the previous seven straight seasons and had collected one NIT and two NCAA titles in the process. The Bluegrass State became so basketball crazed that it began hosting a season-ending high school basketball all-star game against the best players in Indiana—a state always recognized as a powerful basketball producer—in 1940. Kentucky and Indiana would each choose its top ten high school seniors to square off in what became an intense rivalry. Indiana won each of these games up until 1955 except for the 1945 installment that featured Ralph Beard and Wallace Jones for the Bluegrass State. Many of these and the other best preps in the Hoosier State went on to play for Branch McCracken's Indiana teams that had won the 1940 NCAA title and would win it again in 1953 or Ward "Piggy" Lambert's Purdue teams that won thirteen Big Ten titles by 1940 but usually declined postseason bids. Indiana State also captured some of this talent while putting together a run of NAIB success in the late 1940s.[5]

Illinois provided a fine delegation of excellent college basketball teams. The state's namesake university captured national public interest during the 1940s with high-quality, fast-paced, and breathtaking basketball but never received the recognition it deserved because the Illini declined a 1943 postseason bid even though it may have had the best team in the country. Southern Illinois won the 1946 NAIB tournament, and Millikin College finished the 1951 event as a semifinalist. Upstate, however, was where Illinois basketball made its name. Chicago dominates the Land of Lincoln in many ways, and basketball is no exception. While Wheaton College began the prominence with a 1904 Olympic college tournament silver medal, the bigger schools took over from there. Most notably, DePaul and Loyola had been at the forefront of NIT success throughout the 1940s, with the Blue Demons also receiving NCAA District 2 offers. Joliet native George Mikan became a national star in the middle of the decade as he led DePaul to the 1945 NIT championship. Loyola lost in the finals of the 1949 NIT by a single point and would win the NCAA title in 1963.

The region encompassing Missouri, Kansas, and Oklahoma also produced many fine basketball teams. University of Missouri coach George Edwards figured prominently in NAIB and NCAA tournament administration during the 1940s. Yet Edwards's teams only made the NCAA tournament once—in 1944 by default when many other superior District 5 teams declined because of the war. St. Louis University won the 1948 NIT in what became the beginning of a very strong basketball identity. Many of the state's smaller schools also fared well in the AAU National tournament and won the NAIB in 1937, 1938, 1939, 1940, and 1943. The NAIB, not coincidentally, was held in Kansas City, Missouri, every year. And with the NCAA having used Municipal Auditorium since 1940, too, a generation of Kansas City's constituency had now witnessed national-caliber basketball in their hometown.

Phog Allen, who brought the NCAA event to Kansas City, carried the torch that Dr. James Naismith lit in Kansas when he began working at Kansas University. Allen's team placed second in the 1940 NCAA tournament and made the field in 1942. However, the Jayhawks never had an easy time garnering the district selection committee's bid. In-state rival Kansas State won the bid in 1949, but usually Kansas came up against the stiffest competition from south of its border. Oklahoma A&M became the first team to win two consecutive NCAA titles—in 1945 and 1946. Big Bob Kurland had skills never seen before from a man his size. Coach Henry Iba used his big man well, and the Aggies came to national prominence in the middle of the decade. The Oklahoma Sooners and their coach, Bruce Drake, did, too. The young Drake had taken his team to the NCAA tournament three times by 1950. Indeed, with the strength of both the Missouri Valley and Big Seven Conferences within the NCAA's District 5, competition for the lone tournament bid was fierce.

Tournament Growth

With this increase in talented, high-quality teams across the country and the continued popularity of the NCAA tournament, Dutch Lonborg and the tournament committee approved a measure to increase the field of teams. Two years earlier, the NIT had done the same thing. The New York event, which started as a six-team affair before growing to eight in 1941, increased its pool to twelve teams in the days before the 1949 installment. The NCAA saw that this growth had been well received by the ticket-purchasing public and the sports media. The NCAA also realized that over the past three years its net revenue from the tournament had plateaued. Immediately after the war, tournament profits jumped considerably from year to year. However, the event had been waddling between $60,000–$67,000 since 1948. An increase in the size of the tournament seemed like the antidote to this problem.[6]

However, the NCAA's decision to expand was not financially based. The 1950 district selection problems occurring in Districts 3 and 5—in which Kentucky would not engage in a play-off and was therefore denied a bid and Kansas State was left out of its district play-off—put pressure on Lonborg to enhance the tournament selection process. Complaints from coaches when their successful teams did not receive bids or play-off opportunities had certainly occurred in the past. However, the vehement protest from Kansas State and the fact that the two-time defending NCAA champion Kentucky did not receive a bid put this issue on top of the pile on Lonborg's desk. At the 1950 NABC convention, the tournament director and newly named Kansas University athletic director felt the need to address the association on the matter. "There will always be trouble in making selections in certain districts," Lonborg admitted, "However . . . I wish you would withhold your criticism for one year. I am working on a new, and I hope, a more workable formula for selection committees to help them in making selections in the future."[7]

Lonborg and his colleagues decided that for the 1951 championship the association would double its size to host a sixteen-team event. Twice as many teams meant, theoretically, that the tournament could include more of the deserving teams that had ended their seasons dejectedly without a bid. The NCAA's selection of teams would forever change in this format. Previously, each of the eight NCAA districts selected a representative team to send to the event. This was often a difficult decision. Although certain districts such as the 4th (Big Ten) and the 8th (Pacific Coast) had only one major conference within its boundaries, many others such as the 3rd (Southern and Southeastern) and the 5th (Missouri Valley and Big Seven) had more than one. Further complicating matters, most districts included strong teams that were not affiliated with conferences. By 1948, the NCAA listed 318 member schools—a number that rose to 386 by 1952—and most of these schools were conference affiliated. This meant that large numbers of teams across the country were conference independent. District selection committees never had an easy time determining whether the regions' best independent teams deserved the bid over the districts' conference champions. As Lonborg recalled, "I spent many long nights talking to chairmen, telling them I couldn't make a selection (for them)." The tournament director said, "It happened more than once in District 3 where the selection committee from that district would call me and want me to tell them what to do." So the tournament expansion "relieved a lot of problems."[8]

The NCAA's new selection format rectified this problem, or at least limited it. The new method also attempted to encourage conference champions —theoretically among the best in the country— and top independent teams to enter into the NCAA field. The NCAA's new selection format indicated that the champion of ten different conferences would receive "automatic" bids to the event alongside six other "at-large" bids determined by the tournament selection committee. To further promote equal opportunities for all teams to participate, the NCAA announced that only one team from each conference would be allowed into the tournament. This meant that the at-large bids would have to go to either independent teams or those from smaller conferences who had not received automatic bids.[9]

In the East—the area encompassing NCAA Districts 1–4—four conference champions would join four at-large bids. In this area of the country, many prominent schools remained conference independent, and by offering four at-large bids to Eastern teams, the NCAA showed its interest in having these teams compete for its title. The Southern and Southeastern Conference champions would square off against two at-large teams in Raleigh, North Carolina, on Tuesday, March 20, for one night of action. The two winners would then go on to New York City. In the Big Apple, the Big Ten and the Eastern Intercollegiate League champions would face two more at-large teams in first-round action, the winners of which would face the Raleigh first-round winners.[10]

Kansas City maintained its stronghold on Western events, hosting the entire half of the NCAA bracket. Six conferences west of the Mississippi River—the Pacific Coast, the Southwestern, the Missouri Valley, the Skyline, the Border States, and the Big Seven—matched up with two at-large teams to comprise the Western field. All eight of these teams would square off in four consecutive nights of action—Wednesday through Saturday, March 21 to 24.

These dates coincided with the NCAA's Garden dates of Tuesday, Thursday, and Saturday, March 20, 22, and 24.[11]

The Eastern and Western Regional site dates could not have been better. Both regionals had nights of action close together and both culminated with Saturday evening affairs. However, this meant that the NCAA would play its East-West championship game on a Tuesday night. At the Garden this would have been no big deal. NCAA tournament games had been played there to packed houses on every day of the week except Sunday. However, since the tournament committee had chosen the University of Minnesota's new Williams gymnasium—nicknamed "The Barn"—for the final, the Tuesday night date seemed less than desirable. In Minneapolis, far from the entertainment capital and large citizenry of New York City, the Barn likely would have been available any night the NCAA needed. Thus, the Tuesday night choice—which allowed Saturday night capstone games in the Garden and Municipal Auditorium—showed that New York City and Kansas City, to a much lesser extent, still reigned as the tournament's capitals.[12]

The differences between the Barn and the Garden could not have been more appropriate. The Garden, named after America's fourth president, was old. In fact, in 1951 the Madison Square Garden in use was the third venue so named and was built in a different spot in Manhattan from the original two after their demolition. Madison Square Garden, on whichever intersection the facility was located, had a national name and was the premier venue for any type of entertainment imaginable at the time in an indoor facility. It was the crown jewel of arenas, the envy of all others. Every entertainment activity knew it was at the top of its field when it could book the Garden. And when it did, it paid a hefty rental fee. The Garden was under such demand that it could effectively price many events out of the market. However, acts that rented the Garden knew they would usually make large profits back from the cavernous crowd capacities.[13]

The Barn, on the other hand, was a new venue built on the campus of the University of Minnesota for college-related events. No outside promoters benefited in any way from the use of the venue. It was built, maintained, and used by the university. Hosting a national championship basketball game was a big deal in the Twin Cities—a locale far more appropriate for a "Barn" at the time than a "Garden," anyway. An event of national caliber like this would captivate the city much more so than yet another championship game in the Big Apple. But this wholesale captivation would be necessary for the success of the event, for Minneapolis did not have nearly the population of New York City.[14]

The NIT remained a New York City event and, like in 1949, would be the only tournament with a New York City championship game. The fourteenth annual affair would take place before the NCAA tournament. The eight unseeded teams would meet on Saturday, March 10; two of those winners would meet two seeded teams on Monday, March 12; the other two would meet the two remaining seeded teams on Tuesday, March 13; the semifinals would be two days later; and the championship and consolation games would occur on Saturday, March 17. By February 6, Eastern League commissioner and tournament administrator Asa Bushnell noted that, with the increase in talented and high-quality teams, he and his colleagues were considering "at least three dozen" teams for the event.[15]

A New Tournament

Bushnell and his selection committee would need to act quickly and effectively because the NIT would have company during those dates. On February 10, the *Chicago Tribune* announced that Chicago Stadium would host a national invitation basketball tournament "in direct competition with the established national invitation meet at New York's Madison Square Garden." Arthur Morse, who acted on behalf of Chicago Stadium in a capacity much smaller than Ned Irish's role at the Garden, had been in discussions with DePaul to host such an event that would rival what New York City had produced for the past fourteen seasons. Morse told the media that he "was sounding out such teams as Kentucky, Oklahoma A. and M., North Carolina State, Bradley, Arizona, Beloit, and two other ranking quintets to round out an eight-team field." Outside of Beloit, this list included many of college basketball's blue bloods at the time. Corralling all of them to Chicago at the expense of New York City would have been a major blow to the MIBA and the Big Apple's college basketball establishment.[16]

The idea of a "'Siamese Twin' National Invitation basketball tournament" did not sit well with Madison Square Garden officials and the New York City college basketball brass. "Madison Square Garden officials were inclined to give an old-fashioned brush-off to Arthur Morse's plans to hold a tournament out Chicago way on the same dates (March 10–17) as the Garden's NIT," journalist Howard Sigmund wrote in an article picked up in newspapers across the country. Sigmund quoted an unnamed "New York official" who made two arguments: first, that a team winning the Chicago NIT would have little to gain because the tournament is not as prestigious as the established New York event; and second, that teams would not know how much money they would take home from Chicago. In New York, because of the established tradition, teams knew that their parting purse would be large.[17]

CCNY coach Nat Holman spoke surprisingly ambivalently about the proposed event after having a conversation with Morse. Holman mentioned "that western teams might accept a bid to the Chicago tournament if the money proposition was right. They would thus eliminate the long haul to New York." This logic made sense, but it did not overcome the "money angle." Sigmund noted, however, that while much of each team's prize money came from gate attendance—and the Chicago tournament did not know how well it would draw at the gate—television rights had become a notable source of income for the tournaments, too. While the NIT shared little of its television rights sales with its participating teams, Morse's tournament would consider television revenue as part of the gate that it would share with the participating teams.[18]

Gate attendance was, not surprisingly, at the forefront of speculation on this tournament's possible success. The Chicago event would be successful if, as Holman noted, "the money proposition was right." The new tournament would have to draw crowds in comparable numbers to the masses that watched the NIT in Madison Square Garden year in and year out. For if it did, the tournaments could be considered on equal footing. "If Chicago lined up topnotch teams for its tourney" that drew large crowds, Sigmund argued, "could the New York NIT claim that its winner was national champion?" This presumptuous question ignored the reality of the college basketball landscape in which it was far from clear that the NIT was in fact *currently* able to name its winner the national champion. However, attendance figures underscored Sigmund's sentiment. In this metric, the NIT had always reigned supreme. And yet, the landscape had shown signs of change with the growth of the NCAA event. The Chicago tournament's prominence, relatedly, could be determined "by a comparison after the two (NIT) tourneys are held—if they both come off at the same time at all."[19]

The Chicago tournament preparation was off to a good start when it received interest from teams across the country—including those in Philadelphia and Boston. The *Chicago Daily News* reported that a number of the nation's top teams showed interest. The Associated Press poll's #1 team (Kentucky), #2 (Oklahoma A&M), #6 (St. Louis), #7 (Bradley), #9 (North Carolina State), #11 (Arizona), #12 (Brigham Young), #15 (Villanova), and #20 (Beloit) all responded to Morse's feelers with openness. Fifth-ranked Kansas State and seventeenth-ranked Oklahoma had to say no due to the Big Seven's rule against participation in any postseason event other than the

NCAA tournament. A similar rule in the Big Ten kept Morse from contacting #4 Indiana and #10 Illinois.[20]

Many of these schools reported interest because their participation in an NIT event—whether in New York or Chicago—would not preclude them from participating in the newly enlarged NCAA tournament. Indeed, each of the twelve teams that expressed interest in the Chicago NIT still would have been eligible to compete in the NCAA tournament the following week. After CCNY's historic "double" and Bradley's "double" as finalists the previous season, teams competing in both an invitation tournament and the NCAA event no longer seemed uncommon.[21]

With the addition of the eight-team Chicago NIT, the college basketball postseason market had grown to include five "national" tournaments. The NCAA and NIT remained the premier events, with the former—a sixteen-team event—increasing in prestige and popularity at a much quicker rate than the latter—a twelve-team field. The NAIB maintained status as a thirty-two-team Kansas City event theoretically open to all, but it still hosted mostly smaller schools. It had grown from a regional event in 1937 to a fully national affair with a parent organization that included nearly as many members as the NCAA. While it could not shake the reputation as a small school tournament it had certainly become a prominent fixture in the college basketball postseason. The National Catholic Invitational Tournament also continued into its third season in 1951. The original sixteen-team event hosted by Regis College in Denver in 1949 morphed into an eight-team event in Albany, New York, in 1950. The 1951 edition seemed to find comfortable middle ground as a twelve-team gala in Troy, New York. Now that five tournaments dotted the college basketball postseason landscape, as many as eighty teams could participate in games beyond the regular season. Fifteen years prior, that number was zero.[22]

The Growth Comes to a Halt

Each of the tournaments' administrators vied for participating teams and worked diligently to put on shows that would set themselves apart or at least establish a viable identity. However, all of this preparation came to a standstill when New York City legal authorities made an announcement that shook the college basketball world to its core. On February 19, 1951, New York City district attorney Frank Hogan revealed that he had confessions from five college basketball players who had shaved points or thrown games in return for bribery money from gamblers. This was not New York City's first experience with gamblers infiltrating college basketball. In 1945, five

Brooklyn College cagers admitted to accepting bribes to shave points in one of its games. But that was lowly Brooklyn College, a team that never figured into the national—and sometimes even the local—picture.[23]

This was different. Hogan revealed the names of five prominent athletes who had accepted bribes to play less than their best and ensure a particular outcome. Eddie Gard, a 1950 graduate of LIU who starred for Coach Bee's Blackbirds, orchestrated these deals. He secured agreements with NYU's Harvey Schaff and three CCNY players—junior starters Ed Roman, Ed Warner, and Al Roth—during their inconsistent 1949–50 season that ended with an improbable and unprecedented set of "grand slam" championships.[24]

Two days later, Hogan had confessions from one more former LIU player and three current Blackbirds—including the team's African American star, Sherman White, one of the best players in the country. By the end of the month, Hogan had also implicated CCNY's Floyd Layne, the other sophomore starter on the 1950 championship team who had been lauded and named team captain in the wake of the dismissal of his three teammates the previous week.[25]

LIU immediately canceled its entire intercollegiate athletics program. This put Clair Bee out of a job and took the Blackbirds and their Brooklyn-based school off the map. CCNY acted less severely. City College canceled the two remaining games on its schedule and would reevaluate the state of its program in the off-season. The Beavers maintained an athletic program, but heavily de-emphasized their sports by disallowing intersectional games and, at the time, proclaiming to no longer use the Garden for any more than one game a year. As the seat of the scandal, the Garden received a lot of the blame. The amateurism of college basketball, it was argued, had become too professionalized when played in the Garden. It was a business. And putting young, poor boys near the trappings of big money gamblers at the Garden was a recipe for disaster. The Garden administration saw things differently, though, and contemplated dropping basketball from its annual schedule.[26]

In the immediate aftermath of the scandal, most colleges showed their willingness to continue to play games in Irish's venue. Many, for instance, thought Madison Square Garden did nothing wrong. "I don't think you can condemn a playing site because of something like (this)," argued North Carolina State coach Everett Case, because "it could happen any place altho (sic) the tendency is greater in the Garden." Many others seemed to believe that there was no systemic problem—that this scandal was simply the result of a few bad apples showing moral weakness.[27]

Despite efforts to make sense of these transgressions, the scandal had major implications that immediately affected the entire college basketball establishment nationwide. The Chicago NIT's momentum came to a halt and, on February 24 Morse noted that he had abandoned plans for the new meet. Since it had not existed before, this event had no part in the scandal, but its entire concept seemed all too similar to that in New York City, which, at least among midwesterners who inhabited the Windy City and its surrounding region, played a role in fertilizing the landscape for this type of corruption. Arthur Morse's event ended before it even started.[28]

While the scandal played a role in Morse's decision not to continue plans for the Chicago NIT, the DePaul graduate manager of athletics noted publicly that his decision had to do with scheduling. Morse "said that a suitable field could not be worked into available Stadium dates between March 8–16." With the help of DePaul, Morse may have been able to continue its event if enough teams showed interest in participating. And yet that seemed unlikely. Two of the nine teams that originally showed interest in the event had already opted out.[29]

Bradley was one of them. As the previous year's runner-up in both the NCAA and NIT championships, the current #7 team in the country, and a squad located within a few hours of Chicago, Bradley's inclusion in Morse's event was almost a necessity. However, Bradley made a unique decision that became more intuitive a few months later. The Braves decided to forego the Chicago NIT to play "in a Pacific round robin basketball tournament to be sponsored by the University of Hawaii" on the same dates as the proposed Chicago event. Bradley athletic director Arthur Bergstrom noted that the team voted on two separate occasions "to accept the University of Hawaii's invitation in preference to the NIT or the proposed Chicago tournament." Bradley would join Oregon State, the University of Hawaii, and a leading amateur team sponsored by Universal Motors of Hawaii in the event. Bradley president David Owens commented:

> I am glad that our athletic committee and athletic department have honored the wishes of our players. Most of them are seniors and they certainly have earned this wonderful trip. Since Bradley has one of the largest groups of Hawaiian students in the country, in proportion to its enrollment, and since we have a very loyal, enthusiastic group of alumni in the Islands, I know that our boys will receive a royal welcome and that they will make some contacts which will be valuable to us in future years.

Coach Forddy Anderson, who had played college basketball at Stanford under Everett Dean, emphasized the quality of the competition in this new postseason event that seemed to have no intentions of joining the struggle for rights to call its titleholder the national champion. Anderson said, "This is going to be more than a pleasure trip." Bergstrom revealed more about the team's choice, saying, "Bradley players and officials had definitely decided not to accept a bid to the NIT." However, the team had seriously considered the Chicago event. The athletic director noted, "We were afraid that, if we passed up the Hawaiian trip, and if the Chicago tournament did not develop as a major tournament, justifying our participation in it, there would be no post-season play whatever for what all of us believe is the finest basketball team that we have ever had." He also offered a more righteous reason for the decision, that, "under the circumstances existing this year, this college-sponsored tournament in Hawaii is perhaps the best type of post-season activity."[30]

The other team that turned against the Chicago event before it ended was North Carolina State. Wolfpack coach Everett Case had publicly declared his unwillingness to scapegoat Madison Square Garden and therefore had no qualms about his team continuing to compete there. His decision to compete in the New York NIT came only a day before two other potential Chicago NIT squads—Brigham Young and Arizona—also accepted invites to the Garden event. Case wanted his team to compete with the best, and Chicago did not seem to fit that standard.[31]

NCAA Response to the Scandal

On March 3, only one week before the NIT would begin, the NCAA publicly announced a plea for more control of stadiums for intercollegiate basketball events. The association provided six recommendations to those administering college basketball games and tournaments.

1. Member institutions should hold their athletic competition on campus fields and in campus buildings.

2. Where such campus facilities are not adequate, it is recommended that institutions play only on fields or in buildings of which the collegiate institution has effective control, management, and supervision.[32]

These two recommendations aimed to condemn the NIT and its use of the private Madison Square Garden. While the NCAA and NIT events had been battling for supremacy for more than a decade by this time, the NCAA could not and would not miss this opportunity to subtly chastise its peer. But these recommendations represented more than simple finger-pointing. The NCAA had waivered over time on host site policies. In 1939, the NCAA used two off-campus sites to host its inaugural Eastern and Western Regionals. It also sought an off-campus site, Chicago Stadium, for its final game. When that venue could not be scheduled, the next best option was Northwestern's on-campus gymnasium. Therefore, the NCAA tournament began by using off-campus facilities almost exclusively. It only brought the final game on campus because it had no better option. In 1940, the Western Regional and final game remained off-campus but the Eastern Regional occurred in Butler's Fieldhouse in Indianapolis. Wisconsin hosted the Eastern Regional on-campus in 1941 and Tulane did the same in 1942 while the Western Regional and final game remained in Kansas City's Municipal Auditorium. The Garden City's municipality ran this venue and so it operated unlike Madison Square Garden, but it was still an off-campus facility. This subtle difference may have mattered to some, but to others off-campus was anything not owned by a university.

The NCAA likely would have held its Eastern Regional and potentially even the final game in the Garden in the early 1940s if it could have, but Harold Olsen and Ned Irish could never seem to find satisfactory dates. So the NCAA's choice of on-campus venues in 1940–1942 seemed less like a choice and more like a survival tactic—they would play the games wherever they could generate the greatest crowd support. From 1943 to 1948, crowd support was highest at Municipal Auditorium and the Garden, and the NCAA event did not leave these two off-campus facilities during that time. In 1949, when Seattle hosted the championship, it was the University of Washington's on-campus arena that opened its doors.

With this record of using off-campus facilities, the NCAA needed to make more recommendations to ensure that it was absolved of any guilt in this scandal. The NCAA's third suggestion made clear that guilt could be dispersed to other culprits, too.

> 3. Much of the increased emphasis on the sport has been brought about by over-long seasons. Some of the present difficulty apparently had its origin in summer play. In some conferences, organized summer play is prohibited and the penalty is ineligibility. The council encourages this procedure. Where that is impossible, it believes that each institution should redouble its efforts to guide the athletes' pursuits in proper channels during the summer period.[33]

By this time, the summer basketball circuit in upstate New York was well known. Many prominent New Yorkers left the city for long stretches in the summer to vacation in mountain resorts in the Catskill or Adirondack Mountains. These wealthy patrons included a number of the most notorious gamblers in the Big Apple. Many of the summer resorts that hosted these patrons also hired male college students from the city to work for them. Over time, as resorts hired college basketball players on staff, each resort put together a staff basketball team that would challenge other resort staffs in what became known as the Borscht league. This league, often featuring many of the most prominent New York City college cagers, provided a great deal of entertainment for the wealthy vacationers. These games also became the breeding ground for relationships between gamblers and college players. Away from the lights, media, coaches, and school administrators in the city, gamblers and college athletes could rendezvous freely under the guise of staff-patron interaction. The bribes, many believed, had their seeds planted in such relationships in the summer.[34]

The NCAA also wanted to ensure that it covered all of its bases in this series of recommendations, and the final three proposals followed.

4. While we know that coaching staffs now devote much of their attention toward counseling their students . . . (it is) urged that these efforts be redoubled.

5. Because of previously committed contractual and lease arrangements, which it is deemed unwise and impracticable to void at this time, the N. C. A. A. will hold certain of its 1951 basketball tournaments in buildings not on college campuses. However, the N. C. A. A. council is convinced that college sports belong in campus locales and that concentration of them in any other areas contributes to the conditions which have been brought to light in recent weeks.

6. N. C. A. A. future policies shall be definitely guided by these principles.[35]

Coaches, as the most logical adults to oversee the activities of the athletes, needed to be specified in these recommendations. While the coaches did not seem to be at any direct fault for this problem, many saw them as neglecting one of their primary duties—to teach young men about morality. CCNY, over the following years, would struggle most with this issue. The school initially gave Coach Nat Holman administrative leave while it evaluated his role in the scandal. Then they fired him while he was teaching at basketball camps in Europe. However, he successfully fought this action and was reinstated as coach of a program that no longer had any interest in participating on a national stage.[36]

Recommendation #5 came as the most controversial. Did the NCAA have enough time to abandon Municipal Auditorium and Madison Square Garden for on-campus early round sites? The penalty for breaking leases may have been substantial in the Garden because its rental fee—50 percent of the net profits—was so high. But Municipal Auditorium's low rental fee would have meant that their contract could have been voided with potentially little penalty. Clearly, though, this recommendation was not about Kansas City. It was about New York City. And the NCAA was unwilling to put itself in a short-term financial obligation that would result in a major financial loss. Indeed, the issue was not about on- or off-campus facilities at that moment. For the NCAA likely could have found any number of college campus arenas that would have hosted tournament games at a moment's notice. The problem would have been with logistics and paying the Garden a penalty for breach of contract that would result in forfeiting the high profits that the New York facility always generated for the NCAA tournament's bottom line.

Bradley Responds with an Offer

Two schools took these NCAA recommendations very seriously. Bradley and George Washington "came out against playing in the Garden at the present." Bradley took matters even further by offering to host a new tournament. Bradley athletic director Arthur E. Bergstrom announced that his school, as a burgeoning national basketball power, would use its prestige to host a "National Back to Campus" basketball tournament March 24–30— dates that would fall after both the NIT and NCAA events. This tournament came less as a result of the NCAA's recommendations, though, and more as a way to show both the NCAA and NIT that they had it wrong. This event would occur solely on Bradley's campus in the school's gymnasium. "We are not competing with any of these other tournaments," Bergstrom noted, proclaiming that he is "perfectly aware of the fact that no team would pass up the N.C.A.A., which is the official annual tournament of our national athletic body, in favor of this tournament." The Bradley athletic director added that "it is our belief, however, that there is room for at least one major tournament played entirely on a college campus."[37]

Bergstrom sent out twenty-six "feeler invitations" and received positive responses from Colgate, Bowling Green, LaSalle, San Francisco, DePaul, Wyoming, Utah, Duquesne, William and Mary, and Washington and Jefferson. Outside of Colgate and William and Mary, every team in this veritable lineup had played in the NIT or NCAA tournament in recent years. Two more schools, Bergstrom noted, had responded, but conference rules prevented them from entering. The Bradley athletic director used this as his second major argument for the creation of his tournament. "It is possible (based on current NCAA and conference rules)," he mused, "that nearly one-half of the top twenty teams in the United States would not be included in the N.C.A.A., and we feel that these teams, together with other teams having outstanding records this year, should have an opportunity to participate in a national tournament, played under wholesome conditions, with college supervision, and on a college campus."[38]

The Chaos of Team Selection

The Bradley meet, then, added complexity to the tournament selection process that provided great public interest in late February and early March. The frenzy created by this chain of events became a bit like the gold rush and a bit like speed dating—there were a lot of options, there was some risk, not all choices were guaranteed, and yet decisions had to be made quickly. One choice remained simple for the NIT selection committee. With LIU and CCNY out of the picture, St. John's received an early nod. The Redmen were the most prominent New York City team that stayed out of the scandal's wake. North Carolina State, Arizona, and Brigham Young also received early bids. North Carolina State had dominated the Southern Conference ever since Everett Case became coach five years prior, winning a league championship each season the Hoosier was at the helm. Arizona also had a recent stranglehold on its league—the Border Conference. Brigham Young would be a first-time participant. The Cougars won the Skyline Conference and its bid came without argument.[39]

The next three invites raised eyebrows, though. Lawrence Tech of Detroit, Beloit College of Wisconsin, and the University of Dayton all became first-time participants in the NIT, too. While these teams all had good records, they did not offer the national name recognition that most NIT participants usually had. This meant that either MIBA officials worried about whether it could attract big-name teams as a result of the scandal, or the event was interested in opening its doors to new teams emerging on the national stage.[40]

On March 1, Seton Hall accepted an invitation to the NIT. The Pirates and their coach "Honey" Russell—a prominent professional cager in the 1920s—had proven themselves over the past fifteen years to be a very strong program. However, the MIBA often overlooked this team from South Orange, New Jersey, that was often just outside of New York City's eyeshot. Seton Hall had competed in the 1941 event and would bring an integrated and sophomore-heavy squad into this tournament. That same day, Bradley also announced its first official tournament teams. Frequent NIT participants Toledo and Utah agreed to participate with the host Braves.[41]

On March 3, North Carolina State clinched an automatic bid to the

NCAA tournament by defeating Duke for the Southern Conference crown, making the Wolfpack contenders to match CCNY's "grand slam" feat of the previous season. Columbia won the Eastern Intercollegiate League title the following day to take that conference's automatic bid. The Lions entered the tournament as the first team ever undefeated after the regular season to do so. Also on March 4, the National Catholic Invitational Tournament filled its bracket as Iona College of New York accepted the final bid.[42]

On March 6, Asa Bushnell announced the final spots for the NIT. Newcomers Cincinnati and St. Bonaventure entered the fray as relative unknowns with relatively strong records at 17-3 and 18-5, respectively. Cincinnati only received the bid after the number 2 team in the country, Oklahoma A&M, rejected their offer to participate. In Kansas City, Al Duer of the NAIB announced that he had six teams lined up for his thirty-two-team field that would commence seven days later. He also proclaimed that he rejected the recommendation of the New York–New Jersey NAIB district for its representative. This district had sent a team to the tournament over the past few seasons including Brooklyn College in 1949. Duer did not give a reason for why he rejected the recommendation, although it could have been a political move on his part to show disfavor with the gambling scandal based in New York City. The NCIT tournament also opened its tournament field up again, adding a ninth team and expected three more invites.[43]

On March 7, two more teams joined the NCIT—Mount St. Mary's of Maryland and Spring Hill of Alabama. The Maryland squad won the Mason-Dixon Conference and the Alabama quintet won the Gulf States Conference. Syracuse became the fifth team to enter the Bradley tournament, joining the hosts, Wyoming, Utah, and Toledo. The NIT—at that point the only tournament with a full list of entrants—seeded its top four teams. These squads—St. John's, Arizona, Brigham Young, and North Carolina State—all received first-round byes.[44]

Without much coincidence, each of these four teams also qualified for the NCAA field. St. John's received an at-large bid on March 8. Arizona won the Border Conference, Brigham Young the Skyline Conference, and North Carolina State the Southern Conference, giving each of these league titlists an automatic bid. Only six teams had ever played in both events in the same year and never more than two in the same year. With four in both frays all at once, City College's "Grand Slam" would have new suitors. Big Ten champion Illinois, Southeastern Conference champion Kentucky, Big Seven champion Kansas State, and Missouri Valley Conference champion Oklahoma A&M joined those suitors as automatic qualifiers to the NCAA event. Amid a great deal of difficulty and discussion, the NCAA named

Montana State and San Jose State—"one of the strong small college teams in California"—as the two at-large bids in the Western Regional. This left the Pacific Coast and Southwest Conference bids in the air out West and three at-large bids in the East.[45]

By March 9, the NAIB had secured entry from twenty-two teams, leaving only ten spots to be filled within four days before tournament action commenced. The *Kansas City Star* noted that three of the teams had won district play-off games to receive their bids much like the NCAA had done in the past. Participating teams came from as far away as Virginia and Washington.[46]

Tournament Action Begins

The NIT tipped off on March 10 with a four-game docket of unseeded teams to open the five-tournament college basketball postseason. Dayton defeated Lawrence Tech, and Seton Hall won over Beloit in front of 9,200 fans that afternoon; 14,115 watched St. Louis beat LaSalle and St. Bonaventure take down Cincinnati in the NIT's first-ever double overtime game that evening. Despite the relatively sparse crowds for the first-round action, Beloit coach Dolph Stanley reaffirmed the importance of the NIT. After his team's loss, Stanley professed, "Every team should have a goal, and the N.I.T. is the goal of every team in the country . . . This is a fine incentive in intercollegiate sport, which is played cleanly and honestly by the overwhelming majority. The dishonesty of a few should not deprive the many of this goal." After calling the NIT "the rainbow for every college basketball player" and noting that six of his players made the dean's list at Beloit and none are on athletic scholarship, he also sounded off about the big picture of college athletics that had come into question in recent days. "A lot of people have suggested cutting out intercollegiate basketball. It would be silly to do that because a few players are crooked. There are some crooked individuals in almost everything," he opined.[47]

That same night, the NCAA field became clearer. Washington beat UCLA for the Pacific Coast crown, leaving only the Southwest Conference entrant—either Texas or Texas A&M—for the final western spot. The NCAA also leaked that seven teams were being considered for its final three at-large bids out East. The 1947 champion Holy Cross, Villanova, Louisville, Connecticut, Washington and Jefferson, NIT first-round loser Cincinnati, and Bradley tournament entrant Toledo all hoped for the coveted spots.[48]

NIT quarterfinal action and NAIB and NCIT opening-round games tipped off on Tuesday, March 13. In New York City, Brigham Young made easy work of St. Louis in a 75–58 win while St. Bonaventure took St. John's to the limit before succumbing, 60–58. The 10,124 in attendance relished the last-second shot from Johnny center Zeke Zawoluk that broke the tie and gave the locals a semifinal berth. In New York City's other college basketball developments that night, the NCAA announced that Villanova, Louisville, and Connecticut had been selected as the final three at-large bids. The *New York Times* also mentioned that NYU had been considered for a bid. Even though the Violet had one player—star Connie Schayes—implicated in the gambling scandal just weeks before, the school continued its basketball action. And, had the team received an NCAA bid, the Violet would have recovered from the scandal far more quickly than its peers.[49]

On Wednesday, March 14, 9,630 fans witnessed two upsets in the other NIT quarterfinal matches. Dayton took down fourth-seed Arizona, and Seton Hall upset the second-seed North Carolina State. Two teams attempting the "double," then, would not reach that lofty goal. Semifinal action commenced the following night, and local crowd interest finally caught on; 16,815 saw both visiting teams gain berth in the finals. Dayton upset the top seed and local favorite St. John's, 69–62, and Brigham Young beat nearby Seton Hall, 69–59.[50]

Saturday, March 17, 1951, marked the only day in history in which three national basketball championship games were played. Brigham Young downed Dayton in front of 18,379 fans at the Garden for the fourteenth annual NIT championship. The Flyers hung with the Cougars for twenty-six minutes, but then the Utah squad, led by "blond bombshell" Roland Minson, took control for a 62–43 win. Minson scored 26 points, grabbed 15 rebounds, and tallied "numerous interceptions and assists." Brigham Young completed the first leg of its quest for a "double."[51]

Upstate in Troy, New York, NCIT action concluded with St. Francis of New York taking down Seattle University for its fourth win in as many nights and the third annual NCIT crown. The New Yorkers, runners-up in each of the first two NCIT events, finally overcame their championship roadblock to win the tournament. And in Kansas City, Hamline College of Minnesota took home its third NAIB crown by defeating Millikin College of Illinois. The NAIB final attracted a crowd of 9,000 to Municipal Auditorium as the Minnesotans became the first team to win the same national championship tournament three times. However, that feat would be matched soon.[52]

The Expanded NCAA Tournament

NCAA tournament play opened on Tuesday, March 20, in Kansas City, New York City, and Raleigh, North Carolina. A capacity crowd of 12,500 fans jammed into North Carolina State's new William N. Reynolds Coliseum for the double-header. Kentucky, ranked number one in the nation at the end of the regular season, beat Louisville 79–68. The Cardinals held Kentucky's All-American center, sophomore Bill Spivey, in check, but the rest of the Wildcats picked up the slack in the win. The other Raleigh contest featured the home team. In NCAA action, no team had ever lost a tournament game on its official home floor, and the Wolfpack continued this streak by defeating Villanova 67–62. This win was even "more sensational," tournament administrator George Shiebler remarked, "when it is recalled that Villanova won by 68 to 61 and 66 to 64 in regular season contests (with North Carolina State) and while the Wolfpack boasted the All-American Sam Ranzino and Paul Horvath and Vic Bubas. These three four-year men were not eligible for the N.C.A.A. tournament."[53]

Questions about player eligibility remained a contentious issue within the NCAA, a residual effect of the ad hoc wartime policy changes. In late January, the NCAA voted to allow only three years of eligibility for its athletes. Extra years had been permitted during the war and in its aftermath as veterans returned to campus. North Carolina State, a top team all season, knew that this ruling would potentially hit home since Bubas, Horvath, and Ranzino laced up their sneakers as freshmen in the fall of 1947, and so did Bradley University. The 1950 NCAA and NIT runners-up returned four senior starters for the 1950–51 squad, none of whom would be eligible for NCAA postseason play under the new rule. The passage of this legislation further muddied the college basketball postseason waters. Indeed, this ruling may have discouraged certain teams like Bradley from competing in the NCAA event and encouraged them to look elsewhere.[54]

North Carolina State and Kentucky traveled to New York City to join with the Garden's first-round winners. In one opener, Columbia also played without the services of an ineligible player. Sixth man Bob Sullivan, an engineering major at the prestigious institution, fell behind in his grades and would not be allowed to compete with his team. More than 17,000 fans came out to see Columbia and the other local entrant St. John's take on out-of-town teams in first-round action. The Lions fell to Illinois as their "sensational shooting accuracy vanished" in the face of Illinois's "defense perfection." Shiebler also noted that "St. John's enjoyed an easy time with Connecticut due to the latter's bad case of tournament jitters at the start." St. John's jumped out to a 34–19 lead at halftime and coasted to an 11-point victory from there.[55]

In the second round, North Carolina State, without home court advantage in the Big Apple, lost to a fast Illinois squad 84–70 and St. John's, with de facto home court advantage, succumbed to a better Kentucky team, 59–43. Thus the Saturday night Eastern Regional final pitted the Illini and the Wildcats who provided the most evenly matched game of the Eastern tournament. A crowd of almost 17,000 saw a thriller. This seesaw battle had a tie score eleven different times and went down to the wire. Despite fouls costing both teams the services of important players, both squads kept playing aggressively. With a 74–74 tie late in the game, Kentucky's Shelby Linville knocked down a "floor shot." The Illini had seventeen seconds remaining to force another tie, but captain Don Sunderlage's off-balance attempt fell short.[56]

In Kansas City, two District 5 teams—Kansas State and Oklahoma A&M—won their way to the Western Regional final. But neither team looked dominant in doing so. The Kansas State Wildcats had a 23-point lead against the Arizona Wildcats in the first round with nine minutes left, but the southwestern Wildcats fought back to within one with only 1:23 remaining. K-State held on, though, for a 2-point win. The Wildcats again lost a big lead in their second-round matchup against NIT champion Brigham Young. The Cougars had taken down San Jose State in their opener and looked hot for another triumph. However, the Wildcats raced out to a 20-point lead early in the second half before Brigham Young fought back to within four. The Cougars' hopes of a "double" were lost in the final minutes, though, as K-State took control for a 10-point victory.[57]

Oklahoma A&M started with a "snarling" Montana State team and managed only a 4-point victory. The win matched them with a Washington team that had dismantled Texas A&M in the first round. The Aggies eked out another 4-point win over the Huskies in the second round thanks to hot shooting from the field in the first half. And yet the Aggies lost all of their fire in the contest, for it put up little fight against Kansas State in the Western finals. The Wildcats never had less than a 21-point lead in the second half and won by 24. *Kansas City Star* reporter Bob Busby revealed that the teams' overall shooting percentages indicated the outcomes. The Kansas City media, which had made a practice of obtaining and displaying this statistic for the past several years, believed that this previously overlooked data was important in determining which team won. This metric certainly held true throughout the week of NCAA action. Kansas State topped all teams with an overall shooting percentage of 40.8; the "Cowpunchers" of Oklahoma A&M came in next with 36.9 percent; and semifinalists Washington and BYU shot 36.5 percent and 34.5 percent, respectively.[58]

Minnesota's "Barn" hosted two Wildcat teams in the 1951 NCAA finals, played before 15,348 fans on Tuesday, March 27. Kansas State held a 29–27 lead at halftime with center Lew Hitch giving Kentucky's Spivey all he could handle in the pivot. Wily Kentucky coach Rupp, however, made an intermission move that set the game in his team's favor. Sophomore forward Cliff Hagan, who had been bedridden just two days earlier with the flu, came into the game and took much of the pressure off "Poison Ivy" Spivey. With another post player in the fray, Spivey hit on all seven of his second-half shots to end with a game-high 22 points and 21 rebounds. K-State shot 28.7 percent from the floor while Kentucky hit on 40.5 percent of its attempts. Kentucky also won the rebounding edge thanks to Spivey and Hagan, 45–30, helping them to a 68–58 victory and their third NCAA title in four years.[59]

Coach Rupp had put together a major college basketball dynasty that no other team had matched to that point. Over the past six seasons, his team had won the 1946 NIT, the 1948, 1949, 1951 NCAA titles, and the 1948 Olympic gold medal. And the team likely would have won even more were it not for Rupp's stubbornness in turning down an NCAA District 3 play-off game against North Carolina State in 1950 and a fluke loss in the first round of the 1949 NIT. The 1949 team, potentially Rupp's finest ever, could do nothing right in a game it was supposed to win handily. The ultracompetitive coach had no answers in that unique loss amid a six-year span when losses rarely came to the Wildcats. Every other time it mattered, his stars had been able to win, even in the increased NCAA field of 1951.

Since twice as many teams entered the 1951 NCAA tournament as the previous year, the association expected record profits. And, despite fan turn-outs that set new records only in Kansas City, the association did profit greatly, generating $40,000 more take-home than the previous year. The eight-team field in Kansas City made $40,230.86. This included a tourna-ment high $3,650 in radio and television receipts. One night of action in Raleigh profited $14,973.24 thanks to free use of the on-campus facility. The games in Madison Square Garden made $64,575.03, but half of that number went back to Ned Irish and his facility in rental fees. The East-West Final in Minneapolis profited $22,447.52, a total that benefited from no rental price and a $2,285 radio broadcast receipt—almost twice as much as the radio broadcast generated for the same amount of games in Raleigh. In sum, the NCAA made $104,994.03 from the 1951 tournament. Half of this amount went back to the association and the other half went to the participating teams. The finalists each received $5,833.15, a sum much higher than the $1,822.80 that each first-round loser received. This marked the largest differ-ence in prize money between winners and losers, setting more of a premium on tournament success.[60]

Back to Campus

For the first time since its inception in 1939, the NCAA championship was not the season's final tournament. The Bradley "Back to Campus National Championship Tournament" commenced on Tuesday, March 27, with two first-round games. Wyoming led 52–17 at halftime and coasted from there, defeating Duquesne by 17 points. The host Braves downed Western Kentucky by 4 in the other opening night contest. The following night Syracuse beat Toledo by 17, and Utah held off Villanova by 2 in the other opening-round games. Friday night's semifinal action was determined relatively quickly in each game. Syracuse beat Utah by 14, and Bradley beat Wyoming by 17. The following night, Saturday, March 31, Bradley took on Syracuse in the finals in front of a very partisan and raucous home crowd. The Orangemen held a 4-point lead, 70–66, with three minutes left and extended it to 76–68 with a minute and a half remaining. But over the next minute and ten seconds, Bradley scored 6 unanswered points to cut the lead to two, 76–74. With twenty seconds remaining, Syracuse called its sixth timeout of the game. Unfortunately, a team was allowed only five in a game, and this mistake gave the Braves a free throw and the ball. After the successful charity attempt, Bradley worked the ball around and took a long shot that would have given them the lead. The shot fell wide, however, and the Orangemen snuck out with a one-point win and the championship title.[61]

The five-legged postseason had finally come to an end. Indeed, the 1950–51 college basketball season had ended with five different teams enjoying the title of national tournament champions. Siena won the NCIT, Hamline won the NAIB, Brigham Young won the NIT, Kentucky won the NCAA, and Syracuse won Bradley's National Campus Basketball Tournament (NCBT). The NCIT and NAIB events were not recognized as major college tournaments, and their champions were rarely given status as the nation's top team anywhere outside of their home and tournament locales. The Bradley event provided top-notch competition, and its finalists—Syracuse and Bradley—garnered positive publicity at season's end for finishing as well as any team, but it remained a new tournament whose entrants came by invite only. The NIT champion often enjoyed status atop the basketball world, but this season's did not. Champion BYU, in exiting the NCAA tournament in the second round, gave up its claim to the nation's top spot with the loss. NCAA champ Kentucky, who finished the regular season ranked number one, had the best claim to this title.

More Scandal Revelations

The college basketball off-season proved as complex as the postseason, revealing a great deal about college basketball and yet also leaving a lot of questions unanswered. In late July, New York City district attorney Frank Hogan revealed that he had confessions from five Bradley basketball players who had accepted bribes to fix basketball games. Braves star Gene Melchiorre, captain William Mann, and starters Charles "Bud" Grover, Aaron Preece, and James Kelly all admitted to accepting money to "hold down scores in two games." Hogan was also in the process of questioning three other Braves with potential involvement.[62]

Melchiorre and his teammates were offered $500 each to keep the score down in the Braves' NIT third-place game in 1949 against Bowling Green. However, the Falcons won and no payment was made. Bradley players did, however, collaborate with gamblers to shave points in two games played on its campus. Bradley beat Washington State at home on December 21, 1949, but kept the score well under the point spread by eking out a 2-point victory. On December 5, 1950, the Braves also held down their score against Oregon State, winning by only 3 points in a game that could have easily been a blowout victory.[63]

With these devastating revelations, Bradley—the school that had made the most work out of bringing purity back to college basketball by hosting a postseason tournament that remained steadfastly on campus and, therefore, away from the lure of gamblers—took on great shame. With eight players on its roster fixing games or at least trying to over the last three seasons, more Braves tainted college basketball than CCNY, NYU, and Manhattan players combined. Thus, the finger pointing at New York City's college basketball establishment was no longer as focused. Fixing games was no longer a New York City problem, even though the practice still appeared to have its roots in the Big Apple. The fact that Bradley players fixed games meant that this problem was much more widespread. Further, the fact that Braves fixed games played at their campus gym meant that Madison Square Garden was not the only den of this evil and meant that no venue was immune to gambling.

This revelation also makes sense of the Bradley squad's late-season decisions regarding postseason play. Outside of the NCAA event that they did not qualify for because of player eligibility, they could have chosen to play in either the NIT or the proposed Chicago NIT. According to Peoria newspapers, Bradley administrators publicly declared their disgust at the scandal and its roots in New York City. So the team likely would have been discouraged from playing any postseason games at Madison Square Garden that year. The Braves' reasons for not scheduling into the tenuous Chicago event also seemed valid. Despite all of this, athletic director Arthur Bergstrom indicated that the players could choose which postseason invitations to accept.[64]

On the heels of two runner-up finishes in 1950, the competitive instinct in the highly successful Bradley squad would have likely evolved into interest in going back to the NIT or NCAA to settle unfinished business. The NCAA was out unless they wanted to play without the services of their seniors who would have been ineligible by NCAA standards, but their thoughts on the NIT event may have been muddled. A January 11, 1951, visit to the Garden to face St. John's ended poorly for the Braves. Bradley, theretofore the top-ranked team in the country, entered the contest with a fifteen-game winning streak. And 16,937 "screaming onlookers" aided the Redmen defense in holding the visitors to 25 percent shooting—down from their season average of 38 percent at the time. However, Peoria journalists noted other reasons for the loss. The Braves were "unable to fathom the eastern brand of officiating," hearkening back local memories of the "(Gene) Melchiorre Incident" that affected the outcome of the Braves' 1950 NCAA championship game in the Garden. The officiating in question resulted in four Braves being disqualified on fouls against St. John's. Madison Square Garden had become "Heartbreak Hall" for Bradley, a "court that has now definitely established itself as the No. 1 jinx floor to the Peorians."[65]

Thus, Bradley may have felt like it could not win at the Garden after three heartbreaking losses there in ten months. And yet, with St. John's as the only New York team in the 1951 NIT, Bradley could have seen this as a perfect opportunity for redemption on multiple levels. However, the players knew of the gambling scandal that had just surfaced; they knew that prosecuting officials continued to learn more and more about the scope of the scandal; and they knew that they were guilty. Accordingly, they may have looked for any excuse not to travel back to New York City and into the teeth of the growing investigation where the opportunity for their guilt to be disclosed would rise dramatically.

This left the Chicago tournament as the only possibility for Bradley in college basketball's postseason national consciousness. Their reasons for snubbing the Chicago NIT seemed valid—it was not a sure thing—but it certainly would have been a sensible decision to participate. They could have drawn large and adoring local crowds and, before the tournament folded, they could have played against top-notch national competition rivaling any other postseason event. Instead, they chose to take what looked like a late winter vacation to play a few respectable college and amateur teams in a round-robin tournament in Hawaii. This decision seemed to indicate either that the Braves were satisfied with what they had accomplished in the past and were comfortable resting on their laurels and, for the seniors at least, were essentially riding off into the sunset; or they were hiding from something. Potentially both explanations hold some bearing.

Once Bergstrom announced that he would be hosting the NCBT, the Braves had their nationally conscious postseason date. This tournament became, in hindsight, a way in which Bergstrom and fellow administrators on Bradley's campus could condemn the evils of college basketball and a way in which the players could showcase themselves one last time in a credible tournament on a national stage without having to go back to Gotham. However, the fact that Bradley held this on-campus tournament attempting to reinvigorate the college basketball postseason with purity and principles by which it had started, meant that the Peoria campus looked awfully hypocritical once revelations of its implication in the scandal surfaced.

Bradley's success over the past four seasons and its annual trips to New York City gave the Illinois athletes opportunities to connect with the gambling establishment that they seemingly could not pass up. Their success also gave their administration an opportunity to become a leader in college basketball's burgeoning morality movement after the February 1951 revelations of New York City athletes fixing games. Once Melchiorre and his teammates confessed, however, Bradley bowed in shame. Its courage to put college basketball back on moral high ground looked now like nothing more than a sham.

In no way could Bradley host a second annual NCBT. Offering a second annual invite would have generated nothing more than condescending snickers. NIT upstart participant Lawrence Tech of Detroit dropped its entire athletics program due to overemphasis. CCNY and other New York City–run schools heavily de-emphasized basketball, and many other schools reassessed their athletics programs to search for ways to purify the soul of college basketball.[66]

Game fixing in college basketball was not simply a New York City issue. It never had been, but its rumors had become most prominent in games at Madison Square Garden. Thus was the geographic complexity of Bradley's connection to the scandal. The Braves were infiltrated through New York City transplants. Brothers Nick and Tony Englisis grew up in New York City connecting to gamblers before moving to Lexington, Kentucky, so Nick could play football for the Wildcats. The Englisis boys were indicted for bringing Bradley into the fold and, despite the obvious New York City link, their Kentucky connections became ominous.[67]

Even More Scandal

In October 1951, Kentucky took the scrutinizing public eye off Bradley, relieving the Braves of their role as lead goat in this scandal. Although Coach Rupp had come out defiantly against gambling, arguing that he knew everything going on with his players and, in a memorialized quote, saying that, "gamblers couldn't reach my boys with a ten-foot pole," new revelations displayed him as either a liar or simply naïve. Hogan revealed that All-Americans Alex Groza and Ralph Beard along with 1949 team captain Dale Barnstable had fixed games played in the Garden. Thus, the team that took over college basketball with a 1946 NIT championship, NCAA championships in 1948 and 1949, and a 1948 Olympic gold medal had been corrupt.[68]

And the game that Hogan caught these players fixing was obvious in hindsight. The three Wildcats had each accepted $500 to shave points against an underdog Loyola team in the first round of the 1949 NIT. This was the game that had Rupp so confused. The Baron had lost sleep over how his team played so uncharacteristically poorly during a season in which they had been so good and had such realistic hopes of taking home what would have been a theretofore unprecedented "grand slam" championship crown of winning the NIT and NCAA titles. Beard and Groza had also accepted smaller bribes to hold the victory margin down on games played outside New York City, but the NIT loss was the revelation that hit the hardest.[69]

Barnstable, by 1951 a high school basketball coach in Louisville, caught the least of the public's condemnation. After all, he was not an All-American and his playing days were over. Beard and Groza, however, had become household names for their on-court brilliance. They had taken the Wildcats to success that no other college basketball team had matched to that point. Further, upon graduation, they had helped create a new NBA franchise and immediately found success at that level, too. With three other Kentucky teammates, the Indianapolis Olympians with player-owners Groza and Beard made the play-offs each of their first two seasons in the league. After Hogan's revelations, though, Groza and Beard received lifelong suspensions from the NBA by its commissioner Maurice Podoloff. The Olympians folded in 1953.[70]

Matters for Kentucky, unbelievably, got even worse. Coming off the 1951 NCAA title—its third in four years—led by sophomore center Bill Spivey, the Wildcats were in position to continue their dynasty. A Spivey knee injury early in the 1951–52 season derailed Kentucky's thoughts of immediate success. And when surgery was required, Rupp had to reorganize his team's charges. In the wake of this injury, though, rumors of Spivey fixing

The University of Kentucky bench during a 1951 contest. Bill Spivey is third from the left, and Adolph Rupp is fourth from the right. *Courtesy of University of Kentucky Special Collections Research Center.*

games the previous season grew louder. Authorities had credible information that he and a teammate had fixed a game at the 1950 Sugar Bowl. On December 24, 1951, amid the swirling of rumors and speculation, Spivey renounced his eligibility at Kentucky and sought to enter professional basketball immediately. But Spivey's move could not absolve him of guilt. While fixing games was not on the Kentucky state law books as an official crime, this sort of behavior carried a high social penalty. So although Spivey was never jailed like previous Wildcats—fixing games was a crime in New York—he received harsh social penalties. Spivey was kept out of the NBA on Podoloff's orders. Although Spivey found success in the American Basketball League, his ban from the NBA hindered his legacy.[71]

The University of Kentucky basketball team had the book thrown at it. The NCAA came down with its harshest penalty to date without question as it banished the Wildcats from basketball competition for one entire season. The team would not be allowed to play games in the 1952–53 season. While Rupp kept his job and the team intact by playing the role of victim—fooled by Spivey and unfairly penalized by the NCAA—the association acted in a manner that indicated future oversight. New NCAA executive secretary Walter Byers doled out this punishment as the first in his thirty years of association oversight during which the NCAA's power increased drastically.[72]

College basketball had been knocked to its knees with the New York City player confessions. It fell to the ground with Bradley and Kentucky's confessions. And Spivey's revelations just felt like an unnecessary kick in the gut. How much more could the game handle?

New Beginning, with Leverage, 1952–2005

The basketball season in between the scandal and the Kentucky sanctions was tenuous. The scars of the findings were still fresh and became constant reminders of how easily the game could be tainted. Would there be more allegations to come? Was the problem fixed? Any time a team played poorly, suspicion arose that they may be dumping. New revelations from New York City district attorney Frank Hogan had come in January, February, July, and October of 1951, and the college basketball establishment experienced the 1951–52 season bracing all the while for Hogan to make yet another discovery.[1]

The two latest revelations—those of Bradley and Kentucky players fixing games—had been the most difficult to swallow for college basketball's coaches, players, and fans across the country. New York City, from the outside at least, seemed like a den of thieves, a sea of siren calls, a lair of legal shortcomings. To those outside of the Big Apple, it seemed obvious that this scandal came from the big city—the one that drove much of the American social engine, both for better and for worse. Since so many people lived in the five boroughs, the city experienced so much. While there may not have been a larger percentage of "bad apples" in the Big Apple than any other city across the country, the fact that there were so many more people in Gotham meant that more bad could happen.

When the Kentucky players confessed to fixing games, the revelation was shocking but made sense. In Lexington and the small Appalachian or midwestern burgs from which many of these players hailed, they were never tempted in the same ways that the city kids had been. Growing up having to deal everyday with the temptations such as those offered by the gamblers can harden even the most responsible citizens. The city-bred players on LIU, NYU, CCNY, and Manhattan who confessed to fixing games knew what they were getting into. They had been raised around such vices and simply became part of the problem. Social ills such as these in the big city perpetuated themselves through the recruitment of new, young blood to carry the torch. These players were simply the next wave of game fixers.[2]

The Kentucky boys were not. Most of them had been raised in small-town America where mothers served moral biscuits for dinner every evening. And yet, the Wildcats' hometowns in Kentucky and neighboring states were not immune to moral misgivings. Ralph Beard, for example, never experienced the trappings of the big city growing up in Hardinsburg, a small rural community between Evansville and Louisville. After moving to Louisville for high school, though, he entered the horse racing—and horse race betting—capital of the country. Gambling at Churchill Downs was not just customary, it was expected. Beard knew of the connections between big-time sport and gambling. He matriculated at Kentucky, then, as a young, talented, somewhat wide-eyed, and intensely competitive freshman, leading his teammates to the NIT championship with his speed and fearlessness. Alex Groza rejoined the team for Beard's sophomore season, and the Ohio native whose brother was already making money playing professional football would have been much more worldly, hardened, and attuned to the ways of the world after his eighteen-month stint in the military. After leaving New York City that season with no title, they returned as established junior stars who won the NCAA tournament and college portion of the Olympic Trials in 1948. By 1949 they had become nationally recognized. They entered the 1949 postseason having coasted through one of the most successful campaigns a Wildcat team had ever experienced. They knew they were good—well known and respected across the country, to be sure—and they were treated as royalty in Lexington. Beard and Groza both admitted during the investigation that they had been paid monthly stipends for ghost jobs in town—$50 per month from an alcohol distributor for Groza and the same amount from a local pharmacy for Beard. The point guard also admitted to receiving free clothing when he wanted it from local retailers, a claim many other basketball and football players in Lexington also made at the time. Thus, they were accustomed to receiving under-the-table compensation. But as college athletes, they had no way of making legitimate money off their popularity, and many of them wanted—and convinced themselves that they needed and even deserved—even more money. Further, many of their games had been easy victories. They were almost too good when they played together. Winning had become mundane. Their interest in fixing games was understandable, then, even if also repugnant.[3]

The game-fixing revelations that may have been the most inexplicable were those from the Bradley players. Like the Kentucky players but unlike the LIU, NYU, CCNY, and Manhattan players, they were not born and raised in the streets of New York City that always faces a glare from moral trappings. Instead, they were from northern Illinois. Some grew up in Chicagoland and others from greater Peoria—all from the heart of the Midwest that takes pride in its moral decency and the hard work it takes to succeed. Some of the Braves were married by the time they started college and some were military veterans and, like Kentucky, believed that they needed money. But this made them no different from any other college basketball team in the country at the time. Further, they ranked among the top teams in the country but did not have the record, accolades, program history, antagonistic coach, regional domination, or local double standard that may have made Kentucky a bit too comfortable in winning games. In hindsight, the reasons why Gene Melchiorre and teammates colluded with gamblers remain less obvious.[4]

Bradley, a school that as of this writing still refuses to hang Melchiorre's jersey in its gymnasium alongside the school's other highest honorees, demonstrated a good bit of protestant midwestern self-righteousness at the end of the 1951 season by hosting the "Back To Campus National Championship Tournament" that was to display college basketball as it should be played—on campuses, thereby naturally ridding the game of seedy gamblers seeking to infiltrate young and impressionable players. This naïve outlook—that gamblers only infiltrated the games played at off-campus locations and would not or could not get to the players when they played in campus gymnasiums—was shared by many within the college basketball establishment. And the underlying sentiment was that this problem was not systemic, it was simply a New York City issue.[5]

So when Melchiorre and two other Braves of the seven originally indicted confessed to fixing games played outside New York City and did so only four months after Bradley hosted a postseason tournament that was supposed to re-purify college basketball's soul, the paradox was laughable. Melchiorre and his teammates had not only sold out and tainted college basketball, but by covering up their involvement even throughout a home tournament that was only held to serve as an antidote to the other tournaments that had allowed themselves to be infiltrated, these players put their school in an uncomfortable position.

Although the 1951 Bradley tournament had been a success—it had hosted seven schools all of whom had participated in postseason play previously and had attracted large crowds—there was no question that the event could not continue. The Peoria school, like many others that have been caught up in major scandals, was forced to eat humble pie in the wake of the scandal in order for the scars to heal. Indeed, Bradley mentioned nothing publicly about hosting a second annual "Back To Campus" tournament in

1952. No school would take them seriously. Instead, the university focused on getting the Braves back to national prominence with their play. And the steady influx of northern Illinois talent continued. It would not be long before Bradley was back on the national scene.[6]

The Smaller Tournaments

Catholic school administrators hosted the fourth annual National Catholic Invitation Tournament in 1952 in Troy, New York. For the second straight season twelve teams entered the event and the top four received seeds and first-round byes. Siena College of New York became the only team to receive a seed in each of the four years that this tournament had been played. Tournament officials granted the New York school the top seed but it ended the tournament in third place by defeating St. Francis of New York in the consolation game. Marquette, the two-seed, beat St. Francis of Pennsylvania in the finals to take home the crown.[7]

Crowds of 4,000–5,000 filled the Troy gymnasium to watch these games, making the fourth annual NCIT a success. However, the tournament discontinued. What had become the fourth most sustained postseason college basketball tournament folded after the 1952 installment only to be revived a decade later. In 1963, Xavier, St. Bonaventure, Creighton, and Regis College of Colorado participated in the National Catholic College Tour—a tournament that came virtually without context and only occurred once.[8]

The year 1952 marked an opposite trend in the growing NAIB. The late Emil Liston's fifteenth annual event attracted twenty-six conference champions from across the country in its thirty-two-team bracket. Southwest Missouri State took home the prize in a series of contests that elated the local crowd since no local team had won the title since 1943. By winning, the Bears earned a coveted spot in the 1952 Olympic Trials tournament and would play on the college side of the eight-team event alongside the NCAA champion and runner-up and the NIT champion.[9]

The 1952 NAIB gala, however, remains a pivotal event for off-the-court changes. Two structural decisions put the NAIB in position to become a prominent association in college sports for years to come. Al Duer, executive secretary of the association that by then included more than four hundred members, became the visionary and progressive leader for an association that had been rather conservative in the past. In one of the changes, Duer and the executive board agreed to open the NAIB up to more sports than just basketball. The association approved hosting national meets in track, golf, and tennis. However, doing so would require a name change. Duer polled the membership to see if their preference would be the National Association of Intercollegiate Athletics (NAIA) or the National Association of Intercollegiate Sports (NAIS). They chose the former, and the NAIB became the NAIA.[10]

The second change involved the membership of the NAIA. The tournament had excluded black athletes before 1948 and seemingly only dropped this policy so that it would not lose its spot in the 1948 Olympic Basketball Trials. Yet Duer quickly put the association at the forefront of racial integration by encouraging the executive committee to adopt a measure that would create an at-large district made up of historically black colleges that would ensure that one of them would gain entry into the tournament each year. Thus, in 1953, the NAIA became the first national tournament to include a black college among its participants. The association had gone from racial exclusion to required racial integration in five short years.[11]

Duer's impetus to make this progressive change came at the behest of a group of black basketball coaches called the National Athletic Steering Committee (NASC). The legendary John B. McLendon, coach at North Carolina A&T at the time, led this group. McLendon was a native Kansan who, at the age of eighteen in 1933, had the gall to walk into Dr. James Naismith's office on the Kansas University campus to introduce himself. Naismith was the head of the physical education department at the time when the department, like most others at Kansas, was all white. McLendon was not a particularly good athlete and at 5'7" did not have a body well constructed for basketball. But the young man showed great interest in hoops. With the audacity by which he would later be known, McLendon entered Naismith's office and told the "Father of Basketball" that he was coming to Kansas to study physical education and basketball and that Naismith was to be his advisor. Naismith asked the bold youth who had told him this. McLendon answered that his father—a railroad worker who incidentally had no connection to Naismith, Kansas University, or the game of basketball whatsoever—had told him so. Not knowing a thing about Mr. McLendon or his audacious son sitting opposite the director of physical education, Naismith paused for a moment, sighed, and then replied, "Fathers are always right," thus setting off one of the most unusual relationships that sparked the growth of the game of basketball.[12]

McLendon integrated the Kansas physical education department before entering the basketball coaching ranks. He earned a reputation as a top-notch coach at North Carolina A&T and, in 1949, started the NASC with colleagues at other black colleges to seek representation in established post-season events. McLendon and the NASC pleaded with the NIT and NCAA to allow a black school to enter its ranks on a consistent basis but neither one obliged. While both of these events had hosted integrated teams, both were reluctant to offer a predetermined spot in their prestigious events to a black school. Any communication that the NASC had with the MIBA has not been preserved. Black coaches had queried Ned Irish in the past as to why they were never invited to the Garden event, and he said that he did not choose the teams. Likely, since the NIT had included African Americans since its initial event in 1938, the MIBA felt no need to guarantee one spot each year to a black team. After all, it had never guaranteed spots to anyone except for its understandable inclusion of at least one local team each year. The NCAA, however, simply denied the NASC's request. Since the tournament had been geographically determined before 1951, it follows that the NCAA would say no to the NASC. Most black schools resided in District 3 and would have theoretically had to seek an invite through their district. Most schools in District 3 were segregated and, at the time, would not even play against a black player much less a black team. So black schools had no recourse to seek a bid to the NCAA tournament, and the association was not ready to offer an automatic bid to any school or conference at the time. By 1951, the NCAA began offering automatic bids to conference champions and could have included any of the five black college athletic conferences in its list of ten conferences receiving automatic bids. In 1953, this number of automatic bids increased to include sixteen conference champs. But the NCAA did not believe that the quality of play in these black conferences matched what it hosted in its annual season-ending tournament, therefore denying the NASC's request. The NASC consequently referred to the NCAA as "No Colored Athletes Allowed."[13]

Duer and the NAIA finally accepted the NASC's widespread request and allowed the top black college team in the country to enter its tournament beginning in 1953. Within four years, McLendon proved the quality of black basketball. The coach took over the reins at Tennessee State in 1954 and won the NAIA in 1957, 1958, and 1959 with a squad that included two future NBA stars. This three-peat, a feat that no college team had ever accomplished in any tournament to that point, put McLendon on the map and put forth the foundation of his legacy as the "Father of Black Basketball." These wins propelled him into stints coaching Cleveland State, the Cleveland Pipers of the American Basketball League—where he was the first black coach of a team in a major professional sports league—and the Denver Nuggets of the ABA throughout his distinguished career as a basketball leader.[14]

The peak of McLendon's success as three-peat NAIA champions in the late 1950s may have also been the peak of interest in the Kansas City–based tournament. NAIA membership, which reached its highest in this decade, slowly began to wane in subsequent decades. Yet the tournament has survived. The NAIA now hosts a full docket of sports and has split into two divisions: Division I is for larger schools who put a greater emphasis on sports and Division II is for smaller schools who still see sport as a student-based experience that is to be only one aspect of a student's life. The basketball tournaments at both levels remain as weeklong thirty-two-team events just like Liston originally set up.[15]

The Big Tournaments

The NIT has become a thirty-two-team tournament, too. And its evolution parallels that of the NAIA in certain respects—its prestige is not what it once was. Despite the lingering biases against New York City basketball after the 1951 scandal, the NIT was able to put together a strong field for the 1952 event. Although some schools prohibited their teams from entering the Garden tournament and some conferences put a greater emphasis on their champions entering the NCAA and not the NIT, the MIBA event still mattered to many coaches. Duquesne, St. Louis, St. Bonaventure, and St. John's received seeds and first-round byes while Western Kentucky, Louisville, Seton Hall, LaSalle, Dayton, NYU, Holy Cross, and Seattle battled in the first round. At the end of four nights of action, LaSalle came out victoriously. As such, Coach Ken Loeffler's squad earned a spot in the Olympic Basketball Trials alongside the NCAA champion, NCAA runner-up, and the NAIA champion. Many sportswriters indicated that the Olympic Trials would determine the true national champion of college basketball.[16]

The NCAA changed its format slightly for the 1952 event, but the alterations had major impact. The sixteen-team event set up four regional competitions of four teams, and each regional champion would meet at one location for the semifinal and tournament championship. Dutch Lonborg explained the reasons for having four first-round sites. "First, there would be less travel for the teams," he explained diplomatically, "and second, there would be more income with the additional site." NCAA executive director Walter Byers asked Lonborg if he thought each site could make $30,000 profit. They did, and the event netted a record $132,044. The four regional sites also became prescient. "This was a major step for the tournament," Lonborg surmised. Raleigh, North Carolina, hosted first-round games in 1951, and the NCAA selected it to host an entire regional in 1952. Penn State African American sophomore sensation Jesse Arnelle led the Nittany Lions into the Raleigh regional, quickly integrating the tournament's only Dixie venue since Tulane hosted a decade earlier. But Penn State exited just as quickly at the hands of Rupp's Kentucky squad that was in the midst of an NCAA investigation that would include one year's suspension from basketball the following season. The Wildcats made the most of their time in moratorium by embarking on a 29-3 season that ended shortly after the Penn State drubbing. St. John's defeated North Carolina State—playing in its home gym—in the first round before avenging an early season loss to Kentucky by knocking the defending champs out of the tournament in the regional final. The Redmen's guard Solly Walker became the first African American to play in Kentucky's Memorial Coliseum earlier that season in a Wildcat blowout but led his team to victory in the postseason. With the regional championship, St. John's proved that it had suffered no ill effects of the gambling scandal that it somehow avoided. Indeed, while rumors swirled that the powerful New York City diocese pressured the city's prosecutors to steer clear of the Johnnies, Walker and his teammates made the most of their innocence, reaching the NCAA championship game.[17]

The second Eastern Regional site was Chicago Stadium. The site eyed to host the original NCAA tournament's championship game finally made it onto the NCAA docket thirteen years later. The University of Illinois played to the local crowd's passions and won the regional, perpetuating "home crowd" advantage even though North Carolina State provided an exception to this rule. The Illini ended the tournament in third place for the second straight year, and would not return to the Final Four for another thirty-seven years.[18]

For the first time since the 1939 tournament, Kansas City did not host the entire Western half of the bracket. Oregon State, offering one of the most remote locations the NCAA had ever used to that point, brought in four teams with absolutely no geographic proximity to compete for a spot in the national semifinal. Santa Clara defeated John Wooden's UCLA team in the first round and then squeaked by Wyoming in legendary coach Everett Shelton's penultimate NCAA tournament appearance.[19]

Kansas City still hosted the other Western Regional, an event that Coach Allen's Jayhawks won for the first time since it first hosted NCAA tournament games in 1940. After years of lamenting the ways in which skilled big men could unfairly dominate the game, Allen finally succeeded with a giant of his own. Future NBA All-Star Clyde Lovellette finished his Kansas career by leading the Jayhawks to victory over Texas Christian in the first round and St. Louis in the regional final. "Cumulus Clyde," also known as "The Great White Whale of the Planks," went on a rampage throughout the tournament, averaging more than 35 points per game with his deadly hook shot. "His left elbow would come up and clear people out of the way," one teammate noted of the form of this shot, "If they did get in his way, they only did it once."[20]

The NCAA took each of the regional champions to the University of Washington's Edmundsen Arena for the first "final four." This on-campus venue served the association well in 1949 when it hosted the championship game, and the city has since become a part of the association's regular rotation of hosts. The site made sense on a number of levels. New York City was no longer an option. "When we first moved out of the Garden for the 1949 tournament at the University of Washington, we just wanted a change," Lonborg theorized, "Washington always had good crowds." The tournament director also put some cynical speculation to rest, saying, "When we finally left the Garden for good in the early 1950s, it had nothing to do with the gambling scandals there. The main reason was the rental charge. It was very high." Further, he "figured we could make money on campuses. Schools [like Washington] would usually give us the gym at cost . . . (and) there were some good, new arenas springing up that we could use."[21]

At Washington, St. John's edged Illinois in its semifinal matchup while Lovellette and company thrashed Santa Clara in the other game. Kansas's big man finished business in the final by defeating St. John's in yet another lopsided contest. This put the Jayhawks into the 1952 Olympic Trials tournament with good momentum, and it was all they would need. Lovellette brought his coach the final victories he had hoped for since 1936 when basketball became an official Olympic sport. The Jayhawks reached the final of the trials, qualifying for the Olympic team. Allen had finally reached his goal of coaching in the Olympics, and the Americans—led by Lovellette—won yet another gold medal.[22]

Contesting the NIT's Legacy and Another New York City Scandal

St. John's remained a top team the following season. The 1953 NIT concluded with nearby Seton Hall toppling the Redmen for the title. The championship was a highlight of the storied career for the Pirates' legendary coach Honey Russell. The Pirate mentor produced very strong teams throughout the 1930s, 1940s, and 1950s, but rarely figured prominently in the national basketball scene. Unfortunately, his team's campus view of the Manhattan skyline provided a metaphor for its status in metropolitan basketball—the Pirates were on the outside looking in. Seton Hall fans argued that Russell's teams were often overlooked by NIT selection committees. These committees wanted to have a local flavor to the event and so they would always invite

Kentucky's Bill Spivey guards Kansas's "Cumulus" Clyde Lovellette in a late 1951 game. *Courtesy of University of Kentucky Special Collections Research Center.*

at least one and usually more of the MIBA member schools, but they also wanted the tournament to be national in scope and would therefore always invite schools from other regions. The Pirates, as a team just outside of the five boroughs, did not fall into either the local or intersectional categories, giving the selection committees little reason to choose them.[23]

Author Neil D. Isaacs laments that Seton Hall's 1953 NIT championship did not fully exemplify the strength of that team. Nineteen fifty-three, Isaacs argues, was the first year in which the NCAA tournament clearly was above the NIT. Without giving much rationale for this claim, the author notes that by this time the NIT was seen as too New York focused and too Catholic. The composition of the NIT, however, had not changed much from preceding years. It had hosted Catholic and New York City teams virtually every year, and 1953 was no exception. It had also hosted teams from other regions every year in a trait that continued in 1953. This season marked the first time since 1948 that no team participated in both the NIT and NCAA events, and many schools and conferences had rules preventing teams from doing so. In fact, no team would ever play in both events in the same year again. Isaacs, then, may have been referring to the fact that Seton Hall and LaSalle were the only teams ranked in the AP top ten at the end of the regular season to participate in the New York event. Every other ranked team that played in a postseason event chose the NCAA tournament.[24]

Since Associated Press national rankings had only begun in 1948, it is difficult to assess which tournament field—the NCAA's or the NIT's—was stronger before that. In the late 1940s, AP rankings showed that both tournaments included many ranked teams. Indeed, since a few prominent schools entered both tournaments, both fields were strong. In the early 1950s, however, the NCAA tournaments included more prominent and highly ranked teams. Isaacs's sentiment, then, that this was a period of time in which the NCAA's precedence over the NIT became increasingly obvious is correct. Throughout the 1950s, with the NCAA's membership growing rapidly and NCAA member conferences growing in number and size, the association leaned on its conferences to encourage and even mandate its champions to participate in the NCAA tournament and not the NIT. Indeed, throughout the late 1950s, the NABC encouraged the NCAA to levy harsh sanctions on schools that participated in the NIT when an NCAA bid had been proffered. The NCAA did continually put more pressure on its members to shun the NIT, but never with the extreme punishments such as program expulsion that the NABC desired.[25]

In 1961, another series of scandals involving game fixing in college basketball came to light. And this one was more clearly a New York problem than in 1951. Jack Molinas, a star at Columbia in the late 1940s and early 1950s teams that had great success in the Eastern Intercollegiate League and gained two bids to the NCAA event, and a maverick who enjoyed a successful but gambling-shortened NBA career, orchestrated a network of fixed games to satiate his risk-taking habits. Molinas admittedly gambled on many of his own games. The star was so good that he was able to do so without suspicion throughout college. However, when these fixes came to light during his NBA career, he quickly drew the ire of basketball fans and NBA commissioner Maurice Podoloff alike. Podoloff suspended him for life.[26]

Leverage, Power, and Legacy

This scandal déjà vu encouraged the NCAA to reassess its policies regarding basketball postseason play. Unlike the 1951 scandal, the NCAA comfortably watched the Molinas affair unfold without having to publicize its distance from these wrongdoings. In the wake of these revelations, the NCAA University Basketball Committee condescendingly proposed to the MIBA that the NIT become qualifying or first-round action for the NCAA tournament. Not surprisingly, the committee reported after negotiations, "It was generally agreed that a reorganization of the NIT along the lines envisioned would not be accomplished in the immediate future." The NIT would still fight for its existence, even if it was second class.[27]

NCAA executive secretary Walter Byers subsequently negotiated a deal with the NIT that put a clear stamp on the college basketball postseason tournament hierarchy and set in stone the status pattern that had taken shape over the previous twenty years. At the time, the NCAA offered automatic bids to the champions of sixteen different conferences. Those teams would have to accept an NCAA bid if they were to play in the postseason at all. The NCAA also offered between six and nine at-large bids, depending on the year. In the NCAA's 1962 deal with the MIBA, the NCAA got the first shot at inviting at-large teams. The two associations set a date of the Monday after the third Saturday in February as a time at which the NCAA could begin inviting at-large teams and the NIT could begin inviting teams to its event. While the sixteen conference champs—or, if they turned down the offer and ended their seasons prematurely, the next best team in the conference—were committed to the NCAA, the NCAA also had a one-hour window at which it could recruit the best conference independent or nonautomatic bid conference teams in the country. Indeed, in this deal, the NCAA could offer teams at-large bids beginning at nine in the morning on that Monday, giving it the opportunity to fill its entire twenty-two- to twenty-five-team field before the

NIT could invite any team to its event. The NIT had to wait until 10 a.m. on that day and would only be able to invite teams that were not participating in the clearly more powerful NCAA tournament.[28]

While the NIT's agreement to the terms of this deal seems incredulous, the organization seemingly had little choice. The NCAA had become a large and powerful organization because it had accumulated so many members. With size came power. This put the NIT at a distinct disadvantage. Had the NIT not signed this agreement, the NIT feared that the NCAA could have unilaterally chosen to sanction any team that participated in the New York event with such penalties as banishment from competition with NCAA schools. No team would take that risk, and it would have left the NIT with no participants. However, the legality of this type of punishment may have violated the Sherman Antitrust Act, legislation with which the sport industry was slowly becoming acquainted. Thus, in hindsight, signing this agreement was a mistake, for no other administrative action more clearly defined the NCAA's power and the NIT's lack thereof. This legal contract proved that the NCAA had the power to drive the future of college basketball's postseason. How the organization would leverage that power remained to be seen.[29]

This agreement continued into the 1970s with only slight changes. And its clear demarcation of the NCAA's growing power sparked some negative backlash. Because of the association's emphasis on offering bids to conference champions, many independent teams felt like second-class citizens who only received bids when there was enough room to accommodate them. Further, the 1960s became a decade in which the NCAA's growing control over all college sports sparked some resentment. These factors came to a head in 1970 when a Marquette team coached by Al McGuire turned down an NCAA invitation while accepting one to participate in the NIT. McGuire was a New Yorker through and through. He and his older brother Dick played at St. John's before joining forces in the NBA for the New York Knicks. Although Dick was much more talented, Al's hustle, toughness, emotion, and enthusiasm embodied all that city basketball represented. Despite coaching stops in New Hampshire, North Carolina, and Wisconsin, McGuire's heart was always in New York City.[30]

So when Marquette, an independent team even through most of the 1980s, was offered an NCAA at-large bid in 1970 but was asked to play outside its region, McGuire said no. He fought this perceived geographic injustice by risking sanctions or at least being blackballed by entering his team in the New York event. In a measure of some justice, the Milwaukee team won the NIT. Seven years later, McGuire's Marquette squad won the NCAA tournament.[31]

In the meantime, the NIT continued to lose appeal. In 1975, the tournament received a crushing publicity blow. The 1974 NCAA champion North Carolina State—the team that finally dethroned UCLA after seven straight NCAA titles—finished its 1974–75 season well below its lofty expectations. A second-place finish in the Atlantic Coast Conference meant that it would not receive a bid to the NCAA tournament. When it received an NIT invite, All-American David Thompson was quoted in a newspaper article picked up across the country as referring to the New York event as "a loser's tournament." Such was the feeling regarding what had become a distantly second-class affair.[32]

Despite the scandals that scapegoated the NIT in both 1951 and 1961, the New York event likely would not have become "a loser's tournament" were it not for the NCAA's accumulated growth and power. An eight-team event in 1950, the NCAA grew to sixteen in 1951 and in 1953 enlarged its brackets again to include twenty-two teams. The tournament wavered between twenty-two and twenty-five teams each year until 1975. The changes throughout this period came about with the realignment and changes in the strength of conferences that would potentially merit automatic bids. Further, each conference's success in the tournament was quantified together to determine which conferences received first-round byes. For instance, if the Pac Ten conference record in the NCAA tournament over the past ten years was better than that of any other conference, then it would receive a first-round bye for the following season regardless of which Pac Ten team made the tournament.[33]

The NCAA Splits and New Events Emerge

In 1957, the NCAA split itself into two divisions—university and college. The larger schools comprised the university division and the smaller schools made up the college division. The NCAA basketball tournament had historically hosted larger schools almost exclusively, and so this change mattered little to that event. However, a new NCAA event for smaller schools enticed many of the hundreds of small schools around the country to join the NCAA rather than the NAIA. Their own basketball tournament was yet another benefit the NCAA used to entice schools theretofore unaffiliated. To a much lesser extent, this change diverted basketball postseason goals for small schools away from the NIT, too.[34]

Further competition came from other upstart tournaments during this period of time. In 1967, the National Small Colleges Athletic Association hosted a postseason tournament, and in 1968, the National Christian

Colleges Athletic Association hosted a similar event. However, neither of these events seemed to require membership exclusive of any other association like the NCAA and NAIA. In 1969, the first women's postseason basketball championship tournaments commenced. The Association for Intercollegiate Athletics for Women (AIAW) held their inaugural affair in 1969 and so did the NIT, who called their version the National Women's Invitation Tournament (NWIT). The AIAW event lasted until 1982 when the NCAA began hosting women's championship events. Amarillo, Texas, hosted the NWIT each year until it folded in 1996 only to be resurrected in 1998 as the Women's NIT, which continues today under the auspices of Triple Crown Sports—an entity not affiliated with the NCAA.[35]

The Collegiate Commissioners Association Tournament occurred in 1974 and 1975—a short-lived existence that was meant as an alternative option for men's teams at larger schools. Universities not qualifying for the NCAA field could, at this time, receive an invite to this event put on by the NCAA. The lineup for this eight-team event in 1974 included Southern Methodist, Arizona State, Kansas State, Tennessee, Bradley, Toledo, Southern California, and eventual champion Indiana—all second-place teams from prominent conferences around the country. In order to accommodate the conference-independent teams that often bemoaned their second-class status in the NCAA tournament, the organization did not invite more than one team from any of its member conferences—especially those that received automatic bids. These teams had become increasingly competitive—and increasingly frustrated by their inability to get into the main event—and often chose the NIT as a secondary option. Thus, by roping conference runner-up teams into another NCAA-run event, the association further relegated the NIT. In 1975, the NCAA renamed this event the National Commissioners Invitational Tournament. And since this was the year it expanded its main event from twenty-five to thirty-two teams—including, for the first time, multiple teams from the same conference—this secondary event lost much of its luster. Drake defeated a field including Southern California, Bowling Green, Tennessee, Purdue, Missouri, Arizona, and East Carolina for the last such crown.[36]

In 1975, the NCAA made more structural changes, splitting from two membership divisions into three. Division I would become the group of schools who put the greatest emphasis on sports—this included, among other things, offering the most athletic scholarships to athletes. Division II included athletic scholarships, but in lesser numbers. Division III would not include athletic scholarships. Each of these divisions would host an annual national championship tournament, further taking potential candidates away from the other events. And yet again, this change affected the NCAA's top tournament very little. Division II and III was essentially a split of the previous college division along with some university division teams who rarely figured into college basketball's original championship picture.[37]

During this time, the NCAA's top division basketball tournament grew at a continually faster pace. Throughout the late 1940s and 1950s, under the leadership of Dutch Lonborg, the Northwestern coach who became the Kansas athletic director during his years of service to the tournament, and Kentucky athletic director Bernie Shively from 1960 to 1966, the tournament grew in numerous ways. Attendance at the tournament's games continually rose. The inaugural 1939 tournament attracted 15,025 fans to the games of the eight-team field. The 1950 tournament hosted a record 75,464 fans for its eight-team field. The jump to a sixteen-team event in 1951 allowed the attendance numbers to jump to 110,645. In 1956, the first time the tournament hosted twenty-five teams, attendance hit another record 132,513 fans as the University of San Francisco led by Bill Russell and KC Jones finished the first perfect season of any NCAA champion. The 1957 tournament drew only 108,891 fans, but the final game's drama more than made up for the drop in attendance. Sophomore Wilt Chamberlain led the Kansas Jayhawks into the finals against North Carolina. It took the Tar Heels three overtime periods to finally upset the favored Jayhawks, ending as the second undefeated NCAA champion in a row. The following year, attendance jumped to 176,878 as Adolph Rupp coached Kentucky to his fourth and final championship. The next time twenty-five teams entered the event was in 1960, and 155,491 fans came out for the games. Two years later, another twenty-five-team field drew 187,469 fans.[38]

The twenty-four-team draw in 1954 began a standardized Tuesday–Wednesday slate of regional action with the final four ensuing on Friday and Saturday. This season, in which Tom Gola and "the garbage men" took LaSalle to the championship, marked the first time that the championship game was televised nationally. The Philadelphians took down Bradley in the finals—a team that had rehabilitated from the midst of the scandal in a remarkably short period of time. Nine years later, the NCAA inked a five-year contract with Sports Network to televise the championship games nationally. The contract was worth $140,000 to the association.[39]

The NIT, in trying to keep up, grew from twelve to fourteen teams in 1965. Although it struggled to remain relevant, this small change was an attempt to reinvigorate interest in the event. Three years later it grew again, this time to sixteen teams. In 1975, when the NCAA moved to thirty-two teams at the end of John Wooden's UCLA dynasty, the NIT became even further relegated with David Thompson's comments and North Carolina State's snub of their NIT invite. In 1977, NIT executive director Pete Carlesimo decided to move early round NIT games to campus sites to regenerate interest in the event. "Going to campus sites was a matter of survival . . . we had to do it," Carlesimo's successor, Jack Powers, admitted, "we were in trouble. We lost our television contract with CBS, and fan support had fallen off." The first on-campus NIT game sold out in three hours, setting a precedent for the event that continues today. In 1979, with the momentum from the on-campus sites for early round games, the NIT jumped to twenty-four teams and then immediately up to thirty-two for the 1980 event.[40]

Even these major changes could not help the NIT keep pace in what had become an insurmountable disparity. By 1966, the NCAA made more than a half million dollars on its tournament, and television deals continued to increase profits. In 1969, Lew Alcindor's third straight championship at UCLA, the NCAA changed its Friday–Saturday Final Four schedule to Thursday–Saturday, which allowed for more hoopla at the Final Four site and more buildup in anticipation for the finals. After Alcindor and the Bruins took down Rick Mount and Purdue, the NCAA tournament had netted over a million dollars for the first time ever—a total that included $547,500 from television rights.[41]

In 1971, as UCLA was on the road to its fifth straight NCAA title despite talented freshman Bill Walton sitting out to abide by the freshmen ineligibility rule, 9,320,000 homes saw the NBC broadcast of the semifinal night of action on television. With this growth of interest in watching the penultimate games, the NCAA changed its Final Four format from Thursday–Saturday to Saturday–Monday in 1973. That year, television rights topped $1 million for the first time ever and a total television audience of 39 million watched Bill Walton score 44 points on 21-of-22 shooting from the field—one of the most memorable performances in the tournament's history.[42]

In 1974, despite the exponential growth of television viewership of the Final Four, demand for tickets to the semifinal and final games had grown such that the NCAA implemented a public draw to accommodate the over-subscribed orders for Final Four tickets. The lucky winners of this draw got to see a new Final Four format. The East-West split in the bracket that the tournament teams experienced since the inaugural 1939 event had remained even through tournament expansion. However, the 1974 Final Four, in which North Carolina State and David Thompson snapped UCLA's championship streak at seven providing a bitter end to Bill Walton's storied collegiate career, hosted four geographically named regionals. The East Regional champion played that from the West in one semifinal, and the Mideast Regional champion played that from the Midwest in the other semifinal.[43]

In 1975, as John Wooden closed out his unprecedented run of success at UCLA by retiring as his team beat Indiana to win their tenth NCAA title in twelve years, the Bruins did so by overtaking a newly enlarged thirty-two-team field. With this increase in size, the association had to change its method for inviting teams, and the ACC was at the forefront of this movement. In 1974, the North Carolina State–Maryland matchup in the finals of the ACC tournament was a thriller that many believed pitted the top two teams in the nation. Upon the Wolfpack's victory, they entered the NCAA tournament and the Terrapins could not because of the association's rule prohibiting entry of more than one team per conference. The following year, the Wolfpack and their All-American David Thompson found themselves on the losing side of an epic ACC championship game. Their loss and subsequent exclusion from the NCAA tournament (the NCAA invited ACC tournament champion North Carolina and regular season champion Maryland) prompted Thompson's bitter remarks about the NIT being "a loser's tournament." One of Thompson's teammates further gave voice to their perceptions of the postseason, commenting, "The NCAA is the major leagues. The NIT is the minor leagues." In 1976, the second tournament in which the NCAA allowed two entrants from the same conference, two teams from the Big Ten made it to the final round. Indiana capped off a perfect season by taking down Michigan in the first championship game featuring two teams from the same conference, making this band of Hoosiers only the seventh undefeated NCAA titlists.[44]

The 1979 NCAA tournament included forty teams for the first time. The championship game, held in Salt Lake City, featured two budding and contrasting stars. The black, charismatic, flashy Earvin "Magic" Johnson led his Michigan State team to a victory over the white, introspective, downhome Larry Bird and his Indiana State Sycamores. NBC hyped these two stars in their buildup to the championship telecast, and Americans responded with great interest. The game received record television ratings and television share for basketball and set the tournament ablaze. The following year, when Bird and Johnson quickly led their professional teams to the NBA play-offs, the NCAA tournament received further validation of its status. The top college players should take their teams deep into the NCAA tournament, and those players should become the top NBA players who, then, take their teams to NBA championships. This neat and orderly, and probably idealistic, logic provided the NCAA tournament with a platform within the basketball establishment that clearly had no peer. It was the premier event, far and away.[45]

In 1980, the NCAA expanded its bracket to forty-eight teams, and this included twenty-four automatic qualifications to conference champions and twenty-four at-large berths. The selection committee continued to try to provide geographic equality where it could and attempted to keep teams in their geographic locales, but it reserved the right to assign teams to any region to provide the most balance among tournament entrants and among the regions. Underlining these discussions were the difficulties of promoting equality where necessary. Total equality among the tournament entrants was not a goal. Teams who performed best during the regular season would be given an advantage in the tournament. The top sixteen teams received a first-round bye. But the geographic nature of the tournament presented difficulties regarding potential home court or home area advantages to teams that may not have earned this type of advantage. The NCAA created a set of principles by which the selection committee would seed and place teams in the brackets. This system provided rules that sought equality among regions and fairness to conferences more so than overall geographic equality, thus marking one of the larger shifts from geographic focus to a market focus that the tournament had been on since it grew to a sixteen-team event and allowed automatic bids for conference champions in 1951.[46]

In 1983, the tournament expanded to include fifty-two teams, eight of which played in opening-round matchups to secure the last four spots in a forty-eight-team bracket. This event also established the current schedule of early round games the third weekend of March, regional final action the fourth weekend of March, and the Final Four in the first weekend of April. The NCAA also determined that the facilities that would hold each subsequent Final Four must have a minimum of 17,000 seats.[47]

In 1984, the bracket expanded to include fifty-three teams and in 1985 the NCAA hosted a full sixty-four-team tournament that included thirty automatic qualifying conferences—a number that was capped for five years. This growth—the tournament had doubled in ten years—did not sit well with the NIT. The NCAA had wielded its power and popularity in such a way that it had virtually pushed the NIT out of the market of big-time college basketball tournaments. NIT executives began complaining publicly that the NCAA, by expanding its tournament using fear tactics to ensure that teams would accept its bids when offered, had created a monopoly on postseason play. When the NCAA tournament hosted only eight teams, and even when it hosted thirty-two, the NIT felt like it could compete and at least host some quality teams. But with the most recent growth, the NIT felt as if it had been forced into one of its more derogatory nicknames, "The Not Invited Tournament."[48]

The NCAA tournament did not grow in size for another twenty years, but it did grow in popularity and power. In 1987, the NABC endorsed a policy that would allow teams to participate on their home courts in the first and second rounds of competition, but the tournament's growth quickly made that policy unnecessary. In 1989, the NCAA ruled that neutral courts should be used in all rounds of the event, and that the Final Four sites should all be able to accommodate at least 30,000 spectators. A 1991 television contract for seven years that was worth $1 billion and included live coverage of all sessions of the tournament proved most specifically that the NCAA tournament was not only the premier college basketball tournament, but that is was also a premier event in the American sporting landscape.[49]

In 1993, the NCAA required that all pre–Final Four host sites be able to accommodate at least 12,000 spectators. Clearly, live attendance at all sessions continued to grow and the association worked hard to accommodate this demand. In 1994, the NCAA implemented a policy that showed who held the power within the association. Even though no teams seeded number one or two in their regions had ever lost a first-round game to that point in the sixty-four-team era, the tournament committee "agreed to attempt to assign the top four seeds in each region away from a site that may create a 'home-crowd advantage'" for their opponents. The top four seeds in each region usually came from the most powerful conferences in the NCAA and usually matched up against teams from much smaller schools in much less powerful conferences. The top conferences wielded further power by forcing a bracketing policy in 1997 stating that two teams from the same conference would not be placed in the same regional unless there were eight or more teams participating from that conference. This policy came about with what must have been a bit of haughtiness among the power conferences. To think that any one conference could receive eight berths in a sixty-four-team tournament that included thirty automatically qualifying conferences would have meant that the power conferences thought very little of the rest of the conferences. The fact that the proceeds from the tournament's lucrative television contract were divided among conferences based on their order of finish dictated this policy. By separating conference teams into separate regions by policy, it meant that the conferences who received the most bids—the power conferences, usually—had the best chance to take home the most money. In 1998, this policy changed slightly. Instead of the eighth team being able to be matched in a region with the conference's top team, now it was only the sixth conference team invited that could potentially be listed in the top team's region.[50]

In 1995, CBS replaced its $1 billion contract with a new seven-year deal worth $1.725 billion. By 1999, the NCAA inked a deal with CBS for eleven years that was worth $6.2 billion. In comparison, the NIT signed a ten-year

television deal with ESPN in 2000 worth $24.1 million. This type of dispar-
ity and the fact that the NCAA tournament continues to grow, encouraged
the NIT to file a lawsuit against the NCAA claiming that the association
violated antitrust laws by monopolizing college basketball's postseason.[51]

The NIT filed suit in 2001, capping twenty years of public complaints
from the MIBA that the NCAA's growth was prohibiting the NIT from being
a first-rate tournament. In 1982, the NCAA implemented a rule that had
been unspoken and at differing levels of urgency for the previous twenty
years. This rule stated that any team invited to an NCAA postseason event
must accept the "commitment to participate" rule. From 1961 to 1970, eight
college basketball teams—including an Army team coached by Bobby Knight
and Al McGuire's 1970 Marquette squad—turned down NCAA tournament bids. There is no record of teams making such choices after that. The
NCAA's official rule in 1982 spoke to all sports. It solidified basketball's
problem that had been, in reality, already put to rest. But teams in other
sports still needed the regulative motivation.[52]

The NIT's 2001 legal action was based on this 1982 rule. The MIBA,
then comprised of Fordham, Wagner, Manhattan, St. John's, and NCAA
founder NYU believed that the NCAA had created a monopoly and pushed
the NIT out of the postseason major college basketball market. In court,
both sides brought out big guns to testify. The NIT listed coaches Bobby
Knight of Texas Tech, John Calipari of Memphis, Dana Altman of Creighton,
and Lou Carnesecca formerly of St. John's. The NCAA invited Duke's
Mike Krzyzewski, Michigan State's Tom Izzo, Syracuse's Jim Boeheim, and
Kentucky's Tubby Smith to give affidavits. The courts, seeing what could
become endless testimony from coaches, limited each side's presentations,
and so not all coaches took the stand.[53]

In August of 2005, the NCAA and MIBA settled out of court. The
NCAA agreed to pay $56.5 million to the MIBA for the rights to the NIT
with the understanding that the NCAA would continue the event with the
semifinals and finals at Madison Square Garden for at least five years and
would share the profits with the five MIBA schools for ten years. This agreement effectively put to rest any lingering speculation about the relationship
between the two tournaments. The NIT, which had come under the shadows
of the NCAA tournament for decades, was now owned by the larger association. Its second-class status forever solidified in a wholesale buyout that
equaled about a tenth of the amount of money that the NCAA made at the
time in its television deal with CBS each year. The NCAA's March Madness
was not a monopoly, but it had bought out its closest competitor, officially
accomplishing—after sixty-six years—what Harold Olsen, Phog Allen, and

John Bunn set out to do in the inaugural NCAA basketball championship tournament.[54]

Ironically, the escalating market growth of the NCAA tournament since its sixty-four-team era spawned from that which almost killed college basketball in 1951 and, to a lesser extent, again in 1961—gambling. Much of the attraction for fans at 1940s college basketball games in Madison Square Garden was the game within the game. Gambling provided an extra layer of entertainment for fans. Unfortunately, the amounts of money gamblers offered to the college players was high enough compared to the relatively small amounts of money they stood to make as future professional basketball players if they stayed clean. The opportunity cost now is much different from what it was back then.

For now, though, a different sort of gambling has overtaken college basketball's postseason. A sixty-four-team bracket made gambling on the winners of the tournament's sixty-three games a widespread pastime for college basketball diehards, those who never watch the sport, and anyone in between. And even more teams in the NCAA tournament has meant even more intrigue and interest.

While March Madness betting "pools" represent big business in the American economy, the gambling that takes place often seems to have as much to do with camaraderie and pride is it does with financial earnings. This is the new game within the game, and it is seemingly more innocent than the original game within college basketball regarding point spreads, shaving points, and gambling. Bracket pools can become frighteningly high stakes, but the majority of Americans who take part in them do so without malice or pure greed. Indeed, as March Madness has evolved recently with "pool" betting as an inseparable aspect of its interest, this "soft" gambling strikes few as heinous. And yet, the possibility looms that the amounts of money and the stakes that are invested in sports are sowing the seeds of even more destruction and scandal. Hopefully, the NCAA and the professional sports engine have adequately discouraged and dissuaded athletes from tampering with the integrity of their games.

The real reason why point shaving is such an egregious moral shortcoming is because of the drama that sports—basketball in this case—create. We are drawn to sporting events as live theater, action that unfolds as it goes along without anyone knowing for certain what the outcome will be. March Madness, with its series of one-off, win-or-go-home games, has capitalized on this kind of suspense. The upsets, the dramatic finishes, the come-from-behind wins, and the overtime thrillers have and always will be at the center of the madness of March.

Appendix A

AAU National Tournament
Champions, 1897–1952

YEAR	CHAMPION (HOST CITY)
1897	23rd Street YMCA, New York City (New York City)
1898	23rd Street YMCA, New York City (New York City)
1899	New York Knickerbocker Athletic Club (New York City)
1900	New York Knickerbocker Athletic Club (New York City)
1901	Ravenswood YMCA, Chicago (Chicago)
1902	—
1903	—
1904	—
1905	—
1906	—
1907	—
1908	—
1909	—
1910	Company F, Wisconsin National Guard, Portage (Chicago)
1911	—
1912	—
1913	Cornell Armour Square Playground, Chicago (Chicago)
1914	Cornell Armour Square Playground, Chicago (Chicago)
1915	San Francisco Olympic Club (San Francisco)
1916	University of Utah (Chicago)
1917	Illinois Athletic Club, Chicago (Chicago)
1918	—

1919   Los Angeles Athletic Club Blues (Los Angeles)

1920   New York University (Atlanta)

1921   Kansas City Athletic Club (Kansas City)

1922   Lowe and Campbell Athletic Goods, Kansas City (Kansas City)

1923   Kansas City Athletic Club (Kansas City)

1924   Butler University (Kansas City)

1925   Washburn College, Topeka, Kansas (Kansas City)

1926   Hillyard Chemical Company, St. Joseph, Missouri (Kansas City)

1927   Hillyard Chemical Company, St. Joseph, Missouri (Kansas City)

1928   Cook Paint Company, Kansas City (Kansas City)

1929   Cook Paint Company, Kansas City (Kansas City)

1930   Henry Clothiers, Wichita, Kansas (Kansas City)

1931   Henry Clothiers, Wichita, Kansas (Kansas City)

1932   Henry Clothiers, Wichita, Kansas (Kansas City)

1933   Diamond D-X Oilers, Tulsa (Kansas City)

1934   Diamond D-X Oilers, Tulsa (Kansas City)

1935   Southern Kansas Stage Lines, Kansas City (Denver)

1936   Globe Oil Refining Company, McPherson, Kansas (Denver)

1937   Denver Safeway Stores (Denver)

1938   Healy Motors, Kansas City (Denver)

1939   Denver Nuggets (Denver)

1940   Phillips 66 Oilers, Bartlesville, Oklahoma (Denver)

1941   Twentieth-Century Fox Studios, Hollywood (Denver)

1942   Denver American Legion (Denver)

1943   Phillips 66 Oilers, Bartlesville, Oklahoma (Denver)

1944   Phillips 66 Oilers, Bartlesville, Oklahoma (Denver)

1945   Phillips 66 Oilers, Bartlesville, Oklahoma (Denver)

1946   Phillips 66 Oilers, Bartlesville, Oklahoma (Denver)

1947   Phillips 66 Oilers, Bartlesville, Oklahoma (Denver)

1948   Phillips 66 Oilers, Bartlesville, Oklahoma (Denver)

1949   Oakland Bittners (Oklahoma City)

1950   Phillips 66 Oilers, Bartlesville, Oklahoma (Denver)

1951   Stewart Chevrolet, San Francisco (Denver)

1952   Peoria Caterpillar Diesels (Denver)

Appendix B

Retrospective Polls, 1893–1952

YEAR	HELMS	PREMO AND PORRETTA
1893	—	Iowa
1894	—	Hiram
1895	—	Temple
1896	—	Temple
1897	—	Yale
1898	—	Mount Union
1899	—	Yale
1900	—	Yale
1901	Yale	Bucknell
1902	Minnesota	Minnesota
1903	Yale	Minnesota
1904	Columbia	Columbia
1905	Columbia	Columbia
1906	Dartmouth	Wabash
1907	Chicago	Chicago
1908	Chicago	Wabash
1909	Chicago	Chicago
1910	Columbia	Williams
1911	St. John's	St. John's
1912	Wisconsin	Wisconsin
1913	Navy	Navy
1914	Wisconsin	Wisconsin
1915	Illinois	Illinois
1916	Wisconsin	Wisconsin

1917	Washington St.	Washington St.
1918	Syracuse	Syracuse
1919	Minnesota	Navy
1920	Penn	Penn
1921	Penn	Missouri
1922	Kansas	Missouri
1923	Kansas	Army
1924	North Carolina	North Carolina
1925	Princeton	Princeton
1926	Syracuse	Syracuse
1927	Notre Dame	Notre Dame
1928	Pittsburgh	Pittsburgh
1929	Montana St.	Montana St.
1930	Pittsburgh	Alabama
1931	Northwestern	Northwestern
1932	Purdue	Purdue
1933	Kentucky	Texas
1934	Wyoming	South Carolina
1935	NYU	Richmond
1936	Notre Dame	LIU
1937	Stanford	Stanford
1938	Temple	Temple
1939	LIU	LIU
1940	USC	Indiana
1941	Wisconsin	LIU
1942	Stanford	Stanford
1943	Wyoming	Illinois
1944	Army	Army
1945	Oklahoma A&M	Iowa
1946	Oklahoma A&M	Oklahoma A&M
1947	Holy Cross	Kentucky
1948	Kentucky	Kentucky
1949	Kentucky	—
1950	CCNY	—
1951	Kentucky	—
1952	Kansas	—

Appendix C

Continuous College Basketball Postseason Tournaments, 1937–1952

	NAIB	NIT	NCAA
1937	Central Missouri State		
1938	Central Missouri State	Temple	
1939	Southwestern (KS)	LIU	Oregon
1940	Tarkio (MO)	Colorado	Indiana
1941	San Diego State	LIU	Wisconsin
1942	Hamline (MN)	West Virginia	Stanford
1943	Southeast Missouri State	^St. John's	*Wyoming
1944	—	^St. John's	*Utah
1945	Loyola (LA)	^DePaul	*Oklahoma A&M
1946	Southern Illinois	Kentucky	Oklahoma A&M
1947	Marshall	Utah	Holy Cross
1948	Louisville	St. Louis	Kentucky
1949	Hamline (MN)	San Francisco	Kentucky
1950	Indiana State	CCNY	CCNY
1951	Hamline (MN)	Brigham Young	Kentucky
1952	Southwest Missouri State	LaSalle	Kansas

* *Winner of Red Cross War Fund Benefit Game*
^ *Loser of Red Cross War Fund Benefit Game*

Notes

Chapter 1: Prolegomena to the Tournaments, 1901–1937

1. John Dewar, "The Life and Professional Contributions of James Naismith" (Doctoral diss., Florida State University, 1965), 42.

2. A. Leslie Colbeck et al., eds., *The Basketball World* (Munich: International Amateur Basketball Federation, 1972); Allen Guttmann, *Games and Empires: Modern Sports and Cultural Imperialism* (New York: Columbia University Press, 1994); William J. Baker, *Sports in the Western World* (Urbana: University of Illinois Press, 1988).

3. Rob Rains, with Hellen Carpenter, *James Naismith: The Man Who Invented Basketball* (Philadelphia: Temple University Press, 2009), 80, 90.

4. Neil D. Isaacs, *All the Moves: A History of College Basketball*, revised and updated version (New York: Harper Colophon Books, 1984), 19–22.

5. Dewar, "Life and Professional Contributions," 45–46; Alexander M. Weyand, *The Cavalcade of Basketball* (New York: MacMillan Company, 1960), 23.

6. Weyand, Cavalcade of Basketball, 23–27.

7. Weyand, Cavalcade of Basketball, 23–27.

8. Isaacs, *All the Moves*, 21; Peter C. Bjarkman, *Hoopla: A Century of College Basketball* (Indianapolis: Masters Press, 1996), 7–8; Weyand, *Cavalcade of Basketball*, 31–32.

9. Isaacs, *All the Moves*, 21; Bjarkman, *Hoopla*, 7–8; Weyand, *Cavalcade of Basketball*, 31–32.

10. Isaacs, *All the Moves*, 22.

11. Bjarkman, *Hoopla*, 9; Weyand, *Cavalcade of Basketball*, 29.

12. James Naismith, *Basketball: Its Origin and Development* (New York: Associated Press, 1941), 102–5; Weyand, *Cavalcade of Basketball*, 191.

13. Ron Smith, *Sports and Freedom: The Rise of Big-Time College Athletics* (New York: Oxford University Press, 1988), 58–62. The American League existed from 1894 but was not accepted in major league status until 1901.

14. John Sayle Watterson, *College Football: History, Spectacle, Controversy* (Baltimore: Johns Hopkins University Press, 2000), 46.

15. Weyand, Cavalcade of Basketball, 191–92.

16. Weyand, Cavalcade of Basketball, 191.

17. Weyand, *Cavalcade of Basketball*, 192; Rains and Carpenter, *James Naismith*, 84–85;

18. Weyand, *Cavalcade of Basketball*, 192–93; Pedro Escamilla, *The Olympic Basketball History* (Barcelona: Argentaria Foundation Pedro Ferrandiz, 1992), 18–20.

19. Blair Kerkhoff, *Phog Allen: The Father of Basketball Coaching* (Indianapolis: Masters Press, 1996), 10–11.

20. Kerkhoff, *Phog Allen*, 12–13; G. T. Hepbron, "Review of the Season,"

in *Spalding's Official Basket Ball Guide, 1908–9*, ed. G. T. Hepbron (New York: American Sports Publishing Co., 1908), 3–9.

21. Kerkhoff, *Phog Allen*, 13–16.

22. Harry A. Fisher, "Intercollegiate Basket Ball: East vs. West," in *Spalding's Official Basket Ball Guide for 1905–06*, ed. George T. Hepbron (New York: American Sports Publishing Co., 1905), 11–19.

23. Fisher, "Intercollegiate Basket Ball," 11–19.

24. Emmett Dunn Angell, "The Western Intercollegiate Basket Ball Season," in *Spalding's Official Basket Ball Guide for 1905–06*, ed. George T. Hepbron (New York: American Sports Publishing Co., 1905), 43–45.

25. Angell, "The Western Intercollegiate Basket Ball Season."

26. "The Truth behind the Helms Committee," Kentucky Basketball, accessed June 15, 2014, www.bigbluehistory.net/bb/helms/html.

27. Mike Douchant, *Encyclopedia of College Basketball* (Detroit: Visible Ink Press, 1995), 17–18, 23; Kenneth N. Carlson, *College Basketball Scorebook* (Lynnwood, WA: Rain Belt Publications, 1990), 451.

28. Douchant, Encyclopedia of College Basketball, 17–18, 23; Carlson, College Basketball Scorebook, 451.

29. Smith, *Sports and Freedom*, 192–94.

30. Smith, *Sports and Freedom*, 198–208.

31. Douchant, Encyclopedia of College Basketball, 18, 23; Carlson, College Basketball Scorebook, 953.

32. For more on Stagg's career, see Robin Lester, *Stagg's University: The Rise, Decline, and Fall of Big-Time Football at Chicago* (Champaign: University of Illinois Press, 1999).

33. Bjarkman, *Hoopla*, 9, 11; Carlson, *College Basketball Scorebook*, 953; John L. Evers, "Schommer, John Joseph," *Basketball: A Biographical Dictionary*, ed. David L. Porter (Westport, CT: Greenwood Press, 2005), 426–27.

34. Carlson, *College Basketball Scorebook*, 953; Bjarkman, *Hoopla*, 11–12.

35. Bjarkman, *Hoopla*, 12.

36. Joseph E. Raycroft, "The Western Intercollegiate," in *Spalding's Official Basket Ball Guide, 1908–9*, ed. George Hepbron (New York: American Sports Publishing Co., 1908), 27–29.

37. Harry A. Fisher, "The National Championship," *Spalding's Official Basket Ball Guide for 1910–11*, ed. H. A. Fisher (New York: American Sports Publishing Co., 1910), 7.

38. Weyand, Cavalcade of Basketball, 194–95.

39. Douchant, Encyclopedia of College Basketball, 19; Weyand, Cavalcade of Basketball, 195.

40. Douchant, Encyclopedia of College Basketball, 19, 23; Weyand, Cavalcade of Basketball, 74–76; Carlson, College Basketball Scorebook, 953; Edwin C. Caudle, Collegiate Basketball: Facts and Figures on the Cage Sport (Winston-Salem, NC: John F. Blair, Publisher, 1959), 203; Frederick Augustyn Jr., "Meanwell, Walter Earnest 'Doc' 'Little Doctor' 'Napoleon of Basketball' 'the Little Giant' 'the Wizard,'" Basketball: A Biographical Dictionary, ed. David L. Porter (Westport, CT: Greenwood Press, 2005), 320–21.

41. Douchant, Encyclopedia of College Basketball, 19, 23; Weyand, Cavalcade

of Basketball, 74–76; Carlson, College Basketball Scorebook, 953; Caudle, Collegiate Basketball, 203; Augustyn Jr., "Meanwell," 320–21.

42. Douchant, *Encyclopedia of College Basketball*, 19, 23; Weyand, *Cavalcade of Basketball*, 74–76; Carlson, *College Basketball Scorebook*, 953; Caudle, *Collegiate Basketball*, 203; Augustyn Jr., "Meanwell," 320–21; Ralph Morgan, "Review of 1920 Basket Ball Season in the Eastern Colleges," in *Spalding's Official Basket Ball Guide, 1920–1921,* ed. Oswald Tower, A. E. Metzdorf, and William Burdick (New York: American Sports Publishing Company, 1920), 7–11.

43. Weyand, Cavalcade of Basketball, 195–99.

44. Weyand, Cavalcade of Basketball.

45. Kyle Crichton, "Indiana Madness," *Collier's Magazine*, February 6, 1937, 13, 38; Todd Gould, *Pioneers of the Hardwood: Indiana and the Birth of Professional Basketball* (Bloomington: Indiana University Press, 1998), 8, 35–37; "National College Net Meet Here Is Assured," *Indianapolis Star*, February 16, 1922, 10, accessed February 8, 2013, http://search.proquest.com.

46. "Scarlet Tossers Will Represent Indiana in National Intercollegiate Basketball Tourney," *Indianapolis Star*, February 28, 1922, 11, accessed February 8, 2013, http://search.proquest.com.

47. "College Fives of South Fight for Right to Play in National Meet Here," *Indianapolis Star*, March 1, 1922, 15, accessed February 8, 2013, http://search. proquest.com; "Quintets in National College Tourney Here to Hold Drawings Wednesday Night," *Indianapolis Star*, March 3, 1922, 12, accessed February 8, 2013, http://search.proquest.com.

48. "Field of National College Basket Tourney Here May Be Increased Two Teams," *Indianapolis Star*, March 2, 1922, 12, accessed February 8, 2013, http://search.proquest.com.

49. "Naismith: Inventor of Basket Ball Game, Is Invited to Attend National Net Tourney Here," *Indianapolis Star*, March 4, 1922, 13, accessed February 8, 2013, http://search.proquest.com; "Idaho Quintet Starts for College Basket Tourney Here This Week End," *Indianapolis Star*, March 6, 1922, 17, accessed February 8, 2013, http://search.proquest.com.

50. "Grove City Basket Ball Team Selected to Enter Intercollegiate Tourney in This City," *Indianapolis Star*, March 7, 1922, 14, accessed February 8, 2013, http://search.proquest.com; "Idaho Squad Arrives Here for National College Basket Tourney This Week End," *Indianapolis Star*, March 8, 1922, 10, accessed February 8, 2013, http://search.proquest.com.

51. L. M. Stanley, "Little Giants Come through in First Tourney Game," *Indianapolis Star*, March 9, 1922, 14, accessed February 8, 2013, http://search. proquest.com; L. M. Stanley, "Wabash Five Wins National College Basket Ball Meet," *Indianapolis Star*, March 12, 1922, 25, accessed February 8, 2013, http://search.proquest.com.

52. Crichton, "Indiana Madness," 13, 38; Gould, *Pioneers of the Hardwood*, 8, 35–37; "Wabash Wins Tournament," *Boston Globe*, March 12, 1922, 31, accessed February 8, 2013, http://search.proquest.com; "Idaho," 10.

53. For details on the ways in which Harvard and Yale shaped college athletics, see Smith, *Sports and Freedom*.

54. Smith, *Sports and Freedom*, 94, 206–7. In this book, Smith often references

the ways in which the Eastern elites wielded their influence in intercollegiate sport throughout the nineteenth and early twentieth century. He also explains how the Big Ten came into power in the early twentieth century.

55. Weyand, Cavalcade of Basketball, 92–93.

56. Carlson, College Basketball Scorebook, 953; Isaacs, All the Moves, 71–75.

57. Carlson, College Basketball Scorebook, 953; Isaacs, All the Moves, 71–75.

58. Kerkhoff, *Phog Allen*, 96.

59. Kerkhoff, *Phog Allen*.

60. Augustyn Jr., "Meanwell," 320–21; Thomas R. Somerville, "A History of the National Association of Basketball Coaches of the United States" (Doctoral diss., The Ohio State University, 1980), 28–31.

61. Somerville, "History of the National Association," 31–48; Isaacs, *All the Moves*, 24.

62. Somerville, "History of the National Association," 50–51.

63. Somerville, "History of the National Association," 51–53.

64. Bruce J. Dierenfield, "Carlson, Henry Clifford," *Basketball: A Biographical Dictionary*, ed. David L. Porter (Westport, CT: Greenwood Press, 2005), 69.

65. Dierenfield, "Carlson," 69; Isaacs, *All the Moves*, 53.

66. "Hall of Famers: Charles D. 'Chuck' Hyatt," Naismith Memorial Hall of Fame, accessed May 11, 2013, http://www.hoophall.com/hall-of-famers/tag/charles-d-chuck-hyatt; Douchant, *Encyclopedia of College Basketball*, 20, 23; Walter E. Meanwell, "Western Intercollegiate Conference," in *Spalding's Official Basketball Guide, 1930–31*, ed. Oswald Tower (New York: American Sports Publishing Co., 1930), 151–59.

67. Douchant, *Encyclopedia of College Basketball*, 20, 23; Tommy Ray Jones, "Henry Clifford Carlson, MD: His Contributions to Intercollegiate Basketball Coaching" (Master's thesis, University of Pittsburgh, 1965), 18, Dr. Henry C. Carlson Nomination File, Naismith Memorial Basketball Hall of Fame archive, Springfield, Massachusetts (hereafter Naismith Hall of Fame).

68. Roy White, "Tech Plays Host to U.S. Coaches at Meeting Here," *Atlanta Constitution*, March 25, 1934, 4B, accessed February 8, 2013, http://search.proquest.com; H. C. Carlson, *NABC Trial Bulletin*, 1934, 2, Phog Allen Archives, Kansas University Spencer Library, Lawrence, Kansas (hereafter Kansas Archives).

69. Al Smith, "Coaches Delay Rules Action; To Vote Today," *Atlanta Constitution*, March 31, 1934, 13, accessed February 8, 2013, http://search.proquest.com; Somerville, "History of the National Association," 75–76; Jones, *Henry Clifford Carlson*, 19.

70. "'Hallroom Boys,' Pitt Cage Stars, Go 'Hard Way,'" *Atlanta Constitution*, January 31, 1934, 8, accessed February 8, 2013, http://search.proquest.com; Jack Troy, "Two Proposed Rule Changes Demonstrated in Game Here," *Atlanta Constitution*, March 30, 1934, 21, accessed February 8, 2013, http://search.proquest.com.

71. "Rule Changes Would Speed Up Game," *Atlanta Constitution*, March 31, 1934, 13, accessed February 8, 2013, http://search.proquest.com; Douchant, *Encyclopedia of College Basketball*, 20, 23.

72. Jones, *Henry Clifford Carlson*, 19; Wilfrid Smith, "Coaches' Plans for New Rules Tested in Games," *Chicago Tribune*, April 4, 1935, 21, accessed May 11, 2013, http://search.proquest.com.

73. Jones, *Henry Clifford Carlson*, 21–22; Douchant, *Encyclopedia of College Basketball*, 21, 23; "L.S.U. Rallies to Beat Pitt in Cage Tilt, 41–37," *Monroe Morning World* (Monroe, LA), April 14, 1935, 16, accessed June 21, 2015, http://www.newspaperarchive.com.

74. Jones, Henry Clifford Carlson, 22–23.

75. Caudle, Collegiate Basketball, 36; Jones, Henry Clifford Carlson, 22–23.

76. Murray Janoff, "Irish Stepping Down as King of Cage Promoters," *Sporting News*, July 6, 1974, 53, Ned Irish nomination file, Naismith Hall of Fame; Roger Kahn, "Success and Ned Irish," *Sports Illustrated*, March 27, 1961, 39–42, Ned Irish nomination file, Naismith Hall of Fame.

77. Kahn, "Success and Ned Irish," 39–42; "College Basketball Goes Big Time," undated article, Ned Irish nomination file, Naismith Hall of Fame; Janoff, "Irish Stepping Down," 53.

78. Kahn, "Success and Ned Irish," 39–42; Jerry Jaye Wright, "Irish, Edward Simmons 'Ned,'" *Basketball: A Biographical Dictionary*, ed. David L. Porter (Westport, CT: Greenwood Press, 2005), 225; "College Basketball Goes Big Time."

79. Wright, "Irish," 225; "The Horatio Alger of Basketball," *Literary Digest*, March 9, 1935, Ned Irish nomination file, Naismith Hall of Fame; Sandy Padwe, *Basketball Hall of Fame* (Englewood Cliffs, NJ: Prentice-Hall, 1970), 45.

80. Ned Irish, "College Games at Madison Square Garden," in *Spalding's Official Basketball Guide*, ed. Oswald Tower (New York: American Sports Publishing Co., 1936–37), 27.

81. "Olympic Basketball Committee," *Official Program: United States Olympic Basketball Trials* (Madison Square Garden, 1936), 1, Naismith Hall of Fame; Carson Cunningham, *American Hoops: U.S. Men's Olympic Basketball from Berlin to Beijing* (Lincoln: University of Nebraska Press, 2009), 8.

82. Cunningham, American Hoops, 8.

83. Morgan G. Brenner, *College Basketball's National Championships: The Complete Record of Every Tournament Ever Played*, American Sports History Series No. 13 (Lanham, MD: Scarecrow Press, 1999), 675.

84. J. Lyman Bingham, "Olympic Basketball Tryouts," in *The Official Basketball Guide of the National Basketball Committee, 1936–37* (New York: American Sports Publishing Co., 1936), 73–77.

85. Bingham, "Olympic Basketball Tryouts," 675; Kerkhoff, *Phog Allen*, 110.

86. Kerkhoff, *Phog Allen*, 110.

87. Cunningham, *American Hoops*, 9; Bingham, "Olympic Basketball Trials."

88. Cunningham, *American Hoops*, 9.

89. Francis J. O'Riley, "17,623 See Stanford Stop L. I. U. Streak at 43 Games; Georgetown Triumphs," *New York Times*, December 31, 1936, 10, accessed May 11, 2013, http://search.proquest.com.

90. Joe Durso, "The Four Gardens and How They Grew," in *Madison Square Garden: A Century of Sport and Spectacle on the World's Most Versatile Stage*, ed. Zander Hollander (New York: Hawthorn Books, 1973), 31; Ned Irish, "Basketball in Madison Square Garden," in *The 1938–39 Official Spalding Basketball Guide*, ed. Oswald Tower (New York: American Sports Publishing Co., 1938), 36–37.

91. "Sport: Basketball: Midseason," *Time*, February 19, 1934, accessed May 11, 2013, http://content.time.com/time/magazine/article/0,9171,746995,00.html.

92. "The Truth Behind the Helms Committee," Kentucky Basketball.

93. Douchant, Encyclopedia of College Basketball, 18–20, 23.

94. Douchant, Encyclopedia of College Basketball, 18–20, 23.

Chapter 2: Genesis of the Kansas City and New York City Tournaments, 1937–1938

1. For an overview of topics and sources of American sports in the 1930s with special reference to the Great Depression, see Ryan Swanson, "The Interwar and Post-World War II Eras, 1920–1960," in A Companion to American Sport History, ed. Stephen Riess (New York: Wiley-Blackwell, 2014), 60–83.

2. For discussion of the early regionalization of basketball, see Isaacs, All the Moves, 39–184; and Bjarkman, Hoopla, 21–25.

3. For discussions of Indiana basketball, see Randy Roberts, But They Can't Beat Us: Oscar Robertson and the Crispus Attucks Tigers (New York: Skyhorse Publishing, 1999); and Tom Graham and Rachel Graham Cody, Getting Open: The Unknown Story of Bill Garrett and the Integration of College Basketball (New York: Atria Books, 2006). For a discussion of New York City basketball, see Pete Axthelm, The City Game: Basketball in New York City from the World Champion Knicks to the World of the Playgrounds (New York: Harper's Magazine Press, 1970).

4. See Isaacs, All the Moves; and Bjarkman, Hoopla.

5. Padwe, Basketball's Hall of Fame, 45; Adolph H. Grundman, The Golden Age of Amateur Basketball: The AAU Tournament, 1921–1968 (Lincoln: University of Nebraska Press, 2004), 6–8.

6. Grundman, The Golden Age, 6; Kerkhoff, Phog Allen, 15; Rains and Carpenter, James Naismith, 73, 169–71.

7. Dewar, The Life and Professional Contributions, 90. For more on Muscular Christianity, see Clifford W. Putney, Muscular Christianity: Manhood and Sports in Protestant America, 1880–1920 (Cambridge, MA: Harvard University Press, 2001); and Tony Ladd and James Mathisen, Muscular Christianity: Evangelical Protestants and the Development of American Sport (Grand Rapids, MI: Baker Books, 1999).

8. Padwe, Basketball's Hall of Fame, 4; Lester, Stagg's University, 13, 17.

9. Lester, Stagg's University, 13–14; and Rains and Carpenter, James Naismith, 87.

10. Padwe, Basketball's Hall of Fame, 12; Kerkhoff, Phog Allen, 69

11. Kerkhoff, Phog Allen, 22, 71; Padwe, Basketball's Hall of Fame, 12. Kerkhoff lists Naismith's win-loss record as 55-60 (69) while Padwe lists it at 53-55 (12).

12. Kerkhoff, Phog Allen, 1–7, 27.

13. Kerkhoff, Phog Allen, 209–10; Grundman, The Golden Age, 3; Francis Lentz Hoover, "A History of the National Association of Intercollegiate Athletics" (Doctoral diss., Indiana University, 1958), 31.

14. Somerville, "A History of the National Association," 23–24.

15. Somerville, "A History of the National Association," 23–25.

16. Somerville, "A History of the National Association," 26.

17. Somerville, "A History of the National Association," 28–30, 49–50.

18. Somerville, "A History of the National Association," 58.

19. Brundage's legacy is probably most well known for the ways in which he altered American perceptions of Germany in 1936 so the United States would not boycott the Berlin Games. For more on Brundage, Allen, and discussions leading up to the 1936 Olympics, see Adolph H. Grundman, "A.A.U.—N.C.A.A. Politics: Forrest C. 'Phog' Allen and America's First Olympic Basketball Team," *Olympika: The International Journal of Olympic Studies* 5 (1996): 111–26.

20. Padwe, Basketball's Hall of Fame, 64.

21. Grundman, *The Golden Age,* 24–25; Hoover, "History of the National Association," 33.

22. Hoover, "History of the National Association," 31–32. For more information on the AAU tournament from 1921 to 1950, see Grundman, *The Golden Age.*

23. Hoover, "History of the National Association," 33.

24. Danny Stooksbury, *National Title: The Unlikely Tale of the NAIB Tournament* (Bradenton Beach, FL: Higher Level Publishing, 2010), 10–11.

25. Hoover, "History of the National Association," 30.

26. Stooksbury, *National Title,* 11.

27. Hoover, "History of the National Association," 34–35; Stooksbury, *National Title,* 12–13.

28. Hoover, "History of the National Association," 35; "Meet on Tonight," *Kansas City Times,* March 9, 1937, 13.

29. "Meet on Tonight"; "Down to 4 Teams," *Kansas City Star,* March 10, 1937, 12.

30. "Near Cage Climax," *Kansas City Star,* March 10, 1937, 15; "Down to 4 Teams"; "Mules to Finals," *Kansas City Times,* March 11, 1937, 12; "Plan a Cage Meet Here," *Kansas City Times,* March 11, 1937, 12; "Mules Are Victors," *Kansas City Times,* March 12, 1937, 18.

31. Hoover, "History of the National Association," 38–42.

32. Hoover, "History of the National Association," 36–38; Stooksbury, *National Title,* 20. Hoover (4) indicates that certain records of the NAIB tournament have been lost through a 1943 fire at Baker University and through the transit of the records in 1957 from Los Angeles to Kansas City. Thus, certain details, such as Liston's early expense reports, no longer exist.

33. Stooksbury, *National Title,* 24.

34. "Cage Field Set," *Kansas City Times,* March 7, 1938, 13.

35. "Thrill Cage Fans," *Kansas City Times,* March 8, 1938, 12; "Drury Is Beaten," *Kansas City Times,* March 9, 1938, 13; "Washburn by Goal," *Kansas City Times,* March 10, 1938, 11; "Four Teams Left," *Kansas City Times,* March 11, 1938, 15; "Mules vs. Roanoke," *Kansas City Times,* March 12, 1938, 17; Stooksbury, *National Title,* 32.

36. "In Doubt on Cage Fields," *Kansas City Times,* March 3, 1938, 12; "Seven States in Meet," *Kansas City Times,* February 24, 1938, 13.

37. David L. Porter, "Liston, Emil Sycamore," *Basketball: A Biographical Dictionary,* ed. David L. Porter (Westport, CT: Greenfield Press, 2005), 282–83; Kahn, "Success and Ned Irish," 39–46.

38. Everett B. Morris, "Basketball Rebounds: National College Invitation Tourney Slated by Writers in Garden Next Month," *New York Herald-Tribune*, February 2, 1938, 21.

39. Morris, "Basketball Rebounds."

40. "Bushnell, Salmon to Aid in Tourney," *New York Times*, February 16, 1938, 25, accessed January 18, 2012, http://search.proquest.com.

41. "Bid Voted to N.Y.U. or City College," *New York Times*, February 22, 1938, 27, accessed January 18, 2012, http://search.proquest.com.

42. "Field Completed in Court Tourney," *New York Times*, March 7, 1938, 22, accessed January 18, 2012, http://search.proquest.com.

43. "Bradley Tech Drills," *New York Times*, March 8, 1938, 14, accessed January 18, 2012, http://search.proquest.com; "L.I.U. Ranked Superior on Record for Game with N.Y.U. Tonight," *New York Times*, March 9, 1938, 28, accessed January 18, 2012, http://search.proquest.com.

44. Arthur Daley, "13,829 in Garden See N.Y.U. and Temple Fives Triumph in National Tourney," *New York Times*, March 10, 1938, 24, accessed January 18, 2012, http://search.proquest.com; George E. Coleman, "Four-Year-Old Court Debate Faces Settlement," *Brooklyn Daily Eagle*, March 9, 1938, 19, accessed at http://www.newspapers.com; Robert V. Geasey, "Those Deceiving Owls," *1938 National Invitation Tournament Souvenir Program* (Madison Square Garden, 1938), 6, Naismith Hall of Fame.

45. Arthur J. Daley, "Colorado Five Thrills 12,000 in Garden with Last-Minute Victory over N.Y.U.," *New York Times*, March 15, 1938, 26, accessed January 18, 2014, http://search.proquest.com; Arthur Daley, "Temple Crushes Colorado, 60–36," *New York Times*, March 17, 1938, 24, accessed January 18, 2012, http://search.proquest.com; Eddie Dooley, "Colorado Has Its Cage Aces," *1938 National Invitation Tournament Souvenir Program* (Madison Square Garden, 1938), 4, Naismith Hall of Fame.

46. Daley, "Temple Crushes Colorado"; Stooksbury, *National Title*, 32.

47. Douchant, Encyclopedia of College Basketball, 27.

48. Grundman, *The Golden Age*, 60–61; "'Kick' Collegians Out of A.A.U. Cage Tournament," *Chicago Defender* (National edition), March 26, 1938, 9, accessed April 15, 2015, http://search.proquest.umi.

49. "'Kick' Collegians Out"; Grundman, *The Golden Age*, 60–61.

50. Doris Kearns Goodwin, *Team of Rivals: The Political Genius of Abraham Lincoln* (New York: Simon and Schuster, 2005), 141–43. For more on Missouri's battle with slavery, see Robert Pierce Forbes, *The Missouri Compromise and Its Aftermath: Slavery and the Meaning of America* (Chapel Hill: University of North Carolina Press, 2007).

51. "Stars Who Play in National Basketball Tournament Here," *Kansas City Times*, March 5, 1938, 17; "Washburn by Goal"; "Four Teams Left."

52. Hoover, "History of the National Association," 76–78.

53. Hoover, "History of the National Association," 76–78.

54. Dennis Gildea, *Hoop Crazy: The Lives of Clair Bee and Chip Hilton* (Fayetteville: University of Arkansas Press, 2013), 124, 144.

55. Gildea, *Hoop Crazy*, 124, 144.

56. Daley, "13,829 in Garden"; Daley, "Temple Crushes Colorado";

"Basketball Won More Popularity," *New York Times*, December 25, 1938, 54, accessed January 18, 2012, http://search.proquest.com.

57. Daley, "13,829 in Garden"; Daley, "Temple Crushes Colorado"; "Basketball Won More Popularity."

58. Irish, "Basketball in Madison Square Garden," 36.

59. Joseph M. Sheehan, "Honors Garnered by Temple's Five," *New York Times*, March 18, 1938, 25, accessed January 18, 2012, http://search.proquest.com; Irish, "Basketball in Madison Square Garden," 36.

60. "Basketball Won More Popularity"; "Honor Basketball Stars," *New York Times*, April 1, 1938, 20, accessed January 18, 2012, http://search.proquest.com.

61. Sheehan, "Honors Garnered."

Chapter 3: The NABC and the Inaugural NCAA Tournament, 1938–1939

1. Somerville, "History of the National Association," 85.

2. Terry Frei, *March 1939: Before the Madness: The Story of the First NCAA Basketball Tournament Champions* (Lanham, MD: Taylor Trade Publishing, 2014), 44; Somerville, "History of the National Association," 86–87; "Proceedings," *National Association of Basketball Coaches Annual Convention*, April 4–5, 1938, 149, NABC Folder, NCAA Library, Indianapolis, IN (hereafter NCAA Archives).

3. Somerville, "History of the National Association," 85–87.

4. Somerville, "History of the National Association," 85–87; Hoover, "History of the National Association," 44–46.

5. Frei, March 1939, 44.

6. "Proceedings," 149–51.

7. John L. Evers, "Olsen, Harold G.," *Basketball: A Biographical Dictionary*, ed. David L. Porter (Westport, CT: Greenwood Press, 2005), 363; Augustyn Jr., "Meanwell," 320–21.

8. Evers, "Olsen," 363–64; Kenneth L. (Tug) Wilson and Jerry Brondfield, *The Big Ten* (Englewood Cliffs, NJ: Prentice-Hall, 1967), 118.

9. Weyand, *Cavalcade of Basketball*. Weyand notes that this evolution took place on an administrative level, too, as the head of the basketball rules committee from Yale stepped down in 1910 while University of Chicago coach Joseph Raycroft took over.

10. Douchant, Encyclopedia of College Basketball, 17–23.

11. Frei, *March 1939,* 140.

12. George E. Coleman, "Basketball Writers in Dollar Dilemma," *Brooklyn Daily Eagle*, January 25, 1939, 15, accessed June 6, 2015, http://www.newspapers.com.

13. Grundman, "A.A.U.-N.C.A.A. Politics," 111–26.

14. Grundman, "A.A.U.-N.C.A.A. Politics," 111–26.

15. For somewhat varying narratives regarding Brundage's legacy, see Richard D. Mandell, *The Nazi Olympics* (New York: Ballantine Books, 1971); David Clay Large, *Nazi Games: The Olympics of 1936* (New York: W. W. Norton & Company, 2007); and Arnd Kruger, "United States of America: The Crucial

Battle," *The Nazi Olympics: Sport, Politics, and Appeasement in the 1930s,* ed. Arnd Kruger and William Murray (Champaign: University of Illinois Press, 2003).

16. Chad Carlson, "The Motherland, the Godfather, and the Birth of a Basketball Dynasty: American Efforts to Promote Basketball in Lithuania," *International Journal of the History of Sport* 28, no. 11 (August 2011): 1484–85.

17. Grundman, "A.A.U.-N.C.A.A. Politics," 111–26; Chad Carlson, "The Motherland," 1484–85.

18. Grundman, "A.A.U.-N.C.A.A. Politics," 111–26; for more on early American Olympic teams, see Mark Dyreson, *Making the American Team* (Champaign: University of Illinois Press, 1998).

19. Arthur J. Daley, "Awesome Kansas Giants Reverse Basketball Lay-up Shot Process," *New York Times,* March 10, 1936, 29, accessed January 18, 2012, http://search.proquest.com.

20. Kerkhoff, *Phog Allen,* 105.

21. Cunningham, *American Hoops,* 1–28.

22. Harold Olsen to W. B. Owens, 24 March 1938, Forrest C. "Phog" Allen correspondence files, Coach record files, Spencer Research Library, Kansas University, Lawrence, KS (hereafter Kansas Archives).

23. Frei, *March 1939,* 45–46.

24. H. G. Olsen, "General Plans for the Tournament," in *Spalding's Official Basketball Guide, 1939–40* (New York: American Sports Publishing Co., 1940), 9, NCAA Archives.

25. Harold Olsen to John Bunn, 5 November 1938, Kansas Archives; Harold Olsen to Phog Allen, 7 November 1938, Kansas Archives.

26. Phog Allen to Harold Olsen, 16 November 1938, 2, Kansas Archives.

27. Phog Allen to Harold Olsen, 22 November 1938, Kansas Archives.

28. Phog Allen to Clyde E. McBride, 6 December 1938, Kansas Archives; Phog Allen to W. H. Browne, 6 December 1938, Kansas Archives; Phog Allen to E. S. Hickey, 6 December 1938, Kansas Archives.

29. John Bunn to Harold Olsen, 16 December 1938, Kansas Archives; Carl W. Lundquist to Phog Allen, 16 December 1938, Kansas Archives.

30. John Bunn to Harold Olsen, 16 December 1938, Kansas Archives.

31. John Bunn to Harold Olsen, 16 December 1938, Kansas Archives.

32. Harold Olsen to NCAA Basketball Tournament Committee, 26 January 1939, Kansas Archives.

33. Phog Allen to Harold Olsen, 21 January 1939, Kansas Archives; Harold Olsen to NCAA Basketball Tournament Committee, 26 January 1939, Kansas Archives.

34. Editorial Note in "Letters to the Sports Editor," *New York Times,* January 21, 1939, 11, accessed January 18, 2012, http://search.proquest.com.

35. Francis J. O'Riley, "College Invitation Tournament to Be Held in March by Basketball Writers," *New York Times,* January 25, 1939, 29, accessed January 18, 2012, http://search.proquest.com.

36. Philip O. Badger to Harold Olsen, 21 December 1938, "National Collegiate Athletic Association: Basketball Tournament: 1938–1941." Director of Athletics Record Group. The Ohio State University Archive (hereafter Ohio State Archives); Philip O. Badger to Ned Irish, 13 March 1939, Ohio State Archives.

37. In fact, confusion of this continues to linger. See, for instance, the inaccurate quotations from NABC administrators and false conclusions by the author at http://sports.yahoo.com/blogs/ncaab-the-dagger/ncaa-bought-rights-men-basketball-tournament-shocking-bargain-130045967—ncaab.html.

38. Phog Allen to Harold Olsen, 16 November 1938, Kansas Archives; Harold Olsen to Phog Allen, 18 November 1938, Kansas Archives; "Roll Call of Members," in *1939 NCAA Yearbook*, Los Angeles, CA, 28–30 December, 6–15, NCAA Archives; Phog Allen to George Bowles, 21 January 1939, Kansas Archives.

39. F. H. Ewerhardt to Gwinn Henry, 8 December 1938, Kansas Archives.

40. Olsen, "General Plans," 9; Harold Olsen to W. A. Witte, 13 February 1939, Kansas Archives; Harold Olsen to tournament committee, 1 February 1939, Kansas Archives.

41. Frei, *March 1939*, 96.

42. Olsen, "General Plans," 9; Phog Allen to John Bunn, 15 March 1939, Kansas Archives; Phog Allen to District 5 Selection Committee, 9 March 1939, Kansas Archives.

43. Olsen, "General Plans," 9; "Bradley Tech Bid to Tourney Here," *New York Times*, March 10, 1939, 29, accessed January 18, 2012, http://search.proquest.com; Frei, *March 1939*, 108–9.

44. "Teams Set to Go," *Kansas City Times*, March 13, 1939, 13; Whitney Martin, "The Edge to Meet Here," *Kansas City Times*, February 2, 1939, 9.

45. Stooksbury, *National Title*, 39–40.

46. "Big Court Upset," *Kansas City Times*, March 14, 1939, 11; "The Mules Stay In," *Kansas City Times*, March 15, 1939, 11; "Upsets Come Fast," *Kansas City Times*, March 16, 1939, 13; "The Mules Go Out," *Kansas City Times*, March 17, 1939, 19; "For Title Tonight," *Kansas City Times*, March 18, 1939, 15; "So' Western Wins," *Kansas City Star*, March 19, 1939, 12.

47. George E. Coleman, "Writers' Cage Tourney 'Tops,'" *Brooklyn Daily Eagle*, March 10, 1939, 21, accessed June 7, 2015, http://www.newspapers.com; Arthur J. Daley, "L.I.U. and St. John's to Oppose Strong Rivals in Garden Tourney," *New York Times*, March 12, 1939, 74, accessed January 18, 2012, http://search.proquest.com.

48. "'5 Smart Boys' Win Cage Fame," *Brooklyn Daily Eagle*, February 28, 1939, 12, accessed June 7, 2015; Daley, "L.I.U. and St. John's."

49. Louis Effrat, "New Mexico Five to Engage L.I.U.," *New York Times*, March 15, 1939, 32, accessed January 18, 2012, http://search.proquest.com.

50. In 1939, Major League Baseball and the National Football League were both white-only leagues. Further, most college athletic conferences were also white-only at the time.

51. Effrat, "New Mexico Five," *New York Times*; Arthur J. Daley, "14,443 See L.I.U. and St. John's Win as National Tourney Starts," *New York Times*, March 16, 1939, 33, accessed January 18, 2012, http://search.proquest.com; Joseph M. Sheehan, "New Mexico State and Roanoke Paired in Garden Game Monday," *New York Times*, March 17, 1939, 31, accessed January 18, 2012, http://search.proquest.com.

52. Arthur J. Daley, "L.I.U. and Loyola Remain Undefeated in Gaining

Basketball Final," *New York Times*, March 21, 1939, 33, accessed January 18, 2012, http://search.proquest.com.

53. Daley, "L.I.U. and Loyola Remain Undefeated in Gaining Basketball Final."

54. Arthur J. Daley, "18,033 See Unbeaten L.I.U. Five Win National Tourney with 24th Triumph," *New York Times*, March 23, 1939, 32, accessed January 18, 2012, http://search.proquest.com; Arthur J. Daley, "L.I.U. and Loyola Risk Winning Streaks in Tourney Final Tonight," *New York Times*, March 22, 1939, 33, accessed January 18, 2012, http://search.proquest.com; Arthur J. Daley, "Lloyd of St. John's Honored with L.I.U.," *New York Times*, March 24, 1939, 32, accessed January 18, 2012, http://search.proquest.com.

55. Daley, "Lloyd of St. John's."

56. H. Jamison Swarts, "Eastern Play-off, N.C.A.A. Tournament," in *Spalding's Official Basketball Guide, 1939–40*, ed. Oswald Tower (New York: American Sports Publishing Co., 1940), 10–11, NCAA Archives; John W. Bunn, "Western Play-off, N.C.A.A. Tournament," in *Spalding's Official Basketball Guide, 1939–40*, ed. Oswald Tower (New York: American Sports Publishing Co., 1939), 11–12, NCAA Archives; Arthur C. Lonborg, "Championship Game," in *Spalding's Official Basketball Guide, 1939–40*, ed. Oswald Tower (New York: American Sports Publishing Co., 1939), 13, NCAA Archives.

57. Ken Rappoport, *The Classic: The History of the NCAA Basketball Championship* (Kansas City: Lowell Press, 1979), 11; "1500 Students Gather to Pay Tribute to Basketball Squad," *The Ohio State University Lantern*, March 16, 1939, 1.

58. Rappoport, *The Classic*, 9.

59. Ibid., 12.

60. Lonborg, "Championship Game," 13; Earl Luebker, "1939: The Tall Firs," in *NCAA March Madness: Cinderellas, Superstars, and Champions from the NCAA Final Four* (Chicago: Triumph Books, 2004), 2–3.

61. H. G. Olsen et al., "Report of Tournament and Olympic Committee," in *Minutes of the National Association of Basketball Coaches Convention* (Chicago, 1939), 13, NCAA Archives.

62. Olsen et al., "Report of Tournament and Olympic Committee," 13–14.

63. Olsen et al., "Report of Tournament and Olympic Committee," 14.

64. Olsen et al., "Report of Tournament and Olympic Committee," 12.

65. Swarts, "Eastern Play-off," 10–11; Bunn, "Western Play-off," 11–12.

66. "No More Giant Court Players Will Compete," *Dunkirk Evening Observer* (Dunkirk, NY), August 14, 1936, 6, accessed June 6, 2015, http://www.newspapers.com; "Set Height Limit for Cage Players," *Ottawa Journal* (Ottawa, Canada), August 14, 1936, 15, accessed June 6, 2015, http://www.newspapers.com; "I.B.F. Sets Height Limit," *Winnipeg Tribune* (Winnipeg, Canada), August 14, 1936, 11, accessed June 6, 2015, http://www.newspapers.com.

67. "Report of the Treasurer: 1938–39," in *NCAA Yearbook, 1939*, Los Angeles, CA, December 28–30, 116–17, NCAA Archives.

Chapter 4: Toward Sustainability and Financial Solvency, 1939–1940

1. "Proceedings," *1938 Annual Convention,* 149–51.

2. W. B. Owens, "The National Collegiate A.A. Basketball Tournament," in *Spalding's Official Basketball Guide, 1939–40,* ed. Oswald Tower (New York: American Sports Publishing Co., 1939), 8, NCAA Archives; Bunn, "Western Playoff, N.C.A.A. Tournament," 12.

3. Olsen, "General Plans for the Tournament," 9; Bob Gretz, "Phog Allen Helps Save Early Event," *Houston Chronicle,* April 3, 1988, accessed April 15, 2015, http://infoweb.newsbank.com.

4. H. G. Olsen, "Second National Collegiate A.A. Basketball Tournament," in *Spalding's Official Basketball Guide, 1940–41,* ed. Oswald Tower (New York: American Sports Publishing Co., 1940), 16; "Report of the Treasurer," *1939 NCAA Yearbook,* 116–17.

5. Olsen, "Second National Collegiate A.A. Basketball Tournament," 16; "Report of the Treasurer," 116–17.

6. For a history of early NCAA national championships, see Jack Falla, *NCAA: The Voice of College Sports: A Diamond Anniversary History, 1906–1981* (Mission, KS: NCAA, 1981); and Joseph N. Crowley, *In the Arena: The NCAA's First Century* (Indianapolis: NCAA, 2006), 64.

7. These claims are based on the author's perusal of NCAA Yearbooks from 1905 through the 1950s. These yearbooks, found in the NCAA Archives, show the trends identified in the text.

8. Ibid. More specifically, the NCAA Yearbooks from the 1930s and early 1940s demonstrate these trends (NCAA Archives).

9. For more on Allen's thoughts regarding the tournament, see Kerkhoff, *Phog Allen.*

10. Kerkhoff, *Phog Allen,* 124.

11. Hoover, "History of the National Association," 29, 46.

12. Kerkhoff, *Phog Allen,* 124; Harold Olsen to Forrest Allen, 19 April 1939, Kansas Archives.

13. Kerkhoff, *Phog Allen,* 125. The files of the Allen archive at Kansas University include a stack of letters he wrote on behalf of the tournament in 1939 and early 1940.

14. Ned Irish, "Basketball in Madison Square Garden," in *Spalding's Official Basketball Guide, 1940–41,* ed. Oswald Tower (New York: American Sports Publishing Co., 1941), 55–57, NCAA Archives; Philip O. Badger to Harold G. Olsen, 23 February 1940, 1, Ohio State Archives.

15. Walter Williamson, "Basketball in the Metropolitan District: National Invitation College Tournament," in *Spalding's Official Basketball Guide, 1940–41,* ed. Oswald Tower (New York: American Sports Publishing Co., 1941), 53, NCAA Archives; Arthur J. Daley, "On Basketball Courts," *New York Times,* February 9, 1940, 26, accessed December 9, 2013, http://search.proquest.com; Badger to Olsen, 23 February 1940, 2; Arthur J. Daley, "Invitation Tournament," in *NABC Bulletin,* February 17, 1940, 16, Kansas Archives.

16. Smith, *Sports and Freedom,* 134; Badger to Olsen, 23 February 1940; Philip O. Badger to Ned Irish, 13 March 1939, 2, Ohio State Archives.

17. Philip O. Badger to W. B. Owens, 27 January 1939, 2, Ohio State Archives.

18. H. G. Olsen, "General Plans for the Tournament," 9.

19. Arthur J. Daley, "Twin Bills Start at Garden Tonight," *New York Times*, December 16, 1939, 22, accessed December 9, 2013, http://search.proquest.com; Arthur J. Daley, "L.I.U. Five Take Overtime Thriller from Oregon, 56–55," *New York Times*, December 17, 1939, 81, accessed December 9, 2013, http://search. proquest.com.

20. "L.I.U. Five Earned Top Ranking in U.S.," *New York Times*, December 24, 1939, 50, accessed December 9, 2013, http://search.proquest.com; Douchant, *Encyclopedia of College Basketball,* 29.

21. "L.I.U. Five"; Douchant, Encyclopedia of College Basketball, 29.

22. For more on the creation and underlying philosophies of the NAIB tournament, see Hoover, "History of the National Association."

23. Hoover, "History of the National Association," 41–42.

24. Edward Hickox members of the NABC, 12 December 1939, Kansas Archives.

25. Stooksbury, *National Title,* 56–60.

26. Stooksbury, *National Title,* 56–60.

27. Sheehan, "New Mexico State and Roanoke"; Daley, "L.I.U. and Loyola Remain."

28. Brenner, College Basketball's National Championships, 1012; "Open Here Today," Kansas City Times, March 11, 1940, 9.

29. Louis Effrat, "On Basketball Courts," *New York Times*, February 27, 1940, 25, accessed December 9, 2013, http://search.proquest.com; Joseph M. Sheehan, "League Mark of 4 Titles in Row Objective of Dartmouth Quintet," *New York Times*, March 4, 1940, 23, accessed December 9, 2013, http://search. proquest.com.

30. Arthur J. Daley, "City College Snaps Streak of Hitherto Unbeaten N.Y.U. Quintet at 18 Games," *New York Times*, March 6, 1940, 28, accessed December 9, 2013, http://search.proquest.com.

31. Lincoln A. Werden, "Violet Quintet Out of Garden Tourney," *New York Times*, March 7, 1940, 33, accessed December 9, 2013, http://search.proquest.com.

32. Harold Olsen to Philip O. Badger, 26 February 1940, Kansas Archives.

33. "Oklahoma Aggies, Traveling by Plane, to Play Here and in N.C.A.A. Competition," *New York Times*, March 7, 1940, 33, accessed December 9, 2013, http://search.proquest.com.

34. "Oklahoma Aggies."

35. Phog Allen to Harold Olsen, 7 March 1940, Kansas Archives.

36. Arthur J. Daley, "L.I.U. and De Paul Added to Tourney," *New York Times*, March 8, 1940, 30, accessed December 9, 2013, http://search.proquest.com.

37. Daley, "L.I.U. and De Paul."

38. Olsen to Badger, 26 February 1940; Philip O. Badger to Harold Olsen, 1 March 1940, Ohio State Archives.

39. Daley, "L.I.U. and De Paul."

40. Daley, "L.I.U. and De Paul."

41. Daley, "L.I.U. and De Paul."

42. John L. Evers, "Davies, Robert Edris 'Bob' 'The Harrisburg Houdini,'" in *Basketball: A Biographical Dictionary*, ed. David L. Porter (Westport, CT: Greenwood Press, 2005), 106–7; Gildea, *Hoop Crazy*, 10.

43. "Letters to the Sports Editor: Unbeaten and Uninvited," *New York Times*, March 9, 1940, 18, accessed December 9, 2013, http://search.proquest.com.

44. "Close Contests Loom at Garden in National Basketball Tourney," *New York Times*, March 10, 1940, 81, accessed December 9, 2013, http://search.proquest.com.

45. "De Paul's Quintet Will Oppose L.I.U.," *New York Times*, March 11, 1940, 23, accessed December 9, 2013, http://search.proquest.com.

46. Arthur J. Daley, "Duquesne and De Paul Gain Semi-Finals on Garden Court," *New York Times*, March 12, 1940, 32, accessed December 9, 2013, http://search.proquest.com.

47. Louis Effrat, "Colorado and Oklahoma Aggie Quintets Favored in Garden Tonight," *New York Times*, March 13, 1940, 36, accessed December 9, 2013, http://search.proquest.com.

48. Arthur J. Daley, "Colorado and Duquesne Gain Basketball Final," *New York Times*, March 14, 1940, 35, accessed December 9, 2013, http://search.proquest.com.

49. Chad Carlson, "Basketball's Forgotten Experiment: Don Barksdale and the Legacy of the United States Olympic Basketball Team," *International Journal of the History of Sport* 27, no. 8 (May 2010): 1330–59.

50. Daley, "Colorado and Duquesne."

51. Arthur J. Daley, "Duquesne Faces Colorado Tonight in Final of National Basketball," *New York Times*, March 15, 1940, 28, accessed December 9, 2013, http://search.proquest.com; Arthur J. Daley, "Colorado Downs Duquesne in National Basketball Tourney Final at Garden," *New York Times*, March 16, 1940, 17, accessed December 9, 2013, http://search.proquest.com.

52. Arnold Lowenthal, "Letters to the Sports Editor: On N.Y.U.'s Refusal: Officials' Rejection of Tourney Bid to Violet Five Is Hit," *New York Times*, March 16, 1940, 18, accessed December 9, 2013, http://search.proquest.com.

53. James G. Wright, "Letters to the Sports Editor: Spectator Appeal Lacking," *New York Times*, March 16, 1940, 18, accessed December 9, 2013, http://search.proquest.com.

54. "Kansas Prevails, 45–43," *New York Times*, March 17, 1940, 83, accessed December 9, 2013, http://search.proquest.com.

55. "Rice Institute Stars," in *1940 NCAA Western Regional Game Souvenir Program* (Madison Square Garden, 1940), 8, Kansas Archives.

56. Dan Partner, "Western Play-off, N.C.A.A. Tournament," in *Spalding's Official Basketball Guide, 1940–41*, ed. Oswald Tower (New York: American Sports Publishing Co., 1940), 16–18, NCAA Archives.

57. Partner, "Western Play-off, N.C.A.A. Tournament," 16–19.

58. "Protest Over Cage Play," *Kansas City Times*, March 8, 1940, 14.

59. Paul Hinkle, "Eastern Play-off, N.C.A.A. Tournament," in *Spalding's Official Basketball Guide, 1940–41*, ed. Oswald Tower (New York: American Sports Publishing Co., 1940), 21–22, NCAA Archives.

60. Hinkle, "Eastern Play-off, N.C.A.A. Tournament."

61. Hinkle, "Eastern Play-off, N.C.A.A. Tournament," 22; "Appendix III: Financial Reports of Tournaments and Treasurer's Report," *1940 NCAA Yearbook*, 158–60, New York, December 29–31, 1940, NCAA Archives.

62. Dan Partner, "Indiana Wins Feature Event of College Arena—The

N.C.A.A. Annual Tournament," in *Spalding's Official Basketball Guide, 1940–41,* ed. Oswald Tower (New York: American Sports Publishing Co., 1941), 19–21, NCAA Archives.

63. Rappoport, *The Classic,* 15–20; Joe McGuff, "1940: Hail Those Hurryin' Hoosiers," in *NCAA March Madness: Cinderellas, Superstars, and Champions from the NCAA Final Four* (Chicago: Triumph Books, 2004), 4–5.

64. Rappoport, *The Classic,* 15–20; McGuff, "1940," 4–5.

65. Partner, "Indiana Wins Feature Event," 19–21; Rappoport, *The Classic,* 15–20; McGuff, "1940," 4–5.

66. "Parade 'n 2,000 Fans Greet I.U.'s Champions," *Indiana Daily Student,* April 2, 1940, page number unknown (author has copy).

67. Partner, "Indiana Wins Feature Event," 19–21.

68. Olsen, "Second National Collegiate," 15; Dan Partner, "Western Play-off, N.C.A.A. Tournament," in *Spalding's Official Basketball Guide, 1940–41* (New York: American Sports Publishing Co., 1940), 16.

69. Tournament of Champions: The World Series of Basketball: Official Program (Kansas City Municipal Auditorium, 1940), Kansas Archives.

70. "Appendix III," *1940 NCAA Yearbook,* 158–60.

71. "Appendix III," *1940 NCAA Yearbook,* 158–67.

72. Phog Allen to 1940 Western Regional coaches, 12 April 1940, Kansas Archives; Forrest B. Cox to Phog Allen, 22 April 1940, Kansas Archives; Phog Allen to John Bunn, 25 April 1940, Kansas Archives; John Bunn to Phog Allen, 30 April 1940, Kansas Archives; 1940 NCAA Tournament Committee to NCAA Executive Committee, 6 September 1940, Kansas Archives.

73. Major John L. Griffith to Phog Allen, 10 September 1940, Kansas Archives.

74. "Big Ten Votes to Retain Ban on Bowl Games," *Chicago Daily Tribune,* December 8, 1940, B1, accessed December 9, 2013, http://search.proquest.com.

75. "Topsy-Turvy Year for Court Sport," *New York Times,* December 22, 1940, 66, accessed December 9, 2013, http://search.proquest.com.

Chapter 5: Early Peaks and Valleys, 1940–1942

1. Walter Williamson, "National Invitation College Tournament," in *Spalding's Official Basketball Guide, 1940–41,* ed. Oswald Tower (New York: American Sports Publishing Co., 1940), 53–54, NCAA Archives.

2. H. G. Olsen, "The 1941 National Collegiate A.A. Basketball Championship Review," in *The Official National Basketball Committee Basketball Guide, 1941–42,* ed. Oswald Tower (New York: American Sports Publishing Co., 1941), 43, NCAA Archives; "Discontinued NCAA Championships," NCAA, accessed April 15, 2014, http://fs.ncaa.org/Docs/stats/champs_records_book/Discontinued.pdf.

3. "Court Tourney Is Expanded," *New York Times,* December 18, 1940, 36, accessed December 9, 2013, http://search.proquest.com.

4. "Court Tourney Is Expanded."

5. "Court Tourney Is Expanded"; Joseph M. Sheehan, "Basketball Tourney

Invitations to Be Decided at Meeting Today," *New York Times*, March 10, 1941, 25, accessed December 9, 2013, http://search.proquest.com.

6. Stooksbury, *National Title*, 71.

7. "Into Court Play," *Kansas City Times*, March 10, 1941, 9.

8. "Into Court Play"; "Tarkio Is Out," *Kansas City Times*, March 11, 1941, 8; "Two Cage Upsets," *Kansas City Times*, March 12, 1941, 12; "San Diego Wins," *Kansas City Times*, March 13, 1941, 14; "San Diego Again," *Kansas City Times*, March 14, 1941, 12.

9. "West Texas Out," *Kansas City Times*, March 15, 1941, 16; "A Great Tourney Ends," *Kansas City Times*, March 17, 1941, 11; "Santa Barbara College Star Barred from Meet," *Pittsburgh Courier*, March 15, 1941, 17, accessed April 15, 2014, http://search.proquest.com.

10. "16 Double Bills for Garden Court," *New York Times*, October 30, 1940, 32, accessed December 9, 2013, http://search.proquest.com.

11. Louis Effrat, "Rhode Island Quintet Faces St. Francis in Garden Tonight," *New York Times*, January 29, 1941, 11, accessed December 9, 2013, http://search. proquest.com; Gildea, *Hoop Crazy*, 112.

12. Arthur J. Daley, "Fordham to Meet N.Y.U. Five Tonight," *New York Times*, February 19, 1941, 30, accessed December 9, 2013, http://search.proquest. com; Sydney Lane, "Letters to the Sports Editor," *New York Times*, March 1, 1941, 10, accessed December 9, 2013, http://search.proquest.com.

13. Arthur Daley, "17,886 See Beavers Halt N.Y.U. for Metropolitan Honors, 47–43," *New York Times*, March 11, 1941, 31, accessed December 9, 2013, http:// search.proquest.com.

14. "Field Is Completed for Garden Tourney," *New York Times*, March 11, 1941, 31, accessed December 9, 2013, http://search.proquest.com; Joseph M. Sheehan, "College Quintets Await 2 Tourneys," *New York Times*, March 17, 1941, 25, accessed December 9, 2013, http://search.proquest.com.

15. Joseph M. Sheehan, "C.C.N.Y. and Duquesne Quintets Favored in Tourney Games Tonight," *New York Times*, March 18, 1941, 30, accessed December 9, 2013, http://search.proquest.com; Arthur Daley, "Ohio U. and C.C.N.Y. Win as National Invitation Basketball Starts at Garden," *New York Times*, March 19, 1941, 26, accessed December 9, 2013, http://search.proquest.com.

16. George E. Coleman, "St. John's and C.C.N.Y. Choices in Garden Tilts," *Brooklyn Daily Eagle*, March 10, 1941, 13, accessed June 6, 2015, http://www. newspapers.com; Arthur Daley, "Seton Hall and L.I.U. Fives Gain Semi-Finals at Garden," *New York Times*, March 20, 1941, 27, accessed December 9, 2013, http://search.proquest.com.

17. Arthur Daley, "18,357 See Ohio U. Set Back C.C.N.Y. at Garden, 45 to 43," *New York Times*, March 23, 1941, S1, accessed December 9, 2013, http:// search.proquest.com.

18. Arthur Daley, "L.I.U. Halts Ohio U. Five in Garden Final before 18,377," *New York Times*, March 25, 1941, 29, accessed December 9, 2013, http://search. proquest.com.

19. "Basketball Heads Gather Tomorrow," *New York Times*, March 23, 1941, S2, accessed December 9, 2013, http://search.proquest.com.

20. Arthur Daley, "Court Coaches Suggest Change in 3-Second Rule," *New*

York Times, March 26, 1941, 30, accessed December 9, 2013, http://search.
proquest.com.

21. Olsen, "The 1941 National Collegiate," 43; "Friel Praises Cougars,"
Kansas City Times, March 24, 1941, 9; Rappoport, *The Classic*, 21; Mark Cox,
"Western N.C.A.A. Tournament Review," in *The Official National Basketball
Committee Basketball Guide, 1941–42*, ed. Oswald Tower (New York: American
Sports Publishing Co., 1941), 47–51, NCAA Archives.

22. Henry J. McCormick, "Eastern N.C.A.A. Tournament Review," in *The
Official National Basketball Committee Basketball Guide, 1941–42*, ed. Oswald
Tower (New York: American Sports Publishing Co., 1941), 51–54.

23. Rappoport, *The Classic*, 21–25.

24. Rappoport, *The Classic*, 21–25; "In Title Bid Here," *Kansas City Times*,
March 29, 1941, 11.

25. Rappoport, *The Classic*, 21–25.

26. Cox, "N.C.A.A. National Tournament," 44–46.

27. Rappoport, *The Classic*, 21–25.

28. Rappoport, *The Classic*, 21–25.

29. "Appendix III: Financial Reports of Tournaments and Treasurer's Report,"
in *1941 NCAA Yearbook*, Detroit, MI, December 29–31, 1941, 154, NCAA
Archives.

30. "Appendix III: Financial Reports," 155.

31. "Appendix III: Financial Reports," 155–57; Olsen, "1941 National
Collegiate," 43.

32. "L.I.U., Wisconsin Were Acclaimed as Nation's Best in Basketball," *New
York Times*, December 21, 1941, S4, accessed December 9, 2013, http://search.
proquest.com.

33. Fay Young, "The Stuff Is Here: Past-Present-Future," *Chicago Defender*,
April 5, 1941, 22, accessed December 9, 2013, http://search.proquest.com;
Milton S. Katz, *Breaking Through: John B. McLendon, Basketball Legend and
Civil Rights Pioneer* (Fayetteville: University of Arkansas Press, 2007), 33–34.

34. Thomas Harbrecht and Robert Barnett, "College Football during World
War II: 1941–1945," *Physical Educator* (March 1979), 31.

35. Nels Norgren, "Basketball and the War," in *National Association of
Basketball Coaches Bulletin*, January 1942, 2, Kansas Archives.

36. Thomas J. Deegan, "The Golden Jubilee of Basketball," in *The Official
National Basketball Committee Basketball Guide, 1941–42*, ed. Oswald
Tower (New York: American Sports Publishing Co., 1941), 3, NCAA Archives;
Stooksbury, *National Title*, 86–87.

37. "Cage Draw Made," *Kansas City Times*, March 7, 1942, 18; Stooksbury,
National Title, 90–91; "Winners Even in Defeat," *Kansas City Times*, March 13,
1942, 11.

38. Stooksbury, *National Title*, 84–85.

39. Stooksbury, *National Title*, 86–87.

40. Stooksbury, *National Title*, 88–89, 91, 94–95.

41. "Cage Marks Set," *Kansas City Times*, March 10, 1942, 11; "A Scoring
Mark," *Kansas City Times*, March 11, 1942, 11; "Mules Stay In," *Kansas City
Times*, March 13, 1942, 11; "Pittsburg Upset," *Kansas City Times*, March 14,
1942, 17.

42. "Tourney in Garden to Start March 17," *New York Times*, January 22, 1942, 21, accessed December 9, 2013, http://search.proquest.com.

43. Joseph M. Sheehan, "City College Five Bids for Place in National Invitation Tournament," *New York Times*, February 23, 1942, 18, accessed December 9, 2013, http://search.proquest.com; Joseph M. Sheehan, "L.I.U. and C.C.N.Y. in Line for Tourney Bids," *New York Times*, March 2, 1942, 24, accessed December 9, 2013, http://search.proquest.com; "Penn State on Top, 44–30," *New York Times*, February 26, 1942, 24, accessed December 9, 2013, http://search.proquest.com; Joseph M. Sheehan, "On Basketball Courts," *New York Times*, March 3, 1942, 19, accessed December 9, 2013, http://search.proquest.com.

44. "West Texas Accepts Bid," *New York Times*, March 5, 1942, 28, accessed December 9, 2013, http://search.proquest.com; "R.I. State Quintet to Play in Tourney," *New York Times*, March 6, 1942, 24, accessed December 9, 2013, http://search.proquest.com; "L.I.U. Five to Play in National Tourney," *New York Times*, March 11, 1942, 27, accessed December 9, 2013, http://search.proquest.com; "West Virginia Added to Garden Tourney," *New York Times*, March 13, 1942 24, accessed December 9, 2013, http://search.proquest.com.

45. "West Virginia Added."

46. Arthur Daley, "L.I.U. and West Texas Are Upset as Basketball Tournament Starts at Garden," *New York Times*, March 18, 1942, 31, accessed December 9, 2013, http://search.proquest.com; Arthur Daley, "C.C.N.Y. Five Upset by Western Kentucky; Toledo Wins," *New York Times*, March 20, 1942, 27, accessed December 9, 2013, http://search.proquest.com; John Kieran, "Sports of the *Times*: Fifty Years A-Growing," *New York Times*, March 19, 1942, 30, accessed December 9, 2013, http://search.proquest.com; "C.C.N.Y. and Toledo Favored Tonight," *New York Times*, March 19, 1942, 30, accessed December 9, 2013, http://search.proquest.com.

47. Arthur Daley, "West Virginia and Western Kentucky Gain Garden Basketball Final in Upsets," *New York Times*, March 24, 1942, 26, accessed December 9, 2013, http://search.proquest.com.

48. Arthur Daley, "West Virginia Halts Western Kentucky in National Invitation Basketball Final," *New York Times*, March 26, 1942, 28, accessed December 9, 2013, http://search.proquest.com.

49. "Dartmouth and Kentucky Top Three High-Scoring Teams in Tourney Here," *New Orleans Times-Picayune*, March 18, 1942, 15; "Cage Titans Clash Here Tonight in Eastern Eliminations of N.C.A.A. Play," *New Orleans Times-Picayune*, March 20, 1942, 13.

50. Horace Renegar, "N.C.A.A. Eastern Tournament," in *The Official 1942–43 Basketball Guide,* ed. Oswald Tower (New York: A. S. Barnes and Company, 1942), 32–35, NCAA Archives; "Appendix I: Financial Reports of Tournaments and Treasurer's Report," *1942 NCAA Yearbook*, (city and date unknown), 101–3, NCAA Archives (author has copy); Rappoport, *The Classic*, 31.

51. Mark Cox, "N.C.A.A. Western Tournament," in *The Official 1942–43 Basketball Guide,* ed. Oswald Tower (New York: A. S. Barnes Publishing Company, 1942), 35–38, NCAA Archives; "Appendix I," 101–3.

52. Rappoport, *The Classic*, 21–25; Art Rosenbaum, "1942: Those Long-Legged, Gangly Indians," in *NCAA March Madness: The Cinderellas, Superstars, and Champions from the NCAA Final Four* (Chicago: Triumph Books, 2004), 8–9.

53. Rappoport, *The Classic*, 21–25; Rosembaum, "1942," 8–9.

54. Mark Cox, "N.C.A.A. National Championship Tournament," in *The Official 1942–1943 Basketball Guide*, ed. Oswald Tower (New York: A. S. Barnes Publishing Company, 1942), 30–32, NCAA Archives; "Appendix I," 101–3.

55. H. G. Olsen, "N.C.A.A. 1942 Tournament Administration," in *The Official 1942–43 Basketball Guide,* ed. Oswald Tower (New York: A. S. Barnes Publishing Company, 1942), 29–30, NCAA Archives; Cox, "N.C.A.A. National Championship Tournament," 30–32.

56. Jack Coffey, "National Invitation College Tournament," in *The Official 1942–1943 Basketball Guide,* ed. Oswald Tower (New York: A. S. Barnes Publishing Company, 1942), 80–82, NCAA Archives; James McQueeny, "National Intercollegiate Championship Tournament," in *The Official 1942–1943 Basketball Guide,* ed. Oswald Tower (New York: A. S. Barnes Publishing Company, 1942), 79–80, NCAA Archives; Cox, "N.C.A.A. National Championship Tournament," 30–32.

57. "Appendix I," 101–3.

58. Kerkhoff, *Phog Allen*, 121–30.

59. Kerkhoff, *Phog Allen*, 126–27.

60. Kerkhoff, *Phog Allen*, 128; Phog Allen to Earl Foster, 18 February 1941, Kansas Archives.

61. Kerkhoff, *Phog Allen*, 128.

62. "Says Allen Errs," *Kansas City Times*, March 5, 1942, 16.

63. "K.U. Turns Down Bid," *Kansas City Times*, March 7, 1942, 17.

64. John Kieran, "Sports of the *Times*: A Bouncing Game," *New York Times*, February 22, 1942, S2, accessed December 9, 2013, http://search.proquest.com.

65. Kieran, "Sports of the *Times*.

66. Martin Simon, "Letters to the Sports Editor: Why Not C.C.N.Y.-L.I.U.?" *New York Times*, March 21, 1942, 11, accessed December 9, 2013, http://search.proquest.com; Allen M. Teplitz, "Letters to the Sports Editor: L.I.U.-C.C.N.Y. for Charity," *New York Times*, April 4, 1941, 11, accessed December 9, 2013 http://search.proquest.com.

67. "L.I.U. Five to Play C.C.N.Y. Saturday," *New York Times*, March 24, 1942, 26, accessed December 9, 2013, http://search.proquest.com; John Kieran, "Sports of the *Times*: Glancing in All Directions," *New York Times*, March 28, 1942, 12, accessed December 9, 2013, http://search.proquest.com; Arthur Daley, "C.C.N.Y. Quintet Overcomes L.I.U. in Garden, 42–34," *New York Times*, March 29, 1942, S1, accessed December 9, 2013, http://search.proquest.com.

68. E. R. Jessen, "Letters to the Sports Editor: West Virginia's Victory," *New York Times*, April 4, 1942, 21, accessed December 9, 2013, http://search.proquest.com.

69. Irving Braitman, "Letters to the Sports Editor: A Local Fan's Reply," *New York Times*, April 11, 1942, 17, accessed December 9, 2013, http://search.proquest.com; S. Anderman, "Letters to the Sports Editor: A Hollow Argument," *New York Times*, April 11, 1942, 17, accessed December 9, 2013, http://search.proquest.com.

70. "West Virginia Five and Stanford Best," *New York Times*, December 20, 1942, S4, accessed December 9, 2013, http://search.proquest.com.

Chapter 6: New York City and True National Championships, 1942–1945

1. Gary L. Bloomfield, *Duty, Honor, Victory: America's Athletes in World War II* (Guilford, CT: Lyons Press, 2003), 97.

2. V. R. Cardozier, *Colleges and Universities in World War II* (Westport, CT: Praeger, 1993), 130; Bloomfield, *Duty*, 100. For more on sport and the military during World War II, see Wanda Ellen Wakefield, *Playing to Win: Sports and the American Military, 1898–1945* (Albany: State University of New York Press, 1997), 95–110.

3. Olsen to Badger, 26 February 1940; Philip O. Badger to Harold Olsen, 27 February 1940, Ohio State Archives; Gretz, "Phog Allen Helps Save."

4. "N.C.A.A. Court Play at Garden Likely," *New York Times*, January 20, 1943, 26, accessed November 23, 2012, http://search.proquest.com.

5. "N.C.A.A. Court Play at Garden Likely"; "West Virginia Five and Stanford"; Carlson, "Tale of Two Tournaments," 265–67.

6. Kingsley Childs, "N.C.A.A. Will Hold Court Play Here," *New York Times*, January 21, 1943, 28, accessed November 23, 2012, http://search.proquest.com.

7. "Basketball Dates Set," *New York Times*, February 11, 1943, 26, accessed November 23, 2012, http://search.proquest.com. For more on Madison Square Garden history, see Joseph Durso, *Madison Square Garden: 100 Years of History* (New York: Simon & Schuster, 1979). For more on Friday night boxing, see Troy Rondinone, *Friday Night Fighter: Gaspar "Indio" Ortega and the Golden Age of Television Boxing* (Urbana: University of Illinois Press, 2013).

8. "Red Cross Game Listed," *New York Times*, February 19, 1943, 24, accessed November 23, 2012, http://search.proquest.com.

9. "38 Quintets Considered," *New York Times*, February 25, 1943, 28, accessed November 23, 2012, http://search.proquest.com.

10. Louis Effrat, "Push City League for College Fives," *New York Times*, March 2, 1943, 25, accessed November 23, 2012, http://search.proquest.com; "Bid Accepted by Fordham," *New York Times*, March 6, 1943, 18, accessed November 23, 2012, http://search.proquest.com; "Rice's Quintet Invited," *New York Times*, March 7, 1943, S3, accessed November 23, 2012, http://search. proquest.com; Kingsley Childs, "Manhattan, W. and J. Quintets in Invitation Tourney; N.Y.U. in N.C.A.A. Event," *New York Times*, March 12, 1943, 21, accessed November 23, 2012, http://search.proquest.com; "Two Quintets Are Tourney Choices," *New York Times*, March 15, 1943, 17, accessed November 23, 2012, http://search.proquest.com.

11. "Jays Not Coming," *Kansas City Times*, March 4, 1943, 16.

12. Childs, "Manhattan."

13. "Georgetown Five Accepts Bid," *New York Times*, March 10, 1943, 23, accessed November 23, 2012, http://search.proquest.com; Childs, "Manhattan"; "De Paul to Play in N.C.A.A. Meet," *Chicago Tribune*, March 9, 1943, 23, accessed November 23, 2012, http://search.proquest.com.

14. "De Paul to Play"; "Passes Up the N.C.A.A.," *Kansas City Times*, March 9, 1943, 13.

15. "De Paul to Play."

16. "Cage Fans' Week," *Kansas City Times*, March 8, 1943, 11; "A Game for Blood," *Kansas City Times*, March 8, 1943, 11.

17. "Loyola Is Out," *Kansas City Times*, March 9, 1943, 13; "All-State Final," *Kansas City Times*, March 13, 1943, 17.

18. Arthur Daley, "Sports of the *Times*: Basketball, Past and Present," *New York Times*, March 18, 1943, 25, accessed November 23, 2012, http://search.proquest.com.

19. Louis Effrat, "Toledo Five Ousts Manhattan, W. and J. Upsets Creighton in Garden Tourney," *New York Times*, March 19, 1943, 23, accessed November 23, 2012, http://search.proquest.com.

20. Effrat, "Toledo Five Ousts Manhattan," 23.

21. Louis Effrat, "18,135 See St. John's Nip Rice Five, Fordham Top Western Kentucky," *New York Times*, March 23, 1943, 22, accessed November 23, 2012, http://search.proquest.com.

22. Effrat, "18,135 See St. John's," 22.

23. George L. Shiebler, "NCAA Championship Tournament," in *The Official 1943–44 Basketball Guide*, ed. Oswald Tower (New York: A. S. Barnes and Company, 1943), 44–47, NCAA Archives.

24. Shiebler, "NCAA Championship," 44–47.

25. Paul O'Boynick, "Western Playoff," in *The Official 1943–44 Basketball Guide*, ed. Oswald Tower (New York: A. S. Barnes and Company, 1943), 47–49, NCAA Archives.

26. O'Boynick, "Western Playoff," 47–49.

27. O'Boynick, "Western Playoff," 47–49.

28. Louis Effrat, "18,419 See St. John's Rout Fordham Five in Semi-finals, 69–43," *New York Times*, March 28, 1943, S1, accessed November 23, 2012, http://search.proquest.com.

29. Effrat, "18,419 See St. John's," S1.

30. Harold Parrott, "Both Sides," *Brooklyn Daily Eagle*, March 29, 1943, 9, accessed June 6, 2015, http://www.newspapers.com; Louis Effrat, "18,233 See St. John's Five Overwhelm Toledo in National Invitation Final," *New York Times*, March 30, 1943, 25, accessed November 23, 2012, http://search.proquest.com; Louis Effrat, "Wyoming Downs Georgetown to Capture N.C.A.A. Basketball Title," *New York Times*, March 31, 1943, 24, accessed November 23, 2012, http://search.proquest.com.

31. Effrat, "Wyoming Downs Georgetown."

32. Rappoport, *The Classic*, 32–36.

33. Shiebler, "NCAA Championship Tournament," 43; Arthur Daley, "Sports of the *Times*: Horse Haggerty Plays a Return Engagement," *New York Times*, April 1, 1943, 28, accessed November 23, 2012, http://search.proquest.com.

34. For more on the Red Cross charity during World War II, see F. R. Dulles, *The American Red Cross: A History* (Westport, CT: Greenwood Press, 1950); and American National Red Cross (ANRC), *The Greatest Freewill Offering in History* (Washington, DC: American National Red Cross, ca. 1947).

35. John Kieran, "Sports of the *Times*: At Red Cross Purposes," *New York Times*, January 27, 1942, 27, accessed November 23, 2012, http://search.proquest.com.

36. Kieran, "Sports of the *Time*: At Red Cross Purposes," 27.

37. ANRC, Greatest Freewill Offering; Dulles, American Red Cross, 363.

38. Kieran, "Sports of the *Times*: At Red Cross Purposes."

39. "Red Cross Names Sports Committee," *New York Times*, January 19, 1945, 27, accessed November 23, 2012, http://search.proquest.com.

40. Simon Martin, "Letters to the Sports Editor: Why Not C.C.N.Y.-L.I.U.?" *New York Times*, March 21, 1942, 11, accessed December 9, 2012, http://search.proquest.com.

41. Teplitz, "L.I.U.-C.C.N.Y."; John Kieran, "Sports of the *Times*: Glancing in All Directions."

42. Kieran, "Sports of the *Times*: Glancing in All Directions"; Daley, "C.C.N.Y. Quintet Overcomes L.I.U."

43. "Red Cross Names."

44. "N.C.A.A. Court Play."

45. A. J. Ditman to Robert A. Shepard, 9 November 1942, Folder 224: Sports Benefits: Basketball Papers. Central Files, 1881–1982 (1935–1946 segment). Records of the American National Red Cross, Washington, DC (hereafter ANRC Archives).

46. "N.C.A.A. Court Play"; William D. Richardson, "Rhode Island Opposes Tennessee Tonight," *New York Times*, March 17, 1945, 20, accessed November 23, 2012, http://search.proquest.com.

47. Kingsley Childs, "St. John's Faces Wyoming for Red Cross Tonight," *New York Times*, April 1, 1943, 28, accessed November 23, 2012, http://search.proquest.com; Daley, "Sports of the *Times*: Horse Haggerty Plays a Return Engagement"; George E. Coleman, "Redmen Confident They'll Tame Wyoming Cowboy '5,'" *Brooklyn Daily Eagle*, March 31, 1943, 17, accessed June 6, 2015, http://www.newspapers.com.

48. Louis Effrat, "18,316 See Wyoming Quintet Beat St. John's in Overtime," *New York Times*, April 2, 1943, 25, accessed November 23, 2012, http://search.proquest.com; A. J. Ditman to Ned Irish, 2 April 1943, ANRC Archives.

49. Effrat, "18,316 See Wyoming."

50. Effrat, "18,316 See Wyoming"; George E. Coleman, "Wyoming Five Is Real National Champion," *Brooklyn Daily Eagle*, April 2, 1943, 15, accessed June 6, 2015, http://www.newspapers.com.

51. Effrat, "18,316 See Wyoming"; Peter C. Bjarkman, *Big Ten Basketball* (Indianapolis: Masters Press, 1995), 4; Ned Irish and Orlo Robertson, "Busy Wartime Court Season Looms," in *The Official 1943–44 Basketball Guide*, ed. Oswald Tower (New York: A. S. Barnes and Company Publishers, 1943), 14–16, NCAA Archives.

52. Effrat, "18,316 See Wyoming"; "Game Nets $26,244 for Red Cross Here," *New York Times*, April 29, 1943, 24, accessed November 23, 2012, http://search.proquest.com; Eddie Dooley, "Wyoming Cops Benefit Dream Game," in *The Official 1943–44 Basketball Guide*, ed. Oswald Tower (New York: A. S. Barnes and Company Publishers, 1943), 41–42, NCAA Archives.

53. Henry C. Herge, *Navy V-12* (Paducah, KY: Turner Publishing Company, 1996), 20–24.

54. Bloomfield, *Duty*, 93.

55. Louis Effrat, "Garden Dates Set for College Fives," *New York Times*, November 10, 1943, 29, accessed November 23, 2021, http://search.proquest.com.

56. Louis Effrat, "Impressive Western Kentucky Five Arrives and Drills in Garden," *New York Times*, December 23, 1943, 24, accessed November 23, 2012, http://search.proquest.com.

57. John Drebinger, "Sports, Attuned to U.S. War Needs, Had Robust Year," *New York Times*, December 26, 1943, S1, accessed November 23, 2012, http://search.proquest.com.

58. Cardozier, Colleges and Universities, 130.

59. Allison Danzig, "Bingham, Chosen Head of Rules Committee, Opposes Changes in Football Code," *New York Times*, January 7, 1944, 11, accessed November 23, 2012, http://search.proquest.com.

60. Bloomfield, *Duty*, 97.

61. Harbrecht and Barnett, "College Football," 32.

62. "Title Basketball Set for March 16," *New York Times*, February 1, 1944, 16, accessed November 23, 2012, http://search.proquest.com.

63. Stooksbury, *National Title*, 107.

64. Hoover, "History of the National Association," 55; Stooksbury, *National Title*, 110.

65. Arthur Daley, "Sports of the *Times*: Short Shots in Sundry Directions," *New York Times*, February 11, 1944, 14, accessed November 23, 2012, http://search.proquest.com.

66. Daley, "Sports of the *Times*: Short Shots in Sundry Directions."

67. Daley, "Sports of the *Times*: Short Shots in Sundry Directions."

68. Allison Danzig, "Sports Benefits for Red Cross Set," *New York Times*, February 19, 1944, 18, accessed November 23, 2012, http://search.proquest.com.

69. "Kentucky Team to Play in Basketball Tourney," *New York Times*, February 17, 1944, 14, accessed November 23, 2012, http://search.proquest.com; "Utah Five Accepts Garden Invitation," *New York Times*, February 20, 1944, S1, accessed November 23, 2012, http://search.proquest.com.

70. "Utah Five Accepts"; Alexander Wolff and Michael Atchison, "Utah: The First Cinderella," *Sports Illustrated*, March 22, 2010, accessed November 22, 2014, http://www.sivault.com.

71. "St. John's Five Accepts Bid to Garden Tourney," *New York Times*, February 25, 1944, 20, accessed November 23, 2012, http://search.proquest.com.

72. "De Paul Five Will Play in Garden Meet," *Chicago Tribune*, February 27, 1944, A1, accessed November 23, 2012, http://search.proquest.com; "Article 13—No Title," *New York Times*, February 27, 1944, S1, accessed November, 23, 2012, http://search.proquest.com; "Canisius Five in Tourney," *New York Times*, March 3, 1944, 20, accessed November 23, 2012, http://search.proquest.com; "Cornell Crushes Canisius, 51 to 29," *New York Times*, March 5, 1944, S3, accessed November 23, 2012, http://search.proquest.com.

73. Don Leighbur, "Ned Irish Forcing Jim Crow Basketball Play," *Philadelphia Tribune*, March 4, 1944, 12, accessed May 11, 2011, http://search.proquest.com.

74. "Dartmouth Five to Play in N.C.A.A. Tourney," *New York Times*, February 19, 1944, 18, accessed November 23, 2012, http://search.proquest.com.

75. Joseph Declan Moran, *You Can Call Me Al: The Colorful Journey of Basketball's Original Flower Child, Al McGuire* (Madison, WI: Prairie Oak Press, 1999); Louis Effrat, "L.I.U. Counts on Cornell Game to Clinch Garden Tourney

Bid," *New York Times*, February 28, 1944, 21, accessed November 23, 2012, http://search.proquest.com.

76. "Arkansas Five in Tourney," *New York Times*, March 6, 1944, 14, accessed November 23, 2012, http://search.proquest.com; "Iowa State Not to Play," *New York Times*, March 7, 1944, 13, accessed November 23, 2012, http://search.proquest.com; "A Cage Problem," *Kansas City Times*, March 6, 1944, 8; "Iowa State Is In," *Kansas City Times*, March 9, 1944, 15.

77. "Iowa to Play Here," *Kansas City Times*, March 8, 1944, 9; "M.U. in, Iowa Out," *Kansas City Times*, March 14, 1944, 9.

78. "Team in Crash," *Kansas City Times*, March 20, 1944, 8.

79. "De Paul Faces Muhlenberg in Opener Tonight," *Chicago Tribune*, March 16, 1944, 21, accessed November 23, 2012, http://search.proquest.com; "NCAA Draw Pits Dartmouth Five against Catholic U. March 24," *New York Times*, March 14, 1944, 14, accessed November 23, 2012, http://search.proquest.com.

80. Arthur Daley, "Sports of the *Times*: Going Up?" *New York Times*, March 16, 1944, 24, accessed November 23, 2012, http://search.proquest.com.

81. William D. Richardson, "St. John's Upsets Bowling Green Five; De Paul Triumphs," *New York Times*, March 17, 1944, 20, accessed November 23, 2012, http://search.proquest.com.

82. Richardson, "St. John's Upsets Bowling Green Five."

83. Louis Effrat, "Kentucky and Oklahoma Aggies Triumph in Invitation Tourney before 16,273," *New York Times*, March 21, 1944, 22, accessed November 23, 2012, http://search.proquest.com.

84. "Utah Accepts N.C.A.A. Bid," *New York Times*, March 22, 1944, 23, accessed November 23, 2012, http://search.proquest.com.

85. Louis Effrat, "St. John's Upsets Kentucky to Gain Garden Basketball Final; De Paul Victor," *New York Times*, March 23, 1944, 23, accessed November 23, 2012, http://search.proquest.com.

86. William D. Richardson, "N.C.A.A. Quintets in Garden Tonight," *New York Times*, March 24, 1944, 22, accessed November 23, 2012, http://search.proquest.com.

87. H. G. Olsen, "The 1944 Basketball Tournament," in *1944 NCAA Yearbook*, (city and date unknown), 57–59, NCAA Archives (author has copy).

88. Olsen, "The 1944 Basketball Tournament."

89. "Colleges Seek Larger Share of Basket Gate," *Chicago Tribune*, March 24, 1944, 20, accessed November 23, 2012, http://search.proquest.com.

90. Somerville, "History of the National Association," 96–97.

91. George L. Shiebler, "Metropolitan New York Basketball," in *The Official National Basketball Committee Basketball Guide, 1944–45*, ed. Oswald Tower (New York: A. S. Barnes Company Publishers, 1944), 62, NCAA Archives.

92. "Colleges Seek Larger Share."

93. These figures come from perusal of *NCAA Yearbook* Treasury Reports from 1939 to 1944, NCAA Archives (author in possession of copies).

94. Louis Effrat, "18,374 See St. John's Win Invitation Basketball Final Second Year in Row," *New York Times*, March 27, 1944, 22, accessed November 23, 2012, http://search.proquest.com; Louis Effrat, "Utah Upsets Dartmouth in Extra

Period to Take N.C.A.A. Basketball Title," *New York Times*, March 29, 1944, 16, accessed November 23, 2012, http://search.proquest.com.

95. Louis Effrat, "Utah Five to Play in Red Cross Game," *New York Times*, March 28, 1944, 23, accessed November 23, 2012, http://search.proquest.com; Rappoport, *The Classic*, 37–41.

96. Vadal Peterson, "Skyline Basketball," in *The Official National Basketball Committee Basketball Guide, 1944–45*, ed. Oswald Tower (New York: A. S. Barnes Company Publishers, 1944), 16–17, NCAA Archives.

97. Peterson, "Skyline Basketball"; Wolff and Atchison, "Utah."

98. Wolff and Atchison, "Utah."

99. Wolff and Atchison, "Utah."

100. Effrat, "Utah Upsets Dartmouth."

101. William D. Richardson, "St. John's Favored to Beat Utah in Red Cross Basketball Tonight," *New York Times*, March 30, 1944, 25, accessed November 23, 2012, http://search.proquest.com; George Coleman, "Shh, Redmen Should Take Speedy Utes," *Brooklyn Daily Eagle*, March 30, 1944, 14, accessed June 6, 2015, http://www.newspapers.com; George L. Shiebler, "Utah Comes Thru in Red Cross Classic," in *The Official National Basketball Committee Basketball Guide, 1944–45*, ed. Oswald Tower (New York: A. S. Barnes Company Publishers, 1944), 27–29, NCAA Archives; Rappoport, *The Classic*, 37–41.

102. "Top Officials Thrilled by Ute Victory," *Salt Lake Tribune*, March 31, 1944, 19, accessed June 6, 2015, http://www.newspapers.com.

103. Shiebler, "Utah Comes Thru," 27–29.

104. "2 Collegians Bribed by Gamblers to Throw Tourney Basketball Games, Allen Charges," *New York Times*, October 21, 1944, 20, accessed November 23, 2012, http://search.proquest.com.

105. Jimmy Wood, "Sportopics: Whispers," *Brooklyn Daily Eagle*, March 22, 1939, 17, accessed June 6, 2015, http://www.newspapers.com.

106. For more information regarding the college basketball gambling scandals, see Charley Rosen, *The Scandals of '51: How the Gamblers Almost Killed College Basketball* (New York: Seven Stories Press, 1999); and Albert J. Figone, *Cheating the Spread: Gamblers, Point Shavers, and Game Fixers in College Football and Basketball* (Urbana: University of Illinois Press, 2012).

107. "2 Collegians Bribed."

108. "2 Collegians Bribed"; "Allen Furnishes Data on Gambling," *New York Times*, October 22, 1944, S2, accessed November 23, 2012, http://search.proquest.com.

109. "Allen Furnishes Data"; Kerkhoff, *Phog Allen*, 141–51.

110. Kerkhoff, *Phog Allen*, 143; "Coach's Cry of Gaming Peril Draws Rebuke," *Chicago Tribune*, October 22, 1944, A2, accessed November 23, 2012, http://search.proquest.com.

111. Kerkhoff, *Phog Allen*, 143–44.

112. "Allen Furnishes Data"; Stooksbury, *National Title*, 116.

113. Arthur Daley, "Sports of the *Times*: The Passing Scene, or the Year in Review," *New York Times*, December 24, 1944, 40, accessed November 23, 2012, http://search.proquest.com.

114. "Status of Tourneys Not Yet Determined," *New York Times*, February 22, 1945, 33, accessed November 23, 2012, http://search.proquest.com.

115. "N.C.A.A. Plans Unchanged," *New York Times*, January 31, 1945, 24, accessed November 23, 2012, http://search.proquest.com.

116. "N.C.A.A. Plans Unchanged."

117. Louis Effrat, "New Basketball Prize Will Go to Star in College Games Here," *New York Times*, February 20, 1945, 24, accessed November 23, 2012, http://search.proquest.com.

118. Stooksbury, *National Title*, 122–23.

119. "A Cage Field Set," *Kansas City Times*, March 9, 1945, 9; Stooksbury, *National Title*, 122.

120. Louis Effrat, "Three Local Fives on Tentative List," *New York Times*, February 27, 1945, 23, accessed November 23, 2012, http://search.proquest.com.

121. "St. John's Accepts Bid," *New York Times*, March 1, 1945, 24, accessed November 23, 2012, http://search.proquest.com.

122. "Muhlenberg Accepts Bid," *New York Times*, March 3, 1945, 21, accessed November 23, 2012, http://search.proquest.com.

123. "De Paul Accepts Bid to Play in Eastern Meet," *Chicago Tribune*, March 6, 1945, 17, accessed November 23, 2012, http://search.proquest.com; Arthur Daley, "Sports of the *Times*: High Scorer," *New York Times*, March 21, 1945, 29, accessed November 23, 2012, http://search.proquest.com.

124. "N.Y.U. and West Virginia to Play in Court Events," *New York Times*, March 9, 1945, 14, accessed November 23, 2012, http://search.proquest.com; Louis Effrat, "R.P.I. Quintet Completes Field in Invitation Series at Garden," *New York Times*, March 12, 1945, 14, accessed November 23, 2012, http://search.proquest.com; Louis Effrat, "De Paul Five Tops Draw for Tourney," *New York Times*, March 13, 1945, 22, accessed November 23, 2012, http://search.proquest.com.

125. George E. Coleman, "St. John's, NYU May Play for Red Cross Fund," *Brooklyn Daily Eagle*, March 9, 1945, 15, accessed June 6, 2015, http://www.newspapers.com; Effrat, "R.P.I. Quintet."

126. George L. Shiebler, "NCAA Championship Tournament," in *The Official National Basketball Committee Basketball Guide, 1945–46*, ed. Oswald Tower (New York: A. S. Barnes Company, 1945), 23–24, NCAA Archives.

127. Shiebler, "NCAA Championship Tournament," 23–27.

128. "Iowa Season Over," *Chicago Tribune*, March 6, 1945, 17, accessed November 23, 2012, http://search.proquest.com; Shiebler, "NCAA Championship Tournament," 23–27.

129. Arthur Daley, "Sports of the *Times*: Short Shots in Sundry Directions," *New York Times*, March 16, 1945, 19, accessed November 23, 2012, http://search.proquest.com.

130. Daley, "Sports of the *Times*: Short Shots in Sundry Directions."

131. Louis Effrat, "Rhode Island Tops Tennessee, 51 to 44, in Upset at Garden," *New York Times*, March 18, 1945, S1, accessed November 23, 2012, http://search.proquest.com; Louis Effrat, "St. John's Checks Muhlenberg, 34–33," *New York*

Times, March 20, 1945, 24, accessed November 23, 2012, http://search. proquest.com.

132. Effrat, "St. John's Checks Muhlenberg."

133. Louis Effrat, "De Paul Five Beats R.I. State, 97 to 53: Bowling Green's Defense at Its Height in the Garden," *New York Times*, March 22, 1945, 19, accessed November 23, 2012, http://search.proquest.com.

134. Emanuel Strauss, "Mikan's Injury Hits De Paul Hopes of Triumphing in Basketball Final," *New York Times*, March 25, 1945, S1, accessed November 23, 2012, http://search.proquest.com.

135. Shiebler, "NCAA Championship Tournament," 23–27.

136. Shiebler, "NCAA Championship Tournament," 23–27.

137. Paul O'Boynick, "Western Playoff," in *The Official National Basketball Committee Basketball Guide, 1945–46*, ed. Oswald Tower (New York: A. S. Barnes Company, 1945), 28–30, NCAA Archives; "Set Two Marks," *Kansas City Times*, March 24, 1945, 11.

138. O'Boynick, "Western Playoff," 28–30.

139. Louis Effrat, "De Paul Quintet Triumphs by 71–54: A Battle of the Giants in National Final," *New York Times*, March 27, 1945, 27, accessed November 23, 2012, http://search.proquest.com.

140. Rappoport, *The Classic*, 42–48; Shiebler, "NCAA Championship Tournament," 23–24.

141. "Financial Report of the 1945 Basketball Play-offs and Final Game," in *1945 NCAA Yearbook*, (city and date unknown), 165–67, NCAA Archives (author has copies).

142. "Financial Report of the 1945 Basketball Play-offs"; "Cage Inquiry Goes On," *Kansas City Times*, March 29, 1945, 13.

143. Arthur Daley, "Sports of the *Times*: Paging Jack-the-Giant-Killer," *New York Times*, March 29, 1945, 31, accessed November 23, 2012, http://search. proquest.com; William D. Richardson, "Giant Centers Top Court Bill Tonight," *New York Times*, March 29, 1945, 32, accessed November 23, 2012, http://search. proquest.com.

144. Daley, "Sports of the *Times*: Paging Jack-the-Giant-Killer"; Louis Effrat, "Oklahoma Aggies Top De Paul, 52–44," *New York Times*, March 30, 1945, 20, accessed November 23, 2012, http://search.proquest.com; "Basketball Makes Contribution to Red Cross," *New York Times*, April 13, 1945, 20, accessed November 23, 2012, http://search.proquest.com; George E. Coleman, "Battle of Giants Fizzles in Garden," *Brooklyn Daily Eagle*, March 30, 1945, 15, accessed June 6, 2015, http://www.newspapers.com.

145. Carlson, "Tale of Two Tournaments," 260–80.

Chapter 7: Postwar Boom, 1946–1950

1. Austin Bealmear, "Interest in Basketball to Keep Mounting, Leaders Say," *Burlington Daily Times-News* (Burlington, NC), March 22, 1946, 6, accessed June 6, 2015, http://www.newspapers.com.

2. Durso, Madison Square Garden, 106.

3. "Ned Irish Denies Listing Gamblers," *New York Times*, April 3, 1945, 21, accessed November 23, 2012, http://search.proquest.com.

4. "Irish Draws 10% of Games' Profit," *New York Times*, March 29, 1945, 22, accessed November 23, 2012, http://search.proquest.com.

5. "21 Double-Headers Listed for Garden," *New York Times*, November 14, 1945, 28, accessed June 15, 2013, http://search.proquest.com.

6. "Selectors Chosen for Court Tourney," *New York Times*, February 19, 1946, 29, accessed June 15, 2013, http://search.proquest.com.

7. "Kentucky Will Play in National Tourney," *New York Times*, February 26, 1946, 35, accessed June 15, 2013, http://search.proquest.com.

8. "Muhlenberg Accepts Bid," *New York Times*, February 27, 1946, 35, accessed June 15, 2013, http://search.proquest.com; "Bowling Green Is Picked," *New York Times*, February 28, 1946, 33, accessed June 15, 2013, http://search.proquest.com; "N.Y.U., St. John's in Tourneys Here," *New York Times*, March 1, 1946, 26, accessed June 15, 2013, http://search.proquest.com; "Syracuse Five Accepts," *New York Times*, March 2, 1946, 8, accessed June 15, 2013, http://search.proquest.com.

9. Emanuel Strauss, "Basketball Fans Stage Ticket Rush," *New York Times*, March 5, 1946, 30, accessed June 15, 2013, http://search.proquest.com.

10. Strauss, "Basketball Fans Stage Ticket Rush."

11. "Colorado in N.C.A.A. Play," *New York Times*, March 8, 1946, 24, accessed June 15, 2013, http://search.proquest.com; "Arizona Five Accepts," *New York Times*, March 8, 1946, 25, accessed June 15, 2013, http://search.proquest.com; "C.C.N.Y. Protests Choice of R.I. State," *New York Times*, March 9, 1946, 21, accessed June 15, 2013, http://search.proquest.com.

12. "C.C.N.Y. Protests."

13. Emanuel Strauss, "City College's Upset of N.Y.U. Week's Highlight in Basketball," *New York Times*, March 11, 1946, 22, accessed June 15, 2013, http://search.proquest.com.

14. Louis Effrat, "Kentucky Quintet Seeded at Top for National Invitation Tourney," *New York Times*, March 12, 1946, 29, accessed June 15, 2013, http://search.proquest.com.

15. Effrat, "Kentucky Quintet Seeded at Top."

16. Louis Effrat, "Rhode Island Wins in Overtime, 82–79," *New York Times*, March 15, 1946, 16, accessed June 15, 2013, http://search.proquest.com.

17. Effrat, "Rhode Island Wins in Overtime."

18. Louis Effrat, "Kentucky Crushes Arizona by 77–53; Muhlenberg Wins," *New York Times*, March 17, 1946, S1, accessed June 15, 2013, http://search.proquest.com.

19. Louis Effrat, "Kentucky Downs W. Virginia, 59–51," *New York Times*, March 19, 1946, 29, accessed June 15, 2013, http://search.proquest.com.

20. Louis Effrat, "Kentucky Defeats Rhode Island, 46–45," *New York Times*, March 21, 1946, 35, accessed June 15, 2013, http://search.proquest.com.

21. Louis Effrat, "Dartmouth, Ivy League Champion, to Pass Up Post-Season Contests," *New York Times*, February 18, 1946, 29, accessed June 15, 2013, http://search.proquest.com; Emanuel Strauss, "Spotlight on Conference Battles as Basketball Season nears End," *New York Times*, March 4, 1946, 20, accessed

June 15, 2013, http://search.proquest.com; "N.C.A.A. Fives Open Play Here Tonight," *New York Times*, March 21, 1946, 35, accessed June 15, 2013, http://search.proquest.com.

22. George L. Shiebler, "NCAA Championship Tournament," in *The Official National Basketball Committee Basketball Guide, 1946–47*, ed. Oswald Tower (New York: A. S. Barnes Company, 1946), 37–42, NCAA Archives; Carroll Poplin, "Carolina Chatter," *Daily Tar Heel* (Chapel Hill, NC), March 1, 1946, 3, accessed June 6, 2015, http://www.newspapers.com.

23. Shiebler, "NCAA Championship Tournament," 37–42.

24. Shiebler, "NCAA Championship Tournament," 37–42.

25. Dan Partner, "Western Playoff," in *The Official National Basketball Committee Basketball Guide, 1946–47*, ed. Oswald Tower (New York: A. S. Barnes Company Publishing, 1946), 43–46, NCAA Archives.

26. Partner, "Western Playoff."

27. Rappoport, *The Classic*, 47.

28. Shiebler, "NCAA Championship Tournament," 35–37; Rappoport, *The Classic*, 47; Carroll Poplin, "Carolina Chatter," *Daily Tar Heel* (Chapel Hill, NC), March 29, 1946, 3, accessed June 6, 2015, http://www.newspapers.com.

29. Louis Effrat, "Basketball Fans Here Speculate on Fate of Annual Play-Off Game," *New York Times*, January 28, 1946, 24, accessed June 15, 2013, http://search.proquest.com.

30. Effrat, "Basketball Fans Here."

31. "Selectors Chosen"; Effrat, "Kentucky Quintet Seeded."

32. George E. Coleman, "Basketball," *Brooklyn Daily Eagle*, March 19, 1946, 12, accessed June 6, 2015, http://www.newspapers.com; Arthur Daley, "Sports of the *Times*: Short Shots in Sundry Directions," *New York Times*, March 22, 1946, 30, accessed June 15, 2013, http://search.proquest.com.

33. George E. Coleman, "Kentucky Nixes Charity Classic," *Brooklyn Daily Eagle*, March 22, 1946, 17, accessed June 6, 2015, http://www.newspapers.com.

34. George E. Coleman, "Irish Left Juggling Cage Hot Potatoes," *Brooklyn Daily Eagle*, March 26, 1946, 11, accessed June 6, 2015, http://www.newspapers.com.

35. Michael Strauss, "Oklahoma Aggies in Garden Tonight," *New York Times*, March 26, 1946, 33, accessed June 15, 2013, http://search.proquest.com.

36. George E. Coleman, "N.Y.A.C. to Fill in against Oilers," *Brooklyn Daily Eagle*, March 27, 1946, 15, accessed June 6, 2015, http://www.newspapers.com.

37. "Appendix I: Financial Reports of Tournaments and Treasurer's Report," in *1942 NCAA Yearbook*, (city and date unknown), 101–3, NCAA Archives (author has copy); "Appendix I: Financial Reports of Tournaments and Treasurer's Report," in *1943 NCAA Yearbook*, (city and date unknown), 77–80, NCAA Archives (author has copy); "Appendix I: Financial Reports of Tournaments, of Basketball Rules Committee, and of the Treasurer," in *1944 NCAA Yearbook*, (city and date unknown), 165–67, NCAA Archives (author has copy); "Financial Report of the 1945 Basketball Play-offs and Final Game," in *1945 NCAA Yearbook*, (city and date unknown), 165–67, NCAA Archives (author has copy); "Financial Report of the 1946 Basketball Playoffs and Final Game," in *1946 NCAA Yearbook* (city and date unknown), 166–68, NCAA Archives (author has copy).

38. Gretz, "Phog Allen Helps Save."

39. Joseph M. Sheehan, "Oilers Top N.Y.A.C. in Overtime, 69–64," *New York Times*, March 29, 1946, 32, accessed June 15, 2013, http://search.proquest.com.

40. "32 Teams In," *Kansas City Times*, March 9, 1946, 15.

41. Stooksbury, *National Title*, 124, 131; "Marshall Refuses Bid," *Kansas City Times*, February 26, 1946, 8; "Passes Up Tourney Here," *Kansas City Times*, March 6, 1946, 10.

42. Hoover, "History of the National Association," 61–62.

43. Stooksbury, *National Title*, 128–31; Hoover, "History of the National Association," 61–62. Hoover notes that the exhibition game was scored differently in that 3 points were awarded for each field goal. Had the normal 2 points been given, the final score would have been 59–43.

44. Tim Gallagher, "Color Ban Prevented Morningside Player from Competing," *Sioux City Journal*, March 10, 2006, accessed May 11, 2013, http://www.siouxcityjournal.com; "Upset by Drury," *Kansas City Times*, March 13, 1946, 10.

45. "Okla. Aggies Best at .939," *New York Times*, March 29, 1946, 33, accessed June 15, 2013, http://search.proquest.com.

46. Stooksbury, *National Title*, 136–43.

47. John Matthew Smith, *The Sons of Westwood: John Wooden, UCLA, and the Dynasty That Changed College Basketball* (Champaign: University of Illinois Press, 2013), 37–38; Seth Davis, *Wooden: A Coach's Life* (New York: Henry Holt and Company, 2015), 84–85.

48. For more on the racial integration of the Big Ten and college basketball, see Tom Graham and Rachel Graham Cody, *Getting Open: The Unknown Story of Bill Garrett and the Integration of College Basketball* (New York: Atria Books, 2008).

49. Jon P. Scott, "Adolph Rupp Was the Biggest Racist There Was," Kentucky Basketball, accessed May 11, 2013, http://www.bigbluehistory.net/bb/wildcats.html.

50. Charles Martin, Benching Jim Crow: The Rise and Fall of the Color Line in Southern College Sports, 1890–1980 (Urbana: University of Illinois Press, 2010), 215–54.

51. For more on the University of Kentucky, its basketball program, and the racial integration of its athletic department, see Frank Fitzpatrick, *And the Walls Came Tumbling Down: The Basketball Game That Changed American Sports* (New York: Simon & Schuster, 1999).

52. "Basketball Dates Set," *New York Times*, January 26, 1947, S4, accessed June 15, 2013, http://search.proquest.com; Louis Effrat, "St. John's, L.I.U. Quintets Accept Bids to Post-Season Tournament," *New York Times*, March 11, 1947, 34, accessed June 15, 2013, http://search.proquest.com.

53. "Georgetown Ends Duquesne Streak," *New York Times*, March 5, 1947, 32, accessed June 15, 2013, http://search.proquest.com; James D. Whalen and Wayne Patterson, "Cooper, Charles Theodore 'Tarzan,'" in *Basketball: A Biographical Dictionary*, ed. David L. Porter (Westport, CT: Greenwood Press, 2005), 87–88; "N.C. State to Play in Court Tourney," *New York Times*, March 10, 1947, 29, accessed June 15, 2013, http://search.proquest.com; James D. Whalen

and Wayne Patterson, "Case, Everett Norris," in *Basketball: A Biographical Dictionary*, ed. David L. Porter (Westport, CT: Greenwood Press, 2005), 74–75.

54. "C.C.N.Y., Wisconsin Fives Paired in N.C.A.A. Tourney on Thursday," *New York Times*, March 18, 1947, 35, accessed June 15, 2013, http://search. proquest.com; William D. Friedman, "Backtalk: Readers Speak Out on States of College Basketball; Tracing History of Black Presence," *New York Times*, April 11, 1993, accessed May 11, 2013, http://www.nytimes.com.

55. "C.C.N.Y., Wisconsin Fives."

56. Edward J. Garich, "Western Playoff," in *The Official National Basketball Committee Basketball Guide, 1947–48*, ed. Oswald Tower (New York: A. S. Barnes Company, 1947), 43–47, NCAA Archives.

57. Louis Effrat, "No. Carolina State Defeats St. John's in Garden, 61 to 55," *New York Times*, March 16, 1947, S1, accessed June 15, 2013, http://search. proquest.com.

58. Louis Effrat, "Wildcats Conquer L.I.U. Five, 66–62," *New York Times*, March 18, 1947, 35, accessed June 15, 2013, http://search.proquest.com.

59. Louis Effrat, "Wildcats Triumph at Garden, 60 to 42," *New York Times*, March 20, 1947, 34, accessed June 15, 2013, http://search.proquest.com.

60. George R. Edwards, "Basketball," in *1947 NCAA Yearbook*, (city and date unknown), 58–59, NCAA Archives (author has copy); A. C. Lonborg, "The 1947 Basketball Tournament," in *1947 NCAA Yearbook*, (city and date unknown), 60–61, NCAA Archives (author has copy).

61. Lonborg, "1947 Basketball Tournament," 60–61; George L. Shiebler, "Eastern Playoff," in *The Official National Basketball Committee Basketball Guide, 1947–48*, ed. Oswald Tower (New York: A. S. Barnes Company, 1947), 37–43, NCAA Archives; Louis Effrat, "Holy Cross Down City College Five in Garden, 60–45," *New York Times*, March 23, 1947, S1, accessed June 15, 2013, http://search.proquest.com.

62. "Teams Set to Go," *Kansas City Times*, March 21, 1947, 20; "Beavers on the Way Here," *Kansas City Times*, March 19, 1947, 14; Garich, "Western Playoff," 43–47; "Financial Report of 1947 Basketball Playoffs and Final Game," *1947 NCAA Yearbook*, (city and date unknown), 204–7, NCAA Archives (author has copy).

63. Michael Strauss, "Kentucky Opposes Utah Five Tonight," *New York Times*, March 24, 1947, 31, accessed June 15, 2013, http://search.proquest.com.

64. Arthur Daley, "Sports of the *Times*: From Old Kaintuck," *New York Times*, March 24, 1947, 29, accessed June 15, 2013, http://search.proquest.com.

65. Daley, "Sports of the *Times*: From Old Kaintuck."

66. Daley, "Sports of the *Times*: From Old Kaintuck"; Louis Effrat, "Wildcats Toppled by the Utes, 49–45," *New York Times*, March 25, 1947, 32, accessed June 15, 2013, http://search.proquest.com.

67. Effrat, "Wildcats Toppled."

68. Rappoport, *The Classic*, 49–55.

69. Louis Effrat, "Crusaders Annex 23d in Row, 58–47," *New York Times*, March 26, 1947, 33, accessed June 15, 2013, http://search.proquest.com.

70. "Financial Report of 1947 Basketball."

71. Cunningham, *American Hoops*, 29–60; Grundman, "A.A.U.-N.C.A.A. Politics," 111–26.

72. Grundman, *Golden Age*, 112–15; David L. Porter, "Wilke, Louis G. 'Lou,'" in *Basketball: A Biographical Dictionary*, ed. David L. Porter (Westport, CT: Greenwood Press, 2005), 508–9.

73. Cunningham, *American Hoops*, 1–28.

74. "Balk at N.A.I.B. Ruling," *Kansas City Times*, March 4, 1948, 24.

75. Carlson, "Basketball's Forgotten Experiment, 1330–1359"; "Manhattan Accepts N.A.I.B. Bid with Tourney Dropping Negro Ban," *New York Times*, March 6, 1948, 17, accessed June 15, 2013, http://search.proquest.com.

76. Smith, *Sons of Westwood*, 37–38; Davis, *Wooden*, 89–99.

77. "Lift Negro Ban," *Kansas City Times*, March 6, 1948, 20; "Manhattan Accepts"; Hoover, "History of the National Association," 68–69.

78. "A Bid by Titlist," *Kansas City Times*, March 9, 1948, 16; "In Second Tests," *Kansas City Times*, March 10, 1948, 14; "Marshall Is Out," *Kansas City Times*, March 11, 1948, 16; "Only Four Left," *Kansas City Times*, March 12, 1948, 20; "Thrill the Fans," *Kansas City Times*, March 13, 1948, 20; Stooksbury, *National Title*, 144–60.

79. "Basketball Bids Mailed," *New York Times*, February 26, 1948, 31, accessed June 15, 2013, http://search.proquest.com; "Bids Are Accepted by Three Quintets," *New York Times*, February 27, 1948, 29, accessed June 15, 2013, http://search.proquest.com; Leonard Lewin, "Rootin', Tootin', Foul Shootin' Hombres Are These Longhorns from Texas," in *11th Annual Invitation Tournament Quarterfinals Game Program* (Madison Square Garden, March 13, 1948), 24, Naismith Hall of Fame.

80. Sid Friedlander, "N.C. State—A Southern Team with an All-Northern Flavor," in *11th Annual Invitation Tournament Quarterfinals Game Program* (Madison Square Garden, March 13, 1948), 4, Naismith Hall of Fame; "No. Carolina State in Garden Tourney," *New York Times*, February 28, 1948, 11, accessed June 15, 2013, http://search.proquest.com; Michael Strauss, "N.Y.U. and Three Out-of-Town Quintets Complete Invitation Field," *New York Times*, March 6, 1948, 17, accessed June 15, 2013, http://search.proquest.com.

81. Strauss, "N.Y.U. and Three Out-of-Town."

82. A. C. Lonborg, "The 1948 Basketball Tournament," in *1948 NCAA Yearbook*, (city and date unknown), 53, NCAA Archives (author has copy); "The Bears from Baylor," in *Olympic Quarterfinals Game Program* (Madison Square Garden, March 27, 1948), 20, Naismith Hall of Fame.

83. "Marshall Is Out"; "Protest by Utah," *Kansas City Times*, March 10, 1948, 14.

84. "Protest by Utah"; "Rebuff to Utah," *Kansas City Times*, March 11, 1948, 16.

85. Louis Effrat, "St. Louis and Western Kentucky Win as Invitation Basketball Opens," *New York Times*, March 12, 1948, 30, accessed June 15, 2013, http://search.proquest.com.

86. Louis Effrat, "N.Y.U. Tops Texas by 46–43 at Garden on Basket by Kor," *New York Times*, March 14, 1948, S1, accessed June 15, 2013, http://search.proquest.com.

87. Louis Effrat, "N.Y.U. and St. Louis Fives Reach Final of National Invitation Play," *New York Times*, March 16, 1948, 37, accessed June 15, 2013, http://search.proquest.com; Louis Effrat, "St. Louis Conquers N.Y.U. in National

Invitation Basketball Final at Garden," *New York Times*, March 18, 1948, 38, accessed June 15, 2013, http://search.proquest.com.

88. "N.Y.U. Not Yet Out of Olympic Trials," *New York Times*, March 19, 1948, 30, accessed June 15, 2013, http://search.proquest.com.

89. Warren A. Kraetzer, "Eastern Playoff," in *1948 NCAA Yearbook*, (city and date unknown), 55–57, NCAA Archives (author has copy).

90. Kraetzer, "Eastern Playoff."

91. Edward J. Garich, "Western Playoff," in *1948 NCAA Yearbook*, (city and date unknown), 57–59, NCAA Archives (author has copy).

92. Rappoport, *The Classic*, 61; Warren A. Kraetzer, "East-West Championship Game," in *1948 NCAA Yearbook*, (city and date unknown), 54–55, NCAA Archives (author has copy); "Mighty Baylor Bears Facing Kentucky for Championship," *Abilene Reporter-News* (Abilene, TX), March 22, 1948, 3, accessed June 6, 2015, http://www.newspapers.com; Harold V. Ratliff, "If Baylor Cagers Win Rupp Can Take a Bow," *Corpus Christi Caller-Times* (Corpus Christi, TX), March 22, 1948, 4, accessed June 6, 2015, http://www.newspapers.com.

93. "Financial Report of 1948 Basketball Championships," in *1948 NCAA Yearbook*, (city and date unknown), 185–87, NCAA Archives (author has copy).

94. "Financial Report of 1948 Basketball Championships."

95. George R. Edwards, "Basketball," in *1948 NCAA Yearbook*, (city and date unknown), 51–53, NCAA Archives (author has copy).

96. "Sees Campus Site Again for Cage Sport," *Brooklyn Daily Eagle*, January 11, 1948, 25, accessed June 6, 2015, http://www.newspapers.com.

97. "Sees Campus Site Again for Cage Sport."

98. Edwards, "Basketball," 51–53.

99. Carlson, "Basketball's Forgotten Experiment," 1330–59.

100. Carlson, "Basketball's Forgotten Experiment," 1330–59; "Baylor Reaches Semi-Finals in U.S. Olympic Tryouts," *Pampa Daily News* (Pampa, TX), March 28, 1948, 7, accessed June 6, 2015, http://www.newspapers.com; "Baylor, Kentucky Clash Tonight in Cage Semi-Finals," *Brownsville Herald* (Brownsville, TX), March 29, 1948, 5, accessed June 6, 2015, http://www.newspapers.com; Rappoport, *The Classic*, 61.

101. "Oilers Win Olympic Trials," *Brooklyn Daily Eagle*, April 1, 1948, 17, accessed June 6, 2015, http://www.newspapers.com; Carlson, "Basketball's Forgotten Experiment," 1330–59.

102. Rappoport, *The Classic*, 61–62.

103. Rappoport, *The Classic*, 61–62.

104. Rappoport, *The Classic*, 61–62.

105. "Kentucky Quintet Gains Lead in Poll," *New York Times*, February 2, 1949, 39, accessed June 15, 2013, http://search.proquest.com.

106. "St. Louis U. Accepts Bid to Defend Title in National Tourney," *Chicago Tribune*, March 1, 1949, B3, accessed June 15, 2013, http://search.proquest.com; "Kentucky Accepts Two Tourney Bids," *New York Times*, March 2, 1949, 37, accessed June 15, 2013, http://search.proquest.com.

107. "Kentucky Accepts Two Tourney Bids."

108. "Bradley Five Accepts Bid," *New York Times*, March 3, 1949, 35, accessed June 15, 2013, http://search.proquest.com; "Will Invite Local Fives," *New*

York Times, March 5, 1949, 13, accessed June 15, 2013, http://search.proquest.com; Louis Effrat, "City College and San Francisco Accept National Invitation Basketball Bids," *New York Times*, March 8, 1949, 32, accessed June 15, 2013, http://search.proquest.com.

109. Louis Effrat, "N.Y.U., St. John's and Manhattan Accept Bids to Revised 12-Team Tourney," *New York Times*, March 10, 1949, 36, accessed June 15, 2013, http://search.proquest.com.

110. "Invitation Final March 19," *New York Times*, January 27, 1949, 27, accessed June 15, 2013, http://search.proquest.com; Joseph M. Sheehan, "Out-of-Town Fives Choices in Garden," *New York Times*, March 12, 1949, 14, accessed June 15, 2013, http://search.proquest.com.

111. Sheehan, "Out-of-Town Fives"; Michael Strauss, "Afternoon, Night Twin Bills Today on Invitation Court Tourney Slate," *New York Times*, March 14, 1949, 25, accessed June 15, 2013, http://search.proquest.com.

112. Louis Effrat, "Loyola, Bowling Green, San Francisco and Bradley Win," *New York Times*, March 15, 1949, 37, accessed June 15, 2013, http://search.proquest.com; Rappoport, *The Classic*, 66.

113. "Bradley, Loyola in Shape for Clash Tonight," *Chicago Tribune*, March 17, 1949, B1, accessed June 15, 2013, http://search.proquest.com; Louis Effrat, "San Francisco and Loyola Gain National Invitation Basketball Tourney Final," *New York Times*, March 18, 1949, 34, accessed June 15, 2013, http://search.proquest.com; Louis Effrat, "San Francisco Five Trips Loyola, 48–47," *New York Times*, March 20, 1949, S1, accessed June 15, 2013, http://search.proquest.com.

114. Michael Strauss, "Kentucky Favored over Villanova, Illinois Choice over Yale Tonight," *New York Times*, March 21, 1949, 29, accessed June 15, 2013, http://search.proquest.com.

115. A. C. Lonborg, "The 1949 Basketball Tournament," in *1949 NCAA Yearbook*, (city and date unknown), 57–59, NCAA Archives (author has copy).

116. Lonborg, "The 1949 Basketball Tournament"; "Financial Report of 1949 Basketball Championship," in *1949 NCAA Yearbook*, (city and date unknown), 215, NCAA Archives (author has copy).

117. "Illini Quintet Accepts N.C.A.A. Tournament Bid," *Chicago Tribune*, March 7, 1949, B1, accessed June 15, 2013, http://search.proquest.com; Lonborg, "1949 Basketball Tournament," 57–59; "Financial Report of 1949 Basketball," 215–18.

118. Tev Laudeman, "1949: Groza Foiled Iba's Strategy," in *NCAA March Madness: Cinderellas, Superstars, and Champions from the NCAA Final Four* (Chicago: Triumph Books, 2004), 22–23.

119. Laudeman, "1949: Groza Foiled Iba's Strategy."

120. Lonborg, "1949 Basketball Tournament," 57–59; "Financial Report of 1949 Basketball," 215–18.

121. Stooksbury, *National Title*, 162; "Roll Call of Members," in *1952 NCAA Yearbook*, (city and date unknown), 8–23, NCAA Archives (author has copy).

122. Stooksbury, *National Title*, 170–75. Stooksbury incorrectly identifies the Regis team as being from Massachusetts. However, Regis College in Massachusetts did not begin a men's athletic program until the early 1980s (http://www.goregispride.com/sports/Record_Books/RB.Page).

123. "Siena Liked in National Catholic Play," *Portland Press Herald* (Portland, ME), March 20, 1949, 34, accessed June 6, 2015, http://www.newspapers.com; Brenner, *College Basketball's National Championships*, 602–3, 1021.

124. "Top-Seeded Siena Ousted by Ravens in National Catholic Tourney," *Independent Record* (Helena, MT), March 21, 1949, 7, accessed June 6, 2015, http://www.newspapers.com; "Redmen Edged by Late Francis Rally, 57–51," *Winona Republican-Herald* (Winona, MN), March 22, 1949, 13, accessed June 6, 2015, http://www.newspapers.com; "Quarter Finals Set in National Catholic Tourney," *Daily Capital Journal* (Salem, OR), March 23, 1949, 15, accessed June 6, 2015, http://www.newspapers.com; "St. Thomas and Gonzaga Makes Semifinal Bids," *Daily Republic* (Mitchell, SD), March 24, 1949, 12, accessed June 6, 2015, http://www.newspapers.com; "National Catholic Tourney to Semis," *Council Bluffs Nonpareil* (Council Bluffs, IA), March 25, 1949, 23, accessed June 6, 2015, http://www.newspapers.com; "Lacy Sets New Scoring Record," *Daily Mail* (Hagerstown, MD), March 26, 1949, 12, accessed June 6, 2015, http://www.newspapers.com; "Regis College Rangers Win National Catholic Basketball Tourney," *Independent Record* (Helena, MT), March 27, 1949, 14, accessed June 6, 2015, http://www. newspapers.com.

125. Brenner, *College Basketball's National Championships*, 602–3; "Catholic Fives Compete," *Record-Argus* (Greenville, PA), March 28, 1950, 7, accessed June 6, 2015, http://www.newspapers.com; "Lange Paces Siena to 86–49 Rout of Providence in NCIT," *Troy Record* (Troy, NY), March 29, 1950, 20, accessed June 6, 2015, http://www.newspapers.com; "St. Francis Upsets Top-Seeded Creighton in NCIT, 67–66," *Troy Record* (Troy, NY), March 30, 1950, 30, accessed June 6, 2015, http://www.newspapers.com; George Yamin, "Siena Rips Loras, 75–55; Terriers Edge Iona, 62–61 In NCIT," *Troy Record* (Troy, NY), March 31, 1950, 42, accessed June 6, 2015, http://www.newspapers.com; George Yamin, "Siena, Victorious in NCIT, Has Eyes on New Laurels," *Troy Record* (Troy, NY), April 2, 1950, 18, accessed June 6, 2015, http://www.newspapers.com.

126. Hoover, "History of the National Association," 76–78; Stooksbury, *National Title*, 180–81.

127. "Saddened U.N. Players Unpack Suitcases, Tear Up Plane Tickets to Kansas City," *Nevada State Journal* (Reno, NV), March 12, 1950, 4, accessed June 6, 2015, http://www.newspapers.com; "NAIB's Action against Nevada Draws Fire from Californians," *Nevada State Journal* (Reno, NV), March 14, 1950, 11, accessed June 6, 2015, http://www.newspapers.com.

128. Stooksbury, *National Title*, 189–90; "16 Teams to End First Round Play in N.A.I.B. Tourney in K.C.," *Daily Standard* (Sikeston, MO), March 14, 1950, 8, accessed June 6, 2015, http://www.newspapers.com; "NAIB Fives Cut as First Round Marathon Ends," *Daily Capital News* (Jefferson City, MO), March 15, 1950, 3, accessed June 6, 2015, http://www.newspapers.com; Bob Nesbit, "Baldwin-Wallace Is State Foe Tonight in N.A.I.B.," *Terre Haute Tribune* (Terre Haute, IN), March 16, 1950, 20, accessed June 6, 2015, http://www. newspapers.com; Bob Nesbit, "State Battles Tampa in N.A.I.B. Semi-Finals Duel," *Terre Haute Tribune* (Terre Haute, IN), March 17, 1950, 24, accessed June 6, 2015, http://www.newspapers.com; Bob Nesbit, "Indiana State Seeks Initial N.A.I.B. Championship," *Terre Haute Tribune* (Terre Haute, IN), March 18,

1950, 7, accessed June 6, 2015, http://www.newspapers.com; "Gala Welcome for I.S. Squad," *Terre Haute Tribune* (Terre Haute, IN), March 19, 1950, 1, accessed June 6, 2015, http://www.newspapers.com.

129. "Bradley Tops Season's Last Poll with Ohio State Five in 2d Place," *New York Times*, March 8, 1950, 35, accessed June 15, 2013, http://search.proquest.com; "Kentucky in Invitation Tourney; N.C.A.A. Names N. Carolina State," *New York Times*, March 6, 1950, 30, accessed June 15, 2013, http://search.proquest.com.

130. "Kentucky in Invitation"; Oscar Fraley, "Rupp Digs the N.C.A.A.," *Kansas City Star*, March 14, 1950, 18.

131. "Bradley OK's Bid to Garden," *Chicago Tribune*, February 28, 1950, B3, accessed June 15, 2013, http://search.proquest.com; "Bradley Quintet Is Seeded No. 1 for National Invitation Tourney," *New York Times*, March 8, 1950, 35, accessed June 15, 2013, http://search.proquest.com.

132. "12 Fives Will Play in Invitation Here," *New York Times*, February 1, 1950, 34, accessed June 15, 2013, http://search.proquest.com.

133. "Bradley Defeats Kansas Five, 59–57," *New York Times*, March 21, 1950, 37, accessed June 15, 2013, http://search.proquest.com.

134. Michael Strauss, "City College March to Invitation Laurels Highlight of Basketball Campaign," *New York Times*, March 20, 1950, 26, accessed June 15, 2013, http://search.proquest.com.

135. William J. Briordy, "City College, Niagara and Arizona Accept Invitation Tourney Bids," *New York Times*, March 7, 1950, 31, accessed June 15, 2013, http://search.proquest.com; "Bradley Quintet Is Seeded No. 1"; "Bradley Tops Season's Last Poll."

136. "Bradley Quintet Is Seeded No. 1"; "Bradley Tops."

137. "Syracuse Tops Long Island in N.Y. Tourney," *Chicago Tribune*, March 12, 1950, A4, accessed June 15, 2013, http://search.proquest.com; Louis Effrat, "Redmen Set Back W. Kentucky, 69–60," *New York Times*, March 14, 1950, 29, accessed June 15, 2013, http://search.proquest.com; Louis Effrat, "C.C.N.Y. and Duquesne Fives Gain National Invitation Semi-Finals," *New York Times*, March 15, 1950, 36, accessed June 15, 2013, http://search.proquest.com; Louis Effrat, "City College and Bradley Quintets Gain Final Round of National Invitation," *New York Times*, March 17, 1950, 36, accessed June 15, 2013, http://search.proquest.com; Rappoport, *The Classic*, 77.

138. "Records of Tonight's Rivals This Season," in *1950 National Invitation Game Program* (Madison Square Garden, March 13, 1950), 12, Naismith Hall of Fame.

139. "Bradley's Braves Get Wish—Another Crack at Beavers," in *1950 NCAA East-West Finals Game Program* (Madison Square Garden, March 28, 1950), 4, Naismith Hall of Fame.

140. "Basketball Miracle," *New York Times*, March 18, 1950, 12, accessed June 15, 2013, http://search.proquest.com; John Rendel, "C.C.N.Y. Five, Meeting Bradley Tonight, Also Gets N.C.A.A. Bid," *New York Times*, March 18, 1950, 17, accessed June 15, 2013, http://search.proquest.com; for more on CCNY's improbable season and the subsequent fallout from the gambling scandal, see Cohen, *The Game They Played*.

141. Rendel, "C.C.N.Y."; Louis Effrat, "18,000 See C.C.N.Y. Top Bradley, 69–61, in Final at Garden," *New York Times*, March 19, 1950, S1, accessed June 15, 2013, http://search.proquest.com.

142. "Education Board Notes City College Victory," *New York Times*, March 21, 1950, 37, accessed June 15, 2013, http://search.proquest.com; Michael Strauss, "Triumphant Beaver Squad Hailed by Mayor at City Hall Ceremony," *New York Times*, March 21, 1950, 37, accessed June 15, 2013, http://search.proquest.com.

143. Louis Effrat, "Start with Cousy When Picking an All-America Team This Year," in *1950 NCAA Eastern Semi-finals Game Program* (Madison Square Garden, March 23, 1950), 3, Naismith Hall of Fame; Michael Strauss, "C.C.N.Y. Choice in Eastern Final against No. Carolina State Tonight," *New York Times*, March 25, 1950, 22, accessed June 15, 2013, http://search.proquest.com; "Bradley Tops Season's Last Poll"; David Eisenberg, "Getting Down to Cases, It's Everett at North Carolina State, Suh!" in *1950 NCAA Eastern Semi-finals Game Program* (Madison Square Garden, March 23, 1950), 14, Naismith Hall of Fame.

144. Strauss, "C.C.N.Y. Choice"; "Bradley Tops"; "Big 10 Approves 14 Game Basket Slate," *Chicago Tribune*, March 12, 1950, A2, accessed June 15, 2013, http://search.proquest.com.

145. Bob Busby, "Western Playoff," in *1950 NCAA Yearbook*, (city and date unknown), 62–64, NCAA Archives (author has copy).

146. Bob Busby, "Choice of K.U. Touches Off an Angry Blast by Gardner," *Kansas City Star*, March 12, 1950, B1.

147. "Pat on Decision," *Kansas City Star*, March 14, 1950, 18; "New Strategy Planned by Jack Gardner in Future Campaigns," *Kansas City Times*, March 15, 1950, 16.

148. "Bradley Defeats Kansas Five"; Kyle Neddenriep, "All-time Indiana All-Star Countdown: No. 4," *USA Today*, July 18, 2013, accessed June 7, 2015, http://www.usatoday.com.

149. "Bradley Defeats Kansas Five."

150. Busby, "Western Playoff," 62–64; John Wooden with Jack Tobin, *They Call Me Coach: John Wooden* (Chicago: Contemporary Books, 1988), 79.

151. Busby, "Western Playoff," 62–64.

152. George L. Shiebler, "Eastern Playoff," in *1950 NCAA Yearbook*, (city and date unknown), 60–62, NCAA Archives (author has copy).

153. Michael Strauss, "City College Now Favored for N.C.A.A. Title and Basketball Grand Slam," *New York Times*, March 27, 1950, 28, accessed June 15, 2013, http://search.proquest.com.

154. Louis Effrat, "Beavers Confident of Title Triumph," *New York Times*, March 28, 1950, 39, accessed June 15, 2013, http://search.proquest.com.

155. Effrat, "Beavers Confident of Title Triumph."

156. Rappoport, *The Classic*, 74.

157. Louis Effrat, "City College Conquers Bradley for First Sweep of National Basketball Titles," *New York Times*, March 29, 1950, 40, accessed June 15, 2013, http://search.proquest.com; Rappoport, *The Classic*, 74.

158. Irving Spiegel, "C.C.N.Y. Rallies, Parades Hail Basketball Feat," *New York Times*, March 30, 1950, 43, accessed June 15, 2013, http://search.proquest.com.

159. Spiegel, "C.C.N.Y. Rallies."

160. "Rosters," in *NCAA East-West Finals Game Program* (Madison Square Garden, March 28, 1950), 20, Naismith Hall of Fame.

161. Spiegel, "C.C.N.Y. Rallies."

162. "Beavers Honored by Borough Head," *New York Times*, April 7, 1950, 37, accessed June 15, 2013, http://search.proquest.com.

Chapter 8: The Scandal, Damage Control, and Alternate Options, 1950–1951

1. For more on Bee's career, see Gildea, *Hoop Crazy*.

2. For more on Holman, see Cohen, *The Game They Played*.

3. "Brennan Resigns Post as Coach of St. Francis Basketball Team," *New York Times*, March 9, 1948, 29, accessed November 23, 2013, http://search. proquest.com.

4. Irving T. Marsh, "Philly's Taking Title as East's Basket Hub," *New York Herald-Tribune*, January 20, 1964, 21.

5. For more on the Indiana-Kentucky High School All-Star game, see Randy Roberts, *"But They Can't Beat Us": Oscar Robertson and the Crispus Attucks Tigers* (New York: Sports Publishing Co., 1999).

6. A. C. Lonborg, "1950 Basketball Championship," in *1950 NCAA Yearbook*, (city and date unknown), 58, NCAA Archives (author has copy); "Financial Report of 1950 Basketball Championships," in *1950 NCAA Yearbook*, (city and date unknown), 243–45, NCAA Archives (author has copy).

7. Proceedings of the Executive Committee Meeting of the National Association of Basketball Coaches of the United States (March 26, 1950, New York), 136, Naismith Hall of Fame.

8. "28 College Fives in Two Tourneys," *New York Times*, January 28, 1951, S3, accessed June 29, 2013, http://search.proquest.com; Rappoport, *The Classic*, 57; "Roll of Members," *1952–53 NCAA Yearbook*, 8–23.

9. "Revised and Approved N.C.A.A. Basketball Tournament Plan for 1951," in *1950 NCAA Yearbook*, (city and date unknown), 101–4, NCAA Archives (author has copy).

10. "28 College Fives"; "N.C.A.A. Quintets Open Play Tonight," *New York Times*, March 21, 1952, 28, accessed May 11, 2013, http://search.proquest.com.

11. "28 College Fives."

12. "28 College Fives."

13. Zander Hollander, Madison Square Garden: A Century of Sport and Spectacle on the World's Most Versatile Stage (New York: Hawthorn Books, 1973), 1–73.

14. For more information on Williams Gymnasium, originally named Minnesota Field House, see *The Minnesota Alumni Weekly* (ed. Leland F. Leland), 27, no. 17 (February 11, 1928).

15. "28 College Fives"; Peter Brandwein, "Pairings Revised in N.C.A.A. Tourney," *New York Times*, February 6, 1951, 44, accessed June 29, 2013, http://search.proquest.com.

16. "Chicago Plans Tourney to Compete with Garden," *New York Times*, February 11, 1951, 147, accessed June 29, 2013, http://search.proquest.com.

17. Howard Sigmund, "Garden Officials Unimpressed by Proposed Chicago Tourney," *Peoria Journal-Star*, February 14, 1951, page unknown (author has copy).

18. Sigmund, "Garden Officials Unimpressed."

19. Sigmund, "Garden Officials Unimpressed."

20. Bob Russell, "9 Favor Stadium Meet," *Chicago Daily News*, February 21, 1951, page unknown (author has copy).

21. Ed Sainsbury, "Bradley Probable Chicago Entrant," *Peoria Journal-Star*, February 21, 1951, page unknown (author has copy).

22. "St. Michael Is First Foe of LeMoyne," *Syracuse Herald-Journal*, March 10, 1951, 9, accessed June 21, 2015, http://www.newspaperarchive.com.

23. "36 Fives in Running for Invitation Posts," *New York Times*, February 16, 1951, 37, accessed June 29, 2013, http://search.proquest.com; Alexander Feinberg, "3 City College Aces and Gambler Held in Basketball 'Fix,'" *New York Times*, February 19, 1951, 1, accessed June 29, 2013, http://search.proquest.com.

24. Feinberg, "3 City College Aces."

25. "Scandal Forces Long Island from Sports," *Chicago Tribune*, February 21, 1951, B1, accessed June 29, 2013, http://search.proquest.com; Alexander Feinberg, "City College Bans Games as 4th Star Confesses 3 'Fixes,'" *New York Times*, February 28, 1951, 1, accessed June 29, 2013, http://search.proquest.com.

26. "Scandal Forces Long Island"; Feinberg, "City College Bans Games."

27. "Most Colleges Willing to Keep Garden Games," *Chicago Tribune*, February 21, 1951, B1, accessed June 29, 2013, http://search.proquest.com.

28. "Abandon Plans for Chicago Meet," *Peoria Journal-Star*, February 24, 1951, page unknown (author has copy).

29. "Abandon Plans for Chicago Meet."

30. "Bradley Accepts Hawaiian Offer," *Peoria Journal-Star*, February 23, 1951, page unknown (author has copy).

31. "Abandon Plans for Chicago Meet."

32. Wilfrid Smith, "NCAA Asks More Control of Stadiums," *Chicago Tribune*, March 3, 1951, B1, accessed June 29, 2013, http://search.proquest.com.

33. Smith, "NCAA Asks."

34. This speculation is described at length in Rosen, *Scandals of '51*.

35. Smith, "NCAA Asks."

36. Cohen, The Game They Played.

37. "Most Colleges Willing"; "10 Quintets 'Interested' in Bradley Campus Meet," *New York Times*, February 27, 1951, 41, accessed June 29, 2013, http://search.proquest.com; "Eight-Team Meet Starts March 24," *Peoria Journal-Star*, February 25, 1951, page unknown (author has copy).

38. "10 Quintets 'Interested'"; "Eight-Team Meet Starts."

39. Louis Effrat, "St. John's among Four Quintets in National Invitation Tournament," *New York Times*, February 24, 1951, 22, accessed June 29, 2013, http://search.proquest.com.

40. "Fordham Quintet Plays St. John's; Columbia Battles Brown Tonight," *New York Times*, February 28, 1951, 36, accessed June 29, 2013, http://search.proquest.com.

41. "Seton Hall Joins Invitation Play," *New York Times*, March 2, 1951, 29, accessed June 29, 2013, http://search.proquest.com.

42. "N.C. State Checks Duke," *New York Times*, March 4, 1951, 149, accessed June 29, 2013, http://search.proquest.com; "Columbia Quintet in N.C.A.A. Tourney," *New York Times*, March 5, 1951, 25, accessed June 29, 2013, http://search.proquest.com.

43. William Briordy, "Bonaventure Five in Invitation Play," *New York Times*, March 6, 1951, 33, accessed June 29, 2013, http://search.proquest.com; "Garden Pairings Set for Saturday as Cincinnati Quintet Accepts Bid," *New York Times*, March 7, 1951, 47, accessed June 29, 2013, http://search.proquest.com.

44. "Garden Pairings Set for Saturday."

45. "St. John's Quintet in N.C.A.A. Tourney," *New York Times*, March 9, 1951, 34, accessed June 29, 2013, http://search.proquest.com.

46. "St. John's Quintet in N.C.A.A. Tourney."

47. Louis Effrat, "St. Louis Defeats La Salle by 73–61 on Garden Court," *New York Times*, March 11, 1951, 151, accessed June 29, 2013, http://search.proquest.com; "Coach Would Keep Tourneys in Garden," *New York Times*, March 12, 1951, 40, accessed June 29, 2013, http://search.proquest.com.

48. "St. John's to Face Bonaventure Five," *New York Times*, March 12, 1951, 40, accessed June 29, 2013, http://search.proquest.com.

49. Michael Strauss, "Villanova, Louisville, Connecticut Win N.C.A.A. Tournament Berths," *New York Times*, March 13, 1951, 42, accessed June 29, 2013, http://search.proquest.com; Louis Effrat, "St. John's and Brigham Young Advance to Semi-Finals in Invitation Tourney," *New York Times*, March 13, 1951, 42, accessed June 29, 2013, http://search.proquest.com.

50. Louis Effrat, "Seton Hall and Dayton Reach Semi-Finals in Invitation Tourney at Garden," *New York Times*, March 14, 1951, 53, accessed June 29, 2013, http://search.proquest.com; Louis Effrat, "Brigham Young, Dayton Fives Gain Garden Final," *New York Times*, March 16, 1951, 43, accessed June 29, 2013, http://search.proquest.com.

51. Louis Effrat, "Dayton Five Bows to Brigham Young at Garden, 62–43," *New York Times*, March 18, 1951, S1, accessed June 29, 2013, http://search.proquest.com.

52. "St. Francis Wins," *Post-Standard* (Syracuse, NY), March 18, 1951, 37, accessed June 21, 2015, http://www.newspaperarchives.com; "There Was a Wide Gap between Strong and Weak N.A.I.B. Teams," *Kansas City Star*, March 19, 1951, 16.

53. George L. Shiebler, "Eastern Playoffs," in *1951 NCAA Yearbook*, (city and date unknown), 55–59, NCAA Archives (author has copy).

54. "Article IV: Eligibility" (NCAA Bylaws, revised on January 11–12, 1952), in *1951 NCAA Yearbook*, (city and date unknown), 266–67, NCAA Archives (author has copy).

55. Peter Brandwein, "N.C.A.A. Play Opens at Garden Tonight," *New York Times*, March 20, 1951, 49, accessed June 29, 2013, http://search.proquest.com; Shiebler, "Eastern Playoffs," 55–59.

56. Shiebler, "Eastern Playoffs," 55–59.

57. "Kansas State Tops Cougar Team, 64–54," *New York Times*, March 24, 1951, 23, accessed June 29, 2013, http://search.proquest.com; Bob Busby,

"Western Playoffs," in *1951 NCAA Yearbook*, (city and date unknown), 59–63, NCAA Archives (author has copy).

58. Busby, "Western Playoffs," 59–63.

59. George Shiebler, "East-West Championship," in *1951 NCAA Yearbook*, (city and date unknown), 54–55, NCAA Archives (author has copy).

60. "Financial Report of 1951 Basketball Championship," in *1951 NCAA Yearbook*, (city and date unknown), 244–48, NCAA Archives (author has copy).

61. Jack Rosenberg, "3 Refs Noble Experiment?" *Peoria Journal-Star*, March 28, 1951, page unknown (author has copy); Jack Rosenberg, "Parties for NCBT Guests," *Peoria Journal-Star*, March 30, 1951, page unknown (author has copy); "NCBT Sidelights," *Peoria Journal-Star*, March 31, 1951, 4; Brenner, *College Basketball's National Championships*, 601.

62. Alfred E. Clark, "8 Bradley Players Involved in Fixing Basketball Games," *New York Times*, July 25, 1951, 1, accessed June 29, 2013, http://search.proquest.com.

63. Clark, "8 Bradley Players Involved."

64. "Bradley Accepts Hawaiian Offer."

65. LeRoy Chase, "St. John's Snaps Bradley Winning Streak, 68 to 59," *Peoria Journal-Star*, January 12, 1951, B2; Kenneth Jones, "Pot Shots," *Peoria Journal-Star*, January 12, 1951, B2.

66. "Drop Basketball at Lawrence Tech," *New York Times*, August 21, 1951, 43, accessed June 29, 2013, http://search.proquest.com; Rosen, *Scandals of '51*, 195.

67. Rosen, *Scandals of '51*, 157.

68. "3 Basketball Aces on Kentucky Team Admit '49 Fix Here," *New York Times*, October 21, 1951, 1, accessed June 29, 2013, http://search.proquest.com.

69. Rosen, *Scandals of '51*, 183–84, 188–89.

70. Rosen, *Scandals of '51*, 183–84, 188–89; "3 Basketball Aces."

71. Rosen, *Scandals of '51*, 201–4. For more on Spivey's success in the American Basketball League, see Murray Nelson, *Abe Saperstein and the American Basketball League, 1960–63: The Upstarts Who Shot for Three and Lost to the NBA* (Jefferson, NC: McFarland & Co., 2013).

72. Rosen, *Scandals of '51*, 206–7.

Epilogue: New Beginnings, with Leverage, 1952–2005

1. For specific dates of the disclosures, see Rosen, *Scandals of '51*.

2. Rosen, Scandals of '51.

3. "Memorandum for Executive Committee," (date unknown—author has copy), Kirwan SEC file, Hamilton, Horlacher, Jones, and Kirwan Faculty files, 1861–1964, University of Kentucky Special Collections, Lexington, Ky. Rosen, *Scandals of '51*, 166–67.

4. Rosen, *Scandals of '51*, 155–56.

5. Louie Lazar, "For Gene Melchiorre, a Regretful Turn Brought a Unique NBA Distinction," *New York Times*, June 26, 2014, accessed May 11, 2015, http://www.nytimes.com.

6. "NCBT Sidelights." In 1954, Bradley made it to the championship game of the NCAA tournament.

7. "LeMoyne Defeats Providence Quint in N.C.I.T., 67–63," *Syracuse Herald-American* (Syracuse, NY), March 16, 1952, D1, accessed June 21, 2015, http://www.newspaperarchive.com; "Dolphins Play St. Francis Tomorrow in 2d Round of Catholic Tournament," *Post-Standard* (Syracuse, NY), March 17, 1952, 12, accessed June 21, 2015, http://www.newspaperarchive.com; "Terriers Down LeMoyne in Tourney Game, 75–61," *Post-Standard* (Syracuse, NY), March 19, 1952, 31, accessed June 21, 2015, http://www.newspaperarchive.com; "Marquette Five Plays St. Francis for NCIT Title," *Post-Standard* (Syracuse, NY), March 22, 1952, 11, accessed June 21, 2015, http://www.newspaperarchive.com; "Marquette Wins Catholic Tourney at Troy," *Post-Standard* (Syracuse, NY), March 23, 1952, 31, accessed June 21, 2015, http://www.newspaperarchive.com.

8. Brenner, College Basketball's National Championships, 1019, 1021.

9. "NAIB Tournament Opens Today, Winner Shoots for Olympics," *Neosho Daily Democrat* (Neosho, MO), March 10, 1952, 3, accessed June 21, 2015, http://www.newspaperarchive.com; "Springfield Bears Cop NAIB Title," *Sunday News and Tribune* (Jefferson City, MO), March 16, 1952, 7, accessed June 21, 2015, http://www.newspaperarchive.com.

10. Hoover, "History of the National Association," 89–91.

11. Hoover, "History of the National Association," 89–91.

12. Katz, *Breaking Through*, 11–12.

13. Katz, *Breaking Through*, 25–74.

14. Katz, *Breaking Through*, 75–110. For more on McLendon's pioneering efforts with the Cleveland Pipers, see Nelson, *Abe Saperstein*.

15. Hoover, "History of the National Association," 140; Bill Pennington, "N.A.I.A.'s Future Looms Large for Division III," *New York Times*, February 13, 2007, accessed May 11, 2013, http://www.nytimes.com.

16. "N.Y.U. Five Accepts Bid to Tournament," *New York Times*, February 29, 1952, 29, accessed May 11, 2013, http://search.proquest.com; "Tourney Quintets Paired," *New York Times*, March 1, 1952, 11, accessed May 11, 2013, http://search.proquest.com.

17. Bruce Drake, "Basketball," in *1952–53 NCAA Yearbook*, (city and date unknown), 60–62, NCAA Archives (author has copy); Bob Busby, "Eastern Regional No. 1," in *1952–53 NCAA Yearbook*, (city and date unknown), 68–70, NCAA Archives (author has copy); Rappoport, *The Classic*, 84.

18. Bob Busby, "Eastern Regional No. 2," in *1952–53 NCAA Yearbook*, (city and date unknown), 70–72, NCAA Archives (author has copy).

19. Bob Busby, "Western Regional No. 2," in *1952–53 NCAA Yearbook*, (city and date unknown), 66–68, NCAA Archives (author has copy).

20. Bob Busby, "Western Regional No. 1," in *1952–53 NCAA Yearbook*, (city and date unknown), 64–66, NCAA Archives (author has copy); Rappoport, *The Classic*, 82.

21. Rappoport, *The Classic*, 59.

22. Bob Busby, "East-West Championships," in *1952–53 NCAA Yearbook*, (city and date unknown), 62–64, NCAA Archives (author has copy); Cunningham, *American Hoops*, 61–88.

23. Isaacs, *All the Moves*, 84. For more on Coach Honey Russell, see John Russell, *Honey Russell: Between Games, Between Halves* (Washington, DC: Dryad Press, 1986).

24. Isaacs, *All the Moves*, 177; Michael Strauss, "Basketball Upsets Stir Interest in Another Triple-Header Tonight," *New York Times*, March 10, 1952, 28, accessed May 11, 2013, http://search.proquest.com.

25. Carlson, "Tale of Two Tournaments," 273–75.

26. Figone, *Cheating the Spread*, 87–109. For more on the 1961 scandal and Molinas's involvement, see Charley Rosen, *The Wizard of Odds: How Jack Molinas Almost Destroyed the Game of Basketball* (New York: Seven Stories Press, 2003).

27. "NCAA University Basketball Tournament Committee," in *Minutes of the NCAA University Basketball Tournament Committee* (Colorado Springs, CO, July 9–11, 1961), 4, NCAA archives.

28. Carlson, "Tale of Two Tournaments," 273–75.

29. Carlson, "Tale of Two Tournaments," 273–75.

30. Carlson, "Tale of Two Tournaments," 273–75. For more information on Al McGuire's career, see Moran, *You Can Call Me Al*.

31. Leonard Koppett, "Marquette Beats St. John's, 65–53, in N. I. T. Final; U. C. L. A. Tops Jacksonville, 80–69, for N. C. A. A. Title," *New York Times*, March 22, 1970, 193, accessed May 11, 2013, http://search.proquest.com.

32. Carlson, "Tale of Two Tournaments," 273–75.

33. "NCAA Division I Men's Basketball Championship Tournament Facts," NCAA-NABC Affiliation at the Start of the Basketball Tournament File, NCAA Archives.

34. Falla, *NCAA*, 189.

35. Brenner, College Basketball's National Championships, 1011–12, 1024.

36. Brenner, *College Basketball's National Championships*, 1012; Ron Maly, "Bob Ortegel is good for basketball and the game has been good to him," *WHO-TV online*, June 16, 2006, accessed July 1, 2016, http://web.archive.org/web/20070927223855/http://www.whotv.com/.

37. Falla, *NCAA*, 189–90.

38. Falla, *NCAA*, 189–90; "National Collegiate Basketball Championship Founded in 1939 by Hall-of-Famer Olsen," NCAA-NABC Affiliation at the Start of the Basketball Tournament Folder, NCAA Archives.

39. "NCAA Division I Men's Basketball."

40. "NIT Postseason History," NCAA, http://www.ncaa.com/news/basketball-men/article/2010-12-23/nit-postseason-history; "Peter A. Carlesimo," NCAA, http://i.turner.ncaa.com/dr/ncaa/ncaa/release/sites/default/files/files/nit-carlesimo.pdf.

41. "NCAA Division I Men's Basketball."

42. "NCAA Division I Men's Basketball."

43. "NCAA Division I Men's Basketball."

44. Sam Goldaper, "North Carolina State Snubs N. I. T.," *New York Times*, March 10, 1975, 35, accessed May 11, 2013, http://search.proquest.com.

45. "NCAA Division I Men's Basketball"; Seth Davis, *When March Went Mad:*

The Game That Transformed Basketball (New York: Henry Holt and Company, 2009).

46. "NCAA Division I Men's Basketball."

47. "NCAA Division I Men's Basketball."

48. Curtis Eichelberger, "March Madness Swells as NCAA Pumps Up NIT Tournament," *Bloomberg News*, March 14, 2006, accessed May 11, 2013, http://www.bloomberg.com.

49. "NCAA Division I Men's Basketball."

50. "NCAA Division I Men's Basketball."

51. Mark Alesia, "NIT Suggests Smaller NCAA Tourney Field: Opening Statements Start Federal Trial," *Indianapolis Star*, August 3, 2005, August 2005 Folder, NCAA Clip File, NCAA Archives.

52. Alesia, "NIT Suggests Smaller NCAA."

53. Mark Alesia, "NIT's Witness List Includes Knight," *Indianapolis Star*, August 2, 2005, August 2005 Folder, NCAA Clip File, NCAA Archives.

54. Malcolm Moran, "NCAA Buys NIT for $56.5 Million; Event Will Continue," *USA Today*, August 18, 2005, August 2005 Folder, NCAA Clip File, NCAA Archives.

Bibliography

Books

American National Red Cross. *The Greatest Freewill Offering in History*. Washington, DC: American National Red Cross, ca. 1947.

Angell, Emmett Dunn. "The Western Intercollegiate Basket Ball Season." In *Spalding's Official Basket Ball Guide for 1905–6*, edited by George T. Hepbron, 43–45. New York: American Sports Publishing Co., 1905.

Augustyn, Frederick, Jr. "Meanwell, Walter Earnest 'Doc' 'Little Doctor' 'Napoleon of Basketball' 'Little Giant' 'the Wizard.'" In *Basketball: A Biographical Dictionary*, edited by David L. Porter, 320–21. Westport, CT: Greenwood Press, 2005.

Axthelm, Pete. *The City Game: Basketball in New York City from the World Champion Knicks to the World of the Playgrounds*. New York: Harper's Magazine Press, 1970.

Baker, William J. *Sports in the Western World*. Urbana: University of Illinois Press, 1988.

Bingham, J. Lyman. "Olympic Basketball Tryouts." In *National Basketball Committee of the United States and Canada Official Basketball Guide, 1936–37*, edited by Oswald Tower, 73–77. New York: American Sports Publishing Co., 1936.

Bjarkman, Peter C. *Big Ten Basketball*. Indianapolis: Masters Press, 1995.

Bjarkman, Peter C. *Hoopla: A Century of College Basketball*. Indianapolis: Masters Press, 1996.

Bloomfield, Gary L. *Duty, Honor, Victory: America's Athletes in World War II*. Guilford, CT: Lyons Press, 2003.

Brenner, Morgan G. *College Basketball's National Championships: The Complete Record of Every Tournament Ever Played*. American History Series No. 13. Lanham, MD: Scarecrow Press, 1999.

Bunn, John W. "Western Play-off, N.C.A.A. Tournament." In *Spalding's Official Basketball Guide, 1939–40*, edited by Oswald Tower, 11–12. New York: American Sports Publishing Co., 1939).

Cardozier, V. R. *Colleges and Universities in World War II* (Westport, CT: Praeger, 1993).

Carlson, Kenneth N. *College Basketball Scorebook*. Lynnwood, WA: Rain Belt Publications, 1990.

Caudle, Edwin C. *Collegiate Basketball: Facts and Figures on the Cage Sport*. Winston-Salem, NC: John F. Blair, Publisher, 1959.

Coffey, Jack. "National Invitation College Tournament." In *The Official 1942–1943 Basketball Guide,* edited by Oswald Tower, 80–82. New York: A. S. Barnes Publishing Company, 1942.

Cohen, Stanley. *The Game They Played: The story of the only team ever to win the NIT and NCAA tournaments in the same year: The players, the happy hysteria, the scandal.* New York: Carroll & Graf, 1977.

Colbeck, A. Leslie, R. William Jones, Robert Busnel, Witold Szeremeta, and Luis A. Martin, eds. *The Basketball World.* Munich: International Amateur Basketball Federation, 1972.

Cox, Mark. "N.C.A.A. National Championship Tournament." In *The Official 1942–1943 Basketball Guide*, edited by Oswald Tower, 30–32. New York: A. S. Barnes Publishing Company, 1942.

Cox, Mark. "Western N.C.A.A. Tournament Review." In *The Official National Basketball Committee Basketball Guide, 1941–42,* edited by Oswald Tower, 47–51. New York: American Sports Publishing Co., 1941.

Cox, Mark. "N.C.A.A. Western Tournament." In *The Official 1942–43 Basketball Guide,* edited by Oswald Tower, 35–38. New York: A. S. Barnes Publishing Company, 1942.

Crowley, Joseph N. *In the Arena: The NCAA's First Century.* Indianapolis: NCAA, 2006.

Cunningham, Carson. *American Hoops: U.S. Men's Olympic Basketball from Berlin to Beijing.* Lincoln: University of Nebraska Press, 2009.

Davis, Seth. *When March Went Mad: The Game That Transformed Basketball.* New York: Henry Holt and Company, 2009.

Davis, Seth. *Wooden: A Coach's Life.* New York: Henry Holt and Company, 2015.

Deegan, Thomas J. "The Golden Jubilee of Basketball." In *The Official National Basketball Committee Basketball Guide, 1941–42,* edited by Oswald Tower, 3. New York: American Sports Publishing Co., 1941.

Dierenfield, Bruce J. "Carlson, Henry Clifford." In *Basketball: A Biographical Dictionary*, edited by David L. Porter, 69. Westport, CT: Greenwood Press, 2005.

Dooley, Eddie. "Wyoming Cops Benefit Dream Game." In *The Official 1943–44 Basketball Guide,* edited by Oswald Tower, 41–42. New York: A. S. Barnes and Company Publishers, 1943.

Douchant, Mike. *Encyclopedia of College Basketball.* Detroit: Visible Ink Press, 1995.

Dulles, F. R. *The American Red Cross: A History.* Westport, CT: Greenwood Press, 1950.

Durso, Joe. "The Four Gardens and How They Grew." In *Madison Square Garden: A Century of Sport and Spectacle on the World's Most Versatile Stage*, edited by Zander Hollander, 31. New York: Hawthorn Books, 1973.

Durso, Joseph. *Madison Square Garden: 100 Years of History.* New York: Simon & Schuster, 1979.

Dyreson, Mark. *Making the American Team*. Champaign: University of Illinois Press, 1998.

Escamilla, Pedro. *The Olympic Basketball History*. Barcelona: Foundation Pedro Ferrandiz, 1992.

Evers, John L. "Davies, Robert Edris 'Bob.'" In *Basketball: A Biographical Dictionary*, edited by David L. Porter, 106–7. Westport, CT: Greenwood Press, 2005.

Evers, John L. "Schommer, John Joseph." In *Basketball: A Biographical Dictionary*, edited by David L. Porter, 426–27. Westport, CT: Greenwood Press, 2005.

Falla, Jack. *NCAA: The Voice of College Sports: A Diamond Anniversary History, 1906–1981*. Mission, KS: NCAA, 1981.

Figone, Albert J. *Cheating the Spread: Gamblers, Point Shavers, and Game Fixers in College Football and Basketball*. Urbana: University of Illinois Press, 2012.

Fisher, Harry A. "Intercollegiate Basket Ball." In *Spalding's Official Basket Ball Guide for 1905–6*, edited by George T. Hepbron, 11–19. New York: American Sports Publishing Co., 1905.

Fisher, Harry A. "The National Championship." In *Spalding's Official Collegiate Basket Ball Guide for 1910–11*, edited by H. A. Fisher, 7. New York: American Sports Publishing Co., 1910.

Fitzpatrick, Frank. *And the Walls Came Tumbling Down: The Basketball Game That Changed American Sports*. New York: Simon & Schuster, 1999.

Forbes, Robert Pierce. *The Missouri Compromise and Its Aftermath: Slavery and the Meaning of America*. Chapel Hill: University of North Carolina Press, 2007.

Frei, Terry. *March 1939: Before the Madness: The Story of the First NCAA Basketball Tournament Champions*. Lanham, MD: Taylor Trade Publishing, 2014.

Garich, Edward J. "Western Playoff." In *The Official National Basketball Committee Basketball Guide, 1947–48*, edited by Oswald Tower, 43–47. New York: A. S. Barnes Company, 1947.

Gildea, Dennis. *Hoop Crazy: The Lives of Clair Bee and Chip Hilton*. Fayetteville: University of Arkansas Press, 2013.

Goodwin, Doris Kearns. *Team of Rivals: The Political Genius of Abraham Lincoln*. New York: Simon & Schuster, 2005.

Gould, Todd. *Pioneers of the Hardwood: Indiana and the Birth of Professional Basketball*. Bloomington: Indiana University Press, 1998.

Graham, Tom, and Rachel Graham Cody. *Getting Open: The Unknown Story of Bill Garrett and the Integration of College Basketball*. New York: Atria Books, 2008.

Grundman, Adolph H. *The Golden Age of Amateur Basketball: The AAU Tournament, 1921–1968*. Lincoln: University of Nebraska Press, 2004.

Guttmann, Allen. *Games and Empires: Modern Sports and Cultural Imperialism.* New York: Columbia University Press, 1994.

Hepbron, G. T. "Review of the Season." In *Spalding's Official Basket Ball Guide, 1908–9,* edited by G. T. Hepbron, 3–7. New York: American Sports Publishing Co., 1908.

Herge, Henry. *Navy V–12.* Paducah, KY: Turner Publishing Company, 1996.

Hinkle, Paul. "Eastern Play-off, N.C.A.A. Tournament." In *Spalding's Official Basketball Guide, 1940–41,* edited by Oswald Tower, 21–22. New York: American Sports Publishing Co., 1941.

Hollander, Zander, ed. *Madison Square Garden: A Century of Sport and Spectacle on the World's Most Versatile Stage.* New York: Hawthorn Books, 1973.

Irish, Ned. "Basketball in Madison Square Garden." In *The 1938–39 Official Spalding Basketball Guide,* edited by Oswald Tower, 36–37. New York: American Sports Publishing Co., 1938.

Irish, Ned. "Basketball in Madison Square Garden." In *Spalding's Official Basketball Guide, 1940–41,* edited by Oswald Tower, 55–57. New York: American Sports Publishing Co., 1941.

Irish, Ned, and Orlo Robertson. "Busy Wartime Court Season Looms." In *The Official 1943–44 Basketball Guide,* edited by Oswald Tower, 14–16. New York: A. S. Barnes and Company Publishers, 1943.

Isaacs, Neil D. *All the Moves: A History of College Basketball,* revised and updated version. New York: Harper Colophon Books, 1984.

Katz, Milton S. *Breaking Through: John B. McLendon, Basketball Legend and Civil Rights Pioneer.* Fayetteville: University of Arkansas Press, 2007.

Kerkhoff, Blair. *Phog Allen: The Father of Basketball Coaching.* Indianapolis: Masters Press, 1996.

Kruger, Arnd. "United States of America: The Crucial Battle." In *The Nazi Olympics: Sport, Politics, and Appeasement in the 1930s,* edited by Arnd Kruger and William Murray, 44–69. Champaign: University of Illinois Press, 2003.

Ladd, Tony, and James Mathisen. *Muscular Christianity: Evangelical Protestants and the Development of American Sport.* Grand Rapids, MI: Baker Books, 1999.

Large, David Clay. *Nazi Games: The Olympics of 1936.* New York: W. W. Norton & Company, 2007.

Laudeman, Tev. "1949: Groza Foiled Iba's Strategy." In *NCAA March Madness: Cinderellas, Superstars, and Champions from the NCAA Final Four,* 22–23. Chicago: Triumph Books, 2004.

Lester, Robin. *Stagg's University: The Rise, Decline, and Fall of Big-Time Football at Chicago.* Champaign: University of Illinois Press, 1999.

Lonborg, Arthur C. "Championship Game." In *Spalding's Official Basketball Guide, 1939–40,* edited by Oswald Tower, 13. New York: American Sports Publishing Co., 1939.

Luebker, Earl. "1939: The Tall Firs." In *NCAA March Madness: Cinderellas, Superstars, and Champions from the NCAA Final Four*, 2–3. Chicago: Triumph Books, 2004.

Mandell, Richard D. *The Nazi Olympics*. New York: Ballantine Books, 1971.

Martin, Charles. *Benching Jim Crow: The Rise and Fall of the Color Line in Southern College Sports, 1890–1980*. Champaign: University of Illinois Press, 2010.

McCormick, Henry J. "Eastern N.C.A.A. Tournament Review." In *The Official National Basketball Committee Basketball Guide, 1941–42*, edited by Oswald Tower, 51–54. New York: American Sports Publishing Co., 1941.

McGuff, Joe. "1940: Hail Those Hurryin' Hoosiers." In *NCAA March Madness: Cinderellas, Superstars, and Champions from the NCAA Final Four*, 4–5. Chicago: Triumph Books, 2004.

McQueeny, James. "National Intercollegiate Championship Tournament." In *The Official 1942–1943 Basketball Guide,* edited by Oswald Tower, 79–80. New York: A. S. Barnes Publishing Company, 1942.

Moran, Joseph Declan. *You Can Call Me Al: The Colorful Journey of Basketball's Original Flower Child, Al McGuire*. Madison, WI: Prairie Oak Press, 1999.

Morgan, Ralph. "Review of 1920 Basket Ball Season in the Eastern Colleges." In *Spalding's Official Basketball Guide, 1920–1921*, edited by Oswald Tower, 7–11. New York: American Sports Publishing Co., 1920.

Naismith, James. *Basketball: Its Origin and Development*. New York: Associated Press, 1941.

Nelson, Murray. *Abe Saperstein and the American Basketball League, 1960–63: The Upstarts Who Shot for Three and Lost to the NBA*. Jefferson, NC: McFarland & Co., 2013.

O'Boynick, Paul. "Western Playoff." In *The Official 1943–44 Basketball Guide,* edited by Oswald Tower, 47–49. New York: A. S. Barnes and Company, 1943.

O'Boynick, Paul. "Western Playoff." In *The Official National Basketball Committee Basketball Guide, 1945–46*, edited by Oswald Tower, 28–30. New York: A. S. Barnes Company, 1945.

Olsen, H. G. "General Plans for the Tournament." In *Spalding's Official Basketball Guide, 1939–40*, edited by Oswald Tower, 9–10. New York: American Sports Publishing Co., 1939.

Olsen, H. G. "N.C.A.A. 1942 Tournament Administration." In *The Official 1942–43 Basketball Guide,* edited by Oswald Tower, 29–30. New York: A. S. Barnes Publishing Company, 1942.

Olsen, H. G. "Second National Collegiate A.A. Basketball Tournament." In *Spalding's Official Basketball Guide, 1940–41*, edited by Oswald Tower, 16. New York: American Sports Publishing Co., 1940.

Olsen, H. G. "The 1941 National Collegiate A.A. Basketball Championship Review." In *The Official National Basketball Committee Basketball*

Guide, 1941–42, edited by Oswald Tower, 43. New York: American Sports Publishing Co., 1941.

Owens, W. B. "The National Collegiate A.A. Basketball Tournament." In *Spalding's Official Basketball Guide, 1939–40*, edited by Oswald Tower, 8. New York: American Sports Publishing Co., 1939.

Padwe, Sandy. *Basketball Hall of Fame*. Englewood Cliffs, NJ: Prentice-Hall, 1970.

Partner, Dan. "Indiana Wins Feature Event of College Arena—The N.C.A.A. Annual Tournament." In *Spalding's Official Basketball Guide, 1940–41*, edited by Oswald Tower, 19–21. New York: American Sports Publishing Co., 1940.

Partner, Dan. "Western Play-off, N.C.A.A. Tournament." In *Spalding's Official Basketball Guide, 1940–41*, edited by Oswald Tower, 16–18. New York: American Sports Publishing Co., 1940.

Partner, Dan. "Western Playoff." In *The Official National Basketball Committee Basketball Guide, 1946–47*, edited by Oswald Tower, 43–46. New York: A. S. Barnes Company Publishing, 1946.

Peterson, Vadal. "Skyline Basketball." In *The Official National Basketball Committee Basketball Guide, 1944–45*, edited by Oswald Tower, 16–17. New York: A. S. Barnes Company Publishers, 1944.

Porter, David L. "Liston, Emil Sycamore." In *Basketball: A Biographical Dictionary*, edited by David L. Porter, 282–83. Westport, CT: Greenwood Press, 2005.

Porter, David L. "Wilke, Louis G. 'Lou.'" In *Basketball: A Biographical Dictionary*, edited by David L. Porter, 508–9. Westport, CT: Greenwood Press, 2005.

Putney, Clifford. *Muscular Christianity: Manhood and Sports in Protestant America, 1880–1920*. Cambridge, MA: Harvard University Press, 2001.

Rains, Rob, with Hellen Carpenter. *James Naismith: The Man Who Invented Basketball*. Philadelphia: Temple University Press, 2009.

Rappoport, Ken. *The Classic: The History of the NCAA Basketball Championship*. Kansas City: Lowell Press, 1979.

Renegar, Horace. "N.C.A.A. Eastern Tournament." In *The Official 1942–43 Basketball Guide*, edited by Oswald Tower, 32–35. New York: A. S. Barnes and Company, 1942.

Roberts, Randy. *"But They Can't Beat Us": Oscar Robertson and the Crispus Attucks Tigers*. New York: Sports Publishing Co., 1999.

Rondidone, Troy. *Friday Night Fighter: Gaspar "Indio" Ortega and the Golden Age of Television Boxing*. Urbana: University of Illinois Press, 2013.

Rosen, Charley. *The Scandals of '51: How the Gamblers Almost Killed College Basketball*. New York: Seven Stories Press, 1999.

Rosen, Charley. *The Wizard of Odds: How Jack Molinas Almost Destroyed the Game of Basketball*. New York: Seven Stories Press, 2003.

Rosenbaum, Art. "1942: Those Long-Legged, Gangly Indians." In *NCAA March*

Madness: The Cinderellas, Superstars, and Champions from the NCAA Final Four, 8–9. Chicago: Triumph Books, 2004.

Russell, John. *Honey Russell: Between Games, Between Halves.* Washington DC: Dryad Press, 1986.

Shiebler, George L. "Eastern Playoff." In *The Official National Basketball Committee Basketball Guide, 1947–48*, edited by Oswald Tower, 37–43. New York: A. S. Barnes Company, 1947.

Shiebler, George L. "Metropolitan New York Basketball." In *The Official National Basketball Committee Basketball Guide, 1944–45*, edited by Oswald Tower, 62. New York: A. S. Barnes Company Publishers, 1944.

Shiebler, George L. "NCAA Championship Tournament." In *The Official 1943–44 Basketball Guide*, edited by Oswald Tower, 44–47. New York: A. S. Barnes and Company, 1943.

Shiebler, George L. "NCAA Championship Tournament." In *The Official National Basketball Committee Basketball Guide, 1945–46*, edited by Oswald Tower, 23–27. New York: A. S. Barnes Company, 1945.

Shiebler, George L. "NCAA Championship Tournament." In *The Official National Basketball Committee Basketball Guide, 1946–47*, edited by Oswald Tower, 37–42. New York: A. S. Barnes Company, 1946.

Shiebler, George L. "Utah Comes Thru in Red Cross Classic." In *The Official National Basketball Committee Basketball Guide, 1944–45*, edited by Oswald Tower, 27–29. New York: A. S. Barnes Company Publishers, 1944.

Smith, John Matthew. *The Sons of Westwood: John Wooden, UCLA, and the Dynasty That Changed College Basketball.* Champaign: University of Illinois Press, 2013.

Smith, Ronald. *Sports and Freedom: The Rise of Big-Time College Athletics.* New York: Oxford University Press, 1988.

Stooksbury, Danny. *National Title: The Unlikely Tale of the NAIB Tournament.* Bradenton Beach, FL: Higher Level Publishing, 2010.

Suits, Bernard. *The Grasshopper: Games, Life and Utopia.* Boston: David R. Godine Press, 1978.

Swarts, H. Jamison. "Eastern Play-off, N.C.A.A. Tournament." In *Spalding's Official Basketball Guide, 1939–40*, edited by Oswald Tower, 10–11. New York: American Sports Publishing Co., 1939.

Wakefield, Wanda Ellen. *Playing to Win: Sports and the American Military, 1898–1945.* Albany: State University of New York Press, 1997.

Watterson, John Sayle. *College Football: History, Spectacle, Controversy.* Baltimore: Johns Hopkins University Press, 2000.

Weyand, Alexander M. *The Cavalcade of Basketball.* New York: MacMillan, 1960.

Whalen, James D., and Wayne Patterson. "Case, Everett Norris." In *Basketball: A Biographical Dictionary*, edited by David L. Porter, 87–88. Westport, CT: Greenwood Press, 2005.

Whalen, James D., and Wayne Patterson. "Cooper, Charles Theodore 'Tarzan.'"
In *Basketball: A Biographical Dictionary*, edited by David L. Porter, 87–88.
Westport, CT: Greenwood Press, 2005.

Williamson, Walter. "Basketball in the Metropolitan District: National Invitation
College Tournament." In *Spalding's Official Basketball Guide, 1940–41*,
edited by Oswald Tower, 53. New York: American Sports Publishing Co.,
1940.

Williamson, Walter. "National Invitation College Tournament." In *Spalding's
Official Basketball Guide, 1940–41*, edited by Oswald Tower, 53–54. New
York: American Sports Publishing Co., 1940.

Wilson, Kenneth L. (Tug), and Jerry Brondfield. *The Big Ten*. Englewood Cliffs,
NJ: Prentice-Hall, 1967.

Wooden, John, with Jack Tobin. *They Call Me Coach: John Wooden*. Chicago:
Contemporary Books, 1988.

Wright, Jerry Jaye. "Irish, Edward Simmons 'Ned.'" In *Basketball: A Biographical
Dictionary*, edited by David L. Porter, 225. Westport, CT: Greenwood Press,
2005.

Archive Material

0000ua098: "Memorandum for Executive Committee," date unknown, Kirwan
SEC file, Hamilton, Horlacher, Jones, and Kirwan Faculty files, 1861–1964,
University of Kentucky Special Collections, Lexington, Ky.

Alesia, Mark. "NIT Suggests Smaller NCAA Tourney Field: Opening Statements
Start Federal Trial." *Indianapolis Star*, August 3, 2005, August 2005 Folder,
NCAA Clip File.

Alesia, Mark. "NIT's Witness List Includes Knight." *Indianapolis Star*, August 2,
2005, August 2005 Folder, NCAA Clip File.

Allen, Forrest C. "Phog," Papers. Spencer Research Archives. Kansas University
Libraries.

"Appendix I: Financial Reports of Tournaments and Treasurer's Report." In *1942
NCAA Yearbook*, (city and date unknown), 101–3, author has copy.

"Appendix I: Financial Reports of Tournaments and Treasurer's Report." In *1943
NCAA Yearbook*, (city and date unknown), 77–80, author has copy.

"Appendix III: Financial Reports of Tournaments and Treasurer's Report." In *1940
NCAA Yearbook*, 158–60. New York, December 29–31, 1940.

"Appendix III: Financial Reports of Tournaments and Treasurer's Report." In *1941
NCAA Yearbook*, 154. Detroit, MI, December 29–31, 1941.

"Appendix I: Financial Reports of Tournaments, of Basketball Rules Committee,
and of the Treasurer." In *1944 NCAA Yearbook*, (city and date unknown),
165–67, author has copy.

"Article IV: Eligibility" (NCAA Bylaws, revised on January 11–12, 1952). In *1951
NCAA Yearbook*, (city and date unknown), 266–67, author has copy.

"The Bears from Baylor." In *Olympic Quarterfinals Game Program*, 20. Madison Square Garden, March 27, 1948.

"Bradley's Braves Get Wish—Another Crack at Beavers." In *1950 NCAA East-West Finals Game Program*, 4. Madison Square Garden, March 28, 1950.

Busby, Bob. "East-West Championships." In *1952–53 NCAA Yearbook*, (city and date unknown), 62–64, author has copy.

Busby, Bob. "Eastern Regional No. 1." In *1952–53 NCAA Yearbook*, (city and date unknown), 68–70, author has copy.

Busby, Bob. "Eastern Regional No. 2." In *1952–53 NCAA Yearbook*, (city and date unknown), 70–72, author has copy.

Busby, Bob. "Western Playoff." In *1950 NCAA Yearbook*, (city and date unknown), 62–64, author has copy.

Busby, Bob. "Western Playoffs." In *1951 NCAA Yearbook*, (city and date unknown), 59–63, author has copy.

Busby, Bob. "Western Regional No. 1." In *1952–53 NCAA Yearbook*, (city and date unknown), 64–66, author has copy.

Busby, Bob. "Western Regional No. 2." In *1952–53 NCAA Yearbook*, (city and date unknown), 66–68, author has copy.

Carlson, H. C. *NABC Trial Bulletin* (1934), 2.

"College Basketball Goes Big Time." (Undated and unattributed article in Ned Irish nomination file, Naismith Hall of Fame, author has copy.)

Daley, Arthur J. "Invitation Tournament." In *NABC Bulletin*, February 17, 1940, 16.

Dooley, Eddie. "Colorado Has Its Cage Aces." In *1938 National Invitation Tournament Souvenir Program*, 4. Madison Square Garden, 1938.

Drake, Bruce. "Basketball." In *1952–53 NCAA Yearbook*, (city and date unknown), 60–62, author has copy.

Edwards, George R. "Basketball." In *1947 NCAA Yearbook*, (city and date unknown), 58–59, author has copy.

Edwards, George R. "Basketball." In *1948 NCAA Yearbook*, (city and date unknown), 51–53, author has copy.

Effrat, Louis. "Start With Cousy When Picking An All-America Team This Year." In *1950 NCAA Eastern Semi-finals Game Program*, 3. Madison Square Garden, March 23, 1950.

Eisenberg, David. "Getting Down to Cases, It's Everett At North Carolina State, Suh!" In *1950 NCAA Eastern Semi-finals Game Program*, 14. Madison Square Garden, March 23, 1950.

File 224 Sports Benefits Basketball Papers. Central Files, 1881–1982 (1935–1946 segment). Records of the American National Red Cross.

"Financial Report of the 1945 Basketball Play-offs and Final Game." In *1945 NCAA Yearbook*, (city and date unknown), 165–67, author has copy.

"Financial Report of the 1946 Basketball Playoffs and Final Game." In *1946 NCAA Yearbook*, (city and date unknown), 166–68, author has copy.

"Financial Report of 1947 Basketball Playoffs and Final Game." *1947 NCAA Yearbook*, (city and date unknown), 204–7, author has copy.

"Financial Report of 1948 Basketball Championships." In *1948 NCAA Yearbook*, (city and date unknown), 185–87, author has copy.

"Financial Report of 1949 Basketball Championship." In *1949 NCAA Yearbook*, (city and date unknown), 215, author has copy.

"Financial Report of 1950 Basketball Championships." In *1950 NCAA Yearbook*, (city and date unknown), 243–45, author has copy.

"Financial Report of 1951 Basketball Championship." In *1951 NCAA Yearbook*, (city and date unknown), 244–48, author has copy.

Friedlander, Sid. "N.C. State—A Southern Team with an All-Northern Flavor." In *11th Annual Invitation Tournament Quarterfinals Game Program*, 4. Madison Square Garden, March 13, 1948.

Garich, Edward J. "Western Playoff." In *1948 NCAA Yearbook*, (city and date unknown), 57–59, author has copy.

Geasey, Robert V. "Those Deceiving Owls." In *1938 National Invitation Tournament Souvenir Program*, 6. Madison Square Garden, 1938.

Kraetzer, Warren A. "East-West Championship Game." In *1948 NCAA Yearbook*, (city and date unknown), 54–55, author has copy.

Kraetzer, Warren A. "Eastern Playoff." In *1948 NCAA Yearbook*, (city and date unknown), 55–57, author has copy.

Lewin, Leonard. "Rootin', Tootin', Foul Shootin' Hombres Are These Longhorns from Texas." In *11th Annual Invitation Tournament Quarterfinals Game Program*, 24. Madison Square Garden, March 13, 1948.

Lonborg, A. C. "1950 Basketball Championship." In *1950 NCAA Yearbook*, (city and date unknown), 58, author has copy.

Lonborg, A. C. "The 1947 Basketball Tournament." In *1947 NCAA Yearbook*, (city and date unknown), 60–61, author has copy.

Lonborg, A. C. "The 1948 Basketball Tournament." In *1948 NCAA Yearbook*, (city and date unknown), 53, author has copy.

Lonborg, A. C. "The 1949 Basketball Tournament." In *1949 NCAA Yearbook*, (city and date unknown), 57–59, author has copy.

"NCAA Division I Men's Basketball Championship Tournament Facts," NCAA-NABC Affiliation at the Start of the Basketball Tournament File.

"NCAA University Basketball Tournament Committee." In *Minutes of the NCAA University Basketball Tournament Committee*, 4. Colorado Springs, CO, July 9–11, 1961.

"National Collegiate Athletic Association: Basketball Tournament: 1938–1941." Director of Athletics Record Group. The Ohio State University Archives.

"National Collegiate Basketball Championship Founded in 1939 By Hall-of-Famer

Olsen." NCAA-NABC Affiliation at the Start of the Basketball Tournament Folder.

Norgren, Nels. "Basketball and the War." In *National Association of Basketball Coaches Bulletin*, January 1942, 2.

Olsen, H. G. "The 1944 Basketball Tournament." In *1944 NCAA Yearbook*, (city and date unknown), 57–59, author has copy.

Olsen, H. G., John Bunn, and Dr. F. C. Allen. "Report of Tournament and Olympic Committee." In *Minutes of the National Association of Basketball Coaches Convention*. Chicago, 1939. 13.

"Olympic Basketball Committee." *Official Program: United States Olympic Basketball Trials*. Madison Square Garden, 1936. 1.

"Proceedings." In *National Association of Basketball Coaches Annual Convention*, April 4–5, 1938.

Proceedings of the Executive Committee Meeting of the National Association of Basketball Coaches of the United States. March 26, 1950, New York, 136.

"Records of Tonight's Rivals This Season." In *1950 National Invitation Game Program*, 12. Madison Square Garden, March 13, 1950.

"Report of the Treasurer: 1938–39." In *NCAA Yearbook, 1939*. Los Angeles, CA, December 28–30, 116–17.

"Revised and Approved N.C.A.A. Basketball Tournament Plan for 1951." In *1950 NCAA Yearbook*, (city and date unknown), 101–4, author has copy.

"Rice Institute Stars." In *1940 NCAA Western Regional Game Souvenir Program*. Madison Square Garden, 1940. 8.

"Roll Call of Members." In *1939 NCAA Yearbook*. Los Angeles, CA, December 28–30, 1939, 6–15.

"Roll Call of Members." In *1952 NCAA Yearbook*, (city and date unknown), 8–23, author has copy.

"Rosters." In *NCAA East-West Finals Game Program*, 20. Madison Square Garden, March 28, 1950.

Shiebler, George L. "East-West Championship." In *1951 NCAA Yearbook*, (city and date unknown), 54–55, author has copy.

Shiebler, George L. "Eastern Playoff." In *1950 NCAA Yearbook*, (city and date unknown), 60–62, author has copy.

Shiebler, George L. "Eastern Playoffs." In *1951 NCAA Yearbook*, (city and date unknown), 55–59, author has copy.

Tournament of Champions: The World Series of Basketball: Official Program. Kansas City Municipal Auditorium, 1940.

Dissertations/Theses

Dewar, John. "The Life and Professional Contributions of James Naismith." PhD diss., Florida State University, 1965.

Hoover, Francis Lentz. "A History of the National Association of Intercollegiate Athletics." PhD diss., Indiana University, 1958.

Jones, Tommy Ray. "Henry Clifford Carlson, MD: His Contributions to Intercollegiate Basketball Coaching." Master's thesis, University of Pittsburgh, 1965.

Somerville, Thomas R. "A History of the National Association of Basketball Coaches of the United States." PhD diss., The Ohio State University, 1980.

Journal Articles

Carlson, Chad. "A Tale of Two Tournaments: The Red Cross Games and the Early NCAA-NIT Relationship." *Journal of Intercollegiate Sport* 5, no. 2 (December 2012): 260–80.

Carlson, Chad. "Basketball's Forgotten Experiment: Don Barksdale and the Legacy of the United States Olympic Basketball Team." *International Journal of the History of Sport* 27, no. 8 (May 2010): 1330–59.

Carlson, Chad. "The Motherland, the Godfather, and the Birth of a Basketball Dynasty: American Efforts to Promote Basketball in Lithuania." *International Journal of the History of Sport* 28, no. 11 (August 2011): 1479–95.

Grundman, Adolph H. "A.A.U.-N.C.A.A. Politics: Forrest C. 'Phog' Allen and America's First Olympic Basketball Team." *Olympika* 5 (1996): 111–26.

Harbrecht, Thomas, and Robert Barnett. "College Football during World War II: 1941–1945." *Physical Educator* (March 1979): 31–34.

Kretchmar, R. Scott. "On Beautiful Games." *Journal of the Philosophy of Sport* 16 (1989): 34–43.

Newspaper/Magazine Articles

"2 Collegians Bribed by Gamblers to Throw Tourney Basketball Games, Allen Charges." *New York Times*, October 21, 1944, 20. Accessed November 23, 2012, http://search.proquest.com.

"3 Basketball Aces on Kentucky Team Admit '49 Fix Here." *New York Times*, October 21, 1951, 1. Accessed June 29, 2013, http://search.proquest.com.

"'5 Smart Boys' Win Cage Fame." *Brooklyn Daily Eagle*, February 28, 1939, 12. Accessed June 7, 2015.

"10 Quintets 'Interested' in Bradley Campus Meet." *New York Times*, February 27, 1951, 41. Accessed June 29, 2013, http://search.proquest.com.

"12 Fives Will Play in Invitation Here." *New York Times*, February 1, 1950, 34. Accessed June 15, 2013, http://search.proquest.com.

"16 Double Bills for Garden Court." *New York Times*, October 30, 1940, 32. Accessed December 9, 2013, http://search.proquest.com.

"16 Teams to End First Round Play in N.A.I.B. Tourney in K.C." *Daily Standard*

(Sikeston, MO), March 14, 1950, 8. Accessed June 6, 2015, http://www.newspapers.com.

"21 Double-Headers Listed for Garden." *New York Times*, November 14, 1945, 28. Accessed June 15, 2013, http://search.proquest.com.

"28 College Fives in Two Tourneys." *New York Times*, January 28, 1951, S3. Accessed June 29, 2013, http://search.proquest.com.

"32 Teams In." *Kansas City Times*, March 9, 1946, 15.

"36 Fives in Running for Invitation Posts." *New York Times*, February 16, 1951, 37. Accessed June 29, 2013, http://search.proquest.com.

"38 Quintets Considered." *New York Times*, February 25, 1943, 28. Accessed November 23, 2012, http://search.proquest.com.

"1500 Students Gather to Pay Tribute to Basketball Squad." *The Ohio State University Lantern*, March 16, 1939, 1.

"A Bid by Titlist." *Kansas City Times*, March 9, 1948, 16.

"A Cage Field Set." *Kansas City Times*, March 9, 1945, 9.

"A Cage Problem." *Kansas City Times*, March 6, 1944, 8.

"A Game for Blood." *Kansas City Times*, March 8, 1943, 11.

"A Great Tourney Ends." *Kansas City Times*, March 17, 1941, 11.

"A Scoring Mark." *Kansas City Times*, March 11, 1942, 11.

"Abandon Plans for Chicago Meet." *Peoria Journal-Star*, February 24, 1951, page unknown, author has copy.

"All-State Final." *Kansas City Times*, March 13, 1943, 17.

"Allen Furnishes Data on Gambling." *New York Times*, October 22, 1944, S2. Accessed November 23, 2012, http://search.proquest.com.

Anderman, S. "Letters to the Sports Editor: A Hollow Argument." *New York Times*, April 11, 1942, 17. Accessed December 9, 2013, http://search.proquest.com.

"Arizona Five Accepts." *New York Times*, March 8, 1946, 25. Accessed June 15, 2013, http://search.proquest.com.

"Arkansas Five in Tourney." *New York Times*, March 6, 1944, 14. Accessed November 23, 2012, http://search.proquest.com.

"Article 13—No Title." *New York Times*, February 27, 1944, S1. Accessed November, 23, 2012, http://search.proquest.com.

"Balk at N.A.I.B. Ruling." *Kansas City Times*, March 4, 1948, 24.

"Basketball Bids Mailed." *New York Times*, February 26, 1948, 31. Accessed June 15, 2013, http://search.proquest.com.

"Basketball Dates Set." *New York Times*, February 11, 1943, 26. Accessed November 23, 2012, http://search.proquest.com.

"Basketball Dates Set." *New York Times*, January 26, 1947, S4. Accessed June 15, 2013, http://search.proquest.com.

"Basketball Heads Gather Tomorrow." *New York Times*, March 23, 1941, S2. Accessed December 9, 2013, http://search.proquest.com.

"Basketball Makes Contribution to Red Cross." *New York Times*, April 13, 1945, 20. Accessed November 23, 2012, http://search.proquest.com.

"Basketball Miracle." *New York Times*, March 18, 1950, 12. Accessed June 15, 2013, http://search.proquest.com.

"Basketball Won More Popularity." *New York Times*, December 25, 1938, 54. Accessed January 18, 2012, http://search.proquest.com.

"Baylor, Kentucky Clash Tonight in Cage Semi-Finals." *Brownsville Herald* (Brownsville, TX), March 29, 1948, 5. Accessed June 6, 2015, http://www.newspapers.com.

"Baylor Reaches Semi-Finals in U.S. Olympic Tryouts." *Pampa Daily News* (Pampa, TX), March 28, 1948, 7. Accessed June 6, 2015, http://www.newspapers.com.

Bealmear, Austin. "Interest in Basketball to Keep Mounting, Leaders Say." *Burlington Daily Times-News* (Burlington, NC), March 22, 1946, 6. Accessed June 6, 2015, http://www.newspapers.com.

"Beavers Honored by Borough Head." *New York Times*, April 7, 1950, 37. Accessed June 15, 2013, http://search.proquest.com.

"Beavers on the Way Here." *Kansas City Times*, March 19, 1947, 14.

"Bid Accepted by Fordham." *New York Times*, March 6, 1943, 18. Accessed November 23, 2012, http://search.proquest.com.

"Bid Voted to N.Y.U. or City College." *New York Times*, February 22, 1938, 27. Accessed January 18, 2012, http://search.proquest.com.

"Bids Are Accepted by Three Quintets." *New York Times*, February 27, 1948, 29. Accessed June 15, 2013, http://search.proquest.com.

"Big Court Upset." *Kansas City Times*, March 14, 1939, 11.

"Big 10 Approves 14 Game Basket Slate." *Chicago Tribune*, March 12, 1950, A2. Accessed June 15, 2013, http://search.proquest.com.

"Big Ten Votes to Retain Ban on Bowl Games." *Chicago Daily Tribune*, December 8, 1940, B1. Accessed December 9, 2013, http://search.proquest.com.

"Bowling Green Is Picked." *New York Times*, February 28, 1946, 33. Accessed June 15, 2013, http://search.proquest.com.

"Bradley Accepts Hawaiian Offer." *Peoria Journal-Star*, February 23, 1951, page unknown, author has copy.

"Bradley Defeats Kansas Five, 59–57." *New York Times*, March 21, 1950, 37. Accessed June 15, 2013, http://search.proquest.com.

"Bradley Five Accepts Bid." *New York Times*, March 3, 1949, 35. Accessed June 15, 2013, http://search.proquest.com.

"Bradley, Loyola in Shape for Clash Tonight." *Chicago Tribune*, March 17, 1949, B1. Accessed June 15, 2013, http://search.proquest.com.

"Bradley OK's Bid to Garden." *Chicago Tribune*, February 28, 1950, B3. Accessed June 15, 2013, http://search.proquest.com.

"Bradley Quintet Is Seeded No. 1 for National Invitation Tourney." *New York Times*, March 8, 1950, 35. Accessed June 15, 2013, http://search. proquest.com.

"Bradley Tech Bid to Tourney Here." *New York Times*, March 10, 1939, 29. Accessed January 18, 2012, http://search.proquest.com.

"Bradley Tech Drills." *New York Times*, March 8, 1938, 14. Accessed January 18, 2012, http://search.proquest.com.

"Bradley Tops Season's Last Poll with Ohio State Five in 2d Place." *New York Times*, March 8, 1950, 35. Accessed June 15, 2013, http://search. proquest.com.

Braitman, Irving. "Letters to the Sports Editor: A Local Fan's Reply." *New York Times*, April 11, 1942, 17. Accessed December 9, 2013, http://search. proquest.com.

Brandwein, Peter. "N.C.A.A. Play Opens at Garden Tonight." *New York Times*, March 20, 1951, 49. Accessed June 29, 2013, http://search.proquest.com.

Brandwein, Peter. "Pairings Revised in N.C.A.A. Tourney." *New York Times*, February 6, 1951, 44. Accessed June 29, 2013, http://search.proquest.com.

"Brennan Resigns Post as Coach of St. Francis Basketball Team." *New York Times*, March 9, 1948, 29. Accessed November 23, 2013, http://search.proquest.com.

Briordy, William J. "Bonaventure Five in Invitation Play." *New York Times*, March 6, 1951, 33. Accessed June 29, 2013, http://search.proquest.com.

Briordy, William J. "City College, Niagara and Arizona Accept Invitation Tourney Bids." *New York Times*, March 7, 1950, 31. Accessed June 15, 2013, http:// search.proquest.com.

Busby, Bob. "Choice of K.U. Touches Off an Angry Blast by Gardner." *Kansas City Star*, March 12, 1950, B1.

"Bushnell, Salmon to Aid in Tourney." *New York Times*, February 16, 1938, 25. Accessed January 18, 2012, http://search.proquest.com.

"C.C.N.Y. and Toledo Favored Tonight." *New York Times*, March 19, 1942, 30. Accessed December 9, 2013, http://search.proquest.com.

"C.C.N.Y. Protests Choice of R.I. State." *New York Times*, March 9, 1946, 21. Accessed June 15, 2013, http://search.proquest.com.

"C.C.N.Y., Wisconsin Fives Paired in N.C.A.A. Tourney on Thursday." *New York Times*, March 18, 1947, 35. Accessed June 15, 2013, http://search. proquest.com.

"Cage Draw Made." *Kansas City Times*, March 7, 1942, 18.

"Cage Fans' Week." *Kansas City Times*, March 8, 1943, 11.

"Cage Field Set." *Kansas City Times*, March 7, 1938, 13.

"Cage Inquiry Goes On." *Kansas City Times*, March 29, 1945, 13.

"Cage Marks Set." *Kansas City Times*, March 10, 1942, 11.

"Cage Titans Clash Here Tonight in Eastern Eliminations of N.C.A.A. Play." *New Orleans Times-Picayune*, March 20, 1942, 13.

"Canisius Five in Tourney." *New York Times*, March 3, 1944, 20. Accessed November 23, 2012, http://search.proquest.com.

"Catholic Fives Compete." *Record-Argus* (Greenville, PA), March 28, 1950, 7. Accessed June 6, 2015, http://www.newspapers.com.

Chase, LeRoy. "St. John's Snaps Bradley Winning Streak, 68 to 59." *Peoria Journal-Star*, January 12, 1951, B2.

"Chicago Plans Tourney to Compete with Garden." *New York Times*, February 11, 1951, 147. Accessed June 29, 2013, http://search.proquest.com.

Childs, Kingsley. "Manhattan, W. and J. Quintets in Invitation Tourney; N.Y.U. in N.C.A.A. Event." *New York Times*, March 12, 1943, 21. Accessed November 23, 2012, http://search.proquest.com

Childs, Kingsley. "N.C.A.A. Will Hold Court Play Here." *New York Times*, January 21, 1943, 28. Accessed November 23, 2012, http://search.proquest.com.

Childs, Kingsley. "St. John's Faces Wyoming for Red Cross Tonight." *New York Times*, April 1, 1943, 28. Accessed November 23, 2012, http://search.proquest.com.

Clark, Alfred E. "8 Bradley Players Involved in Fixing Basketball Games." *New York Times*, July 25, 1951, 1. Accessed June 29, 2013, http://search.proquest.com.

"Close Contests Loom at Garden in National Basketball Tourney." *New York Times*, March 10, 1940, 81. Accessed December 9, 2013, http://search.proquest.com.

"Coach Would Keep Tourneys in Garden." *New York Times*, March 12, 1951, 40. Accessed June 29, 2013, http://search.proquest.com.

"Coach's Cry of Gaming Peril Draws Rebuke." *Chicago Tribune*, October 22, 1944, A2. Accessed November 23, 2012, http://search.proquest.com.

Coleman, George E. "Basketball." *Brooklyn Daily Eagle*, March 19, 1946, 12. Accessed June 6, 2015, http://www.newspapers.com.

Coleman, George E. "Basketball Writers in Dollar Dilemma." *Brooklyn Daily Eagle*, January 25, 1939, 15. Accessed June 6, 2015, http://www.newspapers.com.

Coleman, George E. "Battle of Giants Fizzles in Garden." *Brooklyn Daily Eagle*, March 30, 1945, 15. Accessed June 6, 2015, http://www.newspapers.com.

Coleman, George E. "Four-Year-Old Court Debate Faces Settlement." *Brooklyn Daily Eagle*, March 9, 1938, 19. Accessed June 6, 2015, http://www.newspapers.com.

Coleman, George E. "Kentucky Nixes Charity Classic." *Brooklyn Daily Eagle*, March 22, 1946, 17. Accessed June 6, 2015, http://www.newspapers.com.

Coleman, George E. "Irish Left Juggling Cage Hot Potatoes." *Brooklyn*

Daily Eagle, March 26, 1946, 11. Accessed June 6, 2015, http://www.newspapers.com.

Coleman, George E. "N.Y.A.C. to Fill in against Oilers." *Brooklyn Daily Eagle*, March 27, 1946, 15. Accessed June 6, 2015, http://www.newspapers.com.

Coleman, George E. "Redmen Confident They'll Tame Wyoming Cowboy '5.'" *Brooklyn Daily Eagle*, March 31, 1943, 17. Accessed June 6, 2015, http://www.newspapers.com.

Coleman, George E. "Shh, Redmen Should Take Speedy Utes." *Brooklyn Daily Eagle*, March 30, 1944, 14. Accessed June 6, 2015, http://www.newspapers.com.

Coleman, George E. "St. John's, NYU May Play for Red Cross Fund." *Brooklyn Daily Eagle*, March 9, 1945, 15. Accessed June 6, 2015, http://www.newspapers.com.

Coleman, George E. "St. John's and C.C.N.Y. Choices in Garden Tilts." *Brooklyn Daily Eagle*, March 10, 1941, 13. Accessed June 6, 2015, http://www.newspapers.com.

Coleman, George E. "Writers' Cage Tourney 'Tops.'" *Brooklyn Daily Eagle*, March 10, 1939, 21. Accessed June 7, 2015, http://www.newspapers.com.

Coleman, George E. "Wyoming Five Is Real National Champion." *Brooklyn Daily Eagle*, April 2, 1943, 15. Accessed June 6, 2015, http://www.newspapers.com.

"College: Fives of South Fight for Right to Play in National Meet Here." *Indianapolis Star*, March 1, 1922, 15. Accessed February 8, 2013, http://search.proquest.com.

"Colleges Seek Larger Share of Basket Gate." *Chicago Tribune*, March 24, 1944, 20. Accessed November 23, 2012, http://search.proquest.com.

"Colorado in N.C.A.A. Play." *New York Times*, March 8, 1946, 24. Accessed June 15, 2013, http://search.proquest.com.

"Columbia Quintet in N.C.A.A. Tourney." *New York Times*, March 5, 1951, 25. Accessed June 29, 2013, http://search.proquest.com.

"Cornell Crushes Canisius, 51 to 29." *New York Times*, March 5, 1944, S3. Accessed November 23, 2012, http://search.proquest.com.

"Court Tourney Is Expanded." *New York Times*, December 18, 1940, 36. Accessed December 9, 2013, http://search.proquest.com.

Crichton, Kyle. "Indiana Madness." *Collier's Magazine*, February 6, 1937, 13, 38.

Daley, Arthur J. "13,829 in Garden See N.Y.U. and Temple Fives Triumph in National Tourney." *New York Times*, March 10, 1938, 24. Accessed January 18, 2012, http://search.proquest.com.

Daley, Arthur J. "14,443 See L.I.U. and St. John's Win as National Tourney Starts." *New York Times*, March 16, 1939, 33. Accessed January 18, 2012, http://search.proquest.com

Daley, Arthur J. "17,886 See Beavers Halt N.Y.U. for Metropolitan Honors, 47–43." *New York Times*, March 11, 1941, 31. Accessed December 9, 2013, http://search.proquest.com.

Daley, Arthur J. "18,033 See Unbeaten L.I.U. Five Win National Tourney with 24th Triumph." *New York Times*, March 23, 1939, 32. Accessed January 18, 2012, http://search.proquest.com.

Daley, Arthur J. "18,357 See Ohio U. Set Back C.C.N.Y. at Garden, 45 to 43." *New York Times*, March 23, 1941, S1. Accessed December 9, 2013, http://search.proquest.com.

Daley, Arthur J. "Awesome Kansas Giants Reverse Basketball Lay-up Shot Process." *New York Times*, March 10, 1936, 29. Accessed January 18, 2012, http://search.proquest.com.

Daley, Arthur J. "C.C.N.Y. Five Upset by Western Kentucky; Toledo Wins." *New York Times*, March 20, 1942, 27. Accessed December 9, 2013, http://search.proquest.com

Daley, Arthur J. "C.C.N.Y. Quintet Overcomes L.I.U. in Garden, 42–34." *New York Times*, March 29, 1942, S1. Accessed December 9, 2013, http://search.proquest.com.

Daley, Arthur J. "City College Snaps Streak of Hitherto Unbeaten N.Y.U. Quintet at 18 Games." *New York Times*, March 6, 1940, 28. Accessed December 9, 2013, http://search.proquest.com.

Daley, Arthur J. "Colorado and Duquesne Gain Basketball Final." *New York Times*, March 14, 1940, 35. Accessed December 9, 2013, http://search.proquest.com.

Daley, Arthur J. "Colorado Downs Duquesne in National Basketball Tourney Final at Garden." *New York Times*, March 16, 1940, 17. Accessed December 9, 2013, http://search.proquest.com.

Daley, Arthur J. "Colorado Five Thrills 12,000 in Garden with Last-Minute Victory over N.Y.U." *New York Times*, March 15, 1938, 26. Accessed January 18, 2014, http://search.proquest.com.

Daley, Arthur J. "Court Coaches Suggest Change in 3-Second Rule." *New York Times*, March 26, 1941, 30. Accessed December 9, 2013, http://search.proquest.com.

Daley, Arthur J. "Duquesne and De Paul Gain Semi-Finals on Garden Court." *New York Times*, March 12, 1940, 32. Accessed December 9, 2013, http://search.proquest.com.

Daley, Arthur J. "Duquesne Faces Colorado Tonight in Final of National Basketball." *New York Times*, March 15, 1940, 28. Accessed December 9, 2013, http://search.proquest.com.

Daley, Arthur J. "Fordham to Meet N.Y.U. Five Tonight." *New York Times*, February 19, 1941, 30. Accessed December 9, 2013, http://search.proquest.com.

Daley, Arthur J. "L.I.U. and De Paul Added to Tourney." *New York Times*, March 8, 1940, 30. Accessed December 9, 2013, http://search.proquest.com.

Daley, Arthur J. "L.I.U. and Loyola Remain Undefeated in Gaining Basketball Final." *New York Times*, March 21, 1939, 33. Accessed January 18, 2012, http://search.proquest.com.

Daley, Arthur J. "L.I.U. and Loyola Risk Winning Streaks in Tourney Final Tonight." *New York Times*, March 22, 1939, 33. Accessed January 18, 2012, http://search.proquest.com.

Daley, Arthur J. "L.I.U. and St. John's to Oppose Strong Rivals in Garden Tourney." *New York Times*, March 12, 1939, 74. Accessed January 18, 2012, http://search.proquest.com.

Daley, Arthur J. "L.I.U. and West Texas Are Upset as Basketball Tournament Starts at Garden." *New York Times*, March 18, 1942, 31. Accessed December 9, 2013, http://search.proquest.com.

Daley, Arthur J. "L.I.U. Five Take Overtime Thriller from Oregon, 56–55." *New York Times*, December 17, 1939, 81. Accessed December 9, 2013, http://search.proquest.com.

Daley, Arthur J. "L.I.U. Halts Ohio U. Five in Garden Final before 18,377." *New York Times*, March 25, 1941, 29. Accessed December 9, 2013, http://search.proquest.com.

Daley, Arthur J. "Lloyd of St. John's Honored with L.I.U." *New York Times*, March 24, 1939, 32. Accessed January 18, 2012, http://search.proquest.com.

Daley, Arthur J. "Ohio U. and C.C.N.Y. Win as National Invitation Basketball Starts at Garden." *New York Times*, March 19, 1941, 26. Accessed December 9, 2013, http://search.proquest.com.

Daley, Arthur J. "On Basketball Courts." *New York Times*, February 9, 1940, 26. Accessed December 9, 2013, http://search.proquest.com.

Daley, Arthur J. "Seton Hall and L.I.U. Fives Gain Semi-Finals at Garden." *New York Times*, March 20, 1941, 27. Accessed December 9, 2013, http://search.proquest.com.

Daley, Arthur J. "Sports of the *Times*: Basketball, Past and Present." *New York Times*, March 18, 1943, 25. Accessed November 23, 2012, http://search.proquest.com.

Daley, Arthur J. "Sports of the *Times*: From Old Kaintuck." *New York Times*, March 24, 1947, 29. Accessed June 15, 2013, http://search.proquest.com.

Daley, Arthur J. "Sports of the *Times*: Going Up?" *New York Times*, March 16, 1944, 24. Accessed November 23, 2012, http://search.proquest.com.

Daley, Arthur J. "Sports of the *Times*: High Scorer." *New York Times*, March 21, 1945, 29. Accessed November 23, 2012, http://search.proquest.com.

Daley, Arthur J. "Sports of the *Times*: Horse Haggerty Plays a Return Engagement." *New York Times*, April 1, 1943, 28. Accessed November 23, 2012, http://search.proquest.com.

Daley, Arthur J. "Sports of the *Times*: Paging Jack-the-Giant-Killer." *New York Times*, March 29, 1945, 31. Accessed November 23, 2012, http://search.proquest.com.

Daley, Arthur J. "Sports of the *Times*: Short Shots in Sundry Directions." *New York Times*, March 22, 1946, 30. Accessed June 15, 2013, http://search.proquest.com.

Daley, Arthur J. "Sports of the *Times*: Short Shots in Sundry Directions." *New York Times*, February 11, 1944, 14. Accessed November 23, 2012, http://search.proquest.com.

Daley, Arthur J. "Sports of the *Times*: Short Shots in Sundry Directions." *New York Times*, March 16, 1945, 19. Accessed November 23, 2012, http://search.proquest.com.

Daley, Arthur J. "Sports of the *Times*: The Passing Scene, or the Year in Review." *New York Times*, December 24, 1944, 40. Accessed November 23, 2012, http://search.proquest.com.

Daley, Arthur J. "Temple Crushes Colorado, 60–36." *New York Times*, March 17, 1938, 24. Accessed January 18, 2012, http://search.proquest.com.

Daley, Arthur J. "Twin Bills Start at Garden Tonight." *New York Times*, December 16, 1939, 22. Accessed December 9, 2013, http://search.proquest.com.

Daley, Arthur J. "West Virginia and Western Kentucky Gain Garden Basketball Final in Upsets." *New York Times*, March 24, 1942, 26. Accessed December 9, 2013, http://search.proquest.com.

Daley, Arthur J. "West Virginia Halts Western Kentucky in National Invitation Basketball Final." *New York Times*, March 26, 1942, 28. Accessed December 9, 2013, http://search.proquest.com.

Danzig, Allison. "Bingham, Chosen Head of Rules Committee, Opposes Changes in Football Code." *New York Times*, January 7, 1944, 11. Accessed November 23, 2012, http://search.proquest.com.

Danzig, Allison. "Sports Benefits for Red Cross Set." *New York Times*, February 19, 1944, 18. Accessed November 23, 2012, http://search.proquest.com.

"Dartmouth and Kentucky Top Three High-Scoring Teams in Tourney Here." *New Orleans Times-Picayune*, March 18, 1942, 15.

"Dartmouth Five to Play in N.C.A.A. Tourney." *New York Times*, February 19, 1944, 18. Accessed November 23, 2012, http://search.proquest.com.

"De Paul Accepts Bid to Play in Eastern Meet." *Chicago Tribune*, March 6, 1945, 17. Accessed November 23, 2012, http://search.proquest.com.

"De Paul Faces Muhlenberg in Opener Tonight." *Chicago Tribune*, March 16, 1944, 21. Accessed November 23, 2012, http://search.proquest.com.

"De Paul Five Will Play in Garden Meet." *Chicago Tribune*, February 27, 1944, A1. Accessed November 23, 2012, http://search.proquest.com.

"De Paul to Play in N.C.A.A. Meet." *Chicago Tribune*, March 9, 1943, 23. Accessed November 23, 2012, http://search.proquest.com.

"De Paul's Quintet Will Oppose L.I.U." *New York Times*, March 11, 1940, 23. Accessed December 9, 2013, http://search.proquest.com.

"Dolphins Play St. Francis Tomorrow in 2d Round of Catholic Tournament." *The Post-Standard* (Syracuse, NY), March 17, 1952, 12. Accessed June 21, 2015, http://www.newspaperarchive.com.

"Down to 4 Teams." *Kansas City Star*, March 10, 1937, 12.

Drebinger, John. "Sports, Attuned to U.S. War Needs, Had Robust Year." *New York Times*, December 26, 1943, S1. Accessed November 23, 2012, http://search.proquest.com.

"Drop Basketball at Lawrence Tech." *New York Times*, August 21, 1951, 43. Accessed June 29, 2013, http://search.proquest.com.

"Drury Is Beaten." *Kansas City Times*, March 9, 1938, 13.

"Education Board Notes City College Victory." *New York Times*, March 21, 1950, 37. Accessed June 15, 2013, http://search.proquest.com.

Effrat, Louis. "18,000 See C.C.N.Y. Top Bradley, 69–61, in Final at Garden." *New York Times*, March 19, 1950, S1. Accessed June 15, 2013, http://search.proquest.com.

Effrat, Louis. "18,135 See St. John's Nip Rice Five, Fordham Top Western Kentucky." *New York Times*, March 23, 1943, 22. Accessed November 23, 2012, http://search.proquest.com.

Effrat, Louis. "18,233 See St. John's Five Overwhelm Toledo in National Invitation Final." *New York Times*, March 30, 1943, 25. Accessed November 23, 2012, http://search.proquest.com.

Effrat, Louis. "18,316 See Wyoming Quintet Beat St. John's in Overtime." *New York Times*, April 2, 1943, 25. Accessed November 23, 2012, http://search.proquest.com.

Effrat, Louis. "18,374 See St. John's Win Invitation Basketball Final Second Year in Row." *New York Times*, March 27, 1944, 22. Accessed November 23, 2012, http://search.proquest.com.

Effrat, Louis. "18,419 See St. John's Rout Fordham Five in Semi-finals, 69–43." *New York Times*, March 28, 1943, S1. Accessed November 23, 2012, http://search.proquest.com.

Effrat, Louis. "Basketball Fans Here Speculate on Fate of Annual Play-Off Game." *New York Times*, January 28, 1946, 24. Accessed June 15, 2013, http://search.proquest.com.

Effrat, Louis. "Beavers Confident of Title Triumph." *New York Times*, March 28, 1950, 39. Accessed June 15, 2013, http://search.proquest.com.

Effrat, Louis. "Brigham Young, Dayton Fives Gain Garden Final." *New York Times*, March 16, 1951, 43. Accessed June 29, 2013, http://search.proquest.com.

Effrat, Louis. "C.C.N.Y. and Duquesne Fives Gain National Invitation Semi-Finals." *New York Times*, March 15, 1950, 36. Accessed June 15, 2013, http://search.proquest.com.

Effrat, Louis. "City College and Bradley Quintets Gain Final Round of National Invitation." *New York Times*, March 17, 1950, 36. Accessed June 15, 2013, http://search.proquest.com.

Effrat, Louis. "City College and San Francisco Accept National Invitation Basketball Bids." *New York Times*, March 8, 1949, 32. Accessed June 15, 2013, http://search.proquest.com.

Effrat, Louis. "City College Conquers Bradley for First Sweep of National Basketball Titles." *New York Times*, March 29, 1950, 40. Accessed June 15, 2013, http://search.proquest.com.

Effrat, Louis. "Colorado and Oklahoma Aggie Quintets Favored in Garden Tonight." *New York Times*, March 13, 1940, 36. Accessed December 9, 2013, http://search.proquest.com.

Effrat, Louis. "Crusaders Annex 23d in Row, 58–47." *New York Times*, March 26, 1947, 33. Accessed June 15, 2013, http://search.proquest.com.

Effrat, Louis. "Dartmouth, Ivy League Champion, to Pass Up Post-Season Contests." *New York Times*, February 18, 1946, 29. Accessed June 15, 2013, http://search.proquest.com.

Effrat, Louis. "Dayton Five Bows to Brigham Young at Garden, 62–43." *New York Times*, March 18, 1951, S1. Accessed June 29, 2013, http://search.proquest.com.

Effrat, Louis. "De Paul Five Beats R.I. State, 97 to 53: Bowling Green's Defense at Its Height in the Garden." *New York Times*, March 22, 1945, 19. Accessed November 23, 2012, http://search.proquest.com.

Effrat, Louis. "De Paul Five Tops Draw for Tourney." *New York Times*, March 13, 1945, 22. Accessed November 23, 2012, http://search.proquest.com.

Effrat, Louis. "De Paul Quintet Triumphs by 71–54: A Battle of the Giants in National Final." *New York Times*, March 27, 1945, 27. Accessed November 23, 2012, http://search.proquest.com.

Effrat, Louis. "Garden Dates Set for College Fives." *New York Times*, November 10, 1943, 29. Accessed November 23, 2021, http://search.proquest.com.

Effrat, Louis. "Holy Cross Down City College Five in Garden, 60–45." *New York Times*, March 23, 1947, S1. Accessed June 15, 2013, http://search.proquest.com.

Effrat, Louis. "Impressive Western Kentucky Five Arrives and Drills in Garden." *New York Times*, December 23, 1943, 24. Accessed November 23, 2012, http://search.proquest.com.

Effrat, Louis. "Kentucky and Oklahoma Aggies Triumph in Invitation Tourney before 16,273." *New York Times*, March 21, 1944, 22. Accessed November 23, 2012, http://search.proquest.com.

Effrat, Louis. "Kentucky Crushes Arizona by 77–53; Muhlenberg Wins." *New York Times*, March 17, 1946, S1. Accessed June 15, 2013, http://search.proquest.com.

Effrat, Louis. "Kentucky Defeats Rhode Island, 46–45." *New York Times*, March 21, 1946, 35. Accessed June 15, 2013, http://search.proquest.com.

Effrat, Louis. "Kentucky Downs W. Virginia, 59–51." *New York Times*, March 19, 1946, 29. Accessed June 15, 2013, http://search.proquest.com.

Effrat, Louis. "Kentucky Quintet Seeded at Top for National Invitation Tourney."

New York Times, March 12, 1946, 29. Accessed June 15, 2013, http://search. proquest.com.

Effrat, Louis. "L.I.U. Counts on Cornell Game to Clinch Garden Tourney Bid." *New York Times*, February 28, 1944, 21. Accessed November 23, 2012, http://search.proquest.com.

Effrat, Louis. "Loyola, Bowling Green, San Francisco and Bradley Win." *New York Times*, March 15, 1949, 37. Accessed June 15, 2013, http://search. proquest.com.

Effrat, Louis. "N.Y.U. and St. Louis Fives Reach Final of National Invitation Play." *New York Times*, March 16, 1948, 37. Accessed June 15, 2013, http://search. proquest.com.

Effrat, Louis. "N.Y.U., St. John's and Manhattan Accept Bids to Revised 12-Team Tourney." *New York Times*, March 10, 1949, 36. Accessed June 15, 2013, http://search.proquest.com.

Effrat, Louis. "N.Y.U. Tops Texas by 46–43 at Garden on Basket by Kor." *New York Times*, March 14, 1948, S1. Accessed June 15, 2013, http://search. proquest.com.

Effrat, Louis. "New Basketball Prize Will Go to Star in College Games Here." *New York Times*, February 20, 1945, 24. Accessed November 23, 2012, http://search.proquest.com.

Effrat, Louis. "New Mexico Five to Engage L.I.U." *New York Times*, March 15, 1939, 32. Accessed January 18, 2012, http://search.proquest.com.

Effrat, Louis. "No. Carolina State Defeats St. John's in Garden, 61 to 55." *New York Times*, March 16, 1947, S1. Accessed June 15, 2013, http://search. proquest.com.

Effrat, Louis. "Oklahoma Aggies Top De Paul, 52–44." *New York Times*, March 30, 1945, 20. Accessed November 23, 2012, http://search. proquest.com.

Effrat, Louis. "On Basketball Courts." *New York Times*, February 27, 1940, 25. Accessed December 9, 2013, http://search.proquest.com.

Effrat, Louis. "Push City League for College Fives." *New York Times*, March 2, 1943, 25. Accessed November 23, 2012, http://search.proquest.com.

Effrat, Louis. "R.P.I. Quintet Completes Field in Invitation Series at Garden." *New York Times*, March 12, 1945, 14. Accessed November 23, 2012, http://search.proquest.com.

Effrat, Louis. "Redmen Set Back W. Kentucky, 69–60." *New York Times*, March 14, 1950, 29. Accessed June 15, 2013, http://search.proquest.com.

Effrat, Louis. "Rhode Island Quintet Faces St. Francis in Garden Tonight." *New York Times*, January 29, 1941, 11. Accessed December 9, 2013, http://search. proquest.com.

Effrat, Louis. "Rhode Island Tops Tennessee, 51 to 44, in Upset at Garden." *New York Times*, March 18, 1945, S1. Accessed November 23, 2012, http://search. proquest.com.

Effrat, Louis. "Rhode Island Wins in Overtime, 82–79." *New York Times*, March 15, 1946, 16. Accessed June 15, 2013, http://search.proquest.com.

Effrat, Louis. "San Francisco and Loyola Gain National Invitation Basketball Tourney Final." *New York Times*, March 18, 1949, 34. Accessed June 15, 2013, http://search.proquest.com.

Effrat, Louis. "San Francisco Five Trips Loyola, 48–47." *New York Times*, March 20, 1949, S1. Accessed June 15, 2013, http://search.proquest.com.

Effrat, Louis. "Seton Hall and Dayton Reach Semi-Finals in Invitation Tourney at Garden." *New York Times*, March 14, 1951, 53. Accessed June 29, 2013, http://search.proquest.com.

Effrat, Louis. "St. John's among Four Quintets in National Invitation Tournament." *New York Times*, February 24, 1951, 22. Accessed June 29, 2013, http://search.proquest.com.

Effrat, Louis. "St. John's and Brigham Young Advance to Semi-Finals in Invitation Tourney." *New York Times*, March 13, 1951, 42. Accessed June 29, 2013, http://search.proquest.com.

Effrat, Louis. "St. John's Checks Muhlenberg, 34–33." *New York Times*, March 20, 1945, 24. Accessed November 23, 2012, http://search.proquest.com.

Effrat, Louis. "St. John's, L.I.U. Quintets Accept Bids to Post-Season Tournament." *New York Times*, March 11, 1947, 34. Accessed June 15, 2013, http://search.proquest.com.

Effrat, Louis. "St. John's Upsets Kentucky to Gain Garden Basketball Final; De Paul Victor." *New York Times*, March 23, 1944, 23. Accessed November 23, 2012, http://search.proquest.com.

Effrat, Louis. "St. Louis and Western Kentucky Win as Invitation Basketball Opens." *New York Times*, March 12, 1948, 30. Accessed June 15, 2013, http://search.proquest.com.

Effrat, Louis. "St. Louis Conquers N.Y.U. in National Invitation Basketball Final at Garden." *New York Times*, March 18, 1948, 38. Accessed June 15, 2013, http://search.proquest.com.

Effrat, Louis. "St. Louis Defeats La Salle by 73–61 on Garden Court." *New York Times*, March 11, 1951, 151. Accessed June 29, 2013, http://search.proquest.com.

Effrat, Louis. "Three Local Fives on Tentative List." *New York Times*, February 27, 1945, 23. Accessed November 23, 2012, http://search.proquest.com.

Effrat, Louis. "Toledo Five Ousts Manhattan, W. and J. Upsets Creighton in Garden Tourney." *New York Times*, March 19, 1943, 23. Accessed November 23, 2012, http://search.proquest.com.

Effrat, Louis. "Utah Five to Play in Red Cross Game." *New York Times*, March 28, 1944, 23. Accessed November 23, 2012, http://search.proquest.com.

Effrat, Louis. "Utah Upsets Dartmouth in Extra Period to Take N.C.A.A. Basketball Title." *New York Times*, March 29, 1944, 16. Accessed November 23, 2012, http://search.proquest.com.

Effrat, Louis. "Wildcats Conquer L.I.U. Five, 66–62." *New York Times*, March 18, 1947, 35. Accessed June 15, 2013, http://search.proquest.com.

Effrat, Louis. "Wildcats Toppled by the Utes, 49–45." *New York Times*, March 25, 1947, 32. Accessed June 15, 2013, http://search.proquest.com.

Effrat, Louis. "Wildcats Triumph at Garden, 60 to 42." *New York Times*, March 20, 1947, 34. Accessed June 15, 2013, http://search.proquest.com.

Effrat, Louis. "Wyoming Downs Georgetown to Capture N.C.A.A. Basketball Title." *New York Times*, March 31, 1943, 24. Accessed November 23, 2012, http://search.proquest.com.

Eichelberger, Curtis. "March Madness Swells as NCAA Pumps Up NIT Tournament." *Bloomberg News*, March 14, 2006. Accessed May 11, 2013, http://www.bloomberg.com.

"Eight-Team Meet Starts March 24." *Peoria Journal-Star*, February 25, 1951, page unknown, author has copy.

Feinberg, Alexander. "3 City College Aces and Gambler Held in Basketball 'Fix.'" *New York Times*, February 19, 1951, 1. Accessed June 29, 2013, http://search.proquest.com.

Feinberg, Alexander. "City College Bans Games as 4th Star Confesses 3 'Fixes.'" *New York Times*, February 28, 1951, 1. Accessed June 29, 2013, http://search.proquest.com.

"Field Completed in Court Tourney." *New York Times*, March 7, 1938, 22. Accessed January 18, 2012, http://search.proquest.com.

"Field Is Completed for Garden Tourney." *New York Times*, March 11, 1941, 31. Accessed December 9, 2013, http://search.proquest.com.

"Field of National College Basket Tourney Here May Be Increased Two Teams." *Indianapolis Star*, March 2, 1922, 12. Accessed February 8, 2013, http://search.proquest.com.

"For Title Tonight." *Kansas City Times*, March 18, 1939, 15.

"Fordham Quintet Plays St. John's; Columbia Battles Brown Tonight." *New York Times*, February 28, 1951, 36. Accessed June 29, 2013, http://search.proquest.com.

"Four Teams Left." *Kansas City Times*, March 11, 1938, 15.

Fraley, Oscar. "Rupp Digs the N.C.A.A." *Kansas City Star*, March 14, 1950, 18.

Friedman, William D. "Backtalk: Readers Speak Out on States of College Basketball; Tracing History of Black Presence." *New York Times*, April 11, 1993. Accessed May 11, 2013, http://www.nytimes.com.

"Friel Praises Cougars." *Kansas City Times*, March 24, 1941, 9.

"Gala Welcome for I.S. Squad." *Terre Haute Tribune* (Terre Haute, IN), March 19, 1950, 1. Accessed June 6, 2015, http://www.newspapers.com.

Gallagher, Tim. "Color Ban Prevented Morningside Player from Competing." *Sioux City Journal*, March 10, 2006. Accessed May 11, 2013, http://www.siouxcityjournal.com.

"Game Nets $26,244 for Red Cross Here." *New York Times*, April 29, 1943, 24. Accessed November 23, 2012, http://search.proquest.com.

"Garden Pairings Set for Saturday as Cincinnati Quintet Accepts Bid." *New York Times*, March 7, 1951, 47. Accessed June 29, 2013, http://search.proquest.com.

"Georgetown Ends Duquesne Streak." *New York Times*, March 5, 1947, 32. Accessed June 15, 2013, http://search.proquest.com.

"Georgetown Five Accepts Bid." *New York Times*, March 10, 1943, 23. Accessed November 23, 2012, http://search.proquest.com.

Goldaper, Sam. "North Carolina State Snubs N. I. T." *New York Times*, March 10, 1975, 35. Accessed May 11, 2013, http://search.proquest.com.

Gretz, Bob. "Phog Allen Helps Save Early Event." *Houston Chronicle*, April 3, 1988. Accessed April 15, 2015, http://infoweb.newsbank.com.

"Grove City: Basket Ball Team Selected to Enter Intercollegiate Tourney in This City." *Indianapolis Star*, March 7, 1922, 14. Accessed February 8, 2013, http://search.proquest.com.

"'Hallroom Boys,' Pitt Cage Stars, Go 'Hard Way.'" *Atlanta Constitution*, January 31, 1934, 8. Accessed February 8, 2013, http://search.proquest.com.

"Honor Basketball Stars." *New York Times*, April 1, 1938, 20. Accessed January 18, 2012, http://search.proquest.com.

"I.B.F. Sets Height Limit." *Winnipeg Tribune* (Winnipeg, Canada), August 14, 1936, 11. Accessed June 6, 2015, http://www.newspapers.com.

"Idaho Quintet Starts for College Basket Tourney Here This Week End." *Indianapolis Star*, March 6, 1922, 17. Accessed February 8, 2013, http://search.proquest.com.

"Idaho Squad Arrives Here for National College Basket Tourney This Week End." *Indianapolis Star*, March 8, 1922, 10. Accessed February 8, 2013, http://search.proquest.com.

"Illini Quintet Accepts N.C.A.A. Tournament Bid." *Chicago Tribune*, March 7, 1949, B1. Accessed June 15, 2013, http://search.proquest.com.

"In Doubt on Cage Fields." *Kansas City Times*, March 3, 1938, 12.

"In Second Tests." *Kansas City Times*, March 10, 1948, 14.

"In Title Bid Here." *Kansas City Times*, March 29, 1941, 11.

"Into Court Play." *Kansas City Times*, March 10, 1941, 9.

"Invitation Final March 19." *New York Times*, January 27, 1949, 27. Accessed June 15, 2013, http://search.proquest.com.

"Iowa Season Over." *Chicago Tribune*, March 6, 1945, 17. Accessed November 23, 2012, http://search.proquest.com.

"Iowa State Is In." *Kansas City Times*, March 9, 1944, 15.

"Iowa State Not to Play." *New York Times*, March 7, 1944, 13. Accessed November 23, 2012, http://search.proquest.com.

"Iowa to Play Here." *Kansas City Times*, March 8, 1944, 9.

"Irish Draws 10% of Games' Profit." *New York Times*, March 29, 1945, 22. Accessed November 23, 2012, http://search.proquest.com.

Janoff, Murray. "Irish Stepping Down as King of Cage Promoters." *Sporting News*, July 6, 1974, 53.

"Jays Not Coming." *Kansas City Times*, March 4, 1943, 16.

Jessen, E. R. "Letters to the Sports Editor: West Virginia's Victory." *New York Times*, April 4, 1942, 21. Accessed December 9, 2013, http://search. proquest.com.

Jones, Kenneth. "Pot Shots." *Peoria Journal-Star*, January 12, 1951, B2.

"K.U. Turns Down Bid." *Kansas City Times*, March 7, 1942, 17.

Kahn, Roger. "Success and Ned Irish." *Sporting News*, March 27, 1961, 39–42.

"Kansas Prevails, 45–43." *New York Times*, March 17, 1940, 83. Accessed December 9, 2013, http://search.proquest.com.

"Kansas State Tops Cougar Team, 64–54." *New York Times*, March 24, 1951, 23. Accessed June 29, 2013, http://search.proquest.com.

"Kentucky Accepts Two Tourney Bids." *New York Times*, March 2, 1949, 37. Accessed June 15, 2013, http://search.proquest.com.

"Kentucky in Invitation Tourney; N.C.A.A. Names N. Carolina State." *New York Times*, March 6, 1950, 30. Accessed June 15, 2013, http://search. proquest.com.

"Kentucky Quintet Gains Lead in Poll." *New York Times*, February 2, 1949, 39. Accessed June 15, 2013, http://search.proquest.com.

"Kentucky Team to Play in Basketball Tourney." *New York Times*, February 17, 1944, 14. Accessed November 23, 2012, http://search.proquest.com.

"Kentucky Will Play in National Tourney." *New York Times*, February 26, 1946, 35. Accessed June 15, 2013, http://search.proquest.com.

"'Kick' Collegians out of A.A.U. Cage Tournament," *Chicago Defender* (National edition), March 26, 1938, 9. Accessed April 15, 2015, http://search.proquest.com.

Kieran, John. "Sports of the *Times*: A Bouncing Game." *New York Times*, February 22, 1942, S2. Accessed December 9, 2013, http://search. proquest.com.

Kieran, John. "Sports of the *Times*: At Red Cross Purposes." *New York Times*, January 27, 1942, 27. Accessed November 23, 2012, http://search. proquest.com.

Kieran, John. "Sports of the *Times*: Fifty Years A-Growing." *New York Times*, March 19, 1942, 30. Accessed December 9, 2013, http://search.proquest.com.

Kieran, John. "Sports of the *Times*: Glancing in All Directions." *New York Times*, March 28, 1942, 12. Accessed December 9, 2013, http://search.proquest.com.

Koppett, Leonard. "Marquette Beats St. John's, 65–53, in N. I. T. Final; U. C. L. A. Tops Jacksonville, 80–69, for N. C. A. A. Title." *New York Times*, March 22, 1970, 193. Accessed May 11, 2013, http://search.proquest.com.

"L.I.U., Wisconsin Were Acclaimed as Nation's Best in Basketball." *New York Times*, December 21, 1941, S4. Accessed December 9, 2013, http://search. proquest.com.

"L.I.U. Five Earned Top Ranking in U.S." *New York Times*, December 24, 1939, 50. Accessed December 9, 2013, http://search.proquest.com.

"L.I.U. Five to Play C.C.N.Y. Saturday." *New York Times*, March 24, 1942, 26. Accessed December 9, 2013, http://search.proquest.com.

"L.I.U. Five to Play in National Tourney." *New York Times*, March 11, 1942, 27. Accessed December 9, 2013, http://search.proquest.com.

"L.I.U. Ranked Superior on Record for Game with N.Y.U. Tonight." *New York Times*, March 9, 1938, 28. Accessed January 18, 2012, http://search. proquest.com.

"L.S.U. Rallies to Beat Pitt in Cage Tilt, 41–37." *Monroe Morning World* (Monroe, LA), April 14, 1935, 16. Accessed June 21, 2015, http://www. newspaperarchive.com.

"Lacy Sets New Scoring Record." *Daily Mail* (Hagerstown, MD), March 26, 1949, 12. Accessed June 6, 2015, http://www.newspapers.com.

Lane, Sydney. "Letters to the Sports Editor." *New York Times*, March 1, 1941, 10. Accessed December 9, 2013, http://search.proquest.com.

"Lange Paces Siena to 86–49 Rout of Providence in NCIT." *Troy Record* (Troy, NY), March 29, 1950, 20. Accessed June 6, 2015, http://www. newspapers.com.

Lazar, Louie. "For Gene Melchiorre, a Regretful Turn Brought a Unique NBA Distinction." *New York Times*, June 26, 2014. Accessed May 11, 2015, http://www.nytimes.com.

Leighbur, Don. "Ned Irish Forcing Jim Crow Basketball Play." *Philadelphia Tribune*, March 4, 1944, 12. Accessed May 11, 2011, http://search. proquest.com.

Leland, Leland F., ed. *Minnesota Alumni Weekly* 27, no. 17 (February 11, 1928).

"LeMoyne Defeats Providence Quint in N.C.I.T., 67–63." *Syracuse Herald-American* (Syracuse, NY), March 16, 1952, D1. Accessed June 21, 2015, http://www.newspaperarchive.com.

"Letters to the Sports Editor" (editorial note). *New York Times*, January 21, 1939, 11. Accessed January 18, 2012, http://search.proquest.com.

"Letters to the Sports Editor: Unbeaten and Uninvited." *New York Times*, March 9, 1940, 18. Accessed December 9, 2013, http://search.proquest.com.

"Lift Negro Ban." *Kansas City Times*, March 6, 1948, 20.

Lowenthal, Arnold. "Letters to the Sports Editor: On N.Y.U.'s Refusal: Officials' Rejection of Tourney Bid to Violet Five Is Hit." *New York Times*, March 16, 1940, 18. Accessed December 9, 2013, http://search.proquest.com.

"Loyola Is Out." *Kansas City Times*, March 9, 1943, 13.

"M.U. in, Iowa Out." *Kansas City Times*, March 14, 1944, 9.

Maly, Ron. "Bob Ortegel Is Good for Basketball and the Game Has Been Good to Him." *WHO-TV online*, June 16, 2006. Accessed July 1, 2016, http://web.archive.org/web/20070927223855/http://www.whotv.com/.

"Manhattan Accepts N.A.I.B. Bid with Tourney Dropping Negro Ban." *New York Times*, March 6, 1948, 17. Accessed June 15, 2013, http://search.proquest.com.

"Marquette Five Plays St. Francis for NCIT Title." *Post-Standard* (Syracuse, NY), March 22, 1952, 11. Accessed June 21, 2015, http://www.newspaperarchive.com.

"Marquette Wins Catholic Tourney at Troy." *Post-Standard* (Syracuse, NY), March 23, 1952, 31. Accessed June 21, 2015, http://www.newspaperarchive.com.

Marsh, Irving T. "Philly's Taking Title as East's Basket Hub." *New York Herald-Tribune*, January 20, 1964, 21.

"Marshall Is Out." *Kansas City Times*, March 11, 1948, 16.

"Marshall Refuses Bid." *Kansas City Times*, February 26, 1946, 8.

Martin, Simon. "Letters to the Sports Editor: Why Not C.C.N.Y.-L.I.U.?" *New York Times*, March 21, 1942, 11. Accessed December 9, 2012, http://search.proquest.com.

Martin, Whitney. "The Edge to Meet Here." *Kansas City Times*, February 2, 1939, 9.

"Meet on Tonight." *Kansas City Times*, March 9, 1937, 13.

"Mighty Baylor Bears Facing Kentucky for Championship." *Abilene Reporter-News* (Abilene, TX), March 22, 1948, 3. Accessed June 6, 2015, http://www.newspapers.com.

Moran, Malcolm. "NCAA Buys NIT for $56.5 Million; Event Will Continue." *USA Today*, August 18, 2005, August 2005 Folder, NCAA Clip File.

Morris, Everett B. "Basketball Rebounds: National College Invitation Tourney Slated by Writers in Garden Next Month." *New York Herald-Tribune*, February 2, 1938, 21.

"Most Colleges Willing to Keep Garden Games." *Chicago Tribune*, February 21, 1951, B1. Accessed June 29, 2013, http://search.proquest.com.

"Muhlenberg Accepts Bid." *New York Times*, February 27, 1946, 35. Accessed June 15, 2013, http://search.proquest.com.

"Muhlenberg Accepts Bid." *New York Times*, March 3, 1945, 21. Accessed November 23, 2012, http://search.proquest.com.

"Mules Are Victors." *Kansas City Times*, March 12, 1937, 18.

"Mules Stay In." *Kansas City Times*, March 13, 1942, 11.

"Mules to Finals." *Kansas City Times*, March 11, 1937, 12.

"Mules vs. Roanoke." *Kansas City Times*, March 12, 1938, 17.

"NAIB Fives Cut as First Round Marathon Ends." *Daily Capital News* (Jefferson City, MO), March 15, 1950, 3. Accessed June 6, 2015, http://www.newspapers.com.

"NAIB Tournament Opens Today, Winner Shoots for Olympics." *Neosho Daily Democrat* (Neosho, MO), March 10, 1952, 3. Accessed June 21, 2015, http://www.newspaperarchive.com.

"NAIB's Action against Nevada Draws Fire from Californians." *Nevada State Journal* (Reno, NV), March 14, 1950, 11. Accessed June 6, 2015, http://www.newspapers.com.

"N.C.A.A. Court Play at Garden Likely." *New York Times*, January 20, 1943, 26. Accessed November 23, 2012, http://search.proquest.com.

"NCAA Draw Pits Dartmouth Five against Catholic U. March 24." *New York Times*, March 14, 1944, 14. Accessed November 23, 2012, http://search.proquest.com.

"N.C.A.A. Fives Open Play Here Tonight." *New York Times*, March 21, 1946, 35. Accessed June 15, 2013, http://search.proquest.com.

"N.C.A.A. Quintets Open Play Tonight." *New York Times*, March 21, 1952, 28. Accessed May 11, 2013, http://search.proquest.com.

"N.C.A.A. Plans Unchanged." *New York Times*, January 31, 1945, 24. Accessed November 23, 2012, http://search.proquest.com.

"NCBT Sidelights." *Peoria Journal-Star*, March 31, 1951, 4.

"N.C. State Checks Duke." *New York Times*, March 4, 1951, 149. Accessed June 29, 2013, http://search.proquest.com.

"N.C. State to Play in Court Tourney." *New York Times*, March 10, 1947, 29. Accessed June 15, 2013, http://search.proquest.com.

"N.Y.U. and West Virginia to Play in Court Events." *New York Times*, March 9, 1945, 14. Accessed November 23, 2012, http://search.proquest.com.

"N.Y.U. Five Accepts Bid to Tournament." *New York Times*, February 29, 1952, 29. Accessed May 11, 2013, http://search.proquest.com.

"N.Y.U. Not Yet Out of Olympic Trials." *New York Times*, March 19, 1948, 30. Accessed June 15, 2013, http://search.proquest.com.

"N.Y.U., St. John's in Tourneys Here." *New York Times*, March 1, 1946, 26. Accessed June 15, 2013, http://search.proquest.com.

"Naismith: Inventor of Basket Ball Game, Is Invited to Attend National Net Tourney Here." *Indianapolis Star*, March 4, 1922, 13. Accessed February 8, 2013, http://search.proquest.com.

"National Catholic Tourney to Semis." *Council Bluffs Nonpareil* (Council Bluffs, IA), March 25, 1949, 23. Accessed June 6, 2015, http://www.newspapers.com.

"National College Net Meet Here Is Assured." *Indianapolis Star*, February 16, 1922, 10. Accessed February 8, 2013, http://search.proquest.com.

"Near Cage Climax." *Kansas City Star*, March 10, 1937, 15.

"Ned Irish Denies Listing Gamblers." *New York Times*, April 3, 1945, 21. Accessed November 23, 2012, http://search.proquest.com.

Neddenriep, Kyle. "All-time Indiana All-Star Countdown: No. 4." *USA Today*, July 18, 2013. Accessed June 7, 2015, http://www.usatoday.com.

Nesbit, Bob. "Baldwin-Wallace Is State Foe Tonight in N.A.I.B." *Terre Haute Tribune* (Terre Haute, IN), March 16, 1950, 20. Accessed June 6, 2015, http://www.newspapers.com.

Nesbit, Bob. "Indiana State Seeks Initial N.A.I.B. Championship." *Terre Haute Tribune* (Terre Haute, IN), March 18, 1950, 7. Accessed June 6, 2015, http://www.newspapers.com.

Nesbit, Bob. "State Battles Tampa in N.A.I.B. Semi-Finals Duel." *Terre Haute Tribune* (Terre Haute, IN), March 17, 1950, 24. Accessed June 6, 2015, http://www.newspapers.com.

"New Strategy Planned by Jack Gardner in Future Campaigns." *Kansas City Times*, March 15, 1950, 16.

"No. Carolina State in Garden Tourney." *New York Times*, February 28, 1948, 11. Accessed June 15, 2013, http://search.proquest.com.

"No More Giant Court Players Will Compete." *Dunkirk Evening Observer* (Dunkirk, NY), August 14, 1936, 6. Accessed June 6, 2015, http://www. newspapers.com.

O'Riley, Francis J. "17,623 See Stanford Stop L.I.U. Streak at 43 Games; Georgetown Triumphs." *New York Times*, December 31, 1936, 10. Accessed May 11, 2013, http://search.proquest.com.

O'Riley, Francis J. "College Invitation Tournament to Be Held in March by Basketball Writers." *New York Times*, January 25, 1939, 29. Accessed January 18, 2012, http://search.proquest.com.

"Oilers Win Olympic Trials." *Brooklyn Daily Eagle*, April 1, 1948, 17. Accessed June 6, 2015, http://www.newspapers.com.

"Okla. Aggies Best at .939." *New York Times*, March 29, 1946, 33. Accessed June 15, 2013, http://search.proquest.com.

"Oklahoma Aggies, Traveling by Plane, to Play Here and in N.C.A.A. Competition." *New York Times*, March 7, 1940, 33. Accessed December 9, 2013, http://search.proquest.com.

"Only Four Left." *Kansas City Times*, March 12, 1948, 20.

"Open Here Today." *Kansas City Times*, March 11, 1940, 9.

"Parade 'n 2,000 Fans Greet I.U.'s Champions." *Indiana Daily Student*, April 2, 1940, page number unknown (author has copy).

Parrott, Harold. "Both Sides." *Brooklyn Daily Eagle*, March 29, 1943, 9. Accessed June 6, 2015, http://www.newspapers.com.

"Passes Up the N.C.A.A." *Kansas City Times*, March 9, 1943, 13.

"Passes Up Tourney Here." *Kansas City Times*, March 6, 1946, 10.

"Pat on Decision." *Kansas City Star*, March 14, 1950, 18.

"Penn State on Top, 44–30." *New York Times*, February 26, 1942, 24. Accessed December 9, 2013, http://search.proquest.com.

Pennington, Bill. "N.A.I.A.'s Future Looms Large for Division III." *New York Times*, February 13, 2007. Accessed May 11, 2013, http://www.nytimes.com.

"Pittsburg Upset." *Kansas City Times*, March 14, 1942, 17.

"Plan a Cage Meet Here." *Kansas City Times*, March 11, 1937, 12.

Poplin, Carroll. "Carolina Chatter." *Daily Tar Heel* (Chapel Hill, NC), March 1, 1946, 3. Accessed June 6, 2015, http://www.newspapers.com.

Poplin, Carroll. "Carolina Chatter." *Daily Tar Heel* (Chapel Hill, NC), March 29, 1946, 3. Accessed June 6, 2015, http://www.newspapers.com.

"Protest by Utah." *Kansas City Times*, March 10, 1948, 14.

"Protest Over Cage Play." *Kansas City Times*, March 8, 1940, 14.

"Quarter Finals Set in National Catholic Tourney." *Daily Capital Journal* (Salem, OR), March 23, 1949, 15. Accessed June 6, 2015, http://www. newspapers.com.

"Quintets in National College Tourney Here to Hold Drawings Wednesday Night." *Indianapolis Star*, March 3, 1922, 12. Accessed February 8, 2013, http://search.proquest.com.

"R.I. State Quintet to Play in Tourney." *New York Times*, March 6, 1942, 24. Accessed December 9, 2013, http://search.proquest.com.

Ratliff, Harold V. "If Baylor Cagers Win Rupp Can Take a Bow." *Corpus Christi Caller-Times* (Corpus Christi, TX), March 22, 1948, 4. Accessed June 6, 2015, http://www.newspapers.com.

"Red Cross Game Listed." *New York Times*, February 19, 1943, 24. Accessed November 23, 2012, http://search.proquest.com.

"Rebuff to Utah." *Kansas City Times*, March 11, 1948, 16.

"Red Cross Names Sports Committee." *New York Times*, January 19, 1945, 27. Accessed November 23, 2012, http://search.proquest.com.

"Redmen Edged by Late Francis Rally, 57–51." *Winona Republican-Herald* (Winona, MN), March 22, 1949, 13. Accessed June 6, 2015, http://www. newspapers.com.

"Regis College Rangers Win National Catholic Basketball Tourney." *Independent Record* (Helena, MT), March 27, 1949, 14. Accessed June 6, 2015, http:// www.newspapers.com.

Rendel, John. "C.C.N.Y. Five, Meeting Bradley Tonight, Also Gets N.C.A.A. Bid." *New York Times*, March 18, 1950, 17. Accessed June 15, 2013, http://search. proquest.com.

"Rice's Quintet Invited." *New York Times*, March 7, 1943, S3. Accessed November 23, 2012, http://search.proquest.com.

Richardson, William D. "Giant Centers Top Court Bill Tonight." *New York Times*, March 29, 1945, 32. Accessed November 23, 2012, http://search. proquest.com.

Richardson, William D. "N.C.A.A. Quintets in Garden Tonight." *New York Times*, March 24, 1944, 22. Accessed November 23, 2012, http://search.proquest.com.

Richardson, William D. "Rhode Island Opposes Tennessee Tonight." *New York Times*, March 17, 1945, 20. Accessed November 23, 2012, http://search.proquest.com.

Richardson, William D. "St. John's Favored to Beat Utah in Red Cross Basketball Tonight." *New York Times*, March 30, 1944, 25. Accessed November 23, 2012, http://search.proquest.com.

Richardson, William D. "St. John's Upsets Bowling Green Five; De Paul Triumphs." *New York Times*, March 17, 1944, 20. Accessed November 23, 2012, http://search.proquest.com.

Rosenberg, Jack. "3 Refs Noble Experiment?" *Peoria Journal-Star*, March 28, 1951, page unknown, author has copy.

Rosenberg, Jack. "Parties for NCBT Guests." *Peoria Journal-Star*, March 30, 1951, page unknown, author has copy.

"Rule Changes Would Speed Up Game." *Atlanta Constitution*, March 31, 1934, 13. Accessed February 8, 2013, http://search.proquest.com.

Russell, Bob. "9 Favor Stadium Meet." *Chicago Daily News*, February 21, 1951, page unknown, author has copy.

"Saddened U.N. Players Unpack Suitcases, Tear Up Plane Tickets to Kansas City." *Nevada State Journal* (Reno, NV), March 12, 1950, 4. Accessed June 6, 2015, http://www.newspapers.com.

Sainsbury, Ed. "Bradley Probable Chicago Entrant." *Peoria Journal-Star*, February 21, 1951, page unknown, author has copy.

"San Diego Again." *Kansas City Times*, March 14, 1941, 12.

"San Diego Wins." *Kansas City Times*, March 13, 1941, 14.

"Santa Barbara College Star Barred from Meet." *Pittsburgh Courier*, March 15, 1941, 17. Accessed April 15, 2014, http://search.proquest.com.

"Says Allen Errs." *Kansas City Times*, March 5, 1942, 16.

"Scandal Forces Long Island from Sports." *Chicago Tribune*, February 21, 1951, B1. Accessed June 29, 2013, http://search.proquest.com.

"Scarlet: Tossers Will Represent Indiana in National Intercollegiate Basketball Tourney." *Indianapolis Star*, February 28, 1922, 11. Accessed February 8, 2013, http://search.proquest.com.

"Sees Campus Site Again for Cage Sport." *Brooklyn Daily Eagle*, January 11, 1948, 25. Accessed June 6, 2015, http://www.newspapers.com.

"Selectors Chosen for Court Tourney." *New York Times*, February 19, 1946, 29. Accessed June 15, 2013, http://search.proquest.com.

"Set Height Limit for Cage Players." *Ottawa Journal* (Ottawa, Canada), August 14, 1936, 15. Accessed June 6, 2015, http://www.newspapers.com.

"Set Two Marks." *Kansas City Times*, March 24, 1945, 11.

"Seton Hall Joins Invitation Play." *New York Times*, March 2, 1951, 29. Accessed June 29, 2013, http://search.proquest.com.

"Seven States in Meet." *Kansas City Times*, February 24, 1938, 13.

Sheehan, Joseph M. "Basketball Tourney Invitations to Be Decided at Meeting Today." *New York Times*, March 10, 1941, 25. Accessed December 9, 2013, http://search.proquest.com.

Sheehan, Joseph M. "C.C.N.Y. and Duquesne Quintets Favored in Tourney Games Tonight." *New York Times*, March 18, 1941, 30. Accessed December 9, 2013, http://search.proquest.com.

Sheehan, Joseph M. "City College Five Bids for Place in National Invitation Tournament." *New York Times*, February 23, 1942, 18. Accessed December 9, 2013, http://search.proquest.com.

Sheehan, Joseph M. "College Quintets Await 2 Tourneys." *New York Times*, March 17, 1941, 25. Accessed December 9, 2013, http://search.proquest.com.

Sheehan, Joseph M. "Honors Garnered by Temple's Five." *New York Times*, March 18, 1938, 25. Accessed January 18, 2012, http://search.proquest.com.

Sheehan, Joseph M. "L.I.U. and C.C.N.Y. in Line for Tourney Bids." *New York Times*, March 2, 1942, 24. Accessed December 9, 2013, http://search. proquest.com.

Sheehan, Joseph M. "League Mark of 4 Titles in Row Objective of Dartmouth Quintet." *New York Times*, March 4, 1940, 23. Accessed December 9, 2013, http://search.proquest.com.

Sheehan, Joseph M. "New Mexico State and Roanoke Paired in Garden Game Monday." *New York Times*, March 17, 1939, 31. Accessed January 18, 2012, http://search.proquest.com.

Sheehan, Joseph M. "Oilers Top N.Y.A.C. in Overtime, 69–64." *New York Times*, March 29, 1946, 32. Accessed June 15, 2013, http://search.proquest.com.

Sheehan, Joseph M. "On Basketball Courts." *New York Times*, March 3, 1942, 19. Accessed December 9, 2013, http://search.proquest.com.

Sheehan, Joseph M. "Out-of-Town Fives Choices in Garden." *New York Times*, March 12, 1949, 14. Accessed June 15, 2013, http://search.proquest.com.

"Siena Liked in National Catholic Play." *Portland Press Herald* (Portland, ME), March 20, 1949, 34. Accessed June 6, 2015, http://www.newspapers.com.

Sigmund, Howard. "Garden Officials Unimpressed by Proposed Chicago Tourney." *Peoria Journal-Star*, February 14, 1951, page unknown, author has copy.

Simon, Martin. "Letters to the Sports Editor: Why Not C.C.N.Y.-L.I.U.?" *New York Times*, March 21, 1942, 11. Accessed December 9, 2013, http://search. proquest.com.

Smith, Al. "Coaches Delay Rules Action; To Vote Today." *Atlanta Constitution*, March 31, 1934, 13. Accessed February 8, 2013, http://search.proquest.com.

Smith, Wilfrid. "Coaches' Plans for New Rules Tested in Games." *Chicago Tribune*, April 4, 1935, 21. Accessed May 11, 2013, http://search. proquest.com.

Smith, Wilfrid. "NCAA Asks More Control of Stadiums." *Chicago Tribune*, March 3, 1951, B1. Accessed June 29, 2013, http://search.proquest.com.

"So' Western Wins." *Kansas City Star*, March 19, 1939, 12.

Spiegel, Irving. "C.C.N.Y. Rallies, Parades Hail Basketball Feat." *New York Times*, March 30, 1950, 43. Accessed June 15, 2013, http://search.proquest.com.

"Sport: Basketball: Midseason." *Time*, February 19, 1934. Accessed May 11, 2013, http://content.time.com/time/magazine/article/0,9171,746995,00.html.

"Springfield Bears Cop NAIB Title." *Sunday News and Tribune* (Jefferson City, MO), March 16, 1952, 7. Accessed June 21, 2015, http://www.newspaper archive.com.

"St. Francis Upsets Top-Seeded Creighton in NCIT, 67–66." *Troy Record* (Troy, NY), March 30, 1950, 30. Accessed June 6, 2015, http://www. newspapers.com.

"St. Francis Wins." *Post-Standard* (Syracuse, NY), March 18, 1951, 37. Accessed June 21, 2015, http://www.newspaperarchives.com.

"St. John's Accepts Bid." *New York Times*, March 1, 1945, 24. Accessed November 23, 2012, http://search.proquest.com.

"St. John's Five Accepts Bid to Garden Tourney." *New York Times*, February 25, 1944, 20. Accessed November 23, 2012, http://search.proquest.com.

"St. John's Quintet in N.C.A.A. Tourney." *New York Times*, March 9, 1951, 34. Accessed June 29, 2013, http://search.proquest.com.

"St. John's to Face Bonaventure Five." *New York Times*, March 12, 1951, 40. Accessed June 29, 2013, http://search.proquest.com.

"St. Louis U. Accepts Bid to Defend Title in National Tourney." *Chicago Tribune*, March 1, 1949, B3. Accessed June 15, 2013, http://search.proquest.com.

"St. Michael Is First Foe of LeMoyne." *Syracuse Herald-Journal*, March 10, 1951, 9. Accessed June 21, 2015, http://www.newspaperarchive.com.

"St. Thomas and Gonzaga Makes Semifinal Bids." *Daily Republic* (Mitchell, SD), March 24, 1949, 12. Accessed June 6, 2015, http://www.newspapers.com.

Stanley, L. M. "Little Giants Come Through in First Tourney Game," *Indianapolis Star*, March 9, 1922, 14. Accessed February 8, 2013, http://search.proquest.com.

Stanley, L. M. "Wabash Five Wins National College Basket Ball Meet," *Indianapolis Star*, March 12, 1922, 25. Accessed February 8, 2013, http://search.proquest.com.

"Stars Who Play in National Basketball Tournament Here." *Kansas City Times*, March 5, 1938, 17.

"Status of Tourneys Not Yet Determined." *New York Times*, February 22, 1945, 33. Accessed November 23, 2012, http://search.proquest.com.

Strauss, Emanuel. "Basketball Fans Stage Ticket Rush." *New York Times*, March 5, 1946, 30. Accessed June 15, 2013, http://search.proquest.com.

Strauss, Emanuel. "City College's Upset of N.Y.U. Week's Highlight in Basketball."

New York Times, March 11, 1946, 22. Accessed June 15, 2013, http://search.proquest.com.

Strauss, Emanuel. "Mikan's Injury Hits De Paul Hopes of Triumphing in Basketball Final." *New York Times*, March 25, 1945, S1. Accessed November 23, 2012, http://search.proquest.com.

Strauss, Emanuel. "Spotlight on Conference Battles as Basketball Season nears End." *New York Times*, March 4, 1946, 20. Accessed June 15, 2013, http://search.proquest.com.

Strauss, Michael. "Afternoon, Night Twin Bills Today on Invitation Court Tourney Slate." *New York Times*, March 14, 1949, 25. Accessed June 15, 2013, http://search.proquest.com.

Strauss, Michael. "Basketball Upsets Stir Interest in Another Triple-Header Tonight." *New York Times*, March 10, 1952, 28. Accessed May 11, 2013, http://search.proquest.com.

Strauss, Michael. "C.C.N.Y. Choice in Eastern Final against No. Carolina State Tonight." *New York Times*, March 25, 1950, 22. Accessed June 15, 2013, http://search.proquest.com.

Strauss, Michael. "City College March to Invitation Laurels Highlight of Basketball Campaign." *New York Times*, March 20, 1950, 26. Accessed June 15, 2013, http://search.proquest.com.

Strauss, Michael. "City College Now Favored for N.C.A.A. Title and Basketball Grand Slam." *New York Times*, March 27, 1950, 28. Accessed June 15, 2013, http://search.proquest.com.

Strauss, Michael. "Kentucky Favored Over Villanova, Illinois Choice Over Yale Tonight." *New York Times*, March 21, 1949, 29. Accessed June 15, 2013, http://search.proquest.com.

Strauss, Michael. "Kentucky Opposes Utah Five Tonight." *New York Times*, March 24, 1947, 31. Accessed June 15, 2013, http://search.proquest.com.

Strauss, Michael. "N.Y.U. and Three Out-of-Town Quintets Complete Invitation Field." *New York Times*, March 6, 1948, 17. Accessed June 15, 2013, http://search.proquest.com.

Strauss, Michael. "Oklahoma Aggies in Garden Tonight." *New York Times*, March 26, 1946, 33. Accessed June 15, 2013, http://search.proquest.com.

Strauss, Michael. "Triumphant Beaver Squad Hailed by Mayor at City Hall Ceremony." *New York Times*, March 21, 1950, 37. Accessed June 15, 2013, http://search.proquest.com.

Strauss, Michael. "Villanova, Louisville, Connecticut Win N.C.A.A. Tournament Berths." *New York Times*, March 13, 1951, 42. Accessed June 29, 2013, http://search.proquest.com.

"Syracuse Five Accepts." *New York Times*, March 2, 1946, 8. Accessed June 15, 2013, http://search.proquest.com.

"Syracuse Tops Long Island in N.Y. Tourney." *Chicago Tribune*, March 12, 1950, A4. Accessed June 15, 2013, http://search.proquest.com.

"Tarkio Is Out." *Kansas City Times*, March 11, 1941, 8.

"Team in Crash." *Kansas City Times*, March 20, 1944, 8.

"Teams Set to Go." *Kansas City Times*, March 13, 1939, 13.

"Teams Set to Go." *Kansas City Times*, March 21, 1947, 20.

Teplitz, Allen M. "Letters to the Sports Editor: L.I.U.-C.C.N.Y. for Charity." *New York Times*, April 4, 1941, 11. Accessed December 9, 2013, http://search.proquest.com.

"Terriers Down LeMoyne in Tourney Game, 75–61." *Post-Standard* (Syracuse, NY), March 19, 1952, 31. Accessed June 21, 2015, http://www.newspaperarchive.com.

"The Horatio Alger of Basketball." *Literary Digest*, March 9, 1935.

"The Mules Go Out." *Kansas City Times*, March 17, 1939, 19.

"The Mules Stay In." *Kansas City Times*, March 15, 1939, 11.

"There Was a Wide Gap between Strong and Weak N.A.I.B. Teams." *Kansas City Star*, March 19, 1951, 16.

"Thrill Cage Fans." *Kansas City Times*, March 8, 1938, 12.

"Thrill the Fans." *Kansas City Times*, March 13, 1948, 20.

"Title Basketball Set for March 16." *New York Times*, February 1, 1944, 16. Accessed November 23, 2012, http://search.proquest.com.

"Top-Seeded Siena Ousted by Ravens in National Catholic Tourney." *Independent Record* (Helena, MT), March 21, 1949, 7. Accessed June 6, 2015, http://www.newspapers.com.

"Top Officials Thrilled by Ute Victory." *Salt Lake Tribune*, March 31, 1944, 19. Accessed June 6, 2015, http://www.newspapers.com.

"Topsy-Turvy Year for Court Sport." *New York Times*, December 22, 1940, 66. Accessed December 9, 2013, http://search.proquest.com.

"Tourney in Garden to Start March 17." *New York Times*, January 22, 1942, 21. Accessed December 9, 2013, http://search.proquest.com.

"Tourney Quintets Paired." *New York Times*, March 1, 1952, 11. Accessed May 11, 2013, http://search.proquest.com.

Troy, Jack. "Two Proposed Rule Changes Demonstrated in Game Here." *Atlanta Constitution*, March 30, 1934, 21. Accessed February 8, 2013, http://search.proquest.com.

"Two Cage Upsets." *Kansas City Times*, March 12, 1941, 12.

"Two Quintets Are Tourney Choices." *New York Times*, March 15, 1943, 17. Accessed November 23, 2012, http://search.proquest.com.

"Upset by Drury." *Kansas City Times*, March 13, 1946, 10.

"Upsets Come Fast." *Kansas City Times*, March 16, 1939, 13.

"Utah Accepts N.C.A.A. Bid." *New York Times*, March 22, 1944, 23. Accessed November 23, 2012, http://search.proquest.com.

"Utah Five Accepts Garden Invitation." *New York Times*, February 20, 1944, S1. Accessed November 23, 2012, http://search.proquest.com.

"Wabash Wins Tournament." *Boston Globe*, March 12, 1922, 31. Accessed February 8, 2013, http://search.proquest.com

"Washburn by Goal." *Kansas City Times*, March 10, 1938, 11.

Werden, Lincoln A. "Violet Quintet Out of Garden Tourney." *New York Times*, March 7, 1940, 33. Accessed December 9, 2013, http://search.proquest.com.

"West Texas Accepts Bid." *New York Times*, March 5, 1942, 28. Accessed December 9, 2013, http://search.proquest.com.

"West Texas Out." *Kansas City Times*, March 15, 1941, 16.

"West Virginia Added to Garden Tourney." *New York Times*, March 13, 1942, 24. Accessed December 9, 2013, http://search.proquest.com.

"West Virginia Five and Stanford Best." *New York Times*, December 20, 1942, S4. Accessed December 9, 2013, http://search.proquest.com.

White, Roy. "Tech Plays Host to U.S. Coaches at Meeting Here." *Atlanta Constitution*, March 25, 1934, 4B. Accessed February 8, 2013, http://search. proquest.com.

"Will Invite Local Fives." *New York Times*, March 5, 1949, 13. Accessed June 15, 2013, http://search.proquest.com.

"Winners Even in Defeat." *Kansas City Times*, March 13, 1942, 11.

Wolff, Alexander, and Michael Atchison. "Utah: The First Cinderella." *Sports Illustrated*, March 22, 2010. Accessed November 22, 2014, http://www. sivault.com.

Wood, Jimmy. "Sportopics: Whispers." *Brooklyn Daily Eagle*, March 22, 1939, 17. Accessed June 6, 2015, http://www.newspapers.com.

Wright, James G. "Letters to the Sports Editor: Spectator Appeal Lacking." *New York Times*, March 16, 1940, 18. Accessed December 9, 2013, http://search. proquest.com.

Yamin, George. "Siena Rips Loras, 75–55; Terriers Edge Iona, 62–61 In NCIT." *Troy Record* (Troy, NY), March 31, 1950, 42. Accessed June 6, 2015, http:// www.newspapers.com.

Yamin, George. "Siena, Victorious in NCIT, Has Eyes on New Laurels." *Troy Record* (Troy, NY), April 2, 1950, 18. Accessed June 6, 2015, http://www. newspapers.com.

Young, Fay. "The Stuff Is Here: Past-Present-Future." *Chicago Defender*, April 5, 1941, 22. Accessed December 9, 2013, http://search.proquest.com.

Index

CHAD CARLSON is assistant professor of kinesiology and an assistant men's basketball coach at Hope College. A former college and semiprofessional basketball player, he now teaches and researches selected topics within the fields of sport history, sport philosophy, and sport and religion.